Minneapolis Star Tribune, Seattle Post-Intelligencer,
History Book Club, *Salt Lake Tribune,*
Mountains and Plains Booksellers,
San Francisco Chronicle, Seattle Times, **Book Sense,**
Portland Oregonian

BOOK OF THE YEAR

Acclaim for Hampton Sides's

BLOOD AND THUNDER

"A magnificent sweeping book, impeccably researched and scrupulously fair to all sides, with the scope and power of *Bury My Heart at Wounded Knee* or *Son of the Morning Star.* This is a story that has been scarcely told at all, and certainly never told this well."
—*Men's Vogue*

"The story that Sides tells contains equal parts of bravery, endurance, ignorance and pure cussedness." —*Pittsburgh Post-Gazette*

"Fascinating. . . . A boldly sweeping account of the winning of the West." —*The Boston Globe*

"A beautifully written, mesmerizing account of the greatest American story between the Revolution and the Civil War: the quarter-century-long quest to explore the Western lands and build an American empire that would span sea to shining sea. Like Shelby Foote, [Sides] has mastered the grand, sweeping style without sacrificing the well-chosen characters, events and minutiae that bring history to life." —*USA Today*

HAMPTON SIDES

BLOOD AND THUNDER

A native of Memphis, Hampton Sides is editor-at-large for *Outside* magazine and the author of the international bestseller *Ghost Soldiers*. *Ghost Soldiers* won the 2002 PEN USA Award for nonfiction and the 2002 Discover Award from Barnes & Noble, and his magazine work has been twice nominated for National Magazine Awards for feature writing. Hampton is also the author of *Americana* and *Stomping Grounds*. A graduate of Yale with a B.A. in history, he lives in New Mexico with his wife, Anne, and their three sons.

BLOOD AND THUNDER

BLOOD AND THUNDER

The Epic Story of Kit Carson and
the Conquest of the American West

Hampton Sides

ANCHOR BOOKS
A Division of Random House, Inc.
New York

FIRST ANCHOR BOOKS EDITION, OCTOBER 2007

Copyright © 2006 by Hampton Sides

The Library of Congress has cataloged the Doubleday edition as follows:
Sides, Hampton.
Blood and thunder: an epic of the American West / Hampton Sides.—1st ed.
p. cm.
1. West (U.S.)—History—19th Century. 2. United States—Territorial expansion.
3. West (U.S.)—History, Military—19th Century. 4. United States Army—
History—19th Century. 5. Frontier and pioneer life—West (U.S.). 6. Carson, Kit,
1809–1868. 7. Indians of North America—Wars—West (U.S.). 8. Indians of
North America—West (U.S.)—History—19th Century. 9. Navajo Indians—
History—19th Century. 10. Southwest, New—History—1848– . I. Title.
F591.S54 2006
978'.02—dc22
2006016579

Anchor ISBN: 978-1-4000-3110-8

Book design by Fritz Metsch
Author photograph © Camille Hewett
Maps by David Cain

www.anchorbooks.com

Printed in the United States of America
10 9 8 7 6 5 4

Anne

CONTENTS

BOOK TWO: A BROKEN COUNTRY

BOOK THREE: MONSTER SLAYER

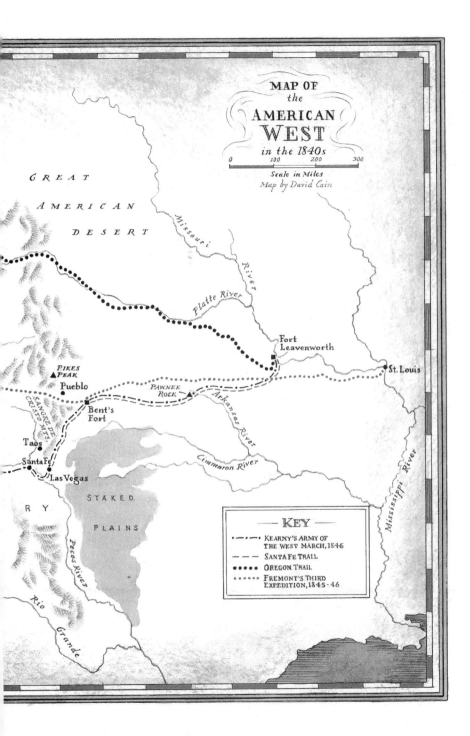

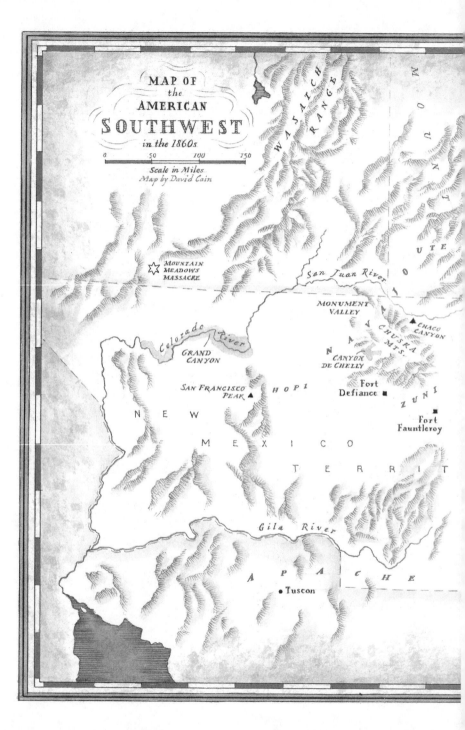

MAP OF
the
AMERICAN
SOUTHWEST
in the 1860s

0   50   100   150
Scale in Miles
Map by David Cain

WASATCH RANGE

MOUNTAINS

UTE

MOUNTAIN
MEADOWS
MASSACRE

San Juan River

MONUMENT
VALLEY

CHACO
CANYON

Colorado River

GRAND
CANYON

N
A
V
A
J
O

CHUSKA MTS.

CANYON
DE CHELLY

Fort
Defiance

ZUNI

SAN FRANCISCO
PEAK

HOPI

Fort
Fauntleroy

N   E   W

M   E   X   I   C   O

T   E   R   R   I   T

Gila River

A   P   A   C   H   E

• Tuscon

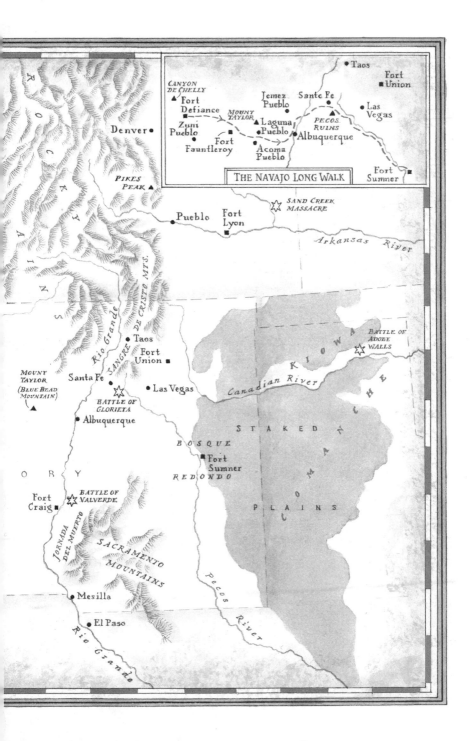

THE NAVAJO LONG WALK

ROCKY MOUNTAINS

Denver

PIKES PEAK

CANYON DE CHELLY
Fort Defiance
MOUNT TAYLOR
Zuni Pueblo
Fort Fauntleroy
Jemez Pueblo
Laguma Pueblo
Acoma Pueblo
Taos
Santa Fe
PECOS RUINS
Albuquerque
Fort Union
Las Vegas
Fort Sumner

Pueblo
Fort Lyon
SAND CREEK MASSACRE
Arkansas River

SANGRE DE CRISTO MTS.
Rio Grande
Taos
Fort Union
Santa Fe
Las Vegas
BATTLE OF GLORIETA
Albuquerque
MOUNT TAYLOR (BLUE BEAD MOUNTAIN)

KIOWA
Canadian River
BATTLE OF ADOBE WALLS
COMANCHE

BOSQUE
Fort Sumner
REDONDO
STAKED
PLAINS

Fort Craig
BATTLE OF VALVERDE
JORNADA DEL MUERTO
SACRAMENTO MOUNTAINS

ORY

Mesilla
El Paso
Rio Grande
Pecos River

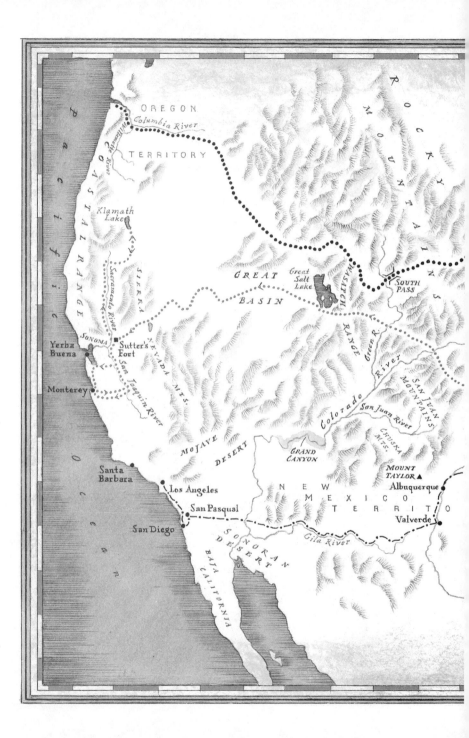

I follow the scent of falling rain
And head for the place where it is darkest
I follow the lightning
And draw near to the place where it strikes

—NAVAJO CHANT

BLOOD AND THUNDER

Prologue   HOOFBEATS

One morning in mid-August 1846, in the cool hours before dawn, the New Mexican villagers of Las Vegas slumbered anxiously. The Americanos were coming. In distant Washington, D.C., for reasons murky to the inhabitants of Las Vegas, the president of the United States had declared war on Mexico. Now scouts had brought word that the invading gringo army was only a few days away, marching steadily westward, and the townspeople were deeply fearful. They had heard from their priest that the United States would outlaw Catholicism, that the soldiers would rape the women in the village and burn the letters "U.S." on their cheeks with branding irons. The villagers even debated among themselves the merits of torching their own church to prevent the Americans from using it as a stable or a barracks.

Las Vegas—"The Meadows" in Spanish—was a hodgepodge of adobe houses, set among rustling cornfields irrigated by a muddy acequia that seeped from the Gallinas River. The town lay at the feet of the Sangre de Cristos—the Blood of Christ Mountains—the magnificent southernmost peaks of the Rockies, which rose more than twelve thousand feet over the prickered plain. Set on the eastern periphery of Spanish settlement, the village was a spore-speck of civilization. Las Vegas was a three-day ride from the capital of the territory, Santa Fe. Its only tie to the larger world was the Santa Fe Trail, which passed along the outskirts of town—the same road the American army would be marching in on. To the east, the prairie seemed to stretch out forever, to the Staked Plains of Texas and the buffalo grasslands beyond—and eventually, if one kept on going, to the land of the American *diablos*.

Hunters from Las Vegas, the *ciboleros,* rode out on the plains in search of antelope and buffalo. Often the villagers made trips to Santa

Fe to buy supplies or confer with the military and religious authorities there. But mostly the people kept to their homes, and to the pageants of their church. Impoverished in every way except faith, they were pioneers, resolute in their battles with nature yet accepting of what they could not control. Although Las Vegas was a new settlement, founded by a land grant only eleven years earlier, most of the frontier families living here were descended from Spanish colonists who had arrived in New Mexico as early as 1598.

The people of New Mexico, especially in rural outposts like Las Vegas, led a defensive, medieval sort of existence, clinging to Catholic folkways ossified by isolation. They labored in the safety of their coyote fences and mud walls, raising peppers and corn, beans, and squash, and tending sheep as their forefathers had in the shadows of the ancient mountains.

August was always a pleasant month in this part of New Mexico. The nights were cool, the mornings golden. Days were hot and dry, the sleepy afternoons frequently doused by thunderstorms that rumbled in from the west. Gardens swelled with vegetables. Flocks grew fat on the grass that greened in the foothills from the new moisture of the monsoonal rains. By all outward appearances, Las Vegas seemed as it always did in this favored season, and yet the people knew that when the Americans arrived, their world would change utterly.

Early on the morning of August 12 the fitful quiet of Las Vegas was punctured by the sound of hoofbeats. By the time the villagers heard the sound and discerned its menace, it was already too late: The invaders had cut across their fields and penetrated the town margins. To the people's surprise, however, these weren't the anticipated American invaders. This was an attack just as dreadful but much more familiar: *Navajos*.

The raiders came boiling out of the mountains, painted for battle. At the last moment they let out a blood-chilling war-whoop that sounded to the villagers something like an owl—*ahuuuuu, ahuuuuuu*. The Navajo warriors rode bareback or on saddles made of sheepskin, and guided their mounts with reins of braided horsehair. They wielded clubs and carried shields made of buckskin layers taken from a deer's hip, where the hide is thickest. They had images of serpents painted on the soles of their moccasins to give them a snakelike sneakiness as they approached their quarry. Their steel-tipped arrowheads were daubed with rattlesnake blood and prickly pear pulp mixed with charcoal taken from a tree that had been struck by lightning. Many of them wore strange, tight-fitting helmets made from the skinned heads of mountain lions.

Before anyone could take up a musket in defense, the Navajos had driven off sheep and goats by the hundreds if not thousands, stolen horses, and killed one adolescent shepherd while kidnapping another.

Then, as fast as they came, the reivers vanished. In the faint light, they drove their herds on networks of tiny trails that spilled into wider trails, and finally into dusty thoroughfares that were permanently worn down by the hooves of driven stock—great trampled highways of theft winding toward the Navajo country far to the west.

BOOK ONE

The New Men

My needle always settles between west and southwest.
The future lies that way to me, and the earth seems
more unexhausted and richer on that side.

—HENRY DAVID THOREAU

Chapter 1 JUMPING OFF

In the two decades he had lived and wandered in the West, Christopher Carson had led an unaccountably full life. He was only thirty-six years old, but it seemed he had done everything there was to do in the Western wilds—had been everywhere, met everyone. As a fur trapper, scout, and explorer, he had traveled untold thousands of miles in the Rockies, in the Great Basin, in the Sierra Nevada, in the Wind River Range, in the Tetons, in the coastal ranges of Oregon. As a hunter he had crisscrossed the Great Plains any number of times following the buffalo herds. He had seen the Pacific, been deep into Mexico, pushed far into British-held territories of the Northwest. He had traversed the Sonoran, Chihuahuan, and Mojave Deserts, gazed upon the Grand Canyon, stood at the life-leached margins of the Great Salt Lake. He had never seen the Hudson or the Potomac, but he had traced all the important rivers of the West—the Colorado, Platte, Sacramento, San Joaquin, Columbia, Green, Arkansas, Gila, Missouri, Powder, Big Horn, Snake, Salmon, Yellowstone, Rio Grande.

Carson was present at the creation, it seemed. He had witnessed the dawn of the American West in all its vividness and brutality. In his constant travels he had caromed off of or intersected with nearly every major tribal group and person of consequence. He had lived the sweep of the Western experience with a directness few other men could rival.

At first glance, Kit Carson was not much to look at, but that was a curious part of his charm. His bantam physique and modest bumpkin demeanor seemed interestingly at odds with the grandeur of the landscapes he had roamed. He stood only five-feet four-inches, with stringy brown hair grazing his shoulders. His jaw was clenched and squarish, his eyes a penetrating gray-blue, his mouth set in a tight little downturned construction that looked like a frown of mild disgust. The skin between his eyebrows was pinched in a furrow, as though permanently creased from constant squinting. His forehead rose high and craggy to a swept-back hairline. He had a scar along his left ear, another one on his right shoulder—both left by bullets. He appeared bowlegged from his years in the saddle, and he walked roundly, with a certain ungainliness, as though he were not entirely comfortable as a terrestrial creature, his sense of ease and familiarity of movement tied to his mule.

He was a man of odd habits and superstitions. He never would take a second shot at standing game if his initial shot missed—this, he believed, was "bad medicine." He never began a project on a Friday. He was fastidious about the way he dressed and cleaned any animal he killed. He believed in signs and omens. When he got a bad feeling about something or someone, he was quick to heed his instincts. A life of hard experience on the trail had taught him to be cautious at all times, tuned to danger. A magazine writer who rode with Carson observed with great curiosity the scout's unfailing ritual as he prepared to bed down for the night: "His saddle, which he always used as a pillow, form[ed] a barricade for his head; his pistols half cocked were laid above it, and his trusty rifle reposed beneath the blanket by his side, ready for instant use. You never caught Kit exposing himself to the full glare of the camp fire." When traveling, the writer noticed, Carson "scarcely spoke," and his eye "was continually examining the country, his manner that of a man deeply impressed with a sense of responsibility."

When he did speak, Carson talked in the twangy cadences of backwoods Missouri—*thar* and *har, ain't* and *yonder, thataway* and *crick* and *I reckon so.* It seemed right that this ultimate Westerner should be from Missouri, the Ur-country of the trans-Mississippi frontier, the mother state.

Out west, Carson had learned to speak Spanish and French fluently, and he knew healthy smatterings of Navajo, Ute, Comanche, Cheyenne, Arapaho, Crow, Blackfoot, Shoshone, and Paiute, among other native tongues. He also knew Indian sign language and, one way or another, could communicate with most any tribe in the West. And yet for all his facility with language, Kit Carson was illiterate. Although he was a mountain man, a fraternity legendary for swilling and creative profanity, Carson was a straight arrow—"as clean as a hound's tooth" as one friend put it. He liked poker and often smoked a pipe, but he drank very little and was not given to womanizing. He was now married to a Hispanic girl from Taos, Josefa Jaramillo. Slender, olive-skinned, and eighteen years his junior, Josefa possessed "a beauty of the haughty, heart-breaking kind" according to one smitten writer from Ohio who got to know her, "a beauty such as would lead a man with the glance of the eye to risk his life for one smile." Only fifteen years old when she married Carson, Josefa was a bit taller than her husband. She was a dark-complected, bright-eyed woman whom one family member described as "very well-built, and graceful in every way." Cristóbal, as Josefa called him, was utterly devoted to her, and to please her family, he had converted to Catholicism.

Especially now that he was a married man, Carson gave off none of the mountain man's swagger. "There was nothing like the fire-eater in his manner," wrote one admirer, "but, to the contrary, in all his actions he was unassuming." An army officer once introduced himself to Carson, saying, "So this is the distinguished Kit Carson who has made so many Indians run." To which Carson replied, "Yes, but most of the time they were running after me." His sense of humor was understated and dry, usually delivered with a faint grin and a glint of mischief in his eyes. When amused, he was prone to "sharp little barks of laughter." He spoke quietly, in short, deliberate sentences, using language that was, according to one account, "forcible, slow, and pointed, with the fewest words possible." A friend said Carson "never swore more'n was necessary."

Yes, Christopher Carson was a lovable man. Nearly everyone said so. He was loyal, honest, and kind. In many pinpointable incidents, he acted bravely and with much physical grace. More than once, he saved people's lives without seeking recognition or pay. He was a dashing good Samaritan—a hero, even.

He was also a natural born killer. It is hard to reconcile the much-described sweetness of his disposition with his frenzies of violence. Carson could be brutal even for the West of his day (a West so wild it lacked outlaws, for no law yet existed to be outside *of*). His ferocious temper could be triggered in an instant. If you crossed him, he would find you. He pursued vengeance as though it were something sacred, with a kind of dogged focus that might be called tribal—his tribe being the famously grudge-happy Scotch-Irish.

When called upon to narrate his exploits, which he did reluctantly, he spoke with a clinical lack of emotion, and with a hit man's sense of aesthetics. He liked to call his skirmishes *pretty*—as in "that was the prettiest fight I ever saw." He spoke of chasing down his enemies as "sport." After participating in a preemptive attack—others called it a massacre—on an Indian village along California's Sacramento River, Carson pronounced the action "a perfect butchery."

By the macabre distinctions of his day, he was regarded not as an Indian killer but as an *Indian-fighter*—which was, if not a noble American profession, at least a venerable one. But Carson did not hate Indians, certainly not in any sort of abstract racial sense. He was no Custer, no Sheridan, no Andrew Jackson. If he had killed Native Americans, he had also befriended them, loved them, buried them, even married them. Through much of his life, he lived more like an Indian than a white man. Most of his Indian victims had died in what he judged to be fair fights, or at least fights that could have gone the other way. It was miraculous he was still alive: He'd had more close calls than he could count.

Because Carson's direct words were rarely written, it's hard to know what he really thought about Indians, or the violence of his times, or anything else. His autobiography, dictated in the mid-1850s (and turned into a biography by a tin-eared writer who has charitably been described as an "ass"), is a bone-dry recitation of his life and leaves us few clues. It was said that Carson told a pretty good story around a campfire, but his book carefully eschews anything approaching an insight. His refusal to pontificate was refreshing in a way—he lived in a golden age of windbags—but at the same time, his reticence in the face of the few big subjects of his life was remarkable. He was, and remains, a sort of Sphinx of the American West: His eyes had seen things, his mind held secrets, but he kept his mouth shut.

∞

Christopher Houston Carson was born in a log cabin in Madison County, Kentucky, on Christmas Eve of 1809, the same year and the same state in which Lincoln was born. A year later the Carson family pulled up stakes and trekked west from Kentucky to the Missouri frontier, with little Christopher, whom they nicknamed "Kit," facing forward in the saddle, swaddled in his mother's arms. The Carsons chose a spot in the wilderness near the Missouri River and hacked their farm from a large tract that had been part of a Spanish land grant bought by the sons of Daniel Boone, prior to the Louisiana Purchase. It was known indelicately as "Boone's Lick," for the salt deposits that attracted wild game and which the Boone family successfully mined. The Boones and the Carsons would become close family friends—working, socializing, and intermarrying with one another.

Kit was a quiet, stubborn, reliable kid with bright blue eyes. Although he had a small frame—a consequence, perhaps, of his having been born two months premature—he was tough and strong, with large, agile hands. His first toy was a wooden gun whittled by one of his brothers. Kit showed enough intellectual promise at an early age that his father, Lindsey Carson, dreamed he would be a lawyer.

Lindsey Carson was a farmer of Scotch-Irish Presbyterian stock who had lived most of his young life in North Carolina and fought in the Revolutionary War under Gen. Wade Hampton. The elder Carson had an enormous family—five children by his first wife and ten by Kit's mother, Rebecca Robinson. Of those fifteen children, Kit was the eleventh in line.

The Boone's Lick country, though uncultivated, was by no means uninhabited. Winnebago, Potawatomi, and Kickapoo Indians, among other tribes, had lived around the Missouri River Valley for many generations, and they were often aggressively hostile to white encroachment. For their own safety the pioneers in the Boone's Lick country had to live huddled together in cabins built near forts, and the men tended the fields with armed sentries constantly patrolling the forest clearings. All able-bodied men were members of the local militia. Most cabins were designed with rifle loopholes so settlers, barricaded within, could defend themselves against Indian attacks. Kit and his siblings grew up with a constant fear of being kidnapped. "When we would go to school or any distance away from our house," Kit's sister Mary Carson Rubey recalled years later, "we would carry bits of red cloth with us to drop if we were captured by Indians, so our people could trace us." Rubey remembered that, even as a little boy, Kit was an especially keen night watchman. "When we were asleep at night and there was the slightest noise outside the house, Kit's little brown head would be the first to bob up. I always felt completely safe when Kit was on guard duty."

One day when Kit was four, Lindsey Carson went out with a small group of men to survey a piece of land when they were ambushed by Sac and Fox Indians. In the attack, Kit's father was nearly killed. The stock of his rifle was shot apart and two fingers on his left hand were blown off. Another man in the party, William McLane, fell in the fight and, according to one vivid account, his Indian attackers cut out his heart and ate it.

Despite many incidents like this, some Missouri tribes were friendly with the settlers, or at least found it pragmatic to strike alliances and keep the peace. As a boy, Carson played with Indian children. The Sac and Fox tribes frequently came into the Boone's Lick settlements and carried on a robust trade. From an early age, Carson learned an important practical truth of frontier life—that there was no such thing as "Indians," that tribes could be substantially and sometimes violently different from one another, and that each group must be dealt with separately, on its own terms.

☒

Before settlers like the Boones and the Carsons arrived, the country along the Missouri River, like so much of North America, was heavily forested. To clear land for planting, pioneers would sometimes "girdle" trees—cutting deep rings around the trunks—to deaden them. But the most expeditious way for farmers to remove dense thickets of timber was to set them afire. One day in 1818, Lindsey Carson was burning the woods nearby when a large limb broke off from a burning tree, killing him instantly.

Kit was only eight at the time, and his life would be profoundly changed. Although some of Lindsey Carson's children had grown up and moved out of the house, Rebecca Carson still had ten children to raise on her own. The Carsons were reduced to a desperate poverty. Kit's schooling ceased altogether, and he spent his time working the fields, doing chores around the cabin, and hunting meat for his family. As Carson put it years later, "I jumped to my rifle and threw down my spelling book—and there it lies."

Briefly, Kit became a ward of a neighbor. Then in 1822, Kit's mother remarried, and the obstreperous boy soon rebelled against his new stepfather. At age fourteen, Kit was apprenticed to a well-known saddler named David Workman in the small settlement of Franklin, Missouri. The boy hated this close and tedious shopwork. For nearly two years he sat at his bench each day, repairing harnesses and shaping scraps of hide with leatherworking tools. Because Franklin was situated on the eastern end of the newly cleared Santa Fe Trail, Workman's clientele largely consisted of trappers and traders, and the shop was often filled with stirring tales from the Far West. This bedraggled tribe of men in their musky animal skins and peltries must have impressed the young boy mightily, and one senses how the worm of his imagination began to turn. Sitting miserably at his station with his shears and his awls and his crimping tools, transfixed by the bold stories of these feral men, Kit began to dream of Santa Fe—the name signifying not so much a specific place as a new kind of existence, a life of expanse and possibility in fresh precincts of the continent.

The Santa Fe Trail had opened only two years earlier, and for young Missourians with any spark of ambition or wanderlust, the burgeoning commerce of the prairies had become a compelling romance. Out west, new fortunes beckoned. For generations, Spain had forbidden all U.S. trade with Santa Fe, and American travelers caught in New Mexico were routinely arrested and treated as hostile spies. But when Mexico won independence in 1821, the new officials in Mexico City were eager for American goods—and the tariffs that could be levied against them. A veil had been lifted; suddenly Americans were welcome. Soon the long road between the ancient capital and the westernmost settlements was creased with traffic. A new term came into vogue for those leaving the settlements for Santa Fe, a term that conveyed the excitement of piercing the unknown: Upon departing the familiar world of Missouri, travelers were said to be "jumping off."

Enchanted by the stories he kept hearing and "anxious to see different countries," Kit resolved to break the contract of his apprenticeship. Although he considered his employer "a good man," Carson found the work suffocating. "The business did not suit me," he said in loud understatement, "and I concluded to leave him." Carson realized that if he stayed with Workman, "I would have to pass my life in labor that was distasteful to me."

⊠

In August of 1826, at the age of sixteen, Carson secretly signed on as a laborer with a large merchant caravan heading west to Santa Fe. "Well, what do you have to say for yourself?" the caravan leader asked Carson when he applied for a job.

"Nothing," Carson replied, "except I can shoot straight."

He was given a slot as a "cavvy boy," the lowliest job on a caravan. The cavvy boy was a hired hand charged with caring for the *caballada*, the herd of spare horses, mules, and oxen that was always brought along to replace those that wore out or died on the long journey. It was menial cowboy work—herding, feeding, and reprimanding the animals—but he loved it. He was grateful to find himself sitting in saddles every day instead of making them.

And so Carson jumped off. As the boy made his way west, David Workman, his employer back in Franklin, posted a notice in the *Missouri Intelligencer,* the local paper, announcing his apprentice's flight. It was the first occasion that Kit Carson's name would ever appear in print—

> Notice is hereby given to all persons that CHRISTOPHER CAR-SON, a boy about 16 years old, small of his age, but thick set; light hair, ran away from the subscriber, living in Franklin, Howard County, Missouri, to whom he had been bound to learn the saddler's trade, on or about the first of September last. He is supposed to have made his way towards the upper part of the state. All persons are notified not to harbor, support, or assist said boy under the penalty of the law. One cent reward will be given to any person who will bring back the boy.

Workman was required by law to report his apprentice's truancy. Reading between the lines, however, it is clear that the saddler was less than zealous in his efforts to secure Carson's return and that, in fact, he may have been aiding the getaway. Workman's advertisement did not appear until a full month after Carson fled. By waiting so long, by providing a false clue as to which direction Carson was headed, and by offering such a conspicuously slim reward, one senses that Workman was smiling on Carson's decision to light out for the West and perhaps wishing him godspeed.

In his autobiography, Carson recalled only one incident from his first trek across the plains. One day as the caravan worked its way along the great bend of the Arkansas River, in present-day southwestern Kansas, a traveler in the party named Andrew Broadus had an accident. The wagon train had passed into buffalo country, which was rife with wolf packs that preyed on the migrating herds. Spotting a wolf in the distance and presumably fearing that it would attack the caravan stock, Broadus reached for his rifle from his wagon. The gun prematurely discharged, and he shot himself point-blank in the right arm.

In a few days the wound became infected and then gangrene set in. No doctors were traveling in the caravan, but it was obvious to everyone that Broadus's arm would have to be amputated if he hoped to live. He was in utter agony now, his pitiful cries going out with each jounce and rattle of his wagon. Still, Broadus would not let the others perform the inevitable, and several more precious days passed, with the line of putrefaction steadily creeping up his arm.

Finally, the party could not take the screaming anymore. They held Broadus down and one of the men sliced through the dead flesh with a razor. Another man then went to work on the arm bone with an old saw while a third cauterized the severed arteries by applying a piping hot king bolt that had been removed from one of the wagons and heated in the fire. As Broadus shrieked, Kit watched in wide-eyed amazement and tried to help out however he could— according to one probably specious account, he volunteered to wield the scalpel and actually made the first cut. Certainly the ordeal gave the sixteen-year-old boy a vivid idea of the sorts of crude and creative expedients to which men on the prairie were often compelled to resort.

At last the operation was complete and Broadus's cries subsided. The men applied a protective plaster to his stump composed of tar taken from a wagon axle. Given the atrocious hygiene common on the caravans, most of the party did not expect Broadus to survive, but the wound soon healed without infection. As Carson put it, Andrew Broadus was "perfectly well" by the time the caravan crossed into New Mexico.

⊠

As fascinated as he was by life on the Santa Fe Trail, Kit Carson did not apparently think much of its namesake city. The caravan groaned into the old capital and created a stir among its bored denizens, but Kit did not linger long in Santa Fe. In his autobiography, Carson scarcely even mentioned the place. As soon as he could, he made his way up to Taos, the mountain village of whitewashed adobe houses some seventy miles north of the capital, and found the rough-and-ready life there much more to his liking. Taos would be his home, sentimentally if not in fact, for the rest of his life.

Spread on the sage plains at the feet of a particularly stunning stretch of the serrated Sangre de Cristo Mountains, Don Fernando de Taos was a cluttered old Spanish settlement of a few thousand souls built close to an even older settlement of Pueblo Indians, who continued to live as they had for centuries in a mud citadel of terraced apartment buildings stacked seven stories high. The town took its name from the thick chokes of willows that lined the stream flowing through the pueblo—*taos* means "people of the red willows" in the Tiwa language. A few miles west of the village, the Rio Grande had cut a deep gorge into the earth, with the cold whitewater spilling through a chasm six hundred feet below the canyon rim.

Taos was also the capital of the Southwestern fur trade. Freetrappers and mountain men associated with various outfits—Hudson's Bay, the American Fur Company, the Rocky Mountain Fur Company—spent their winters in Taos. Here they mended their traps and often blew their summer earnings in sprees of dancing, gambling, lovemaking, and booze. Their poison of choice was a local moonshine known as Taos Lightning, a wheat liquor that had become a form of frontier currency among trappers, Mexicans, and Indians alike. The trappers were a spirited enclave in this remote provincial outpost. The locals resented and at the same time envied these uncouth foreigners who, with their boisterous wanderings and their easy squaw arrangements, lived apart from the stark morality of the padres.

Kit was drawn to the strange fraternity of the mountain men. He was entranced by their freedom, their ready competence, their otherworldly air, and he vowed to become one himself as soon as they would have him. That first winter he was taken in by a trapper and explorer named Mathew Kinkead, who had been an old friend of his father's back in Missouri. From this seasoned frontiersman, Carson absorbed the elements of mountain living. Staying in Kinkead's cabin through the snowy months, sitting before the fire in the gray tang of piñon smoke, Kit began to practice Spanish and several Indian dialects. He learned how to sew his own buckskin clothing, and how to make a good tight bed of cornhusks draped in a buffalo robe. Ventur-

ing on his first bison hunt, he learned how to jerk the meat and turn
it into a fine pemmican, and how to enjoy the Plains Indian delicacy
of the still-hot liver, sliced fresh from the pulsing animal and seasoned
with bile squirted from its gallbladder.

In 1828, after making a caravan journey to El Paso and working
long stretches of the Santa Fe Trail, Kit signed on as a cook for another mountain man named Ewing Young, who had opened a store
in Taos to outfit trapper expeditions. The eighteen-year-old kid apparently was a competent chef, but then these greasy wayfarers, accustomed as they were to such odd field entrées as cougar, dog, mule,
bear, and prairie oysters, were decidedly unpicky eaters known for
their blasé culinary motto, "Meat's meat." (It was said that the trappers' diet was so full of lard that it made a mountain man "shed rain
like an otter, and stand cold like a polar bear.")

By the spring of 1828, Kit had become proficient enough in Spanish to sign on as a translator for a merchant caravan that was bound
for Chihuahua City, a thousand-mile journey round-trip along the
Camino Real. The ancient capital, with its ornate cathedral, its beautiful stone aqueduct, and its stately colonial architecture hewn from
the brutal wealth of Chihuahua's silver mines, was the largest and
most dazzling city Carson had ever visited, and throughout his wildly
peripatetic life, Chihuahua would remain the southernmost extent of
his travels.

Carson returned from his sojourn and took a job as a teamster in
the Santa Rita copper mines of southwestern New Mexico. Then, in
the spring of 1829, Ewing Young asked him to accompany a party of
some forty Taos fur men on a journey deep into unexplored Apache
country to trap the tributaries of the Gila River. Carson had at last received his wish: Although still a greenhorn, he was embarking on his
first full-fledged expedition as a trapper, an occupation that would
hold his interest for the next dozen years.

It was an insanely difficult way to make a living, but, for Carson,
that was no deterrent. A congressional survey of the trapping profession, completed in 1831, described the mountain man existence this
way: "The whole operation is full of exposures and privations . . .

leading to premature exhaustion and disability. Few of those engaged in it reach an advanced stage of life. The labor is excessive, subsistence scanty, and the Indians are ever liable to sudden and violent paroxysms of passion, in which they spare neither friend nor foe."

Although Carson probably did not know it, trapping was already a storied profession in the East. The mountain men became popular avatars of a wild and free life that was romanticized by such writers as Washington Irving and James Fenimore Cooper. The fur trade would produce many legendary names, men like Jim Bridger and Jedediah Smith. But through a peculiar confluence of events, Kit Carson would become the most famous mountain man of them all.

᷂

Carson's first paid voyage into the mountains was an especially ambitious and dangerous one, for in addition to the usual hardships— grizzlies, Indians, hypothermia, the prospect of a killing thirst or starvation—this mission was strictly illegal. Most trapping excursions ventured north into the unclaimed wilderness of the Rocky Mountains, but this time Young planned to trap within the jealously held, if extremely porous, borders of Mexico. The government in Santa Fe rarely issued trapping permits to foreigners, so in order to confuse suspicious officials, Ewing led his party north into the mountains, then doubled back and rode southwest through the country of the Navajo and the Zuni before striking the Gila River. The Gila watershed had scarcely been trapped, and Young's men found it incredibly rich in beaver and other game.

From Young and his international ragtag of mountain men, Carson began to soak up the nuances of the trapping trade—how to read the country and follow its most promising drainages, how to find the "slicks" along the banks where beavers had slithered from their tree stands, how to set and scent the traps with a thick yellow oil called castoreum taken from the beaver's sex glands, how to prepare and pack the pelts, how to cache them safely in the ground to prevent theft and spoilage. And when the traps came up empty, how to invade and dismantle a dam and club the unsuspecting animals in their dark, wet den.

From his new comrades, Carson learned to savor beaver tail boiled to an exquisite tenderness—the trapper's signature dish. He became expert with a Hawken rifle and a Green River skinning knife. He began to pick up the strange language of the mountain men, a colorful patois of French, Spanish, English, and Indian phrases mixed with phrases entirely of their own creation. "Wagh!" was their all-purpose interjection. They spoke of plews (pelts) and fofurraw (any unnecessary finery). They "counted coup" (revenge exacted on an avowed enemy), and when one of their own was killed, they were "out for hair" (scalps). They said odd things like "Which way does your stick float?" (What's your preference?) They met once a year in giant, extended open-air festivals, the "rendezvous," where they danced fandangos and played intense rounds of monte, euchre, and seven-up. Late at night, sitting around the campfires, sucking their black clay pipes, they competed in telling legendary whoppers about their far-flung travels in the West—stories like the one about the mountain valley in Wyoming that was so big it took an echo eight hours to return, so that a man bedding down for the night could confidently shout "Git up!" and know that he would rise in the morning to his own wake-up call.

From these men, too, Carson began to learn how to deal with the Western Indians—how to detect an ambush, when to fight, when to bluff, when to flee, when to negotiate. It is doubtful whether any group of nineteenth-century Americans ever had such a broad and intimate association with the continent's natives. The mountain men lived with Indians, fought alongside and against them, loved them, married them, buried them, gambled and smoked with them. They learned to dress, wear their hair, and eat like them. They took Indian names. They had half-breed children. They lived in tepees and pulled the travois and became expert in the ways of Indian barter and ancient herbal remedy. Many of them were half-Indian themselves, by blood or inclination. Washington Irving, writing about Western trappers, noted this tendency: "It is a matter of vanity and ambition with them to discard everything that may bear the stamp of civilized life, and to adopt the manners, gestures, and even the walk of the Indian.

You cannot pay a freetrapper a greater compliment than to persuade him you have mistaken him for an Indian brave."

The fur trappers knew firsthand that Native Americans were ferocious fighters—some legendarily so, like the Blackfoot and the Comanche. But they also knew that the Indian style of battle was often very different from European warfare, that it was difficult to engage Native Americans in a pitched battle, that their method was consistently one of raid and ambush, attack and scatter, snipe and vanish. The mountain men said that Indians were often like wolves: Run, and they follow; follow, and they run.

The trappers murdered Indians in countless kill-or-be-killed scenarios, and some made a practice of hammering brass tacks into the stocks of their rifles for every native dispatched. But their greater slaughter was unwitting: As the forerunners of Western civilization, creeping up the river valleys and across the mountain passes, the trappers brought smallpox and typhoid, they brought guns and whiskey and venereal disease, they brought the puzzlement of money and the gleam of steel. And on their liquored breath they whispered the coming of an unimaginable force, of a gathering shadow on the eastern horizon, gorging itself on the continent as it pressed steadily this way.

That spring Carson and Ewing Young's party worked along the Gila tributaries, moving into increasingly strange country that had never been mapped. One day Young's camp on the Salt River was approached by Apaches. Sensing hostility, most of Young's men concealed themselves beneath packsaddles and blankets, emboldening the Apaches to swoop down on what they thought was an easy target. Soon "the hills were covered with Indians," as Carson recalled, but when the attackers drew within range, Ewing's men sprang from their hiding places and drew their beads. Aiming his rifle, Carson killed his first Indian, shooting him, as an early biographer put it, "straight through the nipple at which he had aimed—straight through the heart within."

He does not mention it in his autobiography, but according to one account, Carson then removed his sheath knife and pulled back the dead Apache's scalp, as was the common custom among the mountain men.

Carson was nineteen years old.

Chapter 2 THE GLITTERING WORLD

All across New Mexico, the threat of Navajo raiders gave life an undertow of anxiety. The settlers dwelled in a state of vigilance, always half-listening, scanning the sagebrush for movement. Everyone knew some family whose child or mother had been carried off. In the foothills, cairns often studded the pastures. Decorated with crosses or flowers, these markers memorialized shepherds who had been cut down. At a very young age, New Mexicans learned to hate and fear the word "Navajo."

Other tribes preyed upon the New Mexican settlements as well. The Utes in the north, the Kiowas and Comanches in the east, the Apaches in the south. But the Navajos were the strongest, richest, and most creatively adaptable of all the raiding tribes. They were the ancient scourge of an ancient province. As a result of Navajo attacks, the very first Spanish colonial capital of New Mexico, a promising settlement on the Rio Grande called San Gabriel, had been quickly abandoned in 1610 and relocated to the safer remove of present-day Santa Fe. The word "Navajo"—a word of Pueblo Indian origin meaning "people of the great planted fields"—first appeared in a Spanish document in 1626. (The Navajo called themselves "the Diné," which simply means "the people.") An account from the early 1600s by a Spanish friar referred to "the Nabaju" as "a very bellicose people . . . who occupy all frontiers and surround us completely."

In 1659, Fray Juan Ramirez referred to the Navajos as "heathens who kill Christians and carry off others alive to perish in cruel martyrdom." A half century later, Governor Francisco Cuervo y Valdez condemned the Navajos for "their crimes, their audacity, and their reckless depredations upon this kingdom."

The Spanish had tried for a time to Christianize the Navajos— literally chaining them to church pews, according to one account—but they would not tolerate Spanish missionaries. In 1672 a group of Navajos hauled a priest out the doors of his church, ripped off his clothes, then killed him at the base of an outdoor cross by smashing his head in with a bell. By 1750 the Spaniards had given up on all efforts to proselytize among these *indios barbaros*. In that year a priest dolefully noted that the Navajos "could not become Christians or stay in one place because they have been raised like deer."

For centuries the Spanish had mounted retaliatory expeditions into Navajo country, to reclaim stolen livestock as well as to capture women and children to serve as slaves, but these military forays did little to stop the raids. The Navajo lands were so wrinkled, so mazelike, and so huge that the expeditions were scarcely worth the exertion; conquering the Navajos seemed as hopeless as converting them. The Navajo country, noted one Spanish chronicler in the 1630s, "is vaster than all the others . . . In journeying westward through this nation, one never reaches the end of it."

The Navajos lived far away, yet paradoxically they seemed to be close at hand, as though the desert distances did not apply to them, as though miles alone could not check their peregrinations. It was the Navajo menace as much as anything else that made New Mexico so poor, so militarily anemic, and so unready to resist the coming American invasion. Manuel Armijo, the governor and general of New Mexico, said it best in an 1846 letter to his authorities in Mexico City. "The war with the Navajos," he said, "is slowly consuming the Department, reducing to very obvious misery the District of the Southwest."

◨

It was odd, in a way, that the Navajo posed such a threat, for collectively they did not have a reputation for being particularly fierce or effective warriors. They seldom fought in large numbers, and they lacked the highly developed warrior societies typical among many

Plains tribes. The Navajos avoided killing whenever possible, because theirs was a culture that had a deep-seated fear and revulsion of death. They wanted nothing to do with corpses or funerals or anything connected with mortality. When a person died inside a Navajo dwelling—the round, windowless, dome-roofed *hogan* made of mud and timber—the body had to be removed from the structure by bashing a hole in the north wall and pulling the corpse through it; then the hogan had to be destroyed. The taint could never be washed out. The presence of death led to witchcraft, it lured resentful ghosts and evil spirits, it upset the fragile order of things. The Navajos did not have a concept of the devil in any sort of Judeo-Christian sense. There was no single evil spirit permeating the world and counterpoised against good. But the ghosts of the dead were devilish enough. They were vexing and malicious and unimaginably frightening—and they were everywhere. They could even invade a person's dreams.

The Navajos believed in a class of witches called "skinwalkers" who were said to put on wolf pelts and dig up graves. The skinwalkers could be seen prowling around at night on all fours—they had pallid white faces and red glowing eyes and chanted holy prayers backward to invoke evil deities. They desecrated graves and stole funerary trinkets and jewelry. They removed the dead person's flesh and ground it up to make a lethal poison called "corpse powder," which the skinwalkers blew into people's faces, giving them the "ghost sickness." Even a fingernail paring or a strand of hair from a dead person could be used by a skinwalker to perform diabolical things.

A people so unnerved by death could never be great warriors. Then, too, the Navajo social structure was even looser than that of most American Indian tribes. Their absence of any political authority, their lack of a capital or central gathering place, their fractured allegiance to some sixty individual clans and countless local outfits—such factors were not conducive to formulating military strategy on a large scale.

But the Navajos were perhaps the unparalleled masters of the raid. Small-scale warfare suited them. They were an evanescent people, proud thieves on horseback, adroit in the techniques of the swift attack and the quick disappearance. Usually the raids were carried out by young men thirsty for adventure and ambitious to accumulate new wealth. Often these exuberant young warriors rode off against the wishes of their fathers and uncles and the other older men of the tribe, who had already won their wealth and had lived long enough to understand that raids had far-reaching consequences.

Once on the warpath, the young men dismissed such talk and prepared themselves for battle. In the days before a raid, they sat in sweat lodges to cleanse themselves. They sang songs to Monster Slayer, the great war god of Navajo legend, chanting, "Our enemies shall die! The coyote and the crow and the wolves shall carry away every last morsel of their flesh!" They assembled stone clubs and fastened eagle feathers to their shields. They tattooed their bodies with menacing images. To make themselves symbolically invisible to the enemy, they sprinkled corn pollen over their shields. Then they pulled on their buckskin battle-armor and set off on horseback for the Spanish ranches to the east.

Navajo warriors could be quite skittish about their raids, and they sometimes sought the wisdom of hand-tremblers to divine the outcome of a contemplated attack. Other times they visited a stargazer, who would consult the heavens for answers by rubbing under his eyelids a preparation whose recipe included filmy water that had been painstakingly collected from the eyes of an eagle. The wives of warriors were under strict instructions not to leave their hogans until the men had returned, hopefully successful, from their martial adventures abroad—for if the women did stray from their homes, for whatever reason, it was widely believed that their husbands would encounter bad luck. If a coyote crossed their path, the warriors had to turn back. If they stepped on a bear track, if they saw a snake shedding its skin, if they accidentally ate during an eclipse, if they found to their dismay that one of their party was wearing his blanket with the stripes crossways—then the endeavor could be doomed. But if all went well, they reached their target and waited in the early-morning stillness. Just before dawn they descended, sending up the bloodcurdling cry. Within a few minutes they would take horses, cattle, women, children—anything they could drive off or scoop up in their dusty stampede.

Sometimes the purpose of the raid was to steal back a Navajo captive who had been taken by the New Mexicans. Liberating a Navajo slave was always cause for rejoicing—although often the captive, who perhaps had been sold into slavery as a young child and become acclimated to Spanish culture, might be terrified by the attacking horsemen and fearful of returning to a tribal life that existed only as a dim memory.

Mainly, though, the Navajo raiders were interested in obtaining sheep and goats. The Navajo, almost alone among American Indians of the West, were primarily a pastoral people—shepherds, shearers, eaters of mutton, drinkers of goat's milk, master spinners of wool. Navajos followed the slow and watchful life known among anthropologists as *transhumance*, a methodical seminomadism built around the seasonal moving of flocks to higher and lower ground in search of grass. This way of life was, in fact, an ancient and widespread practice throughout the world but nearly unheard of in North America. As pastoralists, the Navajo lifestyle was in some sense more akin to that of ancient Greeks, Hebrews, and Arabs than to contemporary tribes of Native Americans.

The famous loomed wool blankets of the Navajos were among the finest in the world, patterned in bold, crisp geometric designs of red and black, and so tightly woven, it was often said, that they could hold water. (On the Santa Fe Trail, one Navajo blanket was worth ten buffalo robes.)

For the Navajos, everything revolved around the sheep. They talked directly to their flocks, gave them pollen to eat, and sang quaint songs to them on cold winter nights to protect them from freezing. "The sheep is your mother," the Navajos told their children, "the sheep is life." Most of their implements and artifacts were made from the hides, bones, and sinews of sheep and goats. Navajos slept on sheepskins. They made their carrying sacks from wool blankets sewn together with soapweed stalks. They ate every part of the animal—lung and liver, head and heart—even the blood, which they boiled and mixed with corn mush to make a thin, pinkish gruel. A special Navajo delicacy was sheep intestines tightly wound around a string of fat and roasted directly on the coals.

When the Spaniards arrived in the 1500s, the Navajos found that the tough and surefooted *churro* sheep which the conquistadors brought with them was perfectly suited to their harsh rock world. Originally adapted for the spare environment of upland Iberia, the spindly-legged *churro* could eat nearly anything and travel long distances and climb steep cliffs. The *churro*'s wool was tight and coarse, and because it contained little natural oil—other breeds of sheep grew hair often greasy with lanolin—it could be spun without needing washing.

The horse, which also came with the arrival of the Spanish, profoundly changed Navajo life as well. Perhaps most significantly, horses gave the Navajos the speed and mobility to become sheep robbers on a large scale, thinning the flocks of the long and vulnerable Rio Grande Valley with impunity. The horse thus accelerated their pastoral culture. Less than a century after the arrival of the Spanish, the sheep had become the Navajo currency, their mark of status, their food and clothing and livelihood, and the centerpiece of their bedouin life—a form of movable wealth.

But the Navajos were far more than raiders of flocks; they also grew crops, tended orchards, carried on a vigorous trade, staged elaborate rituals, and composed epic stories and songs of a fastidious tonal complexity. The Navajos had a hand in everything, it seemed. They were horse people, cattle people, farmers, hunters, gatherers, weavers. They even occasionally ventured out onto the prairie to hunt bison, like the Plains Indians. They were clear-eyed pragmatists and far-out mystics. They were not sedentary, like the Pueblos, but neither were they strictly nomadic, like the Utes. They were the great in-betweeners, hard to pin down, semiwanderers rooted to their land but moving widely over it from season to season to make the best use of a stark desert topography.

The Navajos, with their linguistic cousins, the Apaches, had ventured down the spine of the Rockies from the bitterness of Athapaska, in what is now northern Canada and Alaska. It's tempting to imagine that they simply held a council in some godforsaken snow-drift beneath the northern lights and decided, once and for all, that they'd had enough of the cold. But in fact, their southward migration does not appear to have been a determined exodus; rather, it was undertaken slowly, in many haphazard and circuitous waves. The Athapaskans began flooding into the Southwest sometime around A.D. 1300. Late arrivals to the region, the Navajos split off from the Apaches and then quickly evolved from a primitive culture of hunter-gatherers to perhaps the most supple and multifarious of all the Southwestern peoples. Over a few short centuries, the Navajos improvised a life that borrowed something from every culture they encountered, spinning it into a society that was entirely their own.

Their creation story, called the Emergence, is thought by some anthropologists to be an allegory for their long migration from Canada. Retold in nightchants and rituals performed during the winter months, the Emergence captures much that is unique about the Navajo—their sense of having been wandering exiles through most of their early history, perpetual outsiders expelled from one country after another, forced to complete a complicated series of journeys through strange dark lands until they finally lit on the "glittering world," as they called their present home; their tendency to view themselves as a tribe apart from others—a kind of chosen people of the Southwest, convinced of their special relationship to the gods and confident in the power of their rituals. And yet simultaneously, a tribe eager to absorb the ideas and implements of others, and to mingle with other peoples. If the Navajo indulged in a tribal pride that bordered on arrogance, it was an arrogance cut with an extraordinary impulse to accept other traditions, a natural ease for ushering in new ways and even new blood.

In a sense, the Navajo were the most "American" of the American Indians: They were immigrants, improvisationists, mongrels. They were mobile and restless, preferring to spread out as far as possible from one another over large swatches of country while still remaining within the boundaries of their land. They inhaled the essence of other cultures, taking what they liked and adapting it to their own ends.

And they were never finished. Navajos hated to complete anything—whether it was a basket, a blanket, a song, or a story. They never wanted their artifacts to be too perfect, or too closed-ended, for a definitive ending cramped the spirit of the creator and sapped the life from the art. So they left little gaps and imperfections, deliberate lacunae that kept things alive for another day. To them, comprehensiveness was tantamount to suffocation. Aesthetically and literally, Navajos always left themselves an out.

Even today, Navajo blankets often have a faint imperfection designed to let the creation breathe—a thin line that originates from the center and extends all the way to the edge, sometimes with a single thread dangling from its border; tellingly, the Navajos call this intentional flaw the "spirit outlet."

In their raids as well, they never completed their work. With an eye on the next season, Navajo warriors were careful not to take *all* the sheep from the Spanish settlements they attacked; they invariably left several ewes and rams behind, to insure that a fine new flock would be there to rob next year.

Chapter 3   THE ARMY OF THE WEST

The volunteers hailed from small towns and villages, places like Independence and Liberty and Excelsior Springs, and from many unnamed crossroads in the central Missouri Valley. They numbered more than sixteen hundred men in all, farm boys and preachers' sons and apprentices from the green hills and river bottoms. In a pique of patriotism, they left their gristmills and their blacksmith shops and their young wives. President Polk in Washington called for volunteers to fight against Mexico, and the men of Missouri resoundingly answered the call. With whatever weapons and horses they might possess, they sped to Fort Leavenworth, the frontier stronghold in far eastern Kansas that was then the remotest outpost of American military power.

Here, in May 1846, they mustered into regiments and camped in the grass not far from the banks of the Missouri River, where whistling steamboats churned the turbid waters, occasionally offloading passengers. Each morning soldiers from the U.S. Dragoons—the mounted infantrymen who were the precursors to the U.S. Cavalry—rode over and conducted martial exercises for the benefit of these volunteers, drilling them in close order, in saber and bayonet techniques, in marching and charging and marksmanship. The dragoons were commanded by a firm, regal man named Stephen Watts Kearny, then a colonel and soon to be a general, and a legendary figure on the Western plains. Kearny's soldiers began to winnow these fresh recruits, a task that at first appeared nearly hopeless. "The raw material is good enough," one lieutenant wrote, despairingly, "but then it is, in truth, *very raw.*" In a few short weeks, however, this ragtag was turned into a semirespectable column of soldiers, which, collectively, would be known as the Army of the West.

On the eve of their departure in June, hundreds of families of the volunteers gathered around Fort Leavenworth to say their good-byes, not knowing if they would ever see their sons and brothers and husbands again. Tearfully, the Missouri ladies presented the assembled companies with American flags to carry into battle, each banner painstakingly sewn by hand. Offering one such flag, a Mrs. Cunningham from Clay County addressed the crowd of volunteers. "We would rather hear of your falling in honorable warfare," she said, "than to see you return disgraced by cowardice." One by one, the leaders of the various companies rose to accept their flags, pledging that their men would not shirk their duty.

"Death before dishonor," one of them declared. "The love of country is the love of God."

Then, the next morning, the Army of the West began to march, the miles of men and animals kicking up plumes of dust along the rutted road. They moved on horseback and on foot in columns stretching across the plains, with yoked teams of oxen pulling Pittsburgh wagons filled with ammunition and salt provisions and hard-tack. Nearly fifteen thousand head of cattle and oxen started out from Fort Leavenworth. Trains of pack mules huffed along, too, burdened with the components of mountain howitzers and other pieces of artillery. With the morning sun at their backs, the Missourians marched under banners of E PLURIBUS UNUM.

Conestoga axles creaked under their loads as the barrels of molasses and bacon and meal rattled in the wagon beds. Drovers cracked their whips at the ox-teams, crying "Catch up! Catch up!" The trail smelled of lathered sweat and fresh excrement and urine, the sour musk of a living army. At the distant head of the column, the report of pistol fire was periodically heard, as the riders in the vanguard cleared the path of rattlesnakes, whose dens were then rife on the prairie.

Kearny's army followed the same grooved highway that Kit Carson had taken twenty years earlier: the Santa Fe Trail. The two-month journey would be arduous and kidney-punishing, but at least the route was sure. This long thread across the prairie, meant for commerce but now invested with military significance, was conveying an army intent on conquering huge sweeps of the West.

Not long out of Fort Leavenworth, the last cornfields and villages of American civilization fell away, and the country opened up. The men would not see another house or settlement for nearly eight hundred miles. They had entered the expanse often marked on maps as "The Great American Desert," a void on the western edge of the country that was thought to have no practical use other than as a preserve for Indians—tribes that had long lived on the prairie as well as those which, like the Cherokee, had been forcibly relocated from the East. In fact, the Great Plains was not considered fully part of the United States at all, properly speaking, but rather a perpetual wilderness, officially designated as the "The Permanent Indian Frontier."

As the men of Missouri marched into this lonely grassland, their sense of isolation deepened, for they had no means of communicating with the world they knew. Although telegraph wires had begun to link the larger cities along the eastern seaboard, no lines came anywhere near the prairie—nor trains, nor even express mail coaches with which to speed urgent messages back home. When a soldier took a fever and died, as happened often during the long march to New Mexico, he was buried in a shallow grave in the fine loess soil of the prairie, not far from the trail itself. The corpse was wrapped in a blanket, and then in an American flag, and as part of a frontier protocol of uncertain origins, the deceased man's saddled horse was brought to the graveside to honor him, with the man's boots dangling upside down in the stirrups. After a three-gun salute, soldiers tamped stones into the burial dirt to discourage wolves, but were careful not to pile them so high as to pique the interest of any wandering Plains Indians, who sometimes desecrated frontier graves.

As the Army of the West followed the trail, the country took on a strange and beautiful spareness. Grasshoppers snapped in the open expanses. Timber grew ever more scarce, until it played out altogether and the men were swallowed in a circumference of primeval grass—rosinweed, bull's-eye, redroot. Occasional slashes of sandbar willow greened along the meandering creeks, but otherwise the land was as featureless as the rolling ocean.

John T. Hughes, a young volunteer from Liberty, Missouri, and a schoolmaster, was moved by the spectacle of the Army of the West as it advanced upon the prairie. He observed that the "boundless plains, lying in ridges of wavy green, seemed to unite with the heavens in the distant horizon. As far as vision could penetrate, the long files of cavalry, the gay fluttering banners, and the canvas-covered wagons of the merchant train, might be seen winding over the undulating surface." But the romance soon wore off for Hughes. A week into the journey the march became "slow and tedious," he said. "The mules and other animals, being mostly unused to the harness, often became refractory and balky. The grass was tall and rank, and the earth in many places so soft that the heavily loaded wagons would sink up to the axle."

☒

Stephen Watts Kearny was the natural candidate to command the Army of the West. Cautious, pragmatic, a stickler for discipline, the fifty-two-year-old colonel (who would learn of his promotion to brigadier general while on the trail to New Mexico) was one of the finest and most intelligent officers in the American army. Kearny had three strenuous decades of experience on the Great Plains, exploring and policing the grassland solitudes that Thomas Jefferson had acquired from Napoleon in the Louisiana Purchase of 1803; Kearny understood the prairie's peculiar hardships, its bizarre weather and wildlife, and its overwhelming sense of isolation. By spurred horse or cordelled keelboat, Kearny had traveled many thousands of miles across the West, navigating the Missouri and the Yellowstone, the Arkansas and the Red. Along the way he'd built forts, completed maps, signed treaties, trained armies. He had served under legendary names of the frontier—among them Col. Henry Dodge and Col. Henry Leavenworth. Kearny was married to the former Mary Radford, stepdaughter of the great explorer William Clark.

Though an Easterner with certain patrician tastes, and a lover of fine wine, Kearny had embraced the rough ways of the frontier. He relished bear meat and badger and elk. He thought nothing of making thousand-mile tramps—the previous year, 1845, he had led an unbelievably brisk march from Fort Leavenworth to the South Pass of the Rocky Mountains and back, a twenty-two-hundred-mile trek that he was able to complete, without a single casualty, in ninety-nine days. He was perfectly content to hunker through the harsh winter at some godforsaken post on the periphery of the known world. He fondly remembered the winter of 1840, at Leavenworth, when the ink in his fountain pen froze solid while he was writing a letter, the thermometer reading 23 degrees below zero. On innumerable occasions he had smoked the pipe with Indians, learning their manner of speaking, their penchant for metaphor; he once flattered a Sioux chief by complimenting him on the "soaring eagle of your fame." During a council with Oglala Indians, he heartily partook of the local delicacies—boiled dog and blood-tinged river water from the paunch of a buffalo.

Kearny perceived, with a clarity rare among frontier soldiers of his generation, that alcohol was destroying the American Indian.

Everywhere he went on the prairies, in his summits with the Plains tribes, he made "firewater" one of his central themes. "You have many enemies about you but this is the greatest of them all," he once said in council with the Sioux. "Open your ears now and listen to me. Whenever you find it in your country, spill it all upon the ground. The earth may drink it without injury but you cannot."

Kearny's experience with Plains Indians was vast and yet, so rare in the brutal history of the West, his encounters were happily uneventful. Among the Plains tribes he was known as Shonga Kahega Mahetonga, Horse Chief of the Long Knives. He'd dealt with the Crows, the Blackfeet, the Chippewa, the Mandan, the Pawnee, the Winnebagos, the Potawatomi, the Sac and Fox, and scores of other tribes and moieties—almost always without bloodshed. Sometimes he fought against them, but more often he tried to referee the various Plains tribes in their time-honored wars against one another—or in their newer wars against the freshly arrived Cherokees, Chickasaws, and other so-called "civilized tribes" that the United States had force-marched from the East in the 1830s to live in the immense, if vaguely defined, Permanent Indian Frontier. Not surprisingly, the tragic U.S. policy of transplanting woodland Indians with an entirely alien culture and grafting them by fiat onto the unfamiliar world of the prairie had pried open a Pandora's box of tensions—tensions that Kearny spent the bulk of his years as a young officer trying to understand and, to the extent possible, resolve. As one historian succinctly put it, Kearny and his contemporaries in the frontier army were charged with the thankless task of "imposing a *Pax Americana* on the entire artificial, ill-amalgamated Indian nation which the government had created."

A diplomat by nature and an officer possessed of a Job-like patience, Kearny was the right man for this kind of work. His career was marked by persistence, discretion, and tolerance. There was about all his actions a distinct "absence of swashbuckling," as biographer Dwight Clarke phrased it. It was that quality, perhaps more than anything else, that kept his invasion of New Mexico in 1846 from devolving into a disaster.

Kearny was a small-statured man with a Roman nose and scrolls of graying hair sweeping back from a high squarish forehead. His discerning eyes, bulging slightly under fleshy hooded lids, seemed to look through his men and out toward a great beckoning future. In his no-nonsense army journals, he wrote precisely in a neat, unflorid hand. An army historian once called Kearny "the strictest disciplinarian in the service—bland in his manners, but of iron firmness." His orders, said one Missourian, "came like claps of thunder in a clear sky." Ulysses S. Grant, who as a young lieutenant served under Kearny in the early 1840s, thought him "one of the ablest officers of the day," a man able to keep discipline "at a high standard but without vexatious rules." Kearny was fond of issuing proclamations that were circulated among his officers and read aloud to his men almost like sermons. "An army," declared one, "is a mob of the worst kind unless properly governed & restrained. Soldiers are commissioned to perform high duties for the glory of our country & such duties can only be performed through rigid discipline."

His training sessions were legendary. During a marching exercise at Jefferson Barracks, near St. Louis, Kearny's horse lost its footing and pinned him to the parade ground, but Kearny, unfazed, continued to bark orders from beneath the horse until the drill was over. As an authority figure, Kearny could be witheringly stern. He once wrote his son Charles a letter imploring him to stick with his schoolwork. "If you do not study so that you can make a living by some profession," he warned, "you will be compelled to starve."

Kearny seemed to reserve his softer emotions for horses. He was, above all, an equestrian. He doted on his mounts and saw to it that they were always immaculately shod and curried. He loved to breed and race them. He abhorred the rough treatment of animals then prevalent in the army. Kearny was the commander of the U.S. Dragoons at Fort Leavenworth, the elite unit of mounted soldiers created in 1833 to police the Western borderlands (the name "dragoon" derived from the so-called "dragon" guns carried by a venerable French mounted outfit on which the dragoons were loosely based). Kearny had personally recruited and shaped this fabled precursor to the

United States Cavalry from its very inception. It is because of this that historians would later call Kearny "the father of the American cavalry." Not surprisingly, the largest part of Kearny's training concerned the care and handling of horses. In the first manual of the U.S. Dragoons, which Kearny wrote, he urged that each soldier always be "very careful to avoid alarming or disturbing his horse." A soft-spoken man by nature, Kearny advised the dragoon to speak to his mount in a low, even voice, almost a whisper.

The frontier was a long way from his roots. Stephen Kearny came from a well-to-do New Jersey family. His father was a successful wine merchant in Newark, and his mother descended from a prominent family of established Knickerbockers; her father, John Watts, was one of the founders of the New York Public Library and the first president of New York Hospital. Kearny studied the classics at Columbia for two years before hurriedly enlisting, in 1810, to fight in the looming war with Britain. His keen rush to join the army before graduating from Columbia may have reflected his desire to expunge the legacy of his father, who, as a British loyalist, had been imprisoned and then lived in humiliating exile during the Revolutionary War. The young Kearny burned to prove his patriotism against the same hated royals to which his father, a generation earlier, had so embarrassingly clung.

In one of the early battles of the War of 1812, at Queenston Heights on the Niagara River, Lieutenant Kearny distinguished himself for bravery during an action that involved clawing up the nearly vertical banks of the Niagara to take a British position on a high hill. In this stirring but ultimately ill-fated battle led by Major General Van Rensselaer, Kearny fought alongside another figure who would become famous during the war with Mexico, Winfield Scott. Years later, General Scott recalled how the young Kearny "gained the peak of the hill" at Queenston Heights and had "driven the enemy from the field," scattering the British and their allies, the Mohawks. It was, Scott said, "one of the most brilliant engagements of the war." The next day, however, Scott and Kearny, along with nine hundred other Americans, were captured by the British. The POWs were marched in disgrace to the old French Citadel in Quebec to serve what proved to be a brief captivity of four months.

One colorful story from Kearny's imprisonment has been passed down. At the Citadel, American officers were occasionally allowed to dine with British officers. During dinner one night, an intemperate Englishman proposed a toast to the president of the United States. "To Mr. Madison, dead or alive!" he shouted, hoisting a glass. To which Lieutenant Kearny is said to have risen and boldly declared, "To the Prince of Wales, drunk or sober!" The dining hall erupted in shouts and near fisticuffs before the British officer who proposed the first toast was carted off and arrested.

After the War of 1812, Kearny decided, apparently against his parents' wishes, to make a career in the military, and as he steadily rose in rank, he ventured ever westward, assigned to a series of increasingly remote posts, first in the Great Lakes region, and then on the Missouri River. Except for a very brief stint in New York City, Kearny would never serve again in the East.

Chapter 4 SINGING GRASS

In the summer of 1835, Kit Carson attended the annual mountain man rendezvous, which that season was held on a large meadow by a languid bend of the Green River in present-day southwestern Wyoming. As always happened at these notorious gatherings, various bands of Indians had also pitched their lodges to trade, gamble, and drink with the mountain men. It was not uncommon for trappers to take squaws for their wives during these monthlong festivals. Carson was twenty-five years old that summer, and during the previous trapping season he'd suffered a near-fatal shoulder wound during a vicious fight with the Blackfoot. Still sore, and perhaps impressed by his brush with mortality, he was in the mood to settle down. Or, as the mountain men liked to say, it was time for him to be "womaned."

One of the more popular women attending the rendezvous was a young Arapaho named Singing Grass (or Waa-ni-beh in her native language, the name suggesting the keening sound of prairie wind whipping through tall grass). The beautiful Singing Grass caught Carson's eye, but another man named Joseph Chouinard was equally smitten. The French-Canadian trapper, known as the "the Bully of the Mountains," was a swaggering, blustering giant and an expert shot. An English adventurer described Chouinard as "a stupid-looking man," while Carson assessed his adversary as "a large Frenchman, one of those overbearing kind and very strong."

There are many versions of the tale—indeed it is one of the most storied incidents in the literature of the mountain men. Apparently it all started over at the Arapaho camp one night when Singing Grass picked Carson, and rejected Chouinard, from a lineup of suitors to be her partner during the ceremonial "soup dance." The jilted Frenchman promptly insulted her and then later, according to one account, tried to rape her. Whatever happened, Carson seems to have felt a keen sense of sexual rivalry with Chouinard. "It was all over a squaw," one of Carson's Taos friends later said, "and the Frenchman got mad about it."

Then, at the fevered height of the rendezvous, Chouinard went on a bender that lasted several days. Fortified by what Carson called "the demon of alcohol," Chouinard began to menace anyone who crossed his path. He was famous for these rampages, however, and everyone tried his best to ignore him—which only got the man more lathered up. Now positively spoiling for a fight, Chouinard shambled over to Carson's camp and disparaged the Americans there, bellowing: "Mewling schoolboys! I could take a switch and switch you!"

Carson had had enough of this drunken thug. "I did not like such talk from any man," he later said, "so I told him that I was the worst American in camp."

Carson wore what one witness called "a peculiar smile, as though he was about to perpetrate some excellent joke." He told Chouinard: "Stop right now, or else I'll rip your guts!"

The two men went in search of weapons while a large crowd of trappers and Indians thronged in the main clearing of the camp. Suddenly Chouinard and Carson came galloping into the grassy arena brandishing guns. They stopped so close to each other that their horses' heads touched. Tense words were exchanged. They raised their hands and fired their guns, point-blank, with such perfect simultaneity that, as Carson later noted, "All present said but one report was heard."

As he did so often throughout his life, Carson had cheated luck: Chouinard's horse jerked as he mashed the trigger. The hot powder of Chouinard's bullet grazed the left side of Carson's face, scorching his eye and hair and leaving a scar under his left ear that he would carry the rest of his life.

Chouinard, on the other hand, was seriously injured. The lead ball from Carson's single-shot pistol had ripped through the Frenchman's right hand and blown away his thumb. Carson went for another pistol to finish him off, but Chouinard, gingerly holding his maimed appendage, begged for his life. In his dictated autobiography, Carson leaves the drama frustratingly open-ended, telling us only that the camp "had no more bother with this bully Frenchman." Some versions of the story have it that Chouinard later died of his wound—as a result of gangrene, perhaps—while others suggest Carson in fact killed Chouinard with a second shot.

The duel became one of the most famous incidents in Carson's life and made him renowned among the mountain men; but in many ways it was uncharacteristic of him. Although he had a lightning temper, Carson was ordinarily a much more calculating risk-taker who certainly knew enough to back out of a fight so obviously fueled by alcohol. Perhaps the incident can be explained by Carson's youth, or by his desire to prove himself among the grizzled fraternity of trappers, or by some chivalric desire to avenge Chouinard's insults to Singing Grass. Whatever the case, the whole hot affair was an aberration for him. He survived less by skill than by thin luck. A newspaper writer said his fight with Chouinard was "the only serious personal quarrel of Kit Carson's life." Certainly Carson had no regrets. Years later a close friend said: "He was pleased with himself for doing it."

⊗

Perhaps the satisfaction had more to do with the romance that blossomed in the incident's aftermath. Now he could pursue Singing Grass in earnest. He asked her father, Running Around, for her hand and offered a "bride price" of three mules and a new gun. The wedding, probably the following year, was a traditional Arapaho ceremony held in her father's tepee. The ritual was complete when Running Around threw a blanket over the couple and gave his blessing. There was a feast and then the Arapaho relatives erected a tepee for the newlyweds. If Carson followed the rest of the Arapaho custom, then he did not immediately consummate the marriage; he and his bride would have slept in the same bed, but for several weeks she would have worn a tight rope cinched about her waist and loins—a chastity belt of sorts—until their probationary period was over.

By most accounts the marriage was a happy one, although we know very few intimate details since Carson neglected even to mention Singing Grass in his memoirs. With certainty, it can be said that the marriage was more than a casual "squaw arrangement." Singing Grass was in every respect his wife. They followed the Arapaho traditions and lived with the tribe's blessing. Singing Grass was his first love, and Carson adored her.

Arapaho relatives told author Stanley Vestal, who spent months interviewing among her band in the 1920s, that Singing Grass was highly regarded within the tribe—"a good girl, a good housewife, and good to look at." Carson learned to speak the strange and sonorous language of the Arapaho, an Algonquin tongue whose "broad vowels, soft liquids, and smooth diphthongs" made it so beautiful, according to Vestal, "that Indians of other tribes preferred to sing Arapaho songs even though they could not understand the words." The Arapaho were also celebrated for their intricate beadwork, and under his wife's careful stitching hand, Carson's clothes—his buckskins, his moccasins, his tobacco pouch and saddlebags—began to take on shiny new patterns of adornment.

With his Arapaho bride following him whenever she could, Carson trapped for two seasons with the Hudson's Bay Company, and then signed on with Jim Bridger's brigades, working the upper Yellowstone, the Powder, and the Big Horn. During these years he moved incessantly throughout present-day Colorado, Utah, Wyoming, Idaho, and Montana. Trapping gave him, he later said, "the happiest days of my life." It was an unimaginably free sort of existence, one that historian David Lavender described as "flitting ghostlike from creek to creek, with no St. Louis board of directors watching behind them and no suspicious clerks checking their balance columns with crabbed fingers." Carson took great pleasure in those seasons spent "in the mountains, far from the habitations of civilized man, with no other food than that which I could procure with my rifle."

Singing Grass helped with the considerable labors of this hard, roving life—and she made the cold nights more eventful. "She was a good wife to me," Carson once told a friend, noting that Singing Grass was always waiting for him in their lodge with a boiling kettle when he returned from the traps, his moccasins soaked in icy river water. "I never came in from hunting," he said, "that she did not have warm water for my feet."

Their first child, a daughter, was born in 1837. Carson named her Adaline after a beloved niece back in Missouri. (Her Arapaho name, whatever it was, is lost to us, although some accounts say that Carson also called his daughter Prairie Flower.) Carson's family life may have been blissful, but economically, times were lean. The nation was in the grip of a serious depression—the Panic of 1837—and the market for Western goods was volatile at best. The same year, a smallpox epidemic worked its way north and west from St. Louis, borne, it was said, on infected blankets. By the time the scourge had passed, whole tribes had been wiped out and one out of every ten Native Americans living along the Missouri River drainage was dead. Carson almost found sympathy for his age-old nemesis, the Blackfoot tribe, which was particularly hard hit by the epidemic. An early Carson biographer vividly described the eerie silence of a pox-ravaged Blackfoot camp that the mountain men once stumbled upon: "Teepees stood smokeless. Wolves ran about the village, fat and impudent. The Indian dead hung in swarms in the trees and brown buzzards sat in rows along the bluffs, gorged with human flesh, drunk with ptomaines."

Meanwhile, the beaver trade was seriously on the wane, in part because of the Panic and in part because of the vicissitudes of high fashion: In an inexplicable turn, silk hats had replaced beaver hats as objects of patrician desire in the cities of the East and all across Europe. And in truth, there weren't very many beaver left. The fur companies had been so successful in penetrating the Western rivers that the beaver population had been pushed to the brink of extinction. Eastern markets were drying up; the summer rendezvous grew smaller and drearier each year. The mountain men, through skillful persistence, were the agents of their own demise, having depleted the very resource that had enriched them. Like most of the trappers, however, Carson seemed only dimly aware of his own role in the phenomenon. "Beaver was getting scarce" was all he said on the subject in his memoirs, adding, "It became necessary to try our hand at something else."

◙

Sometime in 1839, Singing Grass gave birth to their second child, another daughter whose name is not known. Singing Grass developed a fever following childbirth and soon became gravely ill. She lay on her bed of buffalo robes while the medicine men treated her with herbs and tapped a drum to the exact beat of her pulse. It was all in vain—the infection, probably puerperal fever, soon took her. The grieving Carson now realized he would have to raise their two girls on his own. The Arapaho relatives mourned in the self-flagellatory tradition of the tribe—pulling out hanks of their hair, tearing at their own skin, perhaps cleaving a finger. They wondered why Carson was not wailing like they were, and, according to one biographer, "Kit had to explain that he was crying in his heart, after the manner of white men."

We do not know the place or method of burial, but if the Arapaho custom was followed, Singing Grass's body would have been hoisted on a platform high in a tree with some of her favorite personal belongings and then torched, the charred remains left to be consumed by prairie birds.

In the summer of 1840 he somehow managed to attend the summer rendezvous on the Green River—which, as it happened, was the last mountain man gathering ever held. The fur trapper was truly a moribund breed, and at that dismal 1840 gathering, everyone seemed to know it. One participant lamented: "Times was hard, no beaver, and everything dull."

With the death of the trapping trade, Carson was increasingly drawn to Bent's Fort, a teeming mercantile establishment on the Arkansas River in what is now southeastern Colorado. Founded in 1833, the fort was an important nexus for American trappers, traders, mountain men, and assorted other adventurers worming their way into the West. Resembling an ancient Algerian citadel, with adobe walls three feet thick, Bent's Fort was strategically perched on the northern bank of the Arkansas River in the Colorado plain (the Arkansas then defined the border with Mexico). Owner Charles Bent and his brother William were shrewd businessmen, sons of a St. Louis lawyer who had once been surveyor of the Louisiana Territory.

The Bent brothers offered Carson steady employment as a hunter, and he had numerous friends at the fort who helped him look after his girls. As a hunter, Carson ranged widely over the Southern plains, hunting antelope and buffalo not only for their valuable hides but also for meat to sustain the hundreds of people who lived in or worked out of Bent's.

Sometime in 1841, Carson married a Cheyenne woman named Making-Out-Road (the meaning is lost in translation). She was a beautiful but shrewish woman well known around Bent's Fort for her headstrong independence. Carson's union with Making-Out-Road was as miserable as his marriage to Singing Grass had been blessed. His new wife wanted nothing to do with raising his half-Arapaho girls. The couple fought all the time. The marriage lasted only a few months before she evicted him, with all his belongings, from her tepee. (Making-Out-Road went on to marry and divorce a brisk succession of other men, both Native American and Anglo.)

Carson had a brief affair with a Hispanic woman with a loose reputation named Antonia Luna, but by 1842 he had fallen in love with Josefa Jaramillo, the beautiful teenage daughter of a prominent Taos family. The two were soon engaged. Carson decided sometime that year that his daughter Adaline, who at four was now approaching school age, would be better off with his relatives back in Missouri, where she could get a solid education. So in April 1842 he signed on with a merchant caravan captained by Charles Bent and headed east along the Santa Fe Trail with Adaline in tow, having left her little sister with the Bent family in Taos. (He would never see his baby girl again. Shortly thereafter, the toddler was scalded to death when she fell into a boiling vat of soap tallow.)

The Bent train stopped in the small outfitting town of Westport, on the Missouri River, in what is now Kansas City. Carson feared what people in the settlements would say about his having a half-Indian girl, and wanted little Adaline to look clean and pretty. She was primitive-looking in her animal skins, he realized, and her manners left much to be desired. In Westport he bought her new outfits and had them specially tailored to fit her. Susannah Yoacham, the daughter of a Westport tavern owner, recalled Adaline well. "Carson brought this little girl with him to be educated," Yoacham said. "She came to us dressed in buckskin and left dressed in the finest goods [that] could then be bought on the border. She was uncivilized. She pulled up all my mother's vines and was chewing the roots when we found her at it."

Carson went to his former home of Franklin, only to find that it had been washed away in a flood, the town moved to higher ground, its residents scattered. He located his youngest brother, Lindsey, and learned that his mother, Rebecca Carson Martin, had died the previous year. "It had been sixteen years since I had been among civilized people," he said in his memoirs. He knew that some members of the

Carson clan would not understand the outlandish life he'd led in the mountains and would never accept his marriage to an Indian. A first cousin, Thomas Kelly Carson, certainly viewed Kit as a black sheep of the family, judging him "a wild uncouth boy who married, of all things, an Indian squaw and had a little half-breed girl."

But to Carson's relief, most of his immediate family around Franklin was welcoming to Adaline. He was able to leave her with a niece who had a farm not far from a decent country school. He hated to say good-bye, but she was in good hands, among his own people.

Chapter 5 BLUE BEAD MOUNTAIN

Throughout his long lifetime, the esteemed Navajo elder Narbona had always known war. The Navajos had been in nearly perpetual conflict, if not with the Spanish, then with the Utes, the Comanches, or various combinations of the Pueblo tribes—and often with all of these groups at the same time. To be sure, his people had enjoyed times of relative peace, but the cycles of attack and reprisal, escalating and abating with the seasons, had been an aspect of Navajo existence ever since he was a boy.

By the summer of 1846, Narbona was nearing eighty. At his senescent age, he found it increasingly hard to perceive change, let alone react to it. What he knew was that his people were survivors. The ancient rhythms of their culture had persisted through myriad conflicts, through drought and want, since the time of myth and legend. But now a new kind of foe was marching inexorably west across the plains, an enemy he could scarcely imagine.

Narbona was born in 1766 to the Red-Streaked Earth People, his mother's clan. He spent his first years in the embrace of his mother's people, who lived and herded in the Chuska Valley on a sweep of land in present-day northwestern New Mexico that extended from the crest of the Chuska Mountains all the way to the Chaco River. He was not known as Narbona then—that was a Spanish name, given to him many years later. His Navajo name has been lost to history, and subsequent generations of Diné, leery of uttering the names of dead people for fear of stirring up their ghosts, have seemed to prefer that the identity of their greatest patriarch remain comfortably murky. Even when he was alive, the Navajos would not have called him by his own name to his face—the people considered such directness rude.

As a baby in his cradleboard, Narbona probably was not called anything at all, for Navajos, who tended to view early infanthood as an extension of gestation, did not usually give names to their children until specific personal characteristics began to show themselves— Hairy Face, Slim Girl, No Neck, Little Man Won't Do As He's Told. Although Navajo parents followed few hard rules about how to name their children, it was generally agreed that the watershed moment when a baby could definitively be said to have passed from infanthood into something more fully human was the child's "first spontaneous laugh." First laughter was an occasion for much celebration, and it was the time when many Navajos held naming ceremonies for their young; it is likely that this is when Narbona received his original "war name," whatever it might have been.

Strapped to his mother's back like all young Navajo children then were, the infant Narbona saw the world from a jouncing cradleboard that, in lieu of diapers, was lined with shavings of cedar bark. For good luck and protection in case of a fall, his cradleboard may have been festooned with the customary squirrel's tail—the squirrel being an agile animal deft at landing on its feet, unharmed. For his first five years he would have been surrounded mainly by women: aunts and sisters and girl cousins and grandmothers. Raised by so many mothers, Narbona began to learn the singsong language of the Navajo— with its thousand finicky inflections and its delicate glottal stops and its vague echoes of Siberia—while also cultivating the Diné's famous sense of humor, their unslakable appetite for teasing and puns, their delight in any incongruous or absurd situation.

Narbona received his first pony when he was six, and it was at this early age that, like most Navajo boys, he was taken from the daily attentions of the women to spend more time with the men, preparing himself for a life of hunting and war. Before dawn, he would rise and run for miles toward some distant point in the bitter cold, wearing only a leather thong and moccasins stuffed with sand to toughen his feet. To strengthen his wind, he would run with his mouth full of water, breathing only through his nose. He would jump in a freezing spring or roll in the snow, hollering at the top of his lungs to develop his warrior voice. Then, as the morning sun nudged over the horizon, he would race back to the hogan, covered in a rime of ice that cracked with his stride.

With other boys, he wrestled and competed in broad-jumping, stone-throwing, and archery contests. There were all kinds of traditional games of chance and amusement—stick dice, cat's cradle, the moccasin game. Narbona learned to hunt rabbits and other small game. Every day he practiced his horsemanship, the quintessential Navajo skill. The Navajos were always holding races, often gambling on the results. They rightly prided themselves on their riding prowess—a tradition that continues to this day. (A journalist in recent times noted that "getting bucked off a horse is one of the most embarrassing things that can happen to a Navajo.")

When he turned twelve Narbona was given his first sinew-backed bow, and arrows made expressly for him (the bow stood exactly his own height), and he began to range over the country on his first hunts. Narbona's world was defined not by cities, villages, or roads, but rather by many thousands of natural landmarks spreading out haphazardly over many thousands of acres, little quirks of geography with names like Bank Caving Down, Lake Between the Shoulders, White With Reeds, Aspens Coming Down, Two Red Rocks Pointing Together. These were the ordinary places of his life, the places of daily hunting and grazing, but there were larger and more spectacular places, too—immense red buttes and deep gorges, moraines and lava flows. The Dinetah, as the Navajo called their land, was a wrinkled country studded with monumental rock formations that conjured up the shapes of animals or mythic monsters.

Navajo country has moved modern geologists, ordinarily a reserved lot, to adopt a vocabulary of doom: Paradox Basin, Defiance Uplift, the Great Unconformity. Geological maps of the Navajo lands are ominously annotated with "upwarps" and "cinder cones" and "structural disarrays." Not far from Narbona's home lay enormous forests of petrified wood, which the Navajo believed were the bones of Yeitso, a terrible beast slain by the war god Monster Slayer and left to rot on the plains, the creature's blood congealing into lava flows. Throughout Navajo country could be found canyon walls embedded with the fossils of sea organisms—corals, bryozoa, trilobites—that had lived in the ocean more than 300 million years ago.

To the north of Narbona's camp, often visible over the Chuska plain, loomed Tse' Bit' A'i, or the Rock With Wings. This neck of an explosive volcanic vent had eroded over thousands of years into a breathtaking monolith that looked something like the spiny backbone of an enormous dinosaur. In the 1860s, American explorers, fancying that this strange formation resembled a clipper ship, coined the name by which it is more familiarly known today: Shiprock.

But the most conspicuous landmark in Narbona's part of Navajo country was a large dormant volcano that hung magisterially over the sagebrush high country to the south of his family's land. The Navajos called this impressive stand-alone mountain Tsoodzil, or Blue Bead Mountain. Marking the southeastern corner of Navajo country, Blue Bead Mountain rose to eleven thousand feet and was cloaked in ponderosa pines and aspen. Its bald peak was packed with snow during the winter months and green with wild meadow grasses in summer, while the mountain's lower shoulders of piñon and juniper tapered into enormous lava fields of black basalt.

As he grew up, Narbona could look to the south and see this distinctive landmark hovering steadfastly there, a wispy blue mirage. Like all Navajo children, he learned from an early age that Blue Bead Mountain was one of the four sacred mountains that anchored the Navajo country. There was a mountain for each cardinal direction, each one inhabited by different gods, each one figuring prominently in the creation stories. From any place in Navajo country, a person could always see at least one of the four sacred landmarks. Except to make war or go on raids, Navajos were not supposed to venture beyond the borders formed by these great peaks or else they would face sickness or death. For good luck, many Navajos kept prayer bundles in their hogans, little sacks that contained soil taken from each of the four mountains.

The world in which Narbona came of age was one of strict symmetry and balance. The number four held great power. There were four sacred colors, four sacred plants, four sacred gemstones. After a healing ceremony, a patient was not supposed to talk to anyone or engage in sexual relations for four days. Every Navajo was mindful of the four points of the compass. The hogan was always oriented with the doors facing east. Each direction had its own quality and hue—north, for example, was black, and it was considered the direction of death and the supernatural; a Navajo never slept with his head pointing north. Navajo sandpaintings and blankets, for all of their vivid color and originality, adhered to a tight symmetry, the designs usually divided into equal quadrants representing the four directions.

Their ordered world was further divided and defined by gender. Objects, landmarks, even acts of nature could be either "male" or "female." A female rain was a gentle, steady mist; a male rain was an angry black thunderstorm. There were male hogans and female hogans, each constructed of slightly different materials and used for different purposes. The lower Rio Grande, muddy and slow and quiet, was a female river, while the boulder-choked San Juan River, full of froth and rapids, was decidedly male.

◙

The San Juan River traditionally marked the border between Navajo country and the domain of the Utah Indians. The Utes, a fierce tribe of hunter-gatherers, roamed in the mountains north of this thunderous male river. Throughout Narbona's boyhood, the Utes were probably the Navajo's greatest enemy. The two tribes were constantly at war. The Spanish governors in Santa Fe had learned that it was much easier to set the territory's hostile tribes against one another than to fight them outright. And so, with the Spaniards smiling on the situation from afar and promising to stay neutral, the Utes stepped up their long-simmering war with the Navajos. Throughout the 1770s and 1780s they stormed into Navajo camps, stealing children to sell to the Spanish at the slave market in Taos.

For young Narbona and his family it was a time of bloodshed and nearly constant worry. To the Navajos the word "enemy" really meant only one thing: Ute. Narbona grew up with countless stories of Ute outrages, and he longed to go on retaliatory strikes led by his father and other Navajo warriors. By the time he was a teenager he had grown to a formidable height—he was said to stand nearly a head taller than most of his comrades—and he was singled out as a promising warrior. When he was sixteen he went on his first raid, and he found that he was good at it. Returning home from his first fight, Narbona no doubt participated, as most raiders did, in a Nda, the Enemy Way ceremony, an elaborate rite designed to purge any bad spirits or foreign influences a warrior may have unwittingly absorbed while venturing off Navajo lands.

Narbona then began to ride farther afield, striking not only at the Ute camps across the San Juan but also at vulnerable Pueblo settlements and finally, the ultimate prize of all, the Spanish ranches along the Rio Grande. So successful were young Navajo warriors like Narbona in their raids during the late 1770s and early 1780s that the Hispanic villagers finally had to import new horses from Chihuahua—breeding alone could not keep pace with Indian thefts.

When he was in his early twenties, Narbona's parents arranged for him to marry a girl from the Tzith-ah-ni clan named Bikay-djohl. As was the custom, Narbona went to live with his new bride among her people, who lived on the slopes of the Tunicha Mountains, to the north of his own family's outfit. He and Bikay-djohl constructed a hogan close to that of her parents. Most likely, the wedding ceremony was held there in the new hogan. Huddled inside with the family, the medicine man said his prayers and bestowed his blessings, and, upon leaving, advised the young couple, with a bodily frankness that would certainly embarrass most Anglo-American newlyweds back east, to attend immediately to the important community business of procreation—and to that end, instructed them not to leave the hogan for four nights and four days.

Then the couple set up housekeeping, probably surrounded by the hogans of Narbona's mother-in-law and her extended family. Narbona had no choice but to try to get along with his new outfit and acclimate himself to all its disputes and quirks of personality; he was not free to return with his wife to live with his own family's outfit. The Navajos had come up with a system that minimized the possibility of incest— they could marry neither within their own clan nor their own outfit— but the close and complicated living arrangements required of these small seminomadic groups could seem quite incestuous indeed. (Years later an anthropologist would describe the cohesive and geographically isolated Navajo outfits as tending toward "emotional inbreeding.")

Observing an old and curious Navajo taboo, Narbona was not allowed to look at his mother-in-law, nor she at him. It was a custom designed to keep the peace and, apparently, to avoid sexual tension. In fact, many mothers-in-law in Navajo country went so far as to wear little warning bells on their clothing so that a son-in-law would not round a corner and inadvertently find himself staring at her. This was no small thing, especially if he happened to look her in the eye: Even an accidental violation of the mother-in-law taboo might require that the family hire a healer to perform an elaborate—and expensive— nightchant to undo all the harm that had been done.

Sometime in the late 1780s, Narbona took a second wife. His raids of Spanish settlements intensified, and he became known as a great war chief. During one raid Narbona captured a young Zuni woman, and she became one of his wives, by all accounts as loyal and happy a member of his outfit as his two Navajo wives.

He proved to have keen political and diplomatic skills and impressed people as someone who, as the Navajo liked to say, "talks easy." Many young warriors from all over the Chuska Mountains and as far away as Blue Bead Mountain had volunteered to ride and apprentice under him. Over time, the imposing Narbona raised what amounted to a standing army.

The focal point of the fighting was a small fortified village that the Spanish had founded in 1800. The Navajos considered the village, called Cebolleta, an outrageous affront, for it was built on the very flanks of their sacred Blue Bead Mountain, on land the Navajos had controlled for centuries. A group of Spanish settlers fancied the area because of the fine grazing along the mountain's slopes and had won a land grant from the royal governor in Santa Fe to start a new outpost. The Navajos attacked the new village relentlessly. In the escalating conflict, Narbona emerged as the most prominent war leader.

On one occasion in 1804, he organized a force of a thousand warriors and surrounded the tiny settlement. The siege raged for weeks and was marked by desperate hand-to-hand fighting. Spanish accounts of the battle are vivid and brutal. The Cebolletans passed down one story about an elderly grandmother, Antonia Romero, who managed to kill a Navajo attacker by crushing his head with a *metate*—an anvil-sized stone used for grinding corn. Another Cebolletan account tells the story of an intrepid defender named Domingo Baca, who was disemboweled by a Navajo lancer. Undaunted by his injury, Baca strapped a pillow around his belly to hold in his guts, then seized his musket and rejoined the fight. When he removed the pillow that night, writes historian Marc Simmons, Baca's friends "were aghast, and quickly made the sign of the cross as for one already dead. But Baca returned the dangling entrails to their proper place, called for needle and sinew, and sewed up the wound himself. These crude ministrations proved effective, for he recovered and lived to fight again."

Narbona and his thousand warriors might have succeeded in finally dislodging the hated settlers had the Spanish governor not brought in seasoned troops from Sonora. The Spaniards, too, led many counterraids into Navajo country, but few of them made much of an impression on the elusive Diné.

Chapter 6 WHO IS JAMES K. POLK?

The mission on which Kearny led the Army of the West had no precedent in American history. For the first time the U.S. Army was setting out to invade, and permanently occupy, vast portions of a sovereign nation. It was a bald landgrab of gargantuan proportions. President James K. Polk expected Kearny to march nearly one thousand miles and promptly conquer a territory nearly half as large as the existing United States. After reaching Santa Fe and taking New Mexico, he was then to keep moving west, taking all of what is now Arizona and parts of present-day Colorado, Utah, and Nevada, and finally, the greatest prize, California, until the American flag smiled over the blue Pacific. All of the lands in this vast, tattered kingdom were to fall in a single dash.

The war with Mexico was a complex affair with many tentacles of grievance, real and imagined, reaching back many years. Most immediately, the war had to do with Texas. Late the previous year, 1845, the United States had officially annexed the Lone Star Republic, which, a decade earlier, had won its independence from Mexico after the bloody battles at the Alamo Goliad and San Jacinto. But Mexico had never recognized Texas's claim of independence and certainly was not prepared to see it pass into United States possession. President Polk had sent an emissary named John Slidell to Mexico City to negotiate the purchase of Texas, with borders set to the Rio Grande, for some $10 million. While he was at it, Polk instructed Slidell to offer to purchase California and New Mexico, for another $20 million, but this bold overture came to nothing. Realizing that neither diplomacy nor outright bartering would achieve his expansionist ends, Polk was determined to provoke a war. He dispatched Gen. Zachary Taylor to disputed territory, between the Nueces and the Rio Grande, in southern Texas. It was an unsubtle attempt to create the first sparks. In April 1846, Taylor's soldiers were fired upon, and Polk was thus given the pretext he needed to declare war.

"American blood has been spilled on American soil," Polk spluttered with righteous indignation, neglecting to mention that Taylor had done everything within his power to invite attack, and that anyway, it wasn't really American soil—at least not *yet*. Mexico had "insulted the nation," the president charged, and now must be punished for its treachery, beaten back, relieved of vast tracts of real estate it was not fit to govern.

The simple truth was, Polk wanted more territory. No president in American history had ever been so frank in his aims for seizing real estate; it was a curious time in the history of the settlement of North America, a time when the European powers, though fast losing their purchase on the New World, still held dreams of securing the last great unmapped chunks of a wild continent. Britain had designs on the Oregon Territory, and the Russian trappers and sea otter barons, from their bases in Alaska, still maintained a feeble influence along the Northern California coast. Even waning France and Spain nursed various intrigues.

In this competitive environment, President Polk took the position that the United States should aggressively pursue its territorial interests now or else risk forfeiting them forever. Polk especially had his eyes on the ports of California, but he found it hard to resist any of the lands that lay between the existing United States and the Pacific. Nearly from the moment he took office in 1845, Polk had seemed perfectly willing to fight two simultaneous wars—one with Mexico over Texas and California, and another with Great Britain over Oregon—in order to gain the lands he so brazenly coveted.

☒

The eleventh president of the United States was a sly, misanthropic man with long gray hair swept back from his blocky forehead. His jaw was clenched, his countenance grimly determined. He wore a long black coat that was frumpish and out of style, its pockets stuffed with letters. It was impossible to know what the president was thinking. He kept his prim mouth shut, and his gray eyes, hard and jewel-like, gave up nothing.

Perhaps Polk's dour nature had something to do with the excruciating medical condition that he long suffered from as a teenager growing up in Columbia, Tennessee. At seventeen, after years of anguish that seemed to imprint a permanent grimace on his adolescent face, Polk was diagnosed with urinary stones. He was taken by horse-drawn ambulance to a famous Kentucky physician, Dr. Ephraim McDowell, and there underwent what was then a state-of-the-art surgery. With nothing more than brandy for an anesthetic, the future president was strapped naked to the operating table with his legs hoisted high in the air. Dr. McDowell bored through the prostate and into the bladder with a medieval-looking tool called a "gorget." The stones were successfully removed, but the operation is thought to have left Polk sterile and impotent. Polk biographer John Seigenthaler thought that Polk "became a man on Dr. McDowell's operating table. Here, for the first time, were evidences of the courage, grit, and unyielding iron will that Whigs, the British Crown, and the Mexican Army would encounter once he became president."

Polk had been elected in one of the closest contests in American history, one from which many claims of election fraud arose. After the dust of the 1844 campaign settled, no one seemed entirely sure how this small, stern political operative had risen from obscurity to defeat the great Whig candidate Henry Clay. As a speaker Polk was plodding and colorless, a master of the single-entendre. John Quincy Adams said that Polk "has no wit, no literature, no gracefulness of delivery, no elegance of language, no philosophy, no pathos, no felicitous impromptus." Considered the first "dark horse" candidate in presidential history, Polk was nominated on the ninth ballot at the Democratic Party convention in Baltimore. The news of his nomination was shot to Washington by brand-new telegraph lines, the first occasion Samuel Morse's startling invention had been used for a public purpose.

The debonair Clay, sure of his national stature, had underestimated Polk's determination and dismissed the upstart with the mocking campaign slogan "Who is James K. Polk?" But in the end, Polk was elected by a margin of forty thousand votes and became, at age forty-nine, what was then the youngest president in the country's history.

There was about Polk's presidency an acute sense of deadline: As a candidate he vowed that he would seek only one term of office and he would keep his campaign promise. He had four years to accomplish everything and that was it—he would exit the stage. And so everything in Polk's administration was compressed, intensified, accelerated. Extraordinarily, Polk succeeded in achieving nearly all of his goals. Despite his insufferable personality, he was possibly the most effective president in American history—and likely the least corrupt. He outmaneuvered his critics. He established an independent treasury. He confronted the British and conquered Mexico. He seized the western third of the North American continent. By the time he left office, the American land mass would increase by 522 million acres.

Four years was all he needed. Polk would limp home to Tennessee exhausted and seriously ill, suffering from what he called a "derangement of the bowels." In three months he would be dead.

Who was James K. Polk? A stranger, a telegram, a joyless, childless man fueled by an expansionist agenda. A political masochist who gritted his teeth and endured the national growing pains. The populace had picked him to do bold things in a short amount of time. He seemed to spring from nowhere, and there he returned.

◙

Perhaps to dignify the nakedness of Polk's land lust, the American citizenry had got itself whipped into an idealistic frenzy, believing with an almost religious assurance that its republican form of government and its constitutional freedoms should extend to the benighted reaches of the continent then held by Mexico, which, with its feudal customs and Popish superstitions, stood squarely in the way of Progress. To conquer Mexico, in other words, would be to do it a favor.

Mexico's hold on its sparsely populated northern provinces was tenuous at best. Having won independence from Spain in 1821, the young country was poor, disorganized, politically unstable, and hopelessly corrupt. Its army was weak, its people demoralized. The remote territory of New Mexico, nearly two thousand miles from a largely indifferent government in Mexico City, lay withering on the vine. What's more, the Santa Fe Trail had opened up many New Mexican eyes, and pocketbooks, to the benefits of a flourishing commerce with the United States. The Santa Fe trade had convinced many of the superiority of American goods—shoes, textiles, cutlery, tools, rifles—and the burgeoning relationship had bettered their lives in practical ways; for all intents and purposes, much of northern Mexico had already begun to fall within the sphere of American influence.

Whether U.S. expansionism was morally right or wrong, most Americans seemed to believe that it was inevitable—and that there was little point in resisting the tide of history. America and its ideals and institutions were spreading outward, westward, onward. The country could scarcely contain itself. The spirit of expansionism was everywhere in the air, like some beneficent germ. As the volunteers of Missouri marched, they marched with a kind of national giddiness. John Hughes rhapsodized that every soldier in the Army of the West "felt that he was a citizen of the model republic." Possessed of "a high moral sense and a conscious superiority over the Mexican people," Hughes wrote, they were embarked on a mission of high romance—west to the Pacific, south to the Halls of Montezuma!

A few years earlier a young New York editor named John O'Sullivan had coined the self-justifying phrase that captured the righteous new tilt of the country. Writing in the *New York Morning News*, O'Sullivan argued that it was the fate of the United States, necessary and quite inexorable, to sweep westward and settle North America from sea to sea, "to overspread and possess the whole continent allotted by Providence for the free development of our yearly multiplying millions." In order to advance "the great experiment of liberty," the American republic must absorb new lands. It was, O'Sullivan suggested, her "manifest destiny."

At universities across the country, the youth had become smitten with the notion of American exceptionalism, and students began to show their patriotic fervor in a fashionable campus craze called the Young America Movement, which, among other things, unequivocally advocated westward expansion. Even the country's literary elite seemed to buy into Manifest Destiny. Herman Melville declared that "America can hardly be said to have any western bound but the ocean that washes Asia." Walt Whitman thought that Mexico must be taught a "vigorous lesson." Too long had Washington "listened with deaf ears to the insolent gasconnade of [Mexico's] government," Whitman argued; now it was time for "Democracy, with its manly heart and its lion strength to spurn the ligatures wherewith drivellers would bind it." Like Polk, Whitman had his eyes on New Mexico and California, asking, "How long a time will elapse before they shine as two new stars in our mighty firmament?"

At the same time, many critics warned that the war was an enormous mistake. Polk's enemies in the Whig Party opposed the war for all sorts of reasons—some genuine, some cynically political. Other critics, moved by religious or racial concerns, saw great peril in absorbing a Catholic, Hispanic country. Still others brooded over an even more nettlesome question—namely, would the new lands that would likely be gained by the war ultimately become slaveholding or free? Much of the early dissent came out of Massachusetts from a group of abolitionists who called themselves the Conscience Whigs. Led by Charles Francis Adams, son of John Quincy Adams, these critics bemoaned not only "the iniquity of aggression but the iniquity of its purpose—the spread of slavery." Perhaps the most eloquent among the war's opponents was the great Transcendentalist essayist Ralph Waldo Emerson. "The United States will conquer Mexico," he predicted, "but it will be as the man who swallows the arsenic which brings him down in turn. Mexico will poison us."

Still other opponents of the war were critical of the land itself: What was the point, they asked, of conquering a godforsaken desert? Apart from the established value of the Santa Fe trade, New Mexico was not thought to be much of an asset. Kearny had people traveling with him from the Corps of Topographical Engineers, trained scientists like Lt. William Emory, who, in addition to mapping the terrain with state-of-the-art geodetic and astronomical equipment, would be homing in on all sorts of nitty-gritty economic questions, like: Was there coal in New Mexico? Was there good hardwood timber? Was the grazing decent? What were the possibilities for industry, trade, and agriculture—and with agriculture, slavery? How good was the soil in the river bottoms?

Yet most officials back in Washington seriously doubted whether the poor desert province was, in and of itself, worth taking. Expansionists like President Polk, however, believed that the main value of this tract was its contiguity to other, more valuable places: For how could America meaningfully own California without all the country that lay between it and the existing United States? What was the point of having Pacific ports, and the hoped-for trade with China and the rest of the Orient, without also having the intervening lands? Manifest Destiny did not countenance geographical gaps and untidy voids—it was an all-or-nothing concept tied to the free flow of an envisioned commerce.

The tantalizing dream already dancing in the heads of tycoons and politicians back east was a transcontinental railway that would connect New York and Washington to Southern California, quite possibly following the same route the Army of the West had just taken, through Missouri and Kansas, cutting south-by-southwest along the Santa Fe Trail. In his extensive notes, Lieutenant Emory, a perspicacious West Pointer, deemed the route promising thus far. "The road from Leavenworth presents few obstacles for a railway," he wrote, "and, if it continues as good to the Pacific, will be one of the routes to be considered." Emory saw a day when "immense quantities of merchandise will pass into what may become the rich and populous States of Sonora, Durango, and Southern California."

❧

Missouri had long been the portal of American expansion, the pad where great expeditions were outfitted and adventures launched, the place where the westering fever burned at its highest pitch. It was the flash point, the port of embarkation. The state's own senator, the famed Thomas Hart Benton, was perhaps the greatest exponent of westward expansion, and his unapologetic vision of a continental United States animated the Missourians as they pressed toward New Mexico.

The great-uncle of the famous American painter of the same name, Tom Benton was an enormous man with an even more enormous influence. The sixty-five-year-old senator had a long nose and an imposing head nimbused with white hair. In the Senate, as in every other sphere of his life, he was a tenacious fighter. He'd been involved in several duels over the years—one against Andrew Jackson that ended with the future president lying badly wounded, his shoulder shattered, in a pool of his own blood.

Benton was one of the lions of the Senate at a time when the Senate was full of lions—roaring egos like Henry Clay, Daniel Webster, and John C. Calhoun. An ultrahawk, Benton served as chairman of the Senate Military Affairs Committee. He had been in the Senate for more than twenty years, ever since Missouri became a state following passage of the Missouri Compromise of 1820. He was a thoroughly self-made, self-educated man who had cured his boyhood tuberculosis through a regimen of cold showers and vigorous outdoor activity. His daughter Jessie wrote that through his illness he had found an "ally within himself on which he could surely rely—his own will."

He was deaf in one ear from his proximity to a national tragedy that had occurred three years earlier. In February 1844, Benton and a number of other Washington dignitaries had boarded the USS *Princeton* for a Sunday cruise down the Potomac. The ship was captained by Robert Stockton, a flamboyant commodore who would play a prominent role in the American conquest of California. At some point during the excursion, Stockton had ordered his naval gunners to fire a few exhibition rounds from a new cannon that had been placed on board. But something went wrong and the cannon exploded into the assembled crowd of politicians and military officers. A number of dignitaries were killed by shrapnel, including Secretary of State Abel

Upshur and Navy Secretary Thomas Gilmer. Benton survived only by sheer luck—moments before the blast, he had moved a few feet away in search of a better vantage point from which to study the gunner's marksmanship. Still, the blast ruptured his eardrum and left him in such severe shock that it took him several months to recover.

He found his peace in books. An obsessed bibliophile, Senator Benton was said to have the best library west of the Mississippi, and quite possibly, in his third-floor Washington study, the best library *east* of the Mississippi as well. He was especially fond of his rare editions of Plutarch, Herodotus, and the ponderous *British State Trials,* from which he quoted freely and obnoxiously. He was known around Washington as a breathing encyclopedia. Daniel Webster said that Benton "knows more political facts than any other man I have met, even more than John Quincy Adams."

Benton would deliver stem-winding filibusters that might last for twelve hours, full of abstruse facts dressed up in purple layers of grandiloquence. One biographer said Benton "literally smothered listeners with the columns of his research." He would sprinkle not only his formal speeches but even ordinary conversations with lofty allusions from Greek and Roman literature. Another Benton biographer, Teddy Roosevelt, said that the senator, though he had "much erudition," was "grievously afflicted with the rage for cheap pseudoclassicism." Roosevelt went on to capture Benton in a series of pungent fragmentary descriptions: The senator had, he said, a "magnificent physique." He "waxed hot and wrathful" and was "fond of windy orations" in which he "fairly foamed at the mouth." He had an "aggressive patriotism" and an "immense capacity for work," but was "unfortunately deficient in the sense of humor."

Well before the war with Mexico, Benton had kept the long fingers of American settlement steadily curling toward the Pacific. During his first term as senator, in the 1820s, Benton proposed a public works bill that created a true national commerce road from Missouri to New Mexico—the road that became known as the Santa Fe Trail. It was Benton who had pushed for the opening of the Oregon Trail, along which thousands of emigrants were now traveling each year to settle the fertile Willamette Valley. Early on Benton had recognized the necessity of topographical expeditions to map and explore the West, and through his impeccable connections he'd seen to it that his son-in-law John C. Fremont got the choice assignments. More than anyone else in Washington—more than President Polk, even—Tom Benton was the face and voice of Manifest Destiny.

Yet he had arrived at his position by an oblique and unpredictable path, and it was this that made him one of the most interesting men in the Senate. A Southerner by birth, Benton represented a slave state and owned slaves himself. But he did not follow his Southern colleagues in Washington, most of whom favored western expansion primarily as a way to extend slavery into Texas, California, and elsewhere to tip the delicate national balance between slave and free states. Refreshingly, slavery had nothing to do with Benton's designs on the frontier. He regarded the Peculiar Institution as an "incurable evil," one that would cause infinite trouble if Western states attempted to adopt it. "I am Southern in my affections," he once declared, "but I will not engage in schemes for slavery's extension into regions where a slave's face was never seen."

Tom Benton favored westward expansion for altogether different reasons. He was a Unionist, first and foremost, a kind of superpatriot with no patience for men like John C. Calhoun who talked of nullification and secession. Benton believed in the ruddy rightness of American power and American ideals and, especially, American commerce. A staunch advocate of low tariffs and free trade, he was particularly interested in the Orient. He looked forward to the cornucopia of Asian goods that would one day flow through the American ports of San Francisco and Puget Sound. He spoke unabashedly of "the American Empire," and from his wide reading he concocted a theory that all empires in world history had become great by achieving a direct access to Asian trade. He insisted that the nation do everything in its power to blaze a clear path to the Pacific in the interest of establishing what he called "the American road to India." Throughout Benton's long, blustering career, this was his main theme—his "hobby," as Roosevelt put it, a leitmotif he hammered on constantly.

The most significant obstacle to a vigorous Oriental trade, Benton thought, was Great Britain. Having fought in the War of 1812, the senator especially hated the British, who were always sniffing along the coast of California, pushing various intrigues and colonization schemes. With its mighty navy, Britain could thwart America's geopolitical aims in myriad ways. Benton thought President Polk should be more confrontational with London. Although the Polk administration had amicably resolved the Oregon boundary dispute at the 49th parallel, the British still seemed suspiciously interested in California's magnificent ports. Americans, Benton had long thought, should boldly take what was rightly theirs before the British beat them to it.

As a practical matter, of course, Mexico stood in the way—but Stephen Kearny's Army of the West was on the march to remove this annoying impediment.

Chapter 7   WHAT A WILD LIFE!

To an unusual extent, Kit Carson was a person who lived not in words but in action, responding to situations with a preternatural swiftness. Nearly everyone who knew him mentioned this quality. An army doctor who had traveled with Carson remarked on his "shrewdness of perception" and his "promptitude in execution." When telling stories about himself, Carson's favorite phrase was "done so," the words popped off with the clarity of a clean, neutral fact. One of his early biographers, Stanley Vestal, observed that Carson constantly used the construction "Concluded to charge them, done so," noting that he often rendered it in a single sentence. "To Kit," Vestal said, "decision and action were but two steps in the same process."

For all his self-assurance in the heat of a tight moment, Carson had powerful doubts and vulnerabilities. He was deeply embarrassed by his illiteracy and tried to cover it up in various ways, but the fact remained that he could not write his own name. When signing documents he simply scrawled an X (he later learned to write "C. Carson"). At times he showed something of an inferiority complex that manifested itself in an instinctive deference to culturally refined men from back east who were more intellectually accomplished and socially better-connected than he. Falling under the spell of such figures, Carson seemed comfortable playing the role of a loyal lieutenant—or, some might say, a henchman. When people he perceived as his betters told him to do something, he did it, happily and without question.

For Carson, John Charles Fremont was one of those people. Fiercely intelligent but of questionable ethics, Fremont was a man of striking good looks, with a full black beard, hawkish features, and the manic expression of a prophet. Behind his mystic eyes burned the will of a glory hound who saw himself on the path to a fortune far brighter than his rank or talents would immediately suggest. Unlike other leading army topographers, Fremont was not a West Pointer— in fact, he was not even a college graduate, having been expelled from university in South Carolina for "incorrigible negligence." The bastard son of a wandering French *artiste,* Fremont was born in Savannah and grew up in Charleston. Largely self-taught, he had a passion for botany, a reputation as a Lothario, and a penchant for melodrama that could be insufferable.

But Fremont had something else going for him: He was married to Jessie Benton Fremont, the estimable daughter of Sen. Tom Benton. With the senator's constant lobbying behind the scenes, Fremont won an ambitious series of official assignments to explore the great wildernesses of the West.

For his first expedition, in the summer 1842, Fremont's mission was to map and describe the general course of the Oregon Trail all the way to the South Pass in the mountains of present-day Wyoming. The Oregon Trail was a new wagon road that branched off from the Santa Fe Trail in Kansas and worked its way northwest over the Rockies to Oregon, which was then an ill-defined territory occupied jointly by the United States and Great Britain. American emigrant parties, enticed by reports of fertile land in Oregon's Willamette Valley, had been taking to this braided, rutted road in increasing numbers.

But in truth the route was uncertain, its main thoroughfare forked with dangerous detours, its various stages and watering holes poorly understood, the whereabouts of hostile Indian tribes unknown. To all but the stoutest of hearts, the Oregon Trail was simply too forbidding.

And so the proponents of western expansion wanted to do something about this tenuous state of affairs. Hoping to encourage a full-scale wave of emigration, Senator Benton and others realized that what settlers most sorely needed was a foolproof map and guidebook—a manual, almost—one that pioneers could closely follow, mile by mile, stage by stage.

Producing such a handbook would be the task of Fremont's first expedition.

While outfitting his party in St. Louis, Fremont chanced to meet Kit Carson on a Missouri River steamboat. Carson was thirty-two years old then and had been visiting his family in Missouri after his many years working as a trapper in the Rockies.

Leaning against the steamship's railing, Fremont immediately took a liking to this curious little man. "He was broad-shouldered and deep-chested," Fremont wrote, "with a clear steady blue eye." Fremont was particularly impressed with Carson's "modesty and gentleness." He told Carson that he was looking for a guide to lead him to South Pass.

"I've been some time in the mountains," Carson replied. "I could guide you to any point you wish to go."

Fremont hastily inquired after Carson's reputation among other mountain men who happened to be in Missouri—and heard nothing but praise. Carson was hired.

Fremont's "First Expedition," as it came to be called, left Missouri in June 1842 with twenty-five men and the novelty of inflatable rubber boats. The mission took five months and was a success. The weather was fair, no one died on the journey, and the trail was blessedly free of Indian trouble, although false rumors of an impending attack along the North Platte did cause Carson at one point to draw up a will.

Performing splendidly, Carson showed a knack for keeping a traveling party on track and out of trouble. Fremont proved to be a plucky and resourceful explorer—the kind of man who could repair a broken barometer with animal horn and glue from a boiled bison hoof. The expedition reached the South Pass on schedule, and on the way back Fremont made a flamboyant, and ill-considered, dash into the Wind River Range to plant an American flag on the summit of a snowy mountain he erroneously thought to be the highest peak in the Rockies.

All in all, the fates seemed to smile on "Fremont's First." Upon his return to Washington in the fall, he immediately set about writing Benton's hoped-for road manual, complete with maps and botanical sketches. Congress rushed it into print with the ungainly title *A Report on an Exploration of the Country Lying between the Missouri River and the Rocky Mountains on the Line of the Kansas and Great Platte Rivers.*

The report struck a national nerve, and it was soon reprinted in newspapers across the country. The public lapped up Fremont's picaresque descriptions of trail life, of buffalo and grizzly bears and strange Indian customs. The way to Oregon, Fremont seemed to be saying, was not so forbidding after all. The American prairie was not an inhospitable desert, but a beckoning carpet of flowers. Fremont became an instant celebrity, a champion of expansion, a conqueror wielding not a sword but a compass and a transit. "Fremont has touched my imagination," wrote poet Henry Wadsworth Longfellow. "What a wild life, and what a fresh kind of existence! But ah, the discomforts!"

Fremont's expedition narrative did precisely what Senator Benton envisioned it would—it touched off a wave of wagon caravans filled with hopeful emigrants, many of whom held the book in their hands as they bounced down the rutted trail. "Fremont's First" was such a huge success that the next summer he was assigned a follow-up mission. This time it was to map and describe the second half of the Oregon Trail, from South Pass to the Columbia River. It was a considerably longer and more ambitious trek.

Again, Fremont hired Carson to guide him.

Chapter 8 THE RULING HAND OF PROVIDENCE

Kearny's Army of the West marched steadily westward. Climbing imperceptibly into a thinner, drier atmosphere, the men found it harder to judge distances. Sometimes they found themselves tricked by optical illusions—the famous "false ponds." In his journal, Pvt. Jacob Robinson described with astonishment the first mirage he saw. "Nothing appears as it is," he wrote. "About a mile distant from us appeared a crystal lake, studded with numerous islands, so perfectly defined that no one could imagine it to be anything else than a real lake. Though prepared for the illusion, many of the men believed it real, bet upon it, and of course lost their bets."

Pronghorn antelope cropped the short grass, and then sensing something untoward, whisked off like arrows. Prairie dogs sprang from their cratered towns and piped in nervous curiosity. Often the dens were also occupied by rattlesnakes or burrowing owls, predators that lived uninvited in the homes of their prey. At times, Robinson wrote, the ground was so "full of holes and burrows as to make it sound hollow like a bridge when traveled over."

Through most of the month of June 1846, Kearny kept up a blistering pace—averaging twenty-two miles a day but sometimes exceeding thirty. The general could be seen riding up and down the miles of marchers, motivating laggards, instructing greenhorns in the rudiments of horsemanship. The volunteers viewed him with a mixture of resentment and awe. "Nothing could exceed the confidence which every man seems to have in him," wrote one Missourian. "He is, however, fond of rapid marching and keeps us at it steadily." Said another: "He is reputed one of the most expeditious travelers who ever crossed the plains."

It wasn't just a fondness for speed, however. Kearny understood that he was running a race against time and moisture: By late July the plains would lay crisped and brown, without enough good grass to keep his horses, mules, and oxen moving. Not only that, Kearny wanted to intercept the buffalo herds—he was counting on bison meat to feed his men through the middle part of the trek. If his army delayed, he might miss the buffalo altogether, for the herds generally migrated north in midsummer, trending toward the best green grass. Kearny knew enough about prairie travel to appreciate that his window of opportunity was tight.

By early July the animals were depleted. Food grew scarce, forcing Kearny to put the men on half rations. They took to foraging for the black gooseberries and wild plums and cherries that grew along the banks of meandering springs. Teams of marksmen broke off from the caravans to hunt for antelope or deer. On July 4 the Army of the West briefly halted the march to celebrate the birth of their country. "This morning we all took a drink of whiskey in honor of the day," Robinson wrote in his journal, "but are obliged to march on, as the rations we have are nearly gone."

To relieve the boredom of the long day, stories and rumors broke out among the men and traveled haphazardly down the line, evolving in tone and connotation in their endless soldierly repetitions. Kearny was so circumspect—"He is a man who keeps his counsels to himself," wrote one volunteer—that no one seemed to fully understand what the mission was, or precisely where they were going—other than *west*. The men made disparaging remarks about Santa Anna and the Vatican. They sang patriotic songs—"Yankee Doodle" was a favorite—drowning out the grunts of the animals.

Ravens followed the long columns as seagulls would follow a ship, and often they would light on the taut canvas sheets covering the wagons, cawing intently for food. Coyotes and wolves followed the procession, too, packs of them loping along in the grass just beyond rifle range, patiently waiting for a horse to collapse.

The Army of the West was accompanied by its own internal army of attendants and tradesmen contracted to hold the ungainly procession together—wheelwrights, sutlers, laundresses, cooks, stockmen, farriers, teamsters, coopers, foragers, muleteers, hostlers, butchers, liverymen—many of them old hands on the Santa Fe Trail. In anticipation of a creek crossing, a detachment of engineers would bound ahead to study the sandy bottoms and quagmires for the most promising place to ford, bringing shovels and hoes to make small improvements along the banks to ease the passage of the heavy wagons. If the axles were made of a wood too green, they would all too often snap under the burden.

On July 8, Private Robinson's column approached a famous landmark of the Santa Fe Trail, a prominent outcropping known as Pawnee Rock. This promontory was scrawled and chiseled with the names of countless travelers of the Santa Fe trade from decades past. Some of the more elaborate graffiti had been painted on the rock with an ointment of animal fat and black tar. Robinson climbed to the top of the rock, presumably to etch his own name, when he turned west to glimpse, as he put it, "one of the grandest sights ever beheld."

Stretching before him, in the golden light of the afternoon, was a vast herd of buffalo, easily a quarter million strong. "Every acre was covered," Robinson wrote, "until, in the dim distance, the prairie became one black mass from which there was no opening."

As many as 50 million buffalo roamed the Great Plains at this time, a carnival of meat on the hoof migrating north and south with the seasons, wandering west and east with the presence or absence of water, imprinting the plains with intricate capillaries of trails. Robinson joined a party of men and approached the buffalo. They were pitifully easy to shoot—until the beasts actually saw or smelled the source of danger, they would go on stupidly cropping the grass as members of their herd dropped, one by one, all around them. Robinson's party killed forty of them, and the carcasses were immediately butchered and prepared for dinner.

Susan Magoffin, a sprightly eighteen-year-old from Kentucky, was traveling in the midst of the Army of the West with her new husband, a veteran Santa Fe trader. In a diary that has become a classic of

Western literature, Magoffin captured the spectacle of the buffalo hunts. "The men have been out since sun rise," she wrote, "and mules loaded with the spoils of their several victories, are constantly returning to camp. It is a rich sight indeed to look at the fine fat meat stretched out on ropes to dry for our sustenance. Such soup we have made of the hump ribs. I never ate its equal in the best hotels of N.Y. and Philadelphia. And the sweetest butter and most delicate oil I ever tasted is not surpassed by the marrow taken from the thigh bones. If one cannot live and grow fat here, he must be a strange creature."

Robinson's party made camp beneath jumbled cottonwoods along the banks of a small brown river rippling with carp. They circled their wagons and cinched them wheel to wheel with hemp ropes as a defense against Pawnee attack, but also to form natural corrals in which they could unharness their stock. The river bottom was tangled with brown-black hair left by bison that, during the summer shedding season, liked to rub against the roughly ridged trunks of the cottonwoods.

With dusk approaching, the cooks made fires with "prairie fuel"— the dried ordure of buffalo. Robinson and his comrades broiled their steaks and shared pots of bitter coffee—or "black soup," as the definitive beverage of the frontier was sometimes called. The men drew straws to see who would get the fatty ribs from the bison's hump, which was considered the tastiest cut. The dung charcoal, which burned like bricks of peat, imparted a slight bitterness to the flesh, but to famished soldiers the buffalo tasted divine.

Laying out their bedrolls, they stretched beneath the glorious speckling of stars. They turned the tongue of their lead wagon toward the North Star so they would be better oriented in the morning. And in their exhaustion they soon fell asleep to the low growl of buffalo bulls in rut and the cry of the gray wolves, whose "long and doleful bugle-note," as one put it, "makes a night upon the Prairies perfectly hideous."

◌

In the final weeks of July 1846, as the country grew ever more desolate and severe, the Army of the West struck the braided Arkansas

River and marched for many days alongside its cottonwood-skirted banks. Then one day, like an apparition, snow-dusted mountains leapt into view. Off to the northwest the soldiers could see Pikes Peak, vaporous and shimmering and unaccountably huge. And to the southwest loomed the Spanish Peaks, twin conical mountains known to local tribes as Wah-to-Yah, "the Breasts of the World."

The men of Missouri had never seen mountains, real mountains, like these—and they were dumbstruck. One diarist among them wrote that the "jagged peaks are towering in mid-heaven all around us . . . grand beyond description."

By early August, Kearny's troops were spread out over hundreds of miles of the Santa Fe Trail, inching forward in scores of separate caravans. Before making the final push into New Mexico, Kearny decided to pause long enough to concentrate his forces on the Arkansas at Bent's Fort, the adobe citadel where Kit Carson had briefly worked as a hunter back in the early 1840s.

Commanding an impressive vantage along the Santa Fe Trail, the fort's high castle tower was equipped with a nautical spyglass for keeping an eye on hostile Indians. Two live bald eagles held vigil from the rooftop, caged in the belfry. Friendly Plains tribes often pitched their tepees nearby to trade and gamble and drink at the fort. Bent's was a loud and bustling agora, its denizens coarse-mannered but usually friendly when not too drunk, its labyrinths of storerooms stacked with beaver pelts and buffalo robes and barrels of Taos Lightning, the stout New Mexico whiskey.

This outpost of American civilization boasted all sorts of incongruous pleasures and amenities, including peacocks that roamed the compound, a French tailor, white tablecloths in the dining room, ice for the fort's signature mint julep–like drink, which the Bents called a "hailstorm," and the most outlandish luxury imaginable, *a billiards table.*

Kearny's dragoons set up an encampment on the north side of the Arkansas while the legions of Missourians pitched their tents in a sprawling meadow just south of the river. The volunteers picketed their exhausted horses and mules in the pasture, but others were turned loose to graze. Something spooked them—one witnesss claimed it was merely the snap of a falling tree limb—and they began to stampede.

In an instant the constrained horses broke free of their irons and galloped off with the others—with dangling picket pins biting into their flanks and spurring them to greater fury. For miles the prairie swirled with hoofbeats and manic patterns of dust. General Kearny was livid at the volunteers for letting the horses graze loose. On the Santa Fe Trail, stampedes like this were considered a disaster of the first order, and a danger even graver than Indians. In their madness, many horses bolted for the far horizon and were never seen again. The Missourians spent a whole day recapturing their scattered animals, several of which were found more than fifty miles from the fort. Eighty horses were never recovered.

Among the travelers who had taken refuge in one of the fort's many rooms was Susan Magoffin, the young diarist from Kentucky. She had taken ill and was trying in vain to get some rest, but Bent's Fort was no place to be sick. "There is the greatest possible noise," she wrote. "The shoeing of horses, neighing, and braying of mules, the scolding and fighting of men, are all enough to turn my head." Not knowing what was wrong with her, she took her Sappington's Fever and Ague Pills, a popular frontier cure-all containing quinine, and hoped to nurse herself back to health. Magoffin complained of "strange sensations in my head, my back, and hips. I am obliged to lie down most of the time, and when I get up I must hold my hand over my eyes."

But Magoffin's condition progressively worsened. Because she was an unusually well-connected traveler, inquiries were immediately made and a doctor was called for. Her husband, Samuel, had worked the Santa Fe trade for fifteen years and was well known to the Bent brothers. Her brother-in-law, James Magoffin, was also a shrewd old hand on the trail, fluent in Spanish and a popular fixture in Santa Fe.

A few days earlier, in fact, General Kearny had met with James Magoffin at the fort and dispatched him as a kind of shadow envoy to

Santa Fe to conduct secret talks with Gov. Manuel Armijo, whom Magoffin knew well. Kearny hoped Magoffin could persuade Armijo not to fight. Although the details are lost to history, it is also believed that Magoffin was given specific instructions to sweeten the negotiations with considerable bribes. Susan Magoffin, suffering in her room, was oblivious to all of these doings.

Two other notable women had sought haven in Bent's Fort while Kearny's soldiers massed outside. They were two sisters from the prominent Jaramillo family of Taos, Ignacia and Josefa, Kit Carson's young bride. Ignacia was married to Charles Bent, who normally kept his home in Taos when he wasn't on the trail or tending to business at the fort. Fearing that the arrival of the American invaders would cause turmoil in Taos that could jeopardize his wife's safety, he had sent for Ignacia and Josefa, intending to keep them safely ensconced in the fort until the occupation was complete and passions had cooled.

As more and more soldiers trickled in from the trail, Susan Magoffin's illness advanced. She began to suffer "much agony and severest of pains." Finally, around midnight on July 31, a French doctor arrived and gave her morphine. She slumped into her husband's arms and then, as she put it, "I sunk into a kind of lethargy."

Later that night Magoffin had a miscarriage—brought on, the French doctor assumed, by the jolting of the long trail. She had not even known she was pregnant. A few days later she was able to return to her diary. "The mysteries of a new world have been shown to me," she wrote. "In a few short months I should have been a happy mother and made the heart of a father glad, but the ruling hand of Providence has interposed and by an abortion deprived us of the fond hope of mortals." She feared she would not recover, that she would die of some infection in her chamber, and that she would never see "the fair and happy America again."

The night of her miscarriage, her husband told her, a Cheyenne woman, probably the squaw of one of the traders, had given birth to a healthy baby in a room directly below hers. Within a half hour of the birth, the woman, following an ancient tribal custom, ventured out to the Arkansas and bathed herself and her newborn in the river.

While Magoffin was recovering in her bed, she listened to the noises of Kearny's army as it made final preparations for marching one Sunday morning. "Although it was the Sabbath," she wrote, "necessity compelled them to be busily employed. The clang of the blacksmith's hammer was constant. The trumpet sounded oft and loud; swords rattled in their sheaths, while the tinkling spur served as an echo. Ever and anon some military command was heard."

Magoffin, exhausted and probably medicated, lay in her darkened room and reflected on the baser shadings of Kearny's mission. "Though forbidden to rise from my bed, I was free to meditate on the follies and wickedness of man! Of a creature formed for nobler purposes, sinking himself to the level of the beasts, waging warfare with his fellow man, even as the dumb brute. And by his example teaching nothing good, striving for wealth, honour and fame to the ruining of his soul, and losing a brighter crown in higher realms."

Then, at Kearny's command, the Army of the West departed the fort with more than 1,500 wagons and nearly 20,000 animals. The long columns forded the Arkansas River, thus crossing the international border into Mexico, and marched en masse across the high plains to conquer Santa Fe.

Chapter 9 THE PATHFINDER

Fremont's second exploratory expedition, undertaken in 1843, proved an even greater success than the first. En route to Oregon, Fremont and his party lingered beside the Great Salt Lake and, by studying the region's hydrology, correctly surmised that its rivers and streams were strictly inland bodies of water. At the time, a curious and persistent myth, perpetuated in scholarly publications, asserted that the Great

Salt Lake was drained by a monstrous whirlpool that somehow connected, through a network of subterranean rivers, with the Pacific Ocean.

Fremont gradually came to realize that all the country between Utah's Wasatch Mountains and California's Sierra Nevada was landlocked; this was a major contribution to North American geography, and Fremont's term for the desert sink, the Great Basin, graces atlases today.

In the late summer of 1843, Fremont's party reached Oregon, where he mapped the Columbia and its tributaries and caught magnificent glimpses of Mount Rainier, Mount Saint Helens, and Mount Hood. Growing restless, Fremont then strayed from his original assignment and crossed the international border into what was then called Alta California.

Fremont seemed unconcerned that his illegal incursion into Mexican territory might lead not only to his own arrest but also to an international incident that would embarrass government officials in Washington. He was now preoccupied with a hunt that transcended mere borders: He was looking for a mighty waterway that, if it existed, could change the course of history. Many maps of the day showed a major east-west river that led from the Great Lakes all the way across the continent to the Pacific Ocean. This fabled conduit, called the Buenaventura, was widely accepted as a scientific fact even though no known explorer had actually seen it.

With visions of cartographic glory, Fremont was set on finally proving, or disproving, the Buenaventura's existence and thus solving one of the most vexing continental puzzles of his day.

But once he set foot in California, the misadventures began to pile up. He promptly led his party into the winter snowdrifts of the Sierra Nevada, and it was only through luck—and Kit Carson's good judgment—that the expedition was able to avoid the sort of grisly ordeal that would befall the Donner Party a few years later. When they staggered out of the mountains, frostbitten, half naked, and eating scalded dog-meat, they were, Carson thought, "in as poor condition as men could possibly be." One man became "deranged . . . and perfectly wild from the effects of starvation," said Carson, while the ravenous mules ate "one another's tails and the leather of the pack saddles."

Restored with good food provided by American settlers, the party turned south and marched down the full length of California's Central Valley before veering toward the Mojave Desert and points east. Along the way, one of Fremont's men died in a gun accident, another was killed by Indians. Inevitably, Mexican officials got wind of Fremont's uninvited presence in California and threatened to send an army after him.

So Fremont exited the California stage altogether and slinked into Nevada, passing a bucolic watering hole known as Las Vegas. In the desert, Carson chased after a band of Indian horse thieves and showed Fremont how to drink water from a barrel cactus. As the party slowly made its way east toward civilization, Fremont admitted he had never found the fabled Buenaventura River, but that in itself was an important find. Like the Great Salt Lake whirlpool, the Buenaventura was another great hoax that could be consigned to geography's dustbin. The party reached Bent's Fort on July 2, where a July Fourth celebration was held in their honor.

In August 1844, Fremont stumbled into Washington like a ghost; the gaunt explorer was a year late and rumored to be dead. His much-anticipated expedition narrative, which he turned in a few months later, was so well received that the congressional printing office bound the first and second reports in a single volume and published ten thousand copies. Again the newspapers printed excerpts and hailed Fremont as the American Magellan. He was already being touted as a future candidate for president. And why not? Fremont had set in motion one of the great mass migrations of history: The following summer the Oregon Trail saw an even greater hegira of emigrant caravans, with thousands and thousands of pioneers headed west. Many of these emigrants were Mormons. On the strength of Fremont's glowing descriptions of the Great Salt Lake country, Mormon leader Brigham Young decided to move his whole flock from Nauvoo, Illinois, to Utah.

The army, willing to overlook the fact that Fremont had blatantly disobeyed orders by lurching into California, promoted him to captain. The national media, meanwhile, gave him a new sobriquet drawn from James Fenimore Cooper: From then on, John C. Fremont was known as The Pathfinder.

~

If Fremont had become a household name, so had his scout. By 1845, thanks to the expedition reports, Kit Carson's name, with its sturdy alliterative snap, had crossed the threshold of the national imagination. Fremont painted Carson as an explorer of nearly mythic competence and perspicacity on the trail. He consistently came across as courageous but never rash, a person with a sure presence of mind. And also, crucially, a person who seemed to have enormous stores of luck on his side: Time after time, the stars smiled on Kit Carson. In nearly every contretemps Fremont got himself into, Carson found the way out.

The special thing that Carson had couldn't be boiled down to any one skill; it was a panoply of talents. He was a fine hunter, an adroit horseman, an excellent shot. He was shrewd as a negotiator. He knew how to select a good campsite and could set it up or strike it in minutes, taking to the trail at lightning speed. ("Kit waited for nobody," complained one greenhorn who traveled with him, "and woe to the unfortunate tyro.") He knew what to do when a horse foundered. He could dress and cure meat, and he was a fair cook. Out of necessity, he was also a passable gunsmith, blacksmith, liveryman, angler, forager, farrier, wheelwright, mountain climber, and a decent paddler by raft or canoe. As a tracker, he was unequaled. He knew from experience how to read the watersheds, where to find grazing grass, what to do when encountering a grizzly. He could locate water in the driest arroyo and strain it into potability. In a crisis he knew little tricks for staving off thirst—such as opening the fruit of a cactus or clipping a mule's ears and drinking its blood. He had a landscape painter's eye and a cautious ear and astute judgment about people and situations. He knew how to make smoke signals. He knew all about hitches and rope knots. He knew how to make a good set of snowshoes. He knew how to tan hides with a glutinous emulsion made from the brains of the animal. He knew how to cache food and hides in the ground to prevent theft and spoilage. He knew how to break a mustang. He knew which species of wood would burn well, and how to split the logs on the grain, even when an axe was not handy.

These were important skills, all of them, though they were hard to measure and quantify. But in the right person, a person who was also cheerful on a trail he already knew well, who had a few jokes up his sleeve and possessed an absolute honesty—they were invaluable.

Fremont's nickname, The Pathfinder, was a misnomer several times over. For it was Carson, not Fremont, who had usually "found" the path—and often as not he was merely retracing trails that had already been trod by trappers, Indians, or Spanish explorers. In Cooper's Leatherstocking Tales series, the main protagonist, Natty Bumppo, a.k.a. Hawkeye, a.k.a. the Pathfinder, wears buckskins, lives with the Indians and follows their ways. It was Carson, not Fremont, who actually lived a life that resembled Cooper's hero.

Fremont seemed to understand that in curious ways, Carson complemented him. If Fremont was impetuous, visionary, erratic, and at times vainglorious, Carson was cautious, pragmatic, steady, and always humble. Though Fremont brought flourishes of high culture to the trail, the illiterate Carson was versed in a different kind of learning, a practical knowledge that was just as eclectic and even harder won. Fremont described Carson as "prompt, self-sacrificing, and true." He was a man "of great courage; quick and complete perception, taking in at a glance the advantages as well as the chances for defeat." In another passage Fremont fairly sang, "Mounted on a fine horse, without a saddle, and scouring bare-headed over the prairies, Kit was one of the finest pictures of a horseman I have ever seen."

But there was one particular passage in Fremont's second report that crystallized Carson's reputation and forever fixed his name in the public mind. Naturally, the episode had to do with Indians. Somewhere on the Old Spanish Trail, deep in the Mojave Desert, Fremont's men encountered a desperate Mexican man named Andreas

Fuentes and an eleven-year-old boy, both of whom had been ambushed by Indians (which tribe is unknown). The attackers had stolen thirty horses and killed two men Fuentes was riding with, leaving their mangled bodies on the trail. Two women riding with the party had been staked to the ground and badly mutilated before they, too, were killed.

On hearing this tragic tale, Kit Carson and fellow mountain man Alex Godey took pity on Fuentes and vowed to help. For two days Carson and his comrade followed the horse tracks and chased down these "American Arabs," as Fremont called them. Finally Carson and Godey located the thieves and rushed into their crowded encampment. The Indians had already eaten several of the stolen horses. Dodging their arrows, Carson and Godey promptly shot two of the Indians, scattered the rest, and seized the surviving horses. Before leaving the scene, Godey stooped to strip off the scalps of the two slain Indians. But according to Fremont, when Godey raked his knife over the second Indian's scalp, the warrior "sprung to his feet, the blood streaming from his skinned head, and uttered a hideous howl," firing an arrow at Godey that passed through his shirt collar.

Godey raised his rifle and "quickly terminated the agonies of the gory savage."

The following day Fremont was amazed to hear the sound of approaching hoofbeats. It was Carson and Godey returning with Fuentes's recaptured horses. Godey was carrying his rifle like a pole, from which dangled two fresh Indian scalps. Fuentes shed tears of gratitude, and Fremont was in awe. As far as he was concerned, this act was the apotheosis of chivalry. He wrote, "Two men, in a savage desert, pursue day and night an unknown body of Indians into the defiles of an unknown mountain—attack them on sight, without counting numbers—and defeat them in an instant. And for what? To punish the robbers of the desert, and to avenge the wrongs of Mexicans whom they did not know."

Who would do such a thing? Fremont asked rhetorically in his report. "Kit Carson, an American, born in the Booneslick county of Missouri . . . trained to western enterprise from early life."

And so by 1845 the image was already sealed: Kit Carson became a kind of action figure hero, the noble rescuer, righteous avenger, white knight of the West. That his brutality might have an inglorious underside seemed not to cross the adoring public's mind, any more than did the possibility that both the Fremont and Fuentes parties were trespassing on ancestral Indian territory. Fremont could count on his scout to find the way and set things right—and readers could, too. More than any other single factor or incident, this passage from Fremont's second expedition report is where the Kit Carson legend was born; he would have to live down the legend, and respond to the expectations it created, for the rest of his life.

Carson could not read Fremont's glowing words about him, of course, and it is doubtful whether he even knew about them. But Carson's gratitude to Fremont ran deep. The two men had traveled many thousands of miles together and had fought their way out of many scrapes. For all his peculiarities of manner and lapses in judgment, Fremont had proven a brave and tough explorer—and he was never dull. In many situations he had shown flashes of brilliance (although he was usually the first to admit it). There was no questioning his abilities as a field topographer, and in his own fitful, grandiose way he had demonstrated a certain talent for leading and inspiring men.

In any case, Carson genuinely seemed to like his boss and felt much in his debt. Fremont had given him a new lease on life—the promise of a new career just as the trapping profession was drying up—and he'd paid the unheard-of sum of a hundred dollars a month. Carson was the sort of person who, once befriended, was steadfast as a family dog. It was perhaps the sweeter flip side of the Scotch-Irish revenge trait: Like a grudge, he wouldn't let you go. Years later, in praising Fremont in his dictated memoirs, Carson said that he found it "impossible to describe the hardships through which we passed, nor am I capable of doing justice to the credit which Fremont deserves. I can never forget his treatment of me while I was in his employ, and how cheerfully he suffered with his men."

And so for the rest of his life, Carson would always remain in the Fremont camp. The loyalty was mutual. When in the summer of

1845, Fremont set out for yet another assignment to explore the West—this one proving his most ambitious and far-flung odyssey of all—he of course chose Kit Carson to be his guide.

Chapter 10 WHEN THE LAND IS SICK

In 1818, when he was fifty-two, Narbona led another campaign against the Spanish, this one far more successful than the earlier assault on Cebolleta. He made his war plans from atop a Navajo stronghold called Yoo Tsoh, or Beautiful Mountain, where he assembled hundreds of braves to make arrows and shields and other implements of war. He was sure of his timing; most of the Spanish soldiers had left the region to put down a major rebellion deeper in Mexico. When Narbona's warriors were ready, they mounted their horses and swooped down on the valleys, plundering the unprotected ranches and slaughtering anyone who tried to resist.

But Narbona's bloody campaigns of 1818 were successful in a wider sense beyond the great bounty of stolen property they yielded: The following year the Spanish drafted a treaty that for the first time established tribal boundaries and recognized many of the Navajo grievances. The Spaniards, in turn, demanded a stop to all raids. They further insisted that the Navajos convert to Catholicism and build permanent villages so that they might settle down beside their churches and become full-time farmers like the Pueblo Indians—a notion that would crop up over and over again in the Navajos' later dealings with Spanish, Mexican, and American authorities. Narbona would do what he could to halt the raiding, but he knew his people would never agree to this latter sweeping request—which amounted, in the Navajo view, to cultural suicide.

That year, however, Narbona had far bigger concerns than the Spanish. A terrible drought had descended over the Southwest, and the Chuska Valley, semiarid even in good times, turned a crackly brown. The grass dried up and a pall of fine dust hung over the land. On the surrounding mesas, a species of bark beetle began to ravage the shriveling stands of piñon trees that were now unable to produce enough sap to discourage the invading insects. Narbona's sheep and other livestock began to starve.

The situation became so severe that Navajos all over the region were forced to abandon the Chuska Valley. They collected their belongings, wrapped up bundles of seeds, gathered their herds and flocks—and left. For months Narbona and his people wandered westward, looking for a new place they might graze and farm, but everywhere they went, the Navajos were similarly famished. It seemed that the Diné prayers no longer held their magic.

The Navajos always said that "when the land is sick, the people are sick," and it did seem as though the people themselves were now accursed. They began to eye one another suspiciously, wondering who among them had gone astray and displeased the gods and upset the delicate order of things. It must have saddened and humiliated Narbona to see his once affluent outfit reduced to such a desperate refugee existence, leading their dwindling flocks, depending on the generosity of ever more distant circles of friends and relatives, until they had passed out of familiar country altogether and into the red rock wilderness of what is now northern Arizona.

As the drought worsened, Narbona had no choice but to keep moving in search of a better place. The sheep had become so skinny, it was said, that "their bones stuck out like handles for us to carry them by." They were approaching the western periphery of Navajo country—to the southwest they could see the giant peak they called Light Always Glitters on Top. It was another of the four sacred mountains, this one anchoring the southwestern corner of the Navajo lands (the mountain is now known as the San Francisco Peaks, which rise to an elevation of more than twelve thousand feet near present-day Flagstaff, Arizona). For Narbona, the mountain loomed as a forbidding landmark; he realized he could not lead his people farther west without angering the gods.

Here and there Narbona encountered pockets of life, little communities clustered around a feeble river or an underground spring. He found one such place in a well-watered valley below the Hopi settlements of Black Mesa. Narbona climbed up to the mesa to seek the Hopis' permission to squat on their land until the drought had passed. An unchristianized tribe of Pueblo Indian farmers little influenced by the Spanish, the normally peaceful Hopis were ancient foes of the Diné—they called the Navajos the *tasavuh*, or "the head pounders," for their brutal habit of bashing in skulls with stone axes.

Certainly the Hopis had good reason to be skeptical of Narbona's proposed living arrangement. But for some reason the Hopis assented, and Narbona's people settled down. It was a testament to Narbona's diplomatic skills that he was able to secure safe haven among ancestral enemies—he doubtless sweetened the deal with many sheep and goats and other gifts, and promises of more when the drought ended. He may have also floated threats at the Hopis, who perhaps feared that more Navajos were coming to reinforce Narbona's warriors. (Visionary artists and inspired metaphysicians known for their elaborate dances and their fine kachina dolls, the Hopis were inferior fighters; so ingrained was their habit of running that the Navajos called them "little rabbits.")

By whatever methods of persuasion, Narbona lived among the Hopis for much of the 1820s, more than a hundred miles to the west of his beloved Tunicha foothills. During their exile, his people became close friends with the Hopis—learning their elaborate songs and dances—and three of his children even married members of the tribe.

But sometime in the late 1820s, news reached Narbona that the Tunicha Mountains were packed with fresh snow: The drought was over. Soon the people gathered their things and made the happy exodus back to the Chuska Valley.

⊠

The province of New Mexico had seen one major change during their absence: The era of Spanish rule was over. In 1821, Mexico had won its independence from Spain, and now all official affairs were run by a fledgling government out of Mexico City that had no relationship to the crown. The import of this development was lost on most Navajos, and in practical terms they saw no difference between Mexican New Mexicans and Spanish New Mexicans; by whatever name, they were still the enemy.

In fact, while Narbona and his followers were away in Hopi country, the violence between the Hispanic settlers and the eastern Navajos who stayed behind had only escalated. During times of drought the cycles of violence always seemed to intensify, and the drought of the 1820s was particularly harsh. While Narbona was away, some 250 Diné women and children had been stolen in raids and, presumably, sold into slavery.

Certainly the Navajos had struck back wherever and whenever they could. But in March 1822, having grown weary of the bloodshed, a group of sixteen Navajo emissaries had accepted an invitation from the new government in Santa Fe to hold a peace council. Some Navajo leaders understood that the timing was fortuitous—only a month earlier the authorities in Santa Fe had celebrated their independence from Spain. If there were ever a promising moment to strike a chord of peace, it was now, with fresh new leaders lodged in Santa Fe's Palace of the Governors.

The Navajo emissaries set off for the capital with high hopes. But when they passed through the Jemez Pueblo, en route, they walked headlong into a trap set for them by the Mexican commander stationed there. Thomas James, an American trader then living in Santa Fe, documented the episode.

> The [Jemez] commander invited them into the fort, smoked with them, and made a show of friendship. He placed a Spaniard on each side of every Indian as they sat and smoked in a circle, and at a signal each Indian was seized by his two Spanish companions and held fast while others dispatched them by stabbing each one to the heart. A Spaniard who figured in this butchery showed me his knife, which he said had

killed eight of them. Their dead bodies were thrown over the wall of the fort and covered with a little earth in a gully.

A few days afterwards five more of the same nation appeared on the bank of the river opposite the town, and inquired for their countrymen. The Spaniards told them they had gone on to Santa Fe, invited them to come over the river, and said they would be well treated. They crossed, and were murdered in the same manner as the others.

There again appeared three Indians on the opposite bank, inquiring for their chiefs. They were welcomed across, taken into the town under the mask of friendship, and also murdered in cold blood.

In a few days two more appeared, but could not be induced to cross, when some Spanish horsemen went down the river to intercept them. Perceiving this movement, they fled and no more embassies came in.

In all, twenty-four Navajo leaders were treacherously murdered, many of them esteemed elders of the tribe. When news of this three-stage massacre filtered back to the Diné, they prepared for full-scale war. If the Navajos had entertained any vague hopes that the new government in Mexico might treat them any differently than had the Spanish crown, those hopes were shattered. And so that spring of 1822, the Navajos went on an unprecedented rampage of revenge, slaughtering countless Mexican settlers at Valverde, Las Huertas, and many other communities strung along the Rio Grande.

"They killed all of every age and condition, and burned and destroyed all they could not take away with them, and drove away the sheep, cattle, and horses," James wrote, adopting an almost Armageddonish tone. "They came from the South directly towards Santa Fe, sweeping everything before them and leaving the land desolate behind them. They crossed the Rio Grande below Santa Fe and passed to the North, laid bare the country around the town of Taos, and then disappeared, with all their booty."

Chapter 11 THE UN-ALAMO

To call any of Fremont's expeditions purely "scientific," as he often did, would be disingenuous. Ulterior considerations lurked behind nearly all his movements in the West. Overtly or not, his larger purpose was to advance the cause of American emigration, American expansion, American hemispheric hegemony—which is to say, he was carrying out Sen. Thomas Benton's vision like a good and dutiful son-in-law.

But from the beginning, Fremont's third expedition, begun in 1845, was the most political and least scientific of all. He seemed to trust that the third time really was the charm, that this journey would catapult him from the musty studio of a mere mapmaker into another role altogether—that of a glorious conqueror. Before he left Washington, Fremont had met with Polk, and it was clear that the president wanted the Mexican province of Alta California. He was happy to buy it if Mexico would entertain his overtures, but he was willing to fight for it, too.

California was then an errant state, only weakly tied to Mexico City. It had recently been convulsed by a series of revolutions and counterrevolutions. Its Hispanic inhabitants, proud and fiercely independent, had primarily settled along the lush Pacific coast, clustered around a constellation of Spanish missions. Yet other parts of California were slowly and steadily becoming Americanized: For years, a growing trickle of American emigrants had been crossing the Sierra Nevada and settling the fertile Sacramento Valley, and American whalers had been using the fine port of Monterey for a generation. Richard Henry Dana, in his immensely popular *Two Years Before the Mast*, published in 1840, had opened the nation's eyes to California's charms and quickened the popular yearning for American ports on the Pacific.

In 1842 an American commodore named Thomas Catesby Jones, acting on false reports that war was on with Mexico, had actually sailed into Monterey harbor, seized the port, and raised the American flag. (He soon profusely apologized and quit the port with his tail between his legs.) Though it was a ridiculous action, the fact that Commodore Jones was able to take Monterey without the slightest resistance showed leaders back in Washington just how easily the ripe fruit could be plucked.

All the trends were inevitable, Polk felt. It was only a matter of time before California, like Texas, would be fully absorbed by the United States. Why not now?

Such was the pregnant international climate when John Fremont left St. Louis on June 1, 1845, with fifty-five volunteers and headed out for points west on his third exploratory expedition. As far as his immediate superiors at the Corps of Topographical Engineers were concerned, Fremont's mission was quite limited: The assignment they'd given him was to map and explore the eastern slope of the southern Rocky Mountains, tracing the watershed of the upper Arkansas River, and returning to St. Louis by year's end.

But Fremont seems to have been operating under secret orders, or at least some tacit understanding of a wide latitude, afforded by higher authorities (precisely who has never been clear—Benton? Polk? Other officials within the army or navy?). He had no intention of dallying in the Rockies taking dreary measurements. As soon as he reached the Arkansas River in the late summer of 1845, Fremont abandoned his tame-sounding survey project. As though diverted by some pressing appointment with destiny, he made a beeline for California.

Along the way there were the usual sorts of misadventures that often seemed to befall Fremont on his transcontinental jaunts. In the Great Salt Lake Desert, he insisted on routing his men across a fearful *malpais* that local Indians assured him humans had never successfully traversed. His party could have expired from thirst in this dicey passage, but Carson saved the expedition again, this time riding some sixty miles ahead of the others toward a distant mountain, where he quickly located water and grazing grass, and then, by prearranged agreement, built a signal bonfire on the summit as a beacon to Fremont to come on, there was hope ahead.

∞

By early winter 1846, Fremont had crossed the Sierra Nevada and dropped down into the Sacramento Valley. There he made contact with American settlers, taking the political pulse of the province and trying to stir up a nascent patriotic fervor on which he might capitalize. Already Fremont was quietly building alliances with these rough-and-ready expatriots and making bold assurances that, should war break out with Mexico as expected, his party—which, after all, was an official (and reasonably well-armed) expeditionary force of the United States Army—would be there to protect them. Captain Fremont was the only army officer within two thousand miles of California: Should hostilities begin, he was, by default, the commander apparent.

He quietly slipped into Yerba Buena, as the tiny town of San Francisco was then called, making inquiries among Americans there and staying long enough to coin a name for the picturesque mouth of the great bay—the Golden Gate, he called it. Fremont then brought his men south and had them set up camp in the vicinity of the provincial capital of Monterey.

Naturally enough, Mexican authorities took issue with the seemingly bellicose presence of sixty armed American "explorers" insinuating themselves without invitation in their fair province. On March 5, Gen. Jose Castro, the *comandante* in Monterey, issued Fremont an unequivocal demand to leave California at once.

Fremont responded with pure histrionics. He moved his men to Gavilan Peak, a small mountain in the Coastal Range, northeast of Monterey, and there he built a rough-hewn fort. Hunkering down for an Alamo-style defense, he ordered his men to erect a tall sapling on which he hoisted the American flag. It was a brazen if thoroughly half-cocked act of war, and one that could well have gotten his men slaughtered in the face of the thousands of soldiers Castro could easily have organized. Fremont wrote to the American consul in Monterey, in a melodramatic and almost comically dishonest explanation of his actions: "We have in no wise done wrong to the people or the authorities of the country, and if we are hemmed in and assaulted, we will die every man of us, under the Flag of our country."

General Castro issued a passionate proclamation to his people urging them to "lance the ulcer" of the American invasion. He began to muster a response, and in the fields below Gavilan Peak there were rumblings of an imminent battle. In two days Fremont seemed to come to his senses and realized this was a standoff he could not win, one that would only result in certain death and dubious martyrdom. Perhaps Carson injected a note of sanity into his commander's thinking. Conveniently for Fremont, his hastily erected flagpole tumbled to the ground on March 9, and he apparently took the soiling of the flag as a bad omen: "Thinking I had remained as long as the occasion required, I took advantage of the accident to say to the men that this was an indication for us to move camp."

So ended his defiant (and short-lived) stand at Gavilan Peak, the un-Alamo. Fremont slinked away to the safety of the north again, following the course of the Sacramento. By April he had found his way into Oregon and halted on the southern shores of Klamath Lake, where for a time he resumed his role as explorer while keeping a weather eye on California. He seemed to be stalling for time, hovering within striking distance, waiting for something to break.

◎

And then something did. Out of the forest stepped a stranger named Lieutenant Archibald Gillespie, bearing cryptic messages from Washington. He was a gimlet-eyed Marine from New Jersey, sickly but irascible and quite arrogant.

The trek Gillespie had taken to reach this lakeside wilderness has to rank as one of the great solo courier missions in history. He had left Washington in October of the previous year after having met with President Polk and other government officials, including the secretary of the navy, George Bancroft. He took a steamship from New York

City down to Veracruz, Mexico. While on board he committed to memory the texts of his most sensitive dispatches and then destroyed the original documents. From Veracruz, he traveled inland to Mexico City, assuming various disguises and taking copious notes on the turbulent political climate and the nation's disposition toward war.

By December, Gillespie reached Mazatlán, on the west coast of Mexico, and boarded an American whaling ship bound for Hawaii—the Sandwich Islands, as they were then known. From Honolulu he made an about-face, sailing east toward California in an American man-of-war. His ship hove into Monterey in April, and he slipped ashore posing as a merchant. After meeting with the American consul there, Thomas Oliver Larkin, he quietly pushed inland to the Sacramento River, wending his way north along the river until he caught Fremont's scent.

Gillespie, it seemed, was Polk's far-flung secret agent, not just a messenger but someone who had been given considerable discretion to improvise decisions on the ground. History does not know precisely what his dispatches said, or precisely what oral information might have been lodged in his head. Neither Gillespie nor Fremont ever came clean on this question. It remains one of the imponderables of American history just what Fremont knew, when he knew it—and what he chose to ignore.

This much is clear: Polk and others in Washington were worried about California, and they wanted Fremont to return there posthaste to help ensure that the coveted province fell into American hands while simultaneously making certain the British did not try to seize it for themselves.

This fear was not entirely unfounded. England's interest in California dated all the way back to 1579, the year Sir Francis Drake came ashore somewhere north of present-day San Francisco and claimed "Nova Albion," as he called it, for the British crown. In 1846 the British were well ensconced in Oregon. Their ships prowled the Pacific coast of California, and officials in Mexico City were offering to sell California to England in exchange for a war loan. In addition, an Irish priest named Eugene McNamara had secured Mexican permission for a curious scheme (never to reach fruition) that would have brought over boatloads of Catholic immigrants from English-held Ireland to start a new utopian colony in Southern California. Through official and unofficial channels, then, Britain was certainly intrigued by California—the question was how far it was willing to go to antagonize the Americans.

Fremont stayed up talking with Gillespie and reading his dispatches in the flickering firelight. War with Mexico had already broken out, and plans for the grand march of the Army of the West were under way, but Gillespie did not—could not—know that yet; such was the snail's pace of communication then that it would be another month before anyone in California heard the news.

It was perhaps a measure of the national arrogance that in the flushed excitement over the possible intrigues of England and Mexico and the course of empire, the Americans forgot about the *other* inhabitants of the region—the Indians all around them. Fremont was so preoccupied that he neglected to post a watchman that night.

But by the time he drifted off to sleep, Fremont had already made up his mind which path he would take. He later wrote, "The information through Gillespie had absolved me from my duty as an explorer, and I was left to my duty as an officer of the American Army with the future authoritative knowledge that . . . to obtain possession of California was the chief object of the President." Fremont said he now fully appreciated that "the men who understood the future of our country, and who ruled its destinies, regarded the California coast as the boundary fixed by nature to round off our national domain."

Chapter 12 WE WILL CORRECT ALL THIS

On August 14, 1846, two days after the Navajo raid on Las Vegas, General Kearny marched with his Army of the West into the town's central plaza, dismounted from his bay charger, and demanded that the mayor, or *alcalde,* join him in addressing a milling crowd of several hundred shocked villagers.

This was the first village of any size that Kearny's army had encountered, and he wanted to set a certain tone. The people of Las Vegas were fascinated by the Americans, but also afraid. The women cowered in the shadowy edges of the square, drawn up in their shawls and rebozos, some of them nervously smoking cornhusk cigarettes, while the men in their brightly colored serapes and glazed sombreros pushed forward into the open light of the plaza. (Susan Magoffin, who passed through town a few days later, described the Las Vegans as "wild looking strangers" who "constantly stared" and "swarmed around me like bees . . . some of the little ones in a perfect state of nudity.") The village dogs barked incessantly, and pigs could be heard snuffling in their sties, but otherwise the town was silent, the people waiting to hear what the American general had to say.

Kearny and the *alcalde* climbed a rickety ladder to the flat mud roof of one of the adobe buildings facing the plaza. From there, Kearny, wearing a blue flannel frock coat with gold buttons and epaulets and a saber swinging at his side, peered down at the villagers. With the *alcalde* standing awkwardly at his side, Kearny began to speak the will of the United States of America. He did not mince words.

"I have come amongst you by the orders of my government to take possession of your country," Kearny said through an interpreter, his voice even and calm. He pointed to the many hundreds of American troops who were steadily filing past the town on the way to occupy the capital of Santa Fe. "There goes my army. You see but a small portion of it." And yet, the general said, "we come amongst you as friends, not as enemies; as protectors, not as conquerors. Henceforth, I absolve you of all allegiance to the Mexican government."

At this the crowd erupted in a "great sensation," as an American lieutenant put it, a confusion of shouting, cheers, and gasps. Kearny waited for the hubbub to die down, and then continued. "From the

Mexican government," he said, "you have *never* received protection. The Navajos come down from the mountains and carry off your sheep, and even your women, whenever they please."

The people of Las Vegas eyed one another with quickened interest and vigorously nodded. "*Si, si*—it is true," they said.

Kearny sensed that he'd struck a nerve. He had heard about the recent Navajo raid. He realized that he was conquering a people who were already cowed and exhausted by a savage war of the frontier—a war that the United States was now, for better or worse, inheriting. "My government," he said with perfect confidence, "will *correct* all this. It will protect you in your persons and property. Your enemies will become our enemies. We will keep off the Indians."

The villagers were skeptical of this tall promise. The Mexican army, it is true, had never protected them from the Navajo menace, nor had it given the people weapons with which they might defend themselves. All the villagers had to beat back the Indians were lances, bows and arrows, and a few antique muskets dating back to the 1700s. The Spanish had been equally impotent to stop the raids. Navajo predation, it seemed, was part of the order of things in this harsh extremity of the faded Spanish empire, where the echoed idioms of Cervantes were still spoken.

But now the villagers of Las Vegas must have wondered what stout strain of ambition had marched into their midst, this conqueror who called himself a friend. What kind of army was this that presumed to vanquish in an effortless sprint not only their nation but also their nation's sworn enemy? Even if he wanted to, what made this man in the fancy blue uniform think he could "correct all this," reversing the hard pattern of centuries?

Kearny went further. "Not a pepper, not an onion, shall be taken by my troops without pay," he promised. "I will protect you in your persons and property and in your religion. Some of your priests have told you that we would ill-treat your women and brand them on the cheek, as you do your mules on the hip. It is all false."

General Kearny then insisted that the *alcalde* pledge an oath of allegiance to the United States, on the rooftop for all to see. "Look at me in the face," Kearny demanded as the townsfolk watched. The *al-calde* had a hollow expression, but, reluctantly at first, he did as he was told. The short oath ended with a solemnity that was not trivial for a Catholic man swearing before a crowd of staunch Catholics and the glaring village priest. After proclaiming his fealty to the United States of America, he was made to say—*In the name of the Father, the Son, and the Holy Ghost.*

Then Kearny and his men bounded off for Santa Fe, which lay beyond the mountains, some seventy miles to the west. Thus far the conquest of New Mexico had been uneventful. But Kearny's runners learned that the governor of New Mexico was planning to put up a major fight in a canyon fifteen miles outside the city. If Kearny's intelligence was accurate, Armijo had three thousand men already dug into the canyon, waiting to repulse the American invaders.

Chapter 13   N A R B O N A   P A S S

Narbona returned from the Hopi country after the great drought of the 1820s only to hear accounts of the massacre of the chiefs at Jemez, and he understood that little had changed: The old war was very much alive. But Narbona, now sixty-three years old, seemed to understand that ultimately the Navajos would never gain anything from this grinding conflict. The grand old warrior took a different tack— he began to preach peace. In 1829 he was invited to come to Santa Fe for talks, but fearing a trap like the one that had been laid at Jemez, Narbona insisted that the Mexican governor furnish him with a full military escort.

Although suspicious of the Mexicans, he decided that the journey was worth the risk. The ensuing conference in Santa Fe did not achieve any lasting results for the Navajo people, but by establishing himself as a peace leader, he was at least successful in protecting his own outfit—inoculating it, in effect—from further Mexican attacks. He made two other trips to Santa Fe, in 1832 and 1833, and for a time the hostilities seemed to quiet down.

But then in early February 1835, Narbona learned that the Mexicans were mounting a massive campaign against the eastern Navajos. Narbona and his people had kept the peace and refrained from raiding for many years, but certainly an invasion of their homeland called for war. Word reached him that a force of more than one thousand Mexican soldiers and armed civilians had left Santa Fe on February 8 and was aimed toward Navajo country. Among the invaders were a large number of Pueblo Indian warriors.

Narbona hastily gathered together 250 of the best Navajo warriors and raced to a little notch in the Chuska Mountains known as Beesh Lichii'I Bigiizh, or Copper Pass. He knew that the Mexicans would have to pass through this eight-thousand-foot-high rock defile if they were to penetrate Navajo country. When they did, Narbona and his warriors would be waiting for them, hiding in the tall pines on the ridgeline above.

The next morning a dust cloud appeared on the dun floor of the broad flat valley to the east. Soon the Mexican soldiers came into view, a long tattered scarf of men on horseback in the distance, riding along the frozen Rio Chaco. Their silver buttons shone in the morning sun, giving Narbona plenty of time to prepare. On this cold, gusty day in February, the invading army was marching headlong into an ambush. Precisely as Narbona had guessed, it was aiming for Copper Pass.

The long column of Mexicans was led by Capt. Blas de Hinojos, the *comandante general* of New Mexican territory. In raw numbers, his was the largest armed expedition that either Spain or Mexico had ever mounted against the Navajos, and his soldiers were exceedingly confident. But Hinojos's men were an undisciplined band of mostly young men, scarcely more than a rabble. They marched jauntily through the pass without a care, singing songs, laughing, devoid of any sort of military order. American trader Josiah Gregg recorded that the Mexicans were "utterly unconscious of the reception that

awaited them, [and] soon came jogging along in scattered groups, in-
dulging in every kind of boisterous mirth."

Concealed behind large gray rocks at the summit, Narbona told
his men to wait in perfect silence until the Mexicans were right below
them, in the narrowest part of the pass, where they would have to
stretch out in a long, thin column. He compared the vulnerable file
of men to the trunk of a tall tree. When the moment is right, he said,
we will cut the tree into small pieces, just right for firewood. Several
times the impatient younger warriors signaled their eagerness to ini-
tiate the fight, but Narbona calmly held them off. Down in the
canyon, many of the soldiers had to dismount so their horses, already
weary from their trek, could climb the steep path.

Finally the moment came. Narbona gave the signal, and the Navajos erupted in war-whoops, their haunting owl-like call. Arrows
rained down upon the Mexicans. Those Navajos who had guns began
to fire volleys into the startled ranks; others hurled rocks or shoved
boulders down into the gorge. The horses began to scatter and stampede, trampling the men. As Gregg records it, the Mexicans were
"thrown into a state of speechless consternation. Some tumbled off
their horses, others fired their muskets at random; a terrific panic
seized everybody."

Scores, perhaps hundreds, of Mexicans were slain. A historian of
the Mexican-Navajo wars later wrote that "they were felled like deer
trapped in a box canyon." One of the many soldiers killed was the
leader of the expedition, Captain Hinojos. According to Navajo tradition, the captain of Jemez Pueblo, having become cornered by
Navajo warriors, jumped off a precipice to his death rather than face
capture.

In the end the Mexicans were routed. The final tally of casualties
is not known, but by nearly all accounts it was a wholesale slaughter.
Interviewed years after the incident, an elderly Navajo who had been
a warrior at Copper Pass would say only, "We killed plenty of them."

From that day on Copper Pass was known by a different name. Although Navajos seldom named landmarks after individuals, such was
their pride in their resounding victory over the hated Mexicans that

the people made an exception to their custom and gave the great defile a new honorific: Narbona Pass.

Chapter 14   THE UNINVADED SILENCE

Aroused from his sleep at Fremont's camp on the south shore of Klamath Lake, Kit Carson thought he heard something, some random noise in the glade, a snap that seemed out of place. The nearly fifty miles he'd ridden that day should have left him dog-tired and oblivious to such sounds, but Carson was a notoriously light sleeper on the trail, his fears conditioned by experience, his nerves pulled tight as a trip wire.

Carson's eyes quickly scanned the camp. There was Fremont, sitting across the way, reading letters by his own fire. There were the others, spun up in their bedrolls, scattered about the campsite in twos and threes. The party had fourteen men, all told. They snored and snuffled away—greasy, wild-haired expeditioners at home in the wilderness: The French trapper Basil Lajeunesse; a contingent of Delaware Indians, expert trackers who'd been hired back in Kansas; Lucien Maxwell and Alex Godey and Dick Owens, fellow mountain men who were Carson's old friends; and the new arrival, the feisty Marine, Archibald Gillespie, whose dispatches Fremont was now reading, the letters so absorbing that he seemed to ignore the other men.

It was the night of May 9, 1846, and this small group of explorers lay camped in the wilds of southern Oregon. Although they didn't realize it yet, Fremont's men had stumbled upon one of the largest freshwater lakes west of the Mississippi, thirty miles long, its waters teeming with salmon and so saturated with volcanic nutrients that a certain species of algae bloomed along its marshy shores, giving the shallows a strange, blue-green fluorescence. Klamath Lake was the kind of plum assignment a trained geographer like Fremont lived for. For the past week he and his expedition topographers had been sketching the lake country's contours with a camera lucida, clipping plant specimens, taking astronomical readings, consulting their barometers and other instruments, shooting the sun with a sextant at high noon. The Klamath Lake region was "all wild and unexplored," Fremont rhapsodized, "and the uninvaded silence roused our curiosity."

They were in dangerous country now, and Carson was keenly aware of it. A generation earlier, when Jedediah Smith first passed through these precincts, his party of fifteen men was set upon by Indians; only Smith and two others survived with their scalps intact.

Now, on this chilly spring night, Carson was troubled that Fremont had neglected to post a watchman, something he almost always did. But as Carson looked around the tenebrous woods, he saw nothing out of place. The fire ticked and hissed. Smoke curled into the canopy. There was the clean rush of the creek, the wind sighing through the pines, the splash of the waves down on Klamath Lake. The Cascade Mountains, off to the west, were still mantled in spring snow, and their raw peaks gleamed in the moonlight.

Carson said he "apprehended no danger." He rolled himself tight in his saddle blanket and drifted off to sleep.

◎

Later that night, Carson awoke to a distinct sound—a heavy, dull thud. It seemed to come from over by where Lajeunesse lay sleeping. Carson rose up on an elbow and barked, "S'matter over there, Basil?"

The Frenchman gave no answer.

Now Carson clutched his pistol and jumped to his feet. He ran toward his friend Lajeunesse. It was hard to see, but in the shadowy firelight, Carson caught something, a sickening sheen: The Frenchman's head had been cleaved into while he slept. The pale brain glistened, the hairy skull gaped in a widening pool of blood.

"*Indians!*" Carson cried out, firing his pistol into the darkness. The camp was encircled by what appeared to be several dozen attackers, darting in the shadows, plinging arrows.

Everyone sprang to action—everyone, that is, except for Denny, one of the Delaware Indians, a beloved tracker. Carson now saw that he, too, had been attacked in his sleep. He was shot through with arrows. Carson heard Denny give out a groan as he died.

Another Delaware, known as Crane, seized a rifle and snapped vainly away until he realized that it was unloaded. He snatched it by the barrel and swung the gun's stock at his assailants. But Crane was exposed in the firelight, and the enemy bows soon found him. He collapsed with five arrows buried in his chest.

A painted brave, whom Carson judged to be the leader, stole into camp and fought valiantly at close range, managing to hold off Fremont's men for a few long minutes. Carson, Owens, and several others cracked their guns at the warrior, and he stumbled to the ground. Dangling from his wrist was a steel hand ax, presumably the weapon that had killed Lajeunesse.

When the other attackers saw their bravest warrior fall, they receded into the gloom. For a while they mounted occasional charges, attempting to retrieve their leader's body, but Fremont was determined to deny them this reward. Carson and some of the others hung blankets from the boughs of the trees as a kind of screen to blunt the rain of enemy arrows; they held steady, fending off the sorties. Finally the attackers gave up and disappeared for good.

For the rest of the night, Carson and the others nervously guarded the perimeter, wide-eyed, weapons drawn, attuned for another attack. After several anxious hours dawn broke, and the feathery woods opened up. The country seemed clear of Indians, and the lake shone its ghostly turquoise. The three dead men in Fremont's party lay sprawled on the ground. Someone had covered them with blankets.

Carson walked over and inspected the corpse of the fearless Indian warrior who had killed Lajeunesse. He wore a feathered warbonnet and his skin was painted in elaborate patterns. He had forty arrows in his quiver. They were beautiful and finely made, their tips slathered with a poison paste.

This was a Klamath, Carson seemed sure, a lake-land tribe he'd encountered before. They were, he thought, a "mean, low-lived, treacherous race." He and the others concluded that this was the same band of Indians to whom they had given gifts of tobacco, meat, and knives only a few days ago.

Carson examined the ax, which was attached by a leather thong to the warrior's wrist, and recognized it as British-made. Then, too, some of the arrows he found around the camp were headed with lancetlike scraps of iron that could only have come from the Hudson's Bay Company outpost on the Umpqua River, a nearby British concern. Maybe, Carson speculated, the British had put the Klamaths up to this? In the mid-1820s, Hudson's Bay had tried to trap beaver to extinction along the Snake and other interior rivers in order to create what was called a "fur desert," which the company's jealous operatives hoped would discourage American penetration into the more valuable Columbia River country. Any company willing to pursue a policy that ruthless wouldn't think twice about siccing angry Indians on an American exploration party.

It was hard to say, but after closely studying the camp and interpreting the footprints and other signs, he guessed the attack had involved twenty Klamath warriors.

Now he crouched over their leader's bullet-riddled body. Carson had made a career of fighting Indians, but he was particularly impressed by this Klamath. "The bravest Indian I ever saw," he later said. "If his men had been as brave as him, we would all have been killed."

Then Carson removed the ax from the dead warrior's wrist and held it by the handle, testing its heft. The bodies of Lajeunesse, Denny, and Crane lay where they had fallen, their blanketed forms sharpening in the filtered light of dawn. All were "brave, good men," Carson said. They were his friends, and as their guide Carson felt a responsibility for their deaths. He was especially close to Lajeunesse, having ridden thousands of miles with him on Fremont's various expeditions.

The camp was plunged in "an angry gloom," as Fremont put it, yet everyone recognized that the situation could have been much worse, that they all could have been killed. Already the surviving Delawares were engaged in their grieving rites. They smeared themselves in black paint, they wailed and flagellated themselves. "Sick," said one of the mourners, a man named Sagundai. "Very sick now."

Touched perhaps by their sorrow, a wrath began to stir within Carson. Impulsively, he raised the steel ax and sank it into the Klamath warrior's skull.

This did not satisfy his rage. He had lived among Indians for most of his adult life, had absorbed their battle rituals and frenzies of grief. He, too, was mourning now, and he wanted to punish the warrior's spirit with the same ax that had killed Lajeunesse. He hoped this Klamath's comrades would enjoy the full horror of finding him lying here, mutilated and defiled.

And so he hacked away at the corpse's face until it was a sodden tangle—until, as Fremont later put it, "He knocked his head to pieces."

Chapter 15 ON THE ALTAR OF THE COUNTRY

In the blast heat of mid-August, the New Mexicans waited for General Kearny. More than three thousand men had answered their governor's call to patriotism. They had streamed from their villages and ranches and cornfields, rich and poor alike, boys on burros and peasants in their tattered sombreros and old men hobbling on arthritic feet. Chanting *Crush the gringo invaders! Stop the infidels!*—they toted antique muskets, lances, swords, bows and arrows, clubs. They assembled fifteen miles southeast of Santa Fe in a narrow defile called Apache Canyon, so named because the Apaches had for years used it as a place to ambush wagon trains.

Apache Canyon was the eastern gateway to Santa Fe, a parched and rattlesnakey place well suited for defense: As the Santa Fe Trail passed through its tight jaws, the road became so constricted that travelers could enter only one wagon at a time. From the high rock walls, screened behind trees and boulders, a well-positioned army could rain unmerciful fire down upon any invading force. And so, just as the Americans had suspected and feared, the New Mexicans would mount their final defense here.

After weeks of indecisiveness in the face of conflicting rumors about the size and precise intent of the American advance, the New Mexicans now had to work fast. They hauled some old cannons from Santa Fe and set them up in strategic places along the canyon walls. They stockpiled ammunition. They chopped down trees that obstructed the lines of fire and began to dig themselves in.

They were, all in all, an abysmal army, untrained and laughably ill equipped. But they enjoyed one advantage: They loved their country, most of them, and were keen in their desperation to defend it. They had become convinced that the Americans meant to destroy their ancient way of life, to ravage their women, and even to abolish their faith. Santa Fe was plunged into pandemonium. Many of the clergy packed up and fled. Officials proposed destroying the city's churches to prevent the enemy from desecrating them as barracks. Wealthy families boarded up their homes and joined relatives in the south. The rest sent their women into the mountains, and then picked up whatever weapons they could find and made their way to Apache Canyon.

For days, as the canyon's defenders improved their fortifications, dissension brewed in their ranks. No one was quite sure who was in charge, and there were conflicting ideas about how best to hold the canyon. Finally, after many unexplained delays, the governor rode into camp accompanied by a retinue of one hundred presidial soldiers and most of the members of the New Mexican legislative assembly. With his strong presence, it seemed the defenders' efforts would gain new focus.

The governor, Don Manuel Armijo, was a master of court intrigues who had been in and out of power for years. Having risen through cunning from humble peasant origins near Albuquerque, Armijo had a reputation for shameless corruption. He was not above outright stealing: It was said that as a boy he had made his first wealth by robbing a few thousand head of sheep from a prominent man and then selling them back to him. After the Santa Fe Trail opened, he had finagled a post as the collector of customs, and by levying (and personally pocketing) exorbitant tariffs against the American traders, he had amassed a fortune. By charging $500 for every wagon-load that entered Santa Fe, regardless of the contents, Armijo reportedly collected as much as $60,000 per year.

As governor, Armijo was an avid gambler, a secretive breeder of racehorses, and a composer of florid but deeply cryptic proclamations that left the public not quite knowing where he stood. He was arbitrary in his affairs and thought nothing of stealing from his own people without pretext or provocation. "God rules the heavens," he liked to say, "but Armijo rules the earth." One army lieutenant who later investigated him reported that it was "Armijo's practice, in peace or in war, to seize the person or property of anyone who fell under his displeasure." Armijo was called a general, but that was just a bit of title inflation he permitted himself; he had no military training whatsoever. Still, he loved to wear flamboyant uniforms—with bright sashes, glinting swords, and feathery plumes. He was a decorous and gracious host. At the Palace of the Governors he would entertain far into the night, always generous with his imported delicacies and decanters of El Paso brandy. Though married, he kept several mistresses. He had a round, jowly face that was not unhandsome, but he was extremely, almost operatically, obese—"a mountain of fat" in the estimation of one English travel writer who passed through New Mexico.

Armijo was, above all, a survivor, and while he put on a bold face, he could be an impressive coward when cornered. "It is smarter to appear brave," he liked to say, "than to *be* so."

❧

Earlier in the summer, when Armijo first received word that the American army was pressing toward Santa Fe, the "general" behaved strangely. First, he kept to his quarters and did nothing at all. Then he hastily held a meeting of prominent officials in which he called for "a great sacrifice on the altar of the country" while simultaneously indicating that any resistance was doomed. At one point he even asked his own ministers, to their shock, "whether I ought to defend New Mexico . . . or not."

Shortly after that, he secretly entertained an American emissary sent ahead by Kearny, offered him a sumptuous meal, and patiently considered his arguments. The emissary was James Magoffin, brother-in-law of Susan Magoffin, still recovering from her miscarriage back at Bent's Fort. President Polk himself had given the savvy trader what amounted to plenipotentiary powers to negotiate a deal with Armijo. He had come straightaway from Washington to Bent's Fort with high-level orders cloaked in absolute secrecy.

In early August, James Magoffin left Bent's Fort with a small escort of dragoons. A jovial sophisticate, he traveled in style as was his wont, puffing opium and sipping claret in his carriage as he sped to Santa Fe. Behind closed doors at the Palace of the Governors, Magoffin may have offered Armijo a considerable sum of money if he would promise not to take up arms. Whether the governor accepted this outright bribe has never been proven, and the details of their conference are shrouded in conjecture. But given everything that is known about Armijo's rather legendary venality, and his erratic behavior leading up to the American invasion, it seems quite likely that he did.

Even while he was hosting Magoffin, the governor liquidated his own considerable business holdings and cleaned out the church coffers. Then he sent a series of formal letters to Kearny through express runners. These oddly worded messages seemed to float opaquely somewhere between capitulation and tepid defiance. "You have notified me that you intend to take possession of the country I govern," one of Armijo's letters read. "The people of the country have risen en masse in my defense. If you take the country, it will be because you are strongest in battle. I suggest you to stop . . . and we will meet and negotiate on the plains."

Armijo was stalling for time. He was shrewd enough to keep his true intentions to himself. He wrote nothing down—he was, in fact, only half literate. But, truly, he found himself in an impossible situation. His government was bankrupt. His army was a joke. If he put up a fight, the Americans would surely have him hanged. His only slender hope was for his superiors in faraway Chihuahua to send up military reinforcements, and when by mid-August those failed to arrive, he was left in a fretful predicament—"forced," as one historian put it, "to heave from position to position."

Other New Mexican leaders, however, unequivocally insisted that Governor Armijo defend the homeland—to the last man, if necessary. Foremost among these stalwarts was Col. Diego Archuleta, an influential politician and a courageous soldier who was Armijo's second-in-command. In temperament and character, Archuleta was the very opposite of Armijo. For him, it was not a question of whether the war could be won; it was simply a question of honor. Archuleta was astounded that Armijo could even think of deserting the cause. At all costs, the New Mexican people must repulse the invaders, or die trying.

Archuleta had been the prime mover in mustering the volunteers who assembled at Apache Canyon, and he was optimistic about their success. He realized that the American lines of communication, not to mention its supply trains, were now spread out over many hundreds of dismal, Comanche-infested miles. Kearny's troops must surely be hot, hungry, sick, and demoralized, their livestock jaded, their will to fight withering under the high plains sun as they marched a thousand miles from their home. Besides, the New Mexicans outnumbered Kearny's force by more than two-to-one. If they had time to get themselves properly dug in, Apache Canyon would be nearly impossible to breach.

The faithful defenders at Apache Canyon, by and large, were not privy to Armijo's behind-the-scenes vacillations; as far as they knew, their governor remained a staunch protector of the province. That was, at least, the pose he had assumed in public. On August 8, Armijo had circulated a war proclamation that sounded, on its surface, like a clarion call: "Fellow Patriots," it read, "the moment has come at last when the country requires from her sons the bottomless sacrifice which circumstances claim for her salvation." He asked them to show the "highest devotion to homeland," assuring them that "he who actually governs you is ready to sacrifice his life and interests in defense of his beloved country." On the other hand, anyone who closely parsed the governor's call to arms may have detected undertones of equivocation. At one point Armijo urged his subjects to "seek victory . . . *if it be possible*, for no one is obliged to do what is impossible." He told the citizens that, regrettably, they would have to foot the bill themselves, and then basically left the whole matter in their hands: "Your governor is dependent upon your pecuniary resources, upon your decision, and upon your convictions."

On August 16, as the governor rode into the mouth of Apache Canyon, he wore one of his snappiest uniforms and straddled a prized horse that groaned under his staggering weight. He surveyed the breastworks his men were constructing and seemed to like what he saw. He mouthed a few encouraging words about the coming battle. Armijo was a good thespian and knew how to rally a crowd. But even while he bellowed and spluttered and shifted his "mountain of fat" in his beautiful silver-trimmed saddle, restlessly working his horse's ribs with the enormous rowels of his spurs, the governor seemed troubled, his gaze distracted by far-off concerns.

Chapter 16   A PERFECT BUTCHERY

On the morning after the Klamath attack, it was already decided: Fremont would return to California just as he'd been angling to do all along. His scientific expedition would metamorphose more frankly into a military one, and he would meld what he considered his own shining future with that of a soon-to-be-continental nation.

But before he could turn south, Fremont had another, less glorious matter to attend to—avenging the deaths of his three comrades. The

Klamaths must suffer a terrible price, he vowed. It was a matter of honoring Lajeunesse and the two fallen Delawares, but it was also the principle of the thing: No exploring party, now or in the future, should ever have to suffer an unprovoked attack like this again. "For the moment," Fremont wrote, "I threw all other considerations aside and determined to square accounts with these people before I left them."

Fremont decided to make a northward clockwise circuit around the entirety of Klamath Lake, eventually intersecting with the others in his expedition party who were camped on the north shore. As he crept along the timbered shoreline, Fremont planned to search for Indian villages and exact retribution wherever he went. Carson had no problem with this course of action; his outrage over the loss of his old friend Lajeunesse was still keen. "The Indians had commenced the war with us without cause," Carson later said. "I thought they should be chastised in a summary manner."

That morning, May 10, 1846, Carson and the others wrapped the bodies of Denny, Crane, and Lajeunesse in blankets and slung them over the pack animals. Carson wanted to bury them in some nice spot by the lake near the main camp, where they had shovels to dig a proper grave. But as the party threaded through the thick timber, the now-rigid corpses kept thudding and smacking against the trunks of the trees, "becoming much bruised," according to Carson. Realizing they could not in good conscience continue this ghoulish procession, the men scraped a shallow hole with their knives and solemnly buried their friends together, covering the grave with logs and brush to avoid detection. Fremont, exercising the explorer's prerogative, named the nearby brook Denny Creek—a name it still carries to this day.

Fremont's party resumed the march north. The Delaware Indians were the first to detect Klamaths in the bush. They took off in pursuit and in a few moments came the reports of their long rifles. Soon the Delawares returned, bearing two bloody scalps. "Very sick before," one of them said. "Better now."

They kept moving along the shoreline. Fremont picked Carson and ten other men to scout an area where he believed a Klamath settlement was located. Carson's group surged ten miles ahead and soon found the hamlet. They crept up and viewed it from the cattails. It was a large fishing village, named Dokdokwas, built near a marshy place where the Williamson River flowed into Upper Klamath Lake. The village had more than fifty lodges and bustled with life: Dogs yapped, women wove mats out of the lake reeds, fishermen glided about in their dugout canoes. Fillets of salmon and sucker-fish dried in the curing smoke.

Suddenly the villagers became agitated, and Carson realized they'd spotted him. He called for an immediate charge, and although they were greatly outnumbered, the eleven men cantered across the shallows and raced into the now-swarming village. Carson's small party fired away with impunity. Most of the Klamath men were out fishing or hunting, and those few present were armed only with bows and arrows. In a few minutes Carson and his men had killed twenty-one Indians. Frantically the surviving villagers scattered for the hills, and the Delawares slaughtered many of them in their hiding places. Some of the Klamath boys swam away beneath the water, breathing through hollow reeds.

It was, as Carson might say, a perfect butchery—by any standards, pure and literal overkill. "We gave them something to remember," he said. "They were severely punished." Although Carson claimed his men "did not interfere with" women or children, one of his men later wrote that he found at least one "old Indian woman" dead in a canoe. Klamath accounts of the attack on Dokdokwas insist that many women and children were massacred.

Carson then ordered the village destroyed. "I wished to do them as much damage as I could," he later reasoned, "so I directed their houses to be set on fire." His men fanned out and torched the Klamath lodges, semisubterranean hovels made of mud and logs woven together with patterned reeds that, being brittle and dry, were extremely flammable. Soon the whole village was ablaze. It was, Carson thought, "a beautiful sight."

Fremont saw the billowing smoke from a distance and raced to catch up. When he galloped into the burning village, the captain was sorely disappointed to have "arrived too late for the sport." But he seemed immensely satisfied. Said Fremont: "It will be a story for them to hand down while there are any Klamaths still living on their lake."

(True to Fremont's prediction, the massacre at Dokdokwas is indeed a story handed down among the Klamaths—and it still serves as a reminder of what happened in their people's very first encounter with an official party of Americans. The tribe never rebuilt what was then their largest fishing village; today Dokdokwas is a pristine and desolate swath of reedy shoreline, with no markers to indicate what happened there. According to historian David Roberts, who writes perceptively about the curious friendship between Fremont and Carson in his fine study *A Newer World*, the tragedy at Dokdokwas is deepened by the fact that most scholars now agree that Fremont and Carson, in their blind vindictiveness, probably chose the wrong tribe to lash out against: In all likelihood the band of Indians that had killed Lajeunesse and the two Delawares were from the neighboring Modocs, another lake-land tribe centered closer to the Oregon-California border. The Klamaths were culturally related to the Modocs, but the two tribes were bitter enemies.)

Later that day, one of the Klamath warriors returned to Dokdokwas and, realizing his village had been destroyed, drew a bow on Carson in the deep woods. Spying him, Carson raised his gun but it misfired. The Klamath was about to let his poison arrow fly when Fremont—riding a fearless gray warhorse he called Sacramento—glimpsed Carson's predicament. He wheeled Sacramento and trampled the hapless warrior, whose arrow flew awry. Sagundai, a Delaware chief, then descended on the injured Klamath and pummeled him to death with a club. From that moment on, Carson felt he owed Fremont his life. "In all probability, if he had not run over the Indian as he did, I would have been shot," Carson later said. "I owe my life to them two—the captain and Sacramento saved me."

As Fremont and his men completed their long, brutal circuit around Klamath Lake, they continued to kill Indians in a desultory fashion, in ones and twos, but their anger was spent. Even Fremont had reached the bottom of his revenge. "I had now kept the promise I made to myself and had punished these people well for their treachery," he wrote in his memoirs. "Now I turned my thought to the work which they had delayed."

Fremont headed due south now, crossing out of the realm of the Klamaths and on into California. Yet as he and his expedition members dropped out of the Sierras and into the Sacramento Valley, they were nearly continuously hounded by Indians of various tribes—Yahooskins, Modocs, Shastas—whose warriors were clearly riled by reports emanating from Klamath Lake. Carson felt a constant hint of attack, an awareness that the party was being watched. At one point Carson suggested that they bypass a deep gorge where, he rightly suspected, Indians had planned an ambush. Some of those Indians followed Fremont's party, however, and Carson decided to ride into their midst and flush them out. Suddenly one of them emerged from behind a rock. "He came from his hiding place and commenced firing arrows very rapidly," Carson narrates in his autobiography. "I dismounted and fired. My shot had the desired effect."

Carson was impressed by the warrior he had just killed and bore him no ill will: "He was a brave Indian, deserved a better fate, but he had placed himself on the wrong path."

Carson collected the warrior's "fine bow and beautiful quiver of arrows" and presented them as a souvenir to Lieutenant Gillespie. More accustomed to sea travails, Gillespie was exhausted by this nerve-racking existence and was dazzled by trail-savvy men like Carson, who seemed to have the stomach and aptitude for it. "By heaven, this is rough work!" he exclaimed to Fremont. "I'll take care to let them know about it in Washington."

But Fremont's mind was elsewhere. He replied, "It will be long enough before we see Washington again."

Chapter 17   THE FIRE OF MONTEZUMA

By mid-August, Gen. Stephen Watts Kearny's forces were only a few days' march away from Santa Fe. Passing through the tiny towns of Tecolote and San Miguel and then following the bends of the Pecos River, Kearny heard so many rumors about Armijo that he resolved to ignore them all. Apache Canyon might be the Scylla and Charybdis of the Southwest, but he was pressing on—averaging twenty miles a day, a frenetic pace for an army that had already logged eight hundred. Two-thirds of the horses had died along the way, a fact that Kearny, the equine sentimentalist, found hard to bear. Most of his cavalry had become infantry, joining the larger body of Missouri volunteers who had slogged it on foot all the way from Fort Leavenworth.

Kearny's blistered men were now practically starving; they had been on one-third rations since Bent's Fort, and they grumbled about the smiting heat. "Our guns become so hot we cannot handle them," Pvt. Jacob Robinson wrote, "and the sand burns our feet. The dreaded Sirocco blows as from a heated oven, burning us even through our clothes. The discontented men say, 'Let us be anywhere rather than in this desert.' " The land was so parched, wrote another soldier, that "it appeared as though it had not been refreshed by a shower since the day of Noah's flood."

To make matters worse, water on the trail was hardly potable. Marcellus Edwards of Missouri's Company D described a pool of rancid water his thirsty comrades dived into one early August morning: "It was so bad that one who drank it would have to shut both eyes and hold his breath until the nauseating dose was swallowed. Notwithstanding its scarcity, some men allowed their horses to tramp through it, which soon stirred it up to a thick mud. And to give it still greater flavor, we found a dead snake with the flesh dropping from his bones."

Kearny dismissed all such whining and pushed on without a break. He understood the salient fact of invasion, that delays almost always favor a defense. He kept receiving strange letters from Armijo, letters maundering on in elegant phrases that said everything and nothing. Army of the West lieutenant John Hughes described one such letter as "very politely dictated, and so ambiguous in its expressions that it was impossible to know whether it was the Governor's intention to meet Gen. Kearny in council, or in conflict."

Still, Kearny was worried about Apache Canyon. The Santa Fe traders traveling with him knew all about the narrow pass and had been warning him since they were at Bent's Fort that this was the most likely place where the New Mexicans would put up a fight. He sent spies ahead and kept moving as fast as he could.

Another advantage of maintaining a high rate of speed, Kearny believed, was that it kept his forces out of trouble: The pace of their march gave the men focus, it harnessed them to the task at hand, it kept their appetites from wandering. With such a large and unruly army of green volunteers spread out over a hundred miles of trail, there was every opportunity for a devolution of military order. As the war progressed in other provinces of northern Mexico, Gen. Zachary Taylor's volunteers were acquiring a reputation for "sexual terrorism," as one historian put it. But the Army of the West simply had no time or energy for rape or pillage.

Riding up and down the ranks, the stern Episcopalian general set a tone of probity. John Hughes saw Kearny as a "sagacious officer well-fitted for command of veteran troops," but he believed the general unfairly expected the same high standards of "rigid austerity" from the Missourians as he did from his seasoned dragoons. The volunteers, Hughes thought, "are bred to freedom and fired by feeling, principle, and honor" rather than "the study of arms." These young bucks feared and respected Kearny, but they did not much care for his discipline. The punishments Kearny meted out could be severe, even

Sisyphean. One Army of the West diarist reported a case in which a group of five soldiers, having committed some minor infraction, were "court-martialed for insubordination" and then each sentenced to lug forty pounds of sand for a week.

After trekking all this way across the scorched continent, most of the Missourians were itching for a fight. One volunteer wrote that he and his comrades were "full of ardor, burning for the battlefield, and panting for the reward of honorable victory." As rumors of the coming engagement at Apache Canyon spread, a palpable excitement gathered in their ranks. The pace of their march quickened, and they erupted in war songs—*Oh, what a joy to fight the dons and wallop fat Armij-O! So clear the way to Santa Fe, with that we all agree-O!*

In contrast to his hot-blooded volunteers, however, General Kearny did not want to engage the enemy unless he absolutely must. In fact, he preferred not to view the New Mexicans as enemies at all. Kearny hoped to take New Mexico without firing a shot—it would be a "bloodless conquest," he vowed. He understood that if the United States intended to occupy this province and eventually absorb it into the Union, he would have to win the people over.

And so in every settlement he passed, he met with the local leaders and gave some variation of the speech he had delivered from the rooftop in Las Vegas. His men would harm no one, he said. The United States was not hostile to Catholicism. The American army would protect them against the savage tribes. Their women were safe. No one would be branded like a steer. With his interpreters, Kearny wrote up a proclamation in Spanish that conveyed all these points and then sent riders ahead to tack up copies in every town square. In several instances Kearny's troops captured Mexican spies who had been dispatched by Armijo. But rather than hold them as prisoners, the general decided the better course was to show mercy and release them. By doing so, he hoped they might return to Santa Fe and spread stories of American beneficence. More cynically, he trusted that they would report back to Armijo and exaggerate the might of the American forces; Kearny knew from experience that an enemy's size had a way of growing in the excitement of retelling.

⊠

On the night of August 17, Kearny camped near the ruins of the ancient pueblo of Pecos, in a grassy valley where the Pecos River came spilling from a cleft in the mountains. Pecos had been occupied for five hundred years, and until recently it was the largest of all the Pueblo Indian villages. At one time as many as three thousand people had lived there. The pueblo had a legend that concerned the "fire of Montezuma." The Indians believed they were related to the great Aztec leader, and that one day long ago Montezuma instructed them to build a permanent fire in a subterranean chamber. Under no circumstances was the fire to be extinguished until a certain people arrived from the east to liberate them from the tyrannies of Spanish rule.

And so for hundreds of years, as they languished under conquistadors and friars, the Pecos people secretly fed the fire in a special kiva, a round ceremonial room with a smokehole, built underground. Over the patient centuries, tending the fire remained a kind of druidic ritual for them, a symbol of their longing for the prophesied deliverers. The rites were dutifully maintained until the year 1838, when some rash of diseases, doubtless borne on the wagon trains that passed the pueblo on the nearby Santa Fe Trail, decimated the Pecos population. Then a series of Comanche raids nearly finished them off. Facing extinction, the last seventeen Pecos Indians vacated their once-great pueblo and took up residence in the safety of the Jemez Mountains sixty miles to the west, joining a kindred tribe that spoke the same language. The fire was left to die at Pecos, but it was said that a dedicated group of the exiles transported the last embers to their new home in the Jemez and continued the tradition there.

Kearny's soldiers were amazed by the Pecos ruins and liked the sound of the legend—particularly the part about a certain people coming from the east to liberate the long-suffering Indians. Pecos had been a thriving village when the first conqueror, Coronado, passed through these parts in 1540, claiming this kingdom for the Spanish, who were sure that somewhere nearby there existed seven cities of gold, which could be dismantled, melted into ingots, and shipped home to feed the great empire. The golden cities never materialized, however, and the Spaniards turned their attentions to the considerably more prosaic task of winning the souls of Pueblo Indians—while simultaneously enslaving them.

The Americans had their own ideas about New Mexico's worth. If metals could not be teased from the alkaline dirt, then at least wagon roads could be sunk into its barren ribs, connecting the Eastern cities to California, which Kearny was scheduled to conquer next. Perhaps the Americans were not as metal-obsessed as Coronado had been, but they were just as determined to find their own kind of gold.

Though exhausted, many of Kearny's soldiers tramped over the listing walls of the Pecos ruins, blinking at the grandeur of history, and their own place in it. One of the soldiers who kept a journal, Pvt. Frank Edwards from Illinois, was told that the Pecos ruins had been built by a master race of white giants who stood fifteen feet tall. The idea did not seem completely preposterous to Edwards. "The bones which have been dug from the floor of the church are, certainly, of gigantic size," he wrote. "A thigh bone that I saw could never have belonged to a man less than ten feet."

As he was examining the giant's femur, a mule that Edwards had tied up outside broke loose from its picket and clopped into the ruined mission church. "Apparently as anxious to satisfy his curiosity as I was," the mule climbed up to the place where the altar had once stood. "It gravely turned around," Edwards wrote, "and gave vent to his pious feelings in a long EEEhaw."

Chapter 18 YOUR DUTY, MR. CARSON

The windswept grass on the jumbled hills had crisped to a fine summer gold when Kit Carson guided his mule down through the gambrel oak thickets and into the tiny village of Sonoma, California. He rode with Fremont at the head of a ragtag column of 160 volunteers, most of them American settlers from the Sacramento Valley. They were, according to one observer, "very much sunburnt and the most un-uniform and grotesque set of men ever seen."

Cows mashed their cud in the surrounding pastures while the town dogs yipped at the strangers. Sonoma's dirt streets thronged with rabbles of American men drunk on liquor—and drunk on a newfound power. They shouted out "Liberty!" in slurred cries that frightened the local townsfolk, who did not know there was a war on and did not want one.

It was June 25, 1846, and Carson tried to make sense of this chaotic scene. A week and a half earlier, on June 14, a well-armed posse of American hotheads, citing outrages mostly imagined, had risen up against the Mexican authorities and seized this adobe village not far from the shallows of northern San Francisco Bay. Calling themselves *Osos*—Bears—these self-styled revolutionaries took Sonoma's leading citizens as prisoners, cleaned out the modest-sized armory, stole all the horses they could find, and then declared the birth of an independent nation-state: the Bear Flag Republic.

The Osos carried out this spontaneous revolt with a giddy sense of melodrama—as though it were the Boston Tea Party of the West. They called their movement "high and holy," and one of the revolt leaders, a Dr. Semple, said that "the world has not hitherto manifested so high a degree of civilization." But in truth the episode was little more than opera buffa, fueled by impulses that could not be called high-minded. The Osos were little more than a mob, without organization or clear aims. One of Fremont's own men thought that most of the rebels were "moved by nothing but the chance of plunder without the slightest principle of honor."

Using Sonoma as a base, the Bears planned to sweep southward and take over Monterey, Santa Barbara, Los Angeles, and the rest of California. But for now they were content to consolidate their initial victory while savoring their new symbol of solidarity: Over the town plaza a new flag flapped in the breeze, a slightly deformed banner fashioned from scraps of ladies' undergarments, with a grizzly bear (or "something they *called* a bear," as one early historian of the revolt put it) rising on its haunches, the crude image dribbled in berry juice. (Today's state flag of California draws its design from this improbable standard.)

John Fremont's role in this uprising was tangential but nonetheless crucial. His presence in California was the catalyst that made it possible. Ever since he had led his exploring party out of the Oregon wilds and back to the Sacramento River, he had been carefully gauging the unrest among the American expatriates. Constantly entertaining visitors at his camp, Fremont had strongly encouraged the Americans to revolt; at the same time, he stressed that he could not officially intervene in the conflict until the settlers provoked the California authorities into committing a clear act of war. Nor would he permit any of his own men to detach from the expedition.

Still, there was a certain cognitive dissonance to Fremont's moves and positions: The settlers couldn't figure him out. He feared the consequences of his own involvement while also fearing the consequences should accelerating events leave him behind. And so for more than a month he vacillated, brooded, schemed in his tent, sending mixed signals as he waited for the right moment to insert himself into the drama.

Now that moment had arrived. Fremont learned that Gen. Jose Castro in Monterey, as a direct (and understandable) response to the Bear Flag Revolt, had issued an ultimatum demanding that all American foreigners "leave the country or be driven out by force." Not only that, Castro had sent a certain Capt. Joaquin de la Torre north to drive the Bear Flaggers from Sonoma. Here was the provocation Fremont felt he needed: As a U.S. Army officer, he was not authorized to attack the Californians, but he could certainly *defend* American citizens from Californian attack. So Fremont quickly gathered up an army consisting of his exploring expedition plus some one hundred other volunteers and hastened to Sonoma to rebuff de la Torre's offensive.

Fremont's "army" was a strange multinational force of buckskin rogues and filibusterers. One noncombatant observer described them as "Americans, French, English, Swiss, Poles, Russians, Chileans, Germans, Greeks, Austrians, Pawnees. If the Mexicans can whip this crowd they can beat all the world, for Castro will whip all nations, languages and tongues!"

By the time Fremont and Carson rode into Sonoma that fine June day, the Osos had already successfully repulsed Captain de la Torre, and the situation seemed calm. But Fremont was now at last committed to the Bear Flag cause—and impatient to marry it with the larger American cause. Without his help, the army of settlers would face "inevitable disaster," he feared, in the teeth of the more numerous forces the Mexican Californians would soon muster. His own expedition party represented "the Army and the Flag of the United States," a fact that Fremont thought "gave to my movements the national character which must of necessity be respected by Mexico."

Quickly Fremont seemed to undergo a personality transformation. He chucked all pretense of being an explorer and now took to signing his dispatches "Commander of United States Forces in California." He wore a felt hat and more flamboyant garb, surrounded himself with Delaware Indians as bodyguards, and tied natty green ribbons around his horse's tail and neck. He reorganized the various combatants into a unit he called the California Battalion. Employing a bit of chronological legerdemain, he had the Bear Flaggers effectively forward-date the official "start" of the revolt to coincide with the moment he joined it, thus arranging for his leadership to "begin at the beginning," as he later put it. Declaring himself "Oso 1," Fremont began to issue imperious, even ruthless, demands. He told one of his subordinates to "iron and confine any person who shall disobey your orders—shoot any person who shall endanger the safety." When a former ally, a Swiss-born trader and ranch-owner named Johann Sutter, questioned his new authority, Fremont snapped back: "If you don't like what I'm doing, then you can go and join the Mexicans!"

Joaquin de la Torre and his small army of one hundred men had retreated only a few miles from Sonoma. When Fremont learned this, he and his California Battalion gave chase, pursuing the captain to the mission of San Rafael near the shores of San Francisco Bay. But the Californian managed to escape by a clever ruse. He wrote a false note disclosing a plan to outflank Fremont and reattack Sonoma. He sent the dispatch by a courier he deliberately arranged for the Americans to intercept—thus buying him time so that he could sneak with his army across San Francisco Bay in a schooner, vanishing in the fog.

⊠

Then Fremont learned of a tragedy that had befallen a pair of Bear Flag insurrectionists. A few days earlier an American named Fowler and another named Cowie secretly ventured north from Sonoma to secure gunpowder at a small coastal outpost called Bodega. But a band of Mexican guerrillas captured and brutally lynched the two Americans. The two men were tied to trees and slashed with knives, their limbs pulled apart with lariats.

It was an outrageous crime, and the worst bloodshed in what had thus far been a placid and uneventful revolt. But now the Bear Flaggers cried out for retribution, as did Fremont and Carson.

On Sunday, June 28, Fremont spotted a small boat crossing the bay and ordered Carson to intercept it. The boat landed near San Quentin and three men stepped ashore. They were two twenty-year-old twins, Ramon and Francisco de Haro, and their elderly uncle, Jose de los Berreyesa. They were prominent citizens—the two young men were the sons of the mayor of Sonoma.

What happened next is subject to some debate, and different accounts stress different points. But Carson apparently arrested the three men and demanded that they hand over any dispatches they might be carrying. They appeared nervous and uncooperative, but insisted they harbored no messages. Though it was obvious these three men were not soldiers, Carson was suspicious. He called to Fremont and asked him what he wanted to do with them. "Captain, should I take these men prisoner?" he yelled from a distance.

Fremont waved his hand dismissively. "No," he replied, "I have no use for prisoners." Then he added, cryptically, "Do your duty."

Carson was not sure what his commander meant by that. He lingered for a moment, then had a "brief consultation" with some of the other men who had accompanied him to the boat landing. They gradually realized that Fremont intended for these three captives to pay for the deaths of Fowler and Cowie. Fremont would not carry out the deed himself—and later disavowed having any part in it—but he insisted that his loyal scout follow through. He yelled, "Mr. Carson, *your duty.*"

That was good enough for Carson. Without another apparent thought, he turned and gunned down the de Haro twins and their uncle in cold blood. (Some accounts say that several men fired along with Carson.)

Fremont seemed satisfied by the execution and the retribution it afforded. "It is well," he proclaimed after he heard the rifle reports. According to one eyewitness, Carson then searched the bodies and, as he'd suspected, found dispatches on one of them.

Neither Carson nor Fremont mentioned anything about this little atrocity in his memoirs. It remains one of the more unfathomable episodes of Carson's life. One cannot easily attribute his actions to the sort of ignorant racism that animated so many jingoistic soldiers who would fight in the Mexican War: Carson was married to a Hispanic, was a Catholic, spoke Spanish, and had for two decades enjoyed wide circles of Mexican friends. People who otherwise loved Carson had trouble accepting his role in this incident. Years later one of his close friends, W. M. Boggs, would condemn it as "a cold hearted crime."

But in this murder, as in the attack on the Klamath village, a certain troubling pattern had shown itself, one that would recur in Carson's later campaigns. It was a kind of dark symbiosis between authority and action: Fremont needed Carson to carry out his dirty work, and Carson needed Fremont, apparently, to tell him what to do. Modern psychiatry might call these two men codependents. Together they were far more lethal than when apart. Unwilling to disappoint a superior, Carson seemed incapable of resisting an order he personally disagreed with. When given a command, he was the good soldier; in such situations, his trigger-finger did not communicate with his conscience.

⊠

Two weeks later Fremont's California Battalion made its way to the provincial capital of Monterey. Warships of the U.S. Navy's Pacific Squadron had already sailed into the magnificent harbor and, in a bloodless takeover, claimed the town for the United States. Now anchored in the bay were two American transport ships, three frigates, and three sloops—each of which was fixed with forty-four guns. The Stars and Stripes flew uncontested over Monterey's scallop of shoreline.

The new commodore of the Pacific Squadron was Robert Field Stockton, the pompous seaman aboard whose ship Sen. Tom Benton was almost killed by errant cannon fire. A wealthy businessman from New Jersey who had enrolled in Princeton at the precocious age of thirteen, Stockton was a good-looking officer of fifty-one years, with cool, calculating eyes, a determined face, a nest of curly hair, and frizzled scimitars for sideburns. He had sailed much of the world, from the Mediterranean to the horn of South America, and while stationed in West Africa had helped negotiate a treaty that led to the creation of the state of Liberia. When home, he nursed eclectic ventures— canals, real estate, naval architecture, politics (he would later become a U.S. senator from New Jersey, his tendency for long-winded speechmaking earning him the nickname "Gassey Bob"). Ever since he arrived in Monterey and assumed command of the Pacific Squadron, Commodore Stockton held an exaggeratedly high opinion of his status in California. "My word is at present the law of the land," he wrote President Polk. "My person is more than regal."

If it is possible, the commodore nursed even greater ambitions for personal glory than did Fremont: Upon learning from a Mexican newspaper account that the U.S.-Mexican War was officially on, Stockton became impatient to mop up operations in California as soon as feasible so he could stage an amphibious invasion of Acapulco and then march all the way to Mexico City—a project he apparently concocted on his own without authorization from Washington. Restless, ready to bend rules, and forever solicitous of his own immortality, Stockton was a man cut from Fremontian cloth. It was little surprise, then, that the two men should instantly like each other and would become allies.

Stockton proposed to join forces with Fremont's men and quickly conquer Los Angeles and the rest of California. The commodore dashed off an obnoxious declaration of war against Gen. Jose Castro, a document as inflamed as it was untruthful. Stockton claimed that he was receiving "daily reports from the interior of scenes of rapine, blood, and murder." (A lie, of course—Cowie and Fowler were the only known deaths, and, thanks to Carson, they had been more than avenged.) General Castro, Stockton went on, "has violated every principle of international law and national hospitality, by pursuing . . . with wicked intent Capt. Fremont who came here to refresh his men after a perilous journey across the mountains, on a scientific survey." For these "repeated hostilities and outrages," Stockton concluded, "military possession was ordered to be taken of Monterey and San Francisco until redress could be obtained from the government of Mexico."

Stockton soon reorganized Fremont's army as the "Naval Battalion of Mounted Riflemen." Improvising as he went, the commodore designated Fremont a major, Gillespie a captain, and Carson a lieutenant. Although at first most of the expeditioners seemed happy to become regularized, they began to chafe at the restrictions and protocols laid down by Stockton. Fremont writes in his *Memoirs,* "Living an uncontrolled life, ranging prairies and mountains subject to no will but their own, it was a great sacrifice for these border chiefs to lay aside their habits of independence."

By late July the commodore told Fremont to prepare for his first assignment—to sail for San Diego, from which he was then to fan out and conquer Los Angeles and the rest of Southern California. There was some urgency to the assignment, Stockton felt, for the commodore was acutely worried about British meddling. The evidence was not far at hand: Anchored alongside the American ships in Monterey Bay was a single British man-of-war, the *Collingwood,* a formidable vessel armed with eighty guns.

For Stockton and Fremont, the presence of this British flagship was proof enough that the English had planned to take over California and that American Anglophobia had been justified all along. Fremont said he and his men "looked upon the *Collingwood* with the feeling of a racer" who had crossed the finish line a hair ahead of his opponent. In truth, though the British were keenly interested in California, the *Collingwood* had sailed into Monterey primarily to gather intelligence and to ensure that English mercantile interests were not being encroached upon. The *Collingwood*'s commander, Adm. Sir George Seymour, exchanged pleasantries with officers of the U.S. Pacific Squadron and gave no signs of aggression.

The British sailors were intrigued by Fremont's motley army of mountain men. The English seemed to marvel at the trappers as though they were some fabled elite—like French Legionnaires, perhaps, or samurai warriors. One officer aboard the *Collingwood* thought Carson and his comrades were "a curious set . . . who had passed years in the wilds, living upon their own resources." Dressed in "long, loose coats of deerskin," many of them were "blacker than the Indians." The Englishman continued, "One or two enjoy a high reputation in the prairies. Kit Carson is as well known there as the Duke of Wellington is in Europe."

The two groups swapped stories and played games. Carson set up coins at a distance of 150 paces and tested his marksmanship against some of the English sailors—for bets. Early Carson biographer Edwin Sabin notes that his "long, true barrel and remarkable eyesight kept the Britishers poor in pocket."

On July 25, Fremont's battalion boarded the *Cyane,* a navy sloop, and set sail for San Diego. It was an amusing notion to think of Fre-

mont's men as "sailors." Many of them had never seen an ocean before, let alone sailed on one.

Carson, certainly, was a confirmed landlubber. He had been looking forward to the voyage, but soon found that maritime life did not
agree with him. As the *Cyane* heaved in the Pacific swells, with the
headlands of Big Sur shimmering off to port, he grew seasick. For him,
the four-day sail to San Diego was pure hell. He told a friend he would
never again board an oceangoing vessel, "not as long as mules have
backs." Carson said, "I swore it would be the last time I would leave
sight of land," adding: "I'd rather ride on a grizzly than on this boat."

But he wasn't the only one—the decks of the *Cyane* positively
writhed with vomiting, sallow-faced mountain men. A navy chaplain,
the Reverend Walter Colton, found it hilarious that these "wild savages" under whose "heavy tramp the ground seemed to tremble"
should be so helpless at sea. Wrote Colton: "They are laying about
the deck in a spirit of resignation that would satisfy the non-resistant
principles of a Quaker. Two or three resolute old women might tumble the whole lot of them into the sea."

◙

Fremont's men arrived in San Diego harbor on July 29 and were met
with no resistance whatsoever. A brace of Marines marched ashore
and raised the American flag over the town. For a week Fremont was
entertained by the leading citizens of San Diego while Carson went
out to scour the surrounding countryside for horses that would be
needed for the attack on the pueblo of Los Angeles. As they waited
for Commodore Stockton to sail south from Monterey, Fremont lux-
uriated in the Southern California summer. "The days were bright
and hot," "the sky pure and entirely cloudless, and the nights cool and
beautifully serene."

Commodore Stockton tacked out of Monterey Bay on August 1
with 360 sailors aboard the *Congress*. (That same week, Kearny's army
was arriving at Bent's Fort.) Stockton dropped anchor off Santa Barbara only long enough to claim the town and raise the Stars and
Stripes. By the time he arrived in the waters off Los Angeles, General

Castro had already composed a formal letter to Gov. Pio Pico stating that he did not think it was possible to defend the pueblo. General Castro wrote, "After having made on my part every sacrifice that has been in my power to prepare for the defense of the Department and to oppose the invasion that by land and sea has been made by the United States forces, today I find myself in the painful necessity of informing Your Excellency that it is impossible for me to do one or the other."

On August 13, Fremont and Stockton consolidated their forces and marched into Los Angeles without contest. "Our entry," boasted Fremont, "had more the effect of a parade of home guards than of any enemy taking possession of a conquered town." The Americans learned to their delight that Castro had disbanded his army and escaped to the San Bernardino Mountains and then south to Sonora. Governor Pico, meanwhile, had left for Baja California. The Americans were somewhat disappointed that they had no one to fight, and that all the Mexican soldiers had, as Carson put it, "departed to any part of the country where they thought they would not meet with Americans."

Four days later Stockton declared California to be United States soil and named himself both commander in chief and governor. It seemed that the conquest was complete, although, unbeknownst to him, a resistance movement was already quietly building. The commodore sat down and wrote a self-congratulatory letter to President Polk in which he trumpeted that he had "chased the Mexican army more than three hundred miles along the coast, pursued them thirty miles in the interior of their own country, routed and dispersed them and secured the Territory to the United States, ended the war, restored peace and harmony among the people, and put a civil government into successful operation."

Stockton planned to leave California as soon as possible to pursue his planned invasion of the west coast of Mexico proper. Upon his departure, he would name Fremont the new governor of California.

Both Stockton and Fremont were anxious to get the glorious news of the conquest to Washington—and to place their version of events in the hands of President Polk himself. Fremont suggested that they write dispatches and send them overland, placing them in the able hands of none other than Kit Carson.

Carson would "insure the safety and speedy delivery of these important papers," Fremont reasoned, and the plum assignment would be "a reward for his brave and valuable service on many occasions." The journey would route him through New Mexico, allowing him to see his wife, Josefa. "It would be a service of high trust and honor and of great danger also," Fremont said, but Carson would enjoy "going off at the head of his own party with carte blanche for expenses and the prospect of novel pleasure and honor at the end."

Carson accepted the assignment, of course, and pledged to make the journey in sixty days. As usual, the feat would be accomplished on the backs of mules. Cussed though they assuredly were, mules, not horses, were "winning" the West. The sterile cross between a horse mare and a jackass, mules were stronger, sturdier, surer-footed, and less liable to spook. They could carry greater loads longer on less feed—and on feed of a poorer quality. Although they were usually slower and seemed to be designed by committee, they could better withstand temperature extremes and other vagaries of weather.

People like Carson, who had been among them all his life, were superstitious about their mules. Some people insisted mules could detect water five miles away. They could tell if a hailstorm was approaching. They could smell blood. They were even clairvoyant: The literature of the mountain men is rife with stories of mules who saved their owners by sensing the coming attack of hostile Indians—and by clearly communicating their apprehension through one anxious tic or another. Later accounts celebrating Kit Carson's great rides almost invariably place him on a fleet and noble "steed," but that was a bit of equestrian chauvinism; every time Carson aimed for the other side of the continent, he was on a mule.

On the morning of September 5, Stockton and Fremont stuffed his saddlebags with all manner of correspondence. Then Carson, the scout-turned-transcontinental-courier, mounted his mule and headed east toward the sunrise with fifteen men, including six Delaware Indians.

Chapter 19 DAGGERS IN EVERY LOOK

With Kearny only a day away from the capital, Armijo flew into a dither of inspired play-acting at Apache Canyon. As the vital hours slipped by, the governor grew more unpredictable, and at the same time more grandiose. He gathered together the members of the legislative assembly on the steep hills and sat them in the cool shade of the juniper trees. Instead of exhorting them, however, he presented a series of questions.

"*You* tell me what I should do," he said, Pontius-like.

They looked at him with puzzled expressions.

He cast about for the most delicate way to phrase the question. "Should I fight or treat with the enemy?"

One of the legislators stood up and spoke for the others. "The question you have posed is improper," the man resolutely said. "We came here as soldiers, not as legislators. Our duty is to act as such, and obey orders."

This was not the answer Armijo was looking for. He stiffened up and nodded vigorously, grumbling something along the lines of, "Of *course* we are soldiers." With that, he took his leave.

Then he turned to the officers of the militia and floated the same question. Again, the answer failed to satisfy him. "We have assembled to fight," one of his interlocutors stated, "and that is what we should do. That is our only wish."

Armijo again nodded, commending the man for his patriotism. He paced and stewed and sulked, and then suddenly spun around, having worked his actor's face up into a fit of feigned indignation. "With the regular army I would of course meet any enemy," he assured them. "But not with these *volunteers*." He gestured deprecatingly at the peasants and peons working down in the canyon, still slaving away on the

fortifications, felling trees to construct a crude abatis. "Look at them—
they are all *cowards*! I shall not compromise myself by going into battle with people who have no military discipline!"

Then to everyone's mute astonishment, the governor formally
disbanded the defenders of Apache Canyon, the whole lot of them.
As he did so, he affected a look of intense exasperation, as if they
were the ones who had let *him* down. He was, he said, a victim of cir-
cumstance; he had done all that could be done, but it was entirely out
of his hands now. A militia captain vowed to kill him for deserting the
homeland, but the threat came to nothing. For the next several hours
the canyon was a scene of dusty disarray, with people stampeding this
way and that. The three thousand men—bewildered and most of
them, in truth, greatly relieved—hopped on whatever mules or burros immediately presented themselves and scurried toward home to
see to the safety of their families.

Then Armijo sat down and dictated a final letter to Kearny. A
syrup of emotion flowed from his lips to the pen of his mystified
amanuensis. "My heart is grieved with pain on seeing that from my
hands the country in which I first saw light will pass to another nation," he dictated. The governor went on to suggest that Kearny
hadn't seen the last of him, that Armijo would return in due time to
avenge the American conquest. "I do not *deliver* to Your Excellency
the province of New Mexico," he explained. "I only make a temporary military retreat, until I shall receive further orders from my
government."

Finishing the letter, and leaving it in the hands of a messenger,
Armijo assembled his bodyguard of one hundred soldiers and galloped for Santa Fe. From the Palace of the Governors he took all the
money and gold plate he could cram into his trunks and then
mounted his horse. According to one account, an angry throng materialized and tried to prevent him from leaving. Digging into his
overstuffed pockets, the governor tossed out several handfuls of gold
and silver coins, strewing them at the crowd's feet. While the people
jostled for the money, he spurred his horse and sped away toward Chihuahua, never to be seen in Santa Fe again.

At that very moment a large force under Colonel Ugarte was hastening up the Rio Bravo to reinforce Armijo's defenses.

Armijo's second-in-command, Diego Archuleta, did not rise in Armijo's absence to take the reins of the army. James Magoffin, President Polk's secret agent, had met with Archuleta, too, and apparently offered him a separate deal. Magoffin quite disingenuously told Archuleta that Kearny was interested in annexing only *the eastern half* of New Mexico, to the banks of the Rio Grande. The details of their meeting are frustratingly vague, but it appears that Magoffin promised Archuleta that if he acquiesced in the American invasion and did not put up any resistance, he could have all of western New Mexico—an attenuated domain that nonetheless encompassed Arizona and parts of present-day Utah, Nevada, and Colorado. It is not known whether Archuleta accepted this offer, but, like Armijo, the proud soldier declined to defend his country, a tack quite uncharacteristic of him. He retreated to his ranch on the lower Rio Grande, near Albuquerque, to ride out the invasion.

In Santa Fe, the people were left in shock at the realization that their leaders had truly deserted them. The American infidels were coming, and not a thing could be done about it. Women wept in the streets. Valuables were hidden, children sent away. The people battened down their houses as though preparing for a storm. One citizen, mortified by his pusillanimous governor, wrote in disgust, "Mr. Armijo did absolutely nothing. All is lost, including honor."

⊗

While camped along the Pecos River near the great ruins, Kearny's men suddenly heard approaching hoofbeats. They turned from their fires to behold a rider galloping at them, gesticulating wildly, aiming straight for General Kearny. "A large fellow, mounted on a mule, came towards us at full speed, and extending his hand to the general, congratulated him on the arrival of his army," wrote Lt. William Emory. It was the *alcalde* of the nearby Hispanic village of Pecos, and he came bearing important news. "He said, with a roar of laughter, 'Armijo and his troops have gone to hell! The canyon is all clear!'"

Kearny did not necessarily believe the man. He treated the *alcalde*'s news as a rumor, like all the others. The Army of the West rose before dawn on the morning of August 18 and pushed toward Apache Canyon. The news that filtered back from his runners and scouts was encouraging—the *alcalde* apparently spoke the truth. But Kearny cautiously refused to accept his good fortune until he could see it with his own eyes.

When the American forces approached the canyon around noon that day, they were heartened to find that the place was indeed completely deserted. Mexican campfires were still smoldering, the earthworks were half-completed, and trees had been felled this way and that in a manner that suggested both confusion and incompetence. The defenders had quit the canyon in such a hurry that they left their cannons in place, only to be reclaimed by the Americans. Kearny did not waste time studying the nuances of this formidable defile, but it was obvious to him that the New Mexicans could have made the passage murderously difficult for his army. Lieutenant Emory thought that although Armijo's arrangements for defense were "very stupid," Apache Canyon was "a gateway which, in the hands of a skillful engineer and one hundred resolute men, would have been perfectly impregnable." Had Armijo "possessed the slightest qualifications for a general," Emory went on, "he might have given us infinite trouble." Similarly, volunteer George Gibson, a Missouri lawyer who kept a thorough journal, deemed Apache Canyon a place of such "great natural strength [that] a few men could have held off a whole army, for cannon at the mouth could sweep the whole road as it is almost impossible even for infantry to ascend the precipitous sides." A historian would later go further, suggesting, somewhat melodramatically, that had it been defended by an able general, the battle of Apache Canyon "would have proved a second Thermopylae."

Nothing now stood in the way of General Kearny's path to Santa Fe, and he made double time, hoping to have the capital before sundown. It was thirty miles from their morning's campsite to Santa Fe, but the Missourians were excited to get a glimpse of the mythic city. "We marched rapidly on," volunteer George Gibson wrote, "for we were all anxious to see the place about which we had heard so much." The trail made a final bend to the right, skirting the green ridges, climbing over hills covered in chamisa sagebrush and cholla cactus and sprinkled with purple aster. It was monsoon season and the rutted road had recently been doused by a summer shower. Though it left a few wallows, the rain was a welcome thing. It cooled and sharpened the air and dampened the dust. Even now, thunderheads were piled overhead, dropping gray nails of rain that evaporated into vapor as the storms grumbled eastward.

In every direction rose mountains, an embarrassment of them, erupting in incremental shades of blue from the burnt yellow plains—mountains of every description and geological origin, some volcanic, some forged by faults and violent uplifts, some stand-alone monadnocks, others tied to the Rocky Mountain chain. They all had Spanish names and had had them since before the pilgrims sailed to Plymouth Rock: The Sandias. Manzanos. Ortiz. Jemez. Los Cerrillos. Sangre de Cristos. San Mateos. Atalaya. Some seemed so close they could be plucked as effortlessly as pendulous fruit, others were more than a hundred miles off, thin blue phantoms rising from the Navajo country in the hazy west.

Hoping to enter Santa Fe "in an imposing form," Kearny called for frequent halts so that his artillery could catch up. The strain of this final dash sapped the artillery's overworked animals. "Their horses almost gave out," Emory noted, "and during the day mule after mule was placed before the guns, until scarcely one of them was spared."

As Kearny rode the final miles into Santa Fe, the late afternoon sun slanted beneath the clouds, tinting their gauzy undersides in oranges and reds. The high elevation made the atmosphere strangely clarified. Since they had been out on the prairie, the men had been steadily climbing. They were now at seven thousand feet, an altitude that made many of these Missouri flatlanders wheeze and gasp, and gave others nosebleeds and headaches or an anxious tingling at the top of their lungs. Nearly twenty miles to the west lay the muddy Rio Grande, its presence felt by the marching men though they could not see it behind the intervening buttes and ridges. It was the central river toward which all land tilted, the one clear trend in this magnificent jumble of landscapes.

The sagebrush gave way to cornfields and sheep pastures and then scattered houses, and finally the men dropped down into the somber capital—the Royal City of the Holy Faith of Saint Francis of Assisi. Although it had a fabled name with a venerable history—it was founded in 1609—Santa Fe was not a town that sought to impress anyone, numbering at most seven thousand inhabitants. "Our first view of this place was very discouraging—dirt, pigs, and naked children," wrote Frank Edwards. George Gibson dismissed the town as "shabby" and "without taste," offering "nothing to pay us for our long march." Garbage was heaped on the mostly deserted streets, with goats picking among the sour edges. The low mud dwellings, flat-roofed and seemingly random in their cluttered placement, gave Santa Fe the appearance of "an extensive brickyard," one soldier thought. Kearny's men unfurled their pennants and banners and carried them on poles as they filed through the narrow mud streets amid the incessant barking of dogs. They crossed the Santa Fe River, shallow but swollen gray-brown from the rainstorms. The soldiers were still not sure whether they would encounter any resistance, so they struck an exaggeratedly martial pose, with "drawn sabres and daggers in every look," as one lieutenant described it. Behind the courtyard gates and tiny windows pulled taut with oiled rawhide in lieu of glass, the Santa Feans grieved. A few brave young men leaned against a wall, smoking cornhusk cigarettes. Thunder growled in the distant skies.

In sixty days of marching, Kearny's Army of the West had come to the end of the line, for that is what Santa Fe had always been—a geographical and cultural terminus. It was the end of the Santa Fe Trail, the end of the Camino Real, the northern end of the desert, the western end of the prairie, the southern end of the Rockies. It was where Spain stopped and existential wilderness began. The impoverished citizens of this hard outpost, whose families had lived here longer than any Bostonian or Virginian could claim lineage in North America, blinked in disbelief at what was now happening to their ancient city. Lieutenant Elliott of the Missouri volunteers kept noticing

"surly countenances and downcast looks of watchfulness if not terror." Elliott went further than most in sympathizing with their
predicament. "Strange must have been their feelings," he wrote,
"when an invading army was entering their home—all the future
vague and uncertain, their new rulers strangers to their manners, language, and habits, and as they had been taught to believe, enemies of
the only religion they have ever known."

Around five o'clock General Kearny led his army into the plaza. Behind him came his dragoons, smartly dressed and arrogant without
apology, each of his three troop divisions set on mounts of a distinct
color: The first rode black, the second white, and the third sorrel
horses. (Organizing the horses by color, though completely unnecessary, was just the sort of flourish that warmed Kearny's fastidious
heart.) Then came the infantry, that is, whatever foot soldiers had
reached Santa Fe—hundreds of others were still trickling into the outskirts of the city. Kearny made one circle around the plaza and then
stopped in front of the Palace of the Governors, an ancient adobe
building with a long, sagging porch. The provisional governor, a con-
trite and conciliatory man named Juan Bautista y Vigil Alarid, emerged
with a host of New Mexican dignitaries. Over a doorway of the palace
was an inscription that might have been Manuel Armijo's personal
motto. It read VITA FUGIT SICUT UMBRA: Life flees like a shadow.

The American general dismounted and raised his hand, calling for silence. "I, Stephen W. Kearny, General of the Army of the United States,
have taken possession of the province of New Mexico," he declared. "In
the name of the government of the United States I hereby instruct the
inhabitants to deliver their arms and surrender absolutely. Armijo's
power is departed. I am your governor—look to me for protection."

Then the provisional governor essentially offered a reply of no
contest. "I swear obedience to the Northern Republic and tender my
respect to its laws and authority," he said. "No one in this world can
successfully resist the power of him who is stronger. The power of
the Mexican republic is dead." Still, he said, "No matter what her condition, the republic was our mother. What child will not shed abundant tears at the tomb of his parents?"

Later an elderly man emerged from the crowd, his hair white, his eyes watery and perhaps clouded with cataracts. The old-timer threw himself on General Kearny and for a long, awkward moment he shuddered with quiet emotion. The governor admonished the old man to move on. "No, let him remain," Kearny assured him. "Heaven knows the oppressions this man has had to bear."

The governor offered glasses of brandy to Kearny and his staff, and, stiffly, they toasted the bloodless conquest. The brandy was from El Paso and it tasted a bit sharp and resinous, but it went down smoothly enough. "We were too thirsty to judge of its merits," Lieutenant Emory noted. "Anything liquid and cool was palatable."

The buglemen blasted out their notes of triumph as the Stars and Stripes were run up a temporary flagpole fixed to the palace roof. From a distant hill the artillery fired a thirteen-gun salute, and then, as though punctuating the booms, the young men of the Army of the West let out a raucous war-whoop. For the first time in its history, the United States had captured a foreign capital.

In the silence that hung in the air after the rumbling of the guns had subsided, the women of Santa Fe answered the American soldiers with unstifled screams of sorrow and anguish. It was an upwelling both surprising and haunting to the men of Missouri. "Their pent-up emotions could be suppressed no longer," Lieutenant Elliott wrote, "and a wail of grief rose from the depths of the gloomy buildings on every hand."

Chapter 20 MEN WITH EARS DOWN TO THEIR ANKLES

Narbona was worried about the Americans. Throughout the late summer and early fall of 1846, the Navajo leader kept hearing stories about these new conquerors, troubling accounts circulated by messengers from other tribes. Their armies fired lightning bolts, he'd heard. They had magical little boxes that caught the light and allowed them to see things far away. They had overwhelmed the Mexicans without needing to fight them, and now they were building a mighty new fortress on a hill overlooking Santa Fe. They had strong medicine, these people. But Narbona did not understand what they wanted with this part of the world, or why they had bothered to come from such a long distance—from somewhere far to the east, beyond the buffalo plains—to leave their mark in a place so far from their ancestors.

For Narbona, the United States of America was not even the vaguest of abstractions. He had no concept of Washington, D.C., or James K. Polk, or Manifest Destiny. He scarcely had a concept of white men at all and could not fathom that there existed on this earth a people who looked and behaved and spoke and worshiped their gods and organized themselves so differently—a people not quite like the Spanish, or even the Mexicans, indeed not like any other race he had ever encountered. The Navajos came to call the Americans *bilagaana*, a word that apparently derived from their own mispronunciation of the Spanish "Americano."

Along creeks and rivers, Navajo warriors had glimpsed a few strange-looking men with white skin and bushy whiskers—trappers, usually Frenchmen, who had blundered to the edges of Navajo country. Tribes of the Southwest had long held legends and prophesies that told of a new conquering race coming from the east. A few glancing encounters with white men had begun to inspire incredible stories among the Navajos—stories like the one about the giants who had floppy ears that reached down to their ankles.

"A certain people are going to come to us," went the story (later recorded in a classic work of anthropology titled *Navajo Texts*). "From below where the sun rises, they are going to come to us. Their ears are enormous. They extend all the way to their ankles. At night, these people build fires on their knees and cover themselves with those ears of theirs and lie down to sleep."

Other wild variations of these stories abounded. Some Navajos believed white men lacked anuses, and that because of this they could not eat normally—that instead they could only inhale the steam rising off boiling food. Still others believed that white men had a strange growth protuding from their foreheads, almost like a horn, and that they could strike a slender stick on their asses and make fire. "Our country," frets one man in *Navajo Texts,* "is about to be taken away from us by men such as these."

Although Narbona was perhaps the most eminent figure among the Navajos, he was not, in fact, a chief. The Navajos did not have leaders in any official sense. Their style of social order was too fluid, too haphazard, and too relentlessly democratic to allow for a single man to rise to any such vaunted position of authority. The Navajos discussed everything at great and often frustrating lengths, rarely confronting an issue but rather dancing elliptically around its edges until the true topic at hand was struck and some sort of consensus reached.

In the end, everyone had a say. In theory and in practice, Navajo women enjoyed a degree of power unusual among Native Americans. Some of the most important deities in the Navajo pantheon were female—including the benevolent matriarch, Changing Woman, and the wise old hermit Spider Woman, who, among other things, taught the people how to weave. The Navajos were both matrilineal and matrilocal; descent was traced through the mother, and when a girl got married, her husband came to live with *her* people. Women owned property and usually ran the intimate affairs of home life. Children owned things as well (they even had their own livestock) and often were consulted about the minute decisions of daily life. Even the slaves—women and children stolen in raids—could become full citizens, with all the rights of full-blooded Navajos.

In a society this stubbornly egalitarian, it was impossible to designate a single person as *the* chief of even a single clan, let alone of an entire tribe of twelve thousand people that extended over millions of acres of remote land. But if one man held a status that approximated that of "chief," it was Narbona. A tall, slender man with sharp chiseled features and a mane of long white hair, Narbona always presented a fine and formidable appearance, dressed in his beaded buckskins, jeweled in his best silver and turquoise. The great warrior was now the headman of a widely known and extremely prosperous "outfit"—an extended family of relatives working together and living within shouting distance of one another that formed the basic unit of organization in Navajo society. Narbona and his outfit ranged over large stretches of land along the eastern slopes of the Tunicha Mountains.

As a tribe that generously deferred to elders, the Navajos would have revered Narbona for his longevity alone. He had survived many moons, had lived through wars and famines and times of great bounty, had seen with his own eyes the Spanish period, and the Mexican period—and now the coming of the Americans.

Narbona was one of the richest men in all the Navajo country, probably *the* richest. He had thousands of sheep, it was said. He had scores of horses and herds of cattle. He had three wives and many slaves. He was blessed with grandchildren and great-grandchildren and in-laws too numerous to count. His fields in the Chuska Valley rippled with fine corn, and pumpkins and muskmelons swelled on their vines. Stones taken from the wet heat of the sweathouse had been ceremonially set among the plants to prevent them from dying of an early frost. Narbona had many songs, it was said, and he observed all the rites and rituals, taking care to respect the *jhozho,* the sacred balance of life, and that was why he was wealthy and had so many properties.

Narbona was generous with his wealth, too, and was known for taking in children orphaned from the ongoing wars with the Utes and the Mexicans.

His outfit was a loud and lively place, stirring with prayers and songs and horse races, a loose string of hogans spread out on the grassy slopes, smoke tendriling from the central chimney holes, every doorway facing east to greet the day. Instead of doors, mats woven from yucca twine billowed in the wind. Thin strips of drying mutton and venison hung from the surrounding sagebrush bushes and trees. Women worked at their looms, the bright designs of their blankets growing in the sun as they tamped down each new thread of dyed and carded wool and clacked their shuttles smoothly back and forth. They were a resourceful people, making use of nearly everything they found within their reach; they fashioned thread from the fibers of the agave. They snared birds in nooses made from their own hair. They bathed themselves with the suds that could be coaxed from the soapy stalk and root of the yucca. In the foothills, the medicine men gathered willow wands or sprigs of sumac, mint, and sage to use in healing ceremonies.

Adolescent boys led flocks of bleating churro sheep and Angora goats with their large twisted horns toward brush-arbor camps through mountain passes—the mingled animals made distinct to their owners by signifying marks cut into the flaps of their ears. The older men, meanwhile, might be seen heading off to collect salt at ancient seeps, or to hunt mule deer and elk that grazed in the long shadows thrown by ponderosa pines.

⌧

If he had enjoyed a long and abundant life, Narbona now seemed to fear that it all hung in jeopardy. Through couriers sent to him, General Kearny had threatened full-scale war if he did not agree to a peace treaty. The Americans had even stated that they would send a peace emissary into Navajo country to conclude the talks, to save the aged Narbona from having to brave a trip. Narbona was in no position to speak for the entire tribe, but he probably had more powers of suasion than any Navajo alive.

Winter was coming on, the time when Navajos traditionally met in ceremonials and told their stories and discussed their common problems in councils. Winter was the time for conversation, between first frost and first lightning, when the corn had been harvested and stored, when the snakes had gone to bed and the *yeis*, the gods, would be listening. There would be sandpaintings, nightchants, and ceremonies with hand-tremblers. Around campfires, in hogans and sweat lodges, the conversation would surely turn to the Americans, and Narbona would be called on to render his opinion. How should the Navajos respond to the considerable demands of these invaders?

Narbona did not know, but he was certain he needed to see these large-eared Americans for himself. So one day in the fall, probably sometime in late September, he picked a few close comrades and set off on a roundabout journey east. Over the years he had made numerous trips to Santa Fe to talk peace with the Spanish and Mexican authorities on the plaza, and he knew the trails well. But this time the old man took a network of obscure hunting paths that led across the Rio Grande and then well to the north of Santa Fe, up into the Sangre de Cristos.

From the mountains, he and his party dropped down into the foothills that skirted the town, knowing that if they were caught they would likely be shot. Hobbling their horses and leaving them in a protected place, they crouched quietly in the piñon trees and peered down at the ominous stirrings of the new fort that General Kearny was building.

Chapter 21   THE HALL OF FINAL RUIN

On the night of September 24, 1846, bells rang over the city, incessantly, crazily, as they always did when something was afoot. From the six churches they clanked and clanged, filling the streets with a maddening metallic din. The Santa Feans loved their bells and used them to announce every occasion—weddings, masses, even races and fandangos. Their sound was far from dulcet, for most of the bells were decrepit and cracked, some having been forged centuries earlier in Castille and shipped by galleon across the wide ocean and then hauled nearly two thousand groaning miles north from Mexico on the desolate wagon road, the Camino Real, which long served as the town's only umbilicus to the civilized world. Through their long sojourns, the bells had been splashed with brine, dropped in silty arroyos, and pecked by bullets. They had seen revolts and massacres,

and had endured several centuries of a steady faith's ringing in the extremes of a high desert clime. Even though the bells were tarnished
and streaked with verdigris, they remained the pride of the town, enduring relics from a time when the crown of Spain reigned as the
greatest power on earth.

The weather had turned cool and sharp—a storm had dusted the
upper reaches of the mountains with the season's first snow—and on
this brisk evening the clanging of the bells was especially loud. On
one side of town a large funeral was under way—an old man apparently related to half the citizenry had died. And on the other side of
town, over by the plaza, the American merchants were throwing a
formal ball at the Palace of the Governors. The event was a bon voyage party for General Kearny and his dragoons: The next morning
they were leaving for California, to continue the conquest.

Kearny's fete was the largest event of the year. The long, narrow
ballroom was crammed with more than five hundred people, Mexican and American alike, dressed in their finest clothes. They drank
aguardiente and El Paso brandy and performed old dances of the
province as a fiddler and a guitarist scratched out their bittersweet
melodies. The Palace of the Governors' "ballroom" was festive but
decidedly humble in its appointments, its ceiling leaky, its plaster
walls in decay. The floor was made of hard-packed dirt, and the door
panels were fashioned from cured buffalo hide that had been faux-
painted with burls and knots to look like wood. On one wall was a
sweeping mural, painted by a local artist, that depicted General
Kearny unfurling a constitution for a grateful Mexican peasant. LI-
BERTAD, the scroll read, and around it was painted a cross, a plow, and
a cannon festooned in a bunting of American flags. Hung all around
the hall were American company flags and pennants hand-sewn by
the women of Missouri.

The cream of Santa Fe society, such as it was, had turned out to
say its good-byes to the conqueror: government officials, prominent
families, priests, American merchants, officers. Susan Magoffin was at
the ball and described everything in cheerful detail in her journal.
That night she was wearing a Chinese shawl of red crepe as she

danced with several American officers. She noted in her diary that the "ladies were all dressed in silks, satins, ginghams—and decked with showy ornaments, huge necklaces, countless rings. They had large sleeves, short waists, ruffled skirts. All danced and smoked cigarettos." In one corner she was somewhat distressed to see a "dark-eyed senora" from a well-to-do Spanish family who had brought along a "human foot-stool," as Magoffin called it—an Indian servant crouched on the floor for her mistress to use, between dances, "as an article of furniture."

Magoffin was shocked by the boldness of the local ladies, to say nothing of their plunging necklines. "They slap about with their arms and necks bare, their bosoms exposed," she sniffed, wishing she had "a veil drawn closely over my face to protect my blushes." Most of the women wore a bright red rouge on their cheeks that "shone like grease," Magoffin noted, while others were "daubed over with a ghostly flour-paste—a custom they have among them when they wish to look fair and beautiful." The Mexican men, on the other hand, "stand off with crossed arms, and look on with as much wonder as if they were not people themselves."

Magoffin was especially intrigued by a certain redheaded woman who danced and carried herself with a haughty sense of freedom. Her name was Gertrudes Barcelo, but she was universally known around town as Madame La Tules. A Taos native, La Tules had long run a successful tavern in Santa Fe—its gambling rooms and accompanying brothel had been wildly popular among the Missourians. It was rumored that among her many illicit affairs, Barcelo had once been Governor Armijo's mistress. She was a vivacious hostess and a cunning businesswoman; at her establishment the principal amusement was five-card monte—a game, it was said, whose mysteries could be learned only by losing at it. Through her brisk gaming tables, she handled astounding wads of cash for a specie-starved town, and sometimes floated loans to soldiers at usurious rates. Magoffin studied Barcelo as she moved about the ballroom, judging her to be a "stately" woman possessed of "that shrewd sense and fascinating manner necessary to allure the wayward, inexperienced youth to the hall of final ruin."

Kearny's soldiers were also intrigued by the women at the ball, although in a different way. Their diaries are full of prurient compliments. Hughes remarked on their "lustrous, beaming eyes that peer most captivatingly from the folds of their rebozos." Capt. Philip St. George Cooke thought the Santa Fe ladies "remarkable for smallness of hands and feet," but noted that "nowhere is chastity less valued or expected." Private Edwards: "The women are the boldest walkers I know, their step being always free and good, and their bodies have a graceful oscillation. They do not seem to know what modesty is, and are very fond of the attentions of strangers." George Gibson: "As a general thing their forms are much better than the women in the States."

⊠

The wine flowed easily, and the party went far into the night. The tiny ballroom sweltered in the close heat as the guests pressed through a haze of cornhusk cigarette smoke. On the dance floor, the Americans and Mexicans swirled together in "an infinity of petticoats." With the sweep of an eye, Susan Magoffin could see the future of the territory: judges, bankers, engineers, businessmen, the whole new American imprint on the ancient country. In one corner stood the newly appointed governor of New Mexico, the stout and stolid Charles Bent, Kit Carson's old friend. Bent was a bullnecked Missourian with dark features and a massive furrowed brow—"tough as an oak knot" in the words of his biographer David Lavender, "a man of implacable drive." It was Charles Bent who had first tested and then perfected the use of large ox-teams (instead of horses or mules) to pull wagons along the Santa Fe Trail; the success of the slower but far stronger oxen, Lavender suggests, led the way to the "gargantuan freight caravans that came to sinew the West."

General Kearny had picked Bent for the job after careful consideration, but the choice was a controversial one. Bent was an unlovable sort, resented by many Spaniards for arrogances real and imaginary, a hard-driving businessman whose mercantile savvy was often taken for simple greed. He had financial interests spread out from St. Louis to Taos and owned a good number of servants, both Indian and black. But Bent was perceptive and practical-minded; he loved New Mexico and understood its unique problems, and he had already become a towering figure of the Southwest.

Susan Magoffin knew Governor Bent well, and she doubtless spoke with him as she pressed through the milling crowds. His mud fort on the banks of the Arkansas, where her stillborn child lay buried, had already profoundly changed the face of New Mexican life. Traders like Bent had served, in a sense, as the first wave of the American invasion, and so his assumption of political power seemed only a natural progression. He was, thought one historian, "a mighty man whose will was prairie law, who knew Indians and Mexicans as few others did, who had great influence for hundreds of miles . . . and held many tribes in the palm of his hand."

Also circulating in the crowds was Col. Alexander Doniphan, the self-taught country lawyer appointed to replace Kearny as military commander upon the general's exit from Santa Fe the next morning. Magoffin liked Doniphan and accepted his offer to dance. Forty years old, big-boned, a lumbering six-feet two-inches tall, Doniphan towered over her. He was a good-looking man, with bright hazel eyes and a mane of dark hair. The "colonel" had no military training, but he had a reputation for being an unbeatable defense attorney back in Missouri—the sort of man you called if you were in real trouble. He had once defended the Mormon prophet Joseph Smith. At Kearny's command, Doniphan had drawn up a constitution for the new territory that was quite eloquent and forward-thinking. He had a penchant for quoting the classics, yet at the same time he was unpretentious, easygoing, and beloved by the rabble of volunteers who had elected him as their highest officer. He could be coarse—refreshingly so. As one of his subordinates wrote, "The colonel is in the habit of interlarding his language with strong expressions which many Eastern men would call something very like swearing."

Doniphan spun Magoffin around the crowded floor, performing the "cuna," or "cradle"—a kind of frontier waltz. They wrapped arms around each other's waists, leaning "well back," as Magoffin put it, to mimic the rocking of a cradle. Some of the American onlook-ers found the swinging embraces of the dance enticingly sexual: "Such familiarity of position," said one, "would be repugnant to the rules of polite society in our country; but among the New Mexicans, nothing is reckoned a greater accomplishment than passing hand-somely through all the mazes of this waltz."

Magoffin was also taken with Henry Turner, a captain who served as the adjutant of the Army of the West and kept one of the best di-aries of the westward trek. Turner would leave the next day with Kearny and travel all the way to California with him, becoming his second-in-command. Kind, smart, a pious Christian devoted to his wife, Julia, back in St. Louis, Turner was a West Pointer who had stud-ied cavalry tactics at the famous Saumur Military Academy in France. Although he was a cousin of Robert E. Lee and would become a Southern sympathizer during the Civil War, he was a close friend of future Union general William Tecumseh Sherman. Magoffin thought Turner "a gentleman of extensive information, and exceedingly po-lite." He was a fine storyteller, too, a man who "endeavors to make himself agreeable with his interesting narrations."

Mostly, though, Magoffin gravitated toward the guest of honor, Stephen Watts Kearny, the military and civil governor of New Mexico. Enjoying himself on his last night in town, Kearny was turned out in his finest blue uniform, with epaulets, polished boots, and a gleaming sword. His gray hair was swept back, his forehead glistening in the moist heat of the ballroom. Over the past five weeks Kearny had be-come something of a father figure to Susan Magoffin, and it is through her diary that we have our most vivid descriptions of the conquering general. He took her on horseback tours of the city, accompanied her to mass, gently remonstrated her for peccadillos. He kept asking her, half-seriously, to come to California with him. Magoffin was especially fond of the fifty-two-year-old general, finding him "candid and plain-spoken, very agreeable in conversation. He conducts himself with ease, and places himself at my command, to serve me when I wish. United States General No. 1 entirely at my disposal! He speaks to me more as my father would do than any one else."

In truth, General Kearny and Colonel Doniphan weren't the only soldiers smitten with Magoffin—almost all the Army of the West officers were. She was the only American woman in the conquered capital—and quite possibly the first American woman ever to venture all the way down the Santa Fe Trail. As such, she was in high demand: the paragon of American femininity, by default, in a foreign town overrun by roistering young men. She had beautiful long brown hair, dark glistening eyes, and a petite frame. She was intelligent and cultured, with a generous spirit and a bottomless font of good cheer. One historian called her "the belle of the occupation," and the house she and Samuel Magoffin set up not far from the plaza became a kind of salon. Though she was happily married, and devoted to her new husband, visitors came to the house nightly, solicitous young men eager to be in her presence, to remember what American women were like, to catch her smells and ways and inflections. Some came to her excitable and drunk, others came seeking the sustenance of her Christian virtue, and still others came with flames in their hearts and loins. One Missourian rapped on her door, believing that her house was the Madame Tules bordello, and skulked away, mortified and disappointed, when a virtuous young woman from Kentucky answered the door.

Susan Magoffin was mildly shocked by the rough edges of these men—"What an everlasting noise these soldiers keep up—from early dawn till late at night they are blowing their trumpets, whooping like Indians, or making some unheard of sounds, quite shocking to my delicate nerves"—but she recognized the remarkable circumstances of her presence in Santa Fe. And she loved being there, the sole American woman among sixteen hundred American men, eighteen years old and capturing history in her journal. "I am the first American lady who has come under the auspices of the Star-spangled banner," she wrote. "I have entered the city in a year that will always be remembered by my countrymen."

⊠

This farewell ball was perhaps the first occasion General Kearny had had to enjoy himself in public since he marched into the capital five weeks earlier. From his first afternoon in Santa Fe, he had kept himself and his men ceaselessly busy. Kearny was a fastidious man with an uncompromising work ethic, and he kept at it in a quiet fury. He observed an uninterrupted schedule of meetings, junkets, treaties, ceremonies, appointments, construction projects. He was a fine conqueror, firm but beneficent, and the locals seemed to like him. Kearny understood the public relations aspect of conquest, and he went out of his way to show goodwill. He carried a candle during a church processional even though, as he later confessed to Susan Magoffin, "I felt like a fool." He befriended the priests and went to mass. He reduced taxes. He invited delegations from surrounding tribes to come to Santa Fe and smoke the pipe of peace. He took a sojourn down the Rio Grande and visited the pueblos and the haciendas of the rich. At dinners and ceremonies his favorite toast was, "The U.S. and Mexico—they are now united, may no one ever think of separating." He was discreet and diplomatic, and, as one chronicler put it, "he avoided offending a single god."

From the start, Kearny made it clear that things would be done very differently in Santa Fe. A successful democracy required the free flow of information, which depended in turn upon the published word. So he located an antique press up in Taos and had the behemoth hauled down to print Spanish-language circulars and proclamations, and eventually, an English-language newspaper. He kept regular office hours at the Palace of the Governors, opening up the dark, musty rooms and removing all traces of Armijo's cruel regime. In one room of the palace Kearny had found scores of human ears tacked to the wall—ears that had presumably once belonged to Armijo's enemies. The general promptly had the room cleaned up and these grisly trophies buried.

Kearny, an egalitarian at heart, wanted the new government to operate with a simple transparency—and without frills or fanfare. A good example of this no-nonsense style could be found in his reaction to the use of "stamp paper," a clerical practice in Santa Fe that dated back many decades. One day the *alcalde* of Santa Fe explained to Kearny that "an instrument of writing is not legal unless it is drawn up on paper stamped with the government seal and coat-of-arms." All deeds, marriage licenses, death certificates, bills of sale, and other documents had to bear this official imprimatur. The mayor showed the general a copy of the all-important "stamp paper" and explained that it cost eight dollars a sheet—*just for the paper,* quite apart from any clerical fees that might be involved. "It is a very moderate sum to pay," the *alcalde* contended, "for having an important document made strictly legal."

General Kearny stared at the *alcalde* in annoyed disbelief. On the contrary, he thought eight dollars was a scandalous fee, especially for such a poor population. More to the point, it was a ridiculous bit of finery that had no legitimate purpose—Kearny found it offensive on every level. He dashed off a new command with his pen: "The use of 'stamp paper' by the government of New Mexico is hereby abolished. Done by the governor."

Everywhere he went, Kearny preached amnesty and inclusion. No one's property would be harmed, he said. Past wrongs would be forgiven. Even Manuel Armijo was welcome to return—and if he did, Kearny urged the people to greet the old governor and not molest him in any way. Kearny paid a visit to Armijo's wife, Trinidad Gabaldon, in Albuquerque and thought her "a good-looking woman and rather cheerful." (A subordinate traveling with Kearny described her more interestingly: "A comely dame of forty, with the remains of considerable beauty, but quite passe.") Mrs. Armijo indicated that probably her husband would not return to New Mexico. Nearly all his relatives and former friends said the same thing: "The governor has gone to hell."

The constitution that Kearny had Colonel Doniphan draw up was a model of fairness and progressive statecraft. The "Kearny Code," as it was called, had deliberate echoes of the Magna Carta and the Bill of Rights and was so well crafted that it continues as the basis of New Mexico state law to this day. Whether the New Mexicans appreciated all of these doings, in the end, is hard to say. Spanish documents from the period are spotty and circumspect. It was clear that however much the locals might have liked the sound of Kearny's high-minded

documents and lofty pledges, they remained skeptical and still clung
to a national pride, hoping the war in the south would turn in Mexico's favor. Private Gibson said it best when he wrote in his diary,
"The people are civil and well disposed, not being able to resist the
force brought against them. But they are far from receiving us generally as deliverers."

In back of all his goodwill and diplomacy, Kearny's main purpose
remained starkly military—to solidify the American victory and
quash any remaining sentiments of defiance. The larger war was raging deeper in Mexico, and Kearny had almost no knowledge of how
the American armies were faring. He constantly had to sift rumors of
alarming developments to the south, and he had good reason to fear
that Mexican reinforcements might be sent up from Chihuahua or
Durango to retake Santa Fe.

Within days of his arrival in the capital, Kearny ordered the building of a mighty new fortress on a hill overlooking the town. Fort
Marcy, it would be called, in honor of William Marcy, the secretary of
war back in Washington. Looming over the plaza, the fort was laid out
in a complex zigzag pattern like a misshapen star. Buried safely in its
center was a magazine capable of storing many tons of ammunition.
The fort's walls were stuck with cannons and notched with various
loopholes and crenellations. It was built over a large area, with room
enough to garrison a thousand soldiers. One day Kearny took Susan
Magoffin by horseback up to see the construction site, where hundreds of masons were building the enormous walls. "It is the sole master of the entire plain below," Magoffin wrote cheerfully of the
emerging fort. "Every house in the city can be torn by the artillery to
atoms."

⊠

Kearny's orders had been to stay in New Mexico as long as necessary
to thwart any possibility of a revolt, and then to continue on
posthaste to California. The general felt confident he had achieved his
goal—"All is quiet and no armed force of any kind remains in the
field," he reported in mid-September. But this was a somewhat hol-

low statement, he must have realized, for the *real* war in New Mexico was not between the Americans and the Mexicans, but rather between the nomadic Indian tribes and everyone else. He had stumbled into an age-old conflict that showed no signs of abating with the American presence.

Kearny threw himself into the chaos of the Indian conflicts with his characteristic optimism and resolve, but it was clear that the problem was too complex, too multidimensional, and too long-festering for his army to "correct" during its brief stay. Knowledgeable Indian-fighters recognized that the situation with the Southwestern tribes could potentially escalate into the kind of costly, lengthy, messy war the U.S. government had recently fought against the Seminole Indians of Florida—although instead of pursuing their defiant enemy in the swamps of the Everglades, soldiers would have to fight in equally inaccessible desert mountains. Wrote Capt. William McKissack, an assistant quartermaster stationed in Santa Fe: "I fear another Florida War if the Indians desire to protract it."

Kearny, for his part, was much more optimistic. He demanded that representatives of these "wild tribes"—the Utes, the Apaches, the Comanches, and especially the Navajos—come in for council. And if they did not "desist from all robberies and crimes," Kearny said, he would send his soldiers amongst them "and destroy them from the earth."

This tough talk made little impression on most of the Navajos—if they received the import of his message at all. In fact, during her short stay in Santa Fe, Susan Magoffin records that the Navajos descended on the very outskirts of the capital "and carried off some twenty families." Perhaps realizing that she herself could be kidnapped, Magoffin seemed acutely distressed by the news, noting that "there is mourning and lamentation in the streets, for friends who may never again be seen on earth."

In response to the attack, Kearny demanded that the Navajos return all kidnapped prisoners. Susan Magoffin, for one, was optimistic that they would heed his warning, "as the Navajos deem the general almost superhuman since he has walked in so quietly and taken possession of the palace of the great Armijo, their former fear."

Chapter 22 THE NEW MEN

Narbona crouched in the scrub above Santa Fe, looking down upon the battlements and earthworks the Americans had constructed with such haste. He watched the soldiers marching, practicing their marksmanship, drilling in close order. He saw the glint of their guns and swords, the resplendent uniforms of the dragoons. He saw an unfamiliar flag flying over the Palace of the Governors, with crisp stars and bands of red and white. He saw the ambassadors of other Indian tribes trickling into the city to pay homage to the great general, Kearny. On the outskirts of town he could make out the legions of American conquerors quartered in smoky tent cities, erected in the pastures and cornfields of the Mexicans.

The American logic escaped Narbona: How could they make war with the Mexicans and in the next instant not only declare themselves friends with them, but vow to subjugate their enemies? Why would they willingly absorb another people's war? What fickle spirits drove these men?

Then Narbona heard the explosions, the terrific booms of the American guns—the mountain howitzers and other cannons the soldiers periodically shot for artillery practice or for some sort of demonstration. The skies shuddered and the ground shook when these great guns fired. The barrels flashed and seethed smoke. The sounds were terrifying.

Many Native Americans at the time were said to have an overwhelming, irrational fear of artillery—according to one prominent Western historian, Indians often expressed a belief that these big guns "could shoot holes through the earth and kill on the far side of mountains." Whether Narbona shared in this dread is not known, but clearly the howitzers made an impression on him.

Narbona realized that these were a different sort of people. The rumors were correct—their armies really did fire lightning bolts. He saw no point in fighting them, there was nothing to be won. He would make his way back to Navajo country and advocate a permanent peace with the Americans.

A corner had been turned, a fresh era had arrived, and New Mexico was now in the hands of an altogether different race. He called them, with an emphatic simplicity, "the New Men."

Narbona was amazed and troubled by the implications of everything he saw—for if his old enemy had been so quickly and completely vanquished, what lay in store for his own people?

—

BOOK TWO

A Broken Country

The eagle ranges far and wide over the land, farther than
any other creature, and all things there are related simply by
having existence in the perfect vision of a bird.

—N. SCOTT MOMADAY,
HOUSE MADE OF DAWN

Chapter 23   THE GRIM METRONOME

On the morning of September 25—the day after the party—the bells of Santa Fe were tolling again. This time they rang to announce General Kearny's departure and to send the dragoons off in style. Three hundred of his best men assembled at Fort Marcy. Kearny raised his hand in salute, and the column struck out at noon, bearing south by southwest for the Rio Grande. For his guide Kearny had a veteran mountain man, Tom Fitzpatrick, an old friend of Kit Carson's. Most of the Missouri volunteers would be staying behind with Colonel Doniphan, holding down the place until more reinforcements would arrive from Fort Leavenworth—and then they, too, would dash off, for Chihuahua and points south. Most of the Missourians had grown fond of their commander and waved him off with genuine emotion. "We were sorry to part with General Kearny," one wrote. "He had gained the good wishes of every man."

Kearny's dragoons were thrilled finally to be on their way, even if some of them were a bit hungover from the previous night's ball. After spoiling for a fight in New Mexico, none had been forthcoming. Instead they had spent most of their time camping out, getting scurvy from a bad diet, and nursing their sick horses back into shape. They had drunk their share of Taos Lightning and lost innumerable hands of monte over at Madame Tules's place. If they had stayed in Santa Fe much longer, they might well have gone astray in her hall of ruin. Perhaps California would offer something more exciting in the way of battlefield glories.

In truth, no one had liked Santa Fe very much. The soldiers filled their diaries with disparaging descriptions of the place. It was a greasy, smelly, drunken, superstitious little town, they thought, loud with the fulminations of fat friars who scratched their itches and wore the same robe every evening. Santa Fe was a place of goats and chickens, of twisted offshoots of Catholic doctrine, of spiritual and medical guesswork. The axes and hammers and saws were miserable, the apples stunted, the windows did not have glass, the houses lacked furniture, and the doors had leather straps and wood pegs for want of hinges. Sugar came from corn, alcohol from cactus, and the town's only musical instruments were used for fandangos and masses alike. A demented beggar lady picked among the garbage and sucked on old melon rinds. Burros were constantly abused. Wagons did not have true axles or wheels, but rather clumsy trucks hacked from gnarled cottonwood stumps. It seemed an exotically primitive place, one said, as though their hosts had not quite mastered the concept of the wheel.

The soldiers were especially sick of the food, all those chile stews made with mutton fat, and the dubious slop it made on their plates. They were sick of the grit, too, and the goathead thorns and the lice. Lieutenant Emory dutifully reported on the "universal presence of vermin on the bodies of all the inhabitants . . . it is not unusual to see people stop suddenly, expertly hunt, and then cause a sharp sound announcing a tiny death to you—and then the next minute to see them handle the fruit or cheese which they are offering to sell to you."

Santa Fe was indeed a dirty and impoverished place, and yet it had something—some quality of spectacle that Kearny's men would sorely miss as they headed out into the desert. The old city offered odd incongruities of culture and the accrued weight of history. Games of chance were always being played in the streets, and the markets were filled with an interesting babble of Indian tongues. The surrounding land was strange and dramatic, the light danced on the hills, and the mountains were everywhere, in the middle distance, breathing a draught of limitless possibility. The climate was extraordinary, especially in September; all the soldiers' diaries speak soaringly of it: ". . . singularly mild, equable, and salubrious . . . with sunsets as rich as an Italian sky could boast." . . . "The weather continues delightful, as fine as a heart could wish it." . . . "The air is fine and healthy, and the atmosphere perfectly pure."

In the clear air, Kearny and his men could look one hundred miles to the west and see the sacred southeastern mountain of the Navajos, the dormant volcano not far from Narbona's outfit that was called Blue Bead Mountain. The New Mexicans called the mountain San Mateo, but despite the assurance of a good Christian name, it was an especially nagging landmark, a kind of geological rebuke, reminding them that although they had lived hereabouts for three long centuries, they had never entirely conquered this land. The Navajos grazed sheep on the mountain's flanks, sheep they had stolen from the New Mexicans. They thundered across it on stolen horses, and lived all around it, often with women and children they had stolen from New Mexican villages. San Mateo was close enough to see, but too far away to reach safely without mounting an expedition so large as to tip off the Diné encamped there. By the time a party approached the mountain, the stolen horses and sheep and women and children would be long gone with their Navajo captors, scattered into the infinite recesses of Navajo country.

Kearny did not know what to do about the Navajos, and he left the matter in the hands of the new governor, Charles Bent. Bent did not know what to do either, other than to build forts closer to the Navajos to keep a better eye on their movements. Shortly after assuming office, Bent wrote a long and insightful letter to Washington describing the Indian situation in New Mexico—and singling out the Diné as public enemy number one. "The Navajos are an industrious, intelligent and warlike tribe," he wrote, "numbering as many as 14,000 souls. They are the only Indians on the continent having intercourse with white men that are increasing in numbers. Their horses and sheep are said to be greatly superior to those raised by the New Mexicans. A large portion of their stock has been acquired by marauding expeditions against the settlements. Their country consists of high table mountains, difficult of access, and affording them protection against their enemies. Water is hard to find by those not acquainted with their country, affording another natural safeguard against invasion. They have in their possession many prisoners, men, women, and children, taken from the settlements of this Territory, whom they hold and treat as slaves."

Not that the New Mexicans had failed to find ways to make Navajo life miserable. They, too, stole Navajo sheep and horses and women and children. Although slavery was technically illegal, anyone of means in the province had at least one or two Indian *criados* (servants), and a young Navajo woman was considered most valuable of all—in large part because of her assumed talent for weaving.

There were slave markets in Taos and other towns where Indian servants could be purchased for a pittance. Often captives were sold in the town plazas on Sunday afternoons following mass. Other tribes that happened to be enemies of the Diné came to understand their high market value, and so inevitably, Navajo children in ever larger numbers would end up on the auctioning blocks. There was also a phenomenon known as the "New Mexican Bachelor Party," in which a groom and a few of his swashbuckling friends would gamely push into Navajo country and go hunting for a few slaves to give to the bride on her wedding day to help her keep house. Professional slave raiders were part of the ordinary commerce of daily life.

Remarked one disgusted traveler to Santa Fe: "I have frequently seen little Indian children six years of age led around the country like beasts by a Mexican who had probably stolen them from their mother not more than a week before and offered for sale from forty to one hundred and twenty dollars."

Said Lewis Kennon, an American doctor well acqainted with life in New Mexico: "I know of no family which can raise one hundred and fifty dollars but what purchases a Navajo slave. Many families own four or five—the trade in them being as regular as the trade in pigs or sheep."

It has been estimated that of the six thousand people then living in Santa Fe, at least five hundred were Indian slaves or peons. The Mexican families usually baptized their Indian servants in the Catholic faith and often treated them well, like secondary relatives; some even won their freedom. Amado Chaves, son of one famous New Mexico slave raider, wrote: "On arriving home after a slaving expedition, the first thing to do was to take the children to the priest and give them a name. They would naturally take your name and as they grew up they would consider you and your wife as their parents." Certainly the system differed in form and particulars from its agrarian counterpart in the American South, but it was slavery nonetheless.

In general, it was said that the Mexicans were better at stealing people, and the Navajos were better at stealing animals. Whatever the case, the attacks and reprisals were simply part of the grim metronome of life, swinging with the same logic of a feud. In truth there were some on both sides, most of them aggressive young men, who rather liked these cycles of violence: They relieved boredom, they tested courage and resolve, and honed warrior skills. The Navajos and their Mexican adversaries were not accustomed to the concept of all-out war or unconditional surrender or treaties that endured beyond a season—these were European concepts. The combatants in this centuries-old war did not observe tidy declarations or cessations of hostilities. A persistent, low-grade violence was always there, a possibility lurking on the horizon, like San Mateo. It was the only life they had known.

⊠

The Navajos were immediately aware of Kearny's departure from Santa Fe, and they interpreted it as weakness: The Americans were already quitting New Mexico, they thought. These "New Men" would not press their demands; the great general Kearny lacked staying power.

Emboldened, the Navajos began raiding settlements along the Rio Grande, often right under the nose of Kearny's army as it marched south in the last week of September. Between Albuquerque and Polvadera they killed eight settlers and stole thousands of horses, sheep, and cattle. Navajo raiders were even brazen enough to follow Kearny's own beef herd, and near the town of Algodones managed to steal a few head.

Kearny was livid when he heard the news. The Navajos were clearly testing him. It must have seemed to him, in theatrical terms, that the villain was stealing the limelight just as Kearny was exiting the stage. It chafed the general that the Navajos had been the *only* major tribe of New Mexico that had refused to send envoys to Santa Fe to confer with him, and he was embarrassed that he could not make good on his promise to protect the Mexican citizenry from their age-old enemy. But his dragoons could not afford to go hunting after Navajos right now—he was on a tight schedule and had to continue his march to California. Instead, Kearny distributed a proclamation in which he noted the "almost daily outrages committed by the Navajoes" and then "authorized" the people living along the Rio Grande to form their own "war parties, to march into the country of . . . the Navajoes, to recover Property, and to make reprisals and obtain redress for the many insults received from them." Kearny stopped short of urging an all-out war, however: "The Old, the Women, and the Children of the Navajoes," he warned, "must not be injured."

At the same time, Kearny immediately sent back a message to Alexander Doniphan in Santa Fe ordering the colonel to launch a foray into Navajo country as soon as possible. Doniphan, Kearny instructed, was to reclaim New Mexican prisoners and livestock and do whatever the colonel thought necessary to "secure a peace and better conduct from these Indians."

By October 6, Kearny and his three hundred dragoons had marched 150 miles down the Rio Grande. They were eleven days out of Santa Fe and enjoying the crisp radiance of Indian summer. It was a cool, clear day, with the cottonwoods and river willows yellowing in the thick bosque that lined the river. Sandhill cranes and geese flocked overhead—the Rio Grande was a major flyway for waterfowl. They were camped just below the village of Socorro, at a little place called Valverde, which had once been a Spanish village of some importance, but had been abandoned in the wake of Navajo and Apache raids. Kearny's men were bivouacked among the town's adobe ruins. They had come to the end of the first leg of their thousand-mile journey to California. They had been marching straight south, following the river, but from here on they would aim west, eventually striking the

Gila River and crossing the solitudes of the Sonoran and Mojave deserts.

Sometime around midday, a tiny brown cloud appeared on the western horizon. There was a sound of hoofbeats in the distance. Horsemen, a dozen or more, emerged from the contrails of dust. They seemed to be aiming straight for Kearny's camp. The dragoons suspected for a moment that the riders might be Navajos.

As they drew nearer, it became clear that although some were Indians, the party was being led by a group of Americans. It was a meeting of fellow countrymen, and soon the ruins of Valverde erupted in a ruckus of halloos and the tossing of hats.

A small leathery man slid off his mule and greeted the dragoons. Like all of his comrades, he was haggard and sun-beaten and in bad need of food. He indicated that he and his party had come posthaste from California, bearing important messages for the East Coast.

What is your name? someone asked.

The little man grinned as he led his mule into Kearny's camp. "I'm Kit Carson."

⌾

Kearny had never met Kit Carson, but he knew who he was. The general had read about him in Fremont's exploration reports. Carson had a home in Taos, a little adobe not far from the town square, and he was the most famous American then living in the New Mexico territory. He had been away for more than a year, on his various errands in California and Oregon, but nearly everywhere General Kearny's forces had been, they had heard stories about the famed scout. He was a friendly phantom presence: Along the Santa Fe Trail, at Bent's Fort, in the mercantile shops and warehouses of the capital, Carson's name had repeatedly cropped up, usually with a smile and a colorful tale of some wild exploit in the mountains.

Carson and Kearny greeted each other as compatriots. They must have acknowledged the strange serendipity of their encounter. What were the odds that these two men trekking from nearly opposite sides of the continent would meet in this way, that of all the possible routes across the canvas of the West, theirs would intersect?

Carson seemed surprised and puzzled to meet three hundred soldiers of the United States Dragoons, aimed in the same direction from which he had just come. Kearny explained that all of the New Mexico territory had been conquered, without a fight, that the American flag flew over the Palace of the Governors in Santa Fe, and that he was now pushing west to conquer California.

The scout tried to absorb the implications of this news. His home for the past twenty years was now part of America. His wife in Taos and her proud Spanish family had all effectively become Americans. Even now he and the general were standing on American soil. His own brother-in-law was governor.

Carson looked exhausted, and he was thickly coated in dust from a long overland journey. For twenty-six consecutive days Carson and his party of men had ridden more than eight hundred miles from Los Angeles. They had already worn out thirty-four mules, crossing some of the most infernal country imaginable on the Gila Trail, and they still had another two thousand miles to go. They were on their way to Washington City, Carson said, to deliver important dispatches to the president of the United States.

General Kearny was perplexed. Carson went on to explain that he had been given a temporary commission as a lieutenant and was under orders from his commanders in California to ride to Washington in sixty days or less to deliver news on the progress of the war with Mexico. California, he said, was now in American hands; the Stars and Stripes "floated in every port."

Kearny's reaction to this fabulous piece of intelligence was ambiguous. As a patriot he found these developments encouraging, but at the same time he must have been somewhat miffed to learn that his work had already been done for him. New Mexico had fallen without his firing a shot, and now, it seemed, California scarcely needed his services, either. A physician traveling with Kearny, Dr. John S. Griffin, summed up the general reaction to Carson's news. "This created considerable sensation in our party," Griffin wrote, "but the feeling was one of disappointment and regret—most of us hoped on leaving Santa Fe that we might have a little kick-up with the good people of California but this blasted all our hopes."

On the other hand, General Kearny understood that California was a vast realm and that insurgent locals could rise up at any time or place—or worse, that reinforcements might be rushed from Mexico to ignite a widespread resistance. The cautious general wondered whether the dispatches Carson was bearing might convey an overly optimistic assessment of the situation there.

Then Kearny's thoughts began to turn. Whether or not the fighting had ended, his orders were to push on to California and institute a new government there, just as he had done in Santa Fe. The general, however, was seriously concerned about the unmapped desert ahead of him, uncertain which route to take and whether his animals could survive the journey. Carson had just crossed the same withered terrain over which his dragoons would soon be passing. The scout knew the lay of the land and the disposition of the Indians along the route. He knew the watering holes and the grassy spots where his horses and mules might graze. He could tell Kearny which stretches were suitable for wagons and rolling artillery pieces. He knew the best places to ford the creeks and rivers—especially the Colorado, the greatest obstacle before him.

And so Kearny needed Carson. The general recognized something about this man, a certain aura of success, that would be indispensable to his Army of the West. The general ordered him to hand over the dispatches, to be placed in another able courier's saddlebags and taken to President Polk. The great scout had more important work to do: General Kearny wanted him to make an about-face and go back to California, as his personal guide.

This put Carson in a quandary. He had promised Fremont that he would rush the documents to Washington, no matter what. Not being a military man, Carson preferred to ignore the hard dictates of rank—that Fremont was only a Topographical Corps captain whose wishes paled before the will of a brigadier general like Kearny. Carson's simple frontier sense of honor had been offended. His father in

Missouri had always taught him his word was his bond, and here was a man telling him to ignore his earlier promise and give the messages to someone else.

Carson briefly agonized over what to do—agonizing being something he rarely engaged in. He seriously considered a plan to escape from Kearny's forces under cover of nightfall and speed to Washington as planned. He thought of Josefa, whom he had not seen for nearly two years. He had hoped to surprise her for one night in Taos on his way east. If he went west with Kearny, he feared he might not get a chance to see her for yet another year. For her sake, he wanted to get back to Taos and take the pulse of the town.

Mostly, though, he kept thinking of Fremont and Commodore Stockton. "I was pledged to them," he later said, "and could not disappoint them, and besides that I was under more obligations to Captain Fremont than any man alive."

But some of the men in his party persuaded Carson not to attempt an escape. The dragoons would catch up with him, they argued, and even if they didn't, Kearny would have him court-martialed. Besides, the general had already decided to give the messages to a courier Carson knew well and trusted, Tom Fitzpatrick, who had accompanied Fremont on several of his expeditions. Fitzpatrick could blaze the way to "Washington City" just as well as he.

At this, Carson began to soften. Besides, Kearny was a difficult man to say no to—even for someone as stubborn as Carson. Kearny had an iron will, and, as one account put it, he showed "a resolute countenance and cold blue eyes which there was no evading." Carson began to feel the sheer weight of Kearny's rank bearing down on him. "He made me believe," Carson said, "that he had a right to order me." Kearny later recalled that although Carson "was at first very unwilling to turn back," he was "perfectly satisfied" with Fitzpatrick taking the messages, "and so told me."

So Carson relented. He handed over the letters and agreed to accompany the general. The following morning, October 7, 1846, Kearny gave the dispatches to Fitzpatrick and also sent two-thirds of his dragoons back to Santa Fe to reinforce the capital. If Carson's own assessments and the reports in the dispatches were correct, then the situation in California did not require a large force. The general would continue on to Los Angeles leading a leaner, lighter contingent of only one hundred dragoons. Carson would guide them, and he would not look back. Lt. Abraham Johnston, a young officer serving under Kearny, admired Carson's decision. "He turned his face to the west again," Johnston wrote, "just as he was on the eve of entering the settlements, after his arduous trip and when he had set his hopes on seeing his family. It requires a brave man to give up his private feelings thus for the public good; but Carson is one such! Honor to him for it." Capt. Philip St. George Cooke commended Carson: "That was no common sacrifice to duty."

Dr. John Griffin noticed that having Carson on board discernibly improved the morale of all the dragoons. He wrote in his diary, "We put out, with merry hearts & light packs on our long march—every man feeling renewed confidence in consequence of having such a guide. From the way the Genl marched today, I should say he was on his way in Earnest."

Later Carson tersely summed up his decision this way: "Kearny ordered me to join him as his guide. I done so."

Chapter 24   LORDS OF THE MOUNTAINS

The *bilagaana* were coming. Narbona did not know if their intentions were peaceful or not, but according to his scouts, a small, well-armed group of Americans had entered Navajo country on horseback, aiming due west. They would be marching into Narbona's domain in less than a week.

It was now mid-October of 1846. The days were growing short and chilly in the high desert. The brilliant yellow blooms of the chamisa had faded to a drab brown and the aspens were losing their leaves. Frost powdered the ground in the mornings, and higher in the Chuskas fresh snow had fallen. Narbona was not well. Perhaps his recent trip to Santa Fe had taken a toll on his decrepit body. His arthritis had flared up in the biting cold, and he was so sore he could not sit a horse.

He was not sure how to respond to the Americans, but he knew their incursion into Navajo land could not be a good development. Probably he was aware that the younger men had been out on raids over the past few weeks—word of their exploits could not have escaped him. It had been a successful raiding season, and there was much rejoicing in Navajo country. For with so many new sheep now in the tribe's possession, it promised to be a fat and happy winter. The time of the great feasts and nightchants was at hand; now there would be plenty of meat for everyone.

Narbona brooded, however. Like many of the older men, he understood the repercussions of raiding. That the young braves had ventured out and stolen from the hated New Mexicans was of minor concern to him—this was what braves always had done, what he himself had done as a young man. But if the young warriors had stolen from the Americans, too, then that was cause for great worry. He would like to know more, would like to intercept the Americans before they pierced the heart of the Diné territory. But since his health did not permit him to move toward the trouble, he would have to rest in his hogan and await further word from his sentinels.

It must have been a shock for him to learn that these strange white men were now trespassing on the Dinetah, as the Navajo called their ancient lands. During his long lifetime, his wrinkled country had known few interlopers, except for occasional parties of Mexican or Ute raiders bent on some specific mission of theft or reprisal. These raiders typically made superficial incursions, however, creasing only the periphery of Navajo country and then leaving as quickly as they came. Navajo country was a landscape so forbiddingly large that few foreigners risked traversing it, a landscape so harshly intricate that it seemed to swallow up anyone not intimately familiar with its secrets.

But these Americans, whoever they were, appeared to be making a deliberate penetration, as though they had some larger purpose in mind. Narbona was impressed and surprised by their small number: The reports said thirty men. What a tiny, vulnerable party! These Americans must be either extraordinarily brave or else oblivious to the reality that at any moment hundreds of Navajo warriors could descend on them and easily wipe them out.

But now the boundary described by the four sacred peaks had been violated. The *bilagaana* had stolen past Blue Bead Mountain, and Narbona could only wait.

◙

The thirty American soldiers trekking westward were led by a Capt. John Reid. They had come from Santa Fe on a somewhat quixotic mission. In mid-October, Reid's men had broken off from the relative safety of a larger contingent of Missouri volunteers along the Rio Grande and ridden for ninety miles, boring straight into Navajo country. Reid's assignment was to make contact with as many Navajos as possible and impress upon their headmen the importance of meeting in a few weeks for peace talks with the American commander, Alexander Doniphan. They were emissaries, in other words, dispatched to spread the word of the summit that General Kearny had ordered Doniphan to hold. The task seemed straightforward enough, at first, but the deeper they rode into Navajo country, the more Reid and his Missourians realized that this was an absurdly dangerous foray.

People had said as much back on the Rio Grande. Volunteer John Hughes recalled that the New Mexicans they met were "amazed at the temerity of Capt. Reid's proceeding," for "to enter the Navajo country with less than an army was considered by them as certain destruction."

Now hundreds and possibly thousands of Navajo warriors were lurking in the surrounding hills and buttes. With every step of the journey Reid could sense their searching stares, could see them hiding in the shadows or watching from the high remove of the rimrock. Stone-faced and inscrutable, they let the Americans pass through their country, but Reid knew they weren't happy about it. They must have been intensely curious about these intruders. For some, it was a moment of first contact; many of these Navajos had never seen white men before, certainly not on their home ground.

On October 15 a group of Navajos came forward and suggested to Reid through a translator that the person he needed to see was an old man named Narbona, their great leader. Narbona was sick, they said, and could not travel. But the headman's camp was only a day's ride away. Encouraged, Reid decided to stay overnight and push to Narbona's camp the next day.

Soon the Missourians were approached by thirty braves wearing eagle feathers and helmets fashioned from the skinned heads of mountain lions. Jacob Robinson, a volunteer who kept a thorough, perceptive journal of this historic first meeting between the American military and Navajos, thought these men looked like formidable warriors, but their intentions appeared to be peaceful. They were "all well-mounted on beautiful horses," Robinson said, "and had been sent forward to guide us to the heart of their country. They were very active in all their movements, mounting and dismounting their horses in an instant."

With them were ten Navajo women "dressed in splendid Indian attire and fine figured blankets." Robinson found the Navajo women beautiful, with small, delicate feet, long black hair, and brass bracelets jangling on their arms. Impressed with their equestrian skills, he found "the one sex apparently as good at riding as the other . . . The women of this tribe seem to have equal rights with the men, managing their own business and trading as they see fit; saddling their own horses, and letting their husbands saddle theirs."

The following morning these Navajos led Reid's party forward, and as they rode deeper into the Diné country, more and more locals joined the procession. By the end of the day, however, Reid's hosts informed him that Narbona's camp was still another day away. Suspicious but grateful for their seeming hospitality, Reid decided to risk it and continue on. By now the parade of curious Navajos had swelled to several hundred.

After the third day of riding the Diné guides said they *still* hadn't reached their destination, that Narbona's outfit was yet a ways off. Reid now feared a trap but realized he had come too far to turn around now—he was utterly at the Navajos' mercy. This was, Reid said, "the most critical situation in which I ever found myself placed—with only thirty men in the very centre of the most savage and proverbially treacherous people on the continent."

As Reid's volunteers pitched camp on the afternoon of October 18, they realized that they were now surrounded by thousands of Navajo. And then to their horror, they discovered that their horses were nowhere to be seen. The Navajos said they had turned them out to graze in a meadow five miles distant and promised to return them when they were needed. Now the Americans were not only encircled, they had no means of escape. They felt like captives—and maybe they were. The situation was, Reid said, "eminently precarious," and he found it distasteful to have to put "such great confidence in the honesty of . . . these notorious horse stealers." He and his men sat glumly in the sinking October sun, trying hard to keep their faces from registering fear. "To have showed any thing like suspicion," thought Missouri volunteer John Hughes, "would have been insulting to the Indians' pride and wounding to their feelings. It was safer to risk the chances of treachery than to use caution which would serve but to provoke."

▢

Then, to everyone's surprise, Narbona rode into view. The old man was in terrible shape, obviously in great pain and just barely propped on his horse. His camp was only a few miles away, it turned out, but it seemed a matter of pride for him to be initially seen on a horse— and for him to ride the last distance to greet Reid rather than have the visitor come to him. Narbona had white hair down to his shoulders, and his tall, lanky frame was wrapped in his finest animal skins and polished jewels. He was a giant man, standing more than six-feet six-inches tall in his prime, but his body was considerably hunched and twisted by old age. Captain Reid could tell that although Narbona was "held in great reverence by his tribe," he was now "a mere skeleton of a man, being completely prostrated by rheumatism." Reid was amazed and faintly repulsed by Narbona's clawlike fingernails, which he estimated to be nearly two inches long and sharp enough to serve as "formidable weapons."

Someone helped the old headman from his horse, and Reid and Narbona sat down for a long talk, through a Spanish translator, about the recent spate of thefts along the Rio Grande. The captain liked Narbona despite his odd style of manicure, and assessed the leader to be "a mild, amiable man." Narbona said that he was impressed by all that the Americans had done in Santa Fe in such a short time, and that he was ready to meet with Doniphan and hold a council. The meeting would be held a month away at a place well-known to the Navajos called Bear Springs. Reid judged Narbona to be so ill that he thought himself not long for this world and therefore wished to leave a legacy as a diplomat.

"Though he had been a warrior himself," the captain said, "he was very anxious before his death to secure for his people a peace with all their old enemies—as well as with us, the 'New Men,' as he called us."

Some of the other Navajo leaders spoke their minds, and most of them seemed to agree with Narbona: It was time for peace. Robinson records that a headman came forward to declare that he had something special to show Captain Reid. It was a treaty, he said, one that their forefathers had made with American leaders sometime in the distant past. "Seven hundred winters ago," he said with much solemnity and then brought forth a large roll of buckskins that he "commenced unrolling, taking off skin after skin." At last, writes Robinson, the headman "came to a blanket, which he proceeded to unfold" and there lay the precious document carefully preserved inside. "With a grunt," the chief handed the piece of paper to Reid's interpreter. Upon inspection, however, the "treaty" turned out to be nothing but a yellowed receipt from an American trader—an old bill of sale.

Reid's men all erupted in laughter at this odd farce, and then there was a long, awkward moment as the translator tried to explain. It was not altogether clear whether the headman had been spoofed or was himself spoofing—and if it was the latter, then what the point of the joke might have been. Something surely was lost in translation. Robinson writes that "when the chief was informed that the treaty had nothing to do with us, he tucked it away, its value having apparently departed."

Then, according to a Diné account of the meeting, a woman rose to speak. She was one of Narbona's three wives, and the sole woman present at the council. She spoke only in Navajo so that the translator, and thus Captain Reid and his men, could not understand her.

Narbona's wife surveyed the encampment and said she was confused. There were very few of these Americans present, she said, scarcely more than twenty-five. On the other hand, there were several thousand Navajos. These *bilagaana* would be pitifully easy to overpower, she suggested. Then she adopted a shrill tone: Why are you men being such cowards? Why not fall upon these uninvited guests right now and kill every one of them?

Narbona and his wife began to argue about the merits of this proposition. One imagines Reid and his men watching innocently, their heads swiveling as they tried to follow the spirited repartee while remaining oblivious to its deathly import.

Then Narbona angrily told his wife to sit down. What did she know about it? She had not been to Santa Fe, she had not seen their armies. These men here were just messengers, behind them were many thousands more. They had come from beyond the buffalo plains and had conquered Santa Fe without firing a shot. If they were provoked, the New Men could surely obliterate the Diné.

No, he insisted. These *bilagaana* were not to be harmed, but lavished with Navajo hospitality.

⊠

After Captain Reid and Narbona finished their talk, the Diné suddenly seemed in a mood to celebrate. Music erupted in the camp. The warriors stashed their bows in the limbs of a cottonwood tree and began to dance.

Other Navajos descended on the Americans in friendly curiosity, eager to inspect the American clothes and goods—and to barter for their buckles, buttons, forks, straps, lockets, and books. Said Robinson: "The principal chiefs continually exhorted them to come away and not molest us, but we found it impossible to keep the Indians from our encampment. There was almost a continual trading going on between our men and the Indians—a tin cup for a buckskin, a small piece of tobacco for a butcher knife."

The Missouri volunteers eventually traded off most of their clothes, so that in due time, Robinson said, "we had dressed ourselves pretty nearly in the Indian style." Reid noted that the Navajos were "delighted to see our men adopting their costume" and soon the confab took on "much pleasurable excitement."

The Diné seemed intrigued by anything metal—weapons especially. "They were curious to examine our guns," wrote Robinson, "and were astonished when shown the properties of a revolver. One of our men wore a watch, which excited great attention; on placing it to their ears they would start as from a snake."

By late afternoon the Navajo drums began to pound and the piñon bonfires crackled and the scent of roast mutton hung heavy in the air. It seemed that the Missourians and their guests were becoming fast friends. Reid's men were fascinated by the language of the Navajo—with its thousand finicky inflections and throaty pauses. Through clumsy bouts of translation they began to get a vague idea of the Diné's sense of humor, their unslakable appetite for teasing and puns, their delight in any incongruous or absurd situation. Everywhere about the camp the Navajo were lost in traditional amusements—broad-jumping, stone-throwing, archery contests, stick dice. It was as though they were throwing a spontaneous open-air festival for the Americans' benefit.

Reid's men could see that these spirited people, safe in their own domain, were happy, open, and proud. They were at the height of their power, enjoying the fruits of a particularly successful season of raids. John Hughes described the scene as "truly romantic. Contemplate five hundred dancers in the hollow recesses of the mountains,

with the music of shells and timbrels, giving way to the most extravagant joy, and a band of thirty Americans, armed with martial accou-
trements, mingling in the throng!"

Jacob Robinson felt thoroughly at home and almost forgot that he
and his comrades were more than a hundred miles inside sketchy territory with their mounts nowhere in sight. It didn't matter—they
were captivated, smitten almost, by their hosts. They abandoned all
sense of caution. They gnawed greasy lamb shanks together, they
fondled each other's weapons, they danced and sang, they even
swapped clothes. The first American encounter with the Diné had become a love-in.

Later, Robinson looked back on all this naïve revelry with a sort of
what-were-we-thinking incredulity. "It is astonishing," he said, "how
soon our confidence in each other was almost complete. We were in
the midst of a desert, surrounded by a nation of powerful savages,
whose numbers were great, and whose friendship was doubtful; who
had us completely in their power and who might be treacherous.
[But] we mingled in their dance . . . and they appeared much pleased
at our coming to their country."

All in all, Robinson was deeply impressed with the Navajo as a
people, finding them "the most enlightened tribe of wild Indians" he
had yet encountered on the continent. "They are of good stature," he
wrote, "and of fairer complexion than any Indians I have ever seen.
They are well provided with wool and skins and may be considered
wealthy." Robinson was intrigued by the Diné's woven blankets,
which they "look upon with pride, as a badge of national distinction
and superiority."

Watching the Navajos fuss over their flocks and woolen goods,
Captain Reid struck a comparison to the nomadic shepherds of the
Mongolian steppes—an analogy that would crop up frequently in
subsequent accounts by Americans trying to put an Old World frame
of reference on these unfamiliar people so uniquely tied to their
sheep. "They are entirely pastoral," Reid said, "and in their habits very
similar to the Tartars." Above all, the captain observed, the Navajos
were excellent horsemen. "These lords of the mountains," Reid

wrote, "may be said to *live* on horseback. They pay great attention to the breeding of their horses, and think scarcely less of them than do the Arabians."

At one point during the afternoon a rabbit bolted from the underbrush and a group of Navajos on horseback immediately gave chase. Scores of other riders joined in, and, according to Robinson, "the plain was soon covered with these mounted warriors, with their feathers streaming in the wind, their arms raised as for conflict; some riding one way and some another; and in the midst of these exciting scenes they indulged a shout of triumph, as they succeeded in capturing their prey."

The Missourians must have relished their last night in Navajo country. At great risk they had tasted an alien culture and completed their mission without incident. It was learned that the American horses were safe and well fed and ready to be saddled up at dawn. They would leave in the morning, and Narbona would even provide them with an escort from the Navajo lands.

Through their dumb luck and blundering good nature, Reid's volunteers had succeeded in not getting themselves killed. These young farm boys seemed to believe they could do anything, go anywhere, and not get hurt; the ancient cycles of violence did not quite pertain to them.

Chapter 25 THE DEVIL'S TURNPIKE

With Kit Carson now guiding them, General Kearny's one hundred dragoons rose from the Rio Grande on October 7, 1846, and worked their way west until they struck the Gila River and then followed its tortuous canyons through land that was increasingly barren and bleached. As October melted into November, they passed from the realm of the Apache into territory of unknown tribes: the Wolf Eaters, the Dirty

Fellows, the Club Indians, the Pine Forest Dwellers, the Tremblers, the Albinos, the Fools. Such were the informal names gleaned from Spanish interpreters and hastily copied down in official American journals. These remote tribes had never seen Americans, had seldom seen Spaniards, and many were obviously terrified by these strange new warriors boring into their midst. The Tremblers had acquired their name, according to Lt. William Emory, "from their emotions at meeting the whites." Their shaky chief spoke "in a tongue resembling more the bark of a mastiff than the words of a human being."

Carson and Kearny rode together much of the way—the scout in his greasy buckskins, the general in his proud dragoon blues. Fellow Missourians, they shared many friends back home. With laconic good humor, Carson tried to make conversation as they went along, but much of the time he quietly sulked. It wasn't the hard monotony of having to cover, in reverse, the same sun-scoured terrain he had so recently crossed. Nor was it simply that he missed Josefa, nor the nagging distaste he still felt for surrendering to Fitzpatrick the messages that Fremont had formally entrusted to him. He had let go of all those concerns back on the Rio Grande.

Mainly, Carson's stewing had to do with the transcontinental adventure he'd been denied. In all his wide travels, he had never been to the East Coast. Carson had been looking forward to seeing his nation's capital. He was under no illusions that he belonged to that closed world of books and stylish clothes and drawing room manners. Yet he wanted to meet the well-placed men and women who had effectively served as his sponsors, sending him on the errands that had made him nationally famous, writing about him, broadcasting his exploits: not only President Polk, but also Sen. Thomas Hart Benton, and the senator's daughter Jessie Benton Fremont as well as Secretary of State Buchanan, Secretary of War Marcy, and various people connected with the Topographical Engineers.

Carson, who had in effect been a field agent of Manifest Destiny, wanted to meet its prime movers.

The competitor in Carson had also been intrigued by the notion of making a sixty-day trip. To cross the continent in two months' time loomed as a kind of athletic grail. Sixty days was what he had promised Fremont he could do—*coast to coast in sixty days!* The feat he had proposed hung in the air as a mythic goal of doubtful attainability. In 1846 the quickest way to get information or goods from one coast to the other was by ship, via the antipodal tip of Tierra del Fuego—or alternately, to Panama, then overland to another ship waiting on the far shore of the isthmus.

Carson was interested in blazing the continental overland route, thereby proving its merits. He had been right on schedule, by his estimation. Carson's party had spent twenty-six days getting to New Mexico from Los Angeles, but from then on the going would have been easier, riding the well-trod Santa Fe Trail northeast to the Missouri River, then churning by steamboat to St. Louis, then arrowing the final stretches to Washington by rail and stagecoach on good wagon roads.

Now here he was, ingloriously loping along a slow trail with a middle-aged general who'd pointed him toward a land that had already been conquered. Carson did not like it a bit.

◌

In fact, Carson's now-dated information was all wrong; California was *not* conquered. Since he had left Los Angeles with Fremont's triumphant dispatches, the territory had been convulsed by an insurrection. The Americans had been kicked out of Los Angeles, out of Santa Barbara, out of every other coastal settlement south of Monterey. The Mexicans, outraged by the harsh terms clamped on them by Commodore Robert Stockton—including curfews and arbitrary arrests without a hearing—had risen up and attacked American positions. In the words of one historian, the revolt had "blossomed like a crown fire leaping through mountain timber." A manifesto had been circulated among the citizens: "We, all the inhabitants of the department of California, as members of the great Mexican nation, declare that it is and has been our wish to belong to her alone. Therefore, the intrusive authorities appointed by the invading forces of the United

End of the Trail: A Missouri caravan arrives in Santa Fe after a journey of nearly one thousand miles; a lithograph from the 1840s.

"Not so much a place as a new kind of existence": Merchant ox and mule teams crowd the streets of Santa Fe, 1867.

"Nature's Gentleman": One of the earliest known portraits of Kit Carson, taken in the early 1840s.

"It was all over a squaw": An artist's conceptualization of Kit Carson's 1835 duel with the French trapper Chouinard at the Green River mountain-man rendezvous.

CARSON'S INDIAN BRIDE.

"A good girl, a good housewife, and good to look at": An idealized portrait of Carson's first wife, the Arapaho beauty Singing Grass.

"Prompt, self-sacrificing, and true": An illustration depicting Carson and Alex Godey triumphantly returning stolen horses (with the scalps of the Indian horse thieves dangling from Godey's rifle barrel).

"The finest head I ever saw on an Indian": Narbona, Navajo elder, as sketched by expedition artist Richard Kern on August 31, 1849, the same day the great leader was killed by American troops.

The sacred peak of the South: Blue Bead Mountain (a.k.a. Mount Taylor), a landmark of Narbona's country, as sketched by Richard Kern on September 18, 1849.

The great houses of Chaco Canyon, widely considered the most magnificent prehistoric ruins in the American West, as drawn by Kern on August 27, 1849.

"What a wild life!": Army explorer (and notorious glory hound) John Charles Fremont, a.k.a. the Pathfinder.

"The better man of the two": Jessie Benton Fremont, the explorer's gifted—and utterly devoted—wife.

"An aggressive patriotism": Senator Thomas Hart Benton of Missouri, the roaring apostle of Manifest Destiny.

"The hardest-working man in America": President James K. Polk, land-hungry instigator of the Mexican War.

"We will correct all this": General Stephen Watts Kearny, conqueror of New Mexico and California, sometimes called the father of the American cavalry.

"A year that will always be remembered by my countrymen": Susan Magoffin, whose diary of the 1846 conquest has become a Western classic.

"A beauty of the haughty, heart-breaking kind": Josefa Jaramillo Carson with unidentified child.

"Carson's home, sentimentally if not in fact": A lithograph of Taos, New Mexico, from the 1850s.

"My happiness directs me to my home and family": The Kit Carson House, photographed in the 1930s.

Taos Pueblo: One of the oldest continually inhabited villages in North America—originally settled around A.D. 1300—the pueblo was the site of the bloody American siege that ended the 1847 Taos Revolt.

States are held as null and void. All North Americans being foes of Mexico, we swear not to lay down our arms until we see them ejected from Mexican soil."

Now the reversal was nearly complete. The proud Californians again had the upper hand. The only place the Americans still held was San Diego, where Commodore Stockton had a few warships anchored in the bay. But the Mexicans there had him so thoroughly pinned down that he could scarcely come ashore.

General Kearny, with his confident guide and his miserably small and haggard force, was limping toward a trap.

⊠

In early November, Kearny's dragoons reached a world "cracked and drawn into blisters" and uninhabited by man, a world whose only denizens appeared to be tarantulas, scorpions, and skittering lizards. The ground was spongy with saline moisture, and wherever the soldiers' feet pressed the ground, "the salts of the earth effloresced, and gave it the appearance of being covered with frost," Emory wrote. "In this way the numberless tracks of horses were indelible, and could be traced for great distances in long white seams." The men trudged past mesquite and creosote, through ocotillo and paloverde, across dunes of rippled sand. They beheld the splendid weirdness of the century plant and the joshua tree and encountered saguaro cactus for the first time, the giant of the Sonoran desert, with its mighty fluted trunks and sagging humanlike arms. Lieutenant Emory described the land as "beautiful in the extreme," marked by "irregular, fantastic mountains" and "mysterious-looking places."

Capt. Henry Turner said marching over this desert landscape "was a strange existence . . . I constantly feel as though I were in a dream, to be thus surrounded day after day with the wilderness, not one familiar object in nature except the sun, the moon, and the stars. Twere better for it to be blotted out from the face of the earth. It is the veriest wilderness in the world, and then the sad thought comes over me, that I am far away from my little family, and that each day widens the distance."

General Kearny was perhaps less charitable. "It surprised me," he wrote, "to see so much land that can never be of any use to man or beast."

And yet by Kearny's tendriling movement across it, this useless land was now effectively part of the United States. The one hundred men now grunting across the desert did not look like much of an invading force, but that's what they were—a long, slender offshoot of Washington. Kearny's orders from President Polk gave him "a wide discretionary power" to take possession of all of what was then called "Upper California," an unbelievably vast area that included not only the present state of California but also parts of Nevada, Utah, and Arizona. Seldom in history had so much real estate been seized by the simple act of a few men walking over it.

Even as Kearny claimed this sere land, he clearly doubted whether it was worth taking. Although the Spanish had long ago settled large swaths of the lush California coast, they had never been able to make anything of this infernal country on the interior. Spanish explorers crisscrossed it many times, and several crude trails had been stamped out to carry on a feeble intercourse between California and New Mexico's settlements on the Rio Grande. But most of it remained a vague, suppositional country. No Spanish villages, no active missions or presidios dotted these desolate precincts of present-day western Arizona and eastern California—and even the nomadic Indians passed through sparingly.

Blazing by day and freezing at night, the desert march was brutal on Kearny's one hundred dragoons and lethal to their horses and mules. Animals were collapsing almost hourly—in a single day a dozen dropped in their tracks—and the stronger ones were becoming patchy with scabs and saddle sores. Much of the time the animals had only the pods and branches of mesquite shrubs to eat. For hundreds of miles the men walked on foot to spare the mules. Man and beast alike were slashed by serrated yucca leaves and punctured by the needles of prickly pear and barrel cactus.

Increasingly, Kearny spotted the now thoroughly decomposed carcasses of mules that Carson had abandoned on his way east. Eventually Kearny's own magnificent bay, the beloved horse that had been with him ever since Fort Leavenworth, expired. And so even the general, prim equestrian though he was, had to suffer the indignity of mounting a mule.

This terrain was just as Carson had warned Kearny it would be. Back on the Rio Grande, Carson had said that every party that had ever ventured into the Gila had emerged from its stark canyons in an advanced state of starvation. He had advised Kearny that the going would be so rough, there was no point in bringing wagons along; the trail was not passable for them—their axles would quickly snap. Reaching California with supply wagons, Carson estimated, would easily take four months, maybe longer.

The general had taken his scout's advice. He'd sent the wagons back to Santa Fe while summoning more mules. Now, as Kearny led his gaunt men through the rocky goosenecks of the Gila, he was grateful not to be pulling anything other than the two rolling howitzers. There was one particularly grueling stretch that Kearny's men came to call "the Devil's Turnpike," a succession of steep ascents and basalt precipices that alone claimed fifteen mules. Lieutenant Emory described the stygian pass with grim eloquence: "The metallic clinks of spurs, the rattling of the mule shoes, the high black peaks, the deep dark ravines, and the unearthly looking cacti which stuck out from the rocks like the ears of Mephistopheles—all favored the idea that we were now treading on the verge of the regions below. Occasionally a mule gave up the ghost and was left as a propitiatory tribute to the place."

The dragoons began to grumble at their hardships. Captain Turner complained in his journal: "How little do those who sit in their easy chairs in Washington know of the privations we are daily subjected to. Even our anxious friends at home can form no idea of the trials we undergo—wading streams, clambering over rocks, laboring through the valleys [where] the sand causes our animals to sink up to their knees. Then our frugal meals, hard bed, and perhaps wet blankets . . . I have no taste for this mode of life—it contains not a single charm for me. It is *labor, labor* from morning till night. I'm tired of this business. I wish it was over . . . This is a soldier's fare, but I am sick of it."

One of the delicate national issues quietly hovering in the background while the dragoons trudged westward was whether this country would one day be slaveholding should Washington ever fully annex it and grant it statehood. Surveying the desiccated landscapes of present-day Arizona, Lieutenant Emory put an end to such speculation: "No one who has ever visited this country would ever think of bringing his own slaves here with any view to profit. Their labor would never repay the cost of transportation." The only people who might live in this country, thought Henry Turner, were consumptives and other sickly souls attracted to its dry air and pure atmosphere. "Invalids may live here when they might die in any other part of the world," Turner wrote, "but really the country is so forbidding that no one would scarcely be willing to secure a long life at the cost of living in it."

Another issue that Emory's Topographical Corps was supposed to investigate was whether the Gila Trail could be a suitable route for a good wagon road—and ultimately, a transcontinental railway. But Emory blasted that notion as readily as he did the question of slavery: It was impossible, he said, to imagine putting a decent thoroughfare through this ragged rock wasteland. Clearly the crosscountry road, if it was ever to be built, would have to be routed somewhere farther to the south, possibly passing through the Mexican stronghold of Tucson.

Then, out of the black jaws of the Gila, Kearny's column emerged to behold a splendid oasis. They had entered the well-watered land of the peaceful Pimas, and a related tribe called the Maricopas. The Pimas were advanced farmers who had long ago mastered a complex system of dikes and irrigation canals that allowed them to grow abundant corn, beans, squash, tobacco, and cotton, among other crops. Lieutenant Emory's engineering mind was impressed by the "beauty, order, and disposition" of the canals, and was, like most of Kearny's men, thoroughly taken with the whole tribe. They were "frank, confident, peaceful, and industrious," Emory thought, and "in possession of a beautiful and fertile basin." Kearny's men, famished as they were, approached the Pimas and offered money and barter for food, but the Indians refused any sort of payment. "Bread is to eat, not to sell, take what you want," they insisted in Spanish—and promptly invited Kearny's men to a feast.

After they'd had their fill, the dragoons and the Pimas smoked and laughed and traded far into the night. Though they could communicate only through grunts and sign language, the Americans were delighted with their gracious hosts. Henry Turner found the Pimas "a good harmless people and more industrious than I have ever found Indians." They have "kind, amiable expressions," Turner thought. "Never did I look upon a more benevolent face than that of the old chief."

Emory concurred. "It was a rare sight," he wrote in praise of the Pimas, "to be thrown in the midst of a large nation of what is often termed 'wild Indians,' who surpass many of the Christian nations in agriculture, are little behind them in the useful arts, and are immeasurably before them in honesty and virtue."

The Pimas were especially captivated by Lieutenant Emory and his array of surveying tools—his telescopes, sextants, and barometers, his crimped metal tubes and glass bulbs of mercury. In the evening Emory was eager to observe what he called "two occultations of Jupiter's satellites," but as he lamented in his journal, "News got about of my dealings with the stars, and so my camp was crowded the whole time." The Pimas found the lieutenant's spectacles positively frightening. They'd never seen eyeglasses, and seemed to believe that a person wearing them could see right through the Pimas' cotton clothing, as though the lenses imparted X-ray vision. They turned away, embarrassed to be naked in this stranger's presence. "It was a source of much merriment," Emory said. "They would shrink and hide behind each other at my approach. At length, I placed the spectacles on the nose of an old woman, who became acquainted with their use, and explained it to the others."

◫

Entertained, well fed, and restored to a semblance of health, the dragoons reluctantly left the fair land of the Pimas and continued west for California. On November 23 they reached the confluence of the Gila and the mighty Colorado. It was on that day that Lieutenant Emory made a disturbing discovery. He was out surveying the confluence with his staff, tinkering with his equipment as he always did, when he happened to encounter a lone Mexican riding on a horse.

"Where are you going?" he asked through an interpreter.

"I am hunting horses," the Mexican answered nervously.

As he passed by, Emory grew suspicious. The lieutenant noticed that the Mexican rider had packed many bottles of water and other supplies. He appeared to be embarked on a long journey.

"Why don't you follow me to camp?" Emory instructed him.

The Mexican demurred. "I will come in a moment," he protested. "First there is something I must do." And as he said this, he tried to slip away.

Emory's suspicions only intensified. As he later put it, the Mexican's "anxiety increased my determination not to comply with his request." So Emory and his staff effectively arrested the man and led him into Kearny's camp. There Kearny had him searched and found on his person a satchel full of mail, all of it in Spanish.

Interpreters were summoned and immediately set about translating the letters. The rider, it was soon ascertained, was an official courier carrying dispatches from California to Gen. Jose Castro, stationed in Sonora. The deeper the translators dug into these letters, the more troubling was their import. It seemed that there had been a counterrevolution in California. "They all spoke exultingly of having thrown off the 'detestable Anglo-Yankee yoke,' " Emory wrote, "and they congratulated themselves that the tri-color once more floated in California." Further questioning of the courier proved fruitless, for he played his part "so dexterously," according to Emory, that "it was not in our power to extract the truth."

The letters were several weeks old, and likely swollen with braggadocio, but the uniformity of the reports made it clear that the Americans had indeed been kicked out of coastal California. Kearny now understood the full peril of his predicament. He had only a hundred men, and his mounts were in deplorable condition. He cursed his earlier decision to send back two-thirds of his dragoons to Santa Fe. His tiny force was hardly in any shape to fight, but at this point his only recourse was to press on as fast as he could and confront the enemy. It was either fight there, or wither here in the desert.

Carson's reaction to the reversal in California was conflicted. He must have been shocked and surprised to learn that the dispatches he'd been carrying were so full of error. At the same time, he was concerned for his American friends in California, especially Fremont, and wondered how they were faring. California was back on a war footing, and history would be happening there again; at the very least, it would not be dull. Carson knew Southern California, he spoke Spanish, he was already well acquainted with Stockton and the principal players. Now he understood that his services were truly needed. At last he was fully engaged in Kearny's effort and happy to be returning to California.

On November 25, Kearny's force forded the Colorado River. The men plodded westward, now lit with the excitement, mixed with a certain dread, that they were almost certain to meet the enemy in battle. Ever since they had left Fort Leavenworth, the dragoons had wanted a fight and had feared, as one Western writer put it, that "their sabres would be rusted in their scabbards and their muskets foul with idleness." Now it appeared they would get their wish. But they still had several hundred miles of wasteland to cross; the desert country would not let up—if anything it grew even harsher than the Gila wilderness. "Oh this sterile country," Captain Turner wrote, "when shall I say goodbye to you? No earthly power can ever induce me to return." The men had heard so much of California's verdant beauty, but they were beginning to believe it was all the stuff of legend. "We are still to look for the glowing pictures drawn of California," Emory wrote. "As yet, barrenness and desolation hold their reign." The men crossed the sand drifts of the Imperial Valley and passed by the southern reaches of the Sierra Nevada range, whose distant peaks shimmered with fresh snow. The men froze at night. They ate their last rations. Wolves appeared at their flanks. The mules kept on dropping.

By now the dragoons looked like wretches. One officer, a Captain Johnston, inspected his men in camp and despaired at what he saw. "They are a sorry-looking set," he wrote in his journal. "They are well-nigh naked—some of them barefoot." Yet Johnston predicted they would rise to the occasion in battle: "They will be ready for their hour when it comes."

In the dusty chaparral country some fifty miles from San Diego, Kearny encountered an Englishman named Edward Stokes, who had lived and ranched in California for years. Though he was a neutral, Stokes agreed to take a message to Robert Stockton in San Diego. Kearny wrote an urgent letter to the commodore announcing his army's arrival in California. "I come by orders from the President of the United States," Kearny wrote. "We left Santa Fe on the 25th September, having taken possession of New Mexico, and annexed it to the United States." Kearny's letter is notable for its stoic understatement—he never mentions the fact that his men are starving and his few remaining mules are in terrible condition. All he asks is for information: "If you can send a party to open communication with us on the route to this place, and to inform me of the state of affairs in California, I wish you would do so, and as quickly as possible. The fear of this letter falling into Mexican hands prevents me from writing more."

Stokes rushed the letter to San Diego.

☒

Three days later, on the morning of December 5, about twenty-five miles east of San Diego, Kearny's men were amazed to spot an American flag fluttering in the distance over a dust cloud kicked up by an approaching force of United States Marines. The Englishman Stokes had succeeded in getting through to Stockton with Kearny's message. This was the "communication party" Kearny had asked for. Thirty-nine Marines under the command of the intrepid Capt. Archibald Gillespie, he of the epic courier mission to meet Fremont in California, had slipped through the Mexican siege lines ringing San Diego and sped to Kearny's aid.

Of course, Kearny would have preferred to have more than thirty-nine, but he was in no position to complain. Besides, these Marines had a few relatively fresh mounts and a small brass four-pound howitzer—not to mention food. The dragoons and the Marines embraced one another, fellow countrymen united on the far side of the continent. Kearny's spirits lifted.

Captain Gillespie greeted the general and confirmed everything that had been gleaned from the intercepted mail back on the Colorado River: The Americans had indeed been expelled from nearly every coastal town in California except San Diego. Gillespie also informed Kearny that a force of a few hundred well-mounted Californians was camping nearby, at a little Indian village called San Pasqual. These Mexican fighters were led by Capt. Andres Pico, a high-ranking leader of the counterrevolution and brother of the former governor of California. Their camp stood between Kearny and Stockton, directly on the road to San Diego; if the general was going to drive to the Pacific and join forces with the commodore, he would surely have to fight Pico somewhere. Why not here, and now? Gillespie suggested that if Kearny thought it advisable, they should quickly mount a surprise attack against the Mexicans and "beat up their camp."

Kearny liked the sound of this bold adventure. Although taking such risks seemed contrary to his circumspect nature, he thought it far better to shock Captain Pico with an overwhelming predawn strike than to dally and let him learn the truth—that even with Gillespie's reinforcements, the American force was puny, weak, and appallingly mounted. Kearny understood the classic bluff of plains warfare: to disguise weakness in concentrated action, to descend on the enemy and convince him through decisive fury that you're more powerful than you really are. Emory described Kearny's thinking: "The general decided we must be the aggressive party, that he would attack [at] night, and beat them before it was light enough to discover our force."

Carson lent his support to the idea. Based on his previous experience in California, he did not think much of Mexicans as fighters. They were individually brave, he thought, but poorly organized and seldom well equipped. He suggested, "All you have to do is yell, make a rush, and the Californians will run away." Captain Gillespie was similarly disdainful of Mexican military prowess (even though Mexican insurrections had soundly expelled him and his fellow Marines from Los Angeles a month earlier). Gillespie once declared in a report: "Californians of Spanish blood have a holy horror of the American rifle."

It's possible that Kearny, having slogged nearly two thousand miles from Fort Leavenworth in one of the longest marches in American military history, was simply spoiling for a fight. Some historians have certainly leveled this charge at him. Stanley Vestal, for one, argued that Kearny was motivated by a thirst for the glory he imagined his peers were racking up in greater battles deeper in Mexico. "All the other generals had been shooting down Mexicans by the hundreds," Vestal wrote. "He had done nothing but march and read proclamations. Now he would show Fremont how to take California. 'Charge!' "

Kearny's rock-solid record on the plains, and everything that is known about the equanimity of his personality, would seem to discount such an assessment. If he was making an error of judgment, it was not likely for reasons of professional jealousy or personal glory. Besides, there were sound strategic aspects to the contemplated attack. Kearny's main objective here was to seize control of Pico's pastured horses while the Californians were asleep; if he could do that, he realized, the battle would be over before it even began. As the consummate cavalryman, Kearny was mortified by his gaunt animals. If he were to continue on to San Diego and then retake the rest of California, Kearny would have to replace his scrawny, bescabbed mules with strong horses. Here, he felt, was his golden chance.

Carson understood the purpose of the proposed raid perfectly and later described it with his usual directness: "Our object was to get the Californians' animals."

The dragoons and the Marines camped a few hundred yards from each other in a narrow valley only two miles from San Pasqual. It was a rainy night covered in a gelid fog. As most of the men shivered in their heavy wet blankets, Kearny decided to send a small detachment over to Pico's encampment and assess the situation under the cover of darkness. A reconnaissance party was hastily arranged, composed of six dragoons and a Mexican quisling named Rafael Machado who had deserted from the Californian forces.

Around ten o'clock this motley team of spies took off on mules into the mist. Soon they arrived at the outskirts of slumbering San Pasqual. The dragoons sent Machado forward on foot to coax an Indian to come out and provide details about Pico's force: How big was it? Where were the men sleeping? Where were their horses pastured? Machado crept into the village and, sure to the plan, found an Indian who was willing to talk to the Americans. ("The Indians were very inimical to the Californians," one of Kearny's men later wrote, "and always ready to betray them.") But the dragoons thought that Machado was taking too long to accomplish his task. They heard a dog barking, and in their worried impatience they raced toward the village to get a better look. When they did, the jangle of their swords against their saddles alarmed Pico's night watchmen.

The sentries cried out, and the dragoons, having found Machado, spurred away in the fog. But in the confusion of their flight, someone dropped a blue jacket that was stamped "U.S." A Mexican sentinel found the garment and brought it to Pico, who promptly called his men to horses. Soon all the Mexicans were aroused from their sleep. They dashed from the mud huts of the village and ran to their mounts, yelling, "Viva California! Abajo Los Americanos!"

The American reconnoiter had backfired; in a blundered instant, the element of surprise was lost.

Sometime after midnight the dragoons galloped into camp and informed Kearny of the debacle. The general wasted no time—he ordered an immediate attack. If the advantage of surprise had been forfeited, he still had the advantage of darkness; Pico had no idea of the size and strength of Kearny's pitiful army. By first light Pico's spies would be sniffing around, and they would quickly discover Kearny's vulnerability. The time to strike was now, he felt, before a bad situation worsened.

The American camp erupted in wild shouts. It was so cold and damp that the bugler could not get off a note of reveille. The wet blankets were crusty with frost, the men groggy and cold. But once they realized the situation, they sprang to life—as one understated diarist put it, "There was a good deal of excitement and desire for a brush with the enemy." Within fifteen minutes the dragoons were all on their mules and trotting toward San Pasqual. Soon they united with Gillespie and the Marines, and together the two parties marched to war. The bugler had sufficiently warmed his lips to blast a few notes of a battle song called "Charge as Foragers" (a "forage" was an antiquated term for a raid).

When they reached the brow of a hill overlooking the now-stirring hamlet of San Pasqual, Kearny stopped in the scrub and addressed his men. Their country expected much of them, he said. He wanted them to encircle the village and seize the horses. If they had to kill the enemy they should do it, but he wanted to capture as many Californians alive as possible—it was not to be a slaughter. The fight, he suggested, would probably be close-in. Their carbines would not be worth much in the misty darkness, so they should have their swords at the ready.

"Remember," Kearny said, "one point of the saber is far more effective than any number of thrusts."

And then, in the early hours of December 6, 1846, his one hundred dragoons turned their animals toward San Pasqual, which lay a mile off across the low brush country. Soon they were stretched in a long, jumbled column, two abreast. Carson started out near the vanguard with Kearny and Emory, the three men working their way down the steep hill in the filtered gray light of the predawn.

Chapter 26   OUR RED CHILDREN

On the cold, dazzlingly bright morning of November 21, Col. Alexander Doniphan met at Bear Springs with an assembly of fourteen Navajo headmen. Narbona showed up as he said he would, although he was not feeling well enough to speak and entered the encampment borne on a litter. A red rock mesa formed a natural wall, and a cool stream coursed through the gently sloped landscape of piñon and juniper. The site was perfectly familiar to Narbona, for Bear Springs had for centuries been a gathering place of the Diné.

Some five hundred Navajos and three hundred Americans now congregated in the surrounding hills to watch the proceedings.

Colonel Doniphan rose and spoke first. An enormous man with a stentorian voice and the bearing of a poised trial lawyer, he had won over many juries back in his hometown of Liberty, Missouri; this was another trial, of sorts, and he intended to win it.

"The United States," he began, "has taken military possession of New Mexico and her laws now extend over the whole territory. The New Mexicans will be protected against violence and invasion, and their rights will be amply preserved. But the United States is also anxious to enter into a treaty of peace and lasting friendship with you, her red children, the Navajos. The same protection will be given to you that has been guaranteed the New Mexicans. I come with ample powers to negotiate a permanent peace between you, the New Mexicans, and us. If you refuse to treat on terms honorable to both parties, I am instructed to prosecute a war against you. The United States makes no second treaty with the same people; she offers the olive branch, and if that is rejected, then she offers powder, bullet, and steel."

Then a young Navajo headman rose to speak. His Spanish name was Zarcillos Largos, an eloquent man whom John Hughes describes as "very bold and intellectual." Largos represented the younger members of the tribe who thought it dishonorable for the Navajos to relinquish their age-old fight with the New Mexicans. "Americans!" he exhorted. "We have waged war against the New Mexicans for years. We have plundered their villages and killed many of their people and made many prisoners. We had just cause for all this. *You* have lately commenced a war against the same people. You have great guns and many brave soldiers. You have therefore conquered them, the very thing we have been attempting to do for so many years. You now turn upon us for attempting to do what you have done yourselves. We cannot see why you have cause of quarrel with us for fighting the New Mexicans on the west, while you do the same thing on the east."

Colonel Doniphan rose again and tried to explain his country's position. It was clear to him that the Navajos did not understand the American idea of surrender. "It is the custom of the Americans," he said, "that when a people with whom we are at war gives up, we treat them as friends thenceforward. New Mexico has been attached to our government. Now, when you steal property from New Mexicans, you are stealing from us. When you kill them, you are killing our own people, for they have now become ours. This cannot be suffered any longer."

Largos did not like the sound of this, but eventually he relented. "If New Mexico really be in your possession," he said, "and it be the intention of your government to hold it, we will cease our depredations. We will refrain from future wars upon the New Mexican people. For we have no cause of quarrel with you, and do not desire any war with so powerful a nation. Let there be peace between us."

And so the fourteen headmen present were assembled—Narbona, Largos, and the others. Doniphan had prepared a handwritten treaty, five paragraphs long, that proclaimed "permanent peace, mutual trust, and friendship." The names of the fourteen Navajo leaders had been affixed to the bottom. Because none of the Navajos could read or write in any language, Doniphan devised another method for obtaining a signature: He had each man touch the index finger of his right hand to a pen that a soldier held, marking an X alongside each printed signature.

It is doubtful the Navajos had much of an idea what they had signed. Yet it seemed a hopeful time nonetheless, a moment of optimism. The Americans and the Navajos had concluded their first treaty, and nothing terrible had happened. They said they were friends—and seemed to believe it.

Confident that they had more or less solved the Navajo conflict, Colonel Doniphan and his eager Missourians prepared to head south, for Mexico. They were briskly moving on to their next assignment: to invade Chihuahua and take its capital city. Like nearly everything the Missourians had done since leaving Fort Leavenworth, there was a naïve quality to their busy actions in the Navajo country, and at the same time a kind of impudence. They would effortlessly conquer vast lands and fix ancient problems in short order. And, they thought, everyone would love them for it.

Narbona and the other Diné, meanwhile, would go home to sit out the winter season. They would tell their ancient myths and hold their councils and sweat in their lodges. Their world still seemed rich and familiar, and they had plenty to eat.

A treaty had been signed. But so far as the Navajos could tell, not a single thing had changed. Certainly the younger men of the tribe saw it that way. On November 26, less than a week after the treaty had been inked, a band of Navajos killed a New Mexican shepherd not far from Socorro, then ran off with seventeen U.S. government mules and more than eight hundred sheep that had been purchased for American troop consumption. Two poorly armed Missourians, privates Robert Spears and James Stewart, rashly took off after the raiders. Six miles to the west their bodies were found, bristling with twenty-two arrows, their heads hideously smashed in by rocks.

Spears and Stewart were the first American soldiers to be killed by Navajo Indians.

Chapter 27 COLD STEEL

The battle of San Pasqual—generally considered the most significant clash of the Mexican War that took place on what is now U.S. soil—began with an American blunder. About three-quarters of a mile away from the village, Kearny yelled out the command "Trot!" By this time the dragoons were spread out over a long distance, with the officers on fleeter, healthier animals taking the lead. Up in front, Capt. Abraham Johnston of the dragoons misheard Kearny's order as "Charge!" And so Johnston repeated the wrong command, booming it over the valley for his comrades to hear and spurring his horse to a full gallop. All the men around him responded in kind and quickly vanished in the mist.

Kearny instantly saw the peril in this development. "Heavens, I did not mean that!" he cried, but it was too late to correct. The leading third of the command, mostly young officers on the last few good horses, was now charging full-tilt, while the other two-thirds were merely limping along on decrepit mules—with the gap between the two groups growing dangerously large. Kearny lost his place in the vanguard and struggled to keep up, but Carson, because he was riding a horse in relatively good health, was able to push ahead and ride near Johnston at the head of the charge. The army's two howitzers and the Marines' four-pound gun, towed behind mules, were too far in the rear to be of any immediate use.

Capt. Andres Pico and his Californians, all now mounted on their fine horses, had huddled in a ravine beside the town. Wrapped in their serapes, they were quietly conferring amongst themselves when Captain Johnston, Carson, and the other frontrunners suddenly descended on them. Pico's men hastily formed a line and fired their weapons at point-blank range. A musket ball tore into

Johnston's forehead. Killed instantly, the captain tumbled off his horse.

Carson was charging right behind when his horse lost its footing and threw him to the ground. Although he was not seriously injured, Carson's rifle was broken clean in half. Somehow he was able to pick himself up and scurry crabwise from the path of the oncoming animals. "I came very near being trodden to death," he later said, "and finally saved myself by crawling from under them."

The dragoons kept on coming. As they galloped into range of the Mexicans, they snapped off their carbines, but most of the weapons were so damp and corroded, the ammunition so soggy, that their shots had no effect. As Kearny had predicted, they would have to fight "close-in"; they unsheathed their swords and brandished them menacingly as they drove toward the enemy.

In the face of this furious charge, the Californians scuttled their line and executed what at first looked like a retreat. They turned and took off toward the west, following the meandering course of a shallow stream. With Captain Johnston dead, Capt. Ben Moore took charge and ordered the dragoons to follow Pico's fleeing horsemen, and for some distance gave chase. The pursuit was ill advised, however, for it thinned the dragoons out even more, leaving just a few of the men with the strongest animals far out in the lead, left to fight on their own, hopelessly separated from their comrades. (General Kearny and Lieutenant Emory were lagging even farther behind.)

When Pico's *caballeros* got a glimpse of this vulnerable vanguard and saw how diffuse their formations were and how miserable their mounts looked, they made an immediate halt. Smelling weakness, their confidence swelled. With the dexterity of lifelong equestrians, the Californians wheeled their horses and galloped straight at Moore. This time, however, they rode with lances—hefty spears nine feet long and set with sharp metal points.

What is this? the dragoons wondered. It looked like some medieval exercise, with anachronistic weaponry from the days of Cervantes. At first the well-trained cavalrymen scoffed at these oncoming jousters.

But in seconds the Californians expertly surrounded Moore and several of his comrades—"much as they might encircle a herd of cattle," as one historian put it. Recognizing that he was dangerously exposed, Captain Moore charged at Captain Pico himself, ineffectually popping off his pistol and then reaching for his saber. Pico, an excellent swordsman, managed to fend off the attack and slash Moore with his blade. As this was happening, a pair of lancers rushed to the aid of their leader; they made separate charges at Moore and ran him through with their long spears. The captain was knocked from his horse, still alive, blood gouting from numerous gashes and punctures. Moore still clutched his sword in his hand, but in the fall it had broken close to the hilt. He had nothing left to fight with. As Moore lay helpless on the ground near a willow tree, another Californian hurried over with a pistol and finished him off.

Other dragoons arrived and joined the fight. Realizing that their sodden guns were useless, they instead wielded them like clubs, but they found these brutish instruments were no match for the supple Mexican horsemen and their supposedly antiquated fighting technology. The Californians were wickedly precise with their lances, and they deftly stabbed and slashed the dragoons while the absurdly long reach of their weapons kept them unscathed. The sharp staves left deep "slots" in the flesh, as the American doctor later described the wounds. Nearly every dragoon received multiple punctures.

Pico's men were similarly adroit with *reatas*—leather lassos—which they used to yank an unsuspecting dragoon from his saddle while a comrade surged forward to lance the dismounted American as he lay entangled in the twined leather thongs. Wielding the *reata* was said to be a uniquely Californian skill. Throughout Mexico there was an old expression: "A Californian can throw the lasso as well with his foot as any other Mexican can with his hand." A Western historian would write that, to Californians, "the saddle was home, the horse a second self, and the lance and *reata* their manly exercise." On this gray morning, the Americans were discovering the mean truth of such aphorisms.

One of the dragoons who entered the fray was Lt. Tom Hammond, who happened to be the brother-in-law of the fallen Captain

Moore. Wondering what had happened to the other dragoons, he screamed, "For God's sake, men, come up!" He spotted Moore's prone body and darted over to it. Just then a lancer came at him from an unseen angle and thrust a spear into the lieutenant's side. Hammond tumbled off his mount and lay gravely wounded next to his brother-in-law. He would join Moore in death within a few hours.

By this point Kit Carson had managed to sprint ahead from the place where he'd tumbled off his horse. He took a carbine and ammunition from a dead dragoon—probably Johnston—and then he caught a loose horse and took off in the direction of the fight. When he came to the bend in the valley where the dragoons were clashing in full fury and confusion, he instantly assessed the situation and realized it was pointless to try to fight the Californians from the saddle—they were tearing the dragoons to shreds. Every American who'd joined the fight was either dead or seriously wounded. Their swords were no match for the long lances, and their mules and tired horses could not keep pace with the agile Mexican mounts.

And so, perceiving the futility of close-in fighting, Carson did something quite characteristic of him. Quietly, calmly, he dismounted at the edge of the fray and camouflaged himself behind some boulders. From this hiding place, he checked his rifle and cartridges and found that they were not too wet. Then he took careful aim and, one by one, began picking off the Californians as they rode within his range. It was vintage Carson—to sidestep the tumult and romance of a conventional clash and find the cleanest path to efficient fighting.

Now General Kearny and Lieutenant Emory arrived on the scene astride their huffing mules. Kearny immediately joined the action. He was amazed by the skill of the Californian horsemen. "They are the very best riders in the world," he later said. "There is hardly one not fit for the circus." Kearny fought his way through the confusion, parrying with the lancers, yelling commands, displaying admirable swordsmanship. One of the Marines who watched him fight said, "The old general defended himself valiantly, and was as calm as a clock."

But a lancer found him. Kearny was fencing with one of the Californians when another gored him from behind, driving a spear deep into the flesh of his lower back and into his buttock. Another lance slashed through his arm. The general was thrown from his mule and surely would have been killed on the spot had Lieutenant Emory not turned and glimpsed what was happening. Emory dashed over and beat back the attacker with his sword. The general lay seriously wounded on the cold, wet ground, copiously bleeding from multiple punctures.

Capt. Archibald Gillespie was next in line to face the lancers. "Rally, men! For God's sake, rally!" the Marine screamed, and as he did so a lancer slashed the back of his neck and knocked him off his horse. Then came another spear, ripping open his upper lip and bashing out a tooth. And finally a third, stabbing the captain in the sternum and puncturing a lung.

Somehow Gillespie got up and, with shallow, raspy breath, fought his way over to the place where Kearny had fallen—and where the dragoons in larger numbers were now finally flooding in and organizing themselves. They unlimbered a howitzer and succeeded in firing a round or two that set off what appeared to be wholesale retreat of the enemy. Before they fell back, however, a small group of Californians captured the second army fieldpiece. They snagged the howitzer with their *reatas* and hauled it from the battlefield.

The Californians had not actually retreated. They were massing on the surrounding hills, digesting their delicious victory, contemplating how and when to attack next. Captain Pico was enormously pleased with his men. He would later report to his authorities that the Battle of San Pasqual was a fight that had been decided *a pura arma blanca*—entirely by cold steel. The Americans could take comfort only in a slender technicality: They still held the field of battle, which in some West Point textbooks was the definition of a victory.

In the momentary lull, Dr. Griffin, the dragoon surgeon, rushed over to Kearny's side and tried to staunch the bleeding. Kearny told Dr. Griffin, "First, go and dress the wounds of the soldiers who require more attention. When you have done that, come to me."

The general rose up on an elbow and looked around the battlefield. The sun was coming up and the fog had dissipated. He could see bodies strewn in all directions. In fifteen minutes of fighting, twenty-one Americans had died, and many more lay critically wounded. The valley was splattered with gore. Everywhere men moaned in agony. Kearny looked pale, and the hemorrhaging would not stop. As Dr. Griffin attended to other patients, the general fainted.

᠄

For the rest of the day—December 6, 1846—Kearny's forces hardly budged. They concentrated themselves as best they could in a defensive posture, with artillery pieces unlimbered and at the ready. Their situation was looking more and more like a siege. The Americans could see Pico's horsemen pacing in the hills just beyond range, plainly contemplating another attack.

In this tense environment, Dr. Griffin dressed wounds and did his best to comfort the dying. Working with what Emory called "great skill and assiduity," Dr. Griffin was able to revive Kearny, but the general had lost a dangerous amount of blood—so much, in fact, that the doctor feared he would die. Unable to make decisions, Kearny temporarily surrendered command to Capt. Henry Turner.

The immediate task at hand was disposing of the dead. Turner feared that if the dragoons buried the corpses now in plain view of the enemy, the Californians or the local Indians might return later and desecrate the graves. So the captain decided to wait until dark and then secretly bury the dead en masse. At dawn the living would have to break out of their present predicament and bludgeon their way toward San Diego. They had no other choice.

And so the hours ticked away, and the dragoons, bleeding and starving, stayed exposed in the open chaparral country. They readied themselves for battle—drying out their ammunition, cleaning their weapons, sharpening their swords—but the Californians did not mount another sortie.

Finally dusk arrived. Under the stars, the solemn dragoons quietly dug a pit beneath a large willow tree and buried the dead. There were some twenty bodies in all and, according to one account, several corpses of the enemy. Emory noted the "howling of myriads of wolves, attracted by the smell." It was an especially somber occasion, Emory said, because after so many miles of marching, these men had become unusually close. Theirs was a "community of hardships," and it was only fitting that this "band of brave men" should be "put to rest, together and forever." The dragoons led their horses over the site to tamp down the soil, and the men scattered large rocks.

By the next morning Kearny had gained enough strength to resume command from Captain Turner. He looked sallow and gaunt, but somehow Dr. Griffin had patched him up and propped him on a horse. The general cursed through the pain—the big rent in his rump was embarrassing and smarted terribly—but he was determined to move on. As Carson later put it, "Kearny concluded to march on, let the consequences be what they would."

It was decided that other patients who were in worse condition would have to be moved by litters. With the help of the mountain men, the dragoons improvised some sledges—buffalo hides tautly slung between two long willow staves and strapped to the back of the saddles.

Kearny gave the signal and the men began the march in a large procession, with the fieldpieces up front, and riflemen on healthier horses ringing the rear and the flanks. The pack animals moved forward in the safety of the middle—as did the wounded, who bounced uncomfortably on their crude ambulances, with the long travois poles dragging in the dirt. For these unfortunates the ride was agonizing—the sharp jerks and vibrations pulled at their bandages and tore open their wounds. "The ambulances grated on the ground," Emory wrote, "and the sufferings of the wounded were very distressing."

As they inched slowly forward through the dusty scrub, they realized the Californians were following them, watching and hovering in the surrounding hills, waiting for the perfect moment to strike. Sure enough, after a few miles of this slow, cautious advance, the Americans were fired upon. A group of Californians had concealed themselves behind boulders on a nearby hill. Immediately Kearny ordered a charge. A party of dragoons led by Lieutenant Emory succeeded in dislodging the enemy and occupying this higher ground. In the skirmish, five Californians were killed or wounded, but as Emory later described the ac-

tion: "Strange to say, not one of our men fell. . . . The capture of the
hill was but the work of a moment, and when we reached the crest, the
Californians had mounted their horses and were in full flight."

From the top of this cactus-studded eminence—Carson called it
nothing more than a "hill of rocks"—Kearny assessed the situation
and recognized that his men were simply too weak to advance any farther. Dr. Griffin warned that many of the wounded were dangerously
frail and should under no circumstances move another step; he needed
time to re-dress their wounds. San Diego lay only thirty miles off, but
that was just too far for this straggle of invalids. Emory said it was "impossible to move in the open with so many encumbrances, against an
enemy more than twice our number, and all superbly mounted."

So the general decided to make camp on this lonely swell of
blond-colored stones, from which he could at least keep an eye on the
enemy and defend his beleaguered column. The Americans dug
themselves in and prepared for a siege. Along the summit, the able-
bodied men hastily built up fortifications of boulders chinked with
smaller rocks (more than 150 years later, these crude breastworks are
still in place). At dusk the men picked the meatiest of their stringy
mules and slaughtered them for a thin gravy dinner. From that day
on, this forlorn spot would be known as Mule Hill.

Kearny realized his predicament had become truly desperate. If
he could not break through to San Diego, his men would starve. Or
else they would die in a succession of battles they were not prepared
to fight. The Californians were massing in all directions, their numbers growing as Captain Pico rallied fresh recruits to fight the despised Americans, who now seemed such easy prey. Henry Turner
wrote that the Californian forces were now "quadruple our strength"
and firmly believed that Pico would "charge upon us the moment we
descended into the plain." In their present condition, Turner feared
that Pico would not leave "one of us to tell the tale."

Somehow Kearny would have to get word to Stockton about the crippling battle at San Pasqual and request reinforcements. Kearny knew

that Stockton was a ponderous champion of the U.S. Navy and its infallible power, and had nothing good to say about the army. But he was a patriot. If Stockton had any idea how dire the dragoons' situation was, he would surely send more men. The general would make an urgent plea and, he hoped, all petty interservice rivalries would melt away; the navy would promptly come to the army's rescue.

The problem was how to deliver the message: Kearny's camp was now encircled by three cordons of sentries. To make matters worse, the way to San Diego would be similarly policed by Mexican pickets on horseback. According to Emory, "The enemy now occupied all the passes to that town." Though well armed, Commodore Stockton's men were themselves more or less under siege, their backs against the harbor. It would be "an expedition of some peril," Emory fretted, but someone would have to try to sneak through these multiple layers of enemy lines and get to Stockton.

Perhaps inevitably, that person was Carson. Throughout his career, this was precisely the sort of assignment on which he had thrived—focused, small-scale, it was an undertaking with huge stakes and no room for error, a rescue mission that was also a courier mission (for some reason he especially loved to carry information). And so it was no surprise that Carson offered his services immediately. After some initial reluctance, Kearny gave his assent. Carson would leave that night—December 8—accompanied by a twenty-four-year-old naval lieutenant named Edward Beale and a young Diegueno Indian guide known to us only as Chemuctah.

Andres Pico, who was apparently acquainted with Carson's earlier exploits in California and knew he was among Kearny's forces, correctly predicted that the famous guide would try to break free. He admonished his men to stay vigilant. *"Se escapara el lobo,"* he told them: The wolf will escape.

When it was good and dark, Carson and the two other volunteers crouched among the rocks and started sliding down Mule Hill. The slopes were composed of loose scree, and they decided their boots were making too much noise on the gravelly descent. Chemuctah was wearing soft moccasins, but Carson and Beale removed their boots and tucked them under their belts. Carson also worried that their canteens were sloshing and clinking too loudly, so they left them behind.

Now barefoot, Carson and Beale cradled their weapons as quietly as they could and slithered through the brush until they came to the first line of sentinels. They crept right under the noses of the Californians, so close that the enemy horses must have smelled them. Carson could trace the outline of the Mexican lances, held upright to the starry skies. Several times they felt sure they had been spotted. One sentry rode right over to where the Americans were lying prone among the rocks. For what seemed like an eternity the soldier sat on his horse, producing a flint, then lighting and luxuriously smoking a cigaretto. He seemed to be drawing out the act as though he were teasing them; Beale felt sure the sentry knew they were lying there at his horse's feet. The young naval lieutenant was so scared that Carson later swore he "could distinctly hear Beale's heart pulsate."

Finally Beale could endure the suspense no longer. He nudged Carson's thigh and whispered in his ear, "We're gone—let's jump up and fight it out!"

Carson tried to reassure him. "Been in worse places before," he whispered back, and eventually the Californian finished his smoke and ambled away into the darkness.

They heaved a sigh of relief, but then Beale and Carson realized with dismay that during their scrambling descent of Mule Hill, they had lost their boots. Carson knew they couldn't risk going back for them—and besides, the odds of finding the boots in the dark were remote. So the two men skulked on through the night, collecting cactus barbs and needles in their bloody bare feet. Chemuctah, shod in his thin moccasins, fared only a little better.

They stuck to canyons and arroyos, creeping along the low washes, keeping out of sight. By dawn they were clear of Pico's forces: The wolf *had* escaped. By afternoon they had drawn within twelve miles of San Diego and spotted more sentries. All the byways to the town were indeed blocked. Carson decided they should each take a different route in the hope that at least one of them would get through. Carson took the longest path, a roundabout of some twenty miles. (Biographer Edwin Sabin says Carson picked this "more devious course" to "assure success.") Carson, Beale, and Chemuctah bid their farewells and vectored off in separate directions.

Twelve hours later, at around three in the morning, Kit Carson stumbled into Stockton's camp on the Pacific Ocean. His feet were swollen and stiff and so badly lacerated that he wouldn't be able to walk for a week. He had not eaten or drunk water in nearly thirty hours.

To his surprise and relief, Beale and Chemuctah, taking their shorter routes, had made it into camp a few hours earlier. Stockton had already dispatched a rescue force of nearly two hundred well-armed men to relieve Kearny. Beale was so "deranged with fatigue," Carson was told, that he had to be carried into headquarters. After meeting with Stockton, Beale was brought on board the USS *Congress* and led straightaway to the infirmary.

The naval lieutenant would languish there in the sick bay for a month, and it would take him more than a year to fully recover. Historian Stanley Vestal described Beale as "utterly used up" and "out of his head for minutes at a time. To him, the whole world seemed paved with prickly pear." After seeing him, Carson said of Beale: "I did not think he could live." Chemuctah was similarly spent from his journey and, according to some accounts, died soon thereafter.

Carson's barefooted adventure would soon win him further nationwide fame and fulsome commendations in the halls of Washington. Historian Bernard DeVoto ranked Carson's "midnight crawl" to San Diego "high among the exploits of the master mountain man." There was something uncanny about Carson, in the way he popped up from the shadows and impressed his name on the scenes of history. Perhaps it wasn't merely Fremontian exaggeration—he did have a curious knack for making himself present at the critical instant. Whenever an expedition was in trouble—*real* trouble—he was there to bail it out.

After Carson's arrival in San Diego, Kearny's men practically mythologized him. A young sergeant wrote his parents in Hartford,

Connecticut: "Never has there been a man like Kit Carson. All that has been said about him, and more, is true. He is as fearless as the lion, as stealthy as the panther, as strong as the oxen. I believe that Carson would attack a fort filled with Mexicans single-handed and drive them off."

Carson himself seemed unimpressed. In his memoirs he devoted only a few lines to the whole adventure at San Pasqual. "Finally got through," he said, "but had the misfortune to have lost our shoes. Had to travel over a country covered with prickly pear and rocks, barefoot. Got to San Diego the next night."

⊠

While Carson was making his trek to San Diego, Kearny and his men suffered two more miserable days and nights waiting on Mule Hill. Their only fuel for campfires was wild sage, and they managed to find water only by boring deep into the sand and collecting a brown slurry that tasted bitter but possessed the salient quality of wetness. Mules kept turning into dinner.

For the other animals in the fast-dwindling herd, Kearny had to play nourishment against theft: If the mules weren't taken off the hill and turned out to find fresh grass, they would surely starve, but once they were out grazing, the Californians, working on swift mounts, would descend and steal them. The enemy was constantly on the periphery, hectoring, driving wild horses up the hill to try to create a stampede. Pico hoped to fray the gringo general's nerves, to starve him and grind him down; the plan seemed to be working.

Despite the meager food, many of the dragoons were slowly gathering strength and healing from their battle wounds. Dr. Griffin reported to Kearny that nearly all the sick were able to sit a horse—they could dispense with the rickety travois ambulances. Other patients, however, had developed gangrene or horrible infections in the deep punctures left by the lances.

One member of the party, a French trapper named Robideaux who had lost a great amount of blood, was hovering near death. The men had more or less written off the poor fellow, who in his death agonies kept hallucinating that he smelled coffee—a luxury no one traveling with Kearny had seen or tasted in months. "Don't you smell it?" Robideaux beseeched them. "A cup of coffee would save my life!"

Everyone knew that the mountain men were all inveterate coffee addicts—especially the French—so Lieutenant Emory believed that the doomed man was simply exercising a final Gallic nostalgia before passing on to his reward. "I supposed a dream had carried him back to the cafes of St. Louis and New Orleans," Emory said.

But he was soon shocked to find that Robideaux was right—somewhere in the camp a cook was indeed heating up a cup of coffee over a sagebrush fire. Emory went over and persuaded him to give it up to the dying Frenchman. Says Emory: "One of the most agreeable little offices performed in my life, and I believe in the cook's, was to pour this precious draught into the waning body of our friend Robideaux. His warmth returned, and with it hopes of life." Robideaux soon recovered and swore for the rest of his days that he owed his life to coffee.

On the night of December 10, Kearny decided that he had no other choice but to break out early the next morning and try again to push toward San Diego. He had given up on Carson and Beale. Probably they had not made it through to Stockton, Kearny guessed, and thus no reinforcements would be forthcoming. Kearny told his men to prepare for a last desperate march at first light. He ordered them to burn or otherwise destroy all belongings that were not absolutely necessary. This was for two reasons—to lighten the burden for swifter travel, and to deny the enemy any chance at booty. That night the hills danced in the glow of a crackling bonfire as the men consigned their effects to the flames.

A few hours past midnight, the sentinels heard something awful—the deafening shudder of an approaching army's footsteps. "Who goes there?" the guards cried anxiously into the darkness. Out of the shadows emerged a formidable sight: a force of nearly two hundred men marching in close formation up Mule Hill. Some of Kearny's men groggily rose from their sleeping places, thinking they heard the sound of English coming from the valley floor.

"Who goes there?" the sentries demanded again.

"Hold fire!" boomed the reply from below. "We're Americans!"

The camp erupted in cheers. Word had gotten through after all—Stockton had sent reinforcements! One hundred twenty sailors and eighty Marines tramped into the bivouac site bearing tobacco and hardtack—"gallant fellows," Emory thought, "distributing provisions and clothes to our naked and hungry people." As the men whooped and celebrated, a Mexican musket ball sailed through camp but did no damage. It was, thought Kearny biographer Dwight Clarke, "the last mournful shot of disappointment from an enemy robbed of its prey."

In the morning, Kearny found that the enemy had completely vanished. Pico was surprised by the Americans' sudden arrival and intimidated by this newly conjoined force of soldiers, sailors, and Marines—which, all told, numbered more than three hundred men. The siege had been broken.

The newly fortified American forces all left for San Diego the next day and marched unmolested. They arrived in a cold, spitting rain on the afternoon of December 12. Kearny's war was nearly over, though he did not know it yet. Several minor skirmishes would have to be fought before Los Angeles would return at last to American hands, but he would face nothing like his trials at San Pasqual. The reconquest of California was all but complete.

The Army of the West had come as far as it could go, as far as the cardinal direction in its name would take it. Two thousand miles, from Fort Leavenworth, Kansas, to the bitter end of the continent—there had never been a march like it in American history.

The men came to a shaggy bluff and walked to the precipice. And there, for quite some time, they stood gaping at the kelp-strewn shores of an unfamiliar sea. Emory wrote, "The Pacific opened for the first time to our view, the sight producing strange but agreeable emotions. One of the men who had never seen the ocean before opened his arms and exclaimed: 'Lord! There is a great prairie without a tree.'"

General Kearny must have stared at the Pacific with mixed emotions. He wrote his wife Mary: "Take good care of yourself and kiss all my dear little ones for me. We have the ocean in sight and hear the rolling waves which sound like rumbling thunder."

Chapter 28   EL CREPUSCULO

A month after General Kearny reached the California coast, Gov. Charles Bent of New Mexico made his way north on the icy, rutted road to Taos. Under leaden skies, his mules strained up the steep hills on the outskirts of Santa Fe and plunged into arroyos blanketed with snowdrifts. The animals snorted in the crisp desert cold, their nostrils shooting twin plumes of steam. The day was bleak and gusty, and as the governor crept through the small towns north of the capital—Santa Cruz de la Cañada, Chimayo, Trampas—the locals glowered at him. Off to his right, five thousand feet higher up in the winter mists, he and his small entourage could see the sharp triad of the Truchas Peaks, whose snaggled ridges bared themselves like a dog's angry snarl.

Charles Bent was a shrewd, determined man with a round face and a merchant's eye for details. Short and squat and tough, he was forty-seven years old, and his receding hair had gone prematurely gray. Bent always had business to attend to in Taos, but mainly the governor was embarked on a personal errand: He wanted to see his wife, Ignacia, and their three young children. The governor still had his giant mud fort pitched on the edge of the plains, but he rarely went there. Like his friend and brother-in-law Kit Carson, his main home was in the mountain town of Taos, seventy miles north of the capital. Since her husband had become governor, Ignacia rarely ventured down to Santa Fe—she had a busy household to run, a rambling adobe off the Taos plaza, just a stone's throw away from Carson's place. Ignacia always kept her *sala* filled with relatives and the smells of savory Mexican food. Now, in the dead of winter, the governor wanted to be home.

Traveling with Governor Bent were several Taos officials—Sheriff Steve Lee, Circuit Attorney James White Leal, and Ignacia's uncle Cornelio Vigil, who was the Taos prefect. They had been in Santa Fe on official business and decided to ride north with the governor. Also in the party were Ignacia's young brother Pablo Jaramillo, and another teenager named Narciso Beaubien, the bright-eyed son of a U.S. judge who'd just returned from boarding school in St. Louis. The two boys were close friends.

It was January 14, 1847. The United States had occupied Santa Fe for more than four months. Still, Governor Bent knew that the American hold on the territory was extremely tenuous. The weak military garrison back at Fort Marcy was young and inexperienced, the Missouri troops so thoroughly bored they could not be called vigilant. With Kearny and Doniphan gone, the American command was led by an impressively mutton-chopped lawyer-politician, Col. Sterling Price, a stern Missourian who, though by no means incompetent, mistakenly believed that he had a firm handle on things. In truth, the territory was seething with hatred toward the Americans. Bent could feel the spite thickening in the air, could see it in the false grins and narrowed stares of the locals. The Mexicans had failed to fight at first, but they despised these foreigners just as surely as any occupied people must despise their oppressor. Their true feelings, harbored in secret, were now bursting to the surface.

Their defiance was fueled by racial mistrust, religious zeal, and the desire to defend a country they still loved—even if their country, governed corruptly and indifferently from faraway Mexico City, had never particularly loved them. Up and down the Rio Grande the padres had fed the fires of resistance. These gringos sought to outlaw the Catholic religion, the priests warned. They would ban the Spanish tongue, scrap the fiestas and feast days, and jettison all the old ways of doing things. The priests were not above spreading wild untruths, but they had genuine reasons to feel threatened. With the Kearny Code, the Americans had already instituted radical concepts, such as the separation of church and state, and jury trials in which the padres would play no role whatsoever. What was to stop them from going even further? These Americans had godless ideas that sprang from the cold marble halls of a secular republic. The priests now understood that Washington was determined to reform the marooned Catholic world they had run for so long—and this reformation could only mean the steady erosion of their power.

What's more, the Americans were arrogant. They called the Mexican men "greasers," sometimes to their faces, while at the same time they freely consorted with Hispanic women. The Americans brought venereal diseases. They caroused and fought, they mangled the Spanish language, they gorged themselves like hogs. They seemed to have no concept of family or of obligation toward their homes—they just skipped about like flies, rootless, always looking to advance themselves. Their bivouacs on the edge of town were sties of filth. An epidemic of measles, thought to have originated in an American camp, swept through the Mexican and Indian populations alike, infecting thousands and killing hundreds, most of them children. Nearly every day Santa Fe held another juvenile funeral—the dead child carried through the streets on a bier strewn with flowers and borne on the shoulders of four other children, with the grieving adults following behind, drinking brandy and singing doleful songs.

Each week brought new outrages. The longer the Americans stayed, the more the people resented them—not only for the central fact of their conquest, but for the thousand little insults and daily humiliations committed by an uncouth foreigner who considered himself, in every possible way, superior.

It was not entirely surprising, then, that only a few weeks earlier, Governor Bent had discovered a Mexican plot for a full-scale insurrection. The ringleaders were said to be Tomas Ortiz, Augustin Duran, and the ever-proud Diego Archuleta, who nursed an understandable grievance against the Americans that dated back to General Kearny's promise—sweepingly tendered but quickly welched on and then forgotten—to give the colonel control of all of New Mexico west of the Rio Grande. The insurrection plans had called for all Mexicans to rise up on the day after Christmas and murder every American in the territory. The rebellion was to start at midnight with the tolling of church bells. Governor Bent and Colonel Price were to be assassinated, the artillery on the plaza seized, and the garrison at Fort Marcy stormed. In fact, the bloody scheme was only very narrowly foiled. Madame La Tules, the Santa Fe saloon-keeper loyal to the Americans, leaked news of the revolt to the American authorities only a few days before it was set to commence. The Americans soon arrested seven of the insurrectionists, but the three ringleaders managed to escape to the south, one of them disguised as a servant girl. Governor Bent and Colonel Price put the whole province under martial law. American soldiers redoubled their patrols, and impressive guns were strategically mounted along the parapets of the city. Price optimistically wrote to his superiors that "the rebellion appears to be suppressed."

Bent, for his part, was not too sure. Only a few weeks earlier he had issued a proclamation beseeching the people of New Mexico to "turn a deaf ear on all false doctrines and remain quiet, attending to your domestic affairs, so that you may enjoy the blessings of peace." Bent seemed pleased that the insurgents' "treason was discovered in time and smothered at its birth." The governor was sufficiently confident in his own standing among the Hispanic population to believe that he could travel safely without a military guard (although his aides back in Santa Fe thought his trip extremely incautious). He had kept a home in Taos since 1832 and knew practically everyone in the village by virtue of his business dealings and his having married into the prominent Jaramillo family. Among his many other roles—trader, entrepreneur, politician—Bent over the years had established himself in the community as something of a family apothecary; although he had no formal medical training, he had a knack for diagnosing and treating health problems, and through his local store he dispensed medicines and tinctures and herbal cures to the poor of Taos, Hispanic and Indian alike, usually for no charge. Prudently or not, he did not worry for his own safety.

But Governor Bent also recognized that, in general, the Mexicans still felt a "lasting antipathy" toward the Americans. He knew that the Catholic priests of New Mexico found American rule distasteful, and they had the power to stir up trouble among the faithful. There was a particularly influential priest in Taos, in fact, an erudite and some-what Machiavellian man named Padre Antonio Martinez who, among his many endeavors, published a Spanish-language broadsheet called *El Crepusculo de la Libertad* (*The Dawn of Liberty*), the first newspaper printed west of the Mississippi.

So powerful was Padre Martinez in the ecclesiastical affairs and political intrigues of northern New Mexico that he was known as "the Gray Eminence of Taos." Martinez was a bitter enemy of Charles Bent. This animosity dated back many years and was perhaps related to the fact that Bent had neither forsworn his American citizenship nor converted to Catholicism when he married Ignacia. Kit Carson had shown proper deference by becoming Catholic and joining the padre's church; Martinez, consequently, had presided over the marriage of Carson and Josefa and given the couple his formal blessing. But Charles Bent seemed to flout the protocols of the Church entirely and never sought to solemnize his common-law marriage with Ignacia. His children were, in the eyes of the Church, "natural"—that is, illegitimate.

Martinez had other long-standing differences with the governor. For one thing, he was suspicious of the various sub rosa schemes pursued by Bent and other Americans to snatch up large tracts of pristine wilderness in northeastern New Mexico from old land grants that were, Martinez felt, based on dubious historical claims. In the padre's estimation, Bent was just another American opportunist trying to make a fast buck without cultivating any true interest in New Mexico's traditions or people. (Indeed, the governor once wrote in a letter that Mexicans were "stupid, obstinate, ignorant, and vain.") The padre had long viewed Bent's Fort and its trading networks as a corrupting secular force. As a successful Missouri merchant, dealing in whiskey and trinkets and pelts often trapped illegally from Mexican territory, Bent seemed to represent all that was pernicious about American influence years before Kearny ever set foot in New Mexico. What's more, Martinez believed that Bent had sold guns directly to various Indian tribes who used the weapons to raid Spanish settlements.

Bent, for his part, thought Martinez a corrupt and tyrannical man—and a drunk. Bent (who could be an atrocious speller in notes that went unproofread) once wrote of the Padre: "I think he is more sinsearly devoted to Baccus than any of the other gods."

Priests like Martinez were not the only enemies Bent had to keep an eye on. In the south there were many influential landowners who presided over large haciendas on the Rio Grande. They had a good life, by and large, with plenty of Indian peons to do the work and lazy river water oozing into their fields from the acequias. In the relative terms of New Mexico, these landowners in the Rio Abajo (the "Lower River") were wealthy, and they seemed to fear that the coming of the Americans meant that their patrician existence would be forever upset.

With so many potential flash points of discontent, Bent was understandably anxious about the future of the New Mexico territory. He worried that a new revolt might easily sprout, hydralike, from the severed neck of the old. "The principal movers," Bent wrote to Colonel Price on Christmas Day, "may well not leave the country without a last desperate struggle."

☒

If he had any time for reflection as he rode toward Taos, Governor Bent must have wondered why he had accepted this thankless post. He had spent four hard months ensconced in the Palace of the Governors in Santa Fe, fretting over the intricate affairs of this volatile new U.S. territory whose many forms of turmoil were exceeded only by its poverty. He loved New Mexico for its raw beauty and wide-open ways, but it was quite another thing to try to govern this remote and benighted place. The province was a cauldron of conflict, its culture rich and old but stunted by hardship. The population of New Mexico was almost entirely illiterate and swayed by religious passions too potent to gauge, let alone manage.

During its long isolation, New Mexico had preserved archaic traditions, vestigial dialects of Spanish, and fierce strains of a sometimes unorthodox Catholicism that dated back to the most hysterical days of the Inquisition. Throughout New Mexico there were families who carried on curious traditions—lighting nine-lamped candelabras, singing verses of Hebrew, refusing to eat pork. These were the "crypto-Jews," as they've been called, descendants of Spanish Jews who had fled to Mexico in the 1600s to escape the rampant anti-Semitism of the Inquisition, and then had spread to the most isolated and (they hoped) more tolerant precincts of the empire. Heeding a stubborn cultural memory, these families pursued Hebraic customs in semisecrecy, often without knowing why.

In the remote rural areas of the north were secret societies of fla-gellants who called themselves *penitentes*—pious men who went out into the countryside to enact dour passion-play processionals in which they whipped themselves to a bloody pulp and, in certain ex-treme circumstances, even erected wooden crosses and crucified those brethren who wished to know the fullest meaning of Christ's suffering. (To die on the cross, some *penitentes* thought, guaranteed one's place in heaven.) It was said that the floggings and other *peni-tente* rituals had only intensified since the American occupation, as though they feared that the kingdom was at hand—or at least that their religion was now under genuine threat.

As for secular entertainment, the locals had few choices. Aside from horse races and card gaming and fandangos, the chief forms of amusement in this deadly dull province seemed principally to involve chickens. There were cockfights, of course, but also the immensely popular *el gallo,* an old blood sport in which a living fowl was buried up to its neck in the dirt of a hard-packed yard; horsemen would then take turns galloping by and attempt to yank the rooster up by the twitching wattles of its head in a single deft motion. Then, in a final free-for-all, the *caballeros* would fight over the chicken as though it were a football and, in the frenzy, invariably rip their quarry to pieces.

New Mexico officials had long ago learned to accept their sorry lot and make do with very little—and so Governor Bent would also have to resign himself. The day he was appointed governor, Bent wrote a long letter to Secretary of State James Buchanan in which he complained of the sad state of affairs. The whole territory was "im-poverished and undeveloped," he said, and education was "criminally neglected." He warned that "a rude and ignorant people are about to become citizens of the U.S." There was no regular mail service, no law books or stationery, and not enough translators to conduct the work of government. The legal system was a joke, the bench stacked with incompetents. An army lieutenant summed up the primitive state of jurisprudence in a letter home: "All the judges of the New Mexico Superior Court together do not possess the legal knowledge of a single justice of the peace in St. Louis."

Little had changed with the coming of the Americans. Santa Fe had always been a neglected capital, among the last to receive the news of the world and the fruits of invention. It had been the forgotten tongue-tip of the Spanish empire, and now it was a mere outpost of an expansionist American republic. Far to the south, in the agave thickets of Mexico, the war raged, and the Americans were pressing toward the real prize: Mexico City. And out west, in California, Kearny and his dragoons were consummating President Polk's fondest desire to make the United States a continental nation, with American ports on the Pacific. But Santa Fe, true to its forlorn past, had been forgotten again. It had been successfully invaded, but not entirely conquered. Bent's rump government crept along in spite of its conspicuous wants: not enough money, not enough troops, not enough information—an extremity feeling only the feeblest pulse of the nation to which it was newly attached.

And then, there were the Indians. The United States had in no way been able to make good on its promise to check the attacks of the marauding tribes. Every point of the compass brought danger. To the west, the Navajos, emboldened by the disappearance of General Kearny and Colonel Doniphan from New Mexico, had only stepped up their raids. The Apaches in the south, and the Kiowas and Utes in the north, were all testing the will of the Americans. On the east, the Comanches had declared open war, and wagon trains from Missouri were under constant attack along the Santa Fe Trail. The Comanches believed, with good reason, that the epidemics of smallpox and other diseases now running rife through their tribe had been brought by the Americans. As one historian put it, the Comanches blamed the white soldier "for having blown an evil breath on their children, and they were out for revenge."

The only group of Indians that did not seem to worry the governor were the Pueblos. Though they were secretive, they had a reputation for being docile and generally peace-loving. Scattered up and down the Rio Grande, huddled in their mud apartment complexes, they were stolid farmers who loved their corn and their kiva ceremonies and their complicated dances, and they mostly wanted to be left alone. The fact that they were Christians somehow made them seem more understandable, less foreign. They of course had never abandoned their own religion, but had found clever ways to intertwine the new with the old. Their stoic culture was thought to be even-tempered and nearly impervious to change. In 1680, the Pueblos had successfully risen up against the Spanish, ejecting their oppressors from New Mexico in a bloody purge. But when the Spanish returned twelve years later, they established an absolute reign over the Pueblos. Bent believed that at least the Pueblo Indians could be counted on to go along with the new dispensation handed down by America. And of all the Pueblo tribes, officers in the Army of the West thought that the Taos Indians were the most receptive to the Americans. Lieutenant Emory had written that a Taos man "may be distinguished at once by the cordiality of his salutations. That portion of the country seems the best disposed towards the United States. . . . They are our fast friends now and forever."

⊠

So it was with great surprise and some alarm that after four hard days of winter travel Governor Bent crested the brow of the sage-splashed hills and descended into his hometown of Taos, only to be accosted by a mob of hostile Indians from the Taos Pueblo. Fired with whiskey and in an uproar, they surrounded the governor and demanded that he release several Pueblo friends who were now stuck in the Taos jail. Their comrades had been arrested—wrongly, they felt—for theft.

Governor Bent waved them aside, explaining that it was not a matter in which he could intervene. The processes of law were more powerful than any governor, Bent said. The issue would be handled in due time by the courts. Their friends would just have to wait in jail. This only incensed the Taos Indians more. As Bent pushed through the crowds, they shouted their displeasure and cut him sour looks.

The governor safely reached his home and warmed himself by the fire with Ignacia at his side. His house was a foursquare piece of New Mexico architecture, a little gloomy on the inside, its walls three feet thick, its windows small and defensive in posture, paned with sheets of mica. It had an old floor of hard-packed dirt seasoned with ox blood and piñon ash, as was the custom. The flat roof was made of dirt as well, several feet of earth packed above the supporting pine *vigas*. The walls were whitewashed with a plaster fashioned from a local pale clay swirled in a milky liquid of pounded wheat. The Bent children found the chalky mixture so delicious that they had a naughty habit of licking the walls.

Kit Carson's wife Josefa was spending the night at the house, as was another young Hispanic wife of an American, Rumalda Boggs. Bent's children were happy to have their father home, and their laughter filled the rooms. Food simmered on the corner hearth stove, and soon everyone would sit down to a convivial meal.

Beyond Bent's window, however, an unmistakable rancor hung in the air.

◙

Early the following morning, around six o'clock, a mob of Taos Indians and a few New Mexicans appeared outside Bent's house. Roaring drunk and chanting war songs, they pounded on the door. In the crackly cold darkness, just before dawn, the stars shone as pinpricks in a black bowl.

Bent awoke with a start, threw on some clothes, and shuffled out to the porch. "What do you *want!*" he demanded groggily.

"We want your head!" came the answer. "We don't want you to govern us!"

Recognizing the ferocity of their emotions, Bent tried to reason with them. "What have I ever done to you?" he shouted. "When you came to me with your illnesses, I always tried to help. I gave you medicines and cures. I never charged you a cent."

The Indians answered not with words but with their bows. Feathered missiles shot at him from the shadows. It seemed as though they had drawn their weapons laxly, to maim him and make him suffer but not to kill. The governor staggered back into the house with three arrows lodged in his face—one of them buried at a queer angle in the skin of his forehead. He cursed in pain. Blood streamed down his temples and over his cheeks. Bent quickly bolted the door and turned to find Ignacia, wide-eyed with worry, dressed in her nightgown. She, too, had been slightly wounded by an arrow. The couple moved deeper into the safety of their house, trying to decide what to do. The arrows protruding from Bent's head flopped awkwardly as he moved about the rooms. Windows were breaking all around them, and they could scarcely hear each other over the din of the pounding and shouting. *Kill the Americans! The gringo must die!*

Ignacia handed the governor his pistols, but he shook his head. "It's pointless—there's too many out there," he said. "If I use these, they'll massacre all of us."

"Then why don't you jump on one of those and go somewhere?" Ignacia pleaded, pointing out the window at the horses corralled in the courtyard.

"Ignacia, no," Bent said. "It wouldn't do for the governor to run away and leave his family. If they want to kill me, they can kill me here."

Above them, they heard a terrific scraping and digging sound. Some of the mob had clambered onto the parapets; they were trying to tear away the dirt roof and bore through the ceiling. By now everyone in the household had risen—the Bents' daughter Teresina, their son Alfredo, Josefa Carson, Rumalda Boggs, as well as an Indian servant who was probably a kidnapped Navajo. They huddled together, sobbing and shivering in fright.

One of the women devised a plan. The Bent home happened to be connected to another residence by a shared wall of thick adobe bricks. Grabbing whatever tools they could find—a fire poker, large metal spoons—the women scrambled to a back room of the house and be-gan to claw their way through the wall. They pried the bricks apart and scraped at the mortar until they could see light on the other side.

As they worked in a frantic fury, the governor tried to buy time with the rabble outside. Shouting through a broken window, he of-fered them money, but they only laughed in derision. Bent's son Al-fredo appeared at his side. The boy was holding a shotgun in his hands. He peered up at his father with a determined grimace and said, "Let's fight them, Papa." But Bent told the boy: No, it was too late for that, hurry back to the women and help them dig.

The governor resumed his attempts to stall for time. He still clung to the hope that he could pacify the crowd. Bellowing out the win-dow, he promised to set up a committee to hear all Indian grievances, and then offered himself up as a prisoner if they would take him away peaceably.

They would have none of it. "We will start with you," one of them yelled back, "and then we will kill every last American in New Mexico!" A blast of musket fire drilled through the front door. One of the ricocheting bullets pierced the governor in the abdomen, another creased his chin.

By this point the women in the back room had scraped and gouged the hole until it was just big enough for a person to squeeze through. Teresina and Alfredo crawled through first, then Josefa and Rumalda. Realizing that the hordes outside were on the verge of breaking in, Ignacia insisted that Governor Bent go next.

"You're the one they want," she said. "Not me."

Reluctantly, he agreed. But the governor had forgotten about the arrows buried in his head and face, and now they pinched and buck-led and tore at him as he squeezed into the tight passage. In a rage, Bent stood up and plucked the arrows from his head and crushed them against the plaster wall. Then he dived back into the hole, gin-gerly holding his bleeding pate with one hand as he forced his stout body through to the other side.

By then the Taos Indians had broken into the house and were storming through the rooms. They seized Ignacia and one of them raised his rifle to shoot her, but the Navajo servant woman, who had lived as a peon with the Bent family for much of her life and was as loyal as she was brave, stood in front of her mistress in an attempt to shield her—and was promptly gunned down.

The Indian attacker then turned on Ignacia, striking her on the back with the butt of his gun and bringing her to her knees. He and his comrades moved on without causing her further harm. They discovered the hole in the wall and began crawling.

In the house on the other side of the wall, Governor Bent fumbled through his pockets for his memoranda book, with the notion of writing his last words, or possibly a will. He had lost a great deal of blood and was growing faint. Rumalda Boggs cradled him in her arms as he tried to compose his thoughts. He knew the invaders were pressing in on all sides, and that it was only a matter of time. Before he could write anything down, the Taos Indians stole into the building—some streaming in through the passageway from his house, others digging through the dirt roof and dropping down through the *vigas*.

And then, with Teresina, Alfredo, Rumalda, and Josefa watching in horror, they set upon him. The mob's main instigator, a firebrand from the Taos Pueblo named Tomacito Romero, hoisted the governor by his suspenders and hurled him onto the hard dirt floor. They shot more arrows into his body, then riddled him with bullets. The children pleaded for mercy, but, as Teresina Bent later recalled, "Our sobbing had no power to soften their enraged hearts." Tomacito leaned over the governor's still-living form and raked a bowstring over his scalp, pulling away his gray hair in a glistening sheath. As Rumalda described it, the skin was "cut as cleanly with the tight cord as it would have with a knife."

Gloating over their triumphs, crying in a drunken delight, the attackers stripped Governor Bent of all his clothes and then slashed and mutilated him until he ceased to breathe. Someone brought a board and some brass tacks. They stretched out the governor's scalp and nailed it taut to the plank. And then they brought their trophies out into the dawn light and marched toward the town plaza and the mazy mud streets of Taos.

Bent's children were still cringing on the floor with their Aunt Josefa, all of them cursed to be American by blood or marriage—and believing they were next.

⊠

The rampage continued all that day and into the next. The Taos Indians and their Mexican allies had vowed to kill every American in the territory, and they were making good on their promise. The entire party in which Governor Bent had traveled from Santa Fe was now marked. Prefect Cornelio Vigil was hacked to pieces. Sheriff Stephen Lee was killed on the roof of his own house. U.S. Circuit Attorney James Leal was stripped and tortured for hours in broad daylight, and then thrown, blinded but still breathing, into a ditch where he was eaten by hogs.

Next the mob set upon Narciso Beaubien and Pablo Jaramillo, apparently ignoring the fact that these boys were not American. The two young friends were hiding under a straw-covered trough in a stable not far from the Bent house when an Indian servant tipped off the rebels, saying, "Kill the young ones, and they will never be men to trouble us." The Pueblo Indians slashed and pierced the boys with lances until they were unrecognizable.

Now the rebels swarmed in all directions. They broke open the jail and freed the two Pueblo Indian prisoners whose incarceration had sparked their ire. They smashed into Bent's store and picked the place clean. They broke into Kit Carson's house, too, and pillaged everything; if Carson had been home and not off in California, he almost certainly would have been attacked and killed.

The revolt spread to other parts of the north. Mexicans set upon U.S. pack trains and grazing camps, killing all Americans they could find and stealing large herds of animals. Every American trader, merchant, and mountain man was now in mortal danger. Near the town of Mora, some forty miles to the southeast, eight Americans travel-

ing in a caravan were murdered in cold blood. In the tiny settlement
of Arroyo Hondo, north of Taos, a force of several hundred Pueblo
Indians surrounded the house of a well-known American named
Simeon Turley, who ran the distillery that produced Taos Lightning,
the pure-grain alcohol on which many of the Indians were now
drunk. As it happened, nine American trappers were staying at the
Turley mill that day, most of them friends of Charles Bent and Carson. The Indians encircled the place and, after a prolonged siege,
killed all but two of the Americans, who managed to escape under
cover of night.

All told, seventeen Americans were murdered in the opening
hours of the revolt, but the rebels were not yet sated. Now a ragtag
force of nearly a thousand insurrectionists, Indian and Mexican alike,
were clamoring toward Santa Fe, collecting recruits as they marched
south. Delirious from their initial success, they now planned to overtake Fort Marcy and storm the Palace of the Governors, driving out
every trace of the American presence.

What had started as a localized Indian grievance had ignited into
a full-scale Hispanic rebellion of the north. Yet it was not entirely
spontaneous, for the revolution almost certainly was encouraged by
certain Catholic priests around Taos—Padre Antonio Martinez was
widely suspected—and possibly by influential *penitente* leaders as
well. The revolt did not greatly differ in sentiment or design from earlier plots that had been laid for the December insurrection, the one
that Bent and Price had narrowly thwarted just before Christmas.
The Taos rebels had not formulated much of a plan other than to
drive the Americans out, but with so much discontent on which to
feed, that was enough.

For some reason the rebels spared the lives of the women and children huddled inside the Bent home. After stealing nearly everything
from the house, the Indians told the family to stay put, that under no
circumstances should they leave the premises or they would be killed.
As Teresina Bent later recalled, "They ordered that no one should
feed us, and then left us alone with our great sorrow." The Bents only

had their nightgowns to wear, because the mob had taken all their other clothes.

As the revolt fanned out over the north, Spanish women who were married to gringos prepared pastes of mud and spices to daub on their fair-complected half-American children so they might look darker. Whether Ignacia Bent went to these lengths with her own children, the record does not show. But that first night, Josefa Carson disguised herself as an Indian slave and slipped away to live at a friend's house, where she ground corn at a metate and kept to other menial tasks expected of a New Mexico servant.

For two days the Bent family grieved and starved in their bare cold house while the governor's scalped body lay naked on the floor in a congealed pool of blood.

◙

On January 21, 1847, when Sterling Price learned what horrors had transpired in the north, he flew into action, swiftly mustering a force to put down the revolt. The colonel decided not to wait for the Taos rebels to come to him, but rather to meet them head-on, thus stanching their hopes of gathering more recruits as they swarmed south toward Santa Fe. It was a bold decision to leave the capital undefended and thus vulnerable to insurgents who might materialize from other quarters, but Price thought it was worth the risk. He left Fort Marcy on the frigid morning of January 23 with four mountain howitzers and five companies of Missouri soldiers. Also in his party was a company of New Mexico volunteers, commanded by Ceran St. Vrain, a legendary Missouri fur trapper of French-Canadian descent who was Governor Bent's business partner and part owner of Bent's Fort.

St. Vrain was a burly man from St. Louis with great appetites, a connoisseur of good brandy, bawdy stories, and French obscenities. Historian David Lavender describes him as a "convivial figure, with a glossy black beard and wide-set eyes that were quick to crinkle in humor." The volunteers St. Vrain managed to call up were a spirited hodgepodge that included suspenders-wearing American merchants, hirsute mountain men, and a surprising number of Mexicans who had suddenly seen the advantages of demonstrating their allegiance to the United States of America. For his part, St. Vrain's cause was intensely personal: Like his friend Kit Carson, he had learned the frontier code of loyalty and swift reprisal, and now the seasoned mountain man was determined to "count coup" on those who'd murdered one of his own.

Another unlikely enlistee in this ad hoc army was a black man known as Dick Green: He was Charles Bent's slave, whom the governor had left behind in Santa Fe. Apparently moved by genuine sorrow and outrage, Green wanted to do his part to avenge his master's death.

Sterling Price's force, numbering nearly four hundred men, marched northward from the capital, fired by an urgent fury. "We were tiger-like in our craving for revenge," one American trapper recalled. But the thick snow soon stymied their march. Many of Price's men got frostbitten feet as they slogged through the same tiny settlements that Governor Bent and his entourage had passed through a week earlier. This time the villagers did not scowl at the Americans; in fact, they scarcely showed their faces at all. It was plain to see that this army was out for blood—and that little would be required to provoke it. Whatever their true loyalties, the locals were prudent enough to stay out of sight, keeping to their high-walled plazas and adobe compounds.

At half past one on the afternoon of January 24, the Americans met the forward lines of the Taos rebels outside the rural village of Santa Cruz de la Cañada. Price's soldiers mounted a series of ferocious charges, fighting from hilltop to hilltop, and from door to door, until the insurgents were rooted from their holes and thrown back in retreat just before dusk. The American forces at La Cañada suffered only eight casualties. Thirty-six of the enemy lay dead.

Two days later Price's men encountered another line of resistance in a canyon near a place along the Rio Grande called Embudo. "Soon the enemy began to retire, bounding along the rugged mountains," Price reported with pleasure. In the fray, St. Vrain lost only two men while the rebels counted upward of twenty dead and another sixty wounded.

Other than deep snowdrifts, no further obstacles stood in the way of Price's last push into Taos. Scouts brought word to the colonel that the insurgents had all fallen back to the safety of Taos Pueblo, where in their thousands they were barricading themselves behind the massive adobe walls, preparing for a final stand.

◙

First settled around A.D. 1300, Taos Pueblo was one of the oldest continually inhabited places in North America. The pueblo's two enormous apartment complexes lay separated from each other by an icy creek that spilled from the looming Sangre de Cristo Mountains. The source of the people's drinking water, the creek originated in a beautiful alpine lake that figured prominently in the tribe's cosmology. With the two seven-storied buildings rising from the banks as though replying to each other, the village hunkered in an exquisite symmetry. The staggered rooflines were connected by scores of wooden ladders, and the long centuries had left the mud-slathered ramparts gracefully mottled and warped. Piñon smoke issued from the sunken kivas where the men gathered in council. Women scurried about in their bright blankets and doeskin boots, tending to their outdoor ovens, shaped like beehives, in which they baked the soft round bread that was a staple of the tribe. To the immediate east the snowy mountain peaks rose to a crowding height of nearly thirteen thousand feet, slabs and shards of rock arrayed in sublime confusion. Surrounded by high wooden fences and thick defensive walls, the village looked like a medieval Moroccan citadel set against the Atlas Mountains.

At the northwestern corner stood the enormous mission church of St. Jerome, whose twin belltowers rose thirty feet into the gray winter sky. It was a formidable building hugged close by an old graveyard jumbled with crosses. With bulging walls more than six feet thick, the St. Jerome mission offered an obvious refuge, and so it was here where most of the rebels massed. Perhaps the Taos Indians thought the American army would never dare attack a Catholic church—or even if it did, that the numerous holy relics and *santos* stashed along the vestibule walls and niches would protect them. If they had to die, they preferred to die here, closer to God; it was the one place in the world where they felt safe. Inside the dark and draughty cavern, bathed in the guttering light of votive candles, the rebels crudely punched loopholes into the walls from which to fire their weapons. And they waited.

When Colonel Price led his army to the walls of Taos Pueblo on the bitterly cold early morning of February 4, he was immediately impressed and daunted by the pueblo, finding it "a place of great strength, admirably calculated for defence." From a tactical military standpoint, it presented puzzles of complexity he had never faced before. The ladders of the two great houses were all drawn up now, and, as one historian later put it, "their occupants waited within like creatures in burrows listening for a favorable change in the weather." Price had Ceran St. Vrain and his trappers form a half circle around the eastern side of the town "to discover and intercept any fugitives who might attempt to escape toward the mountains." Then the colonel ranged his artillery pieces around the mission and for two hours unleashed an intense bombardment. But the church walls were so thick and at the same time so soft that the shells did scarcely any damage—the friable mud bricks seemed to swallow up the balls and absorb the shock of their detonations.

Frustrated, Price told his artillerymen to cease fire, and then ordered a company of his soldiers under a Capt. J. H. K. Burgwin to charge the western and northern flanks of the church. Burgwin was one of Kearny's best-trained dragoons, "as brave a soldier as was ever seen on the frontier," according to one old trapper who watched him fight. Through withering fire, Burgwin's men ran right up to the mission walls and began hacking into the adobe bricks with hatchets and axes. But Burgwin's sappers were no more effective than the artillery shells had been at breaching the ramparts, so the captain hastened around to the front of the church with some of his men and attempted to break down the immense wooden door.

This sortie proved overly bold, however. Burgwin left himself exposed to direct fire from the rebel loopholes, and he was promptly cut down by a sniper within the church. With their captain slain, Burgwin's men redoubled their efforts and finally managed to chip away a small hole in the wall with their axes. Some lit fused shells with matches and tossed them into the church by hand while others propped crude ladders against the walls and ascended with torches to ignite the roof.

By three o'clock in the afternoon an inferno was blazing from the rooftop. Colonel Price rolled his six-pounder—a howitzer that fired a six-pound shell packed with grapeshot—within fifty yards of the mission. The artillery piece pummeled the building with ten rounds, and when the dust thinned it was discovered that one of the shells had directly struck and enlarged the ragged hole that Burgwin's ax-men had initiated; the breach was now nearly wide enough to admit a person. Encouraged by this, Price had his artillerymen draw the six-pounder within ten yards and blast away at the fissure until it was a yawning gap. This point-blank bombardment resulted in a wholesale slaughter inside; scores of Taos Indians packed in the mission were sliced to pieces by hot shrapnel, and the Americans outside could clearly hear their pitiful cries of agony. As one participant recalled, "The mingled noise of bursting shells and the shrieks of the wounded was most appalling."

Now Price's soldiers stormed through the breach. One of the first to leap inside was Dick Green, Charles Bent's black slave. Inside the mission it was intensely hot and thick with acrid smoke, and mangled forms lay moaning on the floor. Most of the defenders were either dead, wounded, or fast quitting the church through a back door and fleeing east toward the mountains. Those who still dared to put up a fight were soon gunned down or killed in hand-to-hand fighting. There was a suicidally brave Delaware Indian married into the Taos tribe who was, according to one account, "a keen shot and the most desperate of the enemy." The Delaware refused to surrender even as the blackened church rafters creaked and sagged in imminent collapse. The Americans chased him to a back room behind the altar and riddled him with thirty balls.

The church had become a charnel house, the smoke inside "so dense it was impossible to exist in it," wrote one young artillery officer. Eager to declare victory, the troops planted the Stars and Stripes in one of the sturdy mud walls of the church, but several retreating Mexicans stopped long enough to shoot it to tatters.

◙

East of the Pueblo, hidden in the brush, their weapons loaded and cocked, Ceran St. Vrain's volunteers waited. As the insurgents scurried for the foothills, the company slaughtered more than fifty of them, dropping the first wave with well-placed bullets, then chasing down the rest with clubs and knives. One of the men succinctly recalled, "They fled in every direction. Not much quarter was asked or given." St. Vrain himself was nearly killed by an Indian who, playing dead, suddenly sprang upon him with a steel-tipped spear.

Later, one of the escaping Taos Indians emerged from a thicket of sage and cringed before St. Vrain's lynching squads, calling out, "Bueno! Bueno! Me like Americanos."

One of the trappers curtly replied in Spanish, "If you like the Americans, take this sword and return to the brush, and kill all the rebels you find there."

The terrified Indian accepted the sword and disappeared into the sage as he'd been told. A few minutes later he returned with his blade "dripping with gore," according to one trapper account.

"I have killed them," the Pueblo Indian reported, although the blood on the sword may well have been from the body of a fellow countryman—or a Mexican ally—who had already fallen in battle.

The American trapper who had dispatched him on his errand raised his Hawken rifle in disgust and replied, "Well, then you ought to die for killing your own people," and shot the Indian dead.

The battle for Taos raged the rest of the day and into the next. Colonel Price's soldiers went door to door, ransacking the place in search of holdouts. They camped inside the northern pueblo, which the Indians had abandoned, and feasted on the Taos cattle and corn and wheat. They lowered Captain Burgwin into a grave, and then buried thirty other Americans en masse in a long trench near the still-smoldering church, not far from where they'd fallen. Price's lieutenants arrested scores of rebels, Pueblo and Mexican alike, including Tomacito Romero, the man who had scalped Governor Bent alive. Tomacito was confined in a cell to await a formal trial, but an angry dragoon visited him under the pretense of questioning him. The soldier promptly drew his pistol and shot the Indian leader in the head.

Finally, on the third day, the distraught women of the pueblo emerged from the southern apartment complex bearing white flags and sacred relics to offer the Americans. As one witness put it, "They kneeled before the colonel to supplicate for the lives of their surviving friends." Colonel Price accepted their surrender under the condition that these Pueblos turn over other leaders of the insurrection.

Nearly two hundred Pueblo Indians had lost their lives and many more lay wounded. The Pueblos had been utterly defeated. The day after the battle, a young Cincinnati writer named Lewis Garrard walked over the charred and rubbled remains of the village. Garrard, who had traveled to Taos with a group of trappers from Bent's Fort, captured the desolation of the village with pathos. "A few half scared Pueblos walked listlessly about, staring in a state of gloomy abstraction," he wrote. "Their leaders were dead, their grain and cattle gone, their church in ruins, the flower of the nation slain or under sentence of death. In the superstitious belief of the protection afforded by the holy Church, they were astounded beyond measure that they should be forsaken in the hour of need. That *los diablos Americanos* should, within the limits of consecrated ground, trample triumphant, was too much to bear."

▣

A few weeks later a government wagon was parked beneath a leafless cottonwood tree. Two mules were harnessed to the vehicle, and they stood still on this bright cold morning, unaware of their present purpose. A long plank was set across the rear of the wagon, overlapping each side by several feet. From a gnarled gray branch of the tree dangled six rope nooses, recently moistened with soapy water to make them pliable.

People were crowded on the rooftops, trying to get a glimpse of the first public hanging Taos had ever known. A guard of soldiers led the six condemned Pueblo Indians through the town and to the gallows. During the trial, the prisoners had been confined to a cold, dark, filthy room, and now their appearance was deplorable. Lewis Garrard described them as "trembling wretches . . . miserable in dress, ragged, lousy, greasy, and unwashed." They were marched to the tree and told to climb up in the wagon. They had to be careful to balance the plank just right. Two stepped on the middle of the board, while the two other couples offset each other, perching on the overhanging ends. Now the six stood facing the mule-driver, so close together that their arms touched. The sheriff adjusted the nooses around their necks.

"*Mi madre, mi padre*," one of the doomed was heard to mutter. Then another yelled, through gritted teeth: "*Carajo, los Americanos.*"

Their trials had been crude. Judge Carlos Beaubien, whose own son had been murdered in the revolt, presided. Ceran St. Vrain served as court interpreter. And the jury box was packed with vindictive Americans who'd had loved ones die and property stolen.

Ignacia Bent and Josefa Carson had testified convincingly in court, sharing the grisly details of the governor's murder. Yet many of the insurgents had been convicted not for murder, but for treason—quite a feat of legal legerdemain when one considers that Mexico was still at war with the United States. Lewis Garrard, who observed the trials, was puzzled and then incensed by the charge. "To conquer a country and then arraign the revolting inhabitants for treason," Garrard wrote, "certainly was a great assumption. What did these poor devils know about their new allegiance?"

Whatever the charge, the sentences had all come down the same, pronounced by the solemn voice of Judge Beaubien—"*Muerto, muerto, muerto.*"

The massacre of Governor Bent had been instigated by Pueblo Indians, it is true—by several dozen of the most desperate members of the tribe. But the larger revolt, the province-wide revolution, had been smiled upon—and in all likelihood masterminded—by a few well-placed Mexican leaders and Catholic priests who would forever remain in the shadows, their identities unknown, their conspiratorial roles suspected but never proven.

So the Pueblo Indians would pay the price. Precisely what they had been promised for defying the Americans, precisely what they had expected to gain in return, no one knows—the Taos Indians never wrote their own account of the revolt. (Even today, if you visit the lovely Pueblo, with its old mission church still moldering in ruins, the locals will gently admonish you for even asking if such an account exists. "Everything is oral here," they say, the old days are not open for study, and those events of 1847 are never to be spoken of, except perhaps in the smoky safety of the kivas.)

Now the American sheriff gave the signal, and the driver *hawed* the mules forward. The doomed kept their feet on the board until the last possible moment. With a sudden snap, the men fell in unison and the nooses yanked tightly. Garrard described how their bodies swayed back and forth, and how in coming in contact with each other, they shuddered convulsively. "The muscles would relax and again contract," he wrote, "and the bodies writhed most horribly."

But in this random twisting, the hands of two of the Taos Indians found each other. Garrard noticed that their fingers became locked in a firm grip, a handshake of brotherhood, "which they held till the muscles loosened in death."

Chapter 29 AMERICAN MERCURY

St. Louis, the roistering frontier capital, lay at the confluence of the Missouri and the Mississippi, whose snaggy brown waters were filled with steamships. The humid city climbed off the alluvial banks, its streets of dirt and cobblestone crammed with dray wagons and dearborns and lined with locust trees, its huddled neighborhoods radiating west from the wharves in an orderly grid that had been established by the city's French founders. For such a remote city in the hinterlands, St. Louis was a surprisingly cosmopolitan place of more than fifteen thousand souls, a city with its own peculiar Creole culture. Its taverns were filled with French and Spanish and queer Indian tongues—and, more recently, with the tongues of the newer immigrants, the Germans and the Irish, who had come west in droves looking for good work and free land.

The last time Carson passed through here, in 1842, St. Louis was a smallish town perched at the edge of the United States, capital of the westernmost state. Now, in the spring of 1847, the city was almost unrecognizable. Without the residents knowing it, St. Louis had effectively become the geographical center of the country. In only a few short months, through far-flung military events Carson had himself witnessed, the fulcrum of the nation had shifted west more than a thousand miles. The margin had become the middle.

As Carson rode into St. Louis, exhausted after a journey of two months, he was about to change the city's view of itself. It was near the end of May, a month after the trials and executions for the Taos Revolt that marked the final flicker of Mexican resistance to the American conquest of the West. Carson was passing briefly through town, bearing messages from California. The transcontinental courier mission that General Kearny had denied him in the fall of the previous year had finally materialized: After the Mexicans in California had at last capitulated and Los Angeles had returned to American hands, Carson's old friend John C. Fremont, who was serving as governor, had given him a bundle of letters to rush east to the secretary of state, important dispatches on the course of the war. After this short stop in St. Louis, Carson would continue by steamboat, then by train, to Washington City.

It was the kind of assignment that seemed to suit him—riding in a small party, carrying intelligence for people more powerful than he, safeguarding secrets of history as he sped across the continent like some bedraggled Mercury. He was the illiterate bearer of written messages, an irony that probably did not escape him.

To reach St. Louis, Carson had followed the Gila route east from California. He had successfully fended off an attack by Apaches—"them arrers came whizzing along like a raft of geese going south" Carson later said in describing the incident. He had stopped off in Taos long enough to reunite with Josefa, whom he hadn't seen in twenty months. From her, he learned all about the Taos Revolt and that terrifying evening in the Bent home—and became convinced that Padre Antonio Martinez, the Taos priest who'd married Kit and Josefa, was the real mastermind behind the insurrection. Although he was never able to prove it, Carson carried this hunch with him for the rest of his life.

After ten days in Taos, Carson had continued on by way of Bent's Fort and the Santa Fe Trail, passing through Fort Leavenworth. For the whole trip Carson's traveling companion had been his friend Ned Beale, the young navy lieutenant with whom he had trekked barefoot through the California desert to break the siege of San Pasqual. Although the details of the lieutenant's ailments are murky, Beale was still in such excruciating pain from his ordeal in the desert that Carson had to lift him on and off his horse. Beale would be forever grateful to Carson for his kindnesses on their cross-continental odyssey. Years later he thanked "Don Kit" for the time when, under the broiling sun in the mesquite desert, Carson had selflessly removed his own canteen and "poured upon my fevered lips the last drop of water."

(Another anecdote from Beale's long ride illustrated Carson's hair-trigger temper. Stumbling upon an army sergeant hectoring a sick man with a knife—presumably somewhere in California—Carson flashed a pistol and calmly said, "Sergeant, drop that or by the splendor of God, I'll blow your heart out." The story could be exaggerated, but it rang true with other accounts of Carson's reaction to bullies. A small man himself, he had no tolerance for predation and responded with ferocity whenever he encountered it.)

When Carson and Beale loped into St. Louis, the townspeople knew nothing about the battle of San Pasqual or its triumphant aftermath, nor did they know the latest news from the gallows in Taos. Now here was a messenger fresh from the front. Once word spread that Carson had arrived, everyone in town wanted to get a look at the famous mountain man—a fellow Missourian, no less, who had become a national legend.

People didn't just want to gawk, however—they were genuinely anxious to learn what was happening in the West. Nearly everyone in St. Louis had a relative in Kearny's army, or serving with Doniphan's volunteers, but reliable news of how they had fared was almost nonexistent. It is impossible to exaggerate how miserably slow frontier communications were in the 1840s. A soldier's wife in St. Louis was much like a whaler's wife in Boston—she said good-bye to her beloved as he set sail on an ocean of land and then she accepted the voids of silence, the hard nights of not knowing, as the weeks and months became years. In place of solid information, St. Louis buzzed with rumors about the Army of the West: Santa Anna had dispatched an enormous force to retake New Mexico. Colonel Doniphan had been killed by Indians. Kearny's men had all frozen to death in the mountains.

Until now, Carson had never quite realized the extent to which he was a celebrity, or what that meant in a public situation, and he was deeply uncomfortable. People pressed at him in the streets and dram shops, and he soon found himself in what he called "a surround." He was put off by this new impertinence, the way strangers expected something from him. He quickly learned to distrust journalists. "Some of these newspaper fellows," he said, "know more about my affairs than I do." In alleyways and taverns, people would accost him and slap his back as if they knew him. Carson, who was a bit of a claustrophobe anyway and hated crowds, would jerk himself away and gesture awkwardly toward the open street, saying, "I always see folks out in the road."

No one was more impatient to hear Carson's news than Thomas Hart Benton, who happened to be home in St. Louis that May. Some of the dispatches Carson carried in his saddlebags, in fact, were addressed to Benton. The senator offered his house to the cross-country courier and embraced him like a long-lost nephew. Benton of course knew all about Carson from Fremont's expedition reports, but he had never met him.

Throughout his career Benton had befriended nearly all the explorers of the West—the trappers and traders and *voyageurs,* the eccentric English lords who traipsed across the prairies on hunting safaris, the expedition topographers and botanists and Indian-fighters. They all passed through St. Louis eventually, and Benton made it his business to debrief them. Although he had never traveled west of Missouri, he gave off the impression that he had. He seemed to have met everyone connected with the frontier—James Audubon, the Bent brothers, Washington Irving, the explorer William Clark, traveling artist George Catlin, and the great fur trappers Jim Bridger and Jedediah Smith. Benton had also intersected with all the prominent warriors of the West, soldiers like Kearny, Leavenworth, and Dodge, and even the young Robert E. Lee, who served as a captain in St. Louis with the Army Corps of Engineers.

The Benton mansion on the outskirts of the city became something like a clearinghouse—the American Empire's western field office, in effect, where disparate strands of frontier science, commerce, and military intelligence met and mingled in a rough first draft. It was the age of happy dilettantes and gentleman explorers, when disciplines easily blurred, when a soldier might be a geologist, cartographer, botanist, ethnologist, linguist, and artist, all at the same time. American ignorance of the West was so vast that all forms of knowledge, however obtained, were welcome pieces of an emerging puzzle.

Benton's place was where the puzzle came together. Explorers would haul in their dog-eared maps and their field specimens, their Indian relics and their folios of charcoal sketches. Benton would ply them with good food and drink and make them stay up late on the porch, telling stories fresh from the Western wilds.

Carson was no exception. Although he was in a terrific hurry to move on to Washington, he had little choice but to camp out in the

Benton home for a few days and endure a minute cross-examination from the senator on all the latest events in Oregon, California, and New Mexico.

Benton's wife, Elizabeth, a genteel woman from an old Virginia plantation family, was there in the home, but she could speak only in a halting mumble, her face slack and sallow from a paralytic stroke in 1842 that had left her brain-damaged, bedridden, and subject to seizures. The family thought the stroke had been caused by an old family doctor who insisted on bleeding Mrs. Benton whenever she complained of any sort of ailment. (In the years leading up to her stroke, she had been bled thirty-three times.) Benton was devoted to his invalid wife, and since her stroke had scarcely gone out in public. He kept a desk by her bed where he read and scribbled through the nights by the light of a special lamp he had devised—four spermaceti candles burning on a white reflecting screen.

Staying at the Bentons', Carson got a good hot bath, bought some store clothes, and tried to make himself presentable. He was not used to cities, and he was self-conscious about his grimy buckskins and parfleche moccasins. St. Louis, he knew, was only a rehearsal—much more would be expected of him in Washington in the way of fine clothes and manners. He was nervous about what would happen in the nation's capital, the dignitaries he would have to meet, the airs he'd have to put on. But Benton tried to allay his fears. He insisted that when Carson got to Washington, he *must* stay in his home on C Street, not far from the Capitol. He assured Carson that his daughter Jessie, who lived there, would guide him through the tight spots.

Carson was grateful for this new connection and enjoyed his brief stay in St. Louis, although he scarcely mentions it in his autobiography. "I accepted Benton's invitation," Carson allows, "and received the kindest of treatment from him."

Benton was taken with his new guest. The senator thought of Carson as one of the great behind-the-scenes heroes of the Mexican War. "Although he did not enter the army through the gate of the military academy," Benton said, "he is at the head of the principal military successes" in the West. Above all, Benton came to trust Carson's clear sense of judgment. It was not only his honesty, but his attention to concrete details; in an oral culture like that of the American frontier, paramount importance was placed on the hard accuracy of memory, and that was what struck Benton most: Carson's recollections seemed fundamentally reliable. Fremont had once said that his guide was incapable of dissembling, that "Carson and Truth are one." Now Benton saw that same quality. "He is a man," the senator said, "whose word will stand wherever he is known."

The senator was delighted to hear Carson's reports from Los Angeles and San Diego. Carson made it clear that after only a few hiccups and one small, brutal battle with lances, California was now safely in American hands. The British menace, one of Benton's pet terrors, had been averted.

There was one glitch in Carson's narration of events that troubled Benton, however. It had to do with his son-in-law. Apparently Fremont had gotten himself into a terrific row with General Kearny after the final surrender of Los Angeles. By the sound of it, Fremont was caught in the middle of an internecine rivalry between the army and the navy over who would control California. Commodore Stockton insisted that he was in charge, while Kearny claimed that his more recent orders from President Polk clearly trumped Stockton's command. Neither man would back down. To complicate matters, Stockton had named Fremont as his choice to be the new governor, and when Kearny questioned this appointment, Fremont, a mere captain in the Topographical Corps, refused to recognize the general's authority. Brazenly, the new governor said he would not step down until Stockton and Kearny had, as Fremont put it in a tortuous letter to the dumbfounded general, "adjusted the question of rank between yourselves."

Benton, who was well acquainted with all the parties, remained confident from his remove in St. Louis that the dispute could be resolved—especially after he read Fremont's handwritten dispatches carried in Carson's pouch. But the senator also understood the U.S. Army, with its rigid protocols and petty jealousies. A general was not to be trifled with—especially not a general as headstrong as Stephen

Watts Kearny. Benton realized that in the cold light of a court-martial, Fremont's actions could be interpreted as mutiny.

⊗

Having enjoyed Senator Benton's hospitality, Carson had one other matter to attend to before he could resume the trip east to Washington. It was a private errand, an important one that concerned events buried in his personal history: He needed to pay a visit to his daughter.

Five years had passed since he left Adaline. She was ten years old now and could hardly remember her father when he showed up at his niece's farm not far from the town of Fayette, Missouri. The visit must have been as awkward as it was brief. Carson couldn't linger, but he wanted to make sure Adaline was happy, that her education was progressing, that it wasn't too much of a burden for her to grow up as a half-breed so far away from her father.

She was becoming a young woman. He could see a lot of her mother in Adaline. He was satisfied that she felt at home there, and that she was well loved by the Carson clan. It must have tickled him to learn that she could read. Already she had more schooling than he'd ever had. Still, he decided it was time she moved on from the little country school in which he had placed her; he now made arrangements for her to enroll as a boarder in a nearby Catholic school. Education was an understandable sticking point with him; his clumsiness with letters and figures—and the nuanced experiences he'd been denied because of it—remained his greatest humiliation. He wanted to spare his firstborn the lifelong embarrassment he'd felt.

Because his niece refused to take money, he showered the household with gifts and presented the family with a mahogany rocking chair, a sturdy piece of frontier furniture that would last generations. For Adaline, the rocking chair would be part of the architecture of her girlhood, a physical reminder of her kind but emphatically absent father. The family thought his gift was especially apt, for like Kit, the chair was never fully itself unless it was moving.

Chapter 30   TIME AT LAST SETS ALL THINGS EVEN

Jessie Benton Fremont met Carson at the Washington train station late one night near the end of May 1847. Although she had never seen a photograph of his likeness, she recognized him immediately when he stepped off the train. Her husband's descriptions of Carson had been accurate: the dry smile and leathered face, the bandy-legged gait, the twinkle in his gray-blue eyes. How many men in the nation's capital fit that description? She greeted Carson warmly and led him to her carriage.

Jessie Fremont, then twenty-three years old, was not a beautiful woman in the traditional sense. She had her father's overlong nose, her face was round as a moon, her neck stalklike, her shoulders slumpishly sloped. Yet something about Jessie Fremont was immensely attractive to men and women alike. She was exuberant, defiant, opinionated, original. She approached people with a bearing of confidence so complete it was disarming. A friend once parsed her personality as "so much fresh breeze and so much sunlight," but like her father, Jessie also had the musty erudition of a life spent among great books.

She and Carson rode back to her father's house on C Street, and there he stayed for most of his three-week sojourn in Washington. She took him around to the sights, introduced him to her circle of friends, and carted him to dinner parties in which he sat awkwardly in the hotseat of attention and ate unfamiliar continental dishes. He was bewildered and flattered and, at least at first, mildly intrigued.

But in truth, there wasn't much to do in Washington. The nation's capital was then a tiny Southern city that closed up shop in the sultry summer months. L'Enfant's grand plan of broad avenues and circles was very slowly taking shape, but the rutted streets were mires of mud and horse manure. The National Mall was little more than a cow pasture by the swampy margins of the Potomac. The great monuments of today were conspicuously absent—construction on the Washington Monument would not begin until the following year. Only a month before Carson's arrival, crews had broken ground for a new museum to be called the Smithsonian Institution.

Carson liked Jessie Fremont and was grateful to have her escorting him around the town. He found that, temperamentally, she was very similar to her father. Of the four Benton children, Jessie was Tom Benton's favorite, his pet, and the devotion was mutual. Growing up, she never wanted to be away from her father's side. When he enrolled her in a prestigious girl's boarding school in Georgetown, she protested by cutting off her hair so that she would look like the son she thought her father wished her to be. The senator relented, and so Jessie Benton quit "society school" and pursued her education under his tutelage. He set a regimen of books for her to read by lamplight in his formidable study; other times he would "pasture" her, as she liked to say, in the Library of Congress.

She eloped with John C. Fremont at the age of seventeen. Her father fiercely opposed the marriage at first but soon became Fremont's staunchest advocate and sponsor. In an odd way Fremont was the real-life avatar of Benton's designs for the West—a bold young explorer with the training and drive to make the senator's ideas a reality. By marrying Fremont, Jessie had pledged herself to someone whose ambitions were in peculiar alignment with those of her father.

Jessie utterly hitched herself to her husband's career. She furthered Fremont's glory and ran interference for him in Washington while he was off in the wilderness, where, as she once put it, "not even the voice of Fame can reach him." She wrote his letters. She tirelessly pressed and pleaded on his behalf. To a remarkable extent, she grafted her own interests and desires onto her husband's to the point where the couple's ambitions were indistinguishable. She told her husband that she was his "most confirmed worshiper." She kept a daguerreotype of him hanging over her bed. "It is my guardian angel," she once wrote him, "for I could not waste time with that beloved face looking so earnestly at me." Many acquaintances thought her devotion to Fremont unhealthy. Said her closest friend, Lizzie Lee: "She belongs to him body & soul & he does with her as he pleases as much as he does with his own right hand."

Though it was not then widely known, Jessie Fremont had actively collaborated on all his expedition reports. Some said she had actually written them—or at least the best parts. (Carson didn't realize it, but she had, through her skillful pen, done as much as Fremont to make the scout famous.) She was an accomplished phrasemaker, someone who knew how to make an image stick, and she had the desk discipline that her peripatetic husband lacked.

Certainly Jessie was John's intellectual equal—and in some sense his superior. By way of an ambiguous compliment, it was sometimes said around Washington that Jessie was "the better man of the two."

❂

Within a few days, Carson had taken care of his business in Washington: He had met with Secretary of State James Buchanan and Secretary of War William Marcy and placed Fremont's dispatches in their safe hands. Carson was not particularly impressed by either man and scarcely mentioned them in his autobiography.

Wanting to get home to Josefa, Carson packed his things. He had no intention of lingering in Washington. But then he got a message: President Polk wanted Carson to call on him at the White House. The president was quite busy, however, and would not be able to receive Carson until June 14, several weeks away.

So Carson found himself in a miserable holding pattern—more introductions, more newspaper interviews, more society functions. One of the dinners was at Secretary Marcy's home. Many prominent officials, including two generals, were in attendance. It was reported that Carson only "picked at his fish and fowl drenched in rich sauces" but that he "ate all of the vegetables placed before him and appeared to enjoy his ice cream and cake." Carson passed on the fine French wine, though he later accepted one of Marcy's cigars after the ladies had repaired to the drawing room. It was only then, as the men smoked away and drank their brandy, that Carson began to loosen up, relating some of his adventures in California.

Carson's sentence in Washington dragged on. While waiting for President Polk's schedule to open up, he left Jessie's place for a while and spent some time with Ned Beale, whose mother lived in Washington. Beale had grown up in Washington, in fact, and attended Georgetown College. A bon vivant who jerked with odd nervous tics, he dabbled in Islam, wrote verse in the romantic style of Keats and Shelley, and drank to such frequent excess that he created his own recipe for a hangover cure. Beale hailed from a well-established navy family, and he kept Carson busy meeting the leading people of the city. Jessie fondly described Beale as a "witty and eccentric man." (Attesting to both his wit and eccentricity, Beale would in the 1850s preside over a somewhat quixotic U.S. Army experiment that tested—and advocated—the use of camels in the deserts of the American West. When working with the army dromedaries, he studied Arabic so that he could speak to them, he said, "in their native language.")

One day, before some particularly fancy engagement, Beale noticed that Carson became anxious and moody. When he asked his friend what was wrong, Carson confessed that he was worried that the ladies of Washington would find out about Singing Grass. He reminisced about his deceased Arapaho wife and told Beale how much he loved her. He seemed to fear that his former marriage would invite ridicule, that people would cast aspersions not only on him, but on the memory of his dead wife. It seemed an odd thing for him to worry about; but such was the public disapproval of Indians, and the perceived taint of "miscegenation" among certain Eastern circles, that Carson assumed his earlier life would cause a scandal. Once the papers got hold of the story, he feared it might reflect badly on the Bentons and the Fremonts, as well as on Beale's family.

Beale told Carson not to worry, he was getting worked up over nothing. People in Washington would not judge him for this. Society's rules didn't apply on the frontier, and his having lived such a wildly different life only made him more fascinating and impressive to people.

Beale was right, of course. Carson had nothing to fret about: His being a "squaw man" never came up. On the contrary, he was the toast of the city. Foreign ambassadors called on him. Generals and politicians wanted to be seen with him—and so did the ladies. He was an exotic curiosity all the more endearing for his social awkwardness, like some Tarzan figure removed from the jungle and paraded before all the town. The *Washington Union* ran a long, doting profile of him, calling Carson "one of those noble characters that have from time to time sprung up on our frontier." Carson, the *Union* went on, "is modest as he is brave, with the bearing of an Indian, walking even with his toes turned in." (The *Union* profile was the first full-length treatment Carson had ever received in the press; it was widely suspected that Jessie Fremont wrote the article, or at least substantially contributed to it.)

Carson appreciated the welcome reception, but in truth he had come to hate Washington. He disliked and distrusted most of the politicians he met. "They are the princes here in their big houses," he told Jessie, "but out on the Plains, *we're* the princes." He found the city in every way confining. At the Beale house, Carson's bedroom was so stuffy and his mattress so soft that he begged to sleep on the veranda in the open air. He was shocked at the high cost of everything in Washington, and thought it outrageous that carriage operators around the city *charged a fee* for something so basic as transportation. He fussed about this so much that eventually Jessie secured him a horse so he could trot around the city on his own.

Jessie grew close to Carson. She judged him a "perfect Saxon, clear and fair," with "a nature as sweet as a clear winter morning." He was "cool, sagacious, as gentle as he was strong." She thought he had a "merry heart" and "that most lovable combination of a happy and reasoning patience . . . so like the simplicity of the Bible." She discovered to her delight that he liked to be read to. In the Benton library, Carson stumbled upon an illustrated copy of Lord Byron's poems and turned to an engraving depicting "Mazeppa's Ride." The long Romantic poem is based on a supposedly true story taken from Voltaire about a Polish nobleman named Mazeppa who pursued an affair with another man's wife; when the cuckolded husband discovered their dalliances, he stripped Mazeppa naked and bound him helpless to a horse, turning the animal loose on the steppes. Mazeppa ended up hundreds of miles away in the Ukraine, half-dead from hunger and exhaustion—and nursing a righteous revenge.

Carson looked at the startling image of the naked man cinched across the "foaming flank" of a galloping horse. The picture reminded him of some brand of Indian torture he'd seen in the West. "It looks like Blackfoot, sure enough," he told Jessie. "They're devils enough for just such work as that."

He pretended to mouth the words of the poem, then gave up the sham. "You read it to me!" he said. "You can do it so much faster."

And so Jessie started reading stanzas aloud while Carson paced the parlor and tried to absorb the meaning. He was, she later recalled, "intensely stirred." Something about Byron's description of vengeance resonated with Carson.

> *Time at last sets all things even*
> *If we do but watch the hour*
> *There never yet was human power*
> *That could evade, if unforgiven*
> *The patient search, and vigil long*
> *Of him who treasures up a wrong*

Carson became strangely animated over the last line. *Treasures up a wrong.* "Now that's so!" he told Jessie. "That's the word—he knows how it is!"

Then he told her a story from his trapping days of how a band of Blackfeet once stole a season's worth of his pelts. To the mountain men, this was an act of war. As Carson recalled the theft, a latent spite welled inside him. The rage seemed to come out of nowhere, as though the insult had just occurred. This was a side of him Jessie had never seen.

He told her, "It was three years before we could get back and *thank* them. But our time came, and we left mourning in their tribe."

Kit Carson and Jessie Benton were ushered into President James K. Polk's office on the morning of June 14, 1847. The president greeted them as warmly as his mirthless personality would allow. They talked for a time about Carson's exploits in the West and the battles he had witnessed. The president moved the conversation along efficiently, with a few pointed questions. He drank in Carson's news but registered no reaction. The master plan he had set in motion was coming to fruition; the United States had by informal fact if not by formal treaty become a continental nation. Everything he had envisioned at the outset of his presidency was taking place. And yet he seemed to take no pleasure in it.

When the right moment came, Jessie Fremont pressed the president for his thoughts on the emerging conflict between her husband and General Kearny over the governance of California. The president was already well aware of that "unfortunate collision," as he called it. He was willing to hear Carson's version of the story and take receipt of a long letter that Fremont had written describing his own point of view on the controversy. Polk briskly stamped the dispatch and noted, "RECEIVED FROM MR. CHRISTOPHER CARSON."

But the president said nothing of substance on the matter and was careful not to give any indication which way he was leaning. In truth, Polk had already made up his mind that Kearny should rightly be in control of California and that Fremont was "greatly in the wrong" to have questioned the general's authority. He wrote in his diary, "It was unnecessary, however, that I should say so to Fremont's wife, and I evaded giving her an answer."

Polk did have good news for his visitors, however. At the request of Secretary Marcy, he was commissioning Carson as a second lieutenant in the Regiment of Mounted Riflemen. Carson would get a smart new uniform and a stipend. Polk wanted Carson to return posthaste to California with more dispatches, but first he would like the new lieutenant to come that very night to a White House dinner. His wife, Sarah, was planning a little soiree in his honor.

Carson accepted. As he and Jessie were shown the way out, Polk returned to his true love—his deskwork.

Polk had aged dramatically during his two years in office. The conflict with Mexico had proven to be a much more ambitious—and controversial—endeavor than he had bargained for. It was consuming the man, and people in Washington could see it in the haggard lines of his ghostly face. In fairness, he brought most of his hardships on himself. His fussy perfectionism made him impossible to please. He had no faith in his cabinet or his generals, and trusted no one. Consequently, he ended up running most of the war himself from the shadows of his office. Polk was proud to say that he was the "hardest working man in America," and it was probably true. As one biographer put it, he was so worried about Mexico that he had "virtually incarcerated himself in the White House."

He had little reason to be so pessimistic. In fact, the tide of the war was going exactly his way—Zachary Taylor had defeated Santa Anna at Buena Vista, Doniphan had taken Chihuahua, Winfield Scott had staged an amphibious landing at Veracruz and was now marching toward the capital with an army of ten thousand men, while an emissary named Nicholas Trist was already in Mexico City making overtures for a peace negotiation. Yet, as with Carson's news from California, the president took no outward pleasure in any of these developments. He considered Taylor "wholly incompetent," "exceedingly ignorant," and "very ordinary," and Scott he deemed "not fit for command" (even though military historians have consistently given both generals high marks). Nicholas Trist, Polk said, was a "bungling" negotiator with "no ability." If the president did not openly criticize Stephen Kearny, neither could he find many words of praise. If he could, the micromanager-in-chief would have gone down to Mexico and assumed command himself. He confided in his diary, "I am almost ready at times to conclude that there is no reliance to be placed in any of the human race."

America's first war of foreign intervention was uniquely the focused enterprise of a single man; with good reason, it became known as "Mr. Polk's War."

Carson's farewell dinner at the White House went off smoothly enough. Sarah Polk kept the atmosphere informal, having learned from the miscues that seemed to make Carson uncomfortable at Secretary Marcy's party a week earlier. The first lady was a dignified and devout Presbyterian whose poise at social functions did much to make up for her husband's lack of charm. She and the president, both being from Tennessee, knew something about down-home cooking. Instead of rich French dishes, she prepared rare roast beef and had the president carve the meat himself. In lieu of wine she served whiskey, and Carson treated himself to a glass.

Mrs. Polk seemed satisfied that she had put her guest at ease. Still, she could not keep herself from closely analyzing him as he ate.

"His manners at table I found to be faultless," she wrote in a letter to her mother in Nashville the next day. "Lieutenant Carson is courteous, slow-spoken, and with becoming modesty turns aside suggestions that his deeds have been more valiant than those of lesser men. I must confess I watched him to see how he handled his fork, which he used with dexterity."

Sarah Polk observed that while Carson got along fine with Marcy, Buchanan, and the other men, he seemed awkward—tongue-tied even—in his few conversations with the women at the party. Mrs. Polk wrote, "He remained the soul of diffidence with the ladies, and replied to . . . us in so few words as to indicate that our interest disturbed his peace of mind. When I asked him to describe for our edification how he eluded the Mexicans when carrying dispatches to San Diego, he grew red in the face and would not speak."

To his relief, Carson's time in Washington was drawing to a close. Within a few days the lieutenant would be on a train bound for Baltimore, wearing his crisp new uniform, his mail pouches bulging with dispatches addressed to BRIGADIER GENERAL STEPHEN WATTS KEARNY in California.

Chapter 31   A BROKEN COUNTRY

Just after dawn, an army of nearly four hundred troops left Fort Marcy and marched through the slumbering capital of Santa Fe. They were aiming for the blue swell in the western distance, a ragged volcanic massif known as the Jemez Mountains. On this crisp morning in the late summer of 1849, the men moved through high desert air that was radiantly clear and cool, the night monsoons having swept away the atmospheric dust. The Jemez were twenty crow-miles away, rising steeply from the parched mesas beyond the green declivity of the Rio Grande, but in the morning freshness, the mountains seemed close enough to touch. They were splashed with piñon and juniper, and, in the upper reaches, cloaked in distinct bands of ponderosa and quaking aspen. Long fingers of hardened lava reached out from the mountain's eroded flanks, a series of narrow escarpments canted in the runoff patterns of an ancient eruption. For the soldiers now leaving Santa Fe, the Jemez loomed as a magnificent but vaguely unsettling landscape. Summer's lightning storms nearly always came from that direction; in the afternoons the clouds would build and blacken on the Jemez, and then tails of virga would drop from the mounting thunderheads as they snarled east toward Santa Fe, igniting the evenings with jags of electricity.

Beyond the Jemez volcano was a kind of American Canaan, a wilderness, pure and mythic, stretching out for hundreds of miles. It was the country of the Navajo. On this morning—August 16, 1849— the U.S. Army was striking for the first time into the very heart of the Diné world, in what would be the first true reconnaissance of the Navajo lands. Three years had passed since Kearny's conquest and Doniphan's initial foray into the Navajo country, and little had changed in the new territory with respect to the wild tribes. The state of terror that Kearny vowed to "correct" still persisted, even though the United States was spending $3 million a year to maintain an army of Indian-fighters in New Mexico. The raiders continued to come in the night, and they stole with impunity, sometimes right under the noses of American soldiers—Jicarilla Apache, Mescalero Apache, Ute, Comanche, Kiowa, all the wild tribes, either singly or in various shifting alliances.

But the Navajos remained the most cunning and brazen of all. That spring, thefts and murders had reached a new frenzy: Scores of raids were reported up and down the Rio Grande, and many thousands of head of sheep had vanished. (In truth, many of these raids were carried out by Apaches, Utes, and other tribes, but the Navajos usually got the blame.) The new Indian agent to the New Mexico Territory, a Georgian named James Calhoun, attempted to describe the deepening fears to the commissioner of Indian affairs in Washington. "The Navajos commit their wrongs from a pure love of rapine and plunder," Agent Calhoun wrote. "Not a day passes without hearing of some fresh outrage, and the utmost vigilance of the military force in this country is not sufficient to prevent murders and depredations. There are but few so bold as to travel alone ten miles from Santa Fe."

The younger Navajo warriors had apparently decided that Narbona was wrong, that these "New Men" were no different from the Spanish and Mexicans before them, or at least that their differences were of no consequence to the patterns of Navajo life. The conquerors had bigger guns, to be sure, and better organization. But the Americans with their cumbersome equipment and comical uniforms were powerless to stop the fleet raiders. The soldiers couldn't successfully pursue the Navajo horsemen into their mountain hideouts; in most cases the Americans couldn't even find Navajo warriors, let alone punish them.

The Navajos had completely ignored the treaty Alexander Doniphan had concluded at Bear Springs in 1846. Agent Calhoun believed that the Navajos and other "wild Indians of this country have been so much more successful in their robberies since General Kearny took possession of the country that they do not believe we have the power to chastise them." Then Calhoun slyly posed the question: "Is it not time to enlighten them on this subject?"

Apparently it was. Leading this ambitious expedition into Navajo country was the new military governor of New Mexico, a career soldier with the impeccably American name of John Washington. Colonel Washington had arrived in Santa Fe in October, fresh from Monterey, California, where he had been briefly posted. Fifty-three years old, he was a severe Virginian with a taut mouth and wispy eyebrows that sketched across the prominent forehead of his tall, thin face. In the one oil portrait that remains of him, Washington's complexion appears exceedingly fair, and his pale eyes have a quality of hard and frosty perceptiveness. A West Pointer with advanced training as an artilleryman, Washington had fought the Seminoles in Florida, participated in the forced removal of the Cherokee to Oklahoma, and recently won commendations for valor in the Mexican War at the decisive Battle of Buena Vista. He had briefly served as military governor of Saltillo. Little is known about Washington's personality, but he was a seasoned soldier with a sober disposition. In his military correspondence he was given to making stern pronouncements in an incongruously stately English penned in his delicate hand.

❈

The primary purpose of Washington's Navajo expedition was military in nature: to impress the Diné people with the reach and might of the American army, to punish them for their continuing raids, to recover stolen livestock and Mexican slaves, and, if possible, to compel the Navajos to sign a lasting treaty. As he starkly put it in one letter, Washington believed that ultimately the Navajo must learn to "cultivate the earth for an honest livelihood, or be destroyed." He insisted that this tribe of nomadic herders and horsemen would have to settle down in permanent villages and become sedentary farmers, much like the Pueblo Indians. But before that goal could be accomplished, Washington wrote, the Navajos must "become acquainted with our national strength."

Colonel Washington was appalled and frustrated by the spring rampages of the Navajos, and in his army correspondence one can detect his steadily rising ire. "Within the last three weeks," he reported in July, "inhabitants have been murdered, and a considerable quantity of their stock run off. From their numbers and formidable character, greatly increased exertions have become necessary to suppress them." Agent James Calhoun, in a letter to Indian Affairs superiors, wrote that Colonel Washington was determined not to "conciliate the tribes who have caused the recent troubles in this territory. The Indians, presuming upon their knowledge of safe retreats in the mountains, and our entire ignorance of all avenues, are not to be subjected to just restraints until they are properly chastised."

And so the chastisement would begin in earnest. Most of Washington's troops were Missourians, some of the same young volunteers who had left Fort Leavenworth three summers earlier with General Kearny. The Missourians were toughened soldiers now, having marched several thousand miles without respite, and having tasted battle in the thorny chaparrals of Mexico, where they were sent after the conquest of Santa Fe. Schooled by experience rather than any formal training, and still wearing the threadbare gray trousers and blue crush caps they had started out with, this tatterdemalion army of volunteers was, despite all appearances, hardened, disciplined, and skilled. Plowboys had become men—wiser, more cautious, less impressionable. They were proud of their wanderings, and liked to compare their foot slog through hostile country to the march of Xenophon's Ten Thousand Greeks following the Peloponnesian War. Five hundred of the Missourians had returned to Santa Fe in October, marching from Mexico back up the Camino Real, and then into California, and finally, with Colonel Washington, marching for seventy-seven days across the country *back* to New Mexico—yet another journey of a thousand miles to add to their raft of adventures. Several months later, when Col. Washington proposed this march into Navajo country, the expedition must have sounded to them like a mere stroll.

Now on this vivid August morning, as breakfast fires began to issue a low carbon haze over the compounds of Santa Fe, Washington's

men headed west toward the Jemez with four companies of regular infantry, most of whom carried Model 1841 muzzle-loading percussion-
lock rifles. Hundreds of horses and pack mules were burdened with
wooden ammunition chests and all manner of military supplies,
which included linen tents, scores of oil lanterns, medical equipment,
and enough rations to feed five hundred men for a month. Astride his
horse, Colonel Washington wore a long blue jacket and a white cloth
belt set with a gleaming brass buckle, his crisp uniform trimmed in
gold braid. Traveling with Washington and his Missourians were several high-ranking civilian officials, including Indian Agent James Calhoun, who would soon become governor of New Mexico Territory.
The expedition was further reinforced with several companies of
Mexican volunteers and mounted militia, and fifty-five Pueblo Indians who had been selected to serve as guides, picket guards, and
scouts. In his considerable arsenal, Colonel Washington had three
mountain howitzers and one six-pound field gun, the formidable,
bronze-barreled pieces of rolling artillery widely known by Indians as
"thunderwagons."

As the August sun eased over the Sangre de Cristo Mountains to
warm their backs, Washington's men followed the westering course
of the Santa Fe River past the barrio of Agua Fria. The thunderwagons creaked behind them, pulled by straining teams of mules.

⊠

Although it was chiefly a military campaign, Washington's expedition
had a secondary and ultimately far more significant purpose: to survey and explore the Navajo terrain and to piece together its first reliable map. In 1849, Navajo country was terra incognita. Only small
swaths around its edges were known—and they were "known" only
in the heads of a few old traders and trappers who had passed
through in their desultory wanderings, but had rarely written anything down. The Spanish had led punitive raids into Navajo lands, but
had not bothered with making detailed or accurate maps. The Navajo
country was a trackless world as big as New England, with its own
snowy mountain ranges and great drainages, its own nomenclature

and quirks of geology. Because it was so vast and so unknown, many legends had welled up around it over the centuries, of hideous monsters, of beautiful temples and impregnable citadels. Like the people who populated it, Navajo country remained a tantalizing mystery to the United States government, a question mark in a void on a map that did not yet exist.

And so a young West Pointer named James Hervey Simpson, a member of the U.S. Corps of Topographical Engineers, was assigned to Washington's party. Simpson's task was considerable: to map and measure every slow inch of a monthlong reconnaissance. Leaving Santa Fe with his barometers and sextants and viameters, Simpson was to puncture a world that had for centuries been shrouded in mist—to affix miles and temperatures, take soil samples and animal specimens, and generally fill in the vast blanks in the nation's understanding of the strange kingdom it had (on paper, at least) conquered. Simpson was also expected to keep a thorough daily log of the journey; the extraordinary document he would write longhand in pen and ink, *Navaho Expedition: Journal of a Military Reconnaissance*, would become one of the classics of Western exploration literature.

First Lt. James Simpson was a hirsute gnome of a fellow— "dismayingly mousy-looking" in the words of one historian. A devout Episcopalian, Simpson could be, for a young man of thirty-six years, an annoying fuddy-duddy. He had been a child prodigy, entering West Point from his native New Jersey at the age of fifteen. From early on he showed an engineering sensibility and spent much of his young army career undertaking drainage projects in the Florida Everglades and then working on lighthouses and harbor improvements in remote corners of the Great Lakes. Before coming to Santa Fe, he had never been west of the Missouri, and the East was where he preferred to stay. He absolutely hated the Southwest—hated the "nauseating" food, the "nakedness" of the long brown vistas, the untidiness of the Mexican villages, and the fine grit that seemed to work its way into everything. He wrote that the "sickening-colored aspect" of the New Mexico terrain gave him "a sensation of loathing." Perhaps it was because he'd had to leave his new bride back in Buffalo, but throughout Simpson's observations, a distinct whine of petulance is heard.

And yet behind all this fussiness, one is struck by the deepening intensity of Lieutenant Simpson's interest, his slow-blooming fascination over an utterly foreign landscape and its equally foreign inhabitants. In spite of himself, Simpson is amazed by everything he claims to detest—the hard-baked geology, the desert flora and fauna, the odd customs of the people. The more bizarre the country becomes, the more Simpson seems to long for his familiar lighthouses back on the Great Lakes—and yet, at the same time, the more animated his prose becomes. Simpson would later enjoy an eminent career as an army engineer, eventually becoming a brevet general, but the rest of his life story, according to a sympathetic biographer, "frankly makes dull reading." The New Mexico Territory was what Simpson hated most, and yet New Mexico, in the late summer of 1849, was the place where he made his lasting mark.

⊠

Simpson's daunting task was made much easier by the presence of two first-rate explorers who happened to be in Santa Fe when the expedition was getting under way and happily signed on for the ride. The multitalented Richard and Edward Kern were two brothers from a large, prominent family back in Philadelphia. Edward—or "Ned," as he was known—was an expedition artist and topographer whose life had already intersected with the history of westward expansion. Ned had accompanied John Fremont and Kit Carson on Fremont's third exploratory. Later, as a temporary commander of a fort near Sacramento, Kern had played a role in rescuing survivors of the Donner Party after their disastrous sojourn in the Sierra Nevada snowdrifts during the winter of 1846–47.

Ned Kern was a tall, lanky man of twenty-five, with curly red hair and a mercurial temperament to match. In photographs, his face appears drawn and melancholy, but he had a sly sense of humor that expressed itself in endless puns and practical jokes. Ned was an epileptic, and perhaps because of his medical predicament he seemed to find solace in the quiet of his western travels, "away from civilization and brandy," as he put it. Ned Kern seemed happiest when he was in the wilderness, with his lead pencils and his watercolor tins, his transits and chronometers, closely documenting his experiences. At a time when field photography was in its infancy, expedition artists still held great importance; Kern's illustrations, printed in Fremont's reports and in popular journals, provided the reading public with some of the very first images of the American West.

Richard Kern, the older of the two bachelor brothers, was also an artist of note from Philadelphia. Influenced by the Hudson River School of painting, Richard ("Dick," as he was nearly always called) had taught drawing at the prestigious Franklin Institute, and he'd had a number of important exhibitions of his work. Dick Kern also had a scientific cast of mind. An amateur botanist and ornithologist, he had done numerous illustrations for technical and scientific journals, a meticulous skill that had won him membership in the exclusive Philadelphia Academy of Natural Sciences. He was heavier-set than Ned, with long, swept-back hair, a thick beard, and a rogue's smile that was infectious. Dick Kern wasn't much for hygiene or personal tidiness—a friend from Philadelphia sent him a comb by mail to New Mexico, acknowledging Kern's "antipathy to its use" but trusting that "it may gain you favor in the eyes of the senoritas." On his travels, Kern always brought along his flute and liked to drink whiskey. He once described his chief preoccupations as "the library, the festive board, the music room, the rambling study, the love of nature, and the gallery."

One of the weirder projects that Dick Kern wanted to pursue while he was out west was to collect Indian skulls. Back in Philadelphia he was good friends with Dr. Samuel George Morton, an anatomy professor and an eminent physical anthropologist who was among the nation's leading scientists. In his 1839 book *Crania Americana*, Dr. Morton had argued that American Indians constituted a distinct race and that their "aptitude for civilization" was "of a decidedly inferior cast when compared with those of the Caucasian and Mongolian races."

To prove his point, he had been collecting and comparing the crania of Native Americans for many years, often obtaining his specimens by grave-robbing. Although Dr. Morton had amassed more than four hundred skulls from tribes all over the country, his collection had conspicuous gaps: He did not own any examples from the newly conquered Southwest. Dr. Morton had been a generous supporter of Kern at the Philadelphia Academy of Natural Sciences, and he had often invited the young artist to the salon he held every Sunday afternoon at his house. Perhaps it was at one of these convivial sessions that Kern promised his patron that he would bring back a few choice skulls to add to his growing boneyard.

Unlike Lt. James Simpson, Richard Kern loved New Mexico. He delighted in painting its diaphanous horizons, its unexpectedly intense colors, and, in his words, its "mountains high and bold." But as someone who came from a well-to-do family back east, he was dismayed by the prevailing poverty. Often in his picturesque landscapes, whether rendered in oil or washes or pencil, he turned his gaze away from the decrepitude of the villages. "In all New Mexican towns," he wrote, "the distant view is the best, as it swallows all the dirt and misery."

§

The Kern brothers had been holed up in Taos for the summer of 1849, living in a stable and recovering from an ordeal in the mountains that had nearly killed them. Fremont's "fourth expedition," as the ill-fated mission was known, was a wintertime probe into the San Juan Mountains, the craggy range in what is now southern Colorado. The Fremont expedition was a debacle of the first order—"one of the most harebrained exploring expeditions ever undertaken in this country," in the words of one prominent Southwest historian.

The mission was conceived in part as a way to rehabilitate Fremont's tarnished career. In California two years earlier, Stephen Watts Kearny's quarrel with Fremont had escalated into a full-blown standoff. Refusing to recognize Kearny's higher authority and turn the California governorship over to him as ordered, Fremont flagrantly disobeyed the chain of army command—he even challenged one of Kearny's officers to a duel. Finally losing all patience with his subordinate's intransigence, Kearny arrested Fremont and dragged him in irons to Washington, D.C., to stand trial for "mutiny, disobedience, and conduct prejudicial to military discipline." The trial was a feeding frenzy for the media and a political melodrama of the first order. Senator Benton roared his displeasure at the whole affair, arguing that his son-in-law had been unfairly caught in the crossfire of an interservice rivalry between a jealous army and a jealous navy. In the end, Fremont was convicted on all three counts. Heeding the court's recommendation for a lenient sentence, however, President Polk ordered Fremont to return to army service. Fremont refused. Humiliated, depressed, bitter, and in poor health, he resigned in a huff and went on a damage-control offensive to restore his good name.

General Kearny, meanwhile, returned to the front, serving in Veracruz and then ably holding the post of military governor of Mexico City, which the United States occupied in the last lurching months of the war. But Kearny contracted yellow fever—or the *vomito*, as it was more graphically known in Mexico—and soon returned to Missouri to convalesce at home with his pregnant wife, Mary, and their growing family. There is evidence that Fremont, still stewing over his court-martial, visited Kearny in St. Louis with the intention of dueling him, only to find the general on his deathbed. It is not known whether Kearny was dying of the fever itself or complications arising from it, but if it was the former, then Kearny suffered an excruciating death. The whites of his eyes would have turned yellow, his skin a strange luminous gold, and in his last hours he would have bled from his eyes and gums and thrown up a black vomit caused by massive internal hemorrhaging.

Kearny, only fifty-four years old and having recently been promoted to major general, passed away on October 31, 1848, at the Missouri country home of his close friend Meriwether Clark. Only a few weeks earlier, Mary had given birth to their last child, a son named Stephen Watts Kearny.

With his nemesis freshly in the ground, Fremont then hatched his plan for a Fourth Expedition. Goaded as always by Benton, Fremont was determined to find a route across the Rocky Mountains for a transcontinental railway that would connect St. Louis to the Pacific. The only way to demonstrate that such a route was feasible, Fremont insisted, was to traverse it in the dead of winter. He confidently proclaimed that he would find a suitable pass and thus prove to skeptics that the Rocky Mountain snows did not pose an insurmountable obstacle for a railroad.

Fremont's project was fueled by pure hubris; he intended to follow the 39th parallel up and over the serrated San Juan Mountains, which rose more than fourteen thousand feet and were frequently lashed by brutal winter storms. He ignored the large chunks of ice floating in the Arkansas River as he assembled his expedition at Bent's Fort that fall. In November, with thirty-three men in his party, Fremont pressed on toward the San Luis Valley and the snowy San Juan Mountains. By all signs—including the solemn prognostications of friendly tribes they encountered—the winter of 1848 was shaping up to be unusually bitter. Fremont scarcely noticed.

For his guide he had wanted Carson, but instead hired a veteran trapper named Bill Williams, a sixty-two-year-old mountain man who was recovering from a recent Indian fight that had left him with a gunshot wound in the arm. Williams was a likeable crank with vast experience in the Rockies. A former itinerant Methodist preacher legendary for his gambling and drinking binges and his strange and sometimes gruesome eating habits (he especially liked to dine on the raw leg of a fetal calf), Williams claimed to know "every inch" of the San Juans, "better than Fremont knows his own garden." He was a friend of Carson; the two had ridden thousands of miles together during their trapping days. According to one contemporary, Williams had an "old coon's face that was sharp and thin," and he spoke in a "whining voice that left the hearer in doubt whether he was laughing or crying." His rifle, it was said, "cracked away merrily, and never spoke in vain." Williams was skinny as a rail and his red beard glistened with grease. He had an odd habit of mumbling to himself as he bounced along the trail.

Although Williams's intimate knowledge of the mountains could not be gainsaid—indeed, a number of peaks and streams in the

Rockies bore his name—some contemporaries suggested that this outrageous man at times lacked the keen judgment and instinctual caution of Kit Carson. Carson seemed to have an uncanny sixth sense for how to avoid calamity. On this ill-fated mission, he would be sorely missed.

Ned and Dick Kern, caught up in Fremont's peculiar charisma, had happily signed on as expeditionary cartographer and artist, respectively. They had even cajoled their brother Ben, a respected Philadelphia physician, to join them as the expedition's medical doctor. Trusting Fremont, the three Kern brothers failed to see the folly of the expedition for several weeks as they marched headlong into the formidable drifts of the Rockies. But then the Kerns began to entertain doubts. Of Fremont's reckless drive, Dick Kern would later write: "With willfully blind eyes of rashness and self-conceit and confidence, he pushed on." As November slid into December, the snows kept coming. For weeks the party could not budge. "We all looked like Old Winter," Dick wrote. "Icicles an inch long were pendant from our moustache and beard." One night Ned's socks froze so completely that they had to be shaved off his legs.

By late December their predicament turned truly desperate. Fremont's starving mules took to eating one another's manes and leather bridles and then collapsed in the impenetrable drifts. The men ate nothing but their dying pack animals and waited in vain for the weather to break. Ben Kern wrote in his diary that on the morning of December 18, he awoke beneath eight inches of fresh snow piled on his bedroll. "I told Dick the expedition was destroyed," Ben noted, "and if we all got to some settlement with our lives we would be doing well." Finally even Fremont saw that the expedition was hopeless, but by then it was nearly too late. His men had begun to freeze to death, and, with the mules all eaten, they listlessly foraged for odd scraps of protein. Dick Kern jotted in his diary, "Too weak to move. We looked for muscles [sic] & snails & earth worms—found none." Ned Kern later recalled "gradually sinking into a sleep . . . I felt happy and contented sitting nearly all day by the fire in a kind of stupor . . . careless of when my time would come—for I was expecting it and in anticipation of it had written and closed all my business." By the time they were found by a rescue party hastily organized by Kit Carson and other citizens from Taos, eleven of Fremont's thirty-three expeditioners had died, either of starvation or exposure. As in the Donner tragedy, several of the deceased were almost certainly eaten.

The twenty-two frostbitten survivors straggled back to Taos, where some of them stayed at Kit Carson's home. Fremont himself was so exhausted that he had to be carried inside his former guide's house. Carson and Josefa nursed Fremont back to health, plying him with hot chocolate and listening to the shocking story of his disaster in the mountains. The ever-loyal Carson seemed constitutionally incapable of judging his former commander, nor was he disposed to second-guess the decisions of his old friend Bill Williams. But Carson did later suggest, with characteristic wryness, that Williams, with his fiercely strange eating habits, was not a man likely to shy from cannibalism. "In starving times," Carson said, "no man ever walked in front of Bill Williams."

Fremont, however, refused to accept any responsibility for the fiasco, or for the deaths of the eleven men he had led into the mountains—indeed, his letters show not a trace of remorse. Instead, he placed the blame entirely on Williams, while calling many of the subordinate members of the expedition cowards and incompetents. Gathering his energies and his narcissistic pride, Fremont decided to strike out for California using the tried-and-true southern route, along the Gila River to the Colorado—the same route General Kearny and Kit Carson had used in 1846. There would be no railroad through the San Juans; the eventual route would have to pass much farther south.

The three Kern brothers begged off. They'd had enough of John Charles Fremont and his vainglory. They waited in Taos for the Rocky Mountain snowpack to melt. Then, in March, Ben Kern and Bill Williams returned to the San Juan Mountains to recover a cache of valuable paraphernalia they had left behind not far from the frozen headwaters of the Rio Grande—medical equipment, topographical instruments, art supplies, and the like. The two men succeeded in finding their cache, but then were set upon by bandits. The mystery was not entirely solved, but evidence suggests that they were murdered by Ute Indians, among whom some articles of the expedition's equipment were later discovered. According to one account, Williams was "found sitting bolt upright against a tree, frozen stiff and half covered" in snow with a "Ute bullet through his body." Ben Kern's corpse was never recovered.

Still shocked by their brother's probable murder—and despising John Fremont more than ever—Ned and Dick Kern recuperated in Taos, taking lodging for a time in "a suite of rooms that you would say would make capital stabling," Ned wrote in a letter to his sister back in Philadelphia. "But," he reasoned, " 'tis among the best in town, and sociable too for we sometimes receive visits from the Donkeys." In early summer the two destitute brothers walked the seventy miles down to Santa Fe to look for work. Ned described Santa Fe as "a tawny adobe town with a few green trees, set in a half-circle of carnelian-colored hills, that and no more," but he and Dick set to work sketching the strange capital and its six Catholic churches. As luck would have it, the Kerns immediately fell in with Lieutenant Simpson, who employed them as draftsmen and scientific illustrators. Soon they found themselves hired on for another expedition into the wilderness—one on which they hoped the stars this time would smile.

◙

Colonel Washington and his men continued marching west along the Santa Fe River, then turned south, dropping steadily into the broad valley of the Rio Grande. The pack animals were skittish and ornery, as they often were when they first hit the trail. "Many of the mules being wild, much trouble ensued," Dick Kern jotted in his journal. The expeditioners crossed the dry, sandy bed of the Rio Galisteo and established camp at Santo Domingo Pueblo, an old settlement of about eight hundred Indians.

Dick Kern was struck by how "beautiful and fertile" the Rio Grande Valley was around Santo Domingo. "It is harvest time," he noted, "and the Indians are carrying their wheat in bundles on their heads to the thrashing place and singing their wild songs." The Indians at Santo Domingo were friendly to the soldiers and eagerly took them in. Lieutenant Simpson watched a pueblo woman making a kind of tortilla, and she offered him one to eat. Put off by the "perspiration rolling from her face in streams," the fastidious eater reluctantly tasted the freshly baked flat bread. "Although I was exceedingly hungry," he wrote, "it did not fail to leave at the stomach a sensation of nausea."

Washington's men left Santo Domingo the next day and forded the muddy Rio Grande, in which two of their supply wagons became deeply mired. They continued on for twenty-six miles, bearing northwest, through dry country "utterly worthless for cultivation" in Simpson's estimation, until they came to another Indian settlement known as Jemez Pueblo. Lieutenant Simpson was not much impressed with the place. He noted the "unsightly appearance" of the settlement, with its "ragged-looking goat enclosures." The Roman Catholic church was a sagging adobe affair that "was evidently wasting away under the combined influence of neglect and moisture." Inside the musty church flitting and diving from the rafters were innumerable swallows that "seemed to be perfectly at home." Cryptically, a human skull and a pile of bones were placed beside the pulpit. Simpson was impressed, however, by a large painting hanging on the back wall of the chancel, a beatific image depicting San Diego bearing the cross. "At present it is considerably defaced, but the touches of a genuine artist are yet visible upon it," Simpson wrote. "None but a true son of the muse could have thrown into the countenance the expression of beautiful sadness with which it is radiant."

All around Jemez Pueblo, the grounds were covered in orchards of apricot and peach, and along the Jemez River were "patches of good corn and wheat." A few miles from camp Simpson spotted a gray wolf "shying off very reluctantly from us." Curiously, not far from the pueblo, strung along the river, were dozens of empty houses and compounds, even an abandoned copper smelting furnace. According to Simpson's guide, these ruined adobe buildings were "once inhab-

ited by Mexicans who had deserted them from fear of the Navahos."
Less than a month earlier a Catholic pastor, Vicente Garcia, had been
murdered by Navajo raiders.

The precariousness of life here was all too apparent. Jemez was
situated on the front lines of the Navajo wars; over the centuries the
vulnerable pueblo had suffered a disproportionate share of devasta-
tion at the hands of the Navajo raiders. During the latter part of the
sixteenth century, the Navajo had nearly wiped out the Jemez population, and sometime in the seventeenth century a large number of Jemez fled the region altogether, resettling in a safer location many
miles away. Other Jemez Indians joined forces with or were absorbed
by the Navajo and eventually intermarried with them, their offspring
forming the nucleus of a distinct Navajo clan, the *ma-ii deeshgiizhnii*.

Colonel Washington made camp just north of the pueblo. It being
the beginning of harvest season, the Jemez people were celebrating
the Green Corn Dance, and many of Washington's men wandered
over from camp to watch the ceremony from the rooftop of one of
the dwellings. In his journal, Simpson described the movements of
the dancers in minute detail—their feathered headdresses, their
gourd rattles, their costumes of turtle shell, antelope feet, and fox
skin. But, for all its energy and sense of spectacle, the lieutenant was
not much impressed by the Jemez dance, either. "The movements in
the dance," he sniffed, "differed but slightly from those of Indians
generally."

The governor of Jemez, whose name was Hosta, gave Simpson a
tour of the pueblo and led him down into one of its ceremonial kivas, a dark, round chamber without windows entered from the
smokehole in the roof. The kiva's walls were painted with represen-
tations of turkeys, deer, foxes, and wolves. The two men fell into a
conversation about the Jemez religion. Hosta made it clear that his
people had held on to their ancient beliefs even while adopting the
tenets of Roman Catholicism—"which," Simpson noted, "he says has
been forced upon them, and which they do not understand."

Hosta said that both the Jemez and Pecos people believed they
were the direct descendants of Montezuma and the Aztecs, and

that one day they would be delivered from their enemies, the Spanish and the Navajos, and restored to their former glory "by a people who would come from the East." The Jemez Indians, Hosta added, were "beginning to believe that that people had come"—in the form of General Kearny and the Americans. Perhaps it was in part because of flatteries such as these, but Hosta had made quite an impression on Simpson and others in Washington's party. The pueblo chief was invited to accompany Washington's expedition, and he was only too glad to participate in an incursion into the heart of his people's enemy, the Navajo. Before they left Jemez, Dick Kern persuaded Hosta to stand in full warrior regalia for a watercolor portrait. "Hosta," Simpson concluded, "is one of the finest-looking and most intelligent Pueblo Indians I have seen, and on account of his vivacity and offhand graciousness, is quite a favorite among us."

As they left the pueblo behind on the cool morning of August 22, the four hundred men of Washington's expedition pushed into the harsh and beautiful world that sprawled weirdly before them on the back side of the Jemez volcano. The supply wagons could go no farther, the road having petered out in a broiled maze of buttes and gulchy badlands and intervening alkali flats studded with monoliths of rock that suggested the shapes of animals and mythic creatures. It was a fantastical country whose patterns the Americans found more and more difficult to grasp as they worked their way slowly westward.

In his journal, Simpson struggled to find a vocabulary to describe this strange enveloping landscape. Several times he called it "a broken country." Often he resorted to the geological argot of his day, seeming to take comfort in identifying "scoriaceous deposits," "friable sandstones," and "argillaceous rocks burnt to different degrees of calcination." Other times he lapsed into biblical allusions, citing verses from Isaiah and Psalms about the salty desiccation of the Holy Land and suggesting at one point that "the curse of barrenness may be chargeable to the wickedness of the people who inhabit it." Much of this land, he proclaimed, was "a barren waste."

Yet even Simpson was not always entirely immune to the country's charms. He loved its weather, which was favorable to marching—hot and dry in the days, crisp and cool in the star-filled nights, with occasional "fine showers of rain" to clarify the dusty afternoons. Simpson had his first puzzling encounter with petrified wood—"Do not these petrifactions show that this country was once better timbered than it is now?" One morning he was delighted to be entertained by a hummingbird that buzzed into his tent "where it lit for a moment within a foot or two of my person and then disappeared, not to be seen again." Simpson even allowed himself a moment of uncharacteristic poetry. On the morning of August 25, shortly after breaking camp, he looked back with his horizon glass and caught a majestic glimpse of Cabezon Peak, a stand-alone plug of volcanic rock towering two thousand feet over the rolling floor of the Puerco Valley. He wrote, "As the morning sun threw its golden light upon its eastern slope, leaving all the other portions in a softened twilight shadow, I thought I had never seen anything more beautiful and grand."

Inspired by the same vista, Dick Kern did a wash drawing of Cabezon Peak, with the dawn waxing over its fluted shaft. The Navajos, who had been living around Cabezon Peak for centuries, called it Black Rock Coming Down and believed it was the ossified head of an enormous evil giant, Yeitso, chief of the Enemy Gods, whom the great warrior Monster Slayer decapitated in a battle described in Navajo creation stories.

The expedition struck the Rio Puerco, Simpson finding that "rio" was too charitable a term, there being almost no water in it other than a few pools "here and there—the fluid a greenish, sickening color and brackish to the taste." The Puerco's bottom was choked with gumbo mud, and at one point during the crossing a mule bearing a heavy mountain howitzer lost its footing and tumbled into the streambed. The groaning animal fell on its back with its legs trundling helplessly in the air like a capsized beetle, "a scene," Simpson wrote, "that partook both of the painful and ludi-crous."

⊠

After two more days of slow, steady marching, Washington's men crossed the Continental Divide. On August 26 they came to the Chaco Wash and soon found themselves in the presence of what Simpson called a "conspicuous ruin." The Pueblo Indians serving as guides had different words for it. The Pueblo of Montezuma, one of them called it. Another called it the Pueblo of the Rats. In the end, Simpson would call it the Pueblo Pintado, or "Painted Village."

Pintado was the easternmost of the nine "great houses" of Chaco Canyon, the most magnificent prehistoric ruins in the American West. It was apparently not Colonel Washington's conscious inten-tion to route his expedition through this extraordinary place, but since he did, Simpson and the Kern brothers were afforded a great op-portunity. They would be the first Americans to describe and survey the sprawling stone remains of the vanished Anasazi civilization that thrived here around A.D. 1000.

With "high expectations," Simpson, Dick Kern, and a small party of Mexican escorts took off to examine the ruins. This was a once-in-a-lifetime treat for trained surveyors, and a welcome change from the drearier requirements of a military expedition. But they knew they didn't have much time. Washington's troops were moving on, and they would not wait for Simpson and his party to catch up with them. They could not forget that they were in dangerous Navajo country now, and did not want to become separated by too many miles from the protection of the army. And yet they couldn't help themselves; a ruined civilization was too enticing to pass up.

So Simpson and his team worked in a fast fury—taking measure-ments, drawing sketches, collecting artifacts, examining rock art, making excavations, taking compass and astronomical readings. They kept themselves occupied for three long days, moving from one great ruin to another, each structure seemingly larger and more splendid than the last. The vast stone and timber great houses were semicircular, multistoried pueblos, with hundreds of rooms, some of which were "in an almost perfect state of preservation." Most of these pueblos were built on the north side of the wash, back up against the high sandstone wall of the canyon. The largest of all the structures, Pueblo Bonito, had more than seven hundred rooms, stood four stories high, and was oriented almost perfectly along a north-south axis, within fifteen minutes of true north. Simpson marveled at these structures, noting "the grandeur of their design and superiority of their workmanship." They represented, he thought, "a condition of architectural excellence beyond the power of the Indians or New Mexicans of the present day to exhibit."

Dick Kern was having the time of his life, frantically painting watercolors and dashing off wash drawings until the last lumen of light had faded in the sky. He loved being away from the hubbub of the army and having this desolate place to himself, camping among the sagging ramparts. He did a watercolor rendering that offered his best guess of what one of these apartment complexes must have looked like in its day. "The wolfe and lizard and hare are the only inhabitants," Kern wrote in his diary, "and the bright wild flowers fill the open court and halls. Who built them no one knows. . . . But there can be no doubt of their having been built by a race living here in long past ages—Its style is so different from any thing Spanish." He and Lieutenant Simpson could not have been happier—they were boys romping through an enchanted world. They mapped the floor plans of nearly every major structure in the canyon and chiseled their names into the plaster wall of one of the chambers at Pueblo Bonito.

But Simpson realized that they could not do justice to this maze of monuments. Fearing a Navajo ambush, Simpson finally gave the order to pack up the instruments and field books and hastily return to the army. "Had time permitted," he wrote, "we would gladly have remained longer to dig among the rubbish of the past; but the troops having already got some miles in advance of us, we were reluctantly obliged to quit." Circumstances, he concluded, would "not permit us to satisfy our minds."

⌷

Next to nothing was known about the Anasazi at the time of the Washington expedition, and Lieutenant Simpson had almost no information to draw on as he puzzled over these fabulous ruins. Hosta, the Jemez chief, said that the Chaco cities had been built by his ancestor, the Aztec emperor Montezuma, repeating a widely held myth that Simpson seems to have found credible. But in fact, the Chacoans were not directly related to the Aztec civilization, although they almost certainly traded with their predecessors in MesoAmerica. The Chacoans began their rise to prominence around A.D. 950, well before the Aztec ascendancy in central Mexico. Much of their power and affluence was apparently based upon their proficiency with working fine turquoise, a stone highly prized throughout the region for ceremonial purposes. Their superlative skill in milling, shaping, and finishing this fragile stone, mined from the Cerrillos Hills near Santa Fe, seems to have generated a great trade that led, in turn, to a massive concentration of wealth.

For a brief period—little more than a century—the people of Chaco Canyon underwent a sudden explosion in the sophistication of their civilization, a cultural boom that has no parallel in North American prehistory. Archaeologists have come to call it the Chaco Phenomenon. Rapidly, the Chaco Anasazi began to centralize their government, intensify their agriculture, and concentrate their population in these so-called "great houses" strung along the canyon. They fashioned elaborate irrigation systems and dams. They built razor-straight highways radiating outward from their capital. On the tops of far-flung mesas they erected "lighthouses" in which they burned signal fires that broadcast messages over hundreds of miles to outlying Anasazi settlements. Their artifacts and rituals grew in beauty and complexity. They cut down thousands of ponderosa pine trees from mountain stands forty miles distant and dragged them here to build their enormous structures. Soon a powerful priesthood developed, and observatories were designed that allowed these Native American druids, with astonishing precision, to follow the movements of the stars and planets.

North America had never seen such a florescence of culture. But then around A.D. 1150, just as quickly as they had burst upon the scene, the Chacoan culture ebbed. The agent of their demise seems to have been an environmental collapse brought on, in part, by two devastating droughts in 1085 and 1095, and in part by the impact of a dense population living on a marginal desert landscape. Their expansion had been predicated on a kind of meteorological accident; they had been living in a hundred-year cycle of aberrant wetness, and during that brief window the Anasazi in Chaco Canyon had overfarmed, overhunted, and overlogged. In only a few generations their deforested land became eroded, the topsoil depleted, the drainages choked with salt and silt. The river on which they depended for corn and beans dried up. A third major drought, beginning around 1129, delivered the final blow.

This environmental upheaval led, predictably enough, to a social upheaval. In its death agonies, Chaco Canyon was not a pleasant place. People began to starve. They turned their great houses into fortresses, erecting walls, barricading the first-floor windows, retreating to higher stories at night, pulling up their ladders at the slightest hint of danger. Archaeologists have found evidence of widespread civil unrest, witchcraft, and even ritual cannibalism. Finally, the Chaco Anasazi began to leave in large numbers. In many cases they simply walked away from their great apartment complexes, leaving behind beautiful ornamental pottery, sandals and clothing, and large quantities of dried food neatly stored in granaries.

But the Chacoans did not really "vanish." They wandered all over the Southwest, resettling wherever they could find water and safety. The Pueblo Indians were their direct descendants. Hosta and his Jemez people had Chaco blood, not Aztec blood, coursing in their veins, and so did the dozens of other Pueblo tribes whose settlements formed a loose constellation across the New Mexico Territory—the Zuni, the Hopi, the Acoma, the Taos Indians. The architecture of the modern Pueblos, though not as technically sophisticated, was strikingly similar to that of the Chaco great houses, with their multistoried apartments, retreating terraces, and underground kivas. From

Puebloan rock art to their religious ceremonies to the styles of their pottery, the cultural echoes were clear. The Chaco Anasazi remained alive and well; they had simply undergone a diaspora of sorts. In spreading out and regerminating in smaller hunkered settlements, the descendants of the Anasazi learned the final cautionary lesson of Chaco Canyon: the peril of density in the face of the desert. In a meager landscape, civilization must scatter.

Interestingly, about the same time that the Chaco Phenomenon was imploding, the Navajo began to move into the region. For centuries they had been slowly pushing southward from Alaska and northwestern Canada, working their way down the spine of the Rockies. These nomadic warriors were the epitome of a scattered civilization. Supple, adaptive, refusing to tie themselves down to any one place or way of life, they moved freely with the seasons, following the game or their own whimsy.

When the first Navajo saw the ruins at Chaco Canyon, they must have been stunned. Everything about Chaco represented the antithesis of their own life. The Navajo must have instantly recognized that Chaco culture had been advanced beyond anything they had ever seen. But they also intuitively understood that something terrible had happened here, that this ghost city contained the seeds of destruction. They refused to go into the great houses, believing they were places of evil and death. They would never live this way—in cities, clustered in permanent buildings, trapped in a close environment. They would always leave themselves an out.

The timeline is murky, but it is possible that there was some overlap in the two cultures—that is, that the Navajos flooded in just as the Anasazi were leaving, and that for a brief time they had direct dealings with one another. It's also possible that the Navajo's arrival hastened the unraveling of Chaco culture—either through direct warfare or competition for resources. The word *anasazi*, in fact, is a Navajo word, meaning "ancestors of our enemies," and it's a term modern-day Pueblo Indians understandably detest (they prefer the designation "ancestral Puebloans"). Whatever the nature of their relationship, the Navajo clearly filled the void left by the Anasazi departure. They would remain masters of this region, living their roving kind of life in the midst of these crumbling rock cities, incorporating stories about the ruins into their own mythology, but always leaving them alone.

By the time Simpson and Dick Kern wandered through, the Navajo had been the de facto custodians of Chaco Canyon for at least five hundred years. Much of our early understanding of Chaco would be refracted through a Navajo point of view. The word *chaco* is a Spanish approximation of the Navajo *tsekho*—meaning "canyon," or literally, "an opening in the rock." And even as Simpson had been examining the ruins with his men, Navajo scouts had been watching him from afar, puzzling over his intentions, and possibly wondering whether this bewhiskered little man was a witch.

Chapter 32   THE FINEST HEAD
I EVER SAW

Colonel Washington's troops were camped in a bleak, windy dust-bowl near a spot called Badger Springs. The views were sweeping— to the north, the mighty Shiprock could be seen clawing at the sky—but this place was not much of a campsite. They found no wood to burn other than the trunks of a few prickly shrubs. The engineers discovered that they could obtain a little water by digging deep pits in the ground, but it was highly alkaline and had, according to Dick Kern, "very much the taste of a 'bad egg.' " Because Colonel Washington could find no grass or any other suitable forage for his horses and mules, he had earlier in the day ordered his men to cut the green stunted corn from a nearby Navajo field.

Understandably, the Navajos who lived in the vicinity interpreted the theft and trampling of their cornfields as a hostile action. Soon a group of them entered the camp to lodge a complaint with Washington. With them, they brought fifteen horses and mules and a number of sheep to deliver up to the army, as Colonel Washington had gotten the word out that his troops were here to demand the return of stolen property. These Navajos were emissaries of Narbona, and much of the livestock had come directly from Narbona's own flocks and herds. Washington accepted the animals, but the Navajos' protest about their cornfields came to nothing. Among the natives streaming into camp were a number of women, who, Simpson noted, "wore blankets, leggings, and moccasins—the blankets being confined about the waist by a girdle." Simpson seemed mildly shocked that these women "bestrode their horses *a la mode des hommes*." One of them, he observed, "had a child at her breast confined on its back to a board, the upper portion canopied by a frame of willow-work to protect its head from the weather."

The next morning, August 30, Washington's army broke camp and made another westward march, this one of about fifteen miles. Kern noted that as they traveled, there were "multitudes of Indians around us," and it was clear they were growing angry and restless. Most were warriors armed with lances and spears and sinew-backed bows. Simpson thought they were "quite a formidable group," noting that their "helmet-shaped caps were set off with bunches of eagle feathers." Some of the warriors, he observed, "were almost naked— one of them entirely so, excepting his breechcloth, his whole person at the same time looking ghastly on account of a kind of whitewash with which he was covered."

By the middle of the day the Navajo numbers had swelled to several hundred, and they were stirring up huge contrails of dust as they rode in the vanguard. Colonel Washington was growing antsy with all these warriors whooping in his midst, and at one point he ordered his artillerymen to remove two mountain howitzers from the backs of the mules and prepare them for firing in the event of an attack. Lieutenant Simpson had a bad feeling about the day, noting that a "dark, portentous cloud" was hovering over one of the peaks in the distant Chuska Range, with "forked lightning darting vividly athwart it." The thunderclouds continued to mount, and it began to pour.

Washington finally had to halt the march and hunker down for a violent hailstorm.

Washington made camp that afternoon on the north fork of Tunicha Creek, on a piece of land littered with Anasazi potsherds. The valley of the nearby Chuska River was rippling with healthy corn, "extensive and luxuriant fields," as Simpson described them, "finer than any I have seen in this country." Although these fields were not irrigated, they took advantage of water that seeped and trickled under the soft soil. The stalks were planted deeply, not in furrows but in dense clumps—a water-conserving method the Navajos had practiced for centuries.

Feasting his eyes on this bountiful crop, Colonel Washington again ordered his foragers to go out and seize corn from the Navajo fields. When it became apparent that the Navajos intended to resist the troops, Washington sent extra soldiers to "enforce the order." He justified stealing the corn by arguing that the Navajos would eventually have to reimburse the U.S. government for the considerable costs of the expedition now mounted against them, a twist of reasoning that only further infuriated the Navajos, who could only stand by and watch as their winter foodstuffs were ravaged.

Tension was building around the camp. Hundreds of angry Navajos, possibly as many as a thousand, now surrounded the bivouac site, galloping their horses this way and that, thronging in agitation. Washington allowed a few representatives to come into camp for a talk. Once assembled, the colonel told them, through his Spanish interpreter, to go out into the countryside and gather as many chiefs as they could find to represent the Chuska region. He said that his army had entered their territory to chastise them for their constant raids and thefts. But he held out that the United States of America would be their friend as long as they were willing to come back tomorrow and sign a peace treaty. The headmen agreed to meet at noon the next day, noting that the aged Narbona would be present. Before they left, Richard Kern overheard one of the thoroughly miffed and confused Navajo headmen asking Colonel Washington—"If we are friends, why did you take our corn? It is hard, but all we can do is submit."

At midday the next day, several hundred Navajos rode over to Washington's camp. As a whole they were, Simpson thought, "gorgeously decked in red, blue, and white, with rifles erect in hand," presenting a "spectacle that was very imposing." From the milling crowd, three elders emerged and introduced themselves by their Spanish names. They were Archuleta, Jose Largo, and, finally, Narbona.

All eyes fell on Narbona, the most famous of the Navajos. Although he was past eighty, Narbona was still a formidable presence. Simpson described him as "quite old and of a very large frame, having a grave and contemplative countenance not unlike, as many of the officers remarked (I hope the comparison will be pardoned), that of President Washington." That day he wore a handsome chieftain's wool blanket, dyed in the bold geometric patterns of the Navajo. Dick and Ned Kern collaborated on a wash drawing of Narbona, giving him an air of solemn dignity.

Narbona was so decrepit with arthritis that he had to be helped down from his horse and carried to the council place. As a sign of goodwill, he told Washington, he was handing over another herd of animals—several hundred in all. He said that he believed in making peace with the New Men, that his own people, the Chuska Navajos, had never made war on the Americans—although it was true that a state of war had long existed with the New Mexicans, and many wrongs had been committed by both sides. He said that as much as he advocated peace, there were young hotheads and thieves (ladrones, he said) in his tribe whose actions could not always be stopped. Narbona also made it clear that he was not a spokesman for the entire Navajo nation, that no man had such authority, that the Navajo people were comprised of many different bands, and that each had its own autonomy and its own territory.

One of the Navajos present was a young man who could safely be called a hothead and, perhaps, a thief. He was Narbona's son-in-law—proud, strapping, dark-complected, known by the Spanish name of Manuelito. A fierce warrior fast ascending to prominence among the

"God in a war-torn country": Brigadier General James Henry Carleton, commander of New Mexico and architect of the Navajo Long Walk.

"Much is expected of you, both here and in Washington": Colonel Kit Carson, field commander of the Navajo campaign.

Odd fellows: A gathering of Masons in the Santa Fe hall, 1865. Carson (center) is seated beside Carleton (right) in front.

"No command should ever again enter it": The great sandstone chasm of Canyon de Chelly.

Masada of the Southwest: During the winter of 1863–64, starving Navajos took refuge atop Fortress Rock, deep within the Canyon de Chelly complex.

"I have nothing to lose but my life": Navajo headman Manuelito, son-in-law of Narbona, was one of the last to surrender to the American army.

"Severity will be the most humane course": A soldier counts Navajo prisoners at the Bosque Redondo reservation.

"We know this land does not like us": Navajo headman Barboncito, whose passionate eloquence may have swayed Sherman to abandon the Bosque Redondo experiment.

"I believe you have told the truth": General William Tecumseh Sherman decided the fate of the Navajo people.

"Compadre, adios": Kit Carson photographed during an 1868 trip to the East, a few months before his death.

"A class of men as antiquated as Ulysses belonging to a dead past": Kit and Josefa Carson grave site in Taos.

The captain of adventure: Cover of *The Fighting Trapper,* published in 1874, one of the scores of "blood and thunder" dime novels starring a largely fictionalized Kit Carson.

Navajos, Manuelito loved and respected his father-in-law, but he was suspicious of Narbona's calls for peace. A youthful rage boiled within him. Manuelito was tall, with a surly face and smoldering dark eyes. He thought Narbona was going too far in appeasing the white man, and he refused to believe that these new conquerors were any match for the Navajo. Astride his horse, Manuelito watched closely and listened as James Calhoun, the Indian Affairs agent, led the discussion, with Colonel Washington at his side.

CALHOUN: Tell them they are lawfully in the jurisdiction of the United States now, and they must respect that jurisdiction.

INTERPRETER: They say they understand it.

CALHOUN: Tell them that after the treaty is made, their friends will be the friends of the United States, and their enemies the enemies of the United States. Are they willing to be at peace with all the friends of the United States?

INTERPRETER: They say they are willing.

Narbona and his two fellow headmen said they could agree to every point proposed by Calhoun and Colonel Washington, except one. Washington insisted that Narbona come with him to the Navajo stronghold of Canyon de Chelly, where he intended to hold an even bigger council, with representatives from the entire Navajo nation. But Narbona refused, disavowing all connection to the Navajos "over the mountain" while also making it clear that he could not undertake such a long journey in his fragile state of health. After Washington pressed the matter, Narbona finally agreed to appoint two younger chiefs to go to Canyon de Chelly in his stead.

The council broke up to everyone's apparent satisfaction, and for a moment matters between the Navajos and the United States of America seemed hopeful. But then one of the New Mexican militiamen spotted a horse among the Navajo warriors that, he insisted, was his. The militiaman was sure of it, he said. The natives had stolen his horse a few months ago, and now he demanded it back. The Navajos did not dispute that the horse had been stolen, but they indicated that it had passed through so many different hands that it was impossible to ascertain the true owner now—and that, in any case, something like a statute of limitations had taken effect. There was a brief scuffle, and charges were shouted back and forth.

When Colonel Washington got wind of what was happening, he sided with the New Mexican's version of events. The colonel demanded that the Navajo hand over the horse. At this the Navajos "demurred," as Simpson described it. Tempers were flaring all around. After all the abstractions lofted by Colonel Washington, negotiations had finally reached a concrete topic that the Navajos understood with clarity and passion: *a horse.* The situation had become a tense standoff.

"Unless the horse is restored," Washington threatened through an interpreter, "you will be fired upon!"

By this point the accused horse thief had taken off for the hills— riding, of course, the very mount at issue. Not knowing what to do, Washington then told the officer of the guard, a Lieutenant Torrez, to seize another horse in reprisal, any horse he fancied. When Torrez moved toward the throng of mounted Navajos to pick out a horse, the Indians sensed immediately what was happening. In a flash they wheeled about and galloped away—"scampering off," Simpson wrote, "at the top of their speed."

At this, Colonel Washington ordered, *"Fire!"*

Shots ripped through the crowd, as army marksmen posted around the perimeter of the council site fired their muzzle-loading rifles. Artillerymen, meanwhile, turned the enormous bronze barrel of the six-pound field gun—the thunderwagon—and in a close triad of concussions, they blasted the field. Then Washington ordered mounted soldiers to pursue the retreating Navajos, but it was impossible to catch them, for they scattered in all directions and disappeared into a distant ravine.

When the dust settled, Colonel Washington found that none of his own men had been hurt, although Simpson noted with much regret that a few mules had been lost in the "hurry-skurry." The field was now empty but for seven Navajo bodies. Some of them were wounded, some of them apparently lifeless.

Upon closer inspection, Washington learned that one of the writhing forms in the grass was none other than Narbona. The great patriarch was sprawled in a pool of blood. Shrapnel from the thunderwagon had apparently sliced into him, and now he had four or five gaping wounds ranging over his crippled body.

A few minutes later, Narbona lay still.

If their leader's death was not insult enough to the Navajos, then what happened next proved to be the final indignity. A New Mexican souvenir hunter walked up to the old man's corpse, leaned down, and raked a sharp knife across his forehead.

In his diary, Dick Kern did not suggest that Narbona had done anything to cause the attack, but neither did he express any moral outrage over the incident, which may have been one of the most decisive events in the history of Navajo relations with the U.S. government. But Kern did admit that he was furious with himself for not having the presence of mind to secure the head of Narbona for his friend and patron back in Philadelphia, the skull researcher Dr. Samuel George Morton.

"He was the chief of the Nation, and had been a wise man and great warrior," he wrote Dr. Morton a year later. "His frame was immense. I should think his height near 6 ft. 6 in. He was near 90 years old when killed. I very much regret that I had not procured Narbona's cranium, as I think he had the finest head I ever saw on an Indian."

Chapter 33   THE DEATH KNOT

The greatest leader of the Navajos had died, but there would be no funeral. The Navajos did not believe in funerals; when someone died, even a great eminence like Narbona, the important thing was to get the spirit on its way to the underworld as expeditiously as possible. People did not have any desire to linger around the body to pay their respects. The immediate family would handle the messy details of disposing of the corpse and dividing Narbona's considerable possessions. For the many thousands of other Navajos who knew Narbona, and the thousands more who knew *of* him, the mourning would be profound, but it would not be public.

Shortly after he was killed by Colonel Washington's troops, Narbona's body was brought back to the constellation of hogans that formed his outfit on the great slope of the Chuska Mountains. (Some Navajo accounts say Narbona did not die immediately from his wounds; that although he was mortally injured by Washington's troops and then scalped, the aged headman somehow remained alive long enough to be brought back home, where he was able to bid his wives and children and grandchildren farewell.) Outside the hogans, the family prepared the old man's corpse for burial. For them it was a repugnant task, and they went about it quickly, deliberately, alert to any inauspicious signs.

As much as they loathed dealing with death, they knew it was important that the body be handled correctly—according to all the old protocols—or else Narbona's ghost might escape the bonds of mortality and come back to haunt them indefinitely. He would prowl around the hogans at night, whistling in the dark, throwing clods of dirt at people and giving them bad dreams, causing loved ones to become crazy, or to shrivel and die from some strange sickness. He might shoot corpse powder into someone's head, causing a dire condition that would manifest itself only as a faint bump on the victim's scalp. In Navajo thinking, there was no such thing as a good ghost, no matter how kind or gentle the person might have been when he was alive.

If Narbona had simply died of old age—passing happily in his sleep, perhaps—then his family would not have needed to take so many precautions, for it was thought that old people who died of natural causes were incapable of producing ghosts. (The same was said of stillborn babies and infants who died before uttering their first cry.) But Narbona had been killed against his will—murdered, in fact, and then scalped—and now his people had every reason to fear that his ghost would be angry and vengeful. The old man's wrath would naturally be aimed at the Americans, but since a ghost rarely traveled far from his hogans and the immediate world familiar to him when he was alive, Narbona's own people would bear the brunt of his rage; his family feared visitations of a special fury unless they handled the burial with exactitude.

The only fortunate detail about the manner in which Narbona died was that it had happened outside; had he died inside his hogan, by whatever cause, the family would either have had to bury him right there in the floor or else remove the corpse through a hole opened in the north wall. But that was not the end of it: The hogan would then have had to be destroyed—razed and burned—for otherwise it would be considered permanently *chindi,* or bewitched.

◙

When Narbona was alive, some Navajos had wondered whether he might be a witch—at least that was the gossip he sometimes had had to live down. This belief came not from anything Narbona had done or said during his long life, but rather from the simple fact that he was one of the richest men in all the Navajo country—rich in livestock, rich in crops and jewelry and slaves. Some Navajos looked askance at wealth, even as they envied it, and especially among the poorest Diné, speculation often circulated that the only way a person could get rich was by learning witchcraft and breaking into tombs to plunder the treasures inside.

Consequently, a wealthy person had to go to great lengths to counteract this suspicion by constantly sharing his largesse, throwing elaborate and expensive ceremonials attended by many hundreds of hungry people. The expectation that rich men would assume their communal responsibilities and bankroll these extravagant feasts and healing gatherings—ritual meetings that formed the public pulse and political blood of Navajo life—worked as an economic leveler, a kind of tax. The custom encouraged simple generosity, but behind it all was a steadfast need to convince a jealous society that one was not a witch.

Among the Navajos there was an old expression: "You can't grow wealthy if you treat your relatives right." Throughout his life Narbona had done his best to treat his relatives right, yet he must have been acutely conscious of the fine line he was always walking. Now that he was dead, these social obligations surrounding his wealth gave the family all the more reason to follow every last precaution and do the burial properly.

⬛

Narbona's slaves probably performed the most intimate tasks of the body preparation, the abhorrent parts that involved coming in direct contact with the skin. They removed the bloody garments and carefully disposed of them by incineration—for it was thought that a man's blood heedlessly left behind, even a small quantity of it, could be used by a witch for malicious purposes. The attendants then bathed the body and dusted it in corn pollen.

They dressed Narbona in his best clothes, the ones he wore to Blessing Ways and Yeibichei and other ceremonies: lustrous buckskin leggings and a buckskin shirt draped in a brilliant striped blanket, red as blood and black as night. Arms jangling in silver bracelets. A fine turquoise necklace. A belt embedded with silver. Beads of polished coral and abalone shell.

Then they carefully held his scalped head and slipped a feathered helmet over it, so that he looked something like the warrior of old. They placed him on several layers of wool blankets and set one of his long sinew-backed bows by his side with a quiver full of arrows. Other personal objects of value—fetishes, fine pottery, a tobacco pipe—might have been laid with him. Wrapping Narbona up tight in the blankets, the attendants then rolled him in a buffalo pelt, the animal's thick matted fur turned toward the body. With some twine made of horsehair, they tied the bundled corpse until the rope was cinched tight in an intricate pattern the Navajos called "the death knot."

Then, in the late afternoon, two of Narbona's sons assumed their place in the ceremony. They wore their hair untied, their bodies slathered in a gray film of moistened ashes. They hoisted the body and laid it across the sheepskin saddles of Narbona's two favorite horses, a gray stallion and a palomino. Taking a roundabout path, one of the sons led the team slowly on foot while the other son walked alongside, making sure the buffalo-hide sarcophagus did not fall off.

Finally they came to a place called Rock Mesa, and there they found a deep crack in the sandstone. The Navajos rarely buried their dead in the European sense, perhaps because the rocky soil was often too hard to dig. Nor did the Diné follow the tradition of many Plains Indians, who tied the body to a high pole or a tree to be picked apart by birds—the spirit of the dead literally taking flight. Instead, the Navajos placed their dead in high caves and crevices, in the many hidden folds of their red rock world. Tightly wrapped bundles like the one that now contained Narbona were discreetly stashed throughout the pocked and riddled landscape, natural catacombs as dry and hard as the skeletons that moldered inside them.

The Navajos left no cairns or tombstones, no marks of any kind; they did not want anyone to know where the dead were laid to rest for fear that their graves might be desecrated by the skinwalkers or by enemies from other tribes. For the Navajos, the business of burial was to be carried out with a zealous and methodical secrecy.

Carefully, Narbona's sons lowered the body into the crevice with ropes, until they felt it touch the rock surface below. They tossed down juniper branches and the scrub of chamisa sage to obscure the bundle, then a thick dusting of sandy soil. Finally they covered everything with stones of various sizes and shapes, trying to make the site look natural and inconspicuous.

Smudging out their footprints, they led the palomino and the stallion a ways to the north, the direction in which Narbona's spirit, having shed its "shell," would soon be traveling. Then the two men came to a low hill and hobbled the horses and tied them tight, making sure their noses were pointing directly north.

And there, right at sunset, Narbona's sons slaughtered the two steeds, probably by slitting their throats and clubbing the animals to death. This was an old Navajo custom. Those tasked with the burial were supposed to destroy several prized horses of the deceased right beside the tomb site—not only to honor the dead, but also to ensure that he or she would have something to ride into eternity. Certainly Narbona's sons wanted their father to go in style.

Making the long journey happier and easier was the least the living could do for their departed loved ones, for the afterworld was thought to be an uninviting place, a place of desolation. There was nothing radiant about the afterlife—no joyous reunions with the Maker, no glorious white light. On the other hand, neither did the Navajos have a notion of anything resembling the Judeo-Christian concept of hell. They did not believe they would find fire and torments awaiting them; no angry God would judge them for their conduct here on earth.

For them the spirit world was just a realm of drab melancholy where souls eventually went and from which they could never escape; there was no hope of reincarnation, no expectation of a return. Once there, the spirit was there forever.

This afterworld was not a theological construct; it was a real place somewhere off in the distant north, and it was said to be located deep inside the ground. Many Navajos believed it was one of the lower realms from which they had emerged as a people long ago—one of the four netherworlds where they had evolved as a race of chittering insects.

North, of course, was also literally the place from which the Navajos had come. While they did not actually believe they had migrated to the Southwest from Canada (in fact, the theory is still not widely accepted among modern Navajos even in the face of seemingly incontrovertible linguistic, cultural, and DNA evidence), the Diné entertained many dark legends about certain close cousins from the North from whom they had somehow become separated ages ago. The Navajos, spooked by all things too closely associated with cardinal north, seemed unsettled by the notion that they might have direct relatives living in that direction.

There is an extraordinary story about a small delegation of Navajos that was invited to the 1893 World's Fair in Chicago. They were wandering from one exhibit to the next when they stumbled upon a particular pavilion from Canada that struck their fancy. This exhibit was staffed by Indians who happened to be Athapaskans, and the Navajos, to their astonishment, understood nearly every word these oddly familiar-looking Canadians said. Although they could carry on a perfectly intelligible conversation, the Athapaskans were not happy to see the Navajos. "We split up a long time ago," they warned, "and it is said that if we ever saw each other again, the world would be destroyed." The Navajo delegation was similarly unnerved by the encounter, and for their remaining three weeks in Chicago, they never again visited the Athapaskan pavilion.

If not exactly in Canada, the underworld was nonetheless somewhere in that sinister direction. To get there, Narbona's spirit would have to wind down a long, narrow mountain trail with many switchbacks. Near the bottom of the trail stood a rippled sand dune at the base of which he would be greeted by deceased kinfolk who looked just as they had when they were alive. His relatives would guide him on a gloomy trek lasting four hard days. Standing at the gates of the afterworld, vigilant guardians would put Narbona through a series of trials to determine if he was actually dead.

☒

Narbona's sons believed the old man was already on the path.

"You've gone away from us now," they chanted. "You've gone away by yourself."

Having slaughtered the horses and left them on the ground, the two men then ripped the saddles and bridles into shreds so they could not be used by anyone who happened to pass by. They may have also followed the old custom of hurling the ruined tack high up in a tree.

Similarly, whatever tools they had brought with them to perform the burial—an ax, digging sticks, a shovel perhaps—were also destroyed and strewn among the rocks. The Navajos took care to obliterate everything involved with a funeral, as though it had never happened at all. They also obeyed a converse taboo—they were not allowed to break sticks or other objects idly, or to destroy any kind of disused property, or even chop wood at night, for fear that this might be taken as a disrespectful imitation of funeral behavior. Also, the loud snapping and ripping sounds would be extremely vexing to any spirits that might be lurking around.

Narbona's sons then broke into a run, jumping over the scrub and taking erratic paths so no evil spirit could catch them. Around dusk they made a small fire in a sheltered place that enjoyed a commanding view of Rock Mesa. There they stayed for four nights, fasting and chanting songs. During the day they remained in the same place, watching over the mesa and thinking about their father while observing a strict silence, communicating only by sign language.

It must have been difficult for the two men to concentrate on the vigil, knowing as they did that a large force of foreigners—the same people who had killed their father—was even now penetrating deeper into Navajo land, heading for the heart of their country. Possibly the two men could have spotted the plumes of dust kicked up by Washington's expedition as it climbed toward the Chuska Range. Narbona's sons must have burned with hate, must have wondered whether they should be taking up arms against these invaders, the Americans. Their own country was under attack and yet here they were, staring in silence at a rock vista.

But they knew they could not take shortcuts in the burial ritual. They never separated from each other, not even for a minute, for they did not want some evil force "to come between" them. Until the rituals were complete, they felt they were in mortal danger of spiritual infection, and they had to help keep each other strong. Even when one of them had to relieve himself, the other son would go along.

After four nights they were satisfied that Narbona's spirit had reached the underworld and that their father could no longer hear their chants and prayers. So the next morning the two sons headed for home.

On the north bank of the Rio Tunicha, still a good ways from their village, they encountered a mound of rocks that must have made them smile; prior to leaving on their funereal errand they had asked their wives to bring fresh clothes and hide them beneath a rock pile in just this spot. Now here it was, and they were relieved to know they could finally strip out of their dirty, death-tainted clothes.

Beside the cairn the sons constructed a sweat lodge and built a fire and heated river rocks in the coals. Then they crawled inside the close structure, placing the glowing stones in a small pit in the center of the dirt floor. They poured ladles of river water on the rocks so that they sputtered and hissed and then sent up radiant waves of steam. All day and all night they sat and baked in the smarting heat. They wanted to wash off the contamination of death, to make themselves clean again.

The next morning the men buried their old clothes and put on the fresh leggings and shirts their wives had left for them. Purified, their unpleasant but necessary task behind them, they crossed the river and walked toward the smoking breakfast fires of their distant hogans, to eat and drink and sleep among their people. Like all the Navajos of the Chuska Mountains, their hearts were turned away from mourning, and fixed upon a different emotion now—vengeance.

Chapter 34   MEN WITHOUT EYES

While Narbona's sons were burying their father, the Washington Expedition pressed on, north and west, toward the literal and metaphorical heart of Navajo country: the extraordinary sandstone labyrinth known as Canyon de Chelly.

No Americans had ever penetrated this fabulous carved maze, and records left by several Spanish explorers were spotty, describing it ominously as "a fearful chasm" and "a place of awesome grandeur." It was widely believed that the Navajos had built an enormous citadel down in the canyon's recesses—turning what was already a natural stronghold into a kind of Gibraltar of the Southwest. The fortress was reputed to be fifteen stories high and reachable only by a network of ladders. To subdue the Navajos, it was thought, one had to probe the full length of the canyon and destroy their great bastion—something no other army from Santa Fe had ever done. For the Washington Expedition, Canyon de Chelly had an aura of impregnability that, of course, made it irresistible.

The name had a French ring to it, but Canyon *de Chelly* (pronounced *deSHAY*) was neither French nor Spanish in origin. It was derived from the Navajo word *tsegi* ("rock canyon") and was thus redundant: Canyon of the Rock Canyon. Over the centuries Spanish explorers had tried to approximate the unfamiliar sound of the Navajo word, and it came out, in various documents, as Chelli, Chelle, Dechilli, and Chegui, among other renderings—and finally Chelly, which eventually became the preferred spelling.

By whatever name, the canyon—actually a network of several interconnected chasms running nearly one hundred sinuous miles in length—was one of the most splendid landscapes in the American West. Though not as deep as the Grand Canyon, it was, in its own scaled-down way, just as wonderful.

What's more, it was a rock wilderness with a human pulse. Because it did not have a mighty river raging through it but rather a gentle stream percolating beneath its sandy floor, the canyon had long supported culture, with farming and domesticated animals and huddled lodges tucked safely among its myriad notches and alcoves. Before the Navajos took up residence there sometime around 1600, Canyon de Chelly had been continuously inhabited by various other Indian groups for more than two thousand years—including, and especially, the Anasazi. The entire length of it was strewn with ruins, many of them precariously situated on high ledges. In some places the canyon's sheer fluted walls rose nearly a thousand feet from the alluvial floor, and everywhere, painted and pecked and patiently scratched high on the luminous gold rock, could be found the art of the ancients.

James Simpson thrilled at the possibility of being the first American to map and describe Canyon de Chelly. He was intent to make a study of "the fabled Navajo presidio," as he put it, and to puncture the mythology that surrounded the place. The Kern brothers were excited, too, for they had been around Santa Fe long enough to hear the stories about de Chelly. Since no artist, Hispanic or Anglo, had ever captured it on canvas, no one in New Mexico seemed to have the vaguest idea what the canyon looked like. After having stumbled with Simpson on the extraordinary ruins at Chaco, Richard Kern recognized how lucky he was to be heading, only a few weeks later, for another untouched wonder. Lugging their cases of oils and charcoals and sketchbooks, the Kerns itched to get to work.

John Washington aimed to find the Navajo fortress and, if necessary, lay siege to it—and then sign a treaty with any Diné leaders who would present themselves for a council. He was, he insisted, on a mission of peace, not war. But the colonel seems to have had no notion that the recent slaying of Narbona might sour the possibilities of a warm Navajo reception. Washington apparently had nothing to say about the Narbona incident—and certainly he showed no sense of regret. In his brusque report on the expedition, written upon his return to Santa Fe, he would emphatically declare good riddance upon the Navajo leader's passing. He wrote, "Among the dead of the enemy left on the field was Narbona, head chief of the nation, who had been a scourge to the inhabitants of New Mexico for the last thirty years."

Washington failed to grasp the mistake his troops had made. In their first encounter with the Diné, they had met and then promptly killed (and mutilated!) the most eminent Navajo alive, and quite possibly the one man who could have brought about an accord with the United States. An opportunity was not only missed, it was scarcely even perceived—and then in an instant it was gone. One Navajo man, who peacefully approached the Washington Expedition on its march, indicated through a translator that Narbona's death had caused much turmoil among his people. The man claimed he had a cousin who was dying from a gunshot wound sustained in the same fracas that had killed Narbona. "It is regrettable," the Navajo said, "that so much damage has been done and we have lost our greatest warrior, all for so trifling a thing as a horse."

With Narbona slain, angry young warriors of the tribe would gain ascendancy—impatient men like Manuelito who had no use for ac-

commodating these arrogant foreigners. Washington's mission to secure peace had thus ensured its opposite: a new front in an old war,
and one that would last the better part of twenty years. The Navajos
had only expanded their venerable conflict with the Mexicans; now
they were also at odds with the *bilagaana*.

The Washington Expedition, blind to the trouble it left in its wake,
marched blithely onward toward Canyon de Chelly. Predictably, Lieutenant Simpson hated the parched and arroyo-riddled Chuska Valley
through which the soldiers passed. Reading his journal, one can almost see him squinching his nose in distaste. "The country is one extended naked, barren waste," he wrote. Everything was "dead and
lifeless, the soil an all-pervading dull, yellow, buff-color." This land, he
declared, was "under a curse."

Simpson was not unlike most of his countrymen in failing to appreciate such spare terrain. The desert was an unfamiliar—and fur-
thermore, uninviting—world to most Anglo sensibilities. By outlook
if not by profession they were still farmers, most of them; their idea
of beautiful land was never far removed from valuable land, and valuable land was any that could be *used*. Those from back east who
tended to hold more sentimental notions about scenic beauty were in
the thrall of a landscape aesthetic that had been passed down from
European Romanticists and filtered through New England artists,
such as the painters of the Hudson River School. They were used to
finding beauty in greens and blues, in mountain streams, plunging
waterfalls, sailboats, and flowery meadows full of fat cows.

But here was a landscape of upheaval and bright finality, forged in
an unforgiving furnace: *a cursed land*. If the Great Plains was regarded
as the "Great American Desert"—as it was often labeled on maps—
then this stark realm was Hades itself. The scale of it dwarfed a man,
not only spatially but also chronologically; it suggested gulfs of time
that mocked human relevance in the terror of creation. A good Episcopalian (and future deacon) who doubtless believed his Maker had
fashioned the world in six consecutive days not very long ago, Simpson could not understand this land's logic—let alone declare it lovely.
What he did understand, he probably found unsettling.

Even the sketches and lithographs done by the Kern brothers show an awkward uncertainty about how to render the Navajo countryside; the scales and proportions often seem slightly off, the perspectives cramped, the foliage unmistakably Eastern. The Pennsylvanian artists loved the challenge of painting this queer country. They found it endlessly fascinating, clearly, but rarely sublime. It would take many years before American enthusiasts—writers, photographers, and painters—would begin to champion the Navajo land, or indeed any of the desert Southwest, as a place of singular beauty. "Buff" was no color for a country, Simpson's generation apparently felt. It was as though they lacked the retinal nerve that allowed them to see the land for what it was; they could see it only for what it refused to be—namely, the green picturesque scenery and tillable farmland of the settled world from which they had come.

But then the expedition climbed out of the broad desert valley and up into the Chuska Mountains, a jagged ten-thousand-foot-high range where elk grazed in the meadow grasses beneath stands of yellow pine and Douglas fir and quaking aspen. In short order they had entered a distinctly different world, one that Simpson would respond to with something approaching glee. In the desert, the lieutenant was learning, the flora and fauna changes dramatically with even modest gains in elevation, the thickening moisture greening everything (so much so that today, botanists of the Southwest refer to aloof mountain ecosystems like the Chuskas as "sky islands").

The men of the expedition camped beside a clear, swift stream, where they drank "pure, wholesome water" and spotted, to their amazement, a grizzly bear. Lieutenant Simpson was thrilled by "the towering pines and firs, the oak, the aspen, and the willow; and bordering the streams, the hop vine, loaded with its fruit. Flowers of rich profusion, and of every hue and delicacy, are constantly before the eye—upwards of ninety varieties have been picked up, the wild rose being among them." He was surprised and relieved to behold "a rich, well-timbered, and sufficiently watered country, a thing I have not seen since I left the confines of the United States."

To cross the Chuskas, however, the men had to crawl up through the same rocky passage that several Spanish and Mexican military expeditions had squeezed through in generations past. In truth, it was the only practical way to ascend these imposing mountains, and the narrow, winding path had for centuries been a well-trod highway of the Diné. Colonel Washington pronounced it "the most formidable defile I have ever seen." His artillerymen and their animals struggled to pull the mountain howitzers through the tight space. Realizing that they were dangerously exposed, the soldiers marched in fear of a Navajo attack from the high cliffs. Richard Kern wrote that "a fight was expected . . . At nearly every point stones can be rolled on the passers by." The Pueblo Indians who served as Washington's scouts were so worried about an attack that, according to Simpson, they reached into their medicine bags and rubbed warrior herbs "upon their heart, as they said, to make it big and brave." Periodically the soldiers could spot Navajo sentinels watching down on them from high above, but the feared attack never came.

The Navajo strongly associated this place with Narbona, for this was the "Narbona Pass," where in 1835 the great leader's warriors routed a thousand Mexicans in a well-executed ambush.

Lieutenant Simpson, naturally, did not know the Navajo history of this place—but to his thinking, it was the sort of distinctive landmark that cried out for a name. In his journal, Simpson decided to pay his commander an eternal compliment by calling the defile "Pass Washington," and he carefully marked it as such on the official map he was preparing for his superiors back east.

If renaming is the first act of conquest, then Simpson had struck a lasting blow. The new place-name stuck, and today this deep cleft in the Chuska Mountains, Narbona's old stomping ground, is known as Washington Pass. The irony is not lost on the Navajo.

Simpson did not stop with one renaming, however. He took a long look at the great peak to the south, the one the Navajos called Blue Bead Mountain. Perhaps because it was old and craggy and majestic-looking, it reminded Simpson of Zachary Taylor, the Mexican War general who had become such a national hero that he was easily elected president in 1848, succeeding James Polk. Unbeknownst to "Old Rough-and-Ready," who now sat in the White House, an obscure topographer had decided to name a Western peak after him. The name appeared on Simpson's map and continues to this day: Mount Taylor.

◙

On the back side of the Chuskas, the Washington Expedition saw no Navajos for several days, but detected fresh signs of their presence. The Navajos were deft at disappearing and lived in a country riddled with good hiding places—concealed caves, box canyons, high mesas reached by inscrutable paths in the sandstone. Clearly, Navajos far and wide had been forewarned of the expedition's approach, and they had scattered with scarcely a trace. There was something eerie about how completely they and their belongings had vanished from the scene—warriors and women and children and even their herds, all gone—leaving nothing but vacant hogans and strewings of sheep dung.

"Innumerable signs of stock, principally sheep, have been seen along the route," Lieutenant Simpson wrote. "The road we have been traveling looks as if it might be one of the great thoroughfares of the nation." The lieutenant seemed confounded by the Navajo, and their knack for living a life "thoroughly scattered and locomotive." It did not seem to occur to Simpson that the Navajos, having heard the details of Narbona's death, were also terrified of the approaching American army and thought it best to keep themselves scarce.

At night, however, Navajos in small parties were seen and heard—or at least sensed—by Washington's soldiers. The Americans knew they were being watched, could almost feel the bore of Navajo stares. Several times, their pack animals mysteriously disappeared in the night. When it came to livestock, the Diné were incorrigible. Animal theft was the provocation that had brought the American army into their midst in the first place, and, of course, it was a stolen horse that had got Narbona killed. Yet the temptation was irresistible—they kept on stealing, or tried to, yards from Washington's sentries.

The Navajos had no qualms about robbing from the Americans. They had many causes to be angry at these invaders, not the least of which was that everywhere Washington's army went, it helped itself to the Navajo gardens and melon patches and turned its animals loose in the cornfields to devour and trample the Diné's source of winter food. Simpson notes that one night the army camped right in the fields and enjoyed "an abundance of forage for the animals and fine roasting ears for the men." From the Navajo point of view, it was the Americans who were doing the real stealing.

After three more days of determined marching, Washington's troops dropped out of the high timbered mountains and found them-selves at the silty mouth of Canyon de Chelly. Here the stone margins of the canyon were scarcely higher than a man and the soft sand floor was broad and flat. But looking ahead, the soldiers must have felt a sense of imminent claustrophobia, a tingling awareness that the walls were steadily closing in, the sheer faces of rock climbing higher with every coming bend.

Water braided through the canyon, yet most of the flow was sub-terranean, oozing just a few inches beneath the sand. The men had to be extremely wary, for the sloughs were wet and deep enough in places to swallow a horse to its withers. (Even today, Canyon de Chelly is famous for its greedy quicksand, which can cause a pack horse to become so deeply mired that it must be pulled out with a winch, with the animal often breaking a leg in the trauma and having to be put down.) To find water, Washington's thirsty men dug holes in the muck five feet deep and filled their buckets with the turbid brown liquid, which they made potable by repeatedly straining through linen cloth until it was tolerably clear.

As they pushed deeper into the canyon, the expeditioners began to realize that Navajos were watching them from every ledge and out-crop. "The enemy are hovering around us," Simpson wrote, but they would not present themselves. In broad necks of the canyon, the sol-diers encountered hogans clustered around cornfields or peach or-chards, yet the occupants refused to come into the light of day. To flush them out, Washington ordered his troops to set fire to the hogans in his path—yet another action that might have convinced the already skeptical Navajos that this army of peace was actually on the warpath. Simpson found the sight of the burning lodges thrilling. It was "exciting," he wrote, "to observe the huts of the enemy, one after another, springing up into smoke and flame, and their owners scampering off in flight."

Yet the torching may have had its desired effect: The following morning two Navajos came into camp and consented to talk. One of them, who went by the Spanish name of Martinez, wore a great blue coat made of blankets and called himself, absurdly, "the principal chief of the Navajos"—or at least he did not seem to disavow the title when Washington's interpreters suggested it. Colonel Washington was characteristically curt.

WASHINGTON: Are he and his people desirous of peace?

INTERPRETER: He says they are.

WASHINGTON: Tell the chief the stolen property which the nation is required to restore is 1,070 head of sheep, 34 head of mules, 19 head of horses, and 78 head of cattle. When can the chiefs collect here to make a treaty with me?

INTERPRETER: He says the day after tomorrow.

WASHINGTON: Tell him that if they do not enter into a treaty in good faith, it will result in their destruction.

INTERPRETER: His people will do all he has promised.

With an effusive show of emotion, "Chief" Martinez and his companion bid the colonel adieu and vanished into the unseen folds of the canyon, vowing to return in two days.

Then Colonel Washington was visited by a Mexican captive of the Navajos. He was a thirty-year-old man who said he had been kidnapped seventeen years earlier. He had been a boy herding sheep in a field on the outskirts of Santa Fe when the Navajos came spurring out of the west and whisked him away with his flock.

Colonel Washington naturally assumed that the man had come to petition the Americans to take him back home, that he was relieved now to be free of his Indian captors. Several Mexican volunteers on the expedition had apparently recognized the young man, and they wanted to bring him home to his family. But to their disbelief, and then to their frustration and fury, this son of Mexico wanted to remain a savage here in a heathen land. *This* was his home now, the man insisted. Bright and energetic, he spoke and carried himself and dressed like a native-born Navajo. His Spanish had grown thick and faltering.

"He did not wish to be restored to his people again," Simpson records in mild consternation. "Indeed, he did not as much as ask about his friends living at Santa Fe."

⊠

All this time, Lieutenant Simpson seems to have been looking over his shoulder, peering distractedly down the canyon reaches, desperate to explore. Washington's dreary negotiations did not hold his attention. Simpson was not much interested in people anyway—especially not when he had a puzzle of geology spread before him. So on September 8, having a couple of days to kill before the treaty talks were supposed to commence, Lieutenant Simpson pushed east to make the first American reconnaissance of Canyon de Chelly. He brought the Kern brothers with him and, for protection, an escort of about sixty men.

Within a few miles the canyon walls began to "assume a stupendous appearance," Simpson said. "Almost perfectly vertical, they look as if they had been chiselled by the hand of art. . . . They are laid with as much handsome precision as can be seen in the custom-house of the city of New York." He was dazzled by the facets of "red amorphous sandstone" ranged tightly about him and towering over his head, each block cracked and riddled with "imperfect seams of stratification." The immense stone slabs held the day's heat, so that hours after the sun dropped behind the rim, the peach orchards and cornfields on the canyon floor basked in the long-lingering hothouse effect. In many places the golden-pink sandstone was streaked with a brown patina that curled like a witch's fingers down the massive alcoved walls.

Richard Kern immediately set himself to work sketching and would produce the first known illustration of Canyon de Chelly, a work that, if not exactly lovely, comes close to capturing the enveloping grandeur of this natural labyrinth. Kern seemed stunned by the canyon's magnificent intrigues, its whispers of an epochal wrath, with so many twisted monoliths and crumbled heaps of talus testifying to the steady violence of erosion. The "fabulous rocks," as Kern put it, "became wilder at every turn." Simpson, equally amazed, wrote that he was "highly delighted" by "this wonderful exhibition of nature that will always command the admiration of its votaries, as it will the attention of geologists."

The expeditioners pushed nine miles into the canyon, taking rock samples and measurements and making sketches as they went, but then Simpson realized they could go no farther, for Colonel Washington expected them back by the following day. Already the lieutenant was beginning to suspect that the "much-talked about Navajo presidio" was a myth. Although he was premature in saying so—the expedition had explored only a fraction of the one-hundred-mile canyon complex—his suspicions were correct. "The mystery of the Canon of Chelly is now, in all probability, solved," he confidently asserted. "The notion that the canon contains a high fort is exploded."

And yet Simpson kept seeing stone structures everywhere—not fortresses, but formidable-looking cliff dwellings stashed in odd places high along the walls. The structures all appeared to be uninhabited (and indeed the local Navajos never ventured into them, out of respect for the spirits of those who had once lived in them, and out of fear of the corpses that were often buried nearby, in rock fissures and secret caves). The lieutenant correctly surmised that these ruins were built by the same Indians who constructed the marvelous pueblo complexes he and Richard Kern had studied two weeks earlier at Chaco Canyon. He wrote: "I observed upon a shelf fifty feet above the bottom of the canyon a small pueblo ruin of a style and structure similar to that found in the ruins on the Chaco."

But Simpson wrongly assumed that the present Navajos were direct descendants of the builders of these pueblo-like cliff dwellings, which led the lieutenant, perhaps inevitably, to make disparaging comparisons to the crude simplicity of the Navajo lodges seen all about the canyon. Simpson did not think much of hogans. "How is it that they have retrograded in respect to their habitations when they have preserved it in their manufactures?" Simpson wondered. "It seems anomalous to me that a nation living in such miserably constructed mud lodges should, at the same time, be capable of making, probably, the best blankets in the world!"

The "ancient ones" had left other signs of their presence. Scotched into the canyon walls, following faint cracks and meandering fissures, were numerous hand- and toe-hold routes that the Anasazi had cut into the rock many hundreds of years earlier. When the Navajos moved here sometime in the early 1600s, they had made use of these vertiginous routes, too, and had expanded on them, so that now all the various canyon branches were dimpled with improbable paths dotting up the sheer rock hundreds of feet to the rim. At one point Simpson spotted a couple of Navajos standing on a high shelf, and then was astounded to see them "tripping down the almost vertical wall as nimbly and dexterously as minuet dancers." Simpson thought the spectacle of these human crabs scuttling over the rock faces was "one of the most wonderful feats I'd ever witnessed." In general, the Navajos hid from the expeditioners, but on one occasion a woman presented herself and laid out several blankets on the ground for the soldiers. When she unfurled them, they were delighted to find generous piles of ripe peaches from the Navajos' prized orchards.

The canyon walls were scrawled and chipped with untold thousands of petroglyphs and pictographs, often in the unlikeliest of places. For a millennium the canyon had been a canvas for graffiti artists: Basketmaker, Anasazi, Hopi, Navajo. The designs came in a dazzling confusion. Serpents, lightning bolts, elaborate fret patterns, whorls. Star constellations painstakingly inscribed on cave ceilings. Menageries of bizarre creatures—headless birds in flight, humpbacked creatures playing flutes, human figures with insectlike antennae, antelope with crab pincers instead of hooves, bird-headed men, frog-men, turtle-men. Men impaled with arrows, men with enormous dangling penises, alien-humanoid figures with strange protuberances emerging from their left ears. Squatting women with swollen genitalia, giving birth. And everywhere there were palm prints, ancient choruses of hands, hailing from the walls. In places the designs were so densely painted that there seemed to be a kind of frenetic dialogue going on—one such location would later be called Newspaper Rock, for it seemed to archaeologist interpreters to be a gathering place where the ancients came to read the news. Although some of the images had been pecked or chiseled, most had been painted directly onto the rock using mineral dyes mixed with binders made of blood, urine, or the whites of turkey eggs.

If the expeditioners had ventured into another branch of the canyon—an equally spectacular prong known as Canyon del Muerto ("Canyon of Death"), they would have seen a curious tableau scrawled across the walls. Still visible today, it is a quite realistic rendering of a long train of Spanish cavalrymen, wearing flat-brimmed hats, carrying lances and muskets, and riding pinto horses into battle. The ominous-looking figures look like horsemen of the apocalypse, their capes clearly emblazoned with crosses.

The Diné had scratched these haunting images onto the walls some forty years earlier to memorialize a painful event—the only occasion in which the Spanish successfully invaded this Navajo refuge. In January 1805 a force of nearly five hundred soldiers marched all the way from Santa Fe, killing Navajo warriors by the score and collecting prisoners as they rampaged through the canyon's meandering course. In Canyon del Muerto, not far from where these images were painted, the Spanish troops were surprised to hear the shrill voice of a Navajo woman shouting strange invectives at them. "There go the men without eyes!" the voice screamed. "You must be blind!"

Puzzled, one of the soldiers climbed up the talus and spotted a group of more than a hundred women and children crouched in a high recess of the canyon wall (the warriors, including Narbona, were off fighting elsewhere). These Navajo had climbed up to their hiding place by using an ancient trail of toeholds. The hectoring voice, it turned out, was that of an old woman who had once been enslaved by the Spanish. Hidden with the others, and thinking herself safe, she had lost her presence of mind and hurled abuse down on her hated enemies.

The Spanish scout called down to his comrades and reported that the Navajos were hopelessly trapped. Another soldier began to crawl his way up the steep wall with the notion of rounding up prisoners. When he crossed the threshold of the cave, a Navajo woman wrapped her arms around him and dashed for the precipice; the two figures, locked in a desperate grip, plunged several hundred feet to their deaths.

From the canyon floor, the soldiers, who could not see the huddled Navajo forms above but now knew exactly where they were, began to ricochet bullets off the roof of the cave. For hours they kept firing their old muskets and harquebuses into the high recess, expending thousands of rounds of ammunition. Eventually everyone in the cave was killed but an old man, who would repeat the story to other Navajos. More than 150 years later, the victims' bones still lie on the cave floor, layered with bits of Navajo clothing and spent bullets.

Today the spot is widely known as Massacre Cave. But the Navajos have long had their own name for it: The Place Where Two Fell Off.

◙

Although he didn't seem to know it, the treaty that Colonel Washington sought to make with the Navajos was a farce. The man known as Martinez was not the principal chief of the Diné. Only Narbona could have answered to the title, but even that would have been a stretch. What the Navajos wanted was for the Americans to leave as soon as possible, and if putting a mark on a piece of paper would do the trick, they were happy to oblige.

What was paper? Most of the Navajos had never seen it, nor ink pens, nor written words. They had no concept of individual land ownership or constitutions or the rule of law or the delegation of political authority. Their traditions were so radically different that they had no idea what the Americans were really talking about. Nothing would change in their world. The *bilagáana* would leave and go back to wherever they came from, and the raids against the New Mexicans would resume as usual.

So on the appointed day, Martinez and another Navajo "chief" going by the name of Chapitone showed up as promised and sat down with Colonel Washington to hear his treaty. In the distance more than a hundred Navajo warriors waited vigilantly, their metal-tipped lances and thick buckskin shields at the ready. The headmen brought with them four young captives and a herd of 104 sheep, which they conceded they'd stolen from the New Mexicans—and promised to deliver more later.

Washington's treaty had been written down ahead of time, a dense document full of lofty ideals and sprinkled with a few firm demands that sounded fair enough for a conquering army to impose on its subjects. Among the treaty's declarations: "Hostilities between the contracting parties shall cease and perpetual peace and friendship shall exist. . . . The Government of the said States [has] the sole and exclusive right of regulating the trade and intercourse with the said Navahos. . . . Should any citizen of the United States murder, rob, or otherwise maltreat any Navaho Indians, he or they shall be arrested and tried. . . . All American and Mexican captives and stolen property shall be delivered by the Navajo Indians on or before the 9th day of October."

Although it generally tended to take the side of the Mexicans in their age-old conflict with the Navajos, it was, all in all, a reasonable document—and even, in places, a noble one, attesting to the Americans' rockbed faith in republican virtues and the primacy of law.

But, like the Doniphan treaty of three years earlier, it was worthless. As they raced through Washington's various sticking points, one can only imagine how difficult it must have been for either of the two parties to communicate meaningfully with one another—with so many voids in cultural understanding, with the negotiations shifting erratically from English to Spanish to Navajo. From the Americans' perspective, everything about Martinez and Chapitone must have seemed frustratingly vague and indirect—their roundabout style of conversation, their unwillingness to pronounce anyone's name out loud, and their odd refusal to point at anyone except by thrusting out the lips. These strange Indians would not even shake hands. (Washington would never have guessed the reason: The Navajos were afraid these foreigners were witches, and that if the Americans drew too close, they might blow corpse powder into their faces. Even today, many Navajos avoid shaking hands unless they know the person, and the tepid greeting is liable to be of the "limp-fish" variety that most Anglos find unsatisfactory.)

The Navajos, on the other hand, must have found Colonel Washington exceedingly strange with all his high-toned talk about undoing the relationships of their known world. The Navajos did not take much stock in abstractions; they were a determinedly practical people who preferred to deal with matters close at hand. It was a tendency embedded in their own language. Navajo is an extremely precise language in conveying certain things like movement and changing spatial relationships between physical objects, but it can be extremely vague in describing concepts of time. In the same sentence, a Navajo might speak of something that happened today and then effortlessly segue into a story that happened thousands of years ago, in the mists of tribal lore. Given this, Colonel Washington's assumptions about deadlines and jurisdictions, and of legal authority binding from this day forward—all of it must have seemed entirely foreign to the Diné.

Still, they consented. What else were they to do? Washington left them no room for quibbling. Beneath the glowing ochre rocks of Canyon de Chelly, Martinez and Chapitone scrawled their awkward "X"s at the end of the document, alongside J. M. Washington.

James Simpson, who watched the proceedings unfold, seemed satisfied that a "full and complete treaty had been made by which they have put themselves under the jurisdiction of the government of the United States." The lieutenant seemed optimistic that the Navajos understood what they had agreed to, and that they would comply. But if they didn't, the treaty carried another important strategic value in his mind, a rather cynical one.

As Simpson put it in a convoluted but familiar-sounding bit of legalese, the existence of a signed document would help "satisfy the public mind and testify to the whole world that should any future coercion become necessary against the Navahos, it would be but a just retribution and, in a manner of speaking, their own act."

Chapter 35   BLOOD AND THUNDER

In October 1849, a few weeks after the Washington Expedition returned home to its barracks at Fort Marcy, a trader named James M. White was traveling west with his family on the Santa Fe Trail. The Whites had come from Missouri in the company of a well-known merchant named Francis Xavier Aubry, who was leading a large caravan of wagons packed with goods. With only 150 miles left to reach Santa Fe, White decided to break from the slow convoy and push ahead in a faster carriage with his young wife, Ann, and their infant daughter. Believing that they had passed out of the most threatening Indian territory, they bid Aubry and the others in the long train goodbye near a popular stop called Point of Rocks, expecting to reunite with them in Santa Fe in a week's time.

Francis Aubry was a celebrated figure on the trail. A compact French Canadian with intense black eyes and a thick beard, Aubry had made a fortune in the Santa Fe trade. He knew every rutted inch of the road and did not see any problems with his friend James White leapfrogging ahead. White was a veteran of the trail himself, with interests in Santa Fe and El Paso. An unseasonable cold snap had made the going miserable for Mrs. White and her baby girl, and they wanted to get to a warm hotel. White was driving with his family and a black female servant. For protection, Aubry detached three armed men to accompany the Whites in a second carriage.

Francis X. Aubry had won national celebrity a year earlier, when he broke the record for the fastest crossing of the Santa Fe Trail. In September 1848 he had ridden nonstop nearly eight hundred miles from Santa Fe to Independence, Missouri, in five days and sixteen hours—killing several horses in the process, but winning a thousand-dollar bet that he could beat his old record of eight days. Aubry accomplished this feat by stashing fresh horses at relay points every few hundred miles along the route. Many times he dozed off as his mounts galloped eastward, but he took the precaution of cinching himself to his saddle to keep from tumbling. At ten o'clock on the night of September 17, 1848, Aubry and his last horse staggered into Independence, where patrons at a hotel immediately recognized him and lifted him out of his saddle, which was blood-soaked from the more than five days of constant chafing of human against horse. Nearly catatonic from exhaustion, able to speak only in a whisper, Aubry ordered ham and eggs and then was taken upstairs to bed.

His eight-hundred-mile dash made national news and heralded a new age of transport in the last innocent years before construction of the transcontinental railroad, which was then being planned and routed. As his example showed, the physical crossing of the Great Plains was getting to be old hat. The big caravans were still enormous logistical undertakings, and they would always be tediously slow, for there was no way to speed up a train pulled by oxen. But Aubry's record gallop punctured some of the Trail's aura and served to inspire more timid souls who had long been nursing vague ambitions of traveling west. Only a few years after Kearny's conquest of the Southwest, the mother road seemed well trod, its supply points better stocked, the names of its stops and stages burned into the public memory—Switzlow's Creek, Council Grove, Diamond Springs, Pawnee Rock, Cottonwood Fork. New Mexico was still a long way from Missouri, but if a single man could traverse the country in under six days, then the trek was clearly not the impossible adventure it once had been.

Aubry's example made it look too easy, however. People seemed to forget how dangerous the journey still was, particularly in the westernmost stretches, the broiled solitudes where water was scarce and the possibility of Indian attacks high. Every year settlers were murdered by Indians—or kidnapped and mercilessly tortured. The Santa Fe Trail was rife with tales of Indian cruelty. Many of these stories were exaggerated bits of folklore fueled no doubt by racial ignorance if not outright animus, but the mutilation of captives—even corpses—was a documented part of the warrior rituals of many Plains tribes. One authority on the Plains Indians wrote that "as a rule mutilation was inspired by spite after losses, or animated by a superstitious fear that a great fighter—one 'hard to kill'—might come alive again." The hostiles of the Great Plains rarely seemed to hold a special hatred toward white pioneers; in fact, they tended to reserve their most lavish abuses for ancient enemies from other tribes.

Nevertheless, even the most intelligent commentators on the subject tended to assume that the Plains Indians were expressly out to get white folks. William Davis, an astute lawyer and judge who lived in New Mexico for years traveling the circuit court, compared the Plains Indians to the biblical Ishmaelites, "whose hands are turned against every white man, woman, and child." Davis noted that "there are hundreds of captives among the Indians of the Plains, principally women and children. The great majority spend a lifetime with them, and drag out a most miserable existence."

The Comanches were reputed to be the most diabolical in their cruelties to captives. Historian Bernard DeVoto wrote that the Comanches were "practising sadists" who had "great skill in pain" and for whom "cruelty was their catharsis." The authenticated accounts, DeVoto said, "fill thousands of pages, and some are altogether unreadable for men with normal nerves." It was widely reported, for example, that the Comanches liked to take their victims to a remote stretch of the plains and stake their bodies to the ground. Then the Comanches would slit open their bellies and poke their organs with spears, making a slow study of it, delighting in the bloodcurdling screams, sometimes slicing a bit of a victim's liver and eating it right in front of him. Or the Comanches might pry open their captive's eyelids with twigs and leave him, helpless and exposed, to be cornea-scorched by the sun, then eaten alive by wolves.

It was the Comanches who in 1841 killed and scalped twenty-five-year-old Robert Bent, the youngest of the Bent brothers (his scalped body, discovered near the Arkansas River, was buried just outside the walls of Bent's Fort). It was also thought to be the Co-manches who killed Jedediah Smith, probably the greatest explorer of the West, by shooting him in the back and riddling his body with lance wounds. Smith's murder in 1831 occurred on the Cimarron River, not far from the stretch of the Santa Fe Trail where the White party was now riding.

These were the kinds of horrors that were told along the trail, sto-ries that James White had doubtless already heard and discounted when he pulled away from the Aubry caravan and made good time with his family toward Santa Fe.

◙

At that moment, Kit Carson was hard at work in the fields of his new ranch on Rayado Creek, some fifty miles east of Taos and not far from the Santa Fe Trail. By October the corn had all been harvested, but the last patches of squash and beans and peppers were still growing, moistened by the acequia that siphoned cold mountain water from the creek rippling from the Sangre de Cristos. The north-facing crags of the mountains were dusted with snow. Out in the distant fields, clus-ters of cattle, sheep, horses, and mules cropped the blue grama grass. Elsewhere on the property, laid out in erratic jumbles, were various sheds and lean-tos, a blacksmith shop, a slaughterhouse, and a number of pens made of cedar staves wired together to keep the wolves from attacking the stock at night. In the center of it all stood the ranch house, a cabin made of rough-hewn ponderosa logs, reminiscent of the Missouri homesteads of Carson's youth. Surrounding the com-pound was a high adobe wall, to keep the Indians at bay.

At thirty-nine, Christopher Carson had decided, of all things, to become a farmer. He had grown too old for the trail, too weary of the nervous hardship of guiding the U.S. Army. He loved the discipline of working a ranch and took to it immediately. He would head out for the fields at dawn and keep at it until dusk—clearing land, plowing and planting, lambing and shearing, making constant additions and repairs, building his new domain from scratch. There was hay to cut and bundle and sell to government agents as fodder. There were pine logs to whipsaw into lumber and adobe bricks to be molded and baked in the sun. There were vegetables to put up, animals to butcher, hides to tan, mules to shoe, meats to cure. The work was endless.

Yet, as much as he loved it, this sedentary life was against his nature; he had always been a wanderer. As an adolescent runaway, a teamster, a trapper, a hunter, a scout and guide, a soldier, a transcontinental courier—every turn of his career had been characterized by nearly ceaseless movement over the West. In all those years since he left Missouri, he had never stopped.

Taos had been his home, theoretically, a home he kept failing to get back to. It was and would continue to be one of the recurring themes of his life—his desire to settle down to honest labor, to be with his wife and start a family, only to be pulled away again by larger events. He and Josefa had been married six years, but in all that time he had been at home without interruption only a few months. Carson had made several earlier attempts to start a farm near Taos, but something had always come along to disrupt his plans, some unforeseen mission of national import laid at his feet.

After leaving Washington in the summer of 1847 with messages for General Kearny, Carson had sped to California, only to receive further orders *to do it all over again*—that is, to make another trip to Washington bearing another round of important dispatches. Like a good soldier, he accepted the assignment, but all that travel took a toll on him and his family life. Since the start of the Mexican War he had covered nearly sixteen thousand miles—a good percentage of it riding on a mule.

Josefa hated his absences. She missed him, surely, but that was only part of it. Josefa perhaps only dimly knew what Carson was do-

ing all those years and, as a native Mexican, she had no particular reason to share his patriotism for the United States. His fame meant
next to nothing to her. Stories passed down through the Jaramillo
family in Taos have it that she understandably resented her husband
for always being on the go, earning no great sums of money in the
service of an army whose primary relation to her people was one of
subjugation.

So once again Carson was trying to settle down, only this time he
knew he had to make it stick: He was a father. That spring, Josefa,
now twenty-two, had given birth to their first child, a son. They had
named him Charles after Gov. Charles Bent, her sister's late husband,
murdered in his home that horrible night two years earlier. Born prematurely, Little Charles was so sick and fragile that Josefa decided to
stay home with him in Taos that first summer while Kit cleared
ground and established the new ranch.

In this farming operation, Carson had partnered with another famous Taos trapper, named Lucien Bonaparte Maxwell. A native of
Illinois, Maxwell was a stout, swarthy bull of a figure with a vaudevil-
lian mustache. He had been on the first three Fremont expeditions
and knew Carson well. By the happy twist of marriage, Maxwell now
managed, and would soon own, a land grant in northeastern New
Mexico even larger than the state of Delaware. This stupendous piece
of real estate—more than 1.7 million acres—would make Maxwell
the largest private landowner in the United States. It was a kingdom
unto itself, completely undeveloped. From the rugged high country,
promising creeks and rivers dropped into broad, lush valleys. Maps of
the grant showed immense tracts of empty tableland between the
Cimarron and Purgatoire rivers that were marked simply "fine grazing." Maxwell ruled it all, and he had invited Carson and just a few
other acquaintances to develop select parcels of his virgin domain.

Ambitious, dry-humored, lavishly generous to his guests, but
prone to whipping the peons who worked for him, Maxwell "was
king of that whole country," a contemporary said. "He had perfect
control . . . and had Indians and Mexicans just to do what he bid them
to." A soldier who knew him well remembered his "hospitality and

firmness of will." Ranching came naturally to him, for he was already a discerning stockman, ever interested in buying better breeds and improving bloodlines. A contemporary writer said that Maxwell's horses, his cattle, his poultry, even his dogs "were always of the same style—the best that can be had."

Maxwell and Carson had been talking for some time about making a fresh start of it somewhere in this vast land grant. That spring, in 1849, Carson took a thousand dollars saved from his trapping and guiding days and invested in Maxwell's growing operation. It has been written that this was the first large-scale cattle operation ever undertaken by Anglo-Americans in the West—that Maxwell and Carson were, in effect, the first American cowboys. (Hispanic *vaqueros,* of course, had been running cattle for generations throughout the Southwest.) The claim is probably dubious and anyway unprovable, but it is nevertheless true that Carson was again living a step ahead of his time, as he did so often through his protean career in the West.

"We had been leading a roving life long enough," Carson later said in his memoirs, "and now was the time, if ever, to make a home for ourselves. We were getting old. We commenced building and making improvements, and were in a way of becoming prosperous."

The Rayado Valley was a stunning sweep of land on which to settle, an open country of high meadows and brilliant skies where the Sangre de Cristos gave way to the endless plains. Elk and deer and the occasional silvertip grizzly roamed this grassy piedmont, and trout darted in the cold streams. The name Rayado—Spanish for "streaked"—was said to derive from the colorful markings often tattooed on the faces of certain Plains tribes that wandered the area; Rayado was also the name of a prominent Comanche chief from the early 1800s.

Carson's ranch was not far from the Santa Fe Trail, the same road that had brought him here in his youth. His father had been a farmer at the other end of that trail, a thousand miles to the east, in newly cleared forestland that was then the frontier. Now the son was repeating the pattern, one that had been followed by countless other pioneering families in the steady westward crawl of America.

Indians, of course, were part of the old pattern, too. Carson's first memory of life in Missouri was of the men working the fields as sentries patrolled the perimeter with muskets to guard against Indian attack. A constant low-grade fear was imprinted on Carson's psyche from an early age. In that sense the Rayado Valley differed little from Missouri. It was dangerous country. A number of hostile Indian tribes lived and hunted in these high grasslands. Utes and Apaches regularly passed through, as did Comanches, Kiowas, and Cheyennes. The previous summer a band of Ute raiders had shot Maxwell in the neck. Maxwell probably would have died had he not been taken to Santa Fe, where a physician removed the ball in "an extremely difficult and painful operation."

Attacks of this sort were a regular occurrence, and Carson had to remain wary. On the Rayado he kept a guard watching over his cattle by day and by night.

≋

A few days after he pulled away from Aubry's caravan, James White and his party encountered hostile Indians while camped near the Santa Fe Trail at a spot between Rock Creek and Whetstone Branch. The Indians demanded gifts. White was a proud and stubborn man, and considering his party to be well armed, he refused to pay a toll to these highway thieves. In addition to his wife, their daughter, and their servant, White was accompanied by three men—a German named Lawberger, an unknown American, and a Mexican hand. A little later the party was visited by the same Indians, only this time the warriors appeared in much larger numbers, perhaps as many as a hundred. Still, White was adamant—he would offer them nothing. With rifles loaded, he attempted to drive the Indians from his camp. But they descended in a storm of arrows, promptly killing White's Mexican escort, who fell into the burning campfire. The travelers attempted to flee but did not get far. Soon the bodies of White and his two other guides bristled with shafts. The Indians scooped up Ann White, her daughter, and the servant, and stole across the prairie.

Some of the murderers, however, stayed behind with White's carriages. Practicing an old ruse, they hid in the scrub along the road, waiting to ambush the next travelers who might happen along. Soon a party of Mexicans came down the trail. Seeing the dead bodies and the upturned carriages, they began to rummage through White's belongings, taking whatever looked promising. Then the Indians pounced. After a struggle the Mexicans somehow got away, but not before one of their party, a small boy, was pierced with an arrow. Thinking the boy was dead, the marauders quickly gathered up their loot and scattered.

After the horses' hoofbeats had faded, the Mexican boy rose up, frightened and disoriented, and staggered down the trail. The arrow was lodged deeply between the bones of his arm, but he could walk. Later that day he was picked up by a caravan of Americans and taken to Santa Fe, where he was able to communicate the details of his ordeal to the authorities.

Soldiers were dispatched to investigate, and the bodies from White's party were soon found and identified. The abandoned carriages were broken to pieces. Trunks had been pried open and belongings strewn about. It was not altogether clear which tribe of Indians was responsible. The dead had not been scalped or mutilated, which was unusual for a Plains Indian attack. The soldiers buried the bodies by the side of the trail and covered them with rocks to keep the wolves from digging them up. When Francis Aubry learned of the massacre, he immediately put out the word to friends throughout the region, offering a one-thousand-dollar reward for the return of Ann White.

⊠

For some time, Kit Carson had sensed a change in the air. He recognized that the once inexhaustible West was shrinking before his eyes. In the mountains above Taos, the population of silvertip grizzlies had dwindled in just a few short years. The great migratory herds of buffalo roaming the plains were fast succumbing to the new tide of immigrants, many of whom slaughtered the beasts for the sheer sick pleasure of it and left the carcasses to rot on the prairie. Indians across the West were finding that their old hunting grounds were being steadily grabbed up by new settlers. Many tribes had been wiped out by smallpox and other European diseases from which they had no immunity. Homesteads were popping up everywhere, it seemed, and there was an unfamiliar traffic in the narrow mud streets of Taos and Santa Fe. Carson saw the tendrils of civilization creeping in; the America he had left behind was finally catching up with him.

In a literal and even legal sense, it *had* caught up with him. All the West he had known since leaving Missouri as a boy had become, at last, American soil. With the signing of the Guadalupe Hidalgo Treaty in February 1848, the Mexican War officially ended, and the United States officially absorbed 1.2 million square miles of new real estate—increasing the national domain by more than 66 percent. Agreeing to pay the paltry sum of $15 million, Polk had won precisely what he wanted at the outset, a vast, unbroken continental nation with Pacific harbors. Washington's first war of foreign intervention had cost the lives of more than 13,000 Americans—the highest death rate per fighting soldier in U.S. military history—with the Mexican toll soaring far higher, perhaps as high as 25,000 dead. The victory did not come without stout reservations and pangs of somber introspection among many American leaders who could not ignore the war's darker imperial shadings. Ulysses S. Grant, to name one prominent doubter who actually fought in the conflict, would call the Mexican War "one of the most unjust ever waged by a stronger against a weaker nation." Even Sen. John C. Calhoun of South Carolina, who had at first so staunchly supported the war (as a way to extend slavery), began to have his doubts. He told the Senate: "A deed has been done from which the country will not be able to recover for a long time, if ever; it has dropped a curtain between the present and the future, which to me is impenetrable."

Nicholas Trist, the American envoy sent to Mexico City to negotiate the treaty, later recalled sitting down with the Mexican officials and trying to hide his guilt about concluding a treaty that sheared from Mexico nearly half of its territory: "Could those Mexicans have seen into my heart at that moment, they would have known that my feeling of shame as an American was strong. . . . For though it would not have done for me to say so there, that was a thing for every right-minded American to be ashamed of, and I was ashamed of it, most cordially and intensely ashamed of it."

And yet already, it seemed, the great landgrab had paid off: Scarcely before the ink had dried on the Guadalupe Hidalgo Treaty, gold was discovered in California, and now the rush was on. It's remotely possible that Kit Carson played a role in disseminating news of the strike; some accounts have suggested that on his second transcontinental journey to Washington, in 1848, Carson carried in his saddlebags one of the first notices of the placer discoveries in the Sierra Nevada. Almost instantly a dusty exodus of people and goods was set in motion. The Santa Fe Trail, the Oregon Trail, and their tributaries were now virtually choked with determined men—"Forty-Niners," they were called—who had chucked everything for a stake in the California argosy.

From Carson's point of view, the West was filling up fast with what he took to be untrustworthy characters—outlaws, charlatans, religious zealots, opportunists, schemers, boosters, empire-builders. Yet he seemed scarcely to recognize that by guiding Fremont all over the West, he had been an important catalyst in bringing about these changes; in a sense, Carson had unwittingly fouled his own nest, luring to the West the very sorts of people he loathed.

Everything he touched, it seemed, had withered. The beaver he had trapped were on the verge of extinction. The Indians he had lived among had been decimated by disease. Virgin solitudes he once loved had been captured by the disenchanting tools of the topographers. The annual rendezvous of the mountain men was a thing of the past. Even the seemingly indestructible Bent's Fort was no more. One day in August 1849, Charles's brother William decided it was time to start over. Not wanting to sell the great fort to the government, not wanting it to be vandalized and overrun by Indians, he came up with a more dramatic solution: He filled the labyrinthine chambers with kegs of powder and blew parts of his weird, splendid castle to smithereens. If there had been any doubt before, the immolation of Bent's Fort loudly proclaimed the death of an era.

In this diminished new world, Carson was an anachronism, a buckskin curiosity who had, it seemed, no role left to play other than as a beloved symbol. And he *was* beloved: Everyone who encountered him seemed to find him inexplicably endearing. An English writer named George Ruxton, who passed through the West shortly after the American occupation, was intrigued by the contrasts within Carson's personality—his laconic homeliness on the one hand, and his legendary status on the other. Ruxton wrote, "Small in stature, and slenderly limbed, but with muscles of wire, with a fair complexion and quiet, intelligent features, to look at Kit none would suppose that the mild being before him was an incarnate devil in an Indian fight."

William Tecumseh Sherman, then a young army lieutenant, met Carson briefly in California and expressed a similar astonishment at the scout's appearance: "I cannot express my surprise at beholding a small, stoop-shouldered man, with freckled face, soft blue eyes, and nothing to indicate extraordinary courage or daring. He spoke but little, and answered questions in monosyllables." But, Sherman went on, "Carson's integrity was simply perfect. The Indians knew it and would trust him any day before they would us [soldiers], or the president, either!"

"His voice is as soft and gentle as a woman's," wrote George Brewerton in a perceptive article for *Harper's Monthly* after having ridden with Carson on one of his transcontinental treks. "The hero of a hundred desperate encounters, whose life has been mostly spent amid wildernesses where the white man is almost unknown, is one of Dame Nature's gentlemen." For other people, especially women, Carson's humility came across as a disconcerting awkwardness. "He was uncouth . . . a lonely man," recalled Marian Sloan, an Anglo girl who lived in Santa Fe. "His was a great heart and very kind, yet he wore shyness before his face like a veil."

The majority of the public apparently saw something beyond the veil, however, for Carson's fame now spread far and wide. Rivers, lakes, passes, trails, and mountain peaks bore his name. A tiny outpost in

Nevada, eventually to become the territorial and then state capital, would be called Carson City. *Kit Carson,* an elegant steamship launched a year earlier, now threshed the Mississippi and Missouri waters.

Carson was somewhat oblivious to the attention he stirred. Even if it had occurred to him to cash in on his burgeoning fame, he lacked the talents to promote himself, and this only made him more authentic. The man was just plain hard to reach in remote New Mexico and had, up until the summer of 1849, been so constantly on the move that few reporters had gotten a word with him. Keeping himself scarce whetted the public's appetite, for nothing stokes a myth like inaccessibility.

Carson's reticence led people to fill in the gaps and project upon him whatever qualities they wanted a frontier hero to have. Most magazine and newspaper writers couldn't resist the urge to make him taller, stronger, more dashing, and more eloquent than he actually was. Once, on the Oregon Trail, Carson happened to encounter a man from Arkansas who'd heard the famous scout was in the vicinity. "I say, stranger, are you Kit Carson?" he demanded. Carson answered in the affirmative, and the man studied him doubtfully. "Look 'ere," the Arkansan finally said, "you ain't the kind of Kit Carson I'm looking for."

It was only a matter of time before popular novelists would take up the character of Kit Carson and shamelessly fictionalize him. That year, 1849, saw the publication of *Kit Carson: The Prince of the Gold Hunters,* the first pulp fiction paperback featuring Carson as its swashbuckling protagonist. In this forgettable story, written by a hack named Charles Averill, Carson slaughters Indians by the score and predictably rescues a young girl who has been kidnapped by savages. Carson is presented as a great hero who had never lost a battle, a man with "a lynx-like eye and an imperturbable coolness" who is "as little seen as he is widely known." Carson's slight stature has, in Averill's book, swelled to superhuman proportions—he has a "mighty frame," "massive arms," "prodigious strength," and a chest built like "a fortress." Among other twists, the story involves a prairie fire, a treasure-laden cave, a naïve Harvard student pursued west by an evil miserly uncle, and a perilous escape from Indian captors in which Carson frees his party by having one of his comrades hold a torch to his wrists to sizzle away the ropes that bind him.

Averill's twenty-five-cent novel was a "blood and thunder," as the genre was known, a precursor to the modern Western, briskly paced and packed with cliffhangers and hair-raising scrapes. Although he claimed the book was "founded on actual facts," Averill did not make the slightest attempt to learn anything about the real Kit Carson or seek permission to use his name. As one of his actual facts, Averill fabulously asserts that Carson single-handedly "discovered" the goldfields of California. Yet *Prince of the Gold Hunters* became wildly successful, a best-seller as measured by the standards of its day. More important, many other writers would soon copy Averill's formula. His was only the first in what would be a long line of hyperbolic thrillers, pulp novels, and juvenile biographies—some seventy books would be written over the years—starring Kit Carson as avenger, rescuer, horseman, and Indian killer, the "Nestor of the Rockies," the "Happy Warrior," the "Knight of the Prairie," the "Captain of Adventure." He had become an action-figure hero. This lurid body of literature would catapult Carson into a stratosphere of celebrity that few nineteenth-century Americans would ever enjoy.

It was difficult to exaggerate how hungry the nation had become for a single heroic character who could personify the surge of Manifest Destiny that was so dramatically changing the country. Of course, many Americans suspected that stealing land from another sovereign power ran counter to the country's noblest first principles—as did stealing land roamed for millennia by aborigines who just might be human beings. Certainly, there were doubts tugging at the national excitement. Perhaps the public found comfort in the possibility that extraordinary, and yet also quite ordinary, Anglo-Americans already inhabited this new Western world, exalting American accomplishments while simplifying the stickiest themes of the conquest.

Kit Carson, more than any figure on the Western stage, filled the role. Honest, unassuming, wry around a campfire, tongue-tied around the ladies, clear in his intentions, swift in action, a bit of a loner: He was the prototype of the Western hero. Before there were Stetson hats and barbed-wire fences, before there were Wild West shows or Colt six-shooters to be slung at the OK Corral, there was Nature's Gentleman, the original purple cliché of the purple sage.

Carson hated it all. Without his consent, and without receiving a single dollar, he was becoming a caricature.

◙

In late October, about a week after the bodies of the White party were discovered, a group of Pueblo Indians reported that they had visited the encampment of some Jicarilla Apaches somewhere out on the plains to the east of the Santa Fe Trail. In the camp they had seen a white American female and her baby, obviously captives and in some distress. When this news reached Santa Fe, a company of 1st Dragoons was immediately dispatched from Taos under the command of Maj. William Grier. Their mission was to track down the Indians and bring Ann White and her daughter back alive. Grier's mounted soldiers galloped eastward through Taos Canyon to Carson's ranch on the Rayado. After conferring with the tracker and scout, Major Grier persuaded Carson to come along on the rescue.

Carson was intimately acquainted with the Jicarilla tribe. Since setting up the ranch, he'd had several dealings with them. They were a small branch of the Apaches who ranged across northern New Mexico in tight warrior bands. Like all Apaches, they spoke a dialect of the Athapaskan tongue and were ethnically and linguistically related to, though not friendly with, the Navajos. The Jicarillas had few allies. They were overpowered by larger, better-armed, and more cohesive warrior tribes of the plains, especially the Comanches, who made frequent incursions into their territory.

The Jicarillas were a cornered people, living in the interstices, in the shadow of stronger nations. Years later a spokesman of the Jicarillas would remember this dark time when everyone in the tribe seemed plunged in fear. "At the first sound, even a shout, they all made for the brush," he recalled. "And whenever they went out on the plains, they were afraid to stay there."

The tribe's name derived from its proficiency in constructing tight straw baskets—*jicarilla* means "little basket" in Spanish. The name bespoke the tribe's peripatetic lifestyle. The Jicarillas were hunter-gatherers who roamed the watersheds in search of berries, roots, seeds, nuts, and wild plants; as a light and portable means of carrying their foraged foods, baskets were an important part of their culture. Their baskets were reputedly woven so tightly that they could hold liquid. One army account described a raid in which Jicarilla warriors stole a herd of milking cows from the Rayado area; pursuing soldiers found the thieves with the stolen cows surrounded by scores of baskets that were hanging from the trees and filled to their brims with milk. "Evidently," the reporting officer wrote sardonically, "they were planning to go into the dairy business in a big way." The Jicarillas were also expert hunters—pursuing elk, deer, antelope, and mountain sheep as well as small game like jackrabbits, squirrels, and beaver. Occasionally they moved out onto the plains to hunt buffalo, but they did so cautiously, for these expeditions only invited Comanche attack.

The Comanches, in turn, were reacting to new pressures of their own. Pushed steadily westward by the rapid settlement of Texas, the slaughter of the Great Plains buffalo herds, and the creation of new reservations for relocated Eastern tribes in the Indian Territory of Oklahoma, the Comanche warriors had stepped up their attacks on the Jicarillas in recent years. Old borders were changing, and nomadic tribes that had traditionally operated over huge areas were now brushing up against one another as never before. American expansion had set in motion a complex chain reaction of social displacements; even in the immense Southwest, there was only so much land to go around.

Since the American occupation of New Mexico, the Jicarilla hunting grounds had consistently thinned as new settlers moved into their already attenuated territory. Squeezed in this way, the Jicarillas turned to raiding. Their agriculture was limited, and they were finding wild game increasingly scarce. They were understandably angered, and at the same time tantalized by new settlements like Maxwell's growing operation on the Rayado. This was their home turf, and had been for centuries. According to Jicarilla creation stories, their ancestors had emerged into the world not far from here, in a place they broadly referred to as "near the center of the earth." In the early 1700s, Spanish soldiers had explored "La Jicarilla," as they called the wild world beyond the mountains, and they briefly considered building a presidio in its midst but then abandoned the idea as impractical—the area was simply too remote and too overrun with warlike Apaches.

Yet now, a century and a half later, the once-proud Jicarilla tribe was tiny—amounting to no more than 1,000 people, possibly only 500. They were not a twentieth as large or as powerful as their Athapaskan cousins, the Navajos, but they were more desperate. In contrast to the Navajos, who principally stole livestock to increase their already considerable wealth in a risky game of status, the Jicarillas stole to survive. In the three years since the American occupation, the Jicarillas had swiped many thousands of sheep from ranchers in northeastern New Mexico. Carson was not surprised to learn that the Jicarillas were behind the massacre of the James White party and the kidnapping of Ann White, her daughter, and servant. For several years the outrages committed by the Jicarillas had been hotly discussed throughout this part of the territory. An army lieutenant stationed in Taos reported in the summer of 1849 that the Jicarillas were "robbing everywhere throughout the mountains." Col. George A. McGill at the time described the Jicarillas as "troublesome" and "incorrigible," and darkly predicted that they would "continue to rob and murder our citizens until they are exterminated."

When he was governor, Charles Bent characterized the Jicarilla Apaches as "a great annoyance" to life in New Mexico. They were "an indolent and cowardly people," he wrote, "living principally by thefts committed on the Mexicans, there being but little game in the country through which they range, and the fear of other Indians not permitting them to venture on the plains for buffalo."

Whether these assessments from the capital were accurate, the Jicarilla Apache were not an abstract problem for Kit Carson. To make a success of his ranching enterprise, he had to come to terms with the Jicarillas and the changing constellation of other tribes that surrounded him. The Jicarillas would often drop by Rayado for what Carson and his fellow ranchers called "dinner stops." They expected food, tobacco, and other presents, and they always came in sufficiently intimidating numbers to lace their visits with the threat of attack.

In dealing with the Jicarillas, Carson drew on the rough art of frontier diplomacy he had learned as a mountain man, a diplomacy that was entirely pragmatic. He understood the importance of holding peace councils and constantly renewing alliances among tribes, but he did not hesitate to attack any band that had attacked him. He practiced the code of swift reprisal that was almost universally practiced by the Indians themselves: Failure to strike back, he understood, would only be interpreted as weakness and inevitably lead to an even bolder assault.

A few months earlier Carson was briefly visited by a man named Charles Pancoast, a Pennsylvanian traveling the Santa Fe Trail en route to the goldfields of California. Pancoast's diaries leave a vivid portrait of Carson's work on the ranch and his ongoing troubles with the Jicarilla Apaches. Pancoast described Carson as a "Rocky Mountain Hunter" wearing moccasins and buckskins, with shoulder-length hair and a sombrero to block the summer sun. Carson welcomed Pancoast cordially enough, but the visitor was struck by how taciturn and humble the "famous Mountaineer" was; Pancoast had to goad him to talk about himself, but eventually Carson let down his guard and the two men stayed up late around the campfire, discussing Carson's adventures. At one point, at Pancoast's urging, Carson even showed him a few old wounds from his mountain exploits.

Carson was preoccupied with his ranch, which Pancoast said was "not at all stylish." Carson described the difficulties he'd had in protecting his stock from the ravages of the Apaches. He had made a habit of treating all visiting Indians kindly and lavishing them with gifts, but on at least one occasion he had been forced to ask U.S. soldiers to help him pursue raiders. "Being thoroughly acquainted with the haunts of the Indians," Pancoast wrote, "he had punished them so severely that they had found it their best policy to make their peace with him. He now enjoyed their Friendship, and often gave them meat; and they no longer molested his stock, although they continued to steal from others."

Once, Carson brought his family over to the Rayado. Teresina Bent, Charles Bent's daughter, was living with the Carsons then, and years later she recalled a terrifying encounter the family had with an Indian tribe. Carson had left on a business errand of some sort, and while he was away, a band of Indians, probably Jicarilla Apaches, showed up on the property, demanding food. "We women all set to work cooking," Teresina recalled, "coffee and meat and whatever else we had."

The chief of the war party saw me and wanted to buy me to make me his wife. He kept offering horses—ten, fifteen, twenty horses. We acted friendly with the Indians so as not to make the chief angry. My, I was so frightened! And while I carried platters of food from the kitchen, the tears were running down my cheeks. That made the chief laugh. He was bound to buy me, and when they all got through eating he said that they would wait; if I was not delivered to him by the time the sun touched a hill there in the west, he would take me by force. Then he and the warriors went out a little way and camped right in sight of the house. We started to [make] bullets. We were all ready for a siege when, just as the sun touched the hill in the west, Mr. Carson and a company of soldiers came galloping up the valley. The Indians saw them and went away. Then I cried some more, I was so glad. I did not want to go with the dirty chief.

◎

Maj. William Grier and Kit Carson took off from the Rayado ranch with a company of dragoons and sped east some forty miles to the scene of the White massacre. Although it had been several weeks since White and his escorts were slain, Grier and Carson discovered the setting much as the Jicarilla assailants had left it. In his dictated autobiography, he noted that they found "trunks that were broken open, harnesses cut, everything destroyed that the Indians could not carry with them."

Carson studied the scene closely and gazed out over the endless plains, looking for anything that might tell him which way the Jicarillas had ridden. Tracking was his greatest talent. Plenty of mountain men equaled or surpassed him in other skills, but no one was better than Carson at "reading sign," as it was called. There was a narrative on the ground if one had the knack for seeing it. By looking for faint patterns imprinted on the land, by studying the individual blades of grass, by analyzing the dung of the horses he was following, an expert tracker could tease out a story from the most fragmentary of facts. He might look for sheeny compactions in the soil, or tiny cinders blown from a far-off campfire, or curious gaps in the spiderwebs strung between trees. He might notice the broken-off limb of a cholla cactus and see a sticky liquid oozing from the wound; by assaying its amount and the quality of its tackiness, he might judge how long ago someone or something had passed through.

It was early November. The skies were iron gray and touched with the cold breath of winter. The signs were almost impossible to read. Carson said it "was the most difficult trail that I ever followed." Not only were the tracks several weeks old, but they had been further obscured by a light snowstorm. Carson discovered that the Jicarillas had obscured their trail by splitting into different parties after breaking down their camps each morning. These smaller parties, he found, would vector off across the prairie in multiple directions, only to reconvene at some appointed place that evening. Piecing together these byzantine lines was slow and painstaking work, and several times they came close to losing the trail and abandoning the chase. But one day they came upon the residue of a Jicarilla camp, and Carson took heart: Lying in the prairie grass was an article of woman's clothing.

Several days later they passed the next former Jicarilla encampment, and again Carson found a woman's garment. He began to think that Ann White had deliberately left a trail of her belongings, like so many crumbs for her rescuers to follow. Seeing these articles encouraged Carson. As he recalled in a characteristic understatement, "It was the cause of renewed energy."

Major Grier and Carson followed the trail eastward for twelve days, pushing almost to the border of Texas. They passed into the first suggestions of the Staked Plains, a prickly expanse of mesquite, yucca, and cholla cactus. Then Carson spotted fires smoking on the horizon. It was the encampment of several hundred Jicarilla Apaches, under the leadership of a well-known chief named White Wolf, set along the banks of the Canadian River near Tucumcari Butte. As they approached the camp, Grier and his men were spread out over great distances, and a miscommunication occurred. Carson gave the signal to attack, and he started off in a canter toward the encampment. But Grier countermanded Carson's signal and instead ordered his men to wait and confer. Grier thought it was best to approach the Jicarillas in a conciliatory posture and request a parley with White Wolf. Carson, realizing that he was the only one charging the Jicarilla camp, had to stop abruptly and wheel his horse around.

He strongly disagreed with Grier's decision to delay. If Ann White was alive and hidden somewhere in the encampment, the Jicarillas would not turn her over without a fight. Grier's best chance of success, Carson felt, was to surprise the Jicarillas in a lightning assault that gave them no time to react. But now precious minutes were dripping away. The Jicarillas eventually spotted Grier and his men, and began to pack their belongings in haste. The element of surprise had been entirely lost. Several more minutes went by and still the dragoons waited. One of the Jicarillas picked up his rifle and shot Grier in the chest from a distance of several hundred yards. It was an extraordinary bit of marksmanship, but the Jicarilla rifleman was too far away to do much damage. The ball tore through Grier's clothes and knocked the wind out of him but caused only a slight bruise.

Recovering from the shock, Major Grier finally gave the order to charge. Yet, Carson argued, "The order was too late for the desired effect." By the time dragoons reached the camp, the Jicarillas had dispersed, spreading out in all directions. "There was only one Indian in the camp," Carson recalled. "He, swimming into the river hard by, was shot." Some of the dragoons took off in pursuit of the fleeing Jicarillas, killing one and taking several prisoners.

But then Carson spotted something. About two hundred yards from the campsite, a figure was sprawled on the hard-baked plain. The men rode over to inspect and found to their dismay that it was the corpse of an American woman. Ann White had been shot through the heart with a single arrow. "She was perfectly warm," Carson said, "and had not been killed more than five minutes." By the looks of things, she must have known that her rescuers were at hand. She had been running away from the Jicarillas. Carson wrote, "It was apparent that she was endeavoring to make her escape when she received the fatal shot."

Carson studied Ann White's face. It was obvious to him that she had been horribly mistreated. "She was emaciated," he later told a friend, "the victim of a foul disease, and bore the sorrows of a lifelong agony on her face." Probably she had been passed among the warriors and repeatedly raped, Carson said, as "the prostitute of the tribe." A soldier in the party later wrote that Mrs. White was "a frail, delicate, and very beautiful woman, but having undergone such usage as she suffered nothing but a wreck remained; it was literally covered with blows and scratches. Her countenance even after death indicated a hopeless creature. Over her corpse, we swore vengeance upon her persecutors." Carson believed that Ann White had been fatally ill. "She could not possibly have lived long," he said. "Her life, I think, should never be regretted by her friends. She is surely far more happy in heaven, with her God, than among friends of this earth."

Although he kept his opinions to himself, Carson was plainly furious with Major Grier. Carson felt "certain that if the Indians had been charged immediately on our arrival," Ann White might have been saved. The men buried her in the prairie and then began to pick through the various belongings the Jicarillas had left in their camp. One of the soldiers discovered a book that the White family had evidently brought with them from Missouri, a paperback novel starring none other than Kit Carson. Almost certainly it was Charles Averill's blood and thunder, *Kit Carson: The Prince of the Gold Hunters*. Carson could not read it, of course, but later, perhaps over the campfire, one of the soldiers regaled him with passages from the story. *"Kit Carson! His lip, that proud, that determined lip, was compressed with the firmness of a rock between his clenched teeth as he held his devoted hand within the flame, scorching it to the very bone!"*

This was the first time that the real Kit Carson had come in contact with his own myth. "The book was the first of its kind I had ever seen, in which I was made a great hero, slaying Indians by the hundred," Carson said. At first he was vaguely amused by this colorful novel, but then he began to think of Ann White. He imagined her reading it while enduring her miserable captivity. In Averill's story, Kit Carson finds the kidnapped girl and saves the day, fulfilling his vow to her distraught parents back in Boston that he would scour the American West until she was found. But in this instance the real Kit Carson had failed to avert a disaster; he feared Averill's fiction may have given Ann White a false hope. "Knowing that I lived near," Carson said, "I have often thought that as Mrs. White read the book, she prayed for my appearance and that she would be saved." Neither Ann White's daughter nor her servant were ever found.

The White murder would haunt Kit Carson—"I have much regretted the failure to save the life of so esteemed a lady," he wrote a decade later—and he would continue to be troubled by the implications of his growing celebrity. He insisted that everything in Charles Averill's book was a lie. Later, when a friend offered him a copy of his own, Carson threatened to "burn the damn thing."

The *Santa Fe New Mexican* reported the White case's tragic end on November 28, 1849. "We learn," the paper noted dolefully, "that the wife of the late Mr. J.M. White has at last been deprived of her sufferings, having been shot by the Indians." The paper's editors went on to insist that this murder, along with the "recent butchery of Mr. White," called for "a terrible and immediate retribution. The tribes surrounding this Territory should be confined to certain fixed limits and there should be compelled to remain under penalty of utter annihilation. It is folly to think of securing peace by making treaties with these Indians. They must be forced to a complete submission."

BOOK THREE

Monster Slayer

He was a brave Indian, deserved a better fate, but he had
placed himself on the wrong path.

—KIT CARSON

Chapter 36 THE FEARING TIME

The two horses were ready, and so were their riders. The animals flared their nostrils in the desert air and stamped their feet in anticipation. All the bets had been placed. Some five hundred Navajo spectators had taken their spots on the sides of the dusty track outside the American fort. They were splayed out on their bright-patterned blankets, reveling in the carnival atmosphere, shouting out encouragements and the occasional tame invective.

The excitement had been building all day. Since morning the Navajos had been streaming in from the rimrock country, women and children as well as warriors, on horseback and on foot, wearing their finest outfits and bearing serapes and jewelry to trade with the soldiers—whom the Navajos sometimes called "Something-Sticking-Out-From-The-Foreheads" because of the distinct visors protruding from their army-issue caps. There had been bartering and games and feasting through the midday, but in the afternoon the main event—the races—had begun. The Navajos were entranced by the spectacle of the track. Not only were they avid gamblers, they were a tribe with a proud history of horsemanship. Racing ran deep in their blood.

This was to be the last race of the afternoon, the most important race, the one with the fastest horses and the biggest stakes. "Large bets, larger than on the other races, were made on both sides," recalled one witness. "The Indians, some of them mounted on fine ponies, were richly dressed, and all appeared to be there to see the race, and not with any hostile intentions."

In lieu of money, the wagers were made in the form of hard goods: The Indians bet their fine blankets and silver wares, while the soldiers wagered U.S. government property taken from the fort commissary—barrels of bacon, hogsheads of molasses, and the like—an illegal practice that the fort commander, in the interest of entertainment, was willing to overlook. Most of the soldiers were watching from the gates of the fort, but others were mingling with the Indian throngs. Kegs of whiskey had been flowing freely through the day (some Navajos called the great casks "hollow-woods"), and now soldiers and Indians alike were good and drunk.

It was a bright crisp day in Indian country, early fall of 1861. Hints of autumn played on the air. The chamisa had taken on a blazing yellow, and the aspens were just beginning to turn on Mount Taylor, whose broad shoulders rose impressively from the *malpais* in the distant east. The papery dry leaves of the cottonwoods clapped softly in the wind, like a thousand gloved hands at an opera.

Fort Fauntleroy was one of several strongholds that the United States military had built in Navajo country, largely on the basis of information gleaned from the 1849 Washington Expedition and the resulting maps pieced together by army topographer James Simpson. The fort was set in a beautiful spot called Bear Springs—the same ancient gathering place tucked in the Zuni Mountains where Narbona had met with Alexander Doniphan in 1846 to sign the first treaty between the Navajos and the United States government.

The regimental surgeon at the fort, an Irish doctor named F. E. Kavanaugh, owned a fleet thoroughbred that he insisted could not be beaten. Kavanaugh had been racing him all summer and the horse had never lost. In anticipation of today's contest, the soldiers posted at the fort had pampered and trained the champion, making sure it was in top form. To jockey his prized animal, Kavanaugh selected a lithe and small-statured New Mexican lieutenant named Rafael Ortiz, a fierce competitor who was always at home in a saddle.

But the Navajos had their own prized pony—a jittery little sorrel with a spirit for the track. Rumors circulated that Navajo medicine men had performed elaborate ceremonies to ensure victory for their animal, chanting over a fetish shaped in the image of a horse. A young Navajo boy, light and quick of reflex, would ride the sorrel that day, but stories differ about whose horse it was: According to one account the pony was owned by a large Navajo man the Americans called Pistol Bullet. Other accounts say the owner was none other than Manuelito, Narbona's bold and truculent son-in-law, who had emerged as one of the great leaders of the tribe.

Manuelito was an expert horseman, a man attentive to good breeding and rich enough to own the best. If he was indeed there at the fort that day, watching his horse compete, enjoying a moment of peace, it was a rare appearance—and most likely he would have kept himself incognito. For Manuelito was the sworn enemy of the Americans. Consistently, emphatically, categorically, he alone among his tribesmen had advocated war. Known by his countrymen as Hastiin Ch'ilhaajinii, or Black Weeds, Manuelito hated everything about the Americans. They had slaughtered his cattle herds. They had murdered his father-in-law. They had stuck forts in the craw of the Navajo nation. To their every demand, his response was the same uncut rage. The people, he roared, must drive the *bilagaana* from the country.

ȳ

Certainly he had tried. The last few years—1858, 1859, 1860—had been particularly violent ones, and always Manuelito had been at the center of the maelstrom, his steady, implacable voice urging his countrymen not to budge an inch. The Doniphan treaty, signed with so much optimism and goodwill, had proven scarcely worth the paper it was written on, as had the Washington treaty three years later. The old war was still very much alive. If the sheep-rustling Diné had not changed their ways, neither had the New Mexicans, who continued leading freelance raids into Navajo country to steal children and win spoils.

But over the last few years, it seemed, the war had escalated into something else altogether, a conflict of a different order of magnitude. The Diné now had enemies on all sides. They suffered nearly constant attacks not just from New Mexicans, but also from Utes, Comanches, Apaches, and other ancient foes—as well as from their new foe, the American soldiers, who inflicted their punishments with increasing vigor. It seemed to the Navajo that they were surrounded by wolves. Even nature had turned against them—for several seasons the Navajo country had broiled under a terrible drought. People were starving to death, selling their children for food, fighting amongst themselves. Their society was stressed to the breaking point. The medicine men had lost their touch, the old ceremonies didn't seem to work. The Diné had reached the nadir of their tribe's existence, a decade of doubt and struggle that they still call, to this day, the *nahondzod*, "the fearing time."

The American military commanders in Santa Fe, even the more obtuse ones, recognized that the old war between the Navajos and the New Mexicans was a two-sided quarrel, with legitimate grievances flowing in both directions. But they almost always accepted the New Mexican version of the conflict—"chastising" the Navajos for their treaty infractions while looking the other way when Hispanic militias and ragtag vigilante groups marched west. As far as Manuelito was concerned, the Americans had become the bigger problem; if it weren't for them, he thought, the Diné could hold their own in any war against the New Mexicans. Yet there stood the United States government, stubbornly insisting on playing the role of a one-eyed umpire.

Part of the problem was a lack of consistency. From year to year the Navajos had little idea whom they were dealing with; from their point of view, the Great White Father in Washington was restless and fickle, for he kept sending new emissaries to the territory. Since the American occupation of New Mexico, a dizzying succession of commanders had come and gone: Kearny, Doniphan, Price, Washington, Beall, Munroe, Sumner, Garland, Bonneville, Fauntleroy, and now, the current military governor, Col. Edward Canby. Each of these men had attacked the "Navajo problem" in his own way, with lesser or greater degrees of insight and militancy. But the Navajo conflict was a rat's nest, a Gordian knot of troubles, and largely because of it, the 9th Military Department, as New Mexico was known, was considered a hardship post, a shit-hole, a quagmire. The territory's myriad adversities wore a soldier down. Within the army, no one much cared for the place, and few were inclined to stay long enough to really understand the Navajos and the true nature of the conflict—let alone solve it.

If the cast of American leaders had been kaleidoscopic, the main themes were hammered out with an almost monotonous consistency: The Navajos must stop roaming and become sedentary, full-time farmers, working private plots of individually owned land. They must become town-dwellers, and preferably Christians, hewing to clear national boundaries. They must select a single chief to speak for all the Navajo people and answer for all their crimes. In short, the Diné must cease being what they were—an amorphous concatenation of seminomadic bands—and become a single political entity. Over time, the tone with which the American commanders issued their demands became ever more shrill: The Navajos must do all these things, or face extinction.

During the mid-1850s there was perhaps only one bright spot in the American-Navajo relationship. For a few brief years a truly competent man held the office of Indian agent to the Navajo people. His name was Henry Linn Dodge, a perceptive young man from Wisconsin who had lived for years in the territory. Dodge got his first exposure to the Diné in 1849, when he accompanied the Washington Expedition into the Navajo lands. Most Indian agents regarded their posts as mere sinecures, and many were extravagantly corrupt. But Dodge pursued his job with great zeal and a curiosity to match. Soon after his appointment in 1853, he moved his office deep into Diné country. He learned to speak Navajo. He traveled constantly without military escort and befriended all the headmen, attending nightchants and other ceremonials. He brought blacksmiths to teach Navajos metallurgy, bought them wagonloads of hoes and axes often with his own money, led numerous peace delegations to Santa Fe, and lobbied for the creation of schools and the building of mills on Navajo land. He fell in love with the Navajo people—he even married within the tribe (so it was widely said). The Navajos called him "Red Sleeves" and considered him a friend, perhaps the first *bilagaana* who ever bothered to understand them.

His four-year tenure was a testament to the potential power of one-man diplomacy: While Dodge was agent, the Navajos remained substantially at peace, and reports of their raiding were scarce. For a brief time even the tenor of the talk about them changed. William

Davis, a Harvard-trained lawyer and circuit court judge who was also a writer of some note and had made a trip with Dodge and other peace emissaries deep into Navajo country in 1855, theorized that the Diné may well be a remnant of the Lost Tribes of Israel (a fashionable anthropological topic of his day). "In many respects the Navajos are the most interesting tribe of Indians in our country," Davis wrote in his perceptive study of New Mexico, *El Gringo*, published in 1856. "The modern doctrine of 'Women's Rights' may be said to prevail among them to a very liberal extent. Women are admitted into their councils and sometimes control their deliberations. The Navajos are mild in disposition, and very seldom commit murder." They were, Davis concluded, "a superior race of Indians."

With Henry Dodge tirelessly soliciting on their behalf, the Navajos' reputation as the incorrigible thugs of the Southwest was softening. But in 1857 this brief period of amity came to an abrupt end. While hunting in the Zuni Mountains, Red Sleeves was murdered, reportedly by Apache Indians.

Everything Dodge had worked for soon evaporated; the relationship between the Diné and the Americans never recovered.

◻

The conflict between the *bilagaana* and the Navajos came to a flash point in the spring of 1858, when Manuelito insisted on grazing his cattle herds on the grounds of an American fort called Fort Defiance, deep in the Navajo red rock country, on the present-day border between Arizona and New Mexico. From the moment of its construction in 1851, the Americans had intended Fort Defiance, as its name suggests, to be an irritant and a provocation to the Navajos—and it was. When the American soldiers instructed Manuelito to remove his animals from U.S. property, the headman refused. "The water there is mine, not yours," he reportedly said, "and the same with the grass. Even the ground it grows from belongs to me, not to you." And so on May 29, soldiers marched out in the field and shot every last head of Manuelito's cattle herd—some sixty in all—and left the carcasses to rot in the field.

A month after the herd was slaughtered, an anonymous Navajo came to Fort Defiance to trade with the soldiers. When no one was looking, the Navajo turned and fired an arrow into the back of a teenage black slave owned by the American commander, Maj. William Brooks. While the Navajo made a clean getaway, the stricken boy, whose name was Jim, attempted to pull the arrow out himself, but the shaft broke off with the arrowhead lodged deep in his body. Jim died of his wound several days later. Interpreting the incident (probably correctly) as a personal attack, Major Brooks threatened to obliterate the Navajos if they did not produce the murderer at once. A few weeks later the Navajos obliged, hauling in the corpse of the man they said was the culprit. But the fort surgeon conducted an autopsy on the cadaver and determined that the Diné were trying to pull a fast one: The body was that of a Mexican who met almost none of the physical descriptions of the murderer.

After that, the situation escalated into a fairly hot war, with the American army leading multiple forays into Navajo country to hunt down Manuelito. But like a Navajo Rob Roy, the shadowy headman stayed just a few steps ahead of the soldiers. Then in April 1860, Manuelito organized a thousand Navajo warriors and staged a full-frontal assault on Fort Defiance. Striking before dawn and armed primarily with arrows, he and his warriors occupied a number of the fort buildings, killed a United States soldier, and produced numerous casualties. However, Manuelito's near triumph at Fort Defiance did nothing to change American policy in the end, but it cemented his reputation as the preeminent warrior of the Navajo.

By all accounts and photographs, he looked the part: Black Weeds was tall and dark with a distinct air of menace, the sort of man who made people, even other Navajos, edgy. His shoulders were broad, his chest muscular, his torso long and lean. He had a scar on the left side of his chest from a gunshot wound sustained in a fight with Comanches. He carried himself with great confidence, for he was one of the true *ricos* of the tribe, blessed with many thousands of sheep, numerous children, and at least two wives—Narbona's daughter and a Mexican woman named Juanita he had stolen in a raid. His chin was scruffed with a wispy beard, and his facial features, chiseled and vaguely Asian, made him look like a Mongol chieftain. Nearly every photograph of Manuelito shows the scowl of an all-consuming wrath. A biography now taught in Navajo schools describes Black Weeds this way: "An angry fire burned within him, and he refused to put it out."

He was born in 1818, a son of the Bit'ahni, or Folded Arms clan, and grew up in a place called the Bear's Ears, in present-day Utah. Because his homeland was close to the mountain country of the roving Ute Indians, he grew up trilingual, fluent in both Navajo and Ute as well as Spanish. Even as a child he carried himself with a jaunty arrogance that made people notice. His friends teased him that even though he had not been on a single raid, he walked around as though he were a headman.

Young Manuelito replied, "I walk like a headman now so that when I become one, I will already know how to behave."

In 1835, at the age of seventeen, he participated in his first great battle, the ambush on the invading Mexican army at Copper Pass organized by Narbona. He donned a war helmet, carried a buckskin shield, and painted serpents on the soles of his moccasins. He dipped his arrows in a poison made from rattlesnake blood and yucca-leaf juice. During the battle he made a name for himself by attacking and killing a Pueblo Indian in a hand-to-hand fight. He scalped his victim, and later chewed on the bloody skin so that he might draw power from it and become "a true warrior." From his actions that day he won the nom de guerre Hashkeh Naabaah, or Angry Warrior.

He married Narbona's daughter and lived with the great leader's outfit. As a young man he traveled to Santa Fe with Narbona and watched him confer with Mexican leaders in the Palace of the Governors. An account in *Navajo Biographies* notes that during his sojourn in Santa Fe, Manuelito found an unexpected pleasure: "When he stepped boldly into the sunlight, he laughed to himself at the reaction of the timid citizens who jumped in spite of themselves at the sight of the imposing young Navajo. He held his face stern and solemn, never looking to the left or right. He could feel the shock of his appearance and delighted in frightening the passersby. He laughed later, 'Those little Mexicans—they jump around like rabbits!'"

As he grew into full manhood, Manuelito came to think that his father-in-law's efforts at peacemaking were wrongheaded, naïve, and ultimately ruinous for the tribe. He was present at Bear Springs when Narbona and Doniphan signed the first big treaty, and he was present when Col. John Washington's men cut Narbona down.

Through it all, Manuelito had seen where diplomacy led. He had felt his world shrinking. He had watched his people's pride wither under the politics of concession. And so he urged his countrymen: *No more.*

❧

If Manuelito was an absolutist, other Navajos were willing to bend and accommodate. They frequented the American forts to trade and drink, to gather whatever sorry crumbs might be tossed their way. Some Navajo women became whores for the soldiers. Other Navajos hired themselves as quislings, spying on their own people or guiding military expeditions into their homeland. One man in particular, a notoriously clever Navajo traitor named Sandoval, became so good at playing both ends against the middle that his band acquired the name Diné Ana'aii, the Enemy Navajo—an aspersion by which his descendants are known to this day.

Despite what Manuelito said about them, the Americans weren't all bad. In response to the drought, the fort commanders had pursued a policy of mercy (or at least one calculated to deter raiding) by dispensing rations to the hungriest Navajos. It was easier to feed Navajos than fight them, went the new catchphrase. From the gates of the fort, soldiers handed out supplies of meat and flour to the Navajo throngs. Ration day became a festive affair, a day of good cheer—one captain at Fort Fauntleroy sensed a new "friendly feeling" within the tribe. It was only natural that the Navajos and soldiers would hatch the idea of crowning the day with a series of horse races. The spirited contests seemed to symbolize the tentative détente.

Now the moment had come, the day's grand finale. Rafael Ortiz and the young Navajo rider nosed their horses up to the starting line.

As was traditional at the fort, the racers did not wait for a gun to start; instead they relied on an informal honor system in which either rider could call for a restart if he thought his opponent had bolted early. Three times the Navajo boy turned back, but on the fourth attempt, the two riders sprinted across the dusty flats as the liquored crowds roared in delight.

At first the two horses kept pace with each other, but by the end of the first furlong the spectators could tell something was wrong with the sorrel. The Navajo rider was having trouble controlling his mount, and soon he veered completely off the track. Ortiz continued on, his thoroughbred galloping effortlessly across the finish line.

The Navajos were shocked and then outraged. Their inspection of the sorrel suggested foul play: Its bridle had been slashed, they said. Someone had sabotaged the horse. They demanded a rematch.

But the soldiers refused. Dr. Kavanaugh's thoroughbred had won fair and square, they insisted. They collected their wagers and marched around the parade grounds with Kavanaugh's horse, flaunting their victory. Said one participant: "A procession of the winning party went whooping and hallooing" to the sound of "drums beating, and fifes and fiddles screeching."

The Navajos returned to their camp and sulked. Like so many other times since the Americans had arrived, the Diné felt they'd been double-crossed. There was much discussion about what to do next. Most thought they should cut their losses and go home. But a group of hotheads, drunk like their soldier counterparts, had other ideas. They rose up and stormed over to the fort. They swaggered over to the guardhouse, yelling insults and half-audible threats, demanding that their wagers be returned.

Then, from within the gates, the crack of a rifle pierced the afternoon air, and Fort Fauntleroy was plunged into chaos.

❖

The officer in charge of Fort Fauntleroy, Col. Manuel Chaves, was a legendary Indian-fighter hugely admired within the territory, second in reputation only to Kit Carson himself. Short, stocky, and fierce-tempered, Chaves had a crinkled face of olive skin, a thick beard, and long raven hair that skimmed his shoulders. The forty-three-year-old Chaves hailed from a venerable family that dated back to the first colonists of New Mexico, and whose Portuguese and Spanish ancestors had won glory in crucial battles that drove the Moors from the Iberian Peninsula.

Manuel Antonio Chaves was born along the bosque near Albuquerque and grew up in the tiny frontier settlement of Cebolleta on the contested edge of Navajo country (the same isolated village the young warrior Narbona had nearly destroyed in his great siege of 1804). As a young man, Chaves had traveled widely—St. Louis, New Orleans, New York City, even Cuba—but most of his life he spent in the open country of the New Mexican borderlands, living as a sheep rancher, occasional slave-raider, and, when called upon, captain of the local militia. He was a beloved, larger-than-life figure, a favorite son of the province. His bravery in the field of battle had won him a nickname: the Little Lion.

Ironically, the Little Lion had won his fame chiefly for fighting Navajos. Nearly all his life he had lived close to the Diné, had grown up with their outrages, had pursued and killed them. He could name more than two hundred relatives, including two of his own brothers, who had been slain by Indians—most of them at the hands of Navajos.

Chaves had nearly died in a Navajo clash. Only sixteen at the time, the pluck he demonstrated in the incident made him a household name throughout New Mexico. The year was 1834. His older brother Jose decided to lead a slave raid into Navajo country and invited young Manuel along as a kind of initiation rite. (The men from Cebolleta, capitalizing on their geographical proximity to Navajo lands, had long specialized in hunting slaves and had made it a considerable part of their local economy.) Departing from Cebolleta, the small, well-armed party traveled deep into Dinehtah, looking for some unsuspecting woman or child to capture. To their bewilderment they never saw a soul—the country seemed strangely flushed clean of people. But when they came to the rim of Canyon de Chelly and peered down into the great gulch, they found their answer: Thousands of

Navajos were gathered on the sandy floor, reveling in an enormous ceremonial dance, their horses all herded together in a tight branch of the canyon. Alarmed by the large numbers of the enemy, Jose Chaves realized he was tempting fate. He directed the party to turn around and leave at once.

But they were too late. Diné scouts had spotted them, and soon hundreds of warriors appeared. They knew that these invading Nakais, as the Navajos called New Mexicans, had come to hunt slaves. So the warriors attacked with righteous fury. The Chaves party was assailed by a storm of arrows. Young Manuel fought as best he could until he lost consciousness. The Navajos, satisfied that they had killed every last man, finally ceased fire. After taking the party's guns and ransacking the supplies, they returned in triumph to the canyon.

Manuel awoke several hours later to discover that he had seven arrow wounds. He was disoriented and desperately weak from blood loss. Everyone in the party, including his brother, was dead. Manuel took measure of his predicament: He was more than two hundred miles from home, in a hostile country he did not know, sixteen years old and lacking a weapon, with several thousand Navajos encamped close by. Manuel buried his brother in a shallow grave, then started trudging south by southeast. After two days of walking in desolate desert country, he came to a familiar place—Bear Springs, future site of Fort Fauntleroy. In the cool spring water, he washed his wounds and assuaged his hunger by sucking the sour pads of prickly pear cactus. Feverish, his arrow punctures hot and swollen, he somehow summoned the strength to continue walking. At times he lost consciousness and frequently fell into hallucinations, but a few days later young Manuel Chaves staggered into Cebolleta, the sole survivor of the expedition.

Chaves later fought with distinction alongside U.S. troops in the 1847 counteroffensive against the Taos insurrectionists, but he was a volunteer, not a career army regular. In 1861 it was an unusual arrangement for a territorial volunteer, even one as accomplished as he, to command a U.S. fort of such importance. But these were unusual times: Back east, the Civil War had begun. News of Fort Sumter had finally reached New Mexico, and soldiers were steadily departing the territory in droves and heading east for reassignment. To take their place, New Mexican volunteers had been hastily raised to man outposts like Fort Fauntleroy and keep a lid on hostilities as best they could.

While these new Hispanic recruits temporarily solved the manpower crisis, their presence in Navajo country had less-than-savory implications. Professional U.S. soldiers could at least claim some level of objectivity in the conflict. Not so with the New Mexicans. Their hatred of the Navajo was personal, ancestral, seemingly irreconcilable—and the Navajos, of course, felt the same way. The two groups, locked in their age-old antipathy, were the Southwestern equivalent of Jews and Arabs, or Turks and Greeks: There was too much bad blood between them, the patterns too firmly ingrained.

Putting New Mexican recruits in American uniforms, furnishing them with good weapons, and stationing them at a volatile place like Fort Fauntleroy thus had shades of the fox guarding the henhouse: It was only a matter of time before something dramatic would happen, especially with a ferocious fighter like Manuel Chaves left in charge.

⬦

The report of the rifle boomed across the grounds of Fort Fauntleroy and echoed off the distant canyon walls. Alarmed, soldiers seized their weapons and scurried about the grounds of the fort in great confusion. As one witness described it, "Every man ran to arm himself. Companies did not regularly form, but every man ran wherever he thought fit." The word was, one of the drunk Navajos had tried to force his way past the sentinel guarding the entrance of the fort. The sentinel fired and killed the Indian on the spot.

In the field outside the fort, hundreds of Navajos scrambled for cover. It is unclear who gave the order, or if it was simply a spontaneous thing, but the soldiers aimed their rifles and started firing into the crowd, drilling bullets into the backs of the fleeing Indians. In twos and threes, the Navajos dropped in their tracks. Other soldiers chased after their victims on foot and ran them down with bayonets—not only warriors, but women and children.

An eyewitness, Capt. Nicholas Hodt, later described the sickening scene to an investigative committee set up by the U.S. Congress: "I saw a soldier murdering two little children and a woman. I hallooed immediately for him to stop. He looked up but did not obey my order. I ran as quick as I could, but could not get there soon enough to prevent him from killing the two innocent children and wounding severely the squaw."

Outraged, Hodt arrested the soldier and ordered him to hand over his cartridge belts.

Out of the chaos, Col. Manuel Chaves asserted his authority: But instead of calling his troops to order, he only escalated the action. He ordered an artillery sergeant to bring out the mountain howitzers and open fire. Captain Hodt said the sergeant "pretended not to understand the order given, for he considered it unlawful. But being cursed by the officer of the day, and threatened, he had to execute the order or else get himself in trouble."

Howitzer shells arced and exploded over the field, sending shrapnel in all directions. Screaming Navajos ran in wild patterns across the valley below the post. It was a wholesale slaughter: More than twenty Indians, many of them women and children, lay dead in the field. Scores more were wounded, and 112 were taken prisoner.

After the shelling subsided, Captain Hodt brought the man he'd seen murdering the Navajo children to Lieutenant Ortiz (presumably the same lieutenant who had raced Dr. Kavanaugh's thoroughbred). He described to Ortiz the atrocity he had witnessed out in the field and explained why he had disarmed and arrested the man. Ortiz responded by pulling out his own pistol, cocking it, and aiming it at Hodt, shouting: "Give this soldier back his arms, or else I'll shoot you, God damn you!"

He reluctantly obeyed, but reported Ortiz's actions to Colonel Chaves. Hodt received no satisfaction from the Little Lion, however. On the contrary, Chaves said that Lieutenant Ortiz "did perfectly right" and thought the soldier who killed the two children deserved "credit," not censure. Case dismissed.

Later realizing that things had perhaps gotten a bit out of hand,

Chaves went to work on damage control. In his report to authorities in Santa Fe, he stated "with great regret" that the Navajos, without provocation, had "attacked the guard of the post," and that his men were only acting in self-defense. He tried to cover up the incident, or at least control the rumors emanating from it, by not allowing any letters to leave the fort for weeks.

But it was a massacre, pure and simple, and when authorities in Santa Fe found out about it, they suspended Chaves from command of Fort Fauntleroy. Briefly, Chaves was held under house arrest in Albuquerque in preparation for a court-martial hearing, and Kit Carson was sent there to conduct a preliminary investigation. The army, it seemed, was less concerned with the colonel's possible role in the mass slaughter of fleeing Navajos than with the revelation that Chaves had permitted his soldiers to wager government property on horse races.

The trial never came to pass. With the storm clouds of the Civil War looming on the horizon, and with the ranks of the U.S. Army in consequent disarray, the incident at Fort Fauntleroy was all but forgotten. Charges were dropped and, if anything, the Little Lion won public adulation for taking such a hard line against "attacking" Navajos.

Never again would there be horse races at Fort Fauntleroy. The shaky truce was over. The massacre would have a profound influence on the Diné, moving them deeper into the "fearing time." From that point on, the tribe would increasingly see the wisdom of Manuelito's path, especially now that U.S. troops were abandoning the frontier forts to prepare for the invasion of a Confederate army that was rumored to be advancing from San Antonio. The Americans were clearly distracted. Something was pulling them away—Manuelito and the other warriors could sense a new opportunity. Now, they said, was the time to strike.

On a frigid Sunday morning in February, two armies stared at each other across the open plain. A stiff wind blew needles of sleet. Slush formed on the edges of the Rio Grande, and the ghostly cottonwoods rattled along the banks.

The Confederate cavalry had drawn up less than two miles from Fort Craig—and stopped. Their commander, Brig. Gen. Henry Hopkins Sibley, studied the bulwark through his field glasses. He saw the Stars and Stripes snapping in the wind, saw the fresh earthworks and ramparts set with loopholes, saw the smoky encampments of the New Mexico volunteers spread like tattered aprons on the brown grass all about the walls. Originally built to fend off Indian attacks and named after a U.S. Army officer killed while pursuing deserters, Fort Craig was a collection of several dozen adobe buildings set on the west bank of the Rio Grande some 150 miles south of Santa Fe. Nearly four thousand soldiers were dug in around this mud citadel. Ranged along the thick walls, formidable-looking cannons were trained south on the Rebels.

Sibley put away his binoculars in disgust. The general was not feeling well and could barely sit a horse. He was suffering from some undisclosed medical condition—"colic," some speculated—that was certainly being exacerbated by his well-known weakness for the bottle (his troops nicknamed him "the Walking Whiskey Keg"). A Confederate officer said that General Sibley "needs no information" before blundering into battle. "It is enough for him to know that there is to be a quantity of whiskey used in the enterprise." One of his colleagues later wrote that Sibley's "love of liquor exceeded that of home, country, or God." For long stretches at a time he'd been confined to his ambulance, indisposed and apparently incapable of making decisions.

Still, General Sibley could be a commanding presence. Romantic, ambitious, handsomely debonair when he wasn't drunk, the curly-haired West Pointer was a career veteran of the U.S. Army, having served with distinction in both the Mexican War and on the Western frontier. He was also well-known as an inventor; he had patented a design for a conical tent—the Sibley field tent, loosely modeled after the tepee of the Plains Indians—widely used by Union and Confederate armies alike. Perhaps like many inventors, Sibley was a bit dreamy and not very adept at nitty-gritty logistical planning. With good reason, a subordinate declared that he was "too prone to let the morrow take care of itself."

Sibley was intimately familiar with New Mexico. His last post before joining the Confederacy had been in Taos, where he commanded dragoons and led a campaign against the Navajos. He knew Fort Craig well—or at least the old Fort Craig, before it had been reinforced with fresh troops and revetments. He concluded, however, that the new Fort Craig was now too strong to be taken in a frontal assault.

But somehow he *would* have to take the fort, he realized, or else his campaign in New Mexico was doomed. It was an all-or-nothing proposition. His overextended supply line from El Paso flowed in a mere trickle, his army being a thousand lonely miles from its home base and training grounds in San Antonio. The only way he could keep going was to forage off the land, stealing from the Union forces as he conquered them. And he knew that Fort Craig was stuffed with the food, ammunition, and medicine his starved army so desperately needed.

To get it, he would first have to draw the Union troops away from the fort, luring them out by some distraction, and then fight them on the open field beyond the range of their superior artillery. Sibley could not compete with the Union arsenal, which included 12-pounder Napoleon guns and 24-pounder howitzers as well as those mysterious new cannons. But on exposed terrain, Sibley believed, his twenty-five hundred men, most of whom were mounted, would hold a distinct advantage over the Federal forces—which, though more numerous, were primarily infantry.

It was February 16, 1862. As the sun rose like a cold stone over the bosque, Sibley sat for a while, creaking in his saddle, then turned and conferred with his officers about what to do next.

Two miles to the north, the Union commander, Col. Edward Canby, was sitting on his favorite horse, Old Chas, and chomping an unlit cigar. Canby was a tall, clean-shaven Kentuckian, cool and cagey, with enormous fleshy ears. Hardened by decades of fighting Indians, he had cultivated a healthy hatred for this new enemy lately arrived in his midst. He called the Confederates "an arrogant and rapacious invader."

Canby knew his principal adversary all too well. He and Sibley had been classmates together at West Point, and Canby had been best man at Sibley's wedding. They were even related by marriage: Their wives were cousins. In New Mexico the two men had fought Indians together and commiserated on the sorry state of the territory. After news of Fort Sumter reached New Mexico and Sibley quit the U.S. Army for El Paso, he told some of Canby's loyalist colleagues, "Boys, if you only knew it, I am the worst enemy you have!"

Now they *were* enemies, facing each other on this unlikely battlefield, so far from the armies of the East.

Colonel Canby was so taciturn and cautious—"He counsels *no one!*" a subordinate groused—that his men had no idea of his larger strategy for defending New Mexico, or even if he had one. A Union soldier described him as "tall and straight, coarsely dressed, his countenance hard and weather beaten, a cigar in his mouth which he never lights. He certainly has an air of superiority, largely the gift of nature, though undoubtedly strengthened by long habits of command." Descended from a family of Quakers, Canby had nonetheless pursued a military career with gusto—fighting fiercely against the Seminoles of Florida, winning accolades from Gen. Winfield Scott in the Mexican War, and serving with William Tecumseh Sherman in Monterey, California. Though not brilliant—at West Point he graduated thirtieth in his class of thirty-one—Canby's intellect had a certain plodding, tortoiselike consistency that usually carried the day. All descriptions of Canby emphasize his careful, quiet, and sometimes saturnine disposition. One army general later judged Canby "too modest and reserved to win the popular recognition that he merited," but noted that "wherever he went, order, good feeling, and tranquility followed in his footsteps."

With almost no resources to work with, Canby had accomplished near-miracles in preparing Fort Craig for the coming Confederate onslaught. He'd had little more than a month to get the fort supplied and reinforced. Only two days earlier a train of seventy wagons had come from Santa Fe with food, supplies, and ammunition, and now he was well dug in and ready for whatever his former friend the Walking Whiskey Keg had to offer.

But in truth, the fort wasn't nearly as strong as it appeared: Those big artillery pieces ranged along the ramparts were nothing more than decoys—props hewn from pine logs and painted black to look like cannon. "Quaker guns" the men called them, perhaps in deference to Canby's own religious background.

And Canby's four thousand men were not nearly so formidable as they may have looked. Only twelve hundred of them were army regulars. The rest were volunteers or militiamen, mostly Hispanic men from the territory, local boys whose lack of fighting experience was matched only by their lack of a concrete rationale for fighting—understandably, they had little interest and seemingly no stake in the issues of this *Americano* war begun the previous year in some utterly foreign place called South Carolina.

Canby took a dim view of these Spanish-speaking volunteers and considered them "worse than worthless." As he put it, every New Mexican who deserted the ranks "only adds to rather than diminishes our strength." He questioned their loyalty, believing, with good reason, that "the Mexican people have no affection for the institutions of the United States and have a strong, but hitherto restrained hatred for the Americans as a race." Certainly his own racial prejudices entered into his assessment of their military competence—like many U.S.

Army officers who fought in the Mexican War, Canby thought Hispanic soldiers were virtually incapable of organizing an orderly defense. But his concerns were also practical: These New Mexican
paisanos, he knew, were not bred to firearms, had never been around
artillery, and, of course, spoke almost no English. All of which, in the
heat of battle, with American officers shouting commands this way
and that, could make them highly ineffective and prone to confusion
and flight. If possible, Canby intended to keep the volunteers inside,
or at least close to the fort so they would not have to maneuver under direct fire.

Now the two armies formed battle lines on the plain. They sent
out skirmishers and reconnaissance parties, each army initiating gam-
bits to test the resolve and disposition of its foe. Slowly, tentatively,
the Rebels and Federals moved within a thousand yards of each other,
close enough that, in the shifting winds, they could hear bugles blar-
ing and the mingled shouts of the men.

Then Sibley's troops let out a Rebel yell, or at least their best approximation of one; since they had trained in Texas and had never
fought in the East, few of these Confederates had actually heard the
famous battle cry, though they had heard *of* it. Most of the Rebels
were armed with little more than fowling pieces, squirrel guns, pistols, and other frontier weapons—one quixotic unit was composed
entirely of lancers. But they were young and lustful for battle, and
seemed supremely confident that it would all be over soon. One of
their officers, a Major Lockbridge, saw the American flag flying over
the fort and boasted: "I'll make my wife a nightgown out of it!"

⊠

The commander of the 1st New Mexico Volunteers was none other
than Christopher Carson, now a colonel in the Union Army. Encamped near the fort, in the cool shadows of its earthen walls, Carson and his eight companies now prepared for battle. Like Canby,
Carson was personally acquainted with his adversary. Before the war,
he and Sibley had spent time together in Taos—Sibley's post was only
a few miles down the road from Carson's house. A soldier acquain-

tance of both men said that although Sibley had tried to convert many men to the Confederate cause, he never attempted to convert Carson. "I don't think Sibley tried any missionary work," the soldier recalled, "for [Carson] had his opinion on both the North and the South."

Carson, who hated any sort of debate or quarrel, kept his feelings to himself. Said another pro-Union friend in New Mexico: "Kit was loyal, but he was like me and would not argue the point."

Carson reported for duty in Albuquerque, and it was there that he trained his volunteers. Serving in the regular army was a new and trying experience for him; at first he was rather awkward at it. The protocols, the nomenclature, the dress codes seemed to run contrary to his nature. A volunteer from Colorado named Edward Wynkoop recalled that Carson's "uniform did not set well on him at all." Carson's illiteracy caused embarrassment. Once a group of his men asked him to sign a commissary requisition for several kegs of molasses. He happily signed the request, only later to find some of his men good and drunk: The commissary order had been for kegs of *whiskey*. Humiliated by this little prank, Carson from then on never signed a requisition without first having his adjutant read it out loud.

We have no record of how he punished these particular malefactors, but in general Carson was not shy about disciplining his men. Wynkoop thought that he "had the utmost firmness and the best of common sense . . . and could punish a culprit with vigor. He had a beautiful mild blue eye which would become terrible under some circumstances and like the warning of the rattlesnake always sounded the alarm before the spring."

Wynkoop tells another story from Carson's army duty in Albuquerque, an incident that occurred on a day the colonel was away from his post. It was a Sunday morning, and a boat full of "gaily dressed senoritas" was crossing the Rio Grande on the way to mass. From the launching point, "a rough looking Mexican ranchero" hopped aboard. The boatman politely asked the stranger to await his turn, for the boat was now overcrowded and dangerously tippy. The man refused. Wynkoop says that Carson "then approached and in a mild manner pointed out to him his wrong doings, but without avail." Carson then adopted a "peremptory" tone, but the man "was still obstinate." Suddenly Carson sprang into action. "Like a flash of lightning Kit raised his sheathed sabre which he carried in his hand; struck him a tremendous blow along side of the head, knocking him headlong into the turbid waters of the Rio Grande. The fellow sunk like lead." The man would have drowned, but "quicker than thought, Kit plunged after and dragged him out."

It was classic Carson: In an instant he had performed an act of chivalry and then saved the man who gave the ladies offense.

Carson had been chosen to lead the volunteers for his fluency in Spanish and his high standing among the old families of New Mexico. From the start, his greatest challenge had been overcoming the natural apathy of his men. He was able to recruit them and keep them interested in their training only by drawing on an old dread: New Mexicans had long held a fear of and a revulsion for Texans, and, except for Sibley (who was from Louisiana), that was what these attackers were, almost to a man—Texans, having marched from San Antonio with the single-minded intent of claiming New Mexico for the Confederacy. The word "Confederate" meant nearly nothing to Carson's volunteers, but the prospect of an invasion from the south set up a visceral reaction among them and kept them at their guns.

Colonel Carson peered across the plain at the dust clouds being kicked up by the Texans and studied their movements with his field glasses. He'd been hearing about their advance for months and had been trying to convince his men that the coming threat was real. These Texans were an uncommonly brazen people, his in-laws back in Taos had always said. In New Mexico, Texans were like bogeymen: Parents used to tell their children that if they didn't behave, the *Tejanos* would come get them.

The canard was partly true. The "people of the single star" had long nursed an interest in New Mexico—in owning it and having it, on paper and in fact, even though Texans held great disdain for New Mexicans and considered their seared land hardly worth possessing. Their desire to absorb New Mexico was as curious as it was incorrigible. It had something to do with the immaculate tidiness of the Rio Grande as a concept: Ever since Texas became an independent nation in the 1830s, it had claimed, on no particular evidence, that its border extended all the way to the Rio Grande's origins in Colorado, and that most of New Mexico, including the capital of Santa Fe, was thus rightfully part of Texas. In 1841 an armed party of Texans had actually invaded New Mexico in a half-cocked mission of conquest that ended in their prompt capture and brutal imprisonment in a notorious castle-like jail near Mexico City. And in the 1850s, when the New Mexico Territory was being formally established, Texas lawmakers had drawn up new county lines in New Mexico to claim some of the land for the Lone Star state. The Federal government put a stop to it.

But apparently the lust for New Mexico still burned deep in the loins of Texas, like a spurned love that had festered all the more bitterly for the fact that the suitor judged himself superior to his quarry. Sibley's hopefully named "Army of New Mexico" had marched all the way from San Antonio, losing nearly five hundred men to smallpox, pneumonia, exhaustion, and attacks by Apache Indians. One Texan diarist wrote in despair, "The mountains here are full of Indians, and we dread them worse than we do the Lincolnites." (The Texans managed to capture and kill at least one Indian horse thief, an Apache who was so thickly coated in dirt that he looked "like a horned frog"; the body was given over to a team of fascinated brigade surgeons, who fed their anthropological curiosity by dissecting the corpse.) Moving steadily westward, the Texans stole what they could not buy and engulfed Hispanic villages along the way, occasionally "appropriating" the local women, as one participant put it.

Now, here they were in the heart of New Mexico, pressing their old claim once again. It is remarkable the extent to which Sibley misread the mood of the New Mexican population—he truly seemed to expect that the local people would embrace his cause "with a sincere and hearty co-operation," as he put it. In his delusions, Sibley believed that with Hispanic sentiment solidly behind him, his large army could easily "live off the land." The Texans would quickly seize Fort Craig, and then take Socorro, and Albuquerque, and Santa Fe.

After Santa Fe, their designs grew more ambitious, transcending even New Mexico: Sibley's men planned to continue on to Denver and capture the goldfields of Colorado for the specie-starved Confederacy. After that, they hoped to march through Utah to the Pacific, take over the California mining operations, and open up the Golden State to the Peculiar Institution—Cotton plantations on the Sacramento! Slave markets in Los Angeles!—so that Confederate railroads would connect the Confederate ports of Charleston, New Orleans, and Houston to the Confederate port of San Diego. While he was at it, Sibley also wanted to conquer (or purchase) the Mexican states of Sonora, Chihuahua, and Baja California.

As grandiose as it seemed, General Sibley's mission had the blessing of the Confederate high command. In fact, the previous year Sibley had traveled to Richmond to meet with President Jefferson Davis and unfurl his plan for conquering the West. Sibley's optimism and hubris seemed to permeate his entire army. "Our leaders were crazy," one of the Texan volunteers later wrote, "and believed they had the game in their own hands; no enterprise was too rash for them to undertake. Every man, from the general downwards, [was] confident of victory."

For Carson, these territorial schemes must have sounded oddly familiar. The Texans aimed to cover ground that he had already covered for the greater glory of the United States, on routes that he himself had blazed. Theirs was a kind of Empire Retread. It was Manifest Destiny all over again—a Confederate Manifest Destiny.

But now Canby, Carson, and the four thousand men at Fort Craig stood in the way, the first true obstacle in Sibley's singularly bizarre adventure.

◙

Carson's reasons for joining the Yankee fight are not altogether clear. He was from Missouri, a border state violently divided on the issue of secession. The people of Missouri had narrowly decided, after much debate and fighting, to follow the ambiguous course of staying proslavery but also pro-Union. Many if not most of Carson's Missouri relatives were Southern sympathizers, and at least one of his brothers would fight—and die—for the Confederacy. Although New Mexico's barren soil and arid climate had never encouraged agriculture on a scale large enough to make Southern-style slavery profitable, Carson had nonetheless been around enslaved Negroes all his life, both in Missouri and in New Mexico, and he was not known to be openly critical of the institution. (Nor was he an advocate of it—during his roving life as a trapper he had befriended many freed and mixed-race blacks, including the legendary mountain man Jim Beckwourth.)

But certainly Carson was no abolitionist. On the contrary, he owned slaves himself—Indian slaves. He and Josefa had three Navajo servants: a boy named Juan, another named Juan Bautista, and a teenage girl named Maria Dolores. The precise terms and arrangements of their servitude are not known (relatives later suggested that they were actually adopted and considered full-fledged family members). Carson apparently purchased the three Navajos from other Indian tribes who had previously captured them in raids. He had all three baptized in the Catholic faith—"according to the custom of the country," as the local church records state—and they lived in the Carson household for a number of years. Details about Juan Carson's life are sketchy, but it appears that he was raised free like Carson's other children and that he later married a New Mexican woman.

The enslavement of captured Indians was an old convention in New Mexico—as was peonage, another form of servitude in which poor, usually Hispanic workers became indebted to wealthy estate owners. Peonage was a kind of feudal arrangement that kept the landed class rich while the majority of the citizens, illiterate and powerless to improve themselves, stayed mired in a financial misery from which they could rarely escape. William Davis, who as the United States attorney for the territory made a close study of the practice in the 1850s, thought that peonage was "in truth but a more charming name for a species of slavery as abject and oppressive as any found upon the American continent."

Neither Carson nor the better-off New Mexicans he lived among had shown moral qualms about slavery. In fact, the people of the southern part of the New Mexico Territory had, in 1861, seceded from the Union to create their own Confederate state, which they called Arizona. Centered around the towns of Tucson and Mesilla, the population was composed largely of Hispanic landowners who farmed along the Rio Grande, and Anglo Texan transplants who'd moved farther west to try their hand at ranching or mining. (Kit's own brother, Moses Carson, was now a settler living in Mesilla.) Arizonans vigorously cast their loyalty to Richmond and hoped their New Mexico brethren to the north would eventually come over to the Rebel side. The new territory of Arizona was governed by a bold, ruthless man named John Baylor, who sought to import Southern-style Negro slavery while simultaneously pursuing a stated policy of "exterminating all Apaches and other hostile Indians." (Among the more sordid outrages in his career, Baylor was once charged with killing sixty Indians by giving them a sack of poisoned flour.)

Many of the army soldiers who lived in the New Mexico Territory were Southerners. Sibley wasn't the only one who had left the U.S. Army at the first word of war—fully half the officers in the territory had quit New Mexico to fight for the Confederate cause. Officers could resign, but enlisted men in the lower echelons of the department could not without facing charges of desertion (punishable, in some cases, by death). So the ranks of Canby's army on the Rio Grande were sprinkled with regulars who hailed from Southern states—men whose loyalty and motivation he understandably did not trust.

Conceivably, Carson might have been one of them—a Rebel in Union blues—but he wasn't. Most likely, Carson's pro-Union stance grew from a straightforward patriotism, and a straightforward sense of allegiance to his former employer, the United States Army. And also, a devotion to his former commander and friend, John C. Fremont. During the 1850s, Fremont briefly served as U.S. senator from the new state of California while growing immensely wealthy from mining and ranching claims. Fremont *was* an abolitionist, and like his father-in-law Senator Benton (who died in 1858), a staunch Unionist. Fremont had campaigned in large part on an antislavery plank in

1856, when he ran for president of the United States as the first candidate of the new Republican Party. At the outset of the Civil War the Lincoln administration promoted Fremont to general and named him commander of the Western Department, a vast region, headquartered in St. Louis, that included New Mexico. From afar, Fremont was, in a sense, Carson's boss once again.

Unlike Fremont, Carson had gained neither great wealth nor political prominence during the 1850s, but his celebrity status had continued to wax. Much to his chagrin, pulp publishers had continued to churn out the cheesy blood-and-thunder novels, with titles like *Rocky Mountain Kit's Last Scalp Hunt, The Fighting Trapper: Kit Carson to the Rescue,* and *Kit Carson's Bride: The Flower of the Apaches.* A popular play based on Carson's supposed adventures had toured the Eastern cities. Herman Melville had mentioned Carson in *Moby-Dick,* calling him "that brawny doer of rejoicing good deeds" and comparing him favorably to Perseus, Hercules, St. George, and the Hindu god Vishnu. Counties, towns, and rivers bore Carson's name. A sleek clipper ship, *Kit Carson,* was now plying the trans-Horn route between Boston and San Francisco (an amusing irony, since his only ocean voyage had left him green with seasickness).

On an 1853 trip to Northern California, Carson took a new measure of his growing fame. He traveled there on an odd but, as it turned out, extremely lucrative venture: He'd bought more than six thousand sheep in New Mexico and, fighting off wolves and Indians along the route, drove his vast herd all the way to California to sell to the gold miners there. To our cattle-tuned sensibilities it now seems like a wimpy sort of Western idyll—a *sheep* drive?—but in the bargain, Carson made what was to him a fair fortune, netting about seven thousand dollars.

While he was in San Francisco, gawkers overwhelmed him. The papers heralded his arrival; people waylaid him in the streets. Even when strangers didn't recognize him, Carson still heard them talking about him. At restaurants and taverns, according to one account, "men sitting next to him would speak of him and Kit would quietly eat his meal and walk off, signaling his friends not to give him away."

Perhaps hoping to seize some measure of control over his spiraling celebrity, Carson had in 1856 dictated a bare-bones memoir to an amanuensis whose identity is unknown. He then authorized an enterprising friend from Missouri to take the manuscript east to seek out writers who might turn it into a more ambitious narrative. Among others, Washington Irving considered the job but passed. Eventually the project was taken up by DeWitt Peters, a rather fanciful doctor, who in 1859 published what would be the first full-fledged biography of Kit Carson. Peters's book, *The Life and Adventures of Kit Carson, the Nestor of the Rocky Mountains, From Facts Narrated by Himself,* wasn't as bad as the pulp thrillers, but the good doctor couldn't help himself. When Carson finally got around to having the book read to him, his only comment was, "Peters laid it on a little thick."

And yet it was understandable, for in truth Carson had continued to live a life of swashbuckling hyperbole. In 1853, just to take one in a host of exploits, Carson rode a hundred miles east on the Santa Fe Trail in a desperate attempt to warn two traders, whose names were Weatherhead and Brevoort, that the party with whom they were traveling planned to kill them on a remote section of the trail and rob them of the considerable sum of money they were known to be carrying. (One of the conspirators had apparently defected a week earlier and leaked the plot in a Taos tavern.) Carson overran the men just in time to foil the murder. For his trouble, he asked for nothing in return, but the following spring Weatherhead and Brevoort insisted on presenting him with a pair of beautiful silver pistols, which he prized for the rest of his life.

For most of the 1850s, Carson had served as an Indian agent to the Ute tribe, with his own home in Taos serving as the agency office. He gave up most of his ranching interests on the Rayado River so that he could pursue his new official duties while helping Josefa raise their growing family. The Carsons now had four children, plus they were helping Ignacia Bent raise several of her children. By all accounts he was a devoted father, someone who opened up to his children more readily than to adults. He could be whimsical with his kids. A soldier in his volunteers observed that Carson "used to lie down on an Indian blanket with his pockets full of candy and lumps of sugar. His children would then jump on top of him, and take the candy from his pockets. Colonel Carson derived great pleasure from these little episodes."

At last, Carson had achieved the sense of stability he'd longed for during the 1840s. He had become a pillar of the community, a member of the local gentry, a good Catholic, a provider, a diplomat to the Indians. He had even become, of all things, a Mason—having joined the fraternal lodge in Santa Fe, whose membership included nearly all of the most prominent citizens in the territory, tough Western stalwarts wearing funny hats and chanting mantras in a dark hall.

He had slowed down a bit. Now fifty-one years old, Carson was beginning to show signs of his hard life. In 1860 he'd had an accident that nearly killed him. He was hunting elk in the San Juan Mountains of southern Colorado, leading his horse on a steep scree slope, when the animal lost its footing. Somehow Carson became entangled in the reins and he tumbled down the mountain, with the horse apparently rolling over him several times. It's not clear exactly what injuries he sustained in the fall, but he never felt the same again. He had an odd pain in his chest that never left him. His days in the saddle were over, he vowed. He told an Eastern journalist that, having reached the age of fifty, he "designed thenceforward to avoid horseback riding and travel only in carriages."

Still, he didn't waste a minute signing up for the war. The moment that news of Fort Sumter reached Taos, he is said to have joined a group of Union loyalists in marching to the town plaza and hoisting the Stars and Stripes on a cottonwood pole high over town, ignoring the angry shouts of Southern sympathizers. To protect the Union standard, the men took turns guarding the plaza around the clock. (Even now, an American flag flies over the Taos square day and night to commemorate this event.)

As soon as it was possible for him to do so, Carson offered his services to the Union Army—and never looked back.

On the afternoon of February 16, 1862, the battle lines at Fort Craig continued to form and re-form as each side tested the other. Neither of the two leaders could shape the field to his liking. Sibley realized he could not lure Canby from the safety of the fort, while Canby saw that Sibley was too smart to attempt a full frontal attack. They had arrived at a stalemate before the battle had even begun. After a tepid skirmish that resulted in a few casualties, Sibley decided he needed a better plan, that this was not his day to fight. He called for a general retreat from the plain south of the fort, and the Confederates retired to their camp several miles down the Rio Grande.

Then, from the west, a dust storm sailed in from Chihuahua. For nearly two days the wind howled and the cold, brown sky swirled with snow and grit. Visibility shrank to fifty yards. A fine talc pecked at the men and animals and blew into their tents and gear. Both armies hunkered down and waited for the storm to pass. One Texan said the sleet "fell so hard as to almost peel the skin off your face."

It was during this interlude that Sibley's second-in-command, a colonel named Tom Green, hatched an alternate plan of attack. He proposed that their men cross over to the east bank of the river, then march north, bypassing Fort Craig altogether while taking advantage of a large invervening mesa that would hide their movements and afford the Texans good protection from Canby's long-range guns. Then, Green suggested, the Confederates should cross *back* to the west side of the river and seize a critical ford located at Valverde. This ford, just a few hours' march upstream from Fort Craig, was so vital to the Union supply lines that it would surely draw Canby away from his bastion. The Rebels could then finally have the engagement they were hoping for, and on their own terms—away from the big Union artillery and earthworks, out in the open.

Sibley liked the sound of this leapfrog maneuver and gave his immediate approval. It was a promising plan, but also a risky one—by jumping ahead, Sibley would be in the precarious position of having the Union army *between* him and his supply line—a placement that runs counter to the tenets of military thinking. On the morning of February 18, with the dust storm having cleared, the twenty-five hundred Texans forded the icy Rio Grande and followed the course that Green had described. On the nineteenth they passed behind the mesa, slogging up a sand-choked draw, their groaning supply wagons buried up to the axles.

When Colonel Canby got wind of what was going on, he promptly sent Kit Carson and several companies of volunteers to the east bank of the river to occupy a high point from which they could keep a closer eye on the Confederate movements. Canby feared that Sibley's pullout might be an elaborate feint, and that the Rebels were actually planning to veer suddenly, cross the river again, and attack the fort. He needed Carson's forces to check this possible scenario.

Carson took the eminence without incident and from his higher vantage was able to follow Sibley's crawl north. Carson correctly guessed that the Texans were bypassing the fort and instead heading toward Valverde ford—and this was the message, sent via runners and semaphore signals from high points on the mesa, that was relayed to Canby.

Another thing became apparent to Carson: The Texans and their animals, having left the Rio Grande on the eighteenth, were now desperate for water. The rocky topography largely blocked their access to the river, and no other watering holes were to be found for many miles. The Texans, being primarily a cavalry force, were especially vulnerable. In another day, Carson knew, their situation would be critical. The Confederate horses and mules would literally grow mad with thirst. They would become jittery and unpredictable and subject to bolt at the slightest disturbance.

Recognizing the predicament the Texans were in, Colonel Canby authorized a bold mission. The adventure was led by a colorful Irishman—and former saloon-keeper—named James "Paddy" Graydon. For the past several months, Graydon, as the head of a self-styled reconnaissance unit called Graydon's Independent Spy Company, had been gathering intelligence for the Union forces. Known for employing various ruses and disguises, he had once ventured into a Confederate camp as an apple peddler.

A man with a gift for unorthodox solutions and, as one Civil War historian put it, "a widely acknowledged reputation for the spectacular," Graydon came up with a plan for shocking the Confederate animals and setting off a major stampede. He filled two boxes with mountain howitzer shells and improvised two fuses. Then he cinched the boxes to the backs of two mules. Under cover of night, he led the mules across the Rio Grande and crept up to within a few hundred yards of the Confederate camp, close enough that Graydon could hear the Texans talking and laughing around their fires. All around the bivouac site he could make out the silhouettes of the Confederate mules and horses, hundreds of them hobbled or picketed for the night.

Graydon took a deep breath and lit the two fuses. Then with a loud *"Yawwwww!"* he swatted the mules' rumps, sending them off on a suicide gallop toward the Rebel campfires.

The mules arrowed across the field, with the long fuses steadily fizzing on their backs. But as the two animals approached the Texan camp, something stopped them: some unfamiliar smell, perhaps a realization that they did not belong there. In an instant they turned around and started galloping *back toward Graydon.* Spotting this most inconvenient reversal in his plan, Graydon started running for his life. The doomed animals would have overtaken their master, but the fuses ran out.

Boom! Boom! The night skies lit up, and the Confederates turned their heads in panic as mule meat splattered over the chamisa fields.

Amazingly, Graydon's plan seems to have worked: At the noise, the Confederate animals stampeded. Mad for water, wild-eyed and snorting, they broke their pickets and dashed for a gap in the rocky terrain that led down to the river, where Union soldiers were waiting.

After the animals got their fill, the troops easily collected them and led them back to Fort Craig. In just a few bewildering minutes of pyrotechnics, the Texans had been relieved of more than 150 valuable horses and mules—a loss that an invading army so far from home could not afford.

☒

Valverde was a tranquil bend in the Rio Grande choked with copses of willow and cottonwood. In recent years, by the mysterious logic of rivers, the main current had deviated and found a new course, so that at Valverde the Rio Grande curled beside the sandy dry bed of its former channel, like a snake beside its own shed skin. Because the banks here were gently sloped, and the river broad and shallow, Valverde had for centuries been an important ford on the Camino Real. Towering over the ford was an imposing mesa of dark volcanic rock.

Valverde—"green valley" in Spanish—had also been a village of some importance during the colonial period. But in the early 1800s it had fallen on hard times. After repeated attacks by Navajos and Apaches, the settlers abandoned the place. Valverde became a ghost town, and now its walls were listing and cracked, its roofs collapsed, its baked adobe bricks crumbling back into the earth from which they had come.

Kit Carson knew Valverde well and probably detested it—for this was the same spot where he had met General Kearny during the Mexican War, and where the general had so unceremoniously turned him around for California. Once again, the ruined village was about to impress itself upon his career—this time with Carson playing a central role on the westernmost battlefield of the American Civil War.

Early on the cold and cloudy morning of February 21, the Texans struck their camps on the back side of the mesa and began marching toward Valverde. General Sibley was no longer effectively in charge; he was having one of his bouts with "colic," or drunkenness—or both—and once again he confined himself to his ambulance. The Texans were enraged by their general's incapacity in this hour of need—one called him "an infamous coward and a disgrace to the Confederate States."

Sibley's second-in-command, Col. Tom Green, was left to pick up the pieces. Sensing that battle was imminent, Green exhorted his

men: "You've come too far from home hunting a fight to lose now—
you must win or die on the battlefield!"

By eight that morning the Texan vanguard had taken up a position
on the east bank of Valverde, and soon Union troops from Fort Craig
arrived on the west bank to contest the Confederate claim on the
ford. An intense firefight erupted, and the Federals quickly seemed to
gain the upper hand. Among the Union troops was Capt. Alexander
McRae, a stalwart artilleryman who, although a native of North Carolina, "had given his allegiance to country rather than to state," according to Valverde historian John Taylor. McRae's six-gun battery of
howitzers pounded the Texan positions across the river, and his shells
ignited the dry grama grass all around the Confederate artillery. In
the late morning, fighting through intermittent snow flurries, Union
troops crept across the icy-cold river and pursued the enemy into the
bosques on the east side.

Now the cottonwoods pinged with hot lead. The Texans were
able to absorb the Union assault, but not without significant casualties. According to one Union soldier, "Their cavalry was completely destroyed, their horses and men dead and dying on the
field." The Union troops captured a Confederate twelve-pounder
artillery piece, lassoed it "cowboy style," and hauled it back to
Union lines. One Texan who had been shot in the mouth produced
a knife and cut out a large piece of his own tongue that was "hanging ragged."

In desperation, the company of Texan lancers decided to mount a
charge on Union positions. The flamboyant cavaliers carried nine-
foot-long staves fixed with twelve-inch blades from which festive red
pennants were hung, supposedly for the purpose of "drinking the
blood" of impaled enemies. These stubborn horsemen had honed
their skills after recognizing how surprisingly effective lancers were
during the Mexican War. Now they hid with their animals down in
the old river channel and prepared for battle. Bugles sounded, and
suddenly more than fifty of these latter-day knights popped up from
behind the sandy embankment and galloped toward the Union infantry three hundred yards away.

The Federals patiently waited until the Texans had drawn within a hundred yards. Then an officer was heard crying out—"They're Texans—give 'em hell!" The Federal troops fired volley after volley and mowed down the onrushing lancers. Soon the field was a bloody tangle of horses and men. One Union participant wrote that it was "fun to see the Texans fall. On they came and fierce looking fellows they were with their long lances raised, but when they got to us we were loaded again and then we gave them the buck and ball. After the second volley there were but a few of them left. One of them got away. The others were shot and bayoneted."

It lasted only a few minutes, but the Texan assault—widely considered the only lancer charge in the Civil War—ended in a complete slaughter. Nearly every one of the fifty horsemen was killed or wounded. The Texans would later mythologize the action—Colonel Green would call it "one of the most gallant and furious charges ever witnessed in the annals of battle." Yet the surviving lancers recognized the impotence of their weaponry in the face of modern firepower. Enraged and humiliated, they collected their once-beloved lances in a pile and put them to the torch. And then they armed themselves again, with shotguns.

_⊠

When Col. Kit Carson received word, in midmorning, that a withering firefight had broken out at Valverde, he and his volunteers hastened the seven miles to the ford and awaited orders. Carson thought that his unit should wait on the west side of the Rio Grande; if his green troops could stay removed from the fray long enough to study the action in relative calm, Carson suggested to Canby, they would be less likely to panic and bolt when their time came to fight. Canby saw wisdom in the idea, and so for an hour Carson and his men hugged the west bank—and watched.

On the east side of the river the firing raged on through midday. The Union forces seemed to have lost the momentum they had enjoyed in the morning, and for a time the battle smoldered in stalemate. Then Canby devised a plan to turn the tide: Using Alexander

McRae's howitzer battery as a hinge on the Union far left, he would swing the bulk of his forces toward the right like an enormous slamming door, trapping the Confederates in an enfilading fire.

To function as the center-right of his "door," Canby ordered Carson and his men to wade across the river and take up active positions on the battlefield. Carson's idea of waiting in reserve across the river had seemingly paid off: Unlike many of the volunteer and militia units up and down the battlefield, his men were already mentally immersed in the action and now, in their hour, did not flinch. Carson advanced about five hundred yards, swinging toward the right as planned. At one point his men successfully checked a concerted Texan charge on a Union 24-pounder howitzer. Carson described the action: "As the head of the enemy's column came within 80 yards of my right, our whole column poured a volley into them and caused them to break in every direction. Almost at the same time a shell from the 24-pounder was thrown among them with fatal effect."

Through it all, Carson was a calm, unflinching presence. Canby, in his official report, praised him for his "zeal and energy." Carson paced up and down his line of volunteers, yelling, "*Firme, muchachos, firme*"—steady, boys, steady. His volunteers responded magnificently. The column, Carson said, "moved forward to sweep the wood near the hills." Just as Canby had hoped, they had arranged themselves in an enfilade position—one in which they could rake deadly fire across the length of the enemy line. Capt. Rafael Chacon, who fought with Carson's unit, later wrote that the volunteers "fought full of courage and almost in a frenzy, driving the enemy back through blood and fire . . . we put them to flight and drove them clear into the hills."

But on the left, the Union lines were plunged in panic and disarray. Tom Green and the Texans, letting out a Rebel yell, had mounted an assault on Alexander McRae's battery. More than a thousand Confederates charged on foot with what was later described as "wild ardor." It was a frantic sprint, and the Rebels fully expected, as one of them later put it, that "raking fire would slay the last man of us."

The initial Union response was thunderous—one Confederate officer recalled that his men charged into "a driving storm of grape and musket balls." But the Federals were not prepared for the fury of the Rebel onslaught, and many of the New Mexico volunteers began to shrink before "the unsavory diet of canister" being hurled at them from Confederate artillery pieces hidden in the dry riverbed. As the Texans charged in a second wave, and then a third, the Union lines faltered and many Federal troops bolted for the river. Complained one Union soldier: "Down they came upon us, rushing through the fire poured into them, with maddened determination." (Some Texans later admitted that much of their "maddened determination" was born of their desperation for water—many were dying of thirst and were thus willing to risk anything to reach the river.)

In the intense barrage, Union casualties mounted. As Canby surveyed the scene and gnawed his dormant cigar, his beloved warhorse, Old Chas, was shot out from under him.

The men in McRae's six-gun emplacement held on as long as they could, but the Texans finally reached the battery. A fierce hand-to-hand combat commenced. Fighting with bowie knives, clubbed rifles, and revolvers, the Rebels soon overwhelmed the Union gunners. Captain McRae was killed while defending his own artillery piece— according to one account, he and a Texan died simultaneously while struggling over his howitzer, with the blood of the two enemies "mingling on the barrel." A quick-thinking Union gunner, recognizing that capture was inevitable but determined to deny the Texans his stockpile of artillery shells, lit a fuse to his ammunition box and blew it (and everyone in the immediate vicinity) to smithereens.

Canby stood dazed beside the carcass of his horse and watched all this unfold with deepening gloom. Realizing that his crack artillery unit had now been enveloped by the enemy, and perhaps still unnerved by his own brush with death, Canby decided he had risked too much. (For a field commander with a lifetime of battle experience, he seemed unusually sensitive to the sight of his own casualties; a contemporary account noted that later "he went through the ranks of the wounded and wept.") At around five o'clock he called for a general retreat, up and down the line. All Union forces were to cross back to the west bank and return posthaste to Fort Craig.

Kit Carson and his volunteers were dumbfounded by Canby's order—from their point of view on the Union far right, the battle was faring well; in fact, they felt they were on the verge of victory. Capt. Rafael Chacon, fighting with Carson, wrote that he "could not understand the signals to retreat. We had penetrated the enemy zone and considered that our charge had won the battle."

But a command was a command, so Carson called his men back to the river and made sure the crossing was executed in orderly fashion. As the volunteers wallowed across, Chacon recalled that the Texans "were shelling us with our own guns, but their fire fell short and did us no harm."

Elsewhere along the river, however, the retreat took the form of a disorganized rout—"It looked more like a herd of frightened mustangs than men," observed one Texan eyewitness. "We rushed up to the bank and poured a deadly fire upon them. The mortality in the river was terrible. The shot guns came into play and did great execution." So many Union troops were shot dead in the water that, as one Confederate account put it, "the Rio Grande was dyed with Yankee blood."

Even so, as nightfall approached, the Texans in their thirst-crazed legions descended on the river and drank their fill.

Chapter 38   THE SONS OF SOME DEAR MOTHER

The next morning, a raw winter sun crept over the tablelands to reveal a desert battlefield strewn with corpses. On both sides of the cold, brown river, the bodies of men and animals lay mangled. A truce was declared so that both armies might bury their dead. In the morning stillness, the cries of the wounded could be heard up and down the river as surgeons labored in open-air hospitals.

The one-day battle of Valverde had ended in a Confederate victory—at least tactically. Just as they had hoped, the Texans had lured Canby away from his fort and then engaged him on their terms. They had driven the Federals from the field while capturing, in the desperate late afternoon charge, all six guns of Alexander McRae's battery. And over the course of the battle, the Confederates had sustained fewer casualties: Canby's army reported 263 dead, wounded, or missing, while Sibley's total casualties numbered about 200.

On the other hand, Sibley's army had failed to achieve its one vital strategic objective—the capture of Fort Craig. Canby's forces were again safely ensconced behind the fortress walls; their ammunition stockpiles and crammed storerooms lay unharmed so that Canby might fight another day. The Union troops had ample medicine, plenty of fuel to keep them warm, and enough rations for months.

The previous night, some of the men had called Canby a traitor—to his face, even—for so ignominiously quitting the battlefield. But now, in the clarity of morning, the logic behind Canby's retreat impressed itself upon his army. If he had not hastened back to the fort when he did, the Texans, reinvigorated by their successful assault on McRae's battery, might have overrun the Federals and stormed the fort. Canby's much-criticized conservatism had thus paid off: He had cut his losses in order to protect Fort Craig, the only prize that really mattered.

The "victorious" Confederates, camped along the river, were starving, freezing, and running out of ammo. They were also desperately short of horses. What with Paddy Graydon's suicide-bomber stampede, the disastrous lancer charge, and the overall equestrian casualties on the field, the Texans had lost some 350 horses and mules. Prior to the battle the Confederate army had largely been a mounted force—Texans were ferociously proud of their horsemanship. Yet now, almost overnight, Sibley's cavalry had effectively become an infantry.

Still, the Texans were buoyed by their victory at Valverde and optimistic about completing the campaign. Said one of Sibley's officers: "If we can subsist our men and horses, there is very little doubt we will be conquerors of New Mexico, and have it in our power to establish Southern principles in the Territory."

The seldom-seen General Sibley emerged from his ambulance that morning to congratulate the valorous troops he had failed to lead. His men were embarrassed by their apparently craven commander and angry at him for absenting himself in the heat of battle. Under their breath they said that a real Texan, not a Louisianan like Sibley, should be leading the campaign. Some accused Sibley of deliberately trying to lose the battle by colluding with his old pal Canby. Said one critic: "He was the very last man on earth who ought to have been placed in command . . . he had formed too intimate an acquaintance with 'John Barley Corn.' "

Sibley did rise out of his bibulous stupor long enough to issue a demand that verged on the ridiculous. Via subordinate officers sent under a white flag, he instructed Colonel Canby to "capitulate" the fort—even though there were thirty-five hundred well-armed, well-fed Union men behind its thick walls. Sibley grandiosely thought that if he could not take the bastion in battle, then maybe his old friend Canby would just . . . give it up. Canby politely but firmly declined.

In feigned indignation, Sibley pulled together his tattered men and began marching along the river toward Albuquerque—*away* from Fort Craig. Creeping northward, using cow chips for campfire fuel, the famished army swallowed up the tiny villages along the Rio Grande and picked them clean. Finally, the Rebels had abandoned their original (and completely naïve) notion of "living off the land" in the embrace of friendly locals; they had now become an army of looters.

Sibley knew that Albuquerque was a major Union supply station, and he assured his men that they would soon enjoy this "promised land" of ammunition and foodstuffs. But when Sibley reached the outskirts, he was crestfallen to see three enormous columns of black smoke rising over the town: Canby had sent messengers on fast horses ahead of Sibley to instruct Union quartermasters to torch the Albuquerque depots rather than let them fall into Rebel hands.

Now Albuquerque was something of a ghost town, many of its residents having taken to the hills to escape the feared Confederate onslaught. Josefa Carson, who'd been temporarily living in Albuquerque while her husband trained his volunteers, fled with their children and servants back to Taos, where she hid family belongings and heirlooms much as Georgian belles would do, a few years later, in the path of Sherman's despoiling march to the sea. Carson's son Kit Jr. years later recalled how his mother "concealed her valuables in the garments of a faithful Navajo girl servant she had raised from babyhood [probably Maria Dolores]."

Sibley's men entered Albuquerque in triumph and, though disappointed not to have captured Federal stores, proceeded to beg, borrow, or steal from the anxious townsfolk. The ravening army was terrorizing the very citizens whose hearts it needed to win over if the occupation was to have any chance of long-term success. Vaguely aware of this, Sibley issued a proclamation to the people of New Mexico that was equal parts forgiveness and threat. "Those of you who volunteered in the Federal service were doubtless deceived by designing officials," he said. "But the signal victory which crowned our arms at Valverde on the 21st of February proves . . . our powers and ability." He went on to declare "a complete and absolute amnesty to all citizens who have, or may within ten days lay aside their arms. Return with confidence to your homes and avocations, and fear not the result."

Then the Rebels sprinted on toward the capital. On the snowy day of March 13, Sibley's men entered Santa Fe without a fight and hoisted the stars-and-bars over the plaza for the Confederacy, and for Texas. Like Albuquerque, Santa Fe was largely abandoned, its Hispanic residents dreading the prospect of *Tejanos* living in their midst. Most of the Union spouses—including Canby's wife, Louisa Hawkins Canby—had stayed behind in Santa Fe to treat the casualties they expected to come in war's wake. But the territorial government had picked up and moved seventy miles east to Las Vegas (the same tiny high plains village where General Kearny had delivered his rooftop speech upon entering New Mexico in 1846).

Occupying Santa Fe did much for the army's morale—this was the prize Texans had sought for generations—but it did little to satiate the men's hunger. The Rebels were dismayed to find that most of the Federal supplies at Fort Marcy had either been destroyed or transported to another important army stronghold, located twenty-five miles beyond Las Vegas on the Santa Fe Trail, called Fort Union. In anticipation of the Confederate invasion, the Federals had strengthened the battlements of this "star fort" set on the edge of the plains in northeastern New Mexico. An officer stationed at the new and improved Fort Union judged it to be impregnable, boasting that "all Texas can't take it!"

Sibley's army was caught between two isolated forts: Fort Craig to the south, Fort Union to the east. He knew he could not successfully occupy the territory, or advance toward the goldfields of Colorado, without the supplies these two citadels so stingily held. His grand scheme to seize New Mexico seemed to be working magnificently— he held the capital, after all, and had not lost a single battle. But his army was withering from within.

Canby knew this. The Union colonel was still hunkered at Fort Craig, more than 150 miles from Santa Fe. He was happy to turn the defense of the territory into a war of attrition. His plan, cruel in its simplicity, was to stay put at Fort Craig—strategically situated to block the Confederate supply lines coming from Texas. From there, he would let the invaders savor the husks of their victory in Santa Fe until they slowly, surely starved. Periodically, Canby would dispatch guerrilla parties to harass Sibley's advance and tear at his flanks. But otherwise, Canby resolved to withhold the mass of his men—including Carson's unit—and wait.

Meanwhile, Canby requested reinforcements from faraway California and also from Denver, where Union loyalists were raising a sizable volunteer army from the legions of miners who had flooded to Colorado in the 1859 Pikes Peak gold rush. Canby expected these rough-and-ready reinforcements—"Pikes Peakers," they were called—to arrive at Fort Union by mid-March. Once they did, Canby planned finally to emerge from Fort Craig, unite with the Coloradans, and drive Sibley's weakened army from the territory for good.

⊗

The Coloradan volunteers *were* coming, and coming in record speed. Their four-hundred-mile trek from Denver City, through snow and howling winds, across plains and mountain passes, ranks as one of the most spectacular marathons of the Civil War.

The Coloradans, nearly one thousand in number, were already on their way to New Mexico when they received word of the Union defeat at Valverde, and this served to quicken their already brisk pace to forty miles a day. Then they heard that the Rebels had captured Albuquerque, and even Santa Fe—further goads. They knew that whatever happened, they had to get to Fort Union before the Texans did. So the Pikes Peakers marched day and night, wearing out their shoes, wearing out their draft animals until they dropped in their harnesses. Near the end the men jettisoned all unessential belongings to "add wings to our speed," as one private put it. Their pace became truly extraordinary: In a single thirty-six-hour stretch they covered ninety-two miles.

One of the officers leading this sprinting column was Maj. John Milton Chivington, a formidable man who would soon become one of the most notorious figures in the American West. Originally from Ohio, the forty-one-year-old Chivington was a Methodist preacher who brimmed with a sort of muscular Christianity. He had a bull moose physique—standing nearly six-feet five-inches and weighing 260 pounds. A soldier acquaintance once said that the thick-necked, barrel-chested Chivington had the most perfect figure of a man he'd ever seen in a uniform. His doughy face was set with hard, seedlike eyes that seemed to contain a yearning ambition.

Chivington had ability, intelligence, resolve, and stamina—and as a staunch abolitionist who had actively supported the Underground Railroad, he was deeply committed to the Union cause. He possessed ample stores of courage as well. A biographer once said that Chivington was "entirely a stranger to the emotion of fear." But something about the man was distinctly "off." Like most zealots, he was too literal-minded, too uncompromising, too eager to embrace tidy, extreme nostrums. He irritated people. As soon as Chivington came to Colorado in 1860 after a stint performing missionary work among Indians in Kansas, the preacher set about cleaning up the sin he saw everywhere in the mountain mining camps. He seethed and fulminated, he named names and pointed fingers, he cast his disapproving eye on the brothels and gambling halls. As a "circuit rider" traveling about the lawless and violent West, he came to view himself not only as a pastor but also as a one-man vice officer—God's own enforcer.

Once, in Nebraska City, he took it upon himself to destroy the entire liquor supply of a saloon that had, by a perfectly legal deed, located itself in an abandoned church. A shocked witness demanded to know by what authority could he seize and destroy another man's property. Chivington replied: "By the authority of Almighty God!" In one frontier settlement, angry townsfolk literally tried to tar and feather him. The following Sunday, Chivington lumbered to the pulpit brandishing two pistols. He laid them beside his open King James Bible, and then declared: "By the grace of God and these two revolvers, I am going to preach here today."

Having heard stories like this, people in Colorado gave Chivington a wide berth. From him they felt the hot breath of an angry God; if they had no love for Chivington, they at least feared and respected him. He became a fixture around Denver and the goldfields of the Front Range. His sermons were of the fire-and-brimstone variety, his voice booming so loudly it could be heard three blocks away. Aside from his constant rounds of preaching, he founded Denver's first Sunday school.

Everywhere he went, people called him "the Fighting Parson."

When the territorial governor of Colorado called for Union volunteers in 1861, Chivington promptly signed up. Naturally enough, the governor offered him a post as chaplain. But Chivington balked at this—he didn't want a "praying commission," he said; he wanted a "fighting commission."

And so he got one. Now the Fighting Parson was a major in the Colorado 1st Volunteers, racing toward New Mexico with a unit of cussing, irascible miners under his watchful eye.

The overall commander of the Colorado Volunteers, however, was a stern and woolly-bearded lawyer from Denver City named John Potts Slough. A native Ohioan like Chivington, Slough in 1857 made an unsuccessful bid for the governorship of Kansas before moving to Colorado to become the judge of a miner's court. He was the scion of a distinguished military family (during the Revolutionary War one of his uncles was first colonel under George Washington). Perhaps because of his heritage, and the fact that he lacked military training or experience himself, it seemed to many that Slough had a chip on his shoulder—and something dramatic to prove. Whatever the case, he was not in sync with his men. Most of them viewed him as a distant and tyrannical martinet. Their distaste for him was not mild: Once during the march, and several times later in the campaign, his men would conspire to kill him.

On the freezing night of March 11, "with drums beating and colors flying," Slough, Chivington, and their thousand men marched jauntily through the gates of Fort Union to the great relief of the small force of New Mexican volunteers nervously garrisoned there. Their long sprint was, in the estimation of Civil War in the West authority Alvin Josephy, "something of an epic." In just thirteen days the Coloradans had tramped four hundred miles.

Slough wasted no time taking charge of the fort, which was then commanded by an experienced, West Point–educated colonel whom Slough outranked only by some obscure loophole of commission protocol. Showing not the slightest deference to his able predecessor, Colonel Slough announced his intention to march toward Santa Fe to engage the enemy. This contravened higher orders coming from Colonel Canby at Fort Craig. Canby wanted the Coloradans to stay at Fort Union until he gave explicit instructions for a junction of the two Federal armies, a complicated maneuver that would require sound communications, exquisite timing, and a clear chain of command.

But the impatient Slough couldn't suppress the urge to dash ahead and capture the glory he felt was rightfully his—even if it meant facing an irate Canby and a possible court-martial. So on March 22, Slough, Chivington, and their men left the fort and headed west on the Santa Fe Trail.

◙

The Texans, still stationed in the capital, were also spoiling for a fight. Their spies had informed them that a Federal force had left Fort Union, but they did not realize that the oncoming army was composed of recently arrived Coloradan reinforcements. Expecting an easy fight against poorly armed Hispanic volunteers, the Rebels believed they could make quick work of an apathetic enemy and push on to seize Fort Union.

General Sibley would not lead them. Again showing his knack for avoiding a battle, he remained at his headquarters in Albuquerque. Instead, the Rebels would be under the command of Maj. Charles Pyron, an extremely aggressive, no-nonsense Alabama native and veteran of the Mexican War. On March 24, Pyron's small force of four hundred Texans left Santa Fe and soon found themselves in Apache Canyon, the storied defile where, sixteen years earlier, Gov. Manuel Armijo had put up his abortive stand against General Kearny's invading army.

There, inside the canyon's constricted walls early on the crisp afternoon of March 26, the Rebels ran right into Major Chivington, who, with some four hundred infantry and cavalry, was marching west as an advance guard of Slough's force.

A brisk firefight erupted along the old ruts of the Santa Fe Trail. The Coloradans soon gained the upper hand, with Chivington galloping ahead, pistols blazing in each hand. While artillery pieces dueled from the canyon floor, dismounted troops on both sides scurried up the steep rock walls and took positions behind boulders and piñon trees, each army hoping to gain a higher vantage over its enemy. To stymie the Coloradan advance, the Texans destroyed a log bridge that spanned a steep arroyo, but the Pikes Peakers kept spurring on, forcing their horses to jump over the ravine.

By late afternoon Chivington's men had pushed the Rebels back more than a mile and a half toward the western mouth of the canyon. At Chivington's command the Coloradans drew their swords and mounted an audacious cavalry charge, which to one Rebel "looked like so many flying devils." A Texan participant later wrote his wife: "On they came to what I supposed was [their] certain destruction, but no lead or iron seemed to stop them, for we were pouring it into them from every side like hail in a storm."

The two forces fell into a hand-to-hand fight along the road. The Union troops captured so many Texans that Major Pyron thought better of the engagement and withdrew to find more reinforcements.

The canyon fell silent. With dusky light filtering through the ponderosa pines, Major Chivington and his men were left to savor a small turning point. It was only a skirmish, but their stand at Apache Canyon was the first Union victory in the Civil War of the West. Amazingly, they had taken seventy-one rebel prisoners while driving the rest of the Texans from the field.

The skirmish at Apache Canyon was an opening salvo, a sharp and violent throat-clearing before the larger contest could begin. The Federals had won, but the outcome easily could have swung the other way. It was precisely the sort of hot-and-bothered engagement that the prudent Canby would not have countenanced—and when he did learn about it, by messenger several days later, he was furious.

And yet a legend was born that day. In his first brush with battle, the Fighting Parson had distinguished himself as a bold and fearless leader. His men saw something in John Chivington they didn't quite expect from a Sunday school teacher. One account described Chivington this way: "In action, he became the incarnation of war. The bravest of the brave, a giant in stature, and a whirlwind in strife, he had also the rather unusual qualities that go to make soldiers personally love [him], and eager to follow him into the jaws of death."

◙

Two days later the Texan and Coloradan forces regrouped and clashed again, this time a few miles to the east, in much bigger numbers and with far greater fervor. Pyron's small contingent had fallen in with the larger forces of his superior, Col. William Scurry, a chiseled Mexican War veteran turned Texas lawyer, and now the Confederate forces numbered about one thousand. Leaving their supply train of some eighty wagons safely tucked in a protected stretch of canyon, Scurry pushed east in search of the Union troops.

By late morning he had found them: Some fifteen hundred men under Col. John Slough were advancing west along the trail. The main action took place in a pine-feathered mountain pass called Glorieta, a beautiful stretch along the Santa Fe Trail not far from the ancient ruins of Pecos. Bugles sounded, the boulder fields seethed with acrid blue smoke, and artillery shells sliced the tops off the trees. A savage fight raged all day in this stunning gold-green wilderness, with the Confederates driving Slough's men several miles back through the pass to the adobe buildings and corral fencing of a settler's ranch.

By dusk, however, the battle was inconclusive: The Texans had gained the most ground, but the Coloradans still blocked the Confederates' path to Fort Union. The Rebels had lost forty-two killed, sixty-one wounded, and twenty captured; the Union casualties were only slightly higher.

Possibly the most memorable action of the day concerned the widely hated Colonel Slough: At one point in the heat of battle, his own men became so disgusted with him for keeping so far to the rear of the action that they turned a howitzer on him and opened fire, raking the hillside with shrapnel in an attempt to frag him; the colonel barely escaped with his life.

◙

Neither side knew it yet, but the battle of Glorieta *was* conclusive—in fact, the war in New Mexico was all but over. The two field commanders would not discover this spectacular wrinkle until late that

night, and it would take several more days for both armies to comprehend its full import.

John Chivington, again, was at the center of it.

On the morning of the Glorieta battle, Chivington had pulled
away from Colonel Slough at around dawn with a detachment of 490
men. His party was guided by Manuel Chaves, the popular Navajo
fighter recently slapped on the wrist—and then absolved—for his role
in the massacre at Fort Fauntleroy. Quietly climbing into the mountains, Chaves led Chivington's men on a shortcut toward Apache
Canyon, where he was to sneak around the enemy flanks and attack
the Confederate rear. By midafternoon he came to the rim of the
canyon and peered seven hundred feet down into the gorge, where
the Rebels had appropriated an old ranch as a campsite.

"You are right on top of them, Major," Chaves whispered.

Chivington was surprised to find that the valley floor was almost
perfectly quiet; the Confederate camp seemed all but abandoned.
Scurry's men had moved on well east of here, to engage Slough.

Then, through his field glasses, Chivington spied something that
must have made him salivate: Eighty wagons, piled high with supplies, the entire Confederate supply train, lay before him on the
canyon floor. He couldn't believe his eyes. This trove appeared to be
casually guarded by only a hundred men—many of them sick and injured—armed with a single cannon. Not far away, corralled in various
places, were hundreds and hundreds of horses and mules. Here, concentrated in one place, trapped by canyon walls, were the Confederate hopes and dreams: nearly all the rations, ammunition, medicines,
blankets, and other essentials that were meant to sustain the Rebels
all the way to Fort Union and beyond.

Sensing a new opportunity, Chivington abruptly changed his
plans. Instead of dropping into the canyon and heading east to attack
the Confederate rear, he resolved to do something that would prove
infinitely more costly to the Rebels: He would attack here and destroy
everything.

Securing themselves with ropes and leather straps, his men began
to drop over the rim and slip as quietly as possible down into the

gorge. Inevitably someone dislodged a rock, which, in turn, started a small avalanche. The Confederates in the canyon heard the commotion and promptly fired their one cannon, but their shots were ineffectual. Chivington's men reached the floor without incident, seized and spiked the cannon, and then stormed the grounds of the ranch.

The Texans had been caught almost completely off guard. Terrified by the sight of several hundred Colorado miners descending on them from the mesa, most of the Confederates bolted while the others—seventeen, in all—surrendered. Within minutes the ranch was in Union hands.

The shuddering booms coming from the battle at Glorieta could be heard in the distance somewhere to the east, but Chivington couldn't tell how far away the engagement was, or whether it might be moving in his direction. Anxious about the possibility of an ambush, Chivington issued a chilling order: The moment Scurry returned, the moment his vanguard was spotted in the canyon, all Confederate prisoners were to be shot on the spot.

Some of Chivington's men recoiled at the thought of it, but the Fighting Parson was adamant: *Kill every one of them.*

The Texan prisoners heard the order and reeled in fear. Most of them were sick or wounded and had no possible means of escape. One Confederate officer thought that Chivington had "lost all sense of humanity." Harvey Holcomb, a Texas soldier, considered Chivington "a contemptible coward" for issuing an order to have helpless prisoners "shot down like dogs."

Chivington posted pickets to scour the canyon for Rebel movements and then turned to the main business at hand: sabotaging the Confederate supply train. He directed his men to huddle the eighty wagons tightly together and torch them all. Soon a crackling fire licked the air and clouds of thick black smoke billowed from the canyon. One of the ammo wagons exploded in the intense heat of the flames, severely injuring one of the Coloradans. Nothing escaped the torch—tents, flour, Bibles, horsetack, bedrolls, cookware, coffee, clothing, tools, whiskey. Watching their belongings going up in smoke, the prisoners' hopes sank.

Chivington, meanwhile, stood and stared with perverse glee, the ruddy heat of the bonfire spreading over his face. This was a funeral pyre, he must have realized, a cremation. All the Confederate designs on the West were now turning to cinders.

One Coloradan's account characterized the destruction of the baggage train in more romantic terms: "We pierced the Confederate vitals and drew from thence the life blood."

Then Chivington turned to the enemy horses and mules, some five or six hundred of them corralled in various places around the ranch. Without flinching, Chivington ordered his men to kill them all. To save on ammunition, though, he instructed his men to do the work with bayonets. For the next half hour or so the canyon walls echoed with the shrill neighing of horses wild-eyed with fright, with the low groans of stuck animals, and perhaps with the nervous laughter of men lost in this unpleasant errand of slaughter.

In his memoirs, Chivington boasted that his men bayoneted eleven hundred animals that day; it was certainly an inflated number—the Texans insisted it was about half that—but the fact that he would exaggerate shows something of his misplaced pride as well as his remorselessness.

The Texan prisoners watched the massacre of their animals with deepening dread: They figured they were next. Luckily for them, their army never showed itself in the canyon. If it had, Chivington surely would have made good on his vow.

The Confederates were broken. With their supply train destroyed, they had lost the will and the wherewithal to fight. The Texans retreated from the Glorieta battlefield and reconvened in Santa Fe to sift their dwindling options.

In Santa Fe, the casualties from Glorieta began to stream in. Colonel Canby's wife, Louisa, turned her own house into a hospital. When some of her Union friends castigated her for showing generosity to the enemy, she snapped: "Friend or foe, their lives must be saved if it is possible. They are the sons of some dear mother." The Texans were moved by her kindness. One of them wrote of Mrs. Canby: "That Christian lady captured more hearts of Confederate soldiers than her husband ever captured Confederate bodies."

It took General Sibley a week or more to fully appreciate it, but his campaign was over. In his official military correspondence, he tried at first to put the best face on it. Cheerfully noting the tactical successes scored at Glorieta, he wrote his Confederate superior: "I have the honor and pleasure to report another victory." But then he closed his letter with an understated cry for help: "I must have reinforcements."

In a letter to the governor of Texas, however, Sibley was considerably more blunt: "We have been crippled," he said. Sibley's pride would not let him admit that perhaps the Union Army had played a role in the crippling. "We beat the enemy wherever we encountered them," he reasoned. It was, he claimed, "the famished country that beat us." Sibley had grown to loathe New Mexico, asserting that the territory was "not worth one-fourth the blood and treasure we have expended in its conquest." He felt a "dogged, irreconcilable detestation of the country and its people." His great dreams of a Confederate West had withered.

Sibley was already formulating plans for a total exodus from New Mexico. It was not to be a retreat, he euphemized, but rather a "precipitate evacuation."

Canby, meanwhile, decided to act. On April 1 he emerged from Fort Craig with a force of twelve hundred men and headed north along the river. Not yet realizing that Sibley had already resolved to quit New Mexico, Canby's intention was to join forces with the Colorado Volunteers and drive Sibley from the territory. Canby left Kit Carson and ten companies of New Mexico Volunteers at Fort Craig, telling him to defend the stronghold "to the last extremity."

Canby marched north in a welter of emotions. News of the battle at Glorieta had left him both relieved and incensed. Yes, Chivington's raid had hobbled the Confederates, but Colonel Slough had violated Canby's clear orders not to leave Fort Union. As he told Colonel Slough in a series of irate messages, the defense of the territory might have been jeopardized by the Coloradans' rash advance. In truth, Canby could have been tasting sour grapes: It's possible that he resented Slough and his Pikes Peakers for stealing some of the glory that might have been his.

In any case, Canby's withering letters convinced Colonel Slough that he might well face a court-martial. To forestall this humiliating possibility, Slough resigned his commission and absconded to Denver, with Major Chivington replacing him as commander of the 1st Colorado. (In fact, Slough had another, more pressing reason for quitting the service: After the fragging incident at the battle of Glorieta, the unpopular colonel feared that his own men would succeed in killing him. As Slough himself acknowledged in a letter: "I resigned the colonelcy because I was satisfied that a further connection might result in my assassination.")

By April 9, when Canby reached the outskirts of Albuquerque, he began to get a much clearer picture of just how desperately starved and anemic Sibley's army had become. Canby made a brief show of attacking Albuquerque, but this was only a ploy to draw Sibley's forces down from Santa Fe in order to protect the last Confederate reserves of supplies being held along the river. The ruse worked. As soon as Sibley's men arrived in Albuquerque—having completely abandoned the capital—Canby slipped east under cover of night to meet with Chivington and the 1st Colorado.

By executing this little sidestep away from the Rio Grande, Canby had deliberately left the way open for the Rebels to escape. Sibley took the cue, and on April 11 the Confederates began marching south toward Texas.

Now that he was reinforced with the Coloradans, Canby knew he could easily destroy Sibley's retreating army in a final, decisive battle; but he didn't want to. Canby simply wanted the Rebels to leave the territory, quickly and forever. The Union Army could not afford to feed and house the many hundreds of sickly prisoners that would result from another battle. The territory simply didn't have the resources.

So instead of forcing another engagement, Canby resolved merely to "herd" Sibley south along the river—to nag and worry him, to keep a close eye on him, and to make sure he didn't try to attack Carson at Fort Craig as a sort of parting gesture. Sibley's army marched along the west bank of the Rio Grande while Canby marched along the east bank, the two forces proceeding for a hundred miles in a tense and awkward lockstep. Each night they camped across the river from each other, so close they could hear each other's songs and revels and smell each other's food. One Texan thought the sight of the enemy campfires burning so close together was "both grand and awful."

Many of Canby's men hated this inglorious assignment of hounding the enemy without being allowed to fight. One Coloradan ridiculed the colonel's strategy for being too kindhearted: "We do not want to take any unfair advantage of the Texans—that would not be chivalrous. God grant they may never get the same advantage over us."

When Sibley's army drew near to Fort Craig in mid-April, he decided to make a hundred-mile detour into the parched mountains to the west rather than risk a possible engagement with Carson and his garrison. And so one night the Texans secretly burned and buried their last unnecessary belongings and vanished into the desert.

The following morning Canby looked across the river and found to his surprise that the Texans had abandoned their camp, their fires still faintly smoldering. Canby sent scouts to follow them into the mountains, and their reports were grim. Under the unforgiving sun, the Texans were now dying of thirst and disease. Their trail was strewn with discarded clothes, ruined wagons, abandoned weapons, and the corpses of animals and humans alike, with a sprinkling of bones and the appendages of soldiers half-eaten by wolves. Their disgraceful march had become, as one Texan said, "every man for himself." Since the expedition began, their numbers had dwindled by nearly one-third: Of the 3,500 men who marched out of San Antonio the previous year, more than 500 had died in combat or from disease, while another 500 had either deserted or surrendered.

Sibley was now riding in his ambulance, doubtless drunk again, entertaining the wives of Southern sympathizers who were vacating the territory. The general had lost everything, even his sense of shame. As a newspaper back in Austin would later put it: "He was chasing a shadow in a barren land." His campaign was in shambles, his name ruined, his future uncertain, and his men roundly hating him.

It was a pitiful sight—so pitiful that at least one of the Coloradans was moved to feel sorry for the enemy as he dragged homeward, never to be seen again in New Mexico:

Poor fellows! The climate and Uncle Sam's boys have sadly wasted them. They are now fleeing through the mountains with a little more than a third of the number with which they first assaulted us at Fort Craig. Very many softly lie and sweetly sleep low in the ground. Let their faults be buried with them. They are our brothers, erring it may be, still nature will exact a passing tear for the brave dead. And doubt not there are those who will both love and honor their memory if we cannot. Any cause that men sustain to death becomes sacred, at least to them.

Chapter 39 THE ROUND FOREST

The Texans were gone, yet still the war was not over. In the welcome calm, New Mexico awoke to realize that while the army had been preoccupied with ejecting Confederate invaders from the territory's front yard, the Navajos had been attacking from the rear. Manuelito and the other warriors did not understand why the two *bilagaana* armies were fighting each other. They could not have guessed the underlying concepts of secession, or states' rights, or the hovering issue of slavery as it was practiced in a wet, green world that existed somewhere far to the east, beyond the Staked Plains.

But the Diné quickly saw opportunities in the conflict. Many of the American forts were abandoned, and along the Rio Grande the flocks still grazed, ripe for the taking. The chain of logic wasn't complicated: American soldiers were somewhere else, so the Navajos pounced. Emboldened by what they correctly perceived as a power vacuum, and still outraged over the massacre at Fort Fauntleroy, the Diné warriors raided almost without check through the drought-stricken year of 1862. William Arny, a former Indian agent who was now territorial secretary, estimated that New Mexico's property losses to Indian raiders in 1862 amounted to $250,000; more than thirty thousand sheep were stolen by the Navajos that year. James Collins, superintendent of Indian affairs in New Mexico, reported that the record of murders committed by Navajos had become "truly frightful . . . This death list is not made up of a few lives lost. Its number will extend to nearly three hundred for the past eighteen months."

Something had to be done—the people of the territory cried out for retribution as never before. The *Santa Fe Gazette* clamored for all-out war, reminding its readers that "for months the bells of your sacred edifices have tolled the obsequies of your slaughtered citizens."

And so Col. Edward Canby, in his own slow and methodical way, turned his attention to the matter. In the late spring of 1862 he began to formulate plans for a campaign into Navajo country unlike any other. It would be ambitious, it would be decisive, and it would result in the creation of a true Navajo reservation far to the west, carved from Diné land, possibly along the Little Colorado River in what is now northeastern Arizona. As far as Canby was concerned, the time for half measures had passed; this would be the ultimate solution, the endgame. The colonel wrote to his superiors in Washington that "there is now no choice between the Navajos' absolute extermination or their removal and colonization at points so remote from the settlements as to isolate them entirely from the inhabitants of the Territory."

Canby's plan would not come to fruition, not exactly, not in the way he envisioned. History would have played out quite differently, for Edward Canby was above all a practical man, and the campaign he was planning, however ruthless, would have been far better for Navajos and non-Navajos alike than what was to come. But in the summer of 1862, Canby was promoted to general and recalled to serve in the East. His plodding but sensible mind was needed in the frantic halls of wartime Washington. That fall, Canby was replaced by another career frontier soldier, a formidable figure of the West who had his own deeply held notions about the Navajo conflict.

⊠

How to describe the singular personality of Brig. Gen. James Henry Carleton? A pedant, a prig, a man who thought of everything and whose perfectionism seldom gave him an occasion to apologize. But also an officer of rare excellence, rigid ethics, fine manners, and multifaceted competence. An officer with a probing but perhaps overly tidy intellect. In another place, in another time, perhaps in another profession, James Carleton might have been a great man of towering good deeds. Instead, his entrance upon the stage of New Mexico during the late summer of 1862 resulted in one of the most tragic collisions in the U.S. government's long, sorry relationship with Native Americans.

It would be facile to call him, as many have, a villain and a fiend and be done with it. But Carleton was a much more nuanced man than he is usually given credit for. He wasn't an entirely unlikable man—many people found him extremely gracious and kind. As a friend he was steadfast to a fault. His hobbies and interests were refreshingly eclectic. He climbed mountains, collected rare seeds, read voraciously. He had a talent for waltzing. Though he did not attend college, he knew eminent figures of science and literature, men such as Audubon and Longfellow. He penned authoritative articles for the Smithsonian Institution about archaeological ruins, one of his great loves. He wrote the first comprehensive book on perhaps the most crucial engagement of the Mexican War, the Battle of Buena Vista, where he served with distinction under Gen. Zachary Taylor.

Perhaps self-conscious about not being a West Pointer, Carleton had made it his life's work to catch up with his better-connected colleagues by outdoing them in abstrusities of military science, natural history, and other fields befitting a gentleman officer of his day. Whatever it was that drove him, Carleton was a perpetual motion machine, always burrowed in some interesting pet project or cranny of amusement. He was, for example, the nation's foremost military expert on the cavalry tactics of the Russian Cossacks, having made a formal study of the matter at Carlisle Barracks, Pennsylvania. From time to time, during his nearly constant Western travels, he took it upon himself to ship unusual minerals and specimens of flora and fauna to Harvard University. He had a facility for boat design—he was especially fond of building Mackinaws. Perhaps his greatest extracurricular hobby was meteorites, and while in Arizona he discovered an important one, a 632-pound hunk of cosmic metal—"discarded by Vulcan himself"—that he hauled all the way to San Francisco (to this day it's still known as the Carleton Meteorite).

Forty-eight years old, he was a New England Calvinist with the posture of a lamppost. There was a snap and rigor to his movements that fairly telegraphed his titanic work ethic. His sun-crisped face, hedged in a trim topiary of muttonchop sideburns, projected the intellectual pugnacity of Teddy Roosevelt. In photographic portraits, his pronounced jaw is often tensed, his teeth gritted, his lupine eyes trained on something far away, as though he were intensely preoccupied with another, better world. Carleton by all accounts liked the sound of his own voice and had much to say, enunciating with shrill precision in the flinty inflections of his native Maine.

It can't be said that Carleton came out of nowhere. On the contrary, he was a well-established and highly regarded officer, the cream of the frontier army. Carleton seemed to know everyone: U. S. Grant, William Sherman, John C. Fremont, George McClellan, George Crook, the whole pantheon. His wife, Sophia, was the niece of Gen. John Garland. As a young officer, Carleton had trained as a proud dragoon at Fort Leavenworth under the late great Stephen Watts Kearny, and it was General Kearny, that consummate soldier-student of the prairie, whom Carleton seems to have consciously emulated.

Over his long career as a dragoon, Carleton had ridden all over the West—from Oklahoma to Utah to California—and he had dealt with countless Indian tribes. The only place he had lingered for any length of time, however, was New Mexico. For five years during the 1850s, he had been stationed at various forts in the territory, chasing Indians, protecting immigrant trains, and immersing himself in the peculiar problems of the Southwest. In those years he had seemed to hate everything about the place save its magnificent ruins. He once wrote with disgust that the local people of New Mexico were "utterly ignorant of everything beyond their corn fields and *acequias*" and noted a "universal proclivity for rags, dirt, and filthiness. The national expression of *quien sabe* (who knows?) appears deeply written on every face."

Carleton believed that the Navajo conflict was the largest reason for New Mexico's depressing backwardness; the wars sapped resources, rendered enterprise impractical, made travel unsafe, produced a perpetual cycle of enslavement, and gave life in the territory a quality of chronic despair. He recognized that if slavery was the underlying issue of the Civil War as it was being fought in the East, then slavery was also the underlying issue here. As a New England Calvinist from an abolitionist state, he could not countenance the concept of human chattel. There was no hope for any advancement in New Mexico until the citizens confronted what he called "this great evil."

He had been away for five years, and during his absence he'd thought long and hard about how to solve "the Navajo problem." Now, for better or worse, New Mexico would experience the second coming of James Henry Carleton.

To reach the territory, he had marched all the way from California, leading a column of fifteen hundred soldiers and miner volunteers. He had come with the original intention of helping Canby repulse the invading Texans. By the time he reached the Rio Grande, however, the main action was over. Carleton and his California column did successfully flush the territory's southern precincts of avowed Confederates; he instituted martial law and reclaimed Tucson, Mesilla, and other important southern towns for the Union. But he and his men were sorely disappointed to have missed out on the laurels of real battle.

Then, in September 1862, he was named commander of the 9th Military Department, and Carleton rode north to assume his office in Santa Fe.

For the next four years he would preside over New Mexico virtually as a dictator. But he was an uncommon kind of despot: a Puritan schoolmaster with a zeal for social engineering, a martinet of the cod liver oil–dispensing, this-is-for-your-own-good variety. He was a utopian in an odd sense, and a Christian idealist. Carleton saw a perfect world on the horizon but could not imagine the real-world horrors that would be required to reach it. C. L. Sonnichsen, a historian of the Southwest Indian wars, wrote that if Carleton had "never had to function as God in a war-torn and distracted country, his determination and organizing ability might have been put to better use. He had intelligence and foresight, driving energy, and a consuming ambition to do well. His trouble was that he could not admit an error, or take a backward step."

◙

It was his abiding fascination with Indians, with their dying habits and vanishing worlds, that originally brought Carleton to the West.

Born in 1814, the son of a shipmaster who died young, James Henry grew up on Maine's Penobscot Bay in the misty coastal village of Castine. His family was poor, but rich in Yankee blue blood—his mother was a Phelps, a venerable Puritan name, and Carletons had been living in New England since the 1660s. Both lines of his family had mottoes and coats-of-arms and sterling genealogies they were proud to recite.

The time of Carleton's youth was a fragile period in the history of eastern Maine. During the War of 1812, British forces had occupied most of Maine east of the Penobscot River and annexed the territory to New Brunswick. Much of it was an unknown, blackfly-ridden wilderness that had never been properly surveyed and had been in dispute since the Revolutionary War. Like many other American loyalists, the Carleton family became exiles, forced to abandon their original home on what became British-held Moose Island. All through his boyhood the lingering boundary dispute remained a volatile subject, and clouds of war constantly threatened (the border was not finally settled, in fact, until 1842). Some have speculated that it was Carleton's memory of this unpleasant experience from his adolescence—of his family having to endure a bitter, protracted, worrisome dispute along what amounted to a wild frontier—that gave him later in life such an urgent impatience to solve the Navajo problem with clean, stark finality. Whether by constitution or experience, Carleton was a man who hated social messiness.

Apart from the boundary dispute and the early passing of his father (the boy was only fifteen when John Carleton died), James Henry's childhood seems to have been happy. Carleton grew up as a "salt-water Yankee," spending his summers along the Penobscot River and the rocky coastline, fussing with boats, hunting for clams, fishing for quoddies. His friend David Barker (who later became known as the "Robert Burns of Maine") wrote a poem to Carleton about their adolescent years together that captures the mood of those times:

> *When happiness lived up this way*
> *When feet could stroll and hearts could beat*
> *And never feel fatigue*
> *Those times we swam and fished and sailed*
> *Upon old Kenduskeag*

Yet even back in those salad days, Carleton vaguely yearned for the Western frontier and sensed that his destiny lay there. Though his formal schooling was shaky, he had ambitions to be a novelist, and like many aspiring writers of his generation, he was drawn to the narratives of Washington Irving, James Fenimore Cooper, and other American authors who made the frontier a central theme. Carleton was a tireless composer of letters and seems to have made a habit of writing to prominent writers, seeking advice. When he was twenty-four he wrote a letter to Charles Dickens, in which he professed his literary ambitions and his desire to write stories about the "aborigines" of the West. In the letter, he suggested that if he could not make a go of his career in America, he was considering moving to England and trying his hand there. He then somewhat impertinently asked if he might come to London and call on the great novelist as a friend.

To his shock, Dickens actually replied.

The letter, dated March 27, 1839, is quite lengthy. In it, Dickens vehemently suggests that Carleton by all means stay in the United States and write. "I cannot but think that good tales—especially such as you describe, connected with the customs and history of America's aboriginal inhabitants who every day become more interesting as their numbers diminish—would surely find patrons and readers in her great cities." Adopting a tone of paternal kindness cut with just a hint of don't-quit-your-day-job exasperation, Dickens offers very sensible advice: "Satisfy yourself beyond all doubt that you are qualified for the course to which you now aspire . . . and try to achieve something in your own land before you venture on a strange one." Finally, Dickens says that if Carleton came to London, he may or may not call on him as a friend—it was a question he simply could not answer. "To pledge myself to find a friend in a man whom I have never seen and with the whole tenor of whose thoughts and feelings I am unacquainted—as I find them expressed in one enthusiastic letter—would be to prostitute the term."

Ironically, even as Dickens's letter of advice was steaming across the Atlantic, young Carleton was preparing to fight against the countrymen of the famous novelist. Like thousands of Maine youths, Carleton joined the militia to engage a mounting force of English-Canadian troops in what became known as the Aroostook War. This conflict was only the latest chapter of the Northeastern boundary controversy, a crisis that proved bloodless in the end but gave Carleton his first taste of military life.

That same year, Carleton joined the regular U.S. Army and trained at the Cavalry School of Practice, in Carlisle, Pennsylvania. In 1840 he married Henrietta Tracy Loring, a fair young Boston Brahmin with beautiful brown curls. The couple was married only a year, however: In 1841, while stationed with her husband at Fort Gibson on the Arkansas River, Henrietta died, probably of malaria. Her body was shipped back to Massachusetts and buried in Cambridge.

Racked with grief, the widowed Carleton threw himself into his army career. Perhaps because of his prickly personality and his sometimes overzealous desire to fulfill the letter of military protocol, he had a penchant for getting into soldierly altercations—one of which resulted in a brief suspension and reassignment. He was a difficult man to deal with, the sort of man who would not back down.

True to his correspondence with Dickens, Carleton remained fascinated by American Indians and carefully documented his prairie experiences in a series of logbooks that were later published. At Fort Croghan, near Council Bluffs, Carleton was intrigued to interview a tribe of Plains Indians who had a grotesque habit of grinding up the dried remains of their enemies into a lucky powder, which they stored in their medicine bags. He also met a Potawatomi warrior who ate the heart of one of his foes. "Make heap strong," Carleton says the Indian told him. "Like him very much—great medicine."

On the Missouri River, in October 1843, Carleton befriended James Audubon, who was then traveling the West studying and sketching quadrupeds. In his journal, the great naturalist called Carleton "a fine companion and a perfect gentleman" and presented him with a signed plate from a recent study of the Oregon flying squirrel. Carleton, in turn, gave Audubon a bearskin and a fine set of elk horns.

Carleton's years as a young frontier soldier were by all accounts his happiest. Among his many adventures, he accompanied a unit of dragoons, led by Colonel Kearny, on a march of more than two thousand miles from Fort Leavenworth to the South Pass of the Rocky Mountains; the young officer loved every step of the odyssey. Carleton's logbooks are filled with paeans to life in the frontier army. In one passage he rhapsodizes about "the white tents standing in long rows over the green grass, the blue smoke curling upward, the athletic figures of the soldiers intent upon their duties . . . surrounded by nature in all her purity . . . on fields no plough has ever furrowed, in groves no axe has ever sullied." Returning to Fort Leavenworth after a long campaign, Carleton writes that all he can think about is returning to the trail, noting that his heart "would pant with impatience to mount and be away again" with his "staunch and cheerful comrades, the roasted buffalo ribs, the broiled venison and the coffee, the sociable pipe and the accompanying story, joke and song."

But even his pristine prairie was starting to see major changes. Along the Oregon Trail, he marveled at the dusty spectacle of the wagon trains—so many hopeful immigrants pushing West, "all going to the other side of the mountains to bury their bones there and never return." In one passage from his logbooks, Carleton fairly swelled with a national—even racial—pride at the seemingly endless caravans plodding along: "Judging from the way they go on, by the time the leading company reaches the valley of the Columbia, there will be a broad stream of the real Anglo-Saxon stock stretching from the Atlantic to the Pacific, a regular Life-river traveling at a steady three-knot current."

⧉

The Mexican War abruptly ended Carleton's frontier idyll, and he soon found himself fighting under Gen. Zachary Taylor in Monterrey. It was a very different war against a very different enemy. The light and supple dragoon tactics he had honed under Kearny proved irrelevant; in most of the action Carleton witnessed, the fighting was pitched and concentrated, and heavy artillery carried the day.

The battle of Buena Vista, the engagement Carleton fought in and subsequently wrote about, was a turning point of the war—quite possibly *the* turning point. For two murderous days in February 1847, in a mountain pass not far from Saltillo, Taylor's force of five thousand Americans managed to rout an army of fourteen thousand Mexicans serving under Antonio Lopez de Santa Anna, the phoenix-like, one-legged *generalissimo.* In his combat narrative, Carleton describes the morning of the battle as "unusually bright and clear," with the sunlight "seeming to cover with flashing diamonds the burnished Mexican weapons . . . and the fluttering pennons of what appeared to be a countless forest of lances." Carleton vividly recalls the curious quiet in the pass, and then the sudden fury of the battle's opening fusillade: "The sharp rattle of musketry, the sullen reply of the rifle and the bugle-calls, intermingled with the shouts of those who were struggling high up the mountain . . . the rushing sound of the balls as they tore up the ground in the midst of us, or went screaming through the air—all will come back to memory until [we] shall be old men."

The gruff General Taylor is supposed to have acted so coolly during the heat of battle (or so a popular story went) that when he spotted a small cannonball hurtling directly toward him, he nonchalantly rose in his stirrups to let the ball pass between his derriere and his saddle. That one was doubtless apocryphal, but the general did become famous for a command he casually issued during the battle to a young artilleryman, Braxton Bragg. Grumbling in his phlegmy voice, Taylor asked the gunner to pack the howitzers with more lead shot. "Maybe," the general suggested, "you should give 'em a little more grape, Captain Bragg."

Another artillery captain who made a name for himself on the battlefield at Buena Vista was the young John M. Washington, who would, a few years later, put his ordnance acumen to more dubious use in the absurd shelling of the aged Narbona and other fleeing Navajos during the first expedition into Navajo country.

Santa Anna's defeat at Buena Vista marked the beginning of the end of his spirited homeland defense. Leaving their campfires burning, he and his tattered army retreated to Mexico City in semidisgrace and prepared for the inevitable American onslaught. It was said that he brandished his prosthetic cork leg over his head when troops questioned his dedication to the republic.

Many of the officers who fought at Buena Vista—including John Wool, Jefferson Davis, and the aforementioned Braxton Bragg—would swiftly rise in rank and apply the lessons of their hard-won experience, with brutal efficiency, on the battlefields of the Civil War. As for the commanding general, the battle of Buena Vista made Zachary Taylor an almost immediate national hero and catapulted him to the White House with the pitch-perfect campaign slogan "A Little More Grape."

The battle also cemented James Carleton's career: The able young lieutenant was cited for gallantry and double-promoted to major. Contracting a serious illness—possibly dysentery—he was sent back to Washington on sick leave, and it was during his convalescence there and in Boston that he started writing about his war experiences while courting and marrying his second wife, Sophia Garland Wolfe. Carleton's book, *The Battle of Buena Vista,* published by Harper Brothers in 1848, was well received by the popular press and closely read by War Department officials as well as President Taylor himself. Mostly the book is a nitty-gritty battle narrative, clear and concise if a little purple, but at times Carleton lapses into passages of gross hyperbole. "When all is carefully considered," he writes in his gushy conclusion, "the Battle of Buena Vista will probably be regarded as the greatest ever fought on this continent; and it may be doubted if there can be found one that surpasses it in the history of any nation or of any age."

⊠

Glorious though he made it sound, the Mexican War was really only a brief interlude for Carleton, an aberration in a career almost exclusively spent fighting, policing, and studying Indians. He gladly returned to the life he loved as a frontier dragoon and soon found himself stationed in New Mexico. It was there, during the early 1850s, that Major Carleton struck up a lasting and improbable friendship with Kit Carson.

Their first meeting was occasioned by an incident that befell Carson on the Santa Fe Trail in the summer of 1851. Carson was returning from a trip to Missouri to retrieve his now sixteen-year-old daughter Adaline and bring her back to New Mexico to live. He and Adaline were traveling in a small party of about a dozen people that included several Mexican trail hands, Carson's niece Susan, and her new husband, a young man named Jesse Nelson.

Somewhere in western Kansas, the party had a sticky encounter with a village of hostile Cheyenne Indians. Carson was confident at first that trouble could be averted; for he knew the southern Cheyennes well—his second wife had been a member of the tribe—and the Cheyennes were closely tied, by blood and friendship, to the Bent clan. What Carson didn't know was that this particular band had recently been "chastised" by a column of U.S. Army soldiers. Apparently an inebriated American officer had publicly flogged a Cheyenne for some minor infraction, and the man's whole band, which like many Plains tribes did not countenance this sort of physical violence outside of battle, considered the punishment an unforgivable insult. (Days later, when Carson learned about the flogging, he instantly understood its cultural repercussions; in his autobiography he sneers with contempt at the perpetrator: "I presume courage was oozing from his fingertips, and since the Indians were in his power, he wished to be relieved of such a commodity.")

In any case, the humiliated Indian and his band were now on a quest for revenge: *Any* whites would do, preferably the first ones they saw, and Carson's party fit the bill. It didn't matter that Carson was ignorant of the original offense. This was a tribal ethic Carson knew all too well and had practiced himself, as a trapper and as a guide with Fremont. Now Carson uncomfortably found himself on the opposite side of the same retributive code by which he had lived for years.

Sensing from the start that something was seriously wrong, Carson kept his cool and invited the Indians into his camp for a smoke. There, the Cheyenne began talking among themselves, not realizing that Carson understood their language. Carson says in his autobiography that the Cheyenne were plotting to kill him then and there (along with those members of his party they did not choose to kidnap). "I understood them to say that while I was smoking and not on my guard they could easily kill me with a knife," he writes. "As for the Mexicans with me, they could kill them as easily as buffalo."

Carson instantly intervened, glaring at his guests. "I do not know the cause of your wishing my scalp," he says he told them in Cheyenne. "I've done you no injury, and welcomed you as friends. Now you must leave!"

The Indians looked at one another awkwardly, not knowing what to do. According to Jesse Nelson there were a few tense moments, with arrows drawn and guns pointed and one Cheyenne warrior threatening Carson with a tomahawk. Then the Cheyenne rose from the smoke and slinked away toward their horses.

Carson shouted after them, "If you come back, you'll be shot."

He struck his camp and proceeded west on the trail until dusk. Under cover of darkness he dispatched a messenger to ride ahead on his fastest horse to seek assistance from a small garrison of U.S. soldiers stationed near his ranch on the Rayado. The rider took off into the night. The following morning Carson discovered to his dismay that now hundreds of Cheyenne, their faces fairly seething with bad intent, were closely trailing his party.

Carson engaged the Cheyenne in another blunt conversation. "I have sent a rider ahead," he said, confident that his swift messenger had now ridden too far for the Cheyenne to overtake him. "I have many friends among the soldiers. If you kill us, they will know it was you and they will find you. Our deaths will be avenged."

The admonition seems to have worked. The Cheyenne dispersed, though they still followed Carson at a distance.

A few days later a small detachment of well-armed dragoons, led by Maj. James Henry Carleton, came galloping up the trail, rushing to Carson's aid after having ridden more than a hundred lathered miles. And so the two men met for the first time—the crisp, arrogant dragoon and the celebrity hayseed, now vastly relieved, standing perhaps a little bashfully on the plains with his frightened half-breed daughter at his side.

It is possible that in this first encounter, Carleton had saved Carson's life—and the lives of Adaline and the rest of the party. It was the sort of personal indebtedness that Carson, in his very soul, could never forget.

They were an unlikely pair: the odd couple of the West, perhaps even odder than Carson and Fremont had been. But now it was sealed: The two men would be friends for life.

❧

A few months later, Major Carleton had an occasion to venture to the southern part of the territory to survey the Pecos River. Though it seemed a prosaic assignment, it was, for Carleton, a fateful trip—and so it would become for the Navajo.

At the time, the course of New Mexico's second longest and second most important river (after the Rio Grande) was something of a mystery. The Pecos, a crystalline trout stream in its mountainous upper reaches, spilled from the Sangre de Cristo wilderness behind Santa Fe and swirled east past the Pecos ruins and several Mexican villages that drew sustenance from it. Then the river turned south and ran in a straight shot, becoming progressively warmer, slower, and more alkaline as it dropped through red rock mesas and willow-choked sand flats.

The Pecos was known to flow at least as far as the town of Anton Chico. After that, it vanished into oblivion—at least it did on maps. Some called it a "lost river," though it never really went anywhere but south, into precincts of thorny desolation.

In February 1852, Carleton was sent with a contingent of dragoons to follow with precision where the Pecos led, and to learn whether there might be a place, somewhere downriver, to build an army fort.

Carleton and his men traced the river for nearly a hundred unappealing miles, through stingy country of mesquite and cholla cactus, occasionally glimpsing buffalo in the grasslands to the east. They moved across a hard yellow plate of dirt that lay beneath a pitiless sky prone to weird weather, abrupt storms, leveling gusts. He was not far from the border of Texas and the swallowing hopelessness of the Staked Plains, a place so featureless and vast that early Spanish explorers, Theseus-like, were said to hammer stakes into the ground every league they crept along to mark a sure path for their safe return.

Then Carleton began to grow encouraged. The river opened up into a broad valley. Miles of hoary cottonwoods lined the banks. Deer and antelope and wild turkey flitted in the thick timber. One place in the valley especially caught his eye, an abrupt elbow in the river where the soil was chocolate brown. There were duck and beaver and deep pools that promised fine fish. Compared to the blistered country all around, it was an oasis.

The place was an old meeting ground for Indians of the southern plains. Comanches, Kiowas, Mescalero Apaches, and sometimes Spanish buffalo hunters would gather here seasonally to trade and smoke and drink in the cool shade of the big trees. Hemmed by the river's sinuous curve, the cottonwood grove here grew in a thick circular clump, and it was because of this that the Spanish had long called the place Bosque Redondo: The Round Forest.

Carleton was smitten. In his mind's eye, he saw irrigated farms, houses, a meeting hall, a steepled church perhaps—the marks of civilization as he'd known it back east. He studied the soil and pronounced it excellent, comparable if not preferable to the black loam of the Missouri Valley. He noted that the dried stalks of sunflowers, now brittle and clicking in the wind, reached higher than the head of a man mounted on a horse. The surrounding grama grass was rank and luxuriant, and the supply of wood seemingly inexhaustible. One of his men shot a plump turkey, which Carleton found "flavorful."

Carleton reported that Bosque Redondo was "a most excellent point for the establishment of a strong cavalry post," but he seemed to harbor even greater notions about its purpose. In his enthusiasm, he was moved to hack a thick pole out of a cottonwood trunk and drive it into the ground to mark the spot where he thought the fort should go.

The Round Forest—he would never turn loose of the place, or the idea. For years he talked about it when no one would listen. Even though Bosque Redondo lay far from everything, marooned in the meanest Comanche country, he urged his superiors to make something of this Edenic spot. It was his own private vision, the seed of a solution taking root in his mind to problems yet unforeseen, a shimmering place he marked for something grand.

☒

James Carleton's friendship with Kit Carson deepened throughout the major's five-year military tour in New Mexico. Both married, with growing families, the two men didn't have vices to share; they weren't drinking buddies or gamblers, though they did meet every so often as fellow Masons in the new Santa Fe hall. Carson seems to have genuinely liked Carleton and found him a dazzling font of energy. As with Fremont, Kit was impressed by Carleton's erudition, by his high standing in the regular army, and by his connections to the world back east.

Carleton, on the other hand, found Carson a bit rough around the edges for his tastes—at least at first. He suspected that the newspaper accounts of Carson's talents were greatly overblown. But then the major changed his mind. In the spring of 1854 he happened to witness the scout pulling off one of the most storied feats of his career—this one entirely true—and his esteem for Kit Carson was cemented.

In late May of that year, Carleton hired Carson to guide him on a hastily arranged campaign to recover stolen horses from the Jicarilla Apaches, who had been especially restive that spring. The two men left Taos with several companies of dragoons and pushed north into Colorado, crossing the jagged Sangre de Cristo Mountains. When they reached the brink of the prairie, Carson discerned a faint trail—about as faint as the trail he had followed in 1849 while pursuing the kidnapped Ann White and her baby.

Carson was not overly optimistic this time, for the trail was cold and he considered the Jicarillas the hardest of all Southwestern tribes to track. But a few items he found jettisoned on the trail convinced him these were indeed Jicarillas, and after several days of patiently reading sign, the trail grew warm.

One morning over breakfast, Carson confidently told Major Carleton that they would intercept the Jicarillas that very day. Then he went further, saying it would be precisely at two that afternoon.

Carleton was highly doubtful of Carson's specificity—and told him so—but the scout clung to his prediction.

So Carleton proposed a little wager: If the tribe they were following proved to be Jicarillas after all, and if the dragoon party overtook them without incident at two o'clock, he would buy Carson the finest beaver felt hat that could be purchased in New York City. For Carson this was quite a proposition, for not only were beaver hats extremely dear, but in all his years as a beaver trapper, he had apparently never owned the finished product of his cold, wet labors.

The two men shook on it.

That afternoon they spotted the Jicarillas encamped in a natural grass amphitheater in the Raton Mountains, not far from the Santa Fe Trail. Carleton glanced at his watch and cursed under his breath. It was seven minutes past two.

The astounded major later wrote without hesitation that "Kit Carson is justly celebrated as the best tracker among white men in the world." The dragoons attacked, and though most of the Jicarillas escaped, Carleton succeeded in recapturing forty rustled horses and loads of stolen loot.

Carson insisted he had lost the bet by seven minutes, but Carleton said it was close enough. Through the mail he ordered a beaver felt hat from a prestigious haberdasher in New York, and when it arrived in Taos a few months later, Carson could not stifle his grin.

On the inside band, a gilt-lettered inscription read: AT 2 O'CLOCK, KIT CARSON, FROM MAJOR CARLETON.

Chapter 40   CHILDREN OF THE MIST

James Carleton's personality could not have contrasted more starkly with that of Carson. Yet in one respect they were oddly similar: Like his friend in Taos, Carleton had a curious knack for intersecting with history, for popping up in improbable, far-flung places where important things were happening.

In 1859, for example, Carleton happened to play a pivotal investigative role in one of the darkest and most controversial chapters in the settlement of the West. If his life's work as a dragoon had been devoted to fighting and studying the Indian tribes of the frontier, this episode brought him face-to-face with the *other* great tribe of the West—the burgeoning Mormons of Utah.

It was spring of that year, and Carleton was stationed in Southern California, at a place north of Los Angeles called Fort Tejon, when he received orders to proceed with a contingent of dragoons to southwestern Utah to investigate an incident that had happened a little over a year earlier. A large caravan of Arkansas emigrants en route to California had passed through Utah when they mysteriously disappeared at a remote and beautiful stopping point, well known to many travelers, called Mountain Meadows. The caravan—the Fancher Party, as it was known, after one of its Arkansas leaders—numbered more than 120 men, women, and children. It was widely assumed that they had been massacred—by Paiute Indians, Mormon pioneers, or both—but the true facts were not known. No official investigation had been conducted, and no one had been punished for what was surely the most heinous crime, at least in terms of numbers, ever perpetrated on an American immigrant train.

Mountain Meadows was such an isolated spot that it took Carleton and his dragoons weeks of hard riding to reach it, crossing the southern Sierra Nevada and the Mojave Desert, among other obstacles, as he followed the Old Spanish Trail eastward. When he arrived at the site in Utah late that May and began investigating, it was soon obvious to him that all the worst reports were true. Carleton had his men scour the terrain in quadrants, sifting the dirt, painstakingly working inch by inch. The picture that emerged was terrifying: Although most of the very young children had apparently been spared—seventeen juvenile survivors had been placed in foster homes among Mormons living in the area—all of the men, women, and teenage children had been shot, typically in the head, at point-blank range.

Carleton's chilling report to his army superiors was the first reliable source on the tragedy that became known as the Mountain Meadows Massacre—and remains a seminal document in the lingering controversy. By that point in his career, James Carleton was certainly inured to carnage, but he could not hide his shock at the crime scene. It was, he wrote, "horrible to look upon: Women's hair, in detached locks and in masses, hung to the sage bushes and was strewn over the ground in many places. Parts of little children's dresses and of female costume dangled from the shrubbery or lay scattered about; and among these, here and there, on every hand, for at least a mile . . . there gleamed the skulls and other bones of those who had suffered."

Major Carleton began to interview pioneers in the area. Detective work suited him, and he was good at it. The Mormons who lived not far from Mountain Meadows insisted that the massacre had been committed entirely by hostile Paiutes. But Carleton, like the rest of the newspaper-reading nation, was deeply suspicious. The Fancher Party had been extremely well armed and led by experienced Indian-fighters, and the Paiutes were not known to be particularly fearsome warriors. Not only that, but the children survivors of the massacre reported that among the attackers, they saw white men dressed up and painted like Indians.

By cross-examining witnesses and closely studying the site, Carleton was able to determine, at least to his own satisfaction, that the Paiute role was minimal, that in fact the local Mormons had conceived and carried out the whole affair, apparently with the blessing of high-ranking church officials in Salt Lake—possibly Brigham Young himself. Utah had been seething with tension during the months leading up to the massacre; Mormons had good reason to fear that the U.S. Army was on its way from Fort Laramie to occupy Salt Lake City. All-out war seemed imminent. The polygamous Latter-Day Saints, recalling their history of persecution in upstate

New York, Illinois, and Missouri, were in a state of high dudgeon, armed and ready to resist any encroaching Gentiles.

And then, along came the Fancher caravan. To the Mormons, these immigrants were not just *any* Gentiles: They were from Arkansas, and as it happened, a popular prophet within the church, Parley Pratt, had been murdered in Arkansas only a year earlier. Within the Mormon faith there was a doctrine known as "blood atonement"—which sanctioned the killing of Gentiles in situations when the church was threatened. However, Mormon law forbade the murder of "innocents"—which they defined as children up to eight years of age.

Perhaps, Carleton reasoned, this helped explain why the only survivors of the massacre were little children. On the day of the slaughter, the sobbing youngsters, their clothes spattered with the still-wet blood of their murdered parents, were sent temporarily to live among local Mormons—the very people, Carleton believed, who had made them orphans in the first place. These "foster parents" then had the temerity to charge the U.S. government nearly two thousand dollars to recover the costs they claimed to have laid out in "ransoming" the poor children from the Paiute Indians.

Carleton's realization of this latest twist in the crime finally set him off: "Murderers of the parents and despoilers of their property; these relentless, incarnate fiends, dared even to come forward and claim payment for having kept . . . these helpless children. Has there ever been an act which equaled this in devilish hardihood or effrontery?"

The longer he stayed at Mountain Meadows, the more sickened Carleton became. The murderers did not even have the decency to bury their victims. "The remains," he said, "were dismembered by the wolves and the flesh stripped from the bones."

Carleton's men buried the remains of nearly forty members of the Fancher caravan—which was all he was able to find. To mark the site, they cut down several red cedar trees and fashioned a large cross. On the transverse beam, Carleton had his men carve: VENGEANCE IS MINE, SAITH THE LORD: I WILL REPAY.

Then Carleton erected a rock cairn and placed a solid slab of granite in the ground, on which he engraved a brusque inscription: HERE 120 MEN, WOMEN, AND CHILDREN WERE MASSACRED IN COLD BLOOD EARLY IN SEPT. 1857. THEY WERE FROM ARKANSAS.

Carleton's assignment to Mountain Meadows haunted him for the rest of his life. A new fury entered into his writings, his voice now often infused with an apocalyptic tone. The West was a more intractably violent place than he'd ever imagined, with more turmoil and strife, more intricate tribal clashing than his tidy sensibilities could stand.

His lengthy army report, reprinted for the Congress and published in papers all over the country, was an unsparing diatribe against the Mormon Church. "They are an ulcer upon the body-politic," he wrote, "an ulcer which needs more than cautery to cure. It must have excision, complete and thorough." When he returned to duty in California, Carleton had a conversation with a friend in which he went even further: "We might as well look this devil right in the face at once," he said. "Give the Mormons one year, no more; and if after that they still pollute our soil by their presence, then literally make Children of the Mist of them."

For two years Carleton's memorial stood at the site, a raw and eloquent warning to wayfarers. But in 1861, Brigham Young brought an entourage to Mountain Meadows and ordered Carleton's cross and cairn destroyed. As his subordinates took down the monument, rock by rock, the Mormon prophet said, "Vengeance is mine, saith the Lord: I *have* repaid."

                       ◈

Shocked by his experience at Mountain Meadows, Carleton returned to Fort Tejon and remained there another year, immersing himself in California's peculiarly complicated—and bloody—Indian relations. Only a decade had passed since the Gold Rush began, and yet already many California tribes were vanishing, their numbers decimated by disease, displacement, and white militias bent on outright extermination. The massive influx of Anglo-American immigrants, gold-crazed and land-hungry, had accelerated everything in California, including the course of Indian affairs. And so, as would later prove a general truism, California found itself well ahead of the national curve; the rapid demise of the tribes there was only a harbinger of the demise Native Americans would soon suffer throughout the West. The Indians' predicament in the Bear Flag State became so dire so quickly that a number of officials began to show the first signs of an unfamiliar attitude toward the beleaguered tribes—an attitude that might be described as Christian compassion.

A new notion took hold: The tribes of California must be physically separated from white society as an alternative to their own extinction. They must be relocated on some clearly delineated parcel of arable land sufficiently watered by a river. There, they must be taught the rudiments of farming and animal husbandry. The government must not skimp—it must provide the Indians with modern tools, sound stock, and good seeds so that they might finally stop roving and settle down to earn an honest living as self-sufficient farmers, dwelling collectively on what amounted to a kibbutz. This communal farm must be closely guarded by an army fort, not only to prevent the Indians from straying into the white communities but also to keep ill-meaning white folks from venturing onto Indian land, bringing the scourge of alcohol and other vices with them.

The new policy was tantamount to apartheid, to be sure. But if it was predicated on the prevailing racism of the time, it was also fueled by an emerging humanitarian concern that whole tribes were truly on the brink of expiration—becoming, in Carleton's alarming phrase, Children of the Mist.

Fort Tejon, where Major Carleton served, was the site of the first laboratory test of this new agricultural ideal—an experiment that in time would evolve into the United States reservation system. The farm created there was the brainchild of Edward Fitzgerald Beale, the colorful naval officer who had made a name for himself with Carson at the battle of Pasqual and who later accompanied Carson on his first transcontinental trip to Washington (the same man who piloted an ultimately unsuccessful program to introduce U.S. Army camels to the deserts of the American West). In the 1850s, Beale was appointed California's first superintendent for Indian affairs. Progressive for his time, he was appalled by the slow genocide taking place before his eyes. He lamented that California's Indians had been "driven from their fishing and hunting grounds, hunted themselves like wild beasts, lassoed, and torn from homes made miserable by want."

So Beale set aside fifty thousand acres of decent land along a river bottom near Fort Tejon and persuaded nearly three thousand Indians (from the Emigdiano tribe and various other displaced tribes of the southern San Joaquin Valley) to settle there. Beale said he loosely based his idea on the Spanish mission system, which had for centuries kept many thousands of California Indians employed (others would say enslaved) in agricultural pursuits. "Surely," Beale urged, "that which was accomplished by a few poor priests is not too great a task for the mighty republic of the United States."

California newspapers lauded Beale's visionary concept and advocated creating a network of similar reservation-communes up and down the Sierra Nevadas. "Either the whole Indian race in California must be exterminated," argued an editorial in the *California Alta*, "or they must be brought together, organized into a community, made to support themselves by their own labor; and be elevated above the degraded position they now occupy."

By the spring of 1854, Beale had forty plows working the ground every day at Tejon Farm—plows driven by young Indian boys who, after a little training, "showed so much dexterity and skill" that it seemed to Beale as though "they had done nothing else their whole lives." The Indians planted five hundred acres in barley and nearly two hundred acres in corn. They dug irrigation ditches, raised barns, built houses. Beale's dream took off, and for several years Tejon Farm showed great promise.

The experiment wasn't cheap, however. Beale initially requested a federal appropriation of $500,000 and kept asking for more—sums that officials back in Washington considered outlandish. But the California papers, while recoiling at the staggering costs, continued to support Beale's pilot project. The *Alta* argued that through Tejon

Farm, and others like it, the Indians "could be transformed from a state of semi-barbarism, indolence, mental imbecility and moral debasement, to a condition of civilization, Christianity, industry, virtue, frugality, social and domestic happiness, and public usefulness."

Tejon Farm failed, in the end, partly because Superintendent Beale imprudently set the reservation on land whose title was legitimately disputed by Spanish-speaking claimants holding prior land grants, and partly because Beale himself was fired from his post (for reasons of partisan politics) just as his pet project was beginning to take off. Still, Beale had tried something ambitious, and he'd demonstrated, for a short time at least, that a sweeping project in agricultural self-sufficiency *could* work.

⊠

James Carleton was influenced by the ideas being tested at Tejon. After he marched to New Mexico as a newly promoted brigadier general in the early fall of 1862, he almost immediately began to apply the Tejon model to the Navajo problem. Carleton saw a way to harness the anxieties that had been stirred up by the Confederate invasion and the still-hovering fear that the Texans might return. If the territory was already on a war footing, the whole society alert and inflamed, then why not direct all this ramped-up energy toward something useful? Carleton immediately declared a state of martial law, with curfews and mandatory passports for travel, and then brought all his newly streamlined authority to bear on cleaning up the Navajo mess. With a focus that bordered on obsession, he was determined finally to make good on Kearny's old promise that the United States would "correct all this."

"When I came here this time," Carleton wrote, "it not only became my professional business, but my duty to the residents and to the Government, to devise some plan which might, with God's blessing, forever bring these troubles to an end. These Navajo Indians have long since passed that point when talking would be of any avail. They must be whipped and fear us before they will cease killing and robbing the people." He cited William Arny's estimate that in 1862 alone, Navajos had plundered more than thirty thousand sheep from Hispanic and Anglo ranches, with total losses amounting to nearly $250,000. "To cure this great evil from which the territory has been so long a prey," he concluded, "some new remedy must be adopted."

General Carleton's "new remedy" was to re-create the Tejon experiment on a much grander scale—and to do it at Bosque Redondo, the place that had so enchanted him when he surveyed the Pecos River in the early 1850s. The idea seemed to come to him fully formed, like Athena sprung from the head of Zeus, as though he'd been pondering it all his life. Bosque Redondo, he said, would be his "grand work," and he wasted no time getting started. On October 31, 1862, within weeks of arriving in Santa Fe, he ordered the establishment of a new military outpost at the bosque, which he would call Fort Sumner.

A board of army officers sent ahead to study Bosque Redondo reported back to him that the remote site was unsuitable for either a fort or an Indian reservation. As pleasant as this green oasis might be, Bosque Redondo was too far removed "from the neighborhoods that supply forage," they warned. "Building materials will have to be brought from a great distance. A large part of the surrounding valley is subject to inundations by spring floods."

Worst of all, the board said, the Pecos River was alkaline and bitter-tasting, with crackly efflorescences of whitish powder deposited along its banks. "The water of the Pecos," the report emphatically stated, "contains much unhealthy mineral matter."

Carleton was livid when he read this naysaying report. He dismissed the numerous, and seemingly valid, concerns of his lieutenants and forged ahead. In November he ordered the building of Fort Sumner and then began to draw up war plans to conquer the Navajos and move them all to his beloved Round Forest.

"The only peace that can ever be made with them," Carleton wrote superiors at the War Department, "must rest on the basis that they move onto the lands at Bosque Redondo and, like the Pueblos, become an agricultural people and cease to be nomads. Entire subjugation or destruction . . . are the alternatives." His ultimatums sounded eerily similar to his characterization of the Mormon situation in the Mountain Meadows report: *An ulcer upon the body-politic which needs more than cautery to cure. It must have excision, complete and thorough.*

When he wrote about his plan for the Navajos, Carleton fairly effervesced. Bosque Redondo was, he said, "the best pastoral region between the two oceans." The forced removal of twelve thousand people from their homeland might seem cruel at first, he acknowledged, but in the end "severity would be the most humane course." Once the Diné were resettled on the Pecos, good things would happen. The idea, he said, was to gather the Navajos together "away from the hills and hiding places of their country, and there to be kind to them: to teach their children how to read and write: teach them the art of peace: teach them the truths of Christianity. Soon they will acquire new habits, new ideas, new modes of life; the old Indians will die off and carry with them all the latent longings for murdering and robbing: the young ones will take their places: and thus, little by little, they will become a happy and contented people, and the Navajo Wars will be remembered only as something that belongs entirely in the Past." Within a decade, he predicted, the Navajos would be "the most delightfully located pueblo of Indians in New Mexico, perhaps in the United States."

Carleton's optimism was as infectious as it was naïve; almost all of the territorial leaders rallied around his cause. Through all his bloviating, the general was in fact adding a new conceptual layer to the ancient conflict. Before Carleton's arrival, the vocabulary of the Navajo wars was centered almost entirely on the principle of punishment—punishment in a raw Old Testament sense. The army was there to "chastise" and "overawe" them, to make them "feel the power and the sting of the government." But now a certain noblesse oblige had crept into the dialogue, a sense of white man's burden. Instead of punishing the Navajos, Carleton proposed to teach them, to administer a kind of tough love so that they might become "a happy and contented people."

His attempt to apply the Tejon model to the Navajo conflict was a forced endeavor from the start, the social equivalent of cramming square pegs into round holes. Carleton seemed not to perceive the glaring differences in the two situations—or if he did perceive them, to discount them. The Indians who came to Tejon had for the most part been unwarlike hunter-gatherers who had *voluntarily* agreed to take up a new agricultural existence there, at a place not far from their actual homelands. Having lived among the Spanish missions for generations, the methods of intensive cultivation, and the close living arrangements required to support a farm, were not alien to them. What's more, they were a mishmash of small, weak tribes without a clear common past or a clear common future, their numbers dwindling fast. They had nothing to lose, and possibly much to gain, by embracing Beale's experiment.

The Navajos were another matter. Theirs was a sprawling nation, wealthy in stock, obdurate in its ways, open to change but only on its terms. The Navajos were already farmers, it was true, but as sheep-loving seminomads they would never favor the compact methods used at Tejon. Having seen what happened to the Anasazi at Chaco Canyon, they were keenly suspicious of social density.

The main difference, though, was the sheer power of the Diné. Although politically amorphous, much like the tribes at Tejon, the Navajos had a stout and tenacious node of culture whose power radiated outward in all directions—a culture with a shared language and belief system and a sharp sense of identity steeped in myths. The proud Diné were not a people who could be easily coerced into doing anything, let alone starting an entirely new life.

What's more, Bosque Redondo was nearly four hundred miles from Navajo country, set on an enveloping prairie that seemed a world away from the fabulous red rock universe the Navajo knew and loved. Carleton's plan would thus require a forced relocation on a scale not undertaken since the 1830s, when the Cherokee of the Southeastern United States were made to embark on their bitter Trail of Tears exodus to Oklahoma. If Carleton hoped to corral the Navajos and put them on a farm at Bosque Redondo, he would have to fight. The Diné would never leave their land willingly.

History frowned on his project, certainly. Through the ages, battling the Navajos had consistently shown itself to be tricky and ultimately unsatisfying work, like trying to gather up beads of mercury. The Spanish, through all their efforts, had never been able to exact a lasting punishment on the Diné, and neither had the Mexicans. So far the Americans, during their nearly twenty years in power, had proved similarly ineffectual. What made the mutton-chopped schoolmaster general from Maine think he could do any better?

Carleton had spent his life hounding Indians and honing his ideas on how to do the grim business better, more efficiently. He had a notion about how to bring the Navajos to their knees. It would require a different sort of warfare, a kind of persistent guerrilla activity combined with a ruthless scorched-earth policy—to chase and starve them into submission, to burn their crops, kill their animals, and bring the war to every man, woman, and child in every desolate fold and box canyon. The cumbersome, fussily costumed dragoons of Kearny's day would never be effective against the Navajos, Carleton realized. "Those wolves of the mountains," as he called the Diné, would detect a traditional cavalry force many days in advance.

Instead, General Carleton's men would have to move in the shadows. "An Indian," he noted, "is a more watchful and wary animal than a deer. He must be hunted with skill; he cannot be blundered upon; nor will he allow his pursuers to come upon him when he knows it, unless he is the stronger." Carleton had learned much from his study of the Russian Cossacks, and he strenuously argued that the modern U.S. Cavalry should adopt some of the methods of this elite unit in fighting Indians in the West. Like the Cossacks, Carleton insisted that his troops should always travel light and keep after their quarry day and night, moving "not in big bodies, with military noises and smokes, and the gleam of arms by day, and fires, and talks, and comfortable sleeps by night; but in small parties moving stealthily to their haunts and lying patiently in wait for them; or in following their tracks day after day with a fixedness of purpose."

In fighting the Navajos, the central strategy had to shift; no longer was the goal to exact a swift punishment and then leave; rather, it was to hector them constantly through all seasons of the year, to demoralize through relentless pressure. "The purpose now," he wrote, "is never to relax the application of force with a people that can no more be trusted than you can trust the wolves that run through their mountains."

∞

One more rationale, slightly hidden, propelled Carleton's enthusiasm for flushing the Navajos from their country: He smelled gold.

Perhaps he had spent too much time in California watching other men amass great riches. Perhaps he fancied himself competent enough as a geologist that he could, at a mere glimpse of terrain, infer the presence of precious metal. Perhaps he just let his imagination get away from him. Whatever the case, the general got it into his head, on the basis of no particular evidence, that the Navajo country held the next national mother lode.

The fact was, James Carleton was embarrassed by New Mexico—embarrassed by its poverty, its lack of luster, its low standing in the halls of Washington, where no one seemed to favor elevating the territory to the status of a full-fledged state. According to the prevailing sentiment on Capitol Hill, New Mexico, with its Indian troubles and general squalor, was nothing but a drain on the national budget. For years lawmakers had floated serious proposals to return the territory to Mexico: Why squander any more blood and treasure on such a hopeless cause?

If Carleton was ashamed by New Mexico's backwardness, he also must have envied his Union colleagues in the East, who were making frequent appointments with glory on the great battlefields of the Civil War. To get ahead in military circles, Carleton realized he would need to do something fairly spectacular in New Mexico—something that would doubtless come with a high price tag. He would need to find a justification, something tantalizing to convince Washington skeptics, already overburdened by the Civil War, that his ambitious projects were well worth the cost.

What if New Mexico held subterranean value? Colorado and California had both had their strikes, why not here? It wasn't an altogether crazy idea. One had only to look at the territory's severe geology, its dormant volcanoes and thrusted mountains and otherworldly cinder cones to suspect that something valuable might be down there. In truth, people had been mining New Mexico for centuries. The mythic Seven Cities that first attracted Coronado had never materialized, but there were great stores of silver along the Gila, seams of coal and turquoise in the Ortiz Mountains, and large amounts of copper tucked into innumerable wrinkles and drainages.

But it was gold that most interested Carleton, and he was sure New Mexico would provide it. He wrote to Gen. Henry Halleck, "A country as rich if not richer in mineral wealth than California extends from the Rio Grande, northwestwardly, all the way across to Nevada." In other words, Navajo country. It was, Carleton said, "a princely realm . . . a magnificent mineral country. Providence has indeed blessed us, for the gold lies here at our feet to be had by the mere picking of it up."

Where Carleton obtained his evidence for these claims was not clear—he seems to have simply wished it into being. The more salient point was this: There *might* be gold in Navajo country. To ensure the safety of geological exploration, and the inevitable onrush of miners once a strike was made, the Diné would have to be removed. He wrote one of his superiors that among his endeavors since arriving in New Mexico was an effort "to brush back the Indians, so that the people could not only possess themselves of the arable lands . . . of the territory, but, if the country contained veins and deposits of precious metals, they might be found."

In another letter to General Halleck, Carleton went further. On the Gila River, he claimed, there had been found "one of the richest gold countries in the world." The discovery's potential value was so great, Carleton argued, that it would forever redeem the forlorn territory in the eyes of the nation—and might provide the hard bullion needed to help win the Civil War back east. "Do not despise New Mexico, as a drain upon the government," he wrote. "The money will all come back."

In his high position, Carleton understood that it would be unseemly for him to hunt for gold himself, but he encouraged friends and subordinates to head out for Navajo country on their own, to scoop up the riches before news of a big strike would spread to the nation and attract the mining hordes. Carleton wrote a captain named J. G. Walker: "If I can help others to a fortune, it will afford me not quite as much happiness as finding one myself, it is true—but nearly as much. My luck has always been not to be at the right place at the right time for fortunes."

⊠

If Carleton thought it inappropriate for an august general to pan for nuggets, neither did he think it right or necessary for him personally to engage the Navajos in the field. Carleton was odd in this way: A finicky micromanager, a man whose mind swam in details, he had invested heart and soul in his Navajo Plan—and indeed was gambling his whole army career on its success. Yet he showed no interest in directing the details on the ground or witnessing firsthand the historic events he hoped to set in motion. He would be an absentee conqueror, running the war from the safe remove of his Santa Fe headquarters, leaving the drudgeries of battle to his field commander.

And there never was any doubt who his field commander would be: Kit Carson. The two men were friends, of course, and had shared colorful campaigns together. But the truth was, Carleton genuinely needed Carson, just as General Kearny had needed him sixteen years earlier and Fremont had needed him before that. Carleton needed Carson's tracking expertise, his popularity among the territory's inhabitants, his knowledge of the Navajo and their riddled lands, and his good reputation among other tribes of the region. Carson's success at Valverde had proven that he wasn't merely a phenomenal scout; he could actually command troops in the field. Even Carson's fame could be of use, lending an aura of national legitimacy, and a certain storybook sheen, to Carleton's homegrown project.

Carleton regarded Carson as uniquely qualified for the campaign—as a godsend, almost—and he was content to leave the conquest of the Navajos in Carson's able hands. Although Carleton could never be the writer he had aspired to be as a young man, he had ventured west just as Dickens had advised, and now in his lofty position he could write history by making it, with the real-life Kit Carson as his central hero. "The world-wide reputation of Colonel Carson," Carleton gushed in one letter, "gives a good guaranty that anything that may be required of him, which brings into practical operation the peculiar skill and high courage for which he is justly celebrated, will be well done."

※

As a sort of warm-up to the coming Navajo war, the general ordered Carson to lead five companies of the 1st New Mexico Volunteers on a focused campaign to round up a tiny but nettlesome band of Apaches called the Mescaleros. A tribe of nomadic hunter-gatherers centered in the Sacramento and Sierra Blanco mountains of southern New Mexico, the Mescaleros numbered little more than five hundred people. Their name derived from the pulpy, fibrous mescal plant at the core of their diet. But far from being sedate root-diggers, the Mescalero Apaches had a well-deserved reputation for ferocious fighting and expert raiding. Along the principal roadways of southern New Mexico, they had taken advantage of the disarray caused by the Texan invasion, attacking wagon trains and ranches with unprecedented viciousness, committing outrages disproportionate to their numbers. The problem with the Mescaleros bore the hallmarks of the Navajo conflict, on a miniaturized scale.

General Carleton decided that the Mescaleros would be the first captives he would send to the freshly consecrated Bosque Redondo—the guinea pigs, in effect, the first experimental participants in his "grand work." He ordered Colonel Carson to pursue the Mescaleros and give them no quarter until they completely surrendered. They would all have to move to the bosque before winter set in. For the Mescaleros, at least, Bosque Redondo was not an entirely alien place; it was not so very far from the heart of their homeland—less than a hundred miles—and Mescaleros had favored its shady banks for centuries as a summer gathering place.

Carleton made it clear that this precursor to the Navajo campaign was to be an all-or-nothing proposition, and he insisted that Colonel Carson wage it with ruthless efficiency. The Mescaleros, he said, "must be brought to their brutal senses." He gave Carson a chilling order: "All Indian men of that tribe are to be killed whenever and wherever you can find them. The women and children will not be harmed, but you will take them prisoners. If the Indians send in a flag and desire to treat for peace, say that now our hands are untied, and you have been sent to punish them for their treachery and their crimes; that you have no power to make peace; that you are there to kill them wherever you find them."

Carson was appalled by Carleton's shoot-on-sight policy and refused to obey it. In fact, he accepted the surrender of more than a hundred Mescalero warriors who sought refuge with him. Nonetheless he made quick work of the Mescalero Apaches—the campaign was effectively over in a month. In November 1862, Carson sent five of their defeated leaders to Santa Fe to negotiate with General Carleton. One of them, a headman named Cadete, spoke for the delegation in offering an unconditional surrender: "You are stronger than we," Cadete said in a passionate mingling of Spanish and his own tongue. "Your weapons are better than ours. We are worn out. We have no provisions, no means to live. Your troops are everywhere. Our springs and waterholes are occupied by your young men. You have driven us from our last and best stronghold, and we have no more heart. Do with us as may seem good to you, but do not forget we are men and braves."

Carleton promptly ordered the whole tribe to Bosque Redondo—which, in truth, was not entirely a banishment, the bosque being one of their favorite spots on earth. For them, the bitter pill was not the place of their exile, but rather the manner in which they would have to spend it: Carleton informed them that their existence as roving hunters and root-gatherers was over. They were to become farmers now, a fate unimaginably odious to them. Unlike the Navajos, the Mescalero Apaches considered agriculture contemptible work, a form of slavery in itself, a close niggling activity far beneath the dignity of a free mountain people.

But General Carleton gave them no alternative. By late November the vanquished Mescalero Apaches began to spill from the mountains with their few belongings strapped to their backs and marched to their new life on the Pecos. Delighted with how quickly his plans were taking shape, Carleton dashed off an almost jaunty note to his superior in Washington, Adjutant General Lorenzo Thomas: "You will feel pleased to learn that this long dreaded tribe of murderers and robbers has been brought to so promising a condition."

⊠

Carson returned from the Mescalero campaign only to learn that Carleton intended for him to pursue the Navajos without delay. But now that he had seen up close what such a merciless campaign would be like, Carson shied from the assignment. If the Mescalero roundup had been an unqualified success, Carson had taken no pleasure in it. He had joined the Union Army to repulse the Confederates, not to fight Indians. He wanted to be back home in Taos with Josefa and their kids. He wasn't feeling well—his horse accident in the San Juans had taken a toll. He was feeling odd pains in his chest, and found it difficult to sit a horse. He knew that fighting the Navajos would be hard, cold, bitter work, more ambitious by many orders of magnitude than the Mescalero roundup, and he wanted no part of it.

Carson wrote Carleton a letter of resignation dated February 3, 1863. By serving in the army and fighting the Texans at Valverde, Carson said, he had proved his "devotion to that Government which was established by my ancestors." Carson vowed that if the Texans ever returned to New Mexico, it would be his "pride and pleasure" to fight under General Carleton. But, Carson said, "At present I feel that my duty as well as happiness, directs me to my home & family and trust that the General will accept my resignation. . . . I am sorry that I am obliged to dissolve our Official conexion, but it shall ever be my proudest thought that I have had the honor and happiness of serving under Brigadier Genl Carleton."

It was not that Carson disagreed with the basic outlines of Carleton's Indian policy. On the contrary, during his tenure as an agent for the Utes, Carson had increasingly come to see the wisdom of establishing reservations for Native American tribes—physical separation, he felt, was necessary for the Indians' own good.

Carson believed that most of the Indian troubles in the West were caused, as he once flatly put it, "by aggressions on the part of whites." Most of the raids, by Utes and other tribes, were visited upon the settlements only out of desperation—"committed," he argued, "from absolute necessity when in a starving condition." White settlers were increasingly encroaching on Indian hunting grounds. Describing the situation among the Utes and Jicarilla Apache, Carson wrote in a dictated report that "their game is becoming scarce, much of it having been killed by the settlers, and a great deal of it driven from the country . . . they are unable to support themselves by the chase and the hunt."

At the same time, Carson believed there was no stopping the tide of Anglo-American immigration. As historian Tom Dunlay has pointed out, not even in moments of introspection did Carson question the legitimacy of American expansion into the West, a process that he, along with Fremont and a few others, had done more to set in motion than any American alive. Whites were here now—it was simply an irreversible fact. And their presence put the traditional life of all the Western Indians in jeopardy. Native Americans would have to change, he believed, or they would all die out. Predicted Carson, "If permitted to remain as they are, before many years they will be utterly extinct."

And so, more or less in keeping with the Tejon model, Carson had throughout the 1850s advocated with growing vehemence the creation of reservations for the Utes and other tribes, at places located far away from all Anglo or Hispanic settlement, where they might learn the arts of cultivation and husbandry while holding on to their own traditions. As he put it, the Indians must be "set apart to themselves." He truly believed that mingling with whites was ruining their culture. "They should not be allowed to come into the towns," Carson insisted, "for every visit an Indian makes is more or less an injury to him." In their encounters with whites, he said, "Indians generally learn the vices and not the virtues" of settled living. Perhaps the biggest problem was liquor—Carson had seen alcohol rip the soul from whole bands of once-proud Indians. "They become accustomed to the use of ardent spirits," he said, and soon become "a degraded tribe."

If at all possible, though, Carson preferred creating reservations within, or at least in the vicinity of, a given tribe's ancestral lands. "In all cases of locating reservations," he once said, "it would be best to show some deference to the expressed wishes of the tribe." Euro-Americans, particularly in the boom-and-bust West, were relentlessly mobile. They blew about in the wind—deracinated, it seemed, always in search of better fortune. Miners, traders, trappers, merchants, missionaries, they thought nothing of moving great distances and starting all over when new opportunity struck. The hunger to push on, particularly in a westward direction, was an attribute of the (white) American. But Carson knew enough about Indian culture to recognize that even among nomadic tribes, the familiar landmarks of one's homeland were profoundly significant—in fact, they were sacred—and one strayed from them with great trepidation. Homeland was crucial in practical terms, but also in terms of ceremony and ritual, central to a tribe's collective identity and its conception of the universe.

Certainly this was true of the Navajo. They constantly moved about, it was true, but it was a localized nomadism; they seldom traveled far from their outfit. There were taboos against leaving the confines of the four sacred mountains. Carson understood that to uproot the Navajo from their ancient ground and move them hundreds of miles ran the risk of demoralizing the tribe so completely that it could smother all chances of a reservation's success.

Yet, by experience and association, Carson had plenty of other reasons to want the Diné far removed to a reservation. As an Anglo who had happily married into a Hispanic society, he had doubtless adopted some of the biases and perspectives of his in-laws; living as he did in a Spanish-speaking household with many extended relatives under his roof, it would have been difficult for him not to become, in a sense, *Hispanicized* in his outlook. During all his years in New Mexico the Hispanic population had regarded the Navajos, often with good reason, as Public Enemy Number One. The Navajo conflict was, Carson said, "an hereditary warfare" that had "always existed."

As an Indian agent, Carson had become a friend and advocate of the Utes, and the Utes had always considered the Navajo their archenemy. Over the years Carson had also befriended many people from Taos Pueblo, who likewise viewed the Navajo as an age-old nemesis. So in the simplest terms, Carson's tribal fidelities prejudiced him against the Diné. Throughout his life Carson had always been a loyalist, unwavering in his allegiance to any person or group with whom he had, for better or worse, thrown in his lot. One can imagine that the loyalist in him must have welcomed the opportunity that Carleton now laid at his feet: to remove the scourge of his people, to vanquish the foe of his friends.

Still, Carson begged off. He was just plain tired. He didn't have much fight left in him. He wanted some taste of a normal home life.

But James Henry Carleton was not an easy man to turn down, any more than Stephen Watts Kearny had been. Carleton refused Carson's resignation and went to work on him, pulling out all the stops on his peculiarly forceful personality. As a patriot, as a soldier, as a friend, Carson must see this through. It would be the crowning achievement of his career. The people of New Mexico were counting on him.

Chapter 41   G E N E R A L   O R D E R S   N O .   15

The campaign began innocuously enough, with groups of soldiers steadily massing in Santa Fe and in Los Pinos, on the Rio Grande, and then filing slowly westward toward Navajo country. They did not seem in a hurry, nor were they fired with the familiar excitements, the war-whoops and revenge-lust, that ordinarily animated the seasonal slave expeditions into the land of the Diné. These soldiers moved with a solemn and methodical sense of purpose, as though they were conserving their energy. This time they knew they were not making the usual punitive sortie and then returning in shallow triumph with souvenirs and a few slaves. This time they knew they were going away for a long time, and that they were not coming back until they had broken the spirit of an entire nation, forcing twelve thousand people to give up nearly everything they'd ever known.

It was early July 1863. Day after day the sun shone with an impaling brightness, and all along the river the crops were taking shape in the wilting heat. Silty water trickled through the ditches and races to feed the thirsty stalks of beans and corn. It was siesta weather, the middays baking in a torpor that made the inhabitants along the Rio Grande live in the way of lizards, burrowing into the shade of their *portales,* snoozing under brush arbors with their flocks of sheep gathered about them in the shade of the flickering cottonwoods. Now the people roused from their naps and shouted out encouragement, some tipping their sweat-warped sombreros in salute as the soldiers threaded West.

Col. Kit Carson rode at the head of the column, of course. It's not clear what Carleton said to induce him to stay on board, but it worked. Apprehensively, and with some reluctance, Carson was now embarked on the most ambitious assignment of his career.

All told, he would command nearly a thousand men, including U.S. Army officers, New Mexican volunteers, auxiliaries from a number of Pueblo tribes, and scouts recruited from among the Utes. Carson was especially proud of his Ute warriors, many of whom he knew personally from his days as an Indian agent. Hiring them had been his idea. He correctly surmised that the profound hatred the Utes held for the Diné would give them a heightened motivation, while their presence in the field as official allies of the *bilagaana* troops would disturb and demoralize the Navajos. "The Utes," Carson wrote Carleton, "are very brave, and fine shots, fine trailers, and uncommonly energetic in the field. The Navajos have entertained a very great dread of them for many years. I believe one hundred Ute Indians would render more service in this way than double their number of troops." In finally approving Carson's idea, Carleton stipulated that he hire only the cream of the Ute warriors. "We will have none but the best," Carleton insisted. "Our work is to be thorough, and we must have the men to do it."

Carson often preferred riding in the company of the Utes than with either his white or Hispanic comrades. And so on July 7, when Carson left the Rio Grande with his long column of men, he trotted in the vanguard with some of his favorite warriors, including one of their leaders, a man named Kaniache. Carson was hot and uncomfortable in his army blues, the pain in his chest a frequent vexation, his thoughts doubtless clouded by the intricate conquest that lay before him. He was fifty-three years old, and showing his years. It had been especially difficult to pull himself away from Taos this time. During his short leave of absence following the Mescalero campaign, he had savored the pleasures of home in the springtime at the feet of his beloved mountains, the Rio Don Fernando running swift with snowmelt through the town. His family was still growing. Josefa was now pregnant with their sixth child.

Carson's column filed past the pueblos of Laguna and Acoma and bored into the Diné lands. He turned his horses loose among the Navajo fields of corn and wheat and destroyed whatever the animals did not eat. Finally he made his way to Fort Defiance, the abandoned outpost set deep in Navajo country, where his men went to work refurbishing the now ruined buildings that had always been such a stark outrage to Manuelito. Defiance—along with its sister outpost, Fort Wingate—would serve as Carson's headquarters during the long campaign, the place from which he would mount the countless incursions he knew would be required to bring the Navajos to their knees. His men worked long hours to restore the fort, and when it was deemed ready for operation, Carson christened it Fort Canby, after Carleton's stalwart predecessor who, besides checking the Confederate invasion, had done much to lay the groundwork for the present hostilities with the Navajos.

On July 20, while Carson was at Fort Canby, an important if somewhat arbitrary deadline came and went. Six months earlier General Carleton had held a parley at the Palace of the Governors in Santa Fe with some eighteen Navajo headmen. The Diné leaders were apparently quite worried by alarming reports of Carson's Mescalero roundup and rightly feared they would be next. During this summit, General Carleton struck an extremely aggressive pose with the Navajo delegation. The leaders, he said, had until July 20 to return to Santa Fe with assurances that the whole tribe would completely surrender and voluntarily move to Bosque Redondo. If the headmen did not present themselves by that date, Carleton would prosecute a war like none other that had ever been visited upon them, and he would *force* them to move.

Through a Spanish translator, Carleton told the Navajo leaders: "We have no faith in your promises. You can have no peace until you give other guarantees than your word. If you do not return to Santa Fe [by July 20] we will know that you have chosen the alternative of war. After that day every Navajo will be considered as hostile and treated accordingly. After that day the door now open will be closed."

And so now that deadline had passed, and not a single one of the headmen had returned to meet with Carleton. This was all the general needed. Having satisfied the legalistic requirements of his Christian conscience, Carleton had the pretext he wanted for waging total war, a pretext that enabled him to couch the campaign not as an offensive at all, but rather as a diplomatically justified, and indeed almost obligatory, response to the Navajos' failure to heed his explicit warning.

The coming invasion, in other words, would be all their fault. "The consequences," as he later put it, "rested on them."

Carleton drew up a brusque declaration of war bearing the dry, institutional title General Orders No. 15. "For a long time past, the Navajo Indians have murdered and robbed the people of New Mexico," the document read. "It is therefore ordered that Colonel CHRISTOPHER CARSON, with a proper military force proceed without delay to the Navajo country and there . . . to prosecute a vigorous war upon the men of this tribe . . ."

Carleton trusted "the distinguished commander of the expedition," as he called Carson, and gave him carte blanche to purchase supplies "to insure the cardinal requirements of health, food, mobility, and power." But at the same time the impatient general was ever anxious to know all the nitty-gritty facts of the campaign, and to know them as quickly as the mails would permit. As soon as Carson left the Rio Grande and passed into the desolation of Navajo country, Carleton grew antsy for news and found himself unable to stifle his tendency toward micromanagement from afar. A nearly constant stream of letters issued from his goading pen—full of fussy reprimands and minute suggestions written in a formal hand so neat and razor-sharp it seemed turned out by a machine.

Miffed that Colonel Carson had not written him in a while, the general dashed off a note early in the campaign that made it clear he was to send regular, thorough updates. *"Make a note of this,"* Carleton snipped at Carson. "You will send me a weekly report in detail of the operations of your command. Let me know all about the crops destroyed, their extent and location; all about the stock captured; when, where, by whom, and the kind and number; all about the Navajos killed, and the exact number of captured women and children. Be sure and make *timely* requisitions for supplies. The value of time cannot be too seriously considered. Make *every* string draw."

As if Carson wasn't already feeling enough pressure, Carleton concluded his note with a reminder: "Much is expected of you, both here and in Washington."

⊠

There was nothing glorious about Carson's campaign: no great engagements, no fields of honor, no decisive victories. With the American invasion, the Navajos did what they had always done—they scattered, vanished, dropped into their thousand pockets and holes and abided in silence. And so, with no one to fight, Carson's campaign became, of necessity, a war of grinding attrition. The pressure he applied through the summer and fall of 1863 was incremental, cumulative, merciless, and without relent. The goal, pure in its simplicity, was to make the Navajos feel the bitter burn of starvation, on the theory that hunger alone could bring them to accept conditions they would not otherwise entertain. Carson never used the term "scorched earth," but that's what it was, the first systematic use of it in the West—and more than a year before Sherman's march across the South. If there was ever a grandeur or majesty to warfare, surely none could be found here.

On August 5, Carson left Fort Canby on his first scout, an exhausting march under "a broiling sun" that lasted twenty-seven days and covered nearly five hundred miles across the multifingered mesas where the Navajo and Hopi worlds merged. Along the way he captured perhaps a dozen Navajos and killed a like number, but Carson himself thought the expedition failed to inflict "any positive injury" on the Diné and achieved little of military value—other than making Carson appreciate how nearly impossible his task was.

For how could he make the Navajos surrender when he scarcely even saw them? This was a ghost country. Everywhere he went he found fresh evidence of habitation—smoldering fires, ripe animal dung, scattered belongings hanging in trees—but *no people*. Week after week he was reduced to playing an exasperating game of hide-and-go-seek. The long rides were dusty and throat-parching—"thermometer past endurance," noted one soldier. Plainly, it was the kind of work better suited for a younger man. Said one sergeant who rode on one of Carson's epic but ultimately unproductive slogs: "I have seen him reeling in the saddle from fatigue and loss of sleep, still pushing forward and hoping to come upon them."

Usually all he came upon was a horse, or a few goats, or some other stray beast of the elusive Navajos. Almost invariably Carson seized these animals for his own use—or had them shot. One participant in the Navajo campaign recalled sighting a lone white horse on a distant mesa, and then watching a comrade dash up the steep slopes to dispatch the hapless animal. "With straining eyes and beating hearts we watched his career," the diarist wrote. "He reached the unknown animal, halted and soon we heard the report of a Pistol and a poor broken down sore-backed old Navajo pony had gone where his fathers have gone before him—*finis*."

In his frustration over failing to encounter Navajos, Carson redoubled his efforts to achieve stealth. One soldier who served with the New Mexican Volunteers commented that "on the march Carson would never build fires if he wanted to surprise the enemy," but would "creep up cautiously . . . The troops sometimes accused him of cowardice because he was so cautious." Carson ventured out in smaller and smaller parties, hoping to surprise the Diné and flush them out. He would rise before dawn and take his Ute scouts with him, leaving some other officer in charge of the regiment. They would take off in furtive pursuit, and sometimes, if they were lucky, they would engage in a brief and unsatisfying battle. Before the rest of the command caught up, Colonel Carson and his Utes had finished fighting; the skirmish was over.

Capt. Eben Everett, the probable author of the only known diary kept during the campaign, described one of Carson's morning raids. On the morning of August 28, the diary notes, "a party of some thirty men were sent off to go round by way of an Indian village. They joined us at Camp about 3 o'clock bringing with them one scalp of an Indian they had shot. From its appearance the original wearer . . . must have been an *hombre grande*."

It was on one of these sorties that Carson sustained his first—and amazingly, the *only*—casualty of the Navajo campaign. For reasons not entirely clear, Maj. Joseph Cummings, a brave but overly brash young officer, surged alone well ahead of the main column through a desolate canyon. Several hours later his body was found four miles ahead on the canyon floor, a rifle wound in his belly, the bullet apparently having severed his spinal cord. In his report to Carleton, Carson seemed to have little sympathy for Cummings. The major had shown precisely the sort of incautious behavior, blustery and ultimately pointless, that he detested: "Major Cummings left the command alone and proceeded up the cañon" when he was killed "by a concealed Indian," the report dryly announced. In the end the major had acted "against positive orders" and was killed "as a result of rash bravery." For reasons that were never disclosed, Cummings was carrying a rather astounding sum of cash—$4,200—the entire amount found on his person, undisturbed.

In the absence of actual Navajos to fight, Carson turned his men loose on the tribe's unattended wheatfields and cornfields and melon patches. He threw himself into this dark work. His true talents lay more in pursuit than in despoliation, yet once his mind turned in a vandal direction, a certain wicked ingenuity expressed itself. He thought of everything, it seemed. He had his men destroy every pot and basket they stumbled upon, to deprive the Navajos of any means of carrying or storing food. Caches were dug up and plundered, and every stock animal encountered was either killed or appropriated. Carson had his Utes guard all the known watering holes and salt sources of the Navajo country, and in one case he explored the possibility of "turning off" a stream by choking it with boulders so as to divert its flow.

The weekly reports that Carson dutifully dictated to his adjutant for General Carleton's benefit were, for the most part, plodding logbooks of destruction. There was a numbing quality to these accounts. By their droning dreariness one senses that he found as little pleasure reporting the grim deeds as he did performing them. Joyless though they are, Carson's reports make it clear that the crop annihilation was adding up.

From Carson's August logs: "Destroyed about seventy acres of corn." . . . "The Wheat (about fifteen acres) we fed to the animals and the corn (about fifty acres) was destroyed." . . . "Shortly after leaving camp on the 9th, destroyed about twelve acres of corn." . . . "About 12 miles West of Moqui, fed to animals about an acre of corn found there." . . . "While en route on the 16th destroyed about fifty acres of corn." . . . "About five miles from camp, found and destroyed about ten acres of good corn. At the night camp some ten miles farther, found a patch of corn which was fed to the animals." . . . "Packed on the animals all the grain not previously consumed by them or destroyed by the Command." . . . "About 10 A.M., the command arrived at a large bottom containing not less than one hundred acres of as fine corn as I have ever seen. Here I determined to encamp that I might have it destroyed."

And so on, and so on. In the end Carson's men leveled and burned untold thousands of acres of crops—by his estimation nearly 2 million pounds of food, most of it in its prime, ready for harvest. The impact of this obliteration had a built-in time lag; it would not really show itself until the autumn, when the Navajos would face the coming cold in the grip of inevitable famine.

Carson only had to be patient. At one point in his August logs, he pondered the fate of a particular band whose cornfields had just fallen under his blade and torch. "They have no stock," he writes in a tone devoid of either pleasure or remorse, "and were depending entirely for subsistence on the corn destroyed by my command on the previous day." The loss, he predicts, "will cause actual starvation, and oblige them to come in and accept emigration to the Bosque Redondo."

⌧

In fact, a small number of Navajos *did* come to Fort Canby to accept emigration, but unfortunately it was at a time when Carson was still away on his scout. On August 26, four Navajo men appeared outside the fort. According to one eyewitness, they arrived "under a flag of truce" and "represented that they came to sue for peace, and that their tribe or band, numbering from seventy-five to one hundred souls, was outside the Fort and wanted to come in as friends."

But the commanding officer of the post in Carson's absence, an overbearing major named Thomas J. Blakeney, thoroughly bungled this golden opportunity to accept the very first group of Navajos to surrender on Carleton's terms. Instead of offering amnesty and kind passage, Blakeney rudely mistreated the four Diné emissaries. First, they were imprisoned and put to work burying "offal and dead dogs." Then at least one of them was shot dead while two of the others, apparently fearing they would be next, managed to escape for the hills.

Only one of the four Navajos was left at the fort when Carson returned on August 31 from his long reconnaissance. Carson interviewed him, a plainly scared old man of about seventy years named Little Foot, and believed his story. Taking pity, Carson gave Little Foot twelve days to return to the fort with his people—although after what had happened, the colonel saw slim reason for optimism that the Navajo would actually come back. "From all I can learn," Carson reported to Carleton, "these Indians came in with a flag of truce, and I cannot but regret that they were not better received and kept until my arrival. . . . I cannot blame these people for distrusting the good faith of the Troops at this Post, from the manner in which their Messengers have been received. I deplore it the more as I now have only one way of communicating with them—through the barrels of my Rifles."

If he'd had a chance to parley with this first group, Carson firmly believed, he would have been able to patiently explain all of Carleton's terms and win them over with food and other gifts. Had the proceedings gone well, he thought, it might have set off a chain reaction of mass surrenders, possibly obviating the need for a protracted campaign. Instead, Carson was now facing the exact opposite situation: The two emissaries who had escaped were doubtless telling their people, and other bands they met, *not* to surrender, that they would be shot and mistreated if they did—that, in fact, this was a war of extermination.

Carson, for all his strengths, had one serious flaw as a commander: Still unfamiliar with army protocol, he was not an effective disciplinarian. And because he did not have a firm hold on his command, the sort of imbecilic cruelty demonstrated by Blakeney was regrettably more the rule than the exception. In truth, most of the officers Carson had to work with were none too swift. Time and time again they demonstrated themselves to be a uniquely inept and unruly bunch. Overworked and underpaid, many of them drunks, a good number of them immigrants fresh from places like Ireland, England, and the Netherlands, they hated having to do this depressing work in a desert wasteland when they could be digging for gold in California or fighting Rebels back east. Even General Carleton, who had handpicked most of the men of higher rank serving with Carson, admitted that he was "greatly embarrassed for want of good officers."

Lawrence Kelly, who made a thorough study of Carson's command in his excellent book *Navajo Roundup,* noted that nearly half of the officers serving on the Navajo campaign were either court-martialed or forced to resign. Lawrence observes that, among other things, Carson's officers were charged with "murder, alcoholism, embezzlement, sexual deviation, desertion, and incompetence."

Lt. David McAllister was caught in bed with an enlisted man while he was officer of the day at Fort Canby. Capt. Eben Everett was court-martialed for "being so drunk as to be wholly unable to perform any duty properly." Lieutenants Stephen Coyle and William Mortimer were forced to resign after they bloodied each other in "a disgraceful fight" in front of enlisted men. John Caufield was charged with murdering an enlisted man and held in irons until convicted by a military court. Assistant Surgeon James H. Prentiss was charged with stealing most of the "Hospital Whiskey and Wine and applying it to his own use." Lt. Nicholas Hodt was found to be "beastly intoxicated" and "in bed with a woman of bad character." Another officer was found to have offered to secure prostitutes for his men, boasting in all seriousness that he was the "damdest best pimp in New Mexico."

These colorful disciplinary notes go on and on, bearing sad testimony to the morale problems that clearly prevailed among this confederacy of dunces.

To his credit, Carson pursued an investigation into Blakeney's actions, and the officer was soon dismissed, with an examining surgeon claiming that the unpopular major suffered from a "nervous debility" and a bad case of indigestion. When Carson described the Blakeney incident to Carleton in his next report, the general promptly shot back a curt letter: "You are right in believing that I do not wish to have Indians destroyed who are willing to come in. Nor will you permit an Indian prisoner once fairly in your custody to be killed." However, Carson was not to let this minor setback deter him from the main task at hand—nor was the colonel to slacken the ferocity of his rhetoric when he next encountered Navajos willing to talk. Carleton reminded Carson to tell the Navajos that "you have deceived us too often and robbed and murdered our people too long to trust you again at large in your country. . . . This war shall be pursued against you if it takes years, until you cease to exist or move. There can be no other talk on the subject."

In the fall, Carson embarked on two more ambitious scouts, but these, too, were seeming failures. Mules and horses collapsed in alarming numbers while others were cleverly stolen in the night by unseen Navajo rustlers. His Ute warriors deserted upon learning that General Carleton would not permit them to keep the booty or slaves they captured along the way. At one point Carson came very close to catching the great warrior Manuelito—or at least a man described by the Hopis as Manuelito—but the prize refugee slipped away, living with his people on secret stores of corn he had presciently stashed throughout the Navajo lands.

After a series of smaller scouts in late November produced similarly underwhelming results, Carson became truly fed up and not a little embarrassed. He was not a man used to failing, certainly not on this scale. One can sense the undertones of rising frustration in his letters to Carleton. He wrote the general that given the sorry state of his horses, he did not think he could continue to prosecute the campaign through the winter. He thought it more prudent to wait "until the weather opens sufficiently" before resuming "extended operations." At times, it sounded as though he was giving up.

And in fact, he was—at least temporarily. Carson formally requested a two-month leave of absence that would begin on December 15. He wanted to see Josefa, who was approaching her due date. From the field, Carson had been sending her dictated letters whenever he could. One of them survives:

> Beloved Wife—
>
> Do not worry about me, because with God's help we shall see each other again. I charge you above all not to get weary of caring for my children, and to give each one a little kiss in my name. . . . I remain begging God that I return in good health to be with you until death.
>
> > —Your husband who loves you and wishes to see you more than to write to you

In his request for a leave, Carson did not explicitly mention his concern about Josefa's pregnancy; he said only to Carleton that he needed to attend to "some private business of importance." In any case, Carleton denied Carson's request, claiming, "I have not the authority to grant you a leave." Winter was not the season to relax pressure on the Navajos, the general insisted. "Now while the snow is deep is the true time to make an impression on the tribe." Carleton ended his note with a prissy addendum: "Please forward no more applications for leaves of absence."

Carleton was willing to cut a quid pro quo deal with his colonel, however. Carson could come home for a brief visit, the general said, "*as soon as* you have secured one hundred captive Navajo men, women, and children." It was an incentive package that captured the irritating paternalism lodged so deeply within Carleton's personality: Perform your task, and then you can go see your wife.

But there was one more caveat. Through all his exhausting scouts, Carson had carefully stayed away from the stronghold of Navajo country, Canyon de Chelly. Back in September he had paused at the tantalizing western mouth of the canyon, but steadfastly refused to go in. Perhaps he was daunted by the scale of the chasm itself—which he regarded as "stupendous" and "impregnable"—or by the considerable logistics that would be required to mount a campaign through it, something no army had ever successfully done in wartime. Perhaps he was aware of the fact that an American colonel named Dixon S. Miles, after scouting a section of the canyon in 1858, had ominously proclaimed, "No command should ever again enter it." Whatever the reason, Canyon de Chelly was a dread subject for Carson.

Now Carleton had other ideas. Carson would not only have to reach his quota of one hundred captives, but he would have to do it by invading Canyon de Chelly in the dead of winter—and traversing every twisted mile of it.

Chapter 42   FORTRESS ROCK

The Navajos knew that Carson was coming to Canyon de Chelly, perhaps even before Carson did. Or at least they *assumed* that he was coming. Down through the ages, all manner of enemies had trespassed into the great gorge, but usually they would slink home, bewildered by its endless mazes, having caused little harm. The 1805 massacre at The Place Where Two Fell Off was a grotesque exception the Navajos seldom spoke of—a tragedy ascribable to witchcraft, perhaps, or some violated taboo.

In their heart of hearts the Diné had always regarded Canyon de Chelly as their last stronghold and sanctuary, the one place where they felt truly safe. When their wider world was in turmoil, when they could find no relief from pestilence or harrying foes, they had always fallen back here, to hide in the timeless folds.

Along the floor of Canyon de Chelly grew three thousand peach trees, gnarled and scabbed with insect boreholes and now ghostly in the depths of winter, their brittle branches creaking in the wind. These orchards were the pride of the Navajos, the trees hybridized from stock dating back to the Spanish arrival in New Mexico. The succulent fruit they bore helped feed the many hundreds of clansmen who streamed in each fall for elaborate rituals; for nine consecutive nights the people renewed themselves in ceremonial chants, watching their shadows flicker on the thousand-foot-high walls, their lips and fingers sticky with the sour-sweet juice of canyon peaches.

Not only was de Chelly a bountiful place, it was, the Diné believed, protected by supernatural powers no white man could touch. The four *yei* gods lived deep in the canyon, as did Spider Woman, the great Navajo goddess. Spider Woman was a lovable old crone, cryptic but wise, who gave Navajo women the gift of weaving and otherwise amused herself by inflicting harmless and often instructive mischief on her beloved people. She lived atop a nine-hundred-foot-tall pinnacle erupting from the floor of the canyon that is still known today as Spider Rock. From her commanding perch, Spider Woman surely would look out for the Navajos and protect them from any enemies who presumed to invade her realm.

Back in the summer, when Kit Carson was leading his first campaigns across the Navajo country, the Diné who lived in the vicinity of Canyon de Chelly began to prepare themselves for the coming onslaught. Many miles inside the canyon, near an important junction of two lateral gorges, stood a massive anvil of sandstone well known to the Navajos. Fortress Rock, as it was called, soared nearly eight hundred feet and was connected to the main wall of the canyon only by a thin stone bridge sagging from centuries of erosion. To use an urban analogy, it looked rather like a natural rough draft of New York's

Flatiron Building—a thin monolithic wedge standing at the confluence of three sharply angled thoroughfares. Any stranger who happened to pass by Fortress Rock would doubtless find it impressive if
not menacing, but he would scarcely imagine that a path led up its
sheer walls to the tableland at its summit.

Yet it was so: Long ago the Anasazi had chiseled a fretwork of toeholds and handholds, almost invisible, into the face of the rock. On
top they had discovered that there was enough room for hundreds of
people to camp. Various caves and fissures provided welcome places
to hide. Scattered about the surface were pocks and bowls that func-
tioned as cisterns to capture rainwater. Fortress Rock was protected
from all sides; its parapets were invisible from the canyon floor and
too distant from either canyon rim to be within arrow range.

The Anasazi had apparently used Fortress Rock as a secret haven
to hide from their enemies; now the Navajos would do the same.

According to Navajo oral history, the Diné met at the base of
Fortress Rock sometime in the late summer and discussed what to do.
"A frightened feeling had settled among the Navajo people, a feeling
of danger from enemies," says Akinabh Burbank, one of a dozen sto-
rytellers poignantly captured in a 1973 oral history. "Now they were
moving into our territory to search for us and kill us all."

The women began to stockpile foods and supplies—smoked mutton, piñon nuts, wild potatoes, juniper berries, dried grain and
peaches, blankets, and water-bearing vessels of all kinds. The men,
meanwhile, made improvements to the old network of Anasazi toeholds, gouging them deeper, so that children and even elderly Navajos could safely pull themselves up. They shored up a particularly
precarious passage of loose rock by building a sturdy wooden bridge.
As it was related to historian David Roberts, the Navajos then scaled
the last vertiginous heights by laying two trunks of ponderosa pine at
sharp angles—trees they had hauled from stands in the Lukachukai
Mountains, some twenty-five miles away—cutting the bark with
notches to function like rungs on a ladder.

It was a public works project of great ambition as well as peril,
one that took weeks to complete. Fortress Rock had always been a

formidable place, but through their efforts "this thrusting fin," as Roberts puts it, had become "the most sovereign of hideouts, the place of ultimate refuge."

Now that the way up was deemed safe, the Navajos began to haul their supplies and foodstuffs to the top—everything they thought they'd need to get them through a long siege. Then, as winter closed in, the people began to assemble. "You can go to the safe place until the soldiers are gone—we still have time," says Navajo storyteller Teddy Draper, recalling a story passed down from his grandmother. "Kill most of the livestock and prepare the meat. It is getting cold now, so we have to start. We must be on the top before it snows. The men have been working on the trails. The ladders have been put up. Be strong and prepare to defend yourselves."

One day in December, as it started to snow, some three hundred men, women, and children, perhaps tipped off by a sentry that the *bilagaana* army was on its way, ascended to the top and pulled up their ladders and bridges. Hoping the evil might pass beneath them, they planned to dwell in silence for months—and, if necessary, make a last-ditch defense, like the doomed Jewish rebels who defied the Romans from the stone ramparts of Masada.

Some accounts say Manuelito was among the faithful on Fortress Rock, although that is doubtful, because he was also said to be somewhere in the Grand Canyon at that time, and also around Navajo Mountain, and also in the vicinity of Monument Valley. Manuelito, in short, was everywhere—and nowhere—his phantomlike ubiquity made possible by his fame and his great wealth in sheep. His roving defiance was a rallying cry, a source of hope to his people.

As December passed into January, the three hundred Navajos atop Fortress Rock tarried at their now smokeless camps and huddled in their blankets, trying to stay warm. They heard that the American soldiers had been spotted, that the enemy would arrive any day now. They made arrows and sharpened lances while keeping their ears tuned for untoward sounds down in the canyon.

And they waited.

☒

Col. Kit Carson left Fort Canby on the cold, gray morning of January 6, 1864. Six inches of snow powdered the ground. The nearly five hundred men under his command moved slowly, and the oxen groaned at the weight of the wagons. Most of the men were on foot, the snow crunching under their boots. They were draped in blankets or serapes, or buttoned up tight in wool greatcoats, their numb hands thrust deep in the pockets. They hated having to greet the New Year in such bleak surroundings, so far from home, in a wilderness so god-forsaken. To pass the hours they invented their own battle song, a bit of doggerel that they belted out over the winter solitudes—

> *Come dress your ranks, my gallant souls, a standing in a row*
> *Kit Carson he is waiting to crush the savage foe*
> *At night we meet and march o'er lofty hills of snow*
> *We'll first chastise*
> *Then civilize*
> *Bold Johnny Navajo*

Colonel Carson rode up and down the column, his jaws clenched in resolve. A few days earlier Carson had assured Carleton that he had "made all the necessary arrangements to visit the Canon de Chelly" and thought Carleton would be relieved to learn that the expedition he had so long insisted upon was finally happening. "Of one thing the General may rest assured," Carson vowed to Carleton. "Before my return, all that is connected with this canon [canyon] will cease to be a mystery. It will be thoroughly explored [with] perseverance and zeal."

Carson had divided his command into two units. Taking the larger contingent of 375 enlisted men and 14 officers, Carson himself would head toward the western mouth of the canyon, while a smaller party of approximately 100 New Mexico Volunteers under the command of Capt. Albert Pfeiffer would aim for the eastern end. The plan, which General Carleton played a large role in devising, called for executing a kind of pincer movement, with the two separate detachments traversing the chasm from opposite sides and reuniting somewhere in the middle. The idea was to stopper the canyon at both ends so that its denizens could not easily escape. It was a strategy, Carleton hoped, that would also allow him to achieve maximum shock value. He recognized the symbolic power that Canyon de Chelly held for the Navajos. If Carson could sweep the entire length of it, puncturing its aura of impregnability, the maneuver might demoralize the Navajos far more profoundly than the resulting casualties might suggest. In this sense, the thrust of the coming campaign was less purely military than it was psychosocial: By cutting into the soul of the nation, Carleton hoped to break the people's collective will to fight.

The snow was more than Carson had bargained for, however. What should have been a three-day march took six, and the oxen, already weak and straining, began to collapse. Along the way, twenty-seven of the beasts died, their hulking bodies capsizing in the drifts and soon freezing solid, their hooves pitched in the air.

On January 12, Carson arrived at the mouth of the canyon, near the present-day town of Chinle, Arizona, and promptly sent out reconnaissance parties in various directions, both along the rims and down in the canyon itself. Sgt. Andres Herrera, with a detachment of fifty men, intercepted a band of Navajos who were attempting to escape through a side canyon. Herrera attacked and soon the vast ochre walls echoed with gunfire. Herrera's troops killed eleven Navajo warriors and captured two women, two children, and 130 goats and sheep. The battle for Canyon de Chelly had begun.

The next morning Carson began a more ambitious study of the south rim in preparation for his big offensive surge into the canyon, which he planned to undertake in a few days. For many miles he marched along the rim, peering down into the spectral depths, worrying over the puzzling landscape and the ease with which it could conceal snipers or ambushing parties. The idea of taking a party of men through the canyon went against his best mountain man instincts and offended his sense of caution. It looked to him like a trap.

Carson also began to wonder where Albert Pfeiffer and his company might be. Surely Pfeiffer had reached the eastern entrance of the canyon by now and had begun marching westward. Yet as Carson and his men scoured the canyon from its southern rim, they saw no sign of him.

◙

Capt. Albert Pfeiffer was a colorful and somewhat tragic figure. Though a heavy drinker, he was one of Carson's ablest officers. He had kind blue eyes and a stout build, and while he was an immigrant from the Netherlands, he had lived for some time in New Mexico and had, like Carson, married a local woman. Pfeiffer was tranquil by nature, except when he got into a tight situation. The possibility of combat threw him into a blind rage, causing him to curse wildly in Dutch and transforming him, said one contemporary, into "the most desperately courageous fighter in the West."

Captain Pfeiffer was still recovering from a brutal incident that had befallen him several months earlier, down in Apache country, where he had campaigned with Carson in the Mescalero roundup. It seems that Pfeiffer suffered from some sort of skin problem—exacerbated by alcohol—that Carson repeatedly chided him about. "When will you have sense?" Carson admonished the Dutchman in a letter. "Can't you try and quit whiskey for a little while, at least until you get your face cured? If your face ain't well when I next see you, you had better look out."

To cure his dermatological malady, Pfeiffer regularly soaked in a mineral hot spring not far from an army fort where he was stationed. One bright day he and his wife were bathing in the spring when a band of Apaches set upon them. Pfeiffer was seriously wounded by an arrow and his wife was killed. Half naked, Pfeiffer somehow managed to straggle back to camp, becoming badly sunburned in the process. Some accounts have it that the murder of his wife changed Pfeiffer forever, turning him into an inveterate Indian-hater.

Captain Pfeiffer and his company of one hundred rank and file reached the eastern end of Canyon de Chelly without incident on

January 11, a day earlier than Carson entered the western end. Traveling lighter, and with most of his men on horseback, he had been able to keep a brisk pace. Pfeiffer wasted no time—he dropped down into the canyon, following the route of an ice-rimmed creek until it spilled into a deep gorge. Then he started plodding west.

But he had entered the wrong canyon. Somehow he had skirted the main branch of Canyon de Chelly and had instead entered Canyon del Muerto, a secondary though no less awesome artery of the de Chelly complex.

Pfeiffer blundered ahead, employing teams of sappers, equipped with pickaxes, to break trail through ice and snow. It was extremely tough going, and one of the mules bearing a particularly heavy load broke suddenly through the ice and "split completely open." With every turn, the canyon's multifaceted walls bulked larger, enveloping them in an eerie silence. Some men chiseled their names or the letters U.S.A. in the sandstone facades—Kilroys visible to this day. The men found it impossible not to gape at the great opiates of rock and the half-hidden ruins and petroglyphs gracing the walls. But their reveries were quickly punctured when they realized that there were Navajo warriors all around them—perched on the rim, hidden in crannies, watching every move the Americans made. Some of them rose up, Pfeiffer wrote, "and jumped about on the ledges, like Mountain Cats, hallooing at me, swearing and cursing, and threatening vengeance on my command in every variety of Spanish they were capable of mustering."

Along the way the soldiers captured eight Navajo women and children who were clearly surprised by Pfeiffer's sudden appearance from the east and had apparently been expecting soldiers to come from the *other* direction—Carson's direction. Pfeiffer could see they were desperately scared and impoverished—"in an almost famishing condition, half-starved and naked," as he later described them. Elsewhere his men came upon the frozen corpses of several Navajos who had apparently starved to death—further evidence, it seemed, that the Navajos were in truly dire straits and that Carson's long campaign of crop and livestock destruction had exacted a much more serious toll than the Americans realized.

Pushing deeper into Canyon del Muerto, Pfeiffer's men encountered more and more resistance from Navajos who scurried high along the walls. Some of them presented their backsides to the Americans, and others tried unsuccessfully to detour the invaders into cul de sacs and side canyons. Now the Navajos could be seen on both sides of the canyon, "whooping and cursing, firing shots and throwing rocks down upon my command."

Captain Pfeiffer had had enough: He ordered his men to open fire. "A couple of shots from my soldiers with their trusty Rifles caused the Red Skins to disperse and gave me a safe passage," Pfeiffer writes. The volley killed "two Buck Indians and one Squaw who obstinately persisted in hurling rocks and pieces of wood at the soldiers."

The following day, January 12, Pfeiffer and his men passed Fortress Rock and apparently had no inkling that three hundred Navajos were hidden on top—certainly no mention is made of it in Pfeiffer's reports. But as is clear in the oral history of the Navajos, the sight of Pfeiffer's soldiers threading through the canyon left a vivid impression on the refugees camped atop the monolith. Teddy Draper, recounting a story told by his grandmother, says in a published oral history that all the people "were instructed to stay quiet until the soldiers passed us by. From where I was they looked very small, but they were well armed and had good horses. They camped below us at the junction, but our men didn't try to attack them."

The warriors restrained themselves, Draper says, only because their leader, a wealthy headman named Dahghaa 'i, informed them that many more *bilagaana* soldiers had been sighted "at the mouth of the canyon. Their chief commander's name is Bi'ee' Kichii'ii—Kit Carson—a very pure White Man."

As the bleak winter sun slipped behind the canyon walls, the Americans ransacked an old hogan for wood. Bonfires were soon crackling, and the men wrapped themselves in their bedrolls. That night some of the Navajos on Fortress Rock couldn't resist the temptation to harass the sleeping soldiers with a constant stream of catcalls. Wrote Pfeiffer, "At the place where I encamped the curl of the smoke from my fires ascended to where a large body of Indians were resting over my head, but the height was so great that the Indians did not look larger than crows, and as we were too far apart to injure each other, no damage was done except with the tongue."

Pfeiffer's men struck camp early the next morning and kept moving through the bitter cold. At every bend Pfeiffer kept expecting to run into Carson's men—he thought surely by now he would have seen signs of the larger detachment. Seizing more Navajo prisoners as he went—he now had a total of nineteen—Pfeiffer worked his way through Canyon del Muerto until he reached the place where it junctions with the main branch of Canyon de Chelly. It was only then, as he gazed back at this other, even more massive chasm, that he began to suspect his error. Not knowing what else to do, he continued marching west.

The three hundred people sequestered on top of Fortress Rock were safe for the moment—the threat had passed them by. But several weeks later a well-armed party sent by Carson would return and lay siege to the citadel. The soldiers opened fire, killing or wounding some twenty warriors who'd given away their position by hurling stones from an alcove midway up the face. After the battle the Americans camped at the base of Fortress Rock beside a stream called Tsaile Creek and attempted to starve the beleaguered Navajos into final submission. But unknown to the soldiers, the Navajos on top were already slowly perishing from thirst; the snows had melted away and the natural cisterns had run dry.

So one moonlit night in February 1864, the Fortress Rock exiles devised a plan that is frequently described in Navajo oral histories: They formed a human chain along the precarious toehold path, all the way down to Tsaile Creek, where several American guards lay sleeping. A group of warriors crept out onto a ledge twenty feet over the stream and dangled gourds from yucca ropes, dipping the containers into the cold running water. Working through the night, they filled gourd after gourd—right next to the slumbering Americans—and steadily passed the vessels from hand to hand back up the sheer rock face to the summit. By dawn they had replenished their stores.

This legendary effort—which Navajos who live around Canyon de Chelly insist to this day is entirely true—allowed the three hundred refugees on Fortress Rock to outlast the siege and slip from Carson's long reach. They were never captured.

⊠

Carson spent the entire day of January 13 reconnoitering the length of Canyon de Chelly from its southern rim. He ignored several trails that followed lateral gorges down into the canyon. He did not seem at all interested in descending into the deep rift, even to satisfy a passing curiosity, even just to say he'd been in it. His tentativeness could have been a mark of his oft-described sense of military caution, or it could have been, as some have speculated, that Carson was genuinely queasy about the place. In his younger years Carson occasionally had shown a superstitiousness that made him heed odd hunches and omens. He was the kind of wide-open outdoorsman who instinctively steered clear of crowded rooms or constricted places. Perhaps this explained why he had put off for as long as possible the one campaign that most people—Carleton, especially—regarded as imperative. And perhaps it explained, now that he was finally here, why he stuck to the rim: Canyon de Chelly spooked him.

Carson puzzled over the whereabouts of the other detachment. He was "very anxious about the safety of Captain Pfeiffer's command." With morning slipping into a dull gray afternoon, Carson's apprehensions grew. But around dusk, when he returned to his base camp just west of the canyon's wide mouth, Carson was greatly surprised and relieved to find Pfeiffer's company waiting for him. The men embraced each other in camp, comparing notes and drinking coffee around the fires. Although the junction of the two commands hadn't exactly followed the plan, it had at least happened—and without a single American casualty.

And then another piece of good news fell into Carson's lap. A small group of Navajos straggled into camp under a flag of truce and offered themselves up. They were weary, starving, and cold, they said, and they'd had enough of this war. Their spokesman told Carson that all of the people in his band, numbering more than fifty, would like to go to Bosque Redondo.

They were pitiful wretches, and Carson treated them kindly, offering them food and drink. But when he sat down for a council with them, Carson spoke in ultimatums: "You have until tomorrow, when the sun reaches its height," Carson said. "If you do not come in by then, my soldiers will hunt you up and destroy you."

The next morning, well before Carson's deadline, a file of sixty refugees tramped in from the canyon and turned themselves in. They offered their complete submission; they were ready to go wherever Carson wanted them to go.

Carson made sure that they were fed and given blankets. Then he listened to what their spokesmen had to say.

"Because of what your soldiers have done," one of the Navajos said, "we are all starving. Many of our women and children have already died from hunger. We would have come in long ago, but we believed this was a war of extermination."

When Carson assured them this was not so, they seemed "agreeably surprised and delighted." Carson went on to explain what Bosque Redondo was, and why the United States government was moving them there. "The government wants to promote your welfare," Carson told them. "The point is not to destroy you but to save you, if you want to be saved."

Hearing all this, the band of huddled Navajos indicated that they would go farther afield into their country and convince more to come out of hiding. For hundreds of miles in all directions the people were famished, demoralized, and scared. They would gladly give themselves up if they knew they would not be killed by doing so.

Hunger, Carson realized, had been his greatest ally, and it had exacted a mean price. Peering into the squalid crowd of sixty faces, he must have seen the faces of 8,000—10,000—12,000 more. He now recognized the scope of what he had done—and saw for the first time what his soldiers had reduced these people to. The meaning of "scorched earth" was sitting right in front him.

Carson felt no cause for rejoicing—only the beginning of a kind of relief. The Navajo tribe was still a long way from surrendering, but on that cold morning, something had given. The first group of Diné had voluntarily come in for the first important surrender. At last Carson was able to have a face-to-face discussion with Navajos instead of "communicating with them through the barrels of my rifles."

He trusted these Navajos when they promised to go out and persuade their clansmen to surrender. As willing emissaries to their own people, they could be far more effective than any number of military expeditions at turning the tide of the war. He told them to return to Fort Canby within a week with as many people as they could gather. Carson would be there himself to greet them, and they had his word that no one would be harmed.

◈

The following day, Carson prepared to leave for Fort Canby. He wanted to be there to receive the expected influx of prisoners as smoothly and cordially as possible; he understood that a careful diplomacy was of paramount importance now—there could not be a repeat of what had happened a few months earlier under the brutish command of Major Blakeney.

Carson would take only a small detachment with him and leave the bulk of the command at Canyon de Chelly in the able hands of Albert Pfeiffer and Asa Carey. He instructed them to stay in the canyon and clinch the victory. The surrender of the first sixty Navajos had changed his whole outlook. It was as though he'd caught a glimpse of the fighting's end. Fired with a new impatience, he wanted his men to redouble their ruthlessness and press every advantage. Suddenly, it seemed, Carson had got religion—he was almost starting to sound like Carleton. "Now," he wrote, "is the time to prosecute the Campaign with vigor."

Carson ordered Carey and Pfeiffer to proceed through the bowels of Canyon de Chelly—the main branch this time—and lay waste to everything: every hogan, every brush arbor, every animal, every store of grain. It was to be more scorched earth, in other words, only this time the work was to be carried out right in the high church of the Navajos. Any Diné who willingly surrendered was to be treated kindly, but holdouts and those attempting to escape were to be summarily shot.

While they were at it, Carey and Pfeiffer could do a little scouting and exploring and even bring along a field artist to make sketches and maps. By venturing to the far eastern end of the chasm, they would fulfill Carson's earlier promise to Carleton—*". . . all that is connected with this canon will cease to be a mystery."*

Carson seemed especially grateful to delegate this assignment to Pfeiffer and Carey, for he was thereby relieved from having to venture into the canyon himself. Other commanders would have leapt at the chance to be the first American to penetrate the full length of Canyon de Chelly in wartime—and would have insisted on personally leading his troops on a mission with such glorious historical overtones. But Carson was more than happy to give his subordinates all the credit. In fact, even though his name would be forever associated with it, Carson would never set foot in Canyon de Chelly.

Before he left, however, Carson came up with a diabolical idea, a parting gesture of pure aggression. Probably General Carleton had had a hand in suggesting it, but Carson was the one who issued the command: He ordered his captains to chop down every peach tree in Canyon de Chelly.

As it turned out, Pfeiffer and Carey found that destroying the orchards was impractical in the bitter cold weather, but by summertime Carson's men would faithfully execute his order. The fabled orchards came under the saw and the torch. Thousands of peach trees, the pride of the Diné, were hacked down.

It's hard to fathom how this played on the Navajo psyche. To obliterate the grand old orchards was a final thumb in the eye, as if to say, "Everything that you are, everything that you have, is forever disgraced." The Navajos would never forgive him for it.

⊠

Carson swiftly marched back to Fort Canby, and by late January the Navajos started streaming in, first in twos and threes, then by the dozens, and finally by the score. As they'd promised, the sixty Navajos Carson had met in Canyon de Chelly had broadcast the desirability of surrender to their clansmen. Now, they said, thousands more were on their way. "They are arriving almost hourly," Carson wrote Carleton, "and will I believe continue to arrive until the last Indian in this section of the country is en route to the Bosque Redondo."

Carson sat down and dictated his report on the Canyon de Chelly campaign, but his account seems to have been hyped and prettified by his adjutant: "We have thoroughly explored their heretofore unknown stronghold," Carson declared. "We have shown the Indians that in no place, however formidable or inaccessible, are they safe from the pursuit of the troops of this command; and have convinced a large portion of them that the intentions of the Government toward them are eminently humane." Carson ticked off the vital stats of the Canyon de Chelly mission: "*Killed, 23. Prisoners, 34. Voluntarily surrendered, 200 souls. Captured, 200* head of sheep and goats."

Meanwhile, the floodgates had been opened: By the first week of February 1864, more than 800 Navajos had arrived at Fort Canby. In a few weeks the number swelled to 2,500, with thousands more en route. A reporter for the *Weekly New Mexican,* seeing all these prisoners awaiting transfer to the bosque, wrote that "daylight is dawning. . . . Carleton is accomplishing much." The *Santa Fe Gazette* reported that "there are at this moment a hundred campfires sparkling amongst the hills [around Fort Canby] and within five hundred yards of this post. These fires are built by peaceful Navajos who have been arriving daily in large numbers. It is a happy omen."

Actually, the tide of refugees was more than the army could handle. There wasn't enough food at Fort Canby and Fort Wingate to feed the teeming masses. Carson expressed his alarm to Carleton that the Navajos could well starve, and that the meager army ration was not enough. "I would respectfully suggest to you the propriety of giving to the Indians while at the forts and while en route to the Bosque Redondo, a sufficiency to eat," Carson argued. "It is while here that we must convince them of the kind intentions of the Government towards them, otherwise I fear that they will lose confidence in our promises, and desert."

But Carson would not stay long enough at Fort Canby to see the worst of it. Now that he had gathered far more than the general's quota of one hundred prisoners, Carson was entitled to take his leave of absence and return home. The first week of February he departed with an initial convoy of 253 prisoners. Carson, their conqueror and now advocate, escorted them without incident as far as the Rio Grande. From there he turned north for Santa Fe, while armed guards marched the prisoners the remaining three hundred miles to Carleton's new reservation on the Pecos.

In Santa Fe, Carson was greeted as a god. People saluted him, embraced him in the muddy streets. The plaza was thronged with celebrants. In six short months he had done something that no field commander over nearly three hundred years of history had been able to do.

General Carleton was fulsome in his praise, calling Carson's triumph the "crowning act in a long life spent fighting the savages among the fastnesses of the Rocky Mountains." In a glowing report the general sent to superiors in Washington, Carleton pointed out that Canyon de Chelly had been "the great fortress of the Navajo tribe since time out of mind. Colonel [John] Washington and many other commanders have made attempts to go through it, and had to retrace their steps. It was reserved for Colonel Carson to be the first to succeed."

What's more, Carleton was so encouraged by the huge numbers of Navajos streaming into Fort Canby—now four thousand and growing—that he declared a "suspension of arms." On February 27 the general confidently wrote to Washington: "You have doubtless seen the last of the Navajo war." As usual, Carson felt uncomfortable with the public's adulation and was quick to point out that it was

Carey and Pfeiffer who had actually made the historic penetration of Canyon de Chelly.

The truth was, Carson was in no shape to celebrate his victory—even if he was inclined to accept it as such. He was near exhaustion and in increasing pain. He did not know it yet, but something was growing inside his chest that was slowly killing him. His horse accident years ago in the San Juans had apparently caused the formation of an aneurysm on his aorta—a tiny balloon that was steadily expanding and would prove immediately lethal should it burst. He knew something was not right. As Tom Dunlay described it, "An enemy he could neither outwit nor outfight was on his trail."

He wanted no more of the Navajo wars. "The state of my health warns me," Carson wrote, "that I can no longer render my country efficient service." As quickly as he could slip from the clutches of the adoring capital, Carson sped home to Josefa.

Chapter 43   THE LONG WALK

They marched with nothing but the wretched clothes they were wearing. In a column that stretched for many miles, they tramped through the blustery snows of the high desert spring. Before they'd even passed out of Navajo country, tears of homesickness welled in their eyes. Faces that had always known suffering were now filled with new depths of anguish and sorrow—yet many faces were also touched with a faint hope. They trusted that any existence would be better than the life of paranoid squalor they'd been living for the past year. They had little conception of where they were going, or what sort of home to expect once they arrived. All they could do was keep on walking, toward the east.

East was the direction of hope, after all—the direction that every Navajo hogan faced to greet the morning sun. But east was also the direction from which the *bilagaana* had come. There was a paradox to this, and also an admonition: Ever since they could remember, the Diné had been told never to leave the confines of their four sacred mountains. If they did, the ceremonials would cease to work. Ancient chants would become meaningless, and even the best medicine men would lose their touch. And so, as the refugees filed out of Navajo country, past Acoma and Laguna pueblos, and down into the Rio Grande rift, they began to fear the consequences of drawing so close to the land of the sunrise.

For a short time, they could swivel their heads and take comfort in the sight of their familiar Blue Bead Mountain—Mount Taylor— rising over the brown plains, its broad shoulders still shawled in snow. But after another day or two of marching, the mountain began to grow wispier, its bold blues hazing into nothing, until it disappeared altogether. From then on, as they climbed mesas, plunged down *bajadas,* and inched across the prairie, they could see no more vestiges of Navajo country. And still they marched east.

Most of them were guilty of nothing more than being Navajo. The errant young men responsible for most of the raids represented but a small percentage of the tribe. Yet now the many would pay for the malefactions of the few; now all the Diné would finally suffer for the trouble caused by its most incorrigible members. It was the poorest Navajos, the *ladrones,* who had surrendered first. They were the sickest and weakest, the ones who had lacked the wherewithal to hold out. Now they had less than nothing—not their health, not their animals, not even a country.

Men like Manuelito were not among them. Manuelito was one of the *ricos*—he had sheep enough to eat and barter his way across Navajo lands, to keep on the move, to resist. "I shall remain here," he told one army scout who sought his surrender through an intermediary. "I have nothing to lose but my life, and that they can come and take whenever they please." Manuelito was a strong and defiant man, a man of uncommon pride. But he also had something that the *ladrones* did not have when they finally did the unthinkable and gave themselves up: He still had food in his belly.

Now they had food, too, if that's what you called the rations the *bilagaana* provided along the march. The bacon was rancid and caused the Navajos to retch. They had coffee beans but no means to grind them. The daily ration of wheat flour was virtually useless. Although there was nothing particularly wrong with it, most Navajos had never seen flour before and didn't know what to do with it. So they just stuffed it into their mouths, uncooked—and naturally grew sick.

General Carleton ordered his soldiers to treat their charges with "Christian kindness"—and reminded them that the goal was to transport them to Bosque Redondo as swiftly and safely as possible so that soldiers would never have to fight them again. If the guards mistreated them, the Navajos would desert and return to their country, and the wars would begin anew. The Navajos, Carleton said, were now "protégés of the United States—a people who, having given up their country, should be provided for by a powerful and Christian nation."

Kindness may have been the policy, but as almost always happens in the escalating confusion of a refugee evacuation, the best intentions slipped. Army command devolved into chaos. Soldiers raped women, denied rations, and pushed elderly marchers to the brink of death. Cruel guards occasionally shot those who couldn't keep up and left them to rot where they lay. And soldiers looked the other way as old enemies of the Navajos—the Zuni, the Jemez, and the New Mexicans—had their fun with the helpless trains of emigrants, stealing women and children away in the night. The slave raids became so prevalent that an American officer circulated a warning that all guards "must exercise extreme vigilance or the Indians' children will be stolen from them and sold."

Hundreds of Navajos succumbed to sickness, exposure, and exhaustion. The erratic spring weather for which New Mexico is famous only worsened the ordeal. On March 21 a blizzard fell on a party of nearly a thousand marchers. Army quartermasters were not prepared for the storm—they had not procured enough firewood or blankets to go around. Many of the Indians were nearly naked and soon developed frostbite. By the time this unfortunate column reached the bosque, 110 Navajos had died.

◙

There is no indication that the author of all this misery, Gen. James Carleton, ever saw the forced relocation as it was actually happening. For the most part he stayed in his Santa Fe headquarters and kept his tireless pen scribbling. But he received constant updates and descriptions of the hegira that was sweeping across the vast territory he governed. The march was a beautiful metaphor, he thought, an image that epitomized the inevitable last stages of Manifest Destiny—an eastward-moving counterpoint to the greater westward migration of Anglo-Saxons.

"The exodus of this whole people from the land of their fathers is a touching sight," Carleton wrote. "They have fought us gallantly for years on years; they have defended their mountains and their stupendous canyons with heroism; but at length, they found it was their destiny, too, to give way to the insatiable progress of our race."

Carleton was so pleased with the progress of his Navajo campaign that late that summer he allowed himself an uncharacteristic vacation. He had long wanted to climb Baldy Peak, an enormous treeless slab that hovered over Santa Fe. More than twelve thousand feet high, roamed only by mountain sheep and the occasional bear, Baldy was then mistakenly thought by many to be the loftiest point in New Mexico. And yet despite its obvious allure, no white man had ever climbed it—or so Carleton had been informed.

So one day in August, the general and several of his friends set off for the majestic mountain and reached its summit in a few days. There was a beautiful little lake near the top, a cold blue tarn now known as Lake Katherine. From Baldy's lichen-splashed boulders and high meadows of wildflowers, Carleton could gaze west and see the Navajo country. With the sweep of his eye he could take it all in, his newly won domain. He could see the spurred foothills and notched mesas where he was sure gold would be found (and in a few months, in fact, he would give a certain businessman-prospector named Albert Case Benedict the power of attorney to hunt "any ledge, lode, or vein of gold-bearing quartz" in the general's name).

Perhaps, if he looked in the right place with his field glasses, Carleton could also see the "touching sight" of the dust clouds being kicked up by the Navajo refugees as they marched toward their new home at the bosque. Carleton lingered at the breezy summit of Baldy Peak only long enough to do what a conquering U.S. general might be expected to do when perched atop his conquest: He planted an American flag.

☒

For a brief time Carleton seemed indeed to be standing on top of the world. The citizens of New Mexico loved him—they called him the "deliverer of the Southwest." President Lincoln praised his efforts. The territorial governor created a special day of "prayer and thanksgiving" in his honor. The newspapers hailed him as a Roman god.

"Behold him!" one editor wrote, somewhat facetiously. "His martial cloak thrown gracefully around him like a toga, his teeth set firm, his Jove-like front. Carleton rules the land."

The general was pleased to learn that thousands more Navajos were now assembling at Fort Canby and Fort Wingate and preparing to head east. Nearly the entire Navajo nation had surrendered—or was on the verge of doing so. For most of the Navajos the march took about three weeks, depending on the weather, trail conditions, and the exact route followed. It was not a single migration, but a series of them carried out in many stages, the ungainly process stretching out over many months. But taken all together, it was a forced relocation of biblical proportions, one of the largest in American history—second only to the Trail of Tears of the Cherokees. Throughout 1864 and on into 1865, nearly nine thousand Navajos would emigrate to Bosque Redondo; approximately five hundred would die along the way.

The Navajos had their own name for the great exodus, one that was eloquent in its understatement: The Long Walk.

For most of the Navajos, the last desolate stretches of the march were the hardest. In those final miles the land grew sparer and flatter and less like home. The sunbaked ground seemed to crackle underfoot, and the uninviting country, whose elevation was several thousand feet below that of the Navajo lands, was studded only with cholla cactus, mesquite, and creosote. The featureless plain was uninhabited, although in the distance one might see the occasional javelina or pronghorn antelope moving in the heat shimmer. Finally, the marchers dropped down into the valley of the Pecos, and like an apparition, there it was—the bosque, a great clump of shimmering green, guarded over by a new adobe stronghold called Fort Sumner.

It did not look so terrible at first. A shady place along a not inconsiderable river, with loads of firewood and plenty of room to move around. It did not resemble a prison at all—there were no fences or walls, no guard towers, no captives shuffling around in irons. The Diné's movements were to be policed only by "pickets"—small encampments of soldiers placed strategically, but loosely, along the perimeter. And what a perimeter it was: The reservation, the Navajos were told, was a giant parcel of land stretching out on both sides of the river as far as the eye could see. It was, in fact, forty miles square, an area nearly as large as the state of Delaware. The proportions of this alien place were at least familiarly huge—almost Navajoan—in scale.

Within days of their arrival, the Diné were put to work digging a seven-mile-long *acequia madre* on the east side of the river—with numerous lateral ditches—to irrigate the many thousands of acres of fields that Carleton planned to sow. Other Navajos helped army engineers build a dam six miles upriver to control the annual floods, while still others helped the soldiers construct the adobe brick buildings of Fort Sumner—the barracks, the sutler's shop, the officers' quarters, the jail. The Navajos were not unmindful of the fact that by doing so, they were only giving the *bilagaana* a more powerful and luxurious headquarters from which to rule over them.

Carleton wanted a bumper crop that first summer, to get the Navajos on the road to self-sufficiency. And to the soldiers' surprise, the Navajos seemed to throw themselves into the work with relish. They understood what they were doing and why they were doing it.

Agriculture was something they knew and loved. They put in crops of wheat, sorghum, rice, and turnips—but mostly corn, the Navajo staple. By July the cornfields by the river stood lush and tall, the healthy stalks waving brightly in the prairie wind. Carleton was enormously proud to hear about the corn, and he wrote to his superiors that after the harvest "there is no reason why the Navajos will not be the most prosperous and well-provided for Indians in the United States."

⌘

Kit Carson had savored his short leave of absence in Taos. Over the winter, Josefa gave birth to their sixth child, a daughter, whom they named Rebecca. After two months at home, Carson returned to Fort Canby in the spring of 1864 to oversee further mass surrenders of the Navajo. Then, in May, he applied for a new assignment as "superintendent" of the bosque.

Although it was a lackluster administrative post that seemed ill suited to his talents, Carson had in fact campaigned for the job. In a report he wrote at the conclusion of the Navajo campaign, he proposed that the reservation should have a person in charge who was "well versed in Indian character—who knows these people, and by whom he is known, and in whom they have confidence." The superintendent would "supply their wants, settle their disputes, stand between them and the citizens in their limited intercourse, and instruct and direct their labors. One in fact to whom they could look for council and assistance in every and all emergencies." Carson thought this post should be filled by a paternal figure, kind but firm, someone capable of retraining the Navajos "without their being made to feel it." The Navajos, Carson argued, "should not be prematurely forced into the habits or customs of civilized life," but on the other hand, neither should they be "allowed to retrograde." In the end, the superintendent should, by steady example, "teach them to forget the old life [while] reconciling them to the new."

Carson got the job and served as superintendent of Bosque Redondo during its promising early months, when the Navajos were planting their first crops and entering into their new life with at least some measure of hope. He proved a benevolent and fair-minded *co-mandante*. The Navajos were in awe of him. Like their own great war god, Monster Slayer, Kit Carson had accomplished something of legendary proportions, something no Navajo thought possible among mortals. It seemed to them that he had thrown a magical lasso around their people and hauled them in. And so out of fear and respect, they gave Carson a new name: Rope Thrower.

During the summer of 1864, as the corn grew tall and radiant, Carson worked tirelessly on behalf of the Diné, pleading for more supplies and medicines, goading the soldiers, hearing the Navajo grievances. He understood how fragile the bosque idea was and recognized that the first few months would set the tone for the whole tenuous experiment. The Navajos, he knew, were watching him for any sign of bad faith. "It is of utmost importance," he wrote Carleton, "that every promise however trifling should be religiously kept in every particular, else the naturally suspicious mind of the Indian will be alarmed, and distrust will speedily follow."

Despite his good intentions, Rope Thrower proved ineffective in his new post. Carson was many things, but he was not a bureaucrat. He quickly grew to hate his position, chafed at the rules, seethed at the inefficiency and corruption he saw all around him. He missed Josefa terribly, just as much as he had during his campaign in Navajo country. They were still a world away from each other—the bosque lay some two hundred miles from their home in Taos. Sitting at his desk, shuffling papers he could not read, making requests for food and equipment that the financially strapped, war-torn government would seldom honor, he toiled for three months in misery. Not since he was a saddlemaker's apprentice had he felt so trapped in a job for which he had no liking—or competence. It was, he wrote, "not the position I contemplated occupying."

Carson complained to Carleton that he had "no real power or control over the affairs of the Indians, except a moral one." The job required delicacies of domestic politics that were clearly beyond him. He found that he was regularly colliding with other army and civil authorities, especially the post commander of Fort Sumner. "I expected to order where I now have to request," Carson groused, "nor do I think it is a position befitting an officer of my rank in the service." Over the summer Carson tried to resign on several occasions, but Carleton would not accept, assuring him that "there is no disposition to place you in a position beneath your rank."

Part of Carson's hatred of his job, no doubt, stemmed from increasing doubts about the long-term feasibility of the bosque. Already, he was beginning to see cracks in Carleton's shining experiment.

For one thing, the Navajos were not getting along with the Mescalero Apaches, the small tribe with whom they shared the reservation lands. Carleton had put the two tribes together on a mistaken premise: He believed that because they were Athapaskan cousins speaking more or less the same language, they would easily mix. In fact, their hatred for one another had run hot for centuries. Predictably, the Navajos and the Mescaleros soon fell to fighting and had to be constantly policed by armed guards. For Carson, the nearly constant feuding between the two tribes caused endless headaches.

Among other problems, the Mescaleros claimed that at night the Navajos were digging up their graves and clipping fingernails, toenails, and hair, which the Diné medicine men were then using as a powerful shamanic charm. "These nocturnal forays," notes bosque historian Gerald Thompson, "were the cause of serious and repeated complaint."

Then there was the problem of housing. General Carleton insisted that the Navajos build apartment-style dwellings much like those in which Pueblo Indians lived. For Carleton, physical concentration was a paramount goal: The sooner they could be brought close together, the easier it would be to watch them, control them, teach them, *Christianize* them. As with everything else at Bosque Redondo, Carleton personally immersed himself in the nitty-gritty details of the design of these apartments; with all the flower beds and luxuriant courtyards he planned, "no Indian village in the world would compare with it in point of beauty."

But when Carson put them to work building the first of his planned apartments, the Navajos balked. They could not, *would* not, live this way. It went against their very nature. If a person died in one of the rooms, the whole building would have to be abandoned: It was *chindi*. They would prefer to build hogans, but if there wasn't enough wood for true hogans, they would just as soon live in primitive dirt hovels dug into the ground and spread out over many hundreds of acres.

Their refusal to live in a pueblo was so adamant that eventually even the colossally stubborn Carleton abandoned the idea. They could dwell in hovels, he said, but he insisted that they build them close together in long, organized rows. Superintendent Carson proposed to the Navajos that when someone died in one of lodges, the relatives of the deceased could simply vacate the now ghost-haunted structure and build another one at the end of the row. This scheme worked for a time, but really, the Navajos had no interest in living in a grid—a more haphazard pattern was more to their liking. And so, over time, they drifted back to their old nomadic lifestyle, constantly moving around the barren landscape of the reservation in small family groups, living along matrilineal lines. Yet now the wandering was aimless, without its original point of grazing vast herds of sheep. They moved, it seemed, for the sake of moving, for that is what they had always done.

The Navajos were equally adamant in their refusal to embrace Carleton's other "civilizing" schemes. With the help of the Catholic bishop in Santa Fe, Jean Baptiste Lamy, Carleton established a church with a full-time priest as well as a school to teach the Navajos reading, writing, and math. But the Navajos could not understand the Judeo-Christian universe—its male monotheism was forbidding to a tribe with so many female gods, its stories of a chosen people half a world away had no relevance, and rituals like communion and confession seemed beyond strange.

The elementary school, on the other hand, seemed to work—at least at first. The Navajo parents sent their children in droves, but this was only because Carleton gave each pupil a meal ticket for daily attendance. Once this incentive was abolished, however, the children stopped coming. The Navajo saw no use for queer marks on a page or a blackboard—and anyway, most of the parents were skeptical of the purpose of the schooling and instinctively resisted any attempt to indoctrinate their children in the white man's ways.

The failure of the school was a major setback for Carleton, for all along his emphasis had been on the children. The adults he had all but given up on. The traditional life the old folks brought from the Navajo country—"their savage desire to roam about and lead a life of idleness," as he put it—was too deeply ingrained to change. But in "this spacious tribal reformatory," the children could be shaped, he felt, and thus the government owed a special responsibility to them. He often waxed sentimental on the subject of "civilizing" Indian youth. His optimism for their future was nearly as strong as his contempt for the defunct mores of their parents.

Carleton took pity on the children, especially the ones who had been orphaned by Carson's scorched earth campaign. When an order of New Mexico nuns, the Sisters of Loretto, created a new orphanage, he personally brought in the first Navajo child, a little girl. The nuns named her Mary Carleton in his honor.

⊠

A host of other problems began to mount at the bosque, problems that kept Superintendent Carson endlessly busy. Many hundreds of Navajos developed dysentery and other intestinal illnesses as a result of drinking the alkaline waters of the Pecos. Although they had no choice but to drink from it, some Navajos thought the river was poisonous, infected with evil spirits.

The American soldiers also found the water repugnant. "The Rio Pecos," one soldier wrote home to his wife, "is a little stream winding through an immense plain, and the water is terrible, and it is all that can be had within 50 miles; it is full of alkali and operates on a person like castor oil—take the water, heat it a little, and the more you wash yourself with common soap, the dirtier you will get."

Perhaps an even bigger problem than the bad water was the lack of firewood. Within a few short months the great trees of the bosque had been chopped down to construct the various buildings of Fort

Sumner. Now the Navajos had to venture farther and farther away to collect fuel—and usually the only wood they could find was the scrubby, poor-burning mesquite whose deep roots they painstakingly clawed from the ground, often with their bare hands. Later, work details of soldiers and Indians would venture twenty or thirty miles north, cut down stands of piñon, and float the wood downriver.

To control the abuse of food distribution, the army issued paper ration tickets each day, but the Navajos were able to copy the designs printed on them and generate fraudulent tickets by the thousands. Hoping to combat these forgeries, the army then started manufacturing metal tokens. But the young Navajo blacksmiths, who had only recently learned their craft under American tutelage at the bosque, proved singularly adept at counterfeiting the tokens. The army had to send to Washington for coins whose intricate patterns were finally beyond the Navajos' duplication skills.

Syphilis ran rampant throughout the reservation and the army post alike, the epidemic spread by soldiers who found they could enjoy the services of a Navajo girl for the price of a meal ticket or a pint of cornmeal. Symptoms of the disease were everywhere—strange rashes, patchy hair loss, blindness, the sudden ravings of mental illness. Syphilitic sores were so common that many of the soldiers found it difficult to sit on a horse. The 1st California Cavalry, the outfit to which many of the Fort Sumner soldiers were originally attached, reportedly had the highest incidence of venereal disease of any unit during the Civil War, with army surgeons treating at least 50 percent of the ranks each year.

One officer wrote that the Navajo women "lack the slightest idea of virtue" and suggested that they be kept "as far from the fort as possible," but his recommendation came to little avail. Some Navajo parents coerced their young daughters—as young as twelve or thirteen—to prostitute themselves so their families could have something to eat. Over time, many Navajo women who frequented the soldiers' quarters became pregnant; according to Gerald Thompson, a number of these women, ashamed to be carrying the child of a *bilagaana* soldier, "lost their lives in crude attempts at abortion."

Another constant worry for the Navajos was the threat of raids from Comanche Indians. Bosque Redondo was set on the edge of Comanche country, and once these ancient enemies of the Navajo realized how vulnerable the reservation was to attack, they went on the warpath. The Comanches would swoop in the predawn hours and steal sheep, horses, women, and children. And because Carleton would not allow the Navajos to be adequately armed, they were virtually helpless to defend themselves.

It was an odd reversal of fate: Now the Navajos had become victims of the same menace they had once so successfully visited upon the New Mexicans. The soldiers at Fort Sumner sometimes gave chase to the raiding Comanches, but usually to no avail. The problem became so grave that by late summer General Carleton began to draw up plans for a major military expedition against the Comanches.

The one success story, it seemed, was that bumper crop of tasseled corn basking in the summer heat. The great furrowed field, and the promise it held, was the only thing that kept Bosque Redondo together. There lay the pride and future—if there was any—of Carleton's "grand work."

Only a few weeks before harvest, a soldier inspecting the crop noticed something strange. Little worms, fuzzy and writhing, had infested the stalks. Shucking one of the ears, the inspector saw trouble: The kernels were nubbed and stunted almost beyond recognition, the silk lusterless, the ears rotten. Moving down the long rows, he saw that this ravenous pest, whatever it was, had eaten its way over the whole field. "The cursed insects seem to devour all the grain from the ear," one puzzled officer wrote General Carleton.

What made the scourge surprising, and so pernicious, was that the worm did its work out of sight, deep inside the husk, offering no outward clue of the damage it was causing. As the seemingly healthy stalks grew tall, the ears were slowly being destroyed from within.

After more investigation, the insect was determined to be a cutworm, and it spelled disaster. Army agronomists were at a loss to explain where it had come from, and so were the Navajos. It was as though an Old Testament plague had descended upon them. Not uncommon elsewhere in the United States, the cutworm had never been a problem in the West before; it seemed to have arrived suddenly and opportunistically, with the first introduction of large-scale monoculture.

When Carleton learned about the cutworm, he became frantic. He urged the soldiers to go into the fields and try to remove the worms from each individual husk *by hand*—a laborious and of course completely impractical idea born of desperation. He ordered his men to set out pans of molasses at strategic points in the hope that the sweet, sticky liquid would attract the egg-laying moths and drown them.

He tried everything he could think of to arrest this "visitation from God," as he called it, but it was no use. The corn crop of more than three thousand acres was ruined. The first test had failed. And now, with winter around the corner, it seemed likely that the Navajos would starve.

Chapter 44 ADOBE WALLS

Kit Carson would not have to deal with the consequences of the cutworm blight. By mid-September 1864, his short tenure as reservation superintendent was over. Although he had been at the bosque only three months, Carson was called away on an even bigger assignment, in some ways the biggest assignment of his career: General Carleton ordered him to venture east onto the plains of Texas to lead a large-scale expedition against the Comanches.

That year the Comanches, along with their allies the Kiowas, had been wreaking unprecedented havoc. In addition to their nearly constant attacks on the Navajos at the bosque, the Comanches had been preying on emigrant wagon trains and army caravans along the Santa Fe Trail. According to Capt. George H. Pettis, a California volunteer then serving in New Mexico, these "lords of the southern plains" had "held high carnival . . . There was not a week of that whole season, but that some outrage was committed by them."

The Comanches were now expressly targeting Anglo-Americans. At a place called Walnut Creek in western Kansas, a band of Comanches descended on a wagon train and killed ten white men and scalped two boys alive. In August, Comanches murdered five whites leading a caravan across southwestern Kansas; several Hispanic survivors returned to New Mexico to report that, after the attack, the Comanches boasted they would "kill every white man that came on the road." The Comanches even threatened to kill General Carleton himself if he ever sent a force after them. An army colonel then serving in New Mexico wrote: "You cannot imagine a worse state of affairs than exists now on this route."

The stepped-up rampages of the Comanches may have been an echo effect of the Civil War. Army authorities believed, on the basis of credible evidence, that Texas Confederates had incited the Comanches to attack wagon trains in the hope of disrupting Union supply lines. Whether or not Texans were indeed the ultimate source of the trouble, the Comanches by late summer of 1864 had nearly succeeded in halting the mails and cutting off Carleton from his superiors back east. The general fretted: "We have been greatly embarrassed in getting supplies from the States."

Trying to run an enormous military department during the fevered height of the Civil War, Carleton knew that something had to be done to fend off these attacks. And who better to do it than Carson? He had succeeded against the Mescaleros and the Navajos—why wouldn't he also succeed against the Comanches?

So Carleton gave Carson his next assignment, flattering him that "a great deal of my good fortune in Indian matters here—in fact nearly all—is due to you." Now, the general said, Carson must turn his attention to the Comanches and do his utmost "in punishing these treacherous savages before the winter fairly sets in."

In truth, Carson was physically not up to another campaign in the field. He was now constantly in pain. People who knew him commented on the marked change in his appearance. He'd lost weight and his eyesight was steadily worsening. Like a raisin, he appeared to be wrinkling and withering from within. A close acquaintance wrote that "his face seemed haggard and drawn with pain," as though a disease "had fastened itself upon him."

Carson knew that any campaign against the Comanches was likely to be strenuous as well as risky. He had fought several skirmishes with the Comanches over the years and had enormous respect for their prowess in battle. Arriving on the southern plains sometime in the 1700s, this Shoshone-language people had developed elaborate warrior societies and were known to gather and fight in large numbers. Though Comanches had caused nearly constant troubles since the conquest of 1846, the U.S. Army had sent only one modest punitive mission to fight them in the heart of their own country, but the expedition had returned unsuccessful.

It was an encounter with the Comanches that had produced what was perhaps the most colorful story in the whole compendium of Carsonian tall tales. Sometime in the 1830s, while hunting buffalo on the plains east of Bent's Fort, Carson was surrounded by a large band of Comanches on horseback. While still mounted, he reached around his own mule's neck and slashed its throat with his knife. The mule dropped to the ground and promptly expired. Using the carcass as a makeshift barricade, Carson took up his rifle and proceeded to fight off wave after wave of onrushing Comanches. He could not shoot them all, however, and some of the warriors drew perilously near. But when they did, their horses smelled the fresh blood of Carson's mule and became spooked. They halted in their tracks and would advance no farther. Finally, the exasperated Comanches gave up and galloped away across the prairie.

Whether this story is actually true—Carson doesn't mention it in his memoirs—it was widely told and widely believed. And it served to illustrate a larger truth: Like so many men who had lived and traveled in the Southwest, Carson had nearly lost his life fighting Comanches.

With the possible exception of the Blackfeet, he believed they were the fiercest Native American tribe one could encounter. They'd killed Jedediah Smith and Robert Bent, the youngest of the Bent brothers. They'd killed many other men Carson had known over the decades. Carson did not need to be reminded that the only thing worse than being killed by Comanches was being caught by them: Their tortures were too grotesque to contemplate.

Still, Carson did not hesitate to take on the assignment. In some ways it was the same old pattern; his sense of duty all but compelled him to accept General Carleton's call. Yet there was more to it than that. Carson's three months at Bosque Redondo had convinced him that the Comanches were now the greatest menace in the territory. Their attacks on the struggling and virtually defenseless denizens of the bosque threatened to derail the fragile project he had set in motion, while their depredations on the Santa Fe trail threatened to halt the very supplies necessary to ensure the reservation's immediate survival. He felt he had no choice but to go after them.

For Carson, the Indian wars were thus increasingly assuming a vicious, self-perpetuating pattern: Each engagement seemed to beget another. In order to keep the Navajos and Mescaleros safely on the reservation, he needed to pursue their common enemy. In order to preserve his two earlier victories, he now needed to secure a third.

∽

On November 12, 1864, Carson left New Mexico for the plains of the Texas panhandle with some four hundred men, including seventy-five Utes serving as scouts. His well-armed force was composed of two companies of cavalry, one company of infantry, and a battery of two 12-pounder mountain howitzers. Carson rode a beloved racehorse and wore a thick wool greatcoat.

Unlike during the Navajo campaigns, General Carleton had given Carson wide latitude to direct the course of the action. Carleton made it clear that he wanted no women or children killed—at least not "willfully and wantonly"—but otherwise, it was Carson's fight to win or lose and to prosecute as he saw fit. On the subject of strategy,

Carleton offered few words: "You know where to find the Indians, you know what atrocities they have committed, you know how to punish them." Carleton did not want Carson to make peace, only war. "You know I don't believe much in smoking with Indians," the general wrote. "They must be made to fear us or we can have no lasting peace." At this point, Carleton suggested, all treaties with Indians were but "theatricals simply for effect."

The timing of the expedition was deliberate. Through the summer months and on into early fall, the Comanches lived a scattered existence, roaming the plains in small bands in search of migratory buffalo and whatever loot might present itself. But by mid-November they began to concentrate for the winter, setting up their lodges in extended villages along a few creeks and rivers. This was the time to catch them all in one place, Carleton knew. In their villages they could be "easily overtaken," the general wrote, for they would be encumbered "by their families and by their stores of food." They would be, in other words, sitting ducks.

They marched east for nearly two weeks through chilly but not unbearably cold weather, loosely following the course of the Canadian River. Each night as the men set up camp and bedded down, the Utes erupted in war dances. "Their groans and howlings became almost intolerable, it being kept up each night until nearly daybreak," Captain George Pettis writes in a published article that has proven to be the best account of the expedition.

Tramping over the Staked Plains, the column of men passed the spot where in 1849 Carson had found Ann White's still-warm body. He told the story of that sad day to the officers who rode with him, narrating the events in what Pettis described as a "graphic manner." Literally and figuratively, Carson had been over this same ground, and he seemed to have ominous feelings about what was to come. One night on the march, while the Utes danced and keened their war songs, Carson had a dream about a great bloody battle, with the mountain howitzers thundering in the sky. When he woke up the following morning, he sensed that this battle was at hand.

And he was right. It was November 24, a day that President Lincoln had recently declared a new national "Thanksgiving" holiday. The weather was bright and crisp, the atmosphere "rarefied and electrical," by Pettis's description. That morning Carson's Utes caught sight of the Comanche lodges—tepees of bleached buffalo hide shimmering bone-white on the drab plains. The scouts returned in the afternoon and reported to Carson that large encampments—with many hundreds of Comanches and Kiowas—were sprawled on the south bank of the Canadian River. Carson told his officers that "we will have no difficulty finding all the Indians that we desire."

That night Carson ordered a moonlight march. For hours the men crept along in the blackness. Carson would permit no talking or smoking or unnecessary noise. Around midnight they dropped into the rugged gash of the Canadian River, where they found a deep-worn trail freshly left by the Comanche and Kiowa horses. There they waited in silence until the first streaks of dawn broke across the wintry sky. Rallying his men, Carson threw off his heavy overcoat and tossed it in the brush, to be retrieved later. Then he resumed the march, with his Utes now in the lead, decorated in feathers and painted for war.

◙

As they pushed ahead, the thick grass and driftwood clogging the banks slowed the gunners who pulled the mountain howitzers, and they fell behind the rest of the troops. Carson sent Maj. William McCleave ahead with a company of cavalry to attack a smaller Kiowa village of some two hundred tepees, a kind of suburb of the larger Comanche camps farther downriver. As McCleave and his men charged the village, the Kiowa warriors, led by a chief named Little Mountain, held their ground only long enough to allow their women and children to scatter and hide along the river.

Carson's troops destroyed the village, whose tepees, Pettis said, were found to be "full of plunder, including many hundreds of finely finished buffalo robes." The lodges weren't *entirely* empty, it turned out. A chief named Ironshirt refused to leave and was shot at the door of his tepee. Elsewhere, the Utes found four elderly Kiowas cringing in their tepees; the Utes promptly split their heads open with axes.

It was discovered that the Kiowas had been holding at least three American captives: a Colorado woman and her two children, whom the Indians had kidnapped during a recent attack on a wagon train passing through Kansas. The prisoners were nowhere to be found, but as Carson's soldiers ransacked the village, they found the clothing of an American woman as well as children's clothing and photographs of a Caucasian family. Carson's men made a bonfire of all the belongings they did not seize, including a U.S. Army ambulance and a wagon that had been stolen from a government caravan. Soon the village was engulfed in flames.

In the confusion, Kiowa riders had dashed downriver to the larger constellation of Comanche villages to gather reinforcements. Soon several hundred warriors were massing on the plain, their riders bolting this way and that. Periodically they made what McCleave described as "severe charges." Pettis recalled how the warriors rode "with their bodies thrown over the sides, at a full run, and shooting occasionally under their horses." Far outnumbered now, McCleave had clearly bitten off more than he could chew and realized he needed to find a defensive position.

Not far away, only a few hundred yards from the river, stood an old abandoned fort known as Adobe Walls. The Bents had built it years earlier as a satellite outpost of their then extensive empire, using it as a safehouse from which to carry on trade with the Comanches (who, because of their mutual hostility with other Plains tribes like the Arapaho and Cheyenne, were not allowed to camp near Bent's Fort). Now Adobe Walls was nothing but a tumbledown ruin, its ramparts warped and sagging. Still, it was a well-known landmark on the plains, one that helped wayfayers orient themselves as they rode across the featureless solitudes.

Carson, who had joined McCleave's company in the advance, decided to make the old bastion his base. It was a place he knew well from his years spent working for the Bents, a relic of his younger days as a buffalo hunter. Inside its high crumbling walls, he corralled the

horses while his surgeon hastily set up a hospital. All around the ruins, he had his men sprawl in the high grass and fight as skirmishers.

Then, training his field glasses on the horizon, he saw something
terrifying. Behind the Kiowas, a much larger wave of Indians was assembling. Fourteen hundred warriors, perhaps more, most of them
Comanche, had gathered on horseback and seemed poised to make a
great charge.

Luckily for Carson, the mountain howitzers had caught up to the
company. He ordered the gunners to occupy a knobby hill outside
Adobe Walls and unlimber the two artillery pieces. Then, with a
sweeping gesture toward the mustering warriors, Carson told his artillerymen, "Throw a few shell into that crowd over thar."

"Number one—*Fire!* Number two—*Fire!*" The twin howitzers
boomed, and the Comanches and Kiowas rose high in their stirrups
in astonishment. They waited and listened intently as the first shots
lobbed skyward, then exploded wide and short of their mark. The
warriors wheeled their horses and galloped away. By the fourth firing,
they had moved safely out of range of the shells.

The howitzers had done their work, and the immediate danger
had passed. "They won't make another stand," Carson reassured Pettis. In the welcome lull, Carson ordered his men to gather around
Adobe Walls and then to rest and eat—something they hadn't done in
twenty straight hours.

⌧

The soldiers had a meager haversack lunch of dried meat and hard-
tack—"starvation would be averted for a season at least," one allowed. After lunch, Carson planned to push downriver and attack the
Comanche villages, one by one. But then he noticed something
alarming taking shape on the blond plains. He had been wrong: The
Comanche and Kiowa allies *were* massing again, this time in far
greater numbers. As he watched the situation develop from his remove at Adobe Walls, Carson became increasingly anxious. Three
thousand mounted warriors had emerged from the Comanche villages.

In a few short minutes Carson was facing one of the largest engagements of Native American fighters ever gathered in the West. Certainly Carson had never seen such a concentration of warriors. His men were outnumbered nearly ten to one.

Painted for battle and riding what Carson judged to be "first-class horses," most of the warriors were armed with bows and lances, though many had rifles. Wave after wave raced toward Adobe Walls, then circled back and mounted another assault, firing under the necks of their galloping horses as they constantly revised their angle of approach. For hours the battlefield was enveloped in a haunting chorus of ululations, the mingled war cries of Comanches, Kiowas, and Utes "yelling like demons," as Pettis put it. With each sortie, Carson's men fell farther back to the safety of the ruins, defending their position with a furious crack of carbines and a determined shelling from the howitzers.

Still the Indians kept coming, Carson wrote, "repeatedly charging my command from different points, but invariably repulsed with great loss." One howitzer shell passed cleanly through the body of a warrior's mount (killing the horse, but not the man), and then resumed its trajectory, exploding another hundred yards deeper on the plains. Little Mountain, the Kiowa chief, also had his horse shot out from under him, in his case by rifle fire, yet he continued to exhort his men from the ground. Whenever the warriors drew within range of the mountain howitzers, the Indians were now careful to disperse and attack in smaller numbers so as not to present an easy target for shrapnel. Other warriors dismounted and fought lying down in the high grass, "making it hot for most of us by their excellent marksmanship," Pettis writes.

Watching the fighting, Carson was increasingly alarmed. The Comanches and Kiowas had been aroused to a hornetlike fervor. Carson later said that they "acted with more daring and bravery than I have ever before witnessed."

A young man of the New Mexico Volunteers was lying prone and firing in the grass outside the ruins when a rattlesnake bit him in the hand. He was taken to the hospital, where a doctor cleaned the wound and gave the soldier a drink of whiskey. The dazed New Mexican returned to the fight and later killed a Comanche who had sallied too close. Before the comrades of the deceased warrior could circle back and collect the body, the New Mexican scrambled out to the field and took his scalp. Remarkably, it was the only scalp taken that day.

The battlefield was not without its comedy. Months earlier, one of the Kiowa warriors had somehow acquired an army bugle and learned to play it well. Whenever Carson's own cavalry bugler sounded "advance," the Kiowa, unseen in the dusty throngs of horsemen, would sound "retreat." This caused great confusion until Carson's men finally discerned the location of the mysterious second bugler.

The fighting raged into the afternoon, with many Indian casualties—it was, Carson judged, "a great slaughter." The American wounded, however, numbered fewer than a dozen. This astonishing statistic was owed in part to Adobe Walls itself, which had proven to be a superior defensive position. But it also spoke of Carson's coolness under fire. Throughout the day he urged his men to stay calm and steady, to ignore the warriors abroad on the field and focus on each wave as it came. If they had shown any weakness, if the lines had faltered just once, the Comanches would have overrun them with sheer numbers.

But it was the mountain howitzers that made the crucial difference. If not for their presence on the battlefield, Carson said, "few would have been left to tell the tale." Carson biographer Edwin Sabin surmised that "had it not been for the two cannon, this Thanksgiving time fight might have made Josefa a widow."

Through the afternoon the warriors kept pressing in on all sides. Although he enjoyed a temporary advantage in firepower, Carson knew that he could not hold out indefinitely—and that the Indians could.

∞

Then Carson did something singularly intelligent: He retreated. Some of his officers urged him to push forward and attack the Comanche villages as planned, but he now judged such a move to be foolhardy, if not suicidal. "It was impossible for me to chastise them further at present," he euphemized in his official report.

Speaking more frankly, though, he later admitted to a friend: "The Indians whipped me in this fight."

Executing a retreat would be tricky enough. The column would have to vacate Adobe Walls, slink down to the river, and head west like an ungainly centipede, somehow protecting itself as it slowly backpedaled. His troops assembled in a long column, with the horses held in the middle, skirmishers flanking all sides, and the howitzers poised for use and trundling along in the rear.

The Kiowas and Comanches did not let up—on the contrary, Carson said, they "now commenced the most severe fighting of the day." Through the late afternoon, as the column made its crawl along the Canadian, Carson thought the "Indians charged so repeatedly and with such desperation that for some time I had serious doubts for the safety of my rear." The Comanches started a grass fire along the river and used the smoke as a screen to tear at Carson's flanks without being seen. One of his men was shot and lanced, and many others were injured. The smoke and heat grew so intense that Carson and his men had to climb out of the river valley and march on the bluffs, where at least he could clearly see what he was up against.

At dusk the howitzers were put to use again. The shells whistled in the twilit skies, and finally the warriors began to relent. Satisfied that they had taught this white army a lesson, they rode back along the Canadian toward their villages and their families.

The battle of Adobe Walls was the last fight of Kit Carson's life. By most measurements he had been defeated. The Comanche-Kiowa alliance had resoundingly driven him from the field. Had a few things gone differently, the battle could have ended in the total slaughter of his men, a debacle that would have dwarfed Custer's last stand at Little Bighorn twelve years later.

But luckily for his men, Carson was no dashing glory-hunter. Through his caution and good judgment, he shows us just how differently his martial mind worked from that of George Armstrong Custer. Carson understood that the first definition of victory is survival. He was outnumbered ten to one, on a battlefield that lay two hundred fifty miles from his base. These were not good odds.

And yet his casualties were remarkably low: Only three of his men died that day, and twenty-one reported wounded. The Kiowas and Comanches, on the other hand, had lost more than one hundred warriors, with perhaps as many as two hundred wounded, and Little Mountain's village had been utterly destroyed. One Carson biographer thought the battle was a classic "coup" for Carson in the traditional sense understood on the plains—a victory won "exactly in the style the Indians understood: entering enemy territory, inflicting damage, and retiring with little loss."

General Carleton, when he received word of the battle, went so far as to call Adobe Walls "a brilliant affair," and complimented Carson for the "handsome manner in which you all met so formidable an enemy and defeated him." The general said that Carson's campaign added "another green leaf to the laurel wreath which you have so nobly won in the service of your country."

This was plainly an overoptimistic assessment. But if Adobe Walls was a defeat, Carson was at least able to view it as an acceptable one as he limped home to New Mexico during the last cold week of November. In the confusion of his withdrawal, he had completely forgotten about the greatcoat he had tossed on the ground by the Canadian River, so now he rode wrapped in a buffalo robe that had been taken from the destroyed Kiowa village. Fearing that the Comanches and Kiowas might return, he marched all through the night. The following day, when he finally decided the coast was clear, he gave in to his exhaustion and ordered his men to set up camp. He had been in the saddle for four days straight, and his mount was in sorry shape. When he removed the saddle, the horse's skin came with it.

⊠

Four days later, at another remote location on the southern prairie, another American army descended on a village of Plains Indians. A band of Cheyenne led by a chief named Black Kettle had made their winter camp along Sand Creek in southeastern Colorado, not far from the ruins of Bent's Fort. Because Black Kettle had shown peaceful intentions and a willingness to negotiate, U.S. Army officials had promised to afford him protection that winter and even gave him an American flag to fly over his camp.

But on November 29, a force of Colorado Volunteers appeared on the winter plains. They were led by Col. John Chivington, the former minister who had made a name for himself in the battle of Glorieta. Without provocation, Chivington attacked Black Kettle's village at dawn, ignoring both the American flag and the various swatches of white cloth the Indians held up in desperation. The slaughter was beyond horrendous. More than 150 Cheyenne, mostly women and children, were murdered in cold blood that day, in a massacre that is now widely regarded as the worst atrocity committed in all the Indian wars. When someone questioned Chivington's policy of killing children, the "Fighting Parson" is said to have replied, "Nits breed lice."

Chivington returned to Denver in triumph. At a theater his men paraded their war trophies before the cheering crowds: Scalps, fingers, tobacco pouches made from scrotums, purses of stretched pudenda hacked from Cheyenne women. The Denver newspapers praised the Colorado Volunteers for their glorious victory. "Posterity will speak of me as the great Indian fighter," Chivington gloated, adding, "I have eclipsed Kit Carson."

When Carson learned of the massacre upon his return from Adobe Walls, he was appalled. He knew the Cheyennes well and was personally acquainted with many of the victims. Later, he denounced the massacre during a conversation with Col. James Rusling, an army inspector who, though no sentimentalist on the subject of American Indians, faithfully documented Carson's tirade, dialect and all. "Jis to think of that dog Chivington and his dirty hounds, up thar at Sand Creek," Carson told Rusling.

His men shot down squaws, and blew the brains out of little innocent children. You call sich soldiers Christians, do ye? And Indians savages? What der yer 'spose our Heavenly Father, who made both them and us, thinks of these things? I tell you what, I don't like a hostile red skin any more than you do. And when they are hostile, I've fought 'em, hard as any man. But I never yet drew a bead on a squaw or papoose, and I despise the man who would. I've seen as much of 'em as any man livin', and I can't help but pity 'em, right or wrong. They once owned all this country yes, Plains and Mountains, buffalo and everything. But now they own next door to nuthin, and will soon be gone.

Chapter 45   THE CONDITION OF THE TRIBES

General Carleton was alarmed and even panicked by the crop failure of 1864, and he flew into a frenzy of activity to rush more food and supplies to the bosque. For all his character deficits, it cannot be said that the Christian general lacked a conscience. He realized that if he did not do something drastic, he would be responsible for the deaths of thousands. "These Indians are upon my hands," he wrote. "I cannot see them perish either from nakedness or hunger." Through a relentless campaign of personal persuasion and correspondence, Carleton succeeded in shipping tons of emergency foodstuffs to the bosque. Realizing that the whole experiment was in jeopardy, he wrote Adjutant General Lorenzo Thomas in Washington, pleading for more rations and materials. The Navajos, Carleton wrote, "will upbraid us for having taken their birthright and left them to perish. With other tribes we have acquired ever since the Pilgrims stepped on the shore at Plymouth, this has been done too often. For pity's sake, if moved not by any other consideration, for once treat the Indian as he deserves to be treated."

He ordered four thousand sheep and gave specific instructions on how to economize on the meat. "The whole animal, including what the butchers call head and pluck, must be used," he wrote the commanding officer of the camp. The mutton was to be incorporated into stews, soups, blood puddings, and even haggis. When informed that Navajos did not traditionally eat soup, he insisted that they learn: Soup would be their salvation, and it must become their daily ritual. Said Carleton: "It must be inculcated as a religion."

In the meantime, Carleton urged his officers at Bosque Redondo to try to buoy the spirits of the Navajos. "Tell them," he wrote, "to be too proud to murmur at what cannot be helped. Tell them not to be discouraged but to work hard, every man and woman, to put in large crops next year, when if God smiles upon our efforts, they will, at one bound, be forever placed beyond want and be independent."

From his Santa Fe headquarters, Carleton went into a kind of overdrive. He commissioned the planting of more than 12,000 trees. He ordered that every last glop of bacon grease be saved and reused. He requisitioned 13,000 yards of cloth, 7,000 blankets, 20 spinning wheels, 50 corn mills, and thousands of needles and spools of thread. Upon hearing that feral hounds had become a nuisance, he proclaimed that "all dogs found at large will be shot." To make the farms work more efficiently, he arranged for the delivery of an enormous bronze bell; cast in St. Louis and weighing one thousand pounds, the bell was rung throughout the day to call the Navajos to work and mark the hours, much like steam whistles used in Northern factories, or slave horns on Southern plantations.

Carleton's ideas for improvements kept flowing—he couldn't help himself. "You must pardon me, for suggesting all these details," he wrote one beleaguered officer, "but my anxiety is so great. Every idea which comes into my mind I will send to you and believe that you will enter into the spirit that animates me for the good of the Indians."

⊠

Carleton became increasingly preoccupied with locating Manuelito and coaxing—or forcing—him to surrender. If he could nab the most famous Navajo holdout alive, it would signify the end of all resistance and the triumph of the Bosque Redondo idea. In February 1865, General Carleton sent Navajo runners into Diné country to try to convince Manuelito to emigrate to the reservation. He had been hiding with his band of nearly one hundred warriors and a dwindling number of horses and sheep. But when the runners caught up with him near the Zuni trading post, Manuelito told them again that he would never go to Bosque Redondo. "My God and my mother live here in the west," he says, "and I will not leave them. I could never go far from the Chuska Mountains where I was born."

Hearing of Manuelito's continued defiance, Carleton sent a terse dispatch back to the commander of Fort Wingate: "Try to get Manuelito," he said. "Have him securely ironed. It will be a mercy to others whom he controls to capture or kill him at once. I prefer that he should be captured. If he attempts to escape, he will be shot down."

However, a few months later Manuelito made a surreptitious journey to Bosque Redondo to see for himself what conditions were like. He hardly recognized his own people. Everyone seemed listless, melancholy, in a collective state of shock and depression. Among the Navajos, Bosque Redondo was known as Hwelte—their mispronunciation of the Spanish word *fuerte,* or fort—a word now synonymous in the Navajo language with "a place of suffering." Diseases like smallpox and dysentery were rampant, but the Navajos did not know where to turn for treatment; the traditional healers, lacking their familiar herbs, were increasingly powerless, while the army hospital was a fearful place where, as one headman put it, "all who go in never come out."

Crops were failing again, this time as a result of hailstorms and floods. The turnips had dry rot. Out in the fields, the farm machines

sank in the mud. Some of the rations issued were found to be conta-
minated with ground plaster and rat droppings. Navajo urchins could
be seen crawling in the corrals and stables, sifting the manure in
search of undigested corn to eat.

Manuelito conferred with other headmen of the tribe. He spoke
with Barboncito, the short, bewhiskered medicine man from Canyon
de Chelly who was fast emerging as the most prominent leader of the
Navajos at the bosque. Barboncito was in many ways the antithesis of
Manuelito; he was a serene and reflective man, slight and wiry, with
small agile hands, a diplomat by instinct, and an eloquent public
speaker. But he was an old friend of Manuelito and had fought with
him on that early April morning in 1860 when the Navajos attacked
and nearly overran Fort Defiance. Barboncito made it clear to his old
comrade that he saw no future for the people at Hwelte. "Here I own
nothing but my own body," he said. "I have no stock, I have nothing.
In this place, I know the Great Father is a long way off."

Manuelito was repulsed by the truly pathetic state of his people.
He returned straightaway to Navajo country under cover of night,
despite Carleton's orders that soldiers "must kill all Male Indians
found outside the Reservation without a passport." Manuelito burrowed even deeper into the recesses of his homeland and tried to
keep quiet. But his exile was taking its toll on both him and his followers. With so little food and so many spies hounding him from all
sides, he knew he couldn't hold out forever.

◙

Meanwhile, the four hundred Mescalero Apaches sharing the reservation with the Navajos had come to the end of their patience. Outnumbered by Navajos twenty to one, they were especially miserable
at the bosque. They had refused to send their children to Carleton's
school and had completely given up trying to plant corn. Unlike the
Diné, the Mescaleros had no tradition of agriculture and had come to
view the work required to grow crops—while an interesting novelty
at first—as beneath their dignity. At the most basic level, they did not

understand the life Carleton wanted them to live; and to the extent that they did, they abhorred it.

One day at Bosque Redondo, Cadete, the great Mescalero chief, fell into a conversation with Capt. John Cremony about the Mescalero's view of work. With frank eloquence, Cadete explained his people's disdain for the white man's mode of existence. "You desire our children to learn from books, and say, that because you have done so, you are able to build all those big houses, and sail over the sea, and talk with each other at any distance, and do many wonderful things," Cadete told Cremony, who recorded the conversation in an 1868 article published in the magazine *Overland Monthly*:

> Let me tell you what we think. You begin when you are little to work hard. After you get to be men, you build big houses, big towns, and everything else in proportion. Then, after you have got them all, you die and leave them behind. Now, we call that slavery. You are slaves from the time you begin to talk until you die; but we are free as air. The Mexicans and others work for us. Our wants are few and easily supplied. The river, the wood and plain yield all that we require. We will not be slaves; nor will we send our children to your schools, where they only learn to become like yourselves.

When Cremony tried to debate some of Cadete's points, the captain found it "utterly impossible to make him comprehend the other side of this specious argument." The Mescaleros' hatred of the bosque was so palpable, and their rejection of its day-to-day life so complete, that Cremony thought they were unteachable.

One morning in early November 1865, the soldiers at Fort Sumner awoke to discover that the entire tribe of Mescaleros had bolted from the reservation. The Indians had carefully planned their nighttime breakout, scattering in all directions of the compass, then reconvening in the mountains of their homeland. To effect their escape—and also to pay a parting insult to their hated fellow tenants—the Mescaleros absconded with some two hundred horses owned by the Navajos. The army picket guards scarcely bothered to pursue them, and though embarrassed by the episode, Carleton didn't press the matter.

The Mescalero Apaches never returned to the Round Forest.

⊠

Increasingly, officials both in Santa Fe and Washington were beginning to view the experiment at Bosque Redondo as a tragic, and extremely costly, mistake. Carleton was spending nearly $1 million a year and yet the miserable Navajos had not made the slightest progress toward self-sufficiency. The place was cursed, it seemed. Endless bad news seemed to emanate from the bosque: a scurvy outbreak, measles, floods, more attacks by Comanches, more escapes, more crop failures. The alkaline water was now "saturated with animal and vegetable impurities," according to the post surgeon. The soldiers stationed at Fort Sumner plainly hated the place and found Bosque Redondo a hellhole.

The growing consensus was that the Navajos should all be moved to another location, perhaps back to their own lands, but ideally to somewhere in Oklahoma, the preferred dumping ground for all Indians since the time of Andrew Jackson. Clearly the site on the Pecos, with its barren land and putrid water, was not working—it was literally killing the Navajos. Perhaps the most vocal of the critics was Dr. Michael Steck, New Mexico's superintendent of Indian Affairs. An earlier proponent of the bosque, Steck gradually came to see Carleton's policy as "terribly misguided." He stepped up his attacks on Carleton in the press and even traveled to Washington to make his case, saying that the general would be responsible for the deaths of thousands of Navajos. Steck's more sensible suggestion was to create a Navajo reservation on the Little Colorado River, within the old Navajo country itself. This was more or less what General Canby had had in mind in 1860. Steck thought that if Canby's original plans "had not been broken up by the war, I have little doubt the Navajos would this day be at peace, and supporting themselves, instead of being an enormous tax upon the treasury."

A new superintendent of the camp, A. Baldwin Norton, was appointed in early 1865, and upon surveying the premises, rendered his verdict in no uncertain terms. "If they remain on this reservation, they must always be held there by force, and not from choice," Norton wrote. "The sooner it is abandoned and the Indians removed, the better."

But Carleton would not entertain any criticism of his pet project. He was nearly obsessed with the bosque—Gen. William Sherman said he was "half-crazy on the subject." He argued that the future of New Mexico rested on the long-term success of his experiment, and on whether the United States government "has the determination and ability to hold this formidable tribe." Virtually a dictator now, Carleton was able to squelch dissent by maintaining a state of martial law throughout the territory, even though the threat upon which he'd originally justified it—a possible reinvasion by the Texans—had never materialized. Carleton's many arrogances made him more and more enemies, and the newspapers began to attack and ridicule him. The *Santa Fe Weekly New Mexican* called him "this curse, this clog upon the territory."

A satirist in the *Santa Fe Gazette* penned a popular poem that made fun of Carleton's quixotic experiment on the bosque—

> *Fair Carletonia dressed in flowery pride,*
> *Where the swift Pecos rolls its rushing tide,*
> *Here captive tribes no longer sad but gay,*
> *In honest labor pass the lengthened day.*
> *By interest bound; but by the bonds confined,*
> *The once wild Indian curbs his roving mind,*
> *Bends his whole will at once to earnest toil,*
> *And draws abundance from the virgin soil.*

◎

In April 1865, Lee and Grant signed the armistice at Appomattox and the Civil War ended. Suddenly the environment in Washington changed. Political leaders, having focused for four years on the miseries and devastations of the war, awakened to the reality that yet another war was taking place out west. Two months later Sen. James R. Doolittle of Wisconsin, chairman of a committee investigating the hydraheaded muddle that was U.S. Indian policy, led a congressional junket to the Southwest. In large part he was coming to study the Chivington massacre at Sand Creek as well as the spiraling disaster at Bosque Redondo.

Senator Doolittle interviewed Kit Carson at great length and even spent the night in the Carson home. After dinner the senator pressed him for stories from his old trapping days, and though it took some prodding, Carson did not disappoint. He kept the whole entourage up "far into the small hours of the morning," Doolittle said, with tales of being treed by grizzlies and the like. The senator was smitten. "Knowing him as a bear-hunter and an Indian fighter," Doolittle later wrote, "you can hardly imagine the impression which this most unassuming man with a voice almost feminine in accent and expression made upon us."

In their official interviews—recorded by congressional stenographers and later cleaned up into a lofty prose that could not have been his—Carson had much to say on the subject of Indian affairs. Doolittle clung to his every word, and Carson's ideas were prominently featured in the massive report the Doolittle Committee later produced, entitled *The Condition of the Tribes,* now a classic of Western studies. "I came to this country in 1826," Carson began modestly, "and since that time have become pretty well acquainted with the Indian tribes, both in peace and at war."

His thinking on the subject of Indians had evolved over the past several years. He now seemed to believe that most of the troubles "rose from the aggressions of whites." Carson had nothing but criticism for Chivington and his actions at Sand Creek, which apart from being a cold-blooded mass murder had done nothing to make the people of Colorado more secure; on the contrary, it had set off a chain of aggressions among the tribes of the southern plains, threatening to consume the whole region in war. (Doolittle clearly agreed and soon would describe Chivington's attack to the secretary of the interior as a "treacherous, brutal, and cowardly butchery, an affair in which the blame is on our side.") Unable to continue a military career due to his failing health, Carson seemed more interested in playing a role of diplomat to the tribes of the southern plains. "In view of the treatment they have received," he told Doolittle, "I think that justice demands that every effort should be made to secure peace with the Cheyennes and Arapahoes."

As for Bosque Redondo, Carson had little praise for it, but neither did he see an alternative. The conflict between the New Mexicans and the Navajos was "an hereditary war," one that "had about always existed" with "continual thieving back and forth." At least Carleton's reservation at Bosque Redondo had broken the ancient cycle of violence. "If they were sent back to their own country tomorrow," Carson told Doolittle, "it would not be a month before hostilities would commence again."

Carson moved on to discuss other tribes—Comanches, Jicarillas, and his beloved Utes—and through it all sounded a clear note of alarm that Indians as a race were fast heading for extinction, "due in great measure to their intercourse with white men." They had nowhere to go—white settlers were now everywhere, pressing in from all sides. "Civilization," he said, "encircles them."

Doolittle asked why so many New Mexicans were against Carleton's plan to keep the Navajos at the bosque—what was the real source of the growing criticism? Carson answered with what to Doolittle must have seemed a refreshing honesty. It was because the New Mexican slave traders no longer had reservoirs of slaves to draw from, because the markets were drying up—"because they [the New Mexicans] cannot prey on them as formerly," Carson said.

Doolittle could not help noticing, however, that Carson had his own Navajo servants helping out Josefa around the house. And perhaps, Doolittle also saw little Juan Carson, the Navajo boy who seemed to run around the house just like any other family member. During the weeks ahead, the senator would learn that several thousand Navajos were serving as slaves or peons throughout the New Mexico Territory—

nearly one-third of the census of the entire tribe. In Santa Fe alone there were more than five hundred Navajo servants working in both Spanish and Anglo homes. It was New Mexico's dirty little secret. Doolittle was finally absorbing the uncomfortable truth that the United States, having fought a bloody war in large part to banish the evil of chattel slavery, still had slavery flourishing in various pernicious forms in the West.

◙

The congressional entourage moved on to Santa Fe to question Gen. James Carleton. The general was happy to unburden himself of all his theories on Indian affairs, and also to provide the congressional aides with reams of documents and copies of his personal correspondence. Carleton defended his bosque experiment tenaciously, insisting that the Navajos were being treated "with great kindness." Over time their steady exposure to agriculture and sedentary society would show the Navajos "the evils to which their course of life tends."

Reservations—functioning like "islands in a great sea . . . inviolate to the encroachments of whites"—were the only hope of saving the Indian, Carleton said. Although he had so far been unsuccessful in converting the Navajos, he still believed Christianity would play an important role in their transformation. "The natural decay incident to their race must find its remedy in a power above that of mortals," Carleton wrote in a follow-up questionnaire to Doolittle.

However, Carleton was not optimistic about the future of American Indians. Reservations might slow their demise, but ultimately it was their destiny to die out in the divine battle for survival of the fittest. "In their appointed time," Carleton wrote, "God wills that one race of men—as in the races of lower animals—shall disappear off the face of the earth and give place to another race, and so on in the Great Cycle traced out by Himself, which may be seen but has reasons too deep to be fathomed by us. The races of the Mammoths and Mastodons, and the great Sloths, came and passed away: The Red Man of America is passing away!"

Doolittle was impressed by Carleton, if not exactly enamored of him. But during his time in New Mexico, the senator had heard an earful about the serious problems at Bosque Redondo, and before he left the territory, he paid the reservation a visit. Conditions there were alarming enough that he recommended that the Department of the Interior conduct its own separate inquiry into the bosque—which it soon did.

Both at home and within the army, criticism of Carleton began to mount: allegations of financial irregularities, political favoritism, invasions of civil liberties. People had grown weary of his high-and-mighty posturing and his insufferable lectures. Mainly, though, the criticisms centered around his beloved bosque—the spiraling costs, the failed crops, the unwarranted deaths.

Then, in September 1866, the general received notice that he would be removed from his command by early spring. Carleton protested and asked that a board of inquiry review the case, but General Grant denied his request. The territory rejoiced, and the *Weekly New Mexican* fairly screamed good riddance to "this man Carleton, who has so long lorded it amongst us." Two months later, control of the reservation was officially transferred from the military to the Indian Bureau, which fell under the Department of the Interior.

Carleton was to assume a new post in Louisiana, but continued to argue vehemently that the Navajos should stay at Bosque Redondo. Having invested so much in the experiment, he could not turn loose of it, even as he was exiting the stage. In a sad way, it represented his life's work. Until his death, in fact, he seemed blind to the horrors he had wrought. Three thousand Navajos—one out of every three captives held there—died at Bosque Redondo.

Carleton also failed to acknowledge in his correspondence this conspicuous fact: No gold was ever found in Navajo country.

❖

The bosque's architect was gone, but life there crept miserably on for another year. The same week Carleton received his transfer orders, Manuelito—wounded and starving to death—staggered into Fort Wingate on the edge of Navajo country and gave himself up. He and his band of two dozen emaciated followers had been eating berries and sucking on palmilla roots. One of Manuelito's arms had an infected bullet wound and now hung limply at his side. Manuelito was soon removed to Bosque Redondo, the last of the great Navajo headmen to capitulate.

In the spring of 1868 the Navajos refused to plant altogether. The irrigation ditches ran dry, the fields lay fallow. The Diné had given up. They spent their days gathered around the issue house—"like steel filings around a lodestone," according to one account—waiting for the daily dole.

Yet in late May there were rumors circulating through the reservation that an important *bilagaana* was coming to the bosque. He was from the place they called Washington and knew the Great White Father himself. Barboncito, the Navajo medicine man, had been told that this leader, whoever he was, planned to make important decisions about the future of the Navajos.

Their fate would rest in his hands.

Chapter 46   CROSSING PURGATORY

That same week, Kit Carson lay two hundred miles away on a pallet of buffalo robes, on the dirt floor of his doctor's quarters. He was propped up in an awkward, half-sitting posture, one that allowed him to breathe more easily. For the last few days he had been spitting up blood. His physician, Dr. Henry Tilton, had told him that bloody sputum would be the sure sign of his condition's final stages—proof that his aneurysm was leaking into his trachea. And so now, with each raspy cough, Carson could not help studying his own spit, with a kind of dreadful curiosity, to see how much time he had left.

He was at a dreary place called Fort Lyon, an army outpost in southeastern Colorado Territory on the Arkansas River, not far from the site of Bent's Fort. Dr. Tilton, the young post surgeon at Fort

Lyon, had decided to bring Carson here so he could watch him around the clock. Outside the one-room stone house, spring had finally arrived. Along the river, the cottonwoods issued new green leaves. Just a few hundred yards away, the Arkansas ran swollen with Rocky Mountain snowmelt.

Carson could press against his lower neck and feel a bulge steadily growing. His upper chest was under pressure, his heart often raced, and at times he thought he was suffocating. His air passages constantly seized with spasms. To ease his cough, he'd been given a bottle of opium distilled in a syrup of wild cherry, and to regulate his heartbeat he took a tincture of a muscle sedative called veratrum. When the pain became too great, Dr. Tilton knelt at his side to administer chloroform. The doctor warned him that the chloroform itself might kill him, that it was hard to know precisely what dosage might be lethal.

Carson did not care. "He begged me not to let him suffer such tortures," Dr. Tilton later wrote, "and if I killed him by attempting relief, it would be much better than death by suffocation."

"What am I to do?" Carson said at one point. "I can't get along without a doctor."

Dr. Tilton assured him that he would not leave his side. "I'll take care of you."

"You must not think I'm going to live long," Carson said with a smile. "If it wasn't for *this*," he said, thumping his chest, "I might live to be a hundred."

In the intervals when he was feeling better, Carson had spent much of the past few weeks listening to his own story. Dr. Tilton had a copy of *The Life and Adventures of Kit Carson, the Nestor of the Rocky Mountains, From Facts Narrated by Himself.* It was the first Carson biography, published by DeWitt Peters in 1859. Dr. Tilton would read passages from the book, and Carson would lie quietly on his buffalo hides, sometimes smoking his pipe, thinking about the old days. The Peters book was full of gross exaggeration and passages of purple prose—Carson had always said that "Peters laid it on a little thick"— but now he didn't care. He had grown fond of the young surgeon and enjoyed the little ritual they shared.

"With the hero for my auditor," Dr. Tilton wrote, "I read Peters' book . . . and from time to time he would comment on the incidents of his eventful life. It was wonderful to read of the stirring scenes, the thrilling and narrow escapes, and then look at the modest but dignified little man who had done so much."

Though he'd lived a full life, Carson knew he had little to show for it. He had spent the past week drawing up a will, in which he estimated that his assets amounted to nine thousand dollars, mostly in promissories other people owed him. In fact, Carson was destitute, and now he despaired for his family. He had seven living children, three boys and four girls. The youngest, Josefita, was only eleven days old.

The Carson children were happy and spirited enough, but they were, he was embarrassed to admit, quite unruly. Carson had never been much of a disciplinarian, and he regretted it now. A few years earlier General Sherman had visited the Carson household while making an inspection tour of the West and found the Carson kids "as wild and untamed as a brood of Mexican mustangs . . . running through the room half clad and boisterous." Carson confided to Sherman his concern for his children's education; the schools in New Mexico were poor, and he could not afford to send them back east. "I fear I've not done right by them," Carson told Sherman.

His children were only five miles away, but it was hard for his family to visit him. They were staying in the three-room house where he and Josefa had been living for the past year, in a tiny settlement called Boggsville, which was situated near the place where the Purgatory River flows into the Arkansas. To get to Fort Lyon they had to brave the swift, bone-wincingly cold currents of *both* rivers, a trek that was impractical and not a little dangerous. And in truth, Carson found it painful to see his family; he didn't want them to remember him like this.

But one day two of his sons came to visit—William, the oldest at fourteen, and seven-year-old Charles. The boys wanted to see their father one more time before he died.

Carson sat up and gave it his best, but he was soon exhausted. As a parting gift, he sent William and Charles over to the Fort Lyon sutler's store to be outfitted with new hats. The boys said their awkward good-byes and forded the Arkansas. They were proud of their new acquisitions—Little Charles, especially—and cocked them jauntily to their heads.

Then, a few miles to the west, they came to the Purgatory. While they were crossing the river in a wagon, a gust of wind blew Charles's hat off his head and dropped it into the cold river. It shot downstream, spinning like a waterbug on the surface, and drifted away.

Although he now was a pauper on his deathbed, Christopher Carson could take comfort in the fact that he had finally become a general—possibly the only illiterate general in American history. Three years earlier President Lincoln had approved his promotion to the rank of Brevet Brigadier General of Volunteers. It was a well-deserved honorific, but it didn't actually mean much. The "brevet" status conferred neither greater pay nor heightened authority; it just meant that people were supposed to call him "general," which they were more than happy to do, even though Carson found it a little embarrassing. Once, when someone slipped up and called him "colonel," Carson replied, "Oh, call me Kit and be done with it." Carson attributed his rise within the army to good connections and serendipity. "My damn luck—thar's the difficulty," he once said. "It places me in positions I'm no more fit to fill than I'm fit to fill a pulpit."

General Carson had spent the three and a half years since the battle of Adobe Walls almost ceaselessly on the move. He had lived in a succession of cheerless army outposts—Fort Union, Fort Garland, now Fort Lyon. He had led negotiations with various Plains tribes. He had traveled to St. Louis to confer with Gen. John Pope and General Sherman. In his final years, the old warrior had taken on an unfamiliar new role for himself—that of peacemaker. On these and other sojourns, his health did not permit him to ride horseback; he usually traveled in an army ambulance. "I am now quite old and worn out," he wrote a relative, "and hardly my own master."

His most recent trip, in the late winter and early spring of 1868, had taken him to Washington, where he helped negotiate a treaty creating a permanent reservation for the Utes. The trek was extremely difficult for someone in his condition, and Dr. Tilton had warned him against making it. Carson especially hated to leave Josefa, who was seven months pregnant, but Chief Ouray and the other Ute leaders—who called him "Father Kit"—convinced him to be their advocate at the negotiations. Besides, Carson wanted to consult with a prominent doctor back east to seek a definitive diagnosis and, if one existed, a cure.

The general took a series of stagecoaches to Kansas, then rode by train to Washington. The treaty was quickly concluded, and Carson led the Utes all over the capital city. They took Turkish baths, visited President Andrew Johnson in the White House, and gawked at the growing obelisk of the Washington Monument, whose construction had been interrupted by the Civil War. Everywhere he went, people fussed over "the general," but the crowds were more respectful now. They could see he was suffering.

For once, Carson seemed to enjoy the attention. He had come to accept his celebrity and was even a bit amused by it. He had long since given up fighting the fictions of the dime novels. The phenomenon was bigger than he was—why not enjoy it? When offered a copy of a recently published blood and thunder, he put on his spectacles and studied the cover for a minute. It showed an image of Carson with his arm draped around the slender waist of a beautiful buxom girl, surrounded by the corpses of countless freshly killed savages from whose clutches he had just rescued her.

Carson put down the book and said, "Gentlemen, that thar may be true, but I hain't got no recollection of it." And then he winked.

At the War Department, Carson met with generals Phil Sheridan and William Sherman. Sherman was preparing to travel west as part of a special commission to make treaties with numerous tribes. Among other ambitious projects, he and his fellow commissioners would be visiting New Mexico to consider closing down Bosque Redondo. During their visit in Washington, Sherman in all likelihood discussed the Navajo predicament with Carson. They were old friends, after all, and both had led scorched-earth campaigns that would, each in its way, leave long historical wakes.

There is some evidence that Carson had slowly come to recognize the massive failure of the bosque. Having now successfully created a reservation for the Utes in their own homeland, perhaps Carson had come to see the wisdom of allowing the Navajos to return to their native country as well. One writer who kept a diary while accompanying Sherman out west claimed that Carson told Sherman: "General, I'm not so sure the Great Spirit means for us to take over Indian lands. Let me lead them back while they still have the will to live." The possibility that Carson had undergone a complete reversal is tantalizing, but the provenance of this quote seems fishy. Certainly it doesn't sound much like Carson.

One day Carson sat for several portraits with the famous Civil War photographer Mathew Brady in his Washington studio. In the photographs, Carson is dressed in a handsome black suit. He looks like a dignified elder statesman, with a touch of gray in his hair and mustache, but his face is withered, his eyes hardened by pain. There is an unfamiliar tightness in his bearing, as though he is summoning every ounce of energy to pull himself together long enough for the camera shutter to snap.

While staying in Washington, Carson met with his old boss, John C. Fremont, still prominent in Republican Party circles though now financially ruined, his reputation tarnished by shady business deals. Fremont was thrilled to see his beloved scout but found him "greatly altered by suffering." He gave Carson the name of a specialist in New York, Dr. Lewis Albert Sayre, and told him to make an appointment straightaway.

Carson took the train to Manhattan and stayed with some of the Ute chiefs in the Metropolitan Hotel on Broadway. Dr. Sayre had only bad news for Carson: The diagnosis Dr. Tilton had given him back in Colorado—an aneurysm of the aorta—was correct. He could die at any moment, and there was nothing the good doctor could do for him. Dr. Sayre thought the general might postpone his death a little by resting, avoiding excitement, and eschewing alcohol. (Whether they discussed the likely agent of the aneurysm is unclear, but Dr. Sayre would have known that it was most improbable for an aneurysm to have been caused, as Carson always believed, by injuries sustained in that long-ago tumble with his horse. High blood pressure was a more likely cause, though an aneurysm can also be a symptom of syphilis, a disease that Carson might have contracted during his trapping days.)

Shaken by his visit with Dr. Sayre, Carson returned to the Metropolitan. One night, he had a dream that he was dying. He felt his breath leaving him, and the bed seemed to rise, bearing him toward heaven. He woke up in a sweat, with one of the Ute chiefs cradling his head. "You called your Lord Jesus," the chief said. Carson, who had always been private about his beliefs, had no knowledge of having called on Christ. "But," he said, "it's only Him that can help me where I stand now."

Carson was impatient to meet his double deadline—of not only getting home to Josefa alive but getting there in time for her delivery. Before he could leave New York, however, there was one last person he had to see. Jessie Benton Fremont came down from her home on the Hudson and met him in Manhattan at the house of a friend on Madison Square. Carson was so weak he could stand up only by leaning on the shoulder of an escort. "I'm alive yet!" he told Jessie. They embraced and reminisced about old times, but after a few minutes he was out of breath. "If I died out here, it would kill Josefa," he told Jessie. "I must get home, and I think I can do it."

Carson made a short train trip to Boston and possibly consulted another doctor there. Then he rode the new Union Pacific Railroad all the way to Cheyenne, Wyoming, and took a stagecoach to Denver, where he had to stop and rest in a hotel. Each day crowds of well-wishers held vigil outside his window. When he emerged in slightly better health three days later, the general stood up on a dry goods box and thanked the people of Denver for their prayers. Most of the way home he rode in an open wagon, lying in the back wrapped in blankets. Josefa met him with a carriage in the tiny Colorado town of La Junta on April 11, and they hurried home to their three-room house.

Two days later she gave birth to a baby girl. Carson named her Josefita, after her mother.

⊠

Carson was so frail from his cross-country odyssey that he could scarcely hold his new daughter. He spent the next two weeks lying on the floor of his house, on a pallet of blankets, sometimes lost in an opium haze. Dr. Tilton thought the trip had all but killed him. The aneurysm had "progressed rapidly," Tilton wrote, "and the tumor, pressing on the pneumogastric nerves and trachea, caused frequent spasms of the bronchial tubes which were exceedingly distressing."

Josefa was not feeling well, either. She was suffering from complications related to childbirth, an infection of some kind. Her fever would not go away. When Dr. Tilton saw her, he could only describe her as a woman "who had evidently been very handsome," but sickness had leached the beauty from her face.

On the evening of April 27, Josefa must have been feeling better, for somehow she summoned the strength to rise and interact with her children. Teresina, who was thirteen, came to her, and for a few moments she brushed her daughter's hair. Suddenly the bottom dropped from her spirit. "Cristobal, come here!" Josefa cried out. Carson rose from his pallet in another room and shuffled to her as fast as he could.

Her eyes were vacant. "I'm very sick," Josefa said. Then she died in his arms.

She was buried in a garden five hundred yards from the house, near the banks of the Purgatory. Carson was wrecked with grief. "He just seemed to pine away after mother died," Charles Carson recalled years later.

He wrote to Ignacia Bent in Taos and summoned her to come take care of his motherless children. Shortly after Ignacia arrived he began to cough up blood, and Dr. Tilton urged him to cross over to the fort before the rivers rose any higher.

On the afternoon of May 23, Carson rallied. He told Dr. Tilton he was hungry—not for the thin broths and meager gruels he had been subsisting on, but something substantial. He wanted a big buffalo steak like old times, cooked rare, maybe served up with a mess of red chili like he always preferred it. And a big pot of coffee. And after that, a smoke from his clay pipe.

Dr. Tilton got to it, and soon the general had his request. He ate and smoked his fill, there on the floor, sprawled on his buffalo robes. Then, at 4:25 in the afternoon, he started coughing violently, and blood spouted from his lips. The aneurysm had ruptured. Carson yelled out, "Doctor, *compadre, adios!*"

Dr. Tilton rushed to his side. "I supported his forehead on my hand," he wrote, "while death speedily closed the scene."

Other friends appeared in the room. Tilton shook his head. "This is the last of the general," he said.

They took his body across the Arkansas, across the Purgatory, and laid him beside Josefa, the dirt still disturbed from her burial. They were married twenty-five years, and died less than a month apart. At Fort Lyon, a bugler played taps and the flag was flown at half-mast.

Four days later the *Rocky Mountain News* in Denver ran a notice of Carson's death: "Over what an immense expanse of plains, of snow-clad sierras, of rivers, lakes, and seas, has he cut the first paths? His guiding instinct was an innate chivalry. He had in him a personal courage which came forth when wanted, like lightning from a cloud."

And Monster Slayer said, "Some things should be left as they are. Perhaps it is better for all of us in the long run that certain enemies endure."

—FROM *DINÉ BAHANE,*
THE NAVAJO CREATION STORY

Epilogue   IN BEAUTY WE WALK

On a bright morning in late May, the same week that Kit Carson died, several thousand Diné gathered on the plains of Bosque Redondo, away from the Pecos, out on the hard, bright ground where they could all see one another. A chant rose up from their midst, a song that slowly built on itself as the collective energy took hold. Then, the Navajos began to clack stones together, and a clear pulse ran through the tribe.

The sound of the clicking rocks puzzled the soldiers over at Fort Sumner. At first they feared it was the first stirrings of an insurrection, and they climbed to the rooftops of the Issue House to investigate. From there they watched a strange scene unfold.

The Navajos had formed a circle several miles in diameter, so large that any person standing on the circumference could look across the plains and see only tiny human dots on the circle's opposite side. Then, taking small, measured steps, they began to close the ring. As they stepped forward, the Navajos continued to chant and clack their rocks. Slowly, the circle began to shrink on the plain, tightening like a great noose.

In the center, a young coyote stood up and began to run in fright. As the circle closed up, the coyote ran frantically this way and that, until it finally understood it had nowhere to go: It was trapped inside a human corral.

Whether out of sheer terror or an instinct to feign death, the coyote lay down. Then Barboncito, the small, bearded medicine man from Canyon de Chelly, stepped inside the circle and approached the trembling animal. Several others helped him hold the coyote down. Barboncito opened his medicine bag and removed a bead of abalone shell. Carefully, he placed the white bead in the coyote's mouth and began to pray over the animal.

The chanting and the percussion of the rocks stopped, and in the silence, each person on the circumference slowly backpedaled: The great noose was opening up again.

Barboncito was keen to see in which direction the coyote would run. That was the purpose of the ceremony, in fact. It was an ancient ritual, one that Navajo medicine men performed only in extreme circumstances, to look for signs that concerned the future of the tribe.

Suddenly Barboncito and the others pulled away, and the coyote sprang up. It looked confused at first. And then it turned in the direction Barboncito had hoped. The coyote bolted across the thickets of cholla and mesquite, and escaped from the confines of the human circle.

It was running headlong toward the west.

◙

A few days later, on May 28, 1868, Gen. William Sherman arrived at Bosque Redondo with his entourage from the Great Peace Commission. He stepped from his carriage and strode briskly about the reservation, taking mental note of everything he saw. Now forty-eight years old, Sherman was a ruddy, craggy, self-assured figure who moved with the brusque manner of a man who had seen nearly everything there was to see in the department of human misery and could not be easily impressed.

He must have known that his friend Kit Carson had died five days earlier. Everyone in New Mexico had heard the news, and all over the territory, flags were flying at half-mast. Sherman understood that with Carson's passing, an era had ended and a new one had begun. "Kit Carson was a good type of a class of men most useful in their day," Sherman later wrote, "but now as antiquated as Jason of the Golden Fleece, Ulysses of Troy, the Chevalier La Salle of the Lakes, Daniel Boone of Kentucky, all belonging to a dead past."

Carson helped to put the Navajos here, and now Sherman had the authority to undo what his friend had done. He had been given an extraordinary power and was not timid about using it. Navajo women clutched at his coat as he moved about the reservation. Everywhere he went the Navajos struggled to get a glimpse of the great and powerful man.

Sherman was no softhearted advocate for the Indians, but he could see that the reservation was an abject failure, that the Navajos were despondent and the farms fallow. "I found the Bosque a mere spot of grass in the midst of a wild desert," he later wrote, "and that the Navajos had sunk into a condition of absolute poverty and despair."

General Sherman joined the other members of the commission in one of the buildings on the grounds of Bosque Redondo. There they met a small delegation of Navajo headmen, led by Barboncito and Manuelito. Two Spanish interpreters translated the proceedings, and army stenographers recorded everything.

General Sherman rose and spoke first. "The Commissioners are here now for the purpose of learning all about your condition. General Carleton removed you here for the purpose of making you agriculturalists. But we find you have no farms, no herds, and are now as poor as you were four years ago. We want to know what you have done in the past and what you think about your reservation here."

Barboncito stood up to answer for the Navajos. The Diné had finally come to realize the importance the *bilagaana* placed on having a leader, a single representative of the whole tribe. They regarded Barboncito as their most eloquent spokesman. He had great poise, a calmness at the center of his being. But an unmistakable passion also rose from his words and gestures. As he talked, his long whiskers bristled and his tiny hands danced. He spoke for a long time, and Sherman let him go on without interruption.

Barboncito said that he viewed General Sherman not as a man but as a divinity. "It appears to me," he said, "that the General commands the whole thing as a god. I am speaking to you, General Sherman, as if I was speaking to a spirit."

The medicine man continued. "We have been living here five winters," he said. "The first year we planted corn. It yielded a good crop, but a worm got in the corn and destroyed nearly all of it. The second year the same. The third year it grew about two feet high when a hailstorm completely destroyed all of it. For that reason none of us has attempted to put in seed this year. I think now it is true what my forefathers told me about crossing the line of my own country. We know this land does not like us. It seems that whatever we do here causes death."

Barboncito then explained to Sherman his aversion to the prospect of moving to a new reservation in Oklahoma, an idea that the government authorities had lately been floating among the Navajos. "Our grandfathers had no idea of living in any other country except our own, and I do not think it right for us to do so. Before I am sick or older I want to go and see the place where I was born. I hope to God you will not ask me to go to any other country except my own. This hope goes in at my feet and out at my mouth as I am speaking to you."

Sherman was visibly touched by Barboncito's words. "I have listened to what you have said of your people," he told Barboncito, "and I believe you have told the truth. All people love the country where they were born and raised. We want to do what is right."

Then Sherman said something that gave Barboncito his first stab of hope. "We have got a map here which if Barboncito can understand, I would like to show him a few points on." It was a map of Navajo country, showing the four sacred mountains and other landmarks Barboncito immediately recognized.

Sherman continued, "If we agree, we will make a boundary line outside of which you must not go except for the purpose of trading." Sherman carefully showed Barboncito the line he was considering and warned him of the dire consequences of straying beyond it. "You must know exactly where you belong. And you must not fight anymore. The Army will do the fighting. You must live at peace."

Barboncito tried to contain his joy but could not. The tears spilled down over his mustache. "I am very well pleased with what you have said," he told Sherman, "and we are willing to abide by whatever orders are issued to us."

He told Sherman that he had already sewn a new pair of moccasins for the walk home. "We do not want to go to the right or left," he said, "but *straight back to our own country!*"

A few days later, on June 1, a treaty was drawn up. The Navajos agreed to live on a new reservation whose borders were considerably smaller than their traditional lands, with all four of the sacred mountains outside the reservation line. Still, it was a vast domain, nearly twenty-five thousand square miles, an area nearly the size of the state of Ohio. After Barboncito, Manuelito, and the other headmen left their X marks on the treaty, Sherman told the Navajos they were free to go home.

June 18 was set as the departure date. The Navajos would have an army escort to feed and protect them. But some of them were so restless to get started that the night before they were to leave, they hiked ten miles in the direction of home, and then circled back to camp—they were so giddy with excitement they couldn't help themselves.

The next morning the trek began. In yet another mass exodus, this one voluntary and joyful, the entire Navajo Nation began marching the nearly four hundred miles toward home. The straggle of exiles spread out over ten miles. Somewhere in the midst of it walked Barboncito, wearing his new moccasins.

When they reached the Rio Grande and saw Blue Bead Mountain for the first time, the Navajos fell to their knees and wept. As Manuelito put it, "We wondered if it was *our* mountain, and we felt like talking to the ground, we loved it so."

They continued marching in the direction the coyote had run, toward the country they had told their young children so much about. And as they marched, they chanted—

> *Beauty before us*
> *Beauty behind us*
> *Beauty around us*
> *In beauty we walk*
> *It is finished in beauty*

A NOTE ON THE SOURCES

When I began working on this book in early 2002, I had little notion of what a grand and exhausting adventure of research I'd signed on for. Keeping track of the extraordinary Christopher Carson and his movements over the American West is a far-flung enterprise—requiring transcontinental goose chases that are grueling even when you don't have to do them on a mule. Over the past four years I've put something like 20,000 trip miles on my diesel Jetta and consulted approximately 500 sources—contemporary journals and diaries, collections of personal papers, official army reports, frontier post returns, manuscripts, monographs, and academic articles as well as published books—nearly all of which are cited in the Selected Bibliography.

I'm especially indebted to the historical collections housed at the following institutions: the Huntington Library in San Marino, California; the Beinecke Rare Book and Manuscript Library at Yale University; the National Archives in College Park, Maryland; the Library of Congress in Washington, D.C.; the Bancroft Library at the University of California, Berkeley; the Zimmerman Library's Center for Southwest Research at the University of New Mexico in Albuquerque; the Southwest Reading Room of the Santa Fe Library; and the Fray Angelico Chavez History Library and Photographic Archive in Santa Fe. Also of vital importance were the exhaustive Frank McNitt Papers, housed at the State Archives in Santa Fe.

This book is based primarily on firsthand documents and contemporary accounts, but I would like to cite a few of the secondary sources that proved most influential in shaping my narrative. Foremost among these is *Kit Carson and the Indians* by Tom Dunlay, the most thoroughly researched and original work of scholarship on Carson to date. I would urge anyone who seeks to become a student of Carson to start with Dunlay—he's the gold standard. Another eminence in the field, Marc Simmons, has been steadily teasing new details from the Carson story for decades. I especially relied on Simmons's *Kit Carson and His Three Wives*, a study of Carson's strained and sometimes tragic home life.

I also owe a debt of gratitude to Dwight Clarke for his groundbreaking biography of Stephen Watts Kearny, *Soldier of the West*. Kearny is one of the most pivotal, and yet least known, figures of the American West, and Clarke's book has done much to put the general back on the map where he belongs.

With respect to Navajo culture, three books proved especially illuminating: *The Navajo* by Kluckhohn and Leighton, *The Navajos* by Ruth Underhill, and *The Book of the Navajo* by Raymond Friday Locke. One other Navajo book I must mention in a category all by itself: a strange and beautiful (and sexually frank!) gem of oral history called *Son of Old Man Hat*, which comes as close as anything I've read to painting a picture of what Navajo life must have been like before the coming of the Americans.

Only one man has approached the grim subject of the Navajo wars with the sensibility and seriousness of a scholar, and that's Frank McNitt, author of the comprehensive *Navajo Wars*, among other books. For anyone who wants to understand the root causes and cultural nuances of this ancient conflict, all roads lead to McNitt.

On the subject of John C. Fremont: Apart from his memoirs and expedition reports, I leaned heavily on two works of recent vintage: Tom Chaffin's *Pathfinder*, which manages through sound scholarship and clear writing to refract Fremont's melodramas through a modern lens; and David Roberts's *A Newer World*, a fascinating study of Fremont's strange double-helix relationship with Carson.

Finally, I want to cite four books that stand out in the necessarily morose and sometimes overly maudlin literature of the Long Walk experience: *The Army and the Navajo* by Gerald Thompson; *Navajo*

Roundup by Lawrence Kelly; *The Long Walk* by Lynn Bailey; and *Navajo Stories of the Long Walk Period*, an oral history compiled by Ruth Roessel. These books paint an unflinching portrait of a tragic experiment whose impact is lasting and profound—not just for the Navajos, but for the nation's soul.

NOTES

Prologue: Hoofbeats

1 **They had heard from their priest . . .** See Dwight Clarke, *Stephen Watts Kearny: Soldier of the West*, p. 144.

2 **Las Vegas was punctured by the sound of hoofbeats . . .** Reports of the Las Vegas raid appear in several Army of the West diaries, including W. H. Emory's *Lieutenant Emory Reports*, p. 49.

2 **The raiders came boiling out of the mountains . . .** For descriptions of Navajo raid culture, weaponry, and martial dress, see Underhill, *The Navajos*, pp. 76–78; and Kluckhohn and Leighton, *The Navajo*, pp. 34–41.

3 **Many of them wore strange, tight-fitting helmets . . .** Edward Sapir, *Navajo Texts*, p. 413.

3 **they drove their herds on networks of tiny trails . . .** See Lynn Bailey, *The Long Walk*, p. 3.

BOOK ONE: THE NEW MEN

Chapter 1 Jumping Off

8 **He was a man of odd habits and superstitions.** See Vestal, *Kit Carson: The Happy Warrior of the Old West*, p. 119.

8 **"His saddle, which he always used as a pillow . . ."** Brewerton, *Overland with Kit Carson*, pp. 64–65.

9 **"a beauty of the haughty, heart-breaking kind . . ."** Garrard, *Wah-to-yah and the Taos Trail*, p. 181.

9 **"So this is the distinguished Kit Carson . . ."** Tom Dunlay, *Kit Carson and the Indians*, p. 21.

9 **"sharp little barks of laughter . . ."** Ibid., p. 341.

10 **"the prettiest fight I ever saw . . ."** Carson, *Kit Carson's Autobiography*, p. 52.

10 **chasing down his enemies as "sport."** Ibid., p. 101.

10 **"a perfect butchery."** Ibid., p. 95.

12 **"When we would go to school . . ."** *Kansas City Star*, September 13, 1952.

13 **"I jumped to my rifle . . ."** Guild and Carter, *Kit Carson: A Pattern for Heroes*, p. 10.

14 **"anxious to see different countries."** Carson, *Autobiography*, p. 5.

14 **"The business did not suit me."** Ibid., p. 4.

14 "Well, what do you have to say for yourself ?" *Kansas City Star*, September 13, 1952.

15 "Notice is hereby given . . ." Sabin, *Kit Carson Days*, vol. 1, p. 12.

16 Andrew Broadus was "perfectly well." Carson, *Autobiography*, p. 5.

18 the still-hot liver . . . seasoned with bile . . . See Lavender, *Bent's Fort*, p. 98.

18 "Meat's meat." Vestal, *Kit Carson: The Happy Warrior of the Old West*, p. 49.

18 "shed rain like an otter . . ." Lavender, *Bent's Fort*, p. 81.

18 "The whole operation is full of exposures . . ." Ibid., p. 46.

20 they competed in telling legendary whoppers . . . See Vestal, *Kit Carson: The Happy Warrior of the Old West*, p. 61.

20 "It is a matter of vanity and ambition . . ." Washington Irving, *Adventures of Captain Bonneville*, p. 69.

21 Run, and they follow; follow, and they run. Vestal, *Kit Carson: The Happy Warrior of the Old West*, p. 70.

21 "the hills were covered with Indians." Carson, *Autobiography*, p. 10.

21 "straight through the nipple . . ." Vestal, *Kit Carson: The Happy Warrior of the Old West*, p. 47.

Chapter 2 The Glittering World

22 "people of the great planted fields." Locke, *The Book of the Navajo*, p. 164; Underhill, *The Navajos*, p. 4.

22 "a very bellicose people . . . who occupy all frontiers . . ." Frank McNitt, *Navajo Wars*, p. 6.

22 "heathens who kill Christians . . ." Ibid., p. 15.

23 "their crimes, their audacity, . . ." Iverson, *Diné: A History of the Navajos*, p. 28.

23 literally chaining them to church pews . . . *indios barbaros*. Locke, *The Book of the Navajo*, p. 182.

23 "they have been raised like deer." McNitt, *Navajo Wars*, p. 28.

23 "one never reaches the end of it." Ibid., p. 6.

23 "The war with the Navajos is slowly consuming the Department . . ." Ibid., p. 90.

24 The Navajos did not have a concept of the devil . . . See Locke, *The Book of the Navajo*, p. xi.

24 The Navajos believed in a class of witches called "skinwalkers . . ." See Preston, *Talking to the Ground*, pp. 165–69.

25 a preparation . . . collected from the eyes of an eagle . . . Kluckhohn and Leighton, *The Navajo*, p. 313.

25 If a coyote crossed their path, . . . For an excellent compendium of Navajo do's and don'ts, see Ernie Bulow, *Navajo Taboos*.

26 the slow and watchful life known . . . as *transhumance*. Underhill, *The Navajos*, p. 60.

26 On the Santa Fe Trail, one Navajo blanket . . . Lavender, *Bent's Fort*, p. 156.

27 the Navajos found that the tough and surefooted *churro* sheep . . . Underhill, *The Navajos*, p. 38.

27 They were the great in-betweeners, hard to pin down, . . . See Ibid., p. 23.

28 **Their creation story, called the Emergence . . .** For a full English translation from the Navajo, see Paul Zolbrod, *Diné Bahané: The Navajo Creation Story.*

28 **is thought . . . to be an allegory for their long migration from Canada.** See Preston, *Talking to the Ground,* p. 70.

29 **the Navajos call this intentional flaw the "spirit outlet."** Locke, *The Book of the Navajo,* p. 34; and Kluckhohn and Leighton, *The Navajo,* p. 201.

29 **Navajo warriors were careful not to take** *all* **the sheep . . .** Underhill, *The Navajos,* p. 79.

Chapter 3 The Army of the West

30 **"The raw material is good enough, . . ."** Clarke, *Stephen Watts Kearny: Soldier of the West,* p. 110.

30 **"We would rather hear of your falling . . ."** Hughes, *Doniphan's Expedition: Containing an Account of the Conquest of New Mexico,* p. 28.

30 **"Death before dishonor . . ."** Ibid., p. 29.

32 **The corpse was wrapped in a blanket, . . .** For a full description of an Army of the West prairie funeral, see Jacob Robinson, *Sketches of the Great West: A Journal of the Santa Fe Expedition,* p. 15.

32 **"boundless plains, lying in ridges . . ."** Hughes, *Doniphan's Expedition,* p. 30.

33 **when the ink in his fountain pen froze solid . . .** Clarke, *Stephen Watts Kearny,* p. 81.

33 **the "soaring eagle of your fame."** Ibid., p. 66.

34 **"You have many enemies about you but this is the greatest . . ."** Hunt, *Major General James H. Carleton, 1814–1873,* p. 93.

34 **"imposing a** *Pax Americana* **on the entire . . ."** Lavender, *Bent's Fort,* p. 166.

34 **a distinct "absence of swashbuckling."** Clarke, *Stephen Watts Kearny,* p. 38.

35 **"the strictest disciplinarian in the service . . ."** Ibid., p. 73.

35 **"came like claps of thunder in a clear sky."** Hughes, *Doniphan's Expedition,* p. 102.

35 **"one of the ablest officers of the day."** Clarke, *Stephen Watts Kearny,* p. 391.

35 **"An army . . . is a mob of the worst kind . . ."** Gibson, *Journal of a Soldier under Kearny and Doniphan,* p. 243.

35 **"If you do not study . . ."** Clarke, *Stephen Watts Kearny,* p. 103.

36 **be "very careful to avoid alarming . . ."** Ibid., p. 75.

36 **"gained the peak of the hill . . ."** Ibid., p. 13.

37 **"To the Prince of Wales, drunk or sober!"** Ibid., p. 17.

Chapter 4 Singing Grass

38 **known as "the Bully of the Mountains . . ."** Sabin, *Kit Carson Days,* vol. 1, p. 258.

38 **"a large Frenchman, one of those overbearing kind . . ."** Carson, *Autobiography,* p. 42.

38 **"It was all over a squaw . . ."** Marc Simmons, *Kit Carson and His Three Wives,* p. 14.

38 "I did not like such talk from any man . . ." Carson, *Autobiography*, p. 43.

38 "a peculiar smile, as though he was about to perpetrate some excellent joke." Dunlay, *Kit Carson and the Indians*, p. 71.

39 "All present said but one report was heard." Carson, *Autobiography*, p. 43.

39 the camp "had no more bother with this bully Frenchman." Ibid., p. 44.

39 "the only serious personal quarrel of Kit Carson's life." *Washington Daily Union*, June 15, 1847.

40 "He was pleased with himself for doing it." Simmons, *Kit Carson and His Three Wives*, p. 14.

40 a chastity belt of sorts . . . See Lavender, *Bent's Fort*, p. 188; and Vestal, *Kit Carson*, p. 128.

40 "a good girl, a good housewife, and good to look at." Vestal, *Kit Carson*, p. 127.

40 "broad vowels, soft liquids, and smooth diphthongs." Ibid.

41 "the happiest days of my life." Henry Tilton, *The Last Days of Kit Carson*, p. 5.

41 "flitting ghostlike from creek to creek, . . ." Lavender, *Bent's Fort*, p. 60.

41 "in the mountains, far from the habitations of civilized man, . . ." Carson, *Autobiography*, p. 65.

41 "She was a good wife to me." Quoted in John C. Frémont's *Memoirs of My Life*, p. 74.

42 "Teepees stood smokeless . . . drunk with ptomaines." Vestal, *Kit Carson*, p. 132.

42 "Beaver was getting scarce . . ." Carter, *Dear Old Kit*, p. 77.

42 The Arapaho relatives mourned in the self-flagellatory tradition . . . For further descriptions of Plains Indian mourning, see Lavender, *Bent's Fort*, pp. 200–201.

42 "Kit had to explain that he was crying in his heart, . . ." Vestal, *Kit Carson*, p. 179.

43 "Times was hard, no beaver, and everything dull." Dunlay, *Kit Carson and the Indians*, p. 76.

44 The marriage lasted only a few months before she evicted him, . . . Lavender, *Bent's Fort*, p. 220; Vestal, *Kit Carson*, p. 184.

44 Carson had a brief affair with a Hispanic woman with a loose reputation . . . Simmons, *Kit Carson and His Three Wives*, p. 40.

44 "Carson brought this little girl with him to be educated . . ." Ibid., p. 47.

45 "a wild uncouth boy who married . . . an Indian squaw . . ." Ibid., p. 44.

Chapter 5 Blue Bead Mountain

45 Narbona was born in 1766 to the Red-Streaked Earth People, . . . I'm indebted here to Virginia Hoffman for her excellent sketch of the life of Narbona contained in her two-volume work, *Navajo Biographies*, vol. 1, pp. 17–35.

46 cradleboard that, in lieu of diapers, was lined with shavings of cedar bark. See Sapir, *Navajo Texts*, pp. 279–81; and Locke, *The Book of the Navajo*, p. 24.

46 his cradleboard may have been festooned with the customary squirrel's tail . . . Kluckhohn and Leighton, *The Navajo*, p. 203.

47 Narbona received his first pony when he was six, . . . Hoffman, *Navajo Biographies*, p. 18.

47 **Before dawn, he would rise and run for miles . . .** Ibid. See also Walter Dyk, *Son of Old Man Hat,* for similar descriptions of early morning runs and plunges in freezing water as traditional training for a warrior.

47 **There were . . . traditional games of chance and amusement . . .** Locke, *The Book of the Navajo,* p. 29; and Kluckhohn and Leighton, *The Navajo,* p. 96.

47 **"getting bucked off a horse is one of the most embarrassing things . . ."** Preston, *Talking to the Ground,* p. 74.

47 **the bow stood exactly his own height . . .** Hoffman, *Navajo Biographies,* p. 20.

48 **Navajo country has moved modern geologists . . . to adopt a vocabulary of doom . . .** See Halka Chronic, *Roadside Geology of New Mexico;* Robert Julyan, *The Place Names of New Mexico;* and Donald Baars, *Navajo Country: A Geology and Natural History of the Four Corners Region.*

48 **Yeitso . . . the creature's blood congealing into lava flows.** See Preston, *Talking to the Ground,* p. 37; and Kluckhohn and Leighton, *The Navajo,* p. 182.

49 **The . . . San Juan River . . . was decidedly male.** Kluckhohn and Leighton, *The Navajo,* p. 311.

49 **the Utes were probably the Navajo's greatest enemy.** Underhill, *The Navajos,* p. 83.

50 **When he was sixteen he went on his first raid, . . .** Hoffman, *Navajo Biographies,* p. 20.

50 **during the late 1770s . . . villagers finally had to import new horses from Chihuahua . . .** Locke, *The Book of the Navajo,* p. 161.

50 **in his early twenties, Narbona's parents arranged for him to marry . . .** Hoffman, *Navajo Biographies,* p. 20.

50 **advised the young couple, with a bodily frankness that would certainly embarrass . . .** See Locke, *The Book of the Navajo,* p. 23.

51 **"emotional inbreeding."** See Kluckhohn and Leighton, *The Navajo,* p. 237.

51 **Observing an old and curious Navajo taboo, . . .** The Navajo taboo forbidding men from gazing upon their mothers-in-law is vividly explained in Locke, *The Book of the Navajo,* p. 22; and Underhill, *The Navajos,* p. 9.

51 **During one raid Narbona captured a young Zuni woman, . . .** Hoffman, *Navajo Biographies,* p. 20.

51 **He . . . impressed people as someone who . . . "talks easy."** Locke, *The Book of the Navajo,* p. 32.

52 **The Cebolletans passed down one story about an elderly grandmother . . .** Marc Simmons, *The Little Lion of the Southwest,* p. 31.

52 **"were aghast . . . for he recovered and lived to fight again."** Ibid.

Chapter 6 Who Is James K. Polk?

53 **The war with Mexico was a complex affair . . .** For a concise overview of the causes of the Mexican War, see John Eisenhower, *So Far from God.* An excellent Mexican War resource on which I consistently relied is *The United States and Mexico at War* (Donald S. Frazier, ed.). For a particularly vivid oral history of the conflict, I also recommend Smith and Judah (eds.), *Chronicles of the Gringos.*

55 **and there underwent what was then a state-of-the-art surgery.** For an excruciating description of Polk's operation, see John Seigenthaler, *James K. Polk*, p. 21.

55 "**became a man on Dr. McDowell's operating table . . .**" Ibid.

55 "**has no wit, no literature, no gracefulness of delivery . . .**" Sam W. Haynes, *James K. Polk and the Expansionist Impulse*, p. 19.

57 "**felt that he was a citizen of the model republic.**" Hughes, *Doniphan's Expedition*, p. 131.

58 **a fashionable campus craze called the Young America Movement . . .** See Frazier, *The United States and Mexico at War*, p. 487.

58 **Melville declared that "America can hardly be said to have any western bound . . ."** DeVoto, *The Year of Decision: 1846*, p. 26.

58 **Walt Whitman thought that Mexico must be taught a "vigorous lesson."** Ibid., p. 38.

58 "**the iniquity of aggression . . .**" Seigenthaler, *James K. Polk*, pp. 131–32.

58 "**The United States will conquer Mexico, . . . but it will be as the man who swallows . . .**" Ibid., p. 214.

61 **Benton "knows more political facts than any other man . . ."** Theodore Roosevelt, *Thomas H. Benton*, p. 319.

61 "**unfortunately deficient in the sense of humor.**" These descriptions are all taken from Roosevelt's biography of Benton, pp. 47, 83, 221, 223, 235, 286.

62 **He regarded the Peculiar Institution as an "incurable evil."** Ibid., p. 297.

62 "**I am Southern in my affections . . .**" Tom Chaffin, *Pathfinder: John Charles Frémont and the Course of American Empire*, p. 86.

Chapter 7 What a Wild Life!

63 "**Concluded to charge them, done so.**" Vestal, *Kit Carson*, p. 104.

64 **expelled from university . . . for "incorrigible negligence."** David Roberts, *A Newer World*, p. 114.

65 "**He was broad-shouldered and deep-chested . . .**" Frémont, *Memoirs of My Life*, p. 74.

65 "**I've been some time in the mountains . . .**" Carson, *Autobiography*, p. 66.

66 **the kind of man who could repair a broken barometer . . .** See Chaffin, *Pathfinder*, p. 122.

66 "**Fremont has touched my imagination.**" Henry Wadsworth Longfellow, quoted in Ibid., p. 95.

Chapter 8 The Ruling Hand of Providence

67 "**Nothing appears as it is . . .**" Jacob Robinson, *Sketches of the Great West: A Journal of the Santa Fe Expedition*, p. 11.

67 **so "full of holes and burrows as to make it sound hollow . . ."** Ibid.

67 "**Nothing could exceed the confidence which every man seems to have in him . . .**" Clarke, p. 117.

68 "**This morning we all took a drink of whiskey . . .**" Robinson, *Sketches of the Great West*, p. 10.

68 "He is a man who keeps his counsels to himself." Gibson, *Journal of a Soldier*, p. 112.

69 "one of the grandest sights ever beheld . . . Every acre was covered . . ." Robinson, *Sketches of the Great West*, p. 12.

70 "The men have been out since sun rise . . ." Magoffin, *Down the Santa Fe Trail and into Mexico, The Diary of Susan Magoffin*, p. 43.

70 pots of bitter coffee—or "black soup" . . . Lavender, *Bent's Fort*, p. 141.

71 This outpost . . . boasted all sorts of incongruous pleasures . . . Ibid., pp. 146–47, 171, 254.

72 "There is the greatest possible noise . . ." Magoffin, *Diary*, p. 66.

72 "strange sensations in my head, my back, and hips . . ." Ibid.

73 "much agony and severest of pains." Ibid., p. 68.

73 "I sunk into a kind of lethargy." Ibid.

74 "Although it was the Sabbath . . ." Ibid., p. 69.

74 "Though forbidden to rise from my bed, . . ." Ibid.

Chapter 9 The Pathfinder

75 drained by a monstrous whirlpool that somehow connected . . . with the Pacific . . . See Chaffin, *Pathfinder*, p. 168.

75 Fremont's term for the desert sink, the Great Basin, . . . Ibid., pp. 180, 248.

75 This fabled conduit, called the Buenaventura, . . . Ibid., p. 199.

75 "in as poor condition as men could possibly be." Carson, *Autobiography*, pp. 79–81.

77 "Kit waited for nobody . . ." George Brewerton, *Overland with Kit Carson*, p. 66.

77 clipping a mule's ears and drinking its blood. See Lavender, *Bent's Fort*, p. 55.

78 tan hides with a glutinous emulsion made from the brains . . . Ibid., p. 118.

78 "prompt, self-sacrificing, and true." Frémont, *Memoirs*, p. 427.

78 "Mounted on a fine horse, without a saddle, . . ." Frémont, *The Exploring Expedition to the Rocky Mountains*, p. 15.

79 "sprung to his feet, the blood streaming . . ." Frémont, *Memoirs*, p. 374.

79 "quickly terminated the agonies of the gory savage." Ibid.

79 "Two men, in a savage desert, . . ." Ibid.

79 "Kit Carson, an American, born in the Booneslick county . . ." Ibid.

80 "impossible to describe the hardships . . ." Carson, *Autobiography*, pp. 126–27.

Chapter 10 When the Land Is Sick

81 This chapter is primarily drawn from Virginia Hoffman's sketch of the life of Narbona in *Navajo Biographies*, pp. 17–35, and from Frank McNitt's *Navajo Wars*, pp. 66–91.

82 "when the land is sick, the people are sick." Kluckhohn and Leighton, *The Navajo*, p. 155.

83 they called the Navajos the *tasavuh,* or "the head pounders." Locke, *The Book of the Navajo*, p. 7.

84 **some 250 Diné . . . had been stolen in raids . . .** Ibid., p. 189.

84 **The Navajo emissaries set off for the capital . . .** Thomas James, *Three Years among the Indians and Mexicans*, pp. 164–66.

Chapter 11 *The Un-Alamo*

87 **Fremont's mission was quite limited . . .** See Chaffin, *Pathfinder*, p. 254.

88 **the Golden Gate, he called it.** Ibid., p. 283.

88 **Fremont responded with pure histrionics.** For accounts of Fremont's ludicrous stand at Gavilan Peak, see Josiah Royce, *California: A Study of the American Character*, p. 44; and Bernard DeVoto, *The Year of Decision*, pp. 111–14.

89 **urging them to "lance the ulcer" of the American invasion.** Ibid., p. 288.

89 **"Thinking I had remained as long as the occasion required, . . ."** Frémont, *Memoirs*, p. 460.

89 **has to rank as one of the great solo courier missions in history.** For a biographical sketch and a thorough treatment of Gillespie's extraordinary trek, see Werner H. Marti, *Messenger of Destiny*, pp. 1–49.

91 **"The information . . . had absolved me from my duty as an explorer, . . ."** Frémont, *Memoirs*, p. 488.

Chapter 12 *We Will Correct All This*

92 **The people of Las Vegas were fascinated by the Americans . . .** My description of the Army of the West's arrival in Las Vegas is adapted from diaries and other firsthand accounts, primarily Emory, Gibson, Edwards, Robinson, and John Hughes.

92 **"wild looking strangers" who "constantly stared" and "swarmed . . ."** Magoffin, *Diary*, p. 92.

92 **"I have come amongst you . . . to take possession of your country."** The most thorough account of Kearny's rooftop speech, and the one I quote from here, is found in Emory, *Lieutenant Emory Reports*, pp. 49–51.

93 **"Look at me in the face."** Emory, *Lieutenant Emory Reports*, p. 51. See also Clarke, *Stephen Watts Kearny*, p. 135.

Chapter 13 *Narbona Pass*

95 **"utterly unconscious of the reception that awaited them, . . ."** Josiah Gregg, *Commerce of the Prairies*, p. 200.

96 **When the moment is right . . . we will cut the tree into small pieces . . .** Hoffman, *Navajo Biographies*, p. 25.

96 **"thrown into a state of speechless consternation . . ."** Gregg, *Commerce of the Prairies*, p. 200.

96 **"they were felled like deer trapped in a box canyon."** McNitt, *Navajo Wars*, p. 74.

96 **According to Navajo tradition, the captain of Jemez . . .** Ibid.

96 **"We killed plenty of them."** Locke, *The Book of the Navajo*, p. 192.

Chapter 14 The Uninvaded Silence

98 **"all wild and unexplored, . . . and the uninvaded silence roused our curiosity."** Frémont, *Memoirs*, p. 490.

98 **Carson . . . "apprehended no danger."** Carson, *Autobiography*, p. 98.

99 **They were . . . a "mean, low-lived, treacherous race."** Ibid., p. 78.

100 **the arrows . . . were headed with lancetlike scraps of iron . . .** See Chaffin, *Pathfinder*, p. 313.

100 **"The bravest Indian I ever saw . . ."** Carson, *Autobiography*, p. 97.

100 **All were "brave, good men."** Ibid.

100 **The camp was plunged in "an angry gloom."** Frémont, *Memoirs*, p. 492.

101 **"Sick" . . . "Very sick now."** Ibid.

101 **"He knocked his head to pieces."** Ibid.

Chapter 15 On the Altar of the Country

101 My description of Armijo's aborted stand at Apache Canyon is based on soldier eyewitness accounts as well as primary documents found in William Keleher's *Turmoil in New Mexico* and Ralph Emerson Twitchell's *The Story of the Conquest of Santa Fe*.

103 **"a mountain of fat."** George Ruxton, quoted in DeVoto, *The Year of Decision*, p. 276.

103 **"It is smarter to appear brave . . . than to *be* so."** Clarke, *Stephen Watts Kearny*, p. 105.

104 **"whether I ought to defend New Mexico . . . or not."** Paul Horgan, *Great River: The Rio Grande in North American History*, p. 720.

105 **"forced . . . to heave from position to position."** Ibid., p. 719.

105 **"Fellow Patriots . . . the moment has come . . ."** Keleher, *Turmoil in New Mexico*, p. 10.

106 **"he who actually governs you is ready to sacrifice . . ."** Horgan, *Great River*, p. 720.

Chapter 16 A Perfect Butchery

107 **"For the moment . . . I threw all other considerations aside . . ."** Frémont, *Memoirs*, p. 492.

107 **"I thought they should be chastised . . ."** Carson, *Autobiography*, p. 101.

108 **It was . . . "a beautiful sight."** Ibid., p. 100.

109 **Fremont and Carson . . . probably chose the wrong tribe . . .** David Roberts, *A Newer World*, pp. 161–62.

109 **"I owe my life to them two . . ."** Carson, *Autobiography*, p. 102.

110 **"he had placed himself on the wrong path."** Ibid., p. 104.

110 **"It will be long . . . before we see Washington . . ."** Frémont, *Memoirs*, p. 495.

Chapter 17 The Fire of Montezuma

111 "It was so bad that one who drank it . . ." DeVoto, *The Year of Decision,* p. 272.

112 "sagacious officer well-fitted for command . . ." Hughes, *Doniphan's Expedition,* p. 105.

113 *Oh, what a joy to fight the dons and wallop fat Armij-O!* Marc Simmons, *New Mexico: An Interpretive History,* p. 124.

Chapter 18 Your Duty, Mr. Carson

116 "very much sunburnt and the most un-uniform . . ." Chaffin, *Pathfinder,* p. 331.

116 "high and holy" . . . "so high a degree of civilization." Royce, *California,* pp. 51–52.

117 "something they *called* a bear." Ibid., p. 48.

118 "gave to my movements the national character . . ." Frémont, *Memoirs,* p. 520.

120 "I have no use for prisoners . . ." Dunlay, *Kit Carson and the Indians,* p. 120.

120 "a cold hearted crime." Ibid., p. 121.

121 "My word is at present the law of the land . . ." Chaffin, *Pathfinder,* p. 354.

123 "as well known there as the Duke of Wellington . . ." Dunlay, *Kit Carson and the Indians,* pp. 121–22.

124 "I'd rather ride on a grizzly . . ." Roberts, *A Newer World,* p. 172.

125 "Our entry . . . had more the effect of a parade . . ." Chaffin, *Pathfinder,* p. 354.

125 "departed to any part of the country . . ." Carson, *Autobiography,* p. 108.

Chapter 19 Daggers in Every Look

130 "a gateway which, in the hands of a skillful engineer . . ." Emory, *Lieutenant Emory Reports,* p. 55.

130 "possessed the slightest qualifications . . ." Ibid., p. 58.

130 "We marched rapidly on . . . for we were all anxious . . ." Gibson, *Journal of a Soldier,* p. 204.

131 "Their horses almost gave out . . ." Emory, *Lieutenant Emory Reports,* p. 56.

132 "Our first view of this place was very discouraging . . ." Frank Edwards, *A Campaign in New Mexico,* p. 45.

132 "nothing to pay us for our long march." Gibson, *Journal of a Soldier,* p. 205.

132 "an extensive brickyard." John Hughes, *Doniphan's Expedition,* p. 91.

132 "drawn sabres and daggers in every look." Gibson, *Journal of a Soldier,* p. 205fn.

133 VITA FUGIT SICUT UMBRA . . . Horgan, *Great River,* p. 728.

133 "I, Stephen W. Kearny, . . ." Keleher, *Turmoil in New Mexico,* p. 15.

133 "I swear obedience to the Northern Republic . . ." Ibid., p. 16.

134 "No, let him remain . . . Heaven knows the oppressions . . ." Gibson, *Journal of a Soldier,* p. 86.

134 **"We were too thirsty to judge of its merits . . ."** Emory, *Lieutenant Emory Reports,* p. 56.

134 **"Their pent-up emotions could be suppressed no longer . . ."** Lieutenant Elliott in the *Weekly Reveille,* September 28, 1846. Quoted in Gibson, *Journal of a Soldier,* p. 205fn.

Chapter 20 Men with Ears Down to Their Ankles

135 **"A certain people are going to come to us . . ."** Edward Sapir, *Navajo Texts,* p. 331.

135 **Some Navajos believed white men lacked anuses . . .** Ibid.

136 **"Our country . . . is about to be taken away from us . . ."** Ibid.

137 **"outfit"—an extended family . . . living within shouting distance . . .** For a concise description of Navajo living arrangements, see Locke, *The Book of the Navajo,* pp. 16–19; and Kluckhohn and Leighton, *The Navajo,* p. 109.

138 **"Winter was the time for conversation, between first frost and first lightning . . ."** Locke, *The Book of the Navajo,* p. 49.

Chapter 21 The Hall of Final Ruin

139 **The Santa Feans loved their bells . . .** Nearly all the soldier journals mention the incessant clanging of the bells, including Edwards, *Campaign in New Mexico,* p. 64. See also Horgan, *Great River,* p. 730; and Magoffin, *Diary,* p. 103.

141 **"ladies were all dressed in silks, . . ."** Magoffin, *Diary,* p. 124.

141 **a "dark-eyed senora" . . . who had brought along a "human foot-stool."** Ibid., p. 123.

141 **"They slap about with their arms and necks bare, . . ."** Ibid., p. 95.

141 **"stand off with crossed arms, . . ."** Ibid., p. 150.

141 **"that shrewd sense and fascinating manner . . ."** Ibid., p. 120.

142 **"lustrous, beaming eyes . . ."** Hughes, *Doniphan's Expedition,* p. 93.

142 **"remarkable for smallness of hands . . ."** Philip St. George Cooke, *Conquest of New Mexico and California,* pp. 49–50.

142 **"The women are the boldest walkers . . ."** Edwards, *Campaign in New Mexico,* p. 52.

142 **"As a general thing their forms are much better . . ."** Gibson, *Journal of a Soldier,* p. 224.

142 **"an infinity of petticoats."** Edwards, *Campaign in New Mexico,* p. 52.

142 **"a man of implacable drive."** Lavender, *Bent's Fort,* p. 131.

142 **"gargantuan freight caravans that came to sinew the West."** Ibid., p. 136.

143 **"a mighty man whose will was prairie law, . . ."** DeVoto, *The Year of Decision,* p. 267.

143 **"The colonel is in the habit of interlarding . . ."** Edwards, *Campaign in New Mexico,* p. 76.

144 **"Such familiarity of position . . . would be repugnant . . ."** John Hughes, *Doniphan's Expedition,* p. 94.

144 **"a gentleman of extensive information, . . ."** Magoffin, *Diary,* p. 125.

144 **"candid and plain-spoken, very agreeable . . ."** Ibid., p. 106.

145 **belle of the occupation.**" DeVoto, *The Year of Decision*, p. 330.

145 **"What an everlasting noise these soldiers keep up . . ."** Magoffin, *Diary*, p. 114.

146 **"The U.S. and Mexico—they are now united, . . ."** DeVoto, *The Year of Decision*, p. 332.

146 **"an instrument of writing is not legal . . ."** Hughes, *Doniphan's Expedition*, p. 98.

148 **"The people are civil and well disposed, . . ."** Gibson, *Journal of a Soldier*, p. 210.

148 **"It is the sole master of the entire plain below . . ."** Magoffin, *Diary*, p. 140.

149 **"desist from all robberies and crimes . . ."** John Hughes, *Doniphan's Expedition*, p. 128.

149 **"and carried off some twenty families."** Magoffin, *Diary*, p. 110.

149 **"as the Navajos deem the general almost superhuman . . ."** Ibid., p. 111.

Chapter 22 The New Men

150 **"Many Native Americans . . . irrational fear of artillery . . ."** See Kupke, *The Indian and the Thunderwagon*.

151 **He called them . . . "the New Men."** McNitt, *Navajo Wars*, p. 110.

BOOK TWO: A BROKEN COUNTRY

Chapter 23 The Grim Metronome

155 **"We were sorry to part with General Kearny . . ."** Edwards, *Campaign in New Mexico*, p. 70.

156 **the "universal presence of vermin . . ."** Ibid., p. 51.

156 **"singularly mild, equable, and salubrious . . ."** Gibson, *Journal of a Soldier*, p. 260.

156 **"The weather continues delightful, . . ."** Ibid., p. 230.

156 **"The air is fine and healthy, . . ."** Magoffin, *Diary*, p. 115.

157 **"The Navajos are an industrious, intelligent and warlike tribe . . ."** Charles Bent, quoted in Keleher, *Turmoil in New Mexico*, p. 71.

158 **There was also a phenomenon known as the "New Mexican Bachelor Party,"** . . . See Locke, *The Book of the Navajo*, p. 182.

158 **"On arriving home after a slaving expedition, . . ."** Simmons, *The Little Lion of the Southwest*, p. 35.

162 **"This created considerable sensation in our party . . ."** Clarke, *Stephen Watts Kearny*, p. 169.

165 **"He turned his face to the west again, . . ."** Sabin, *Kit Carson Days*, p. 273.

165 **"We put out, with merry hearts . . ."** Clarke, *Stephen Watts Kearny*, p. 170.

165 **"Kearny ordered me to join him . . ."** Carson, *Autobiography*, p. 109.

Chapter 24 Lords of the Mountains

167 **"amazed at the temerity of Capt. Reid's proceeding . . ."** John T. Hughes, *Doniphan's Expedition*, p. 169.

168 "all well-mounted on beautiful horses . . ." Robinson, *Sketches of the Great West*, p. 36.

168 "dressed in splendid Indian attire . . ." Ibid., p. 35.

169 "To have showed any thing like suspicion . . ." John T. Hughes, *Doniphan's Expedition*, p. 175.

170 "held in great reverence by his tribe . . ." See McNitt, *Navajo Wars*, p. 108.

170 "Seven hundred winters ago . . ." Robinson, *Sketches of the Great West*, pp. 36–37.

171 Why not . . . kill every one of them? Hoffman, *Navajo Biographies*, p. 29. See also Locke, *The Book of the Navajo*, p. 205.

172 "truly romantic . . . mingling in the throng!" John T. Hughes, *Doniphan's Expedition*, p. 170.

173 "It is astonishing . . . how soon our confidence . . ." Robinson, *Sketches of the Great West*, p. 38.

173 "They are entirely pastoral . . ." Captain Reid's report, quoted in John T. Hughes, *Doniphan's Expedition*, pp. 170–72.

Chapter 25 The Devil's Turnpike

175 "in a tongue resembling more the bark of a mastiff . . ." Emory, *Lieutenant Emory Reports*, p. 114.

175 The competitor in Carson had also been intrigued . . . See Lavender, *Bent's Fort*, p. 289.

176 "blossomed like a crown fire . . ." Sabin, *Kit Carson Days*, p. 522.

177 "beautiful in the extreme . . ." Emory, *Lieutenant Emory Reports*, p. 98.

177 marching over this desert landscape "was a strange existence . . ." Clarke, *The Original Journals*, pp. 90–91.

178 "It surprised me . . . to see so much land . . ." Clarke, *Soldier of the West*, p. 185.

179 "The metallic clinks of spurs, . . ." Emory, *Lieutenant Emory Reports*, p. 108.

179 "How little do those who sit in their easy chairs . . ." Clarke, *The Original Journals*, p. 106.

179 "No one who has ever visited this country . . ." Emory, *Lieutenant Emory Reports*, p. 155.

180 "Invalids may live here . . ." Clarke, *The Original Journals*, p. 90.

181 "a good harmless people and more industrious . . ." Ibid., p. 108.

181 "It was a source of much merriment . . ." Emory, *Lieutenant Emory Reports*, p. 138.

182 "anxiety increased my determination . . ." Ibid., p. 151.

183 "sabres would be rusted in their scabbards . . ." Sabin, *Kit Carson Days*, p. 526.

183 "Oh this sterile country, . . . when shall I say goodbye to you?" Clarke, *The Original Journals*, pp. 96–97.

184 "They are a sorry-looking set, . . ." Clarke, *Stephen Watts Kearny*, p. 189

185 "The general decided we must be the aggressive party, . . ." Emory, *Lieutenant Emory Reports*, p. 148.

186 "All the other generals had been shooting . . ." Vestal, *Happy Warrior*, p. 234.

186 "Our object was to get the . . . animals." Carson, *Autobiography*, p. 111.

187 "The Indians were very inimical . . ." Clarke, *Stephen Watts Kearny*, p. 200.
188 "Remember, . . . one point of the saber . . ." Ibid., p. 202.

Chapter 26   Our Red Children

189 "The United States . . . has taken military possession . . ." John T. Hughes, *Doniphan's Expedition*, p. 177.
190 "very bold and intellectual." Ibid., p. 178.
190 "Americans! . . . while you do the same thing on the east." McNitt, *Navajo Wars*, p. 118.
191 Spears and Stewart were the first American soldiers . . . Ibid., p. 122.

Chapter 27   Cold Steel

192 My account of the Battle of San Pasqual is drawn from the following sources: *The Battle of San Pasqual* by Jonreed Lauritzen, *The Battle of San Pasqual Dec. 6, 1846 & the Struggle for California* by Peter Price, Emory's *Lieutenant Emory Reports*, Clarke's *The Original Journals*, Marti's *Messenger of Destiny*, Clarke's *Stephen Watts Kearny*, and Carson's *Autobiography*.
192 "Heavens, I did not mean that!" Clarke, *Stephen Watts Kearny*, p. 203.
193 "I came very near being trodden to death . . ." Carson, *Autobiography*, p. 112.
194 "much as they might encircle a herd of cattle." Clarke, *Stephen Watts Kearny*, p. 208.
194 "A Californian can throw the lasso as well with his foot . . ." Emory, *Lieutenant Emory Reports*, p. 153.
195 "There is hardly one not fit for the circus." Clarke, *Stephen Watts Kearny*, p. 208.
196 "Rally, men! For God's sake, . . ." Marti, *Messenger of Destiny*, p. 97.
196 entirely by cold steel. Sabin, *Kit Carson Days*, p. 531.
196 "First, go and dress the wounds of the soldiers . . ." Clarke, *Stephen Watts Kearny*, p. 216.
198 a "community of hardships" . . . "band of brave men." Emory, *Lieutenant Emory Reports*, p. 170.
198 "Kearny concluded to march on, . . ." Carson, *Autobiography*, p. 115.
198 "The ambulances grated on the ground . . ." Emory, *Lieutenant Emory Reports*, p. 171.
199 "quadruple our strength" . . . "the moment we descended into the plain." Clarke, *The Original Journals*, p. 130.
200 "an expedition of some peril." Emory, *Lieutenant Emory Reports*, p. 172.
200 "Se escapara el lobo." Sabin, *Kit Carson Days*, p. 537.
201 "Been in worse places before." Ibid., p. 538.
202 "midnight crawl" . . . "high among the exploits . . ." DeVoto, *The Year of Decision*, p. 370.
203 "Never has there been a man like Kit Carson . . ." Noel Gerson, *Kit Carson: Folk Hero and Man*, pp. 139–40.
203 "Got to San Diego the next night." Carson, *Autobiography*, p. 116.

204 **"One of the most agreeable little offices . . ."** Emory, *Lieutenant Emory Reports,* p. 173.
205 **"the last mournful shot of disappointment . . ."** Clarke, *Stephen Watts Kearny,* p. 228.
205 **"The Pacific opened for the first time . . ."** Emory, *Lieutenant Emory Reports,* p. 175.
205 **"Take good care of yourself . . . like rumbling thunder."** Clarke, *Stephen Watts Kearny,* p. 235.

Chapter 28 El Crepusculo

208 **Nearly every day Santa Fe held another juvenile funeral . . .** For vivid descriptions of these doleful processionals, see Gibson, *Journal of a Soldier,* p. 242; and Edwards, *Campaign in New Mexico,* p. 48.
210 **an erudite and somewhat Machiavellian man . . .** For further reading on the intriguing and influential Padre Martinez, see David J. Weber, *On the Edge of Empire: The Taos Hacienda of Los Martinez;* and also Fray Angelico Chavez, *But Time and Change: The Story of Padre Martinez of Taos, 1793–1867.*
212 **These were the "crypto-Jews."** For a thorough, scholarly look at this fascinating phenomenon, see Stanley Hordes, *To the End of the Earth: A History of the Crypto-Jews of New Mexico.*
212 *penitentes*—**pious men who went out into the countryside . . ."** There are several excellent works on the New Mexico *penitentes.* See Marta Weigle, *The Penitentes of the Southwest;* Alice Henderson, *Brothers of Light: The Penitentes of the Southwest;* and Thomas Steele and Rowena Rivera, *Penitente Self-Government: Brotherhoods and Councils, 1797–1947.*
212 *el gallo,* **an old blood sport . . .** See Lavender, *Bent's Fort,* p. 107.
214 **"for having blown an evil breath on their children, . . ."** Lavender, *Bent's Fort,* p. 298.
214 My account of the Taos Massacre is drawn from multiple sources, but among the best are James Crutchfield, *Tragedy at Taos: The Revolt of 1847;* John Durand, *The Taos Massacres;* Michael McNierney, *Taos 1847: The Revolt in Contemporary Accounts.*
218 **"cut as cleanly with the tight cord . . ."** Unpublished reminiscences of Teresina Bent, a copy of which I obtained at the Bent home bookstore in Taos.
220 **"They ordered that no one should feed us, . . ."** Ibid.
221 **"convivial figure, with a glossy black beard . . ."** Lavender, *Bent's Fort,* p. 64.
222 **"We were tiger-like in our craving for revenge."** McNierney, *Taos 1847,* p. 58.
223 **Taos Pueblo . . . one of the oldest continually inhabited . . .** For a good general source on the background and culture of the extraordinary Taos Pueblo, see John Bodine, *Taos Pueblo: A Walk through Time.*
224 **"a place of great strength, . . ."** Colonel Price, quoted in McNierney, *Taos 1847,* p. 50.
224 **"like creatures in burrows listening . . ."** Paul Horgan, *Great River,* p. 767.
225 **"The mingled noise of bursting shells . . ."** McNierney, *Taos 1847,* p. 67.
227 **"A few half scared Pueblos walked listlessly . . ."** Lewis Garrard, *Wah-to-yah and the Taos Trail,* p. 187.

228 "trembling wretches . . . miserable in dress, . . ." Ibid., p. 194.
228 *"Mi madre, mi padre . . ."* Ibid., p. 197.
229 "The muscles would relax and again contract . . ." Ibid., p. 198.

Chapter 29 American Mercury

231 "poured upon my fevered lips" . . . "I'll blow your heart out." Sabin, *Kit Carson Days*, p. 557.
232 "I always see folks out in the road." Ibid., p. 567.
234 In the years leading up to her stroke, . . . Chaffin, *Pathfinder*, p. 139.
234 "Although he did not enter the army through . . . military academy . . ." Thomas Hart Benton, *Thirty Years View: A History of the Working of the American Government, 1820 to 1850*, p. 718.
235 "He is a man . . . whose word will stand wherever he is known." Ibid.
236 a private errand . . . to pay a visit to his daughter. See Dunlay, *Kit Carson and the Indians*, pp. 60–61; and Marc Simmons, *Kit Carson and His Three Wives*, p. 77.

Chapter 30 Time at Last Sets All Things Even

237 "so much fresh breeze and so much sunlight." Pamela Herr and Mary Lee Spence, *The Letters of Jessie Benton Fremont*, p. xviii.
238 his "most confirmed worshiper." Ibid., p. 25.
239 "She belongs to him body & soul . . ." Ibid., p. xxiii.
239 "the better man of the two." Ibid., p. xviii.
239 "picked at his fish and fowl . . ." Noel Gerson, *Kit Carson: Folk Hero and Man*, p. 143.
240 A bon vivant who jerked with odd . . . My descriptions of Beale are primarily drawn from Gerald Thompson, *Edward F. Beale and the American West*.
241 "one of those noble characters that have . . . sprung up on our frontier." From the *Washington Union*, June 15, 1847, a copy of which I viewed at the Beinecke Rare Book and Manuscript Library, Yale University.
241 "but out on the Plains, *we're* the princes." My descriptions of Carson's visit with Jessie Fremont are primarily drawn from Pamela Herr, *Jessie Benton Frémont*, pp. 152–53, 156; and Jessie Fremont, *Will and the Way Stories*, pp. 39–42.
244 the "hardest working man in America." John Seigenthaler, *James K. Polk*, p. 121.
244 "virtually incarcerated himself in the White House." Ibid., p. 103.
245 "His manners at table I found to be faultless . . ." Gerson, *Kit Carson: Folk Hero and Man*, pp. 144–45.
245 "He remained the soul of diffidence . . ." Ibid.

Chapter 31 A Broken Country

247 "The Navajos commit their wrongs from a pure love of rapine . . ." Keleher, *Turmoil in New Mexico*, p. 52.

247 **"wild Indians of this country have been so much more successful . . ."** Ibid., p. 53.

249 **"The Indians . . . until they are properly chastised."** Keleher, *Turmoil in New Mexico*, p. 45.

250 **most of whom carried Model 1841 muzzle-loading . . .** My description of the Washington Expedition's equipment and weaponry is drawn primarily from Frank McNitt's introduction to *Navaho Expedition*, by Lt. James Simpson, pp. lxvi–lxix.

251 **"dismayingly mousy-looking."** McNitt, introduction to *Navaho Expedition*, p. lx.

252 **"frankly makes dull reading."** Ibid.

253 **"antipathy to its use"** . . . **"favor in the eyes of the senoritas."** David Weber, *Richard Kern: Expeditionary Artist in the Far Southwest*, p. 122.

253 **Dr. Samuel George Morton, an anatomy professor** . . . See Dunlay, *Kit Carson and the Indians*, p. 54, and Weber, *Richard Kern*, p. 24.

254 **"mountains high and bold"** . . . **"swallows all the dirt and misery."** Weber, *Richard Kern*, p. 116.

254 **"one of the most harebrained exploring expeditions ever undertaken . . ."** McNitt, introduction to Simpson's *Navaho Expedition*, p. xxxii.

255 **Kearny suffered an excruciating death.** For further details on the advanced stages of yellow fever, see *American Plague*, by Molly Crosby.

256 **His rifle . . . "cracked away merrily, and never spoke in vain."** Vestal, *Kit Carson: The Happy Warrior*, p. 150.

257 **"We all looked like Old Winter . . ."** Weber, *Richard Kern*, p. 39.

257 **"I told Dick the expedition was destroyed . . ."** Roberts, *A Newer World*, p. 213.

257 **"gradually sinking into a sleep . . ."** Weber, *Richard Kern*, p. 45.

258 **"In starving times . . . no man ever walked . . ."** DeVoto, *The Year of Decision*, p. 341.

259 **"But . . . 'tis among the best in town, . . ."** Weber, *Richard Kern*, p. 67.

260 **"Although I was exceedingly hungry . . ."** McNitt, *Navaho Expedition*, p. 10.

260 **"At present it is considerably defaced, . . ."** Ibid., p. 18.

261 **Other Jemez Indians joined forces** . . . Ibid., p. 15fn.

262 **"Hosta . . . is one of the finest-looking . . ."** Ibid., p. 24.

263 **Much of this land . . . was "a barren waste."** Ibid., p. 70.

263 **"where it lit for a moment within a foot or two of my person . . ."** Ibid., p. 25.

263 **"a scene . . . that partook both of the painful and ludicrous."** Ibid., p. 29.

265 **The largest of all the structures, Pueblo Bonito, . . .** See Preston, *Talking to the Ground*, p. 56.

265 **"and the bright wild flowers fill the open court . . ."** Weber, *Richard Kern*, p. 88.

265 **"Had time permitted, . . . we would gladly have remained . . ."** McNitt, *Navaho Expedition*, pp. 39, 47.

266 **Archaeologists have come to call it the Chaco Phenomenon.** For a concise description of the Chaco Phenomenon, see Preston, *Talking to the Ground*, pp. 56–58, 268–78.

267 **North America had never seen such a florescence . . .** My description of the Anasazi rise and fall is primarily adapted from James Judge, *New Light on Chaco*

Canyon; David Roberts, *In Search of the Old Ones;* and Preston, *Talking to the Ground.*

269 **wondering whether this bewhiskered little man was a witch.** See Preston, *Talking to the Ground,* p. 269.

Chapter 32 The Finest Head I Ever Saw

270 **"bestrode their horses *a la mode des hommes."*** McNitt, *Navaho Expedition,* p. 62.
270 **a "dark, portentous cloud" was hovering . . .** Ibid., p. 63.
271 **"If we are friends, . . ."** McNitt, *Navajo Wars,* p. 143.
272 **"gorgeously decked in red, blue, and white, . . ."** McNitt, *Navaho Expedition,* p. 67.
272 **"quite old and of a very large frame, . . ."** Ibid., p. 63.
273 **"CALHOUN: Tell them they are lawfully . . ."** Ibid., p. 66.
274 **negotiations had finally reached a concrete topic . . .** See Underhill, *The Navajos,* p. 99.
275 **A New Mexican souvenir hunter . . .** McNitt, *Navajo Wars,* p. 145.
275 **"He was the chief of the Nation . . ."** Weber, *Richard Kern,* p. 96.

Chapter 33 The Death Knot

277 **The hogan would then have had to be destroyed . . .** Sapir, *Navajo Texts,* p. 431, and Locke, *The Book of the Navajo,* p. 15.
277 **some Navajos had wondered whether he might be a witch . . .** Ibid., pp. 118, 247.
277 **feasts and healing gatherings . . . worked as an economic leveler . . .** Kluckhohn and Leighton, *The Navajo,* p. 227.
278 **"You can't grow wealthy if you treat your relatives right."** Locke, *The Book of the Navajo,* p. 32, and Kluckhohn and Leighton, *The Navajo,* p. 100.
278 **Narbona's slaves probably performed . . . the abhorrent parts . . .** Locke, *The Book of the Navajo,* p. 30, and Hoffman, *Navajo Biographies,* p. 34.
279 **Those tasked with the burial were supposed to destroy several prized horses . . .** Sapir, *Navajo Texts,* p. 431, and Hoffman, *Navajo Biographies,* p. 34.
280 **There was nothing radiant about the afterlife . . .** Locke, *The Book of the Navajo,* p. 29.
280 **Navajos . . . invited to the 1893 World's Fair in Chicago.** Ibid., p. 10.
281 **the two men then ripped the saddles and bridles into shreds . . .** After they were destroyed, these objects became known as "ghost's belongings." See Sapir, *Navajo Texts,* p. 431.
282 **There they stayed for four nights . . .** Ibid.

Chapter 34 Men Without Eyes

284 **It was derived from the Navajo word *tsegi* . . .** Grant, *Canyon de Chelly: Its People and Rock Art,* p. 3.

285 "It is regrettable . . . that so much damage . . ." McNitt, *Navaho Expedition*, p. 73.

286 "The country is one extended naked, barren waste . . ." Ibid., p. 70.

287 "pure, wholesome water" . . . "the towering pines . . ." Ibid., p. 78.

288 "a fight was expected . . . At nearly every point . . ." Weber, *Richard Kern*, p. 96.

288 Simpson decided to pay his commander an eternal compliment . . . McNitt, *Navaho Expedition*, p. 75.

289 "The road we have been traveling looks as if . . ." Ibid., p. 86

291 It was "exciting . . . to observe the huts of the enemy, . . ." Ibid., pp. 86–87.

291 WASHINGTON: Are he and his people desirous of peace? Ibid., pp. 88–89.

292 "Almost perfectly vertical . . . the custom-house of the city of New York." Ibid., p. 93.

293 The "fabulous rocks . . . became wilder at every turn." Weber, *Richard Kern*, p. 102.

293 "The mystery of the Canon of Chelly is now . . . solved." McNitt, *Navaho Expedition*, p. 95.

294 "It seems anomalous to me that a nation . . ." Ibid., p. 96.

294 "tripping down the almost vertical wall as nimbly . . ." Ibid., p. 92.

294 The designs came in a dazzling confusion. Grant, *Canyon de Chelly*, pp. 153–268.

295 a curious tableau scrawled across the walls. My account of the 1805 massacre is drawn from McNitt, *Navajo Wars*; Grant, *Canyon de Chelly*, pp. 84–89; and Underhill, *The Navajos*, pp. 72–73.

297 "Hostilities between the contracting parties . . ." McNitt, *Navajo Wars*, pp. 150–51.

298 their unwillingness to pronounce anyone's name out loud, . . . See Locke, *The Book of the Navajo*, p. 25.

298 Navajo is an extremely precise language . . . See Kluckhohn and Leighton, *The Navajo*, pp. 253–93.

299 "satisfy the public mind and testify to the whole world . . ." McNitt, *Navaho Expedition*, p. 100.

Chapter 35 Blood and Thunder

299 Francis Aubry was a celebrated figure on the trail. David Dary, *The Santa Fe Trail: Its History, Legends, and Lore*, p. 201.

300 Aubry ordered ham and eggs and then was taken upstairs . . . Ibid., p. 207.

301 "whose hands are turned against every white man, . . ." William Davis, *El Gringo*, p. 251.

301 "practising sadists" who had "great skill . . ." DeVoto, *The Year of Decision*, p. 250.

302 the Comanches who in 1841 killed and scalped . . . Robert Bent, . . . Lavender, *Bent's Fort*, p. 203.

304 another famous Taos trapper, named Lucien . . . See Harriet Freiberger, *Lucien Maxwell: Villain or Visionary*; and Lawrence R. Murphy, "Master of the Cimarron."

304 "king of that whole country . . . He had perfect control . . ." Ibid.

305 "We had been leading a roving life long enough, . . ." Carson, *Autobiography*, p. 130.

306 "an extremely difficult and painful operation." See Murphy, "Rayado."

308 the highest death rate per fighting soldier . . . Eisenhower, *So Far from God*.

308 "A deed has been done from which the country will not . . . recover . . ." DeVoto, *The Year of Decision*, p. 214.

308 "Could those Mexicans have seen into my heart . . ." Robert Drexter, *Guilty of Making Peace: A Biography of Nicholas P. Trist*, p. 139.

309 He filled the labyrinthine chambers with kegs of powder . . . For a full description of William Bent's destruction of the old fort, see Lavender, *Bent's Fort*, pp. 338–39.

310 "Small in stature, and slenderly limbed, . . ." George Ruxton, *In the Old West*, 286–87.

310 "I cannot express my surprise at beholding . . ." Dunlay, *Kit Carson and the Indians*, p. 13.

310 "The hero of a hundred desperate encounters, . . ." George Brewerton, *Overland with Kit Carson*, p. 38.

310 "He was uncouth" . . . "yet he wore shyness . . . like a veil." Dunlay, *Kit Carson and the Indians*, p. 191.

311 "I say, stranger, are you Kit Carson?" Ibid., p. 10.

311 "a lynx-like eye and an imperturbable coolness . . ." Charles Averill, *Kit Carson: The Prince of the Gold Hunters*, p. 26, a microfilm copy of which I viewed at the Library of Congress.

313 "At the first sound, even a shout, . . ." Veronica Tiller, *The Jicarilla Apache*.

314 *jicarilla* means "little basket" Ibid., p. 5.

315 "an indolent and cowardly people . . ." Keleher, *Turmoil in New Mexico*, p. 71.

316 a "Rocky Mountain Hunter" wearing moccasins . . . Dunlay, *Kit Carson and the Indians*, pp. 136–37.

316 "Being thoroughly acquainted . . ." Ibid.

319 "The order was too late for the desired effect." Carson, *Autobiography*, p. 133.

320 "She was perfectly warm . . ." Ibid.

321 "*Kit Carson! His lip, that proud, that determined lip . . .*" Charles Averill, *Kit Carson, The Prince of the Goldhunters*, p. 98.

321 "The book was the first of its kind I had ever seen . . ." Carson, *Autobiography*, p. 135.

321 "I have much regretted the failure to save the life . . ." Ibid.

321 "burn the damn thing." Dunlay, *Kit Carson and the Indians*, p. 140.

BOOK THREE: MONSTER SLAYER

Chapter 36 The Fearing Time

325 the Navajos sometimes called "Something-Sticking-Out-From-The-Foreheads . . ." Maurice Frink, *Fort Defiance and the Navajos*, p. 47.

325 "Large bets, larger than on the other races, were made on both sides." Nicholas Hodt, testimony recorded in United States, *Condition of the Indian Tribes: Report of the Joint Special Committee*, p. 314.

326 some Navajos called the great casks "hollow-woods." See Lavender, *Bent's Fort*, p. 156.

327 Other accounts say the owner was . . . Manuelito, . . . Locke, *The Book of the Navajo*, p. 343.

329 a truly competent man held the office of Indian agent . . . For more on the remarkable Henry Linn Dodge, see McNitt, *Navajo Wars*, p. 267; and Underhill, *The Navajos*, pp. 103–11.

330 "a superior race of Indians." Davis, *El Gringo*, pp. 411–12.

330 "The water there is mine, not yours . . ." See Hoffman, *Navajo Biographies*, p. 99.

331 Major Brooks threatened to obliterate the Navajos . . . For a full account of the attack on Brooks's slave and its aftermath, see McNitt, *Navajo Wars*, p. 325.

331 in April 1860, Manuelito organized a thousand Navajo warriors . . . See Frink, *Fort Defiance and the Navajos*, p. 51, Hoffman, *Navajo Biographies*, p. 100, and McNitt, *Navajo Wars*, p. 380.

332 "An angry fire burned within him . . ." Hoffman, *Navajo Biographies*, p. 93.

332 "I walk like a headman now . . ." Ibid., p. 90.

332 He scalped his victim, and later chewed on the bloody skin . . . Ibid., p. 91.

333 *"they jump around like rabbits!"* Ibid., p. 88.

333 Now the moment had come, the day's grand finale. For more details on the massacre at Fort Fauntleroy, see McNitt, *Navajo Wars*, p. 422; Marc Simmons, *The Little Lion of the Southwest*, p. 165; and Marc Simmons, "Horse Race at Fort Fauntleroy: An Incident of the Navajo War," in the journal *La Gaceta* 5(3) (1970).

334 "A procession of the winning party . . ." Nicholas Hodt testimony in United States, *Condition of the Indian Tribes*, p. 314.

335 The forty-three-year-old Chaves hailed from a venerable . . . My biographical sketch of Manuel Chaves is drawn from Marc Simmons, *The Little Lion of the Southwest*.

335 Chaves had nearly died in a Navajo clash. Ibid., pp. 38–42.

338 "I saw a soldier murdering two little children . . ." Nicholas Hodt testimony in United States, *Condition of the Indian Tribes*, p. 314.

338 "Give this soldier back his arms, . . ." Ibid.

Chapter 37 People of the Single Star

340 two armies stared at each other . . . My account of the battle of Valverde is based primarily on the following sources: John Taylor, *Bloody Valverde: A Civil War Battle on the Rio Grande*; Max Heyman, *Prudent Soldier: A Biography of Major General E. R. S. Canby*; Alvin Josephy, *The Civil War in the American West*; Charles Carroll and Lynne Sebastian, eds., *Fort Craig: The United States Fort on the Camino Real*; and Martin Hall, *Sibley's New Mexico Campaign*.

341 "too prone to let the morrow take care of itself." Martin Hall, *Sibley's New Mexico Campaign*, p. 38.

343 Those big artillery pieces . . . were nothing more than decoys . . . Taylor, *Bloody Valverde*, p. 105.

344 "I'll make my wife a nightgown out of it!" Ibid., p. 25.

345 "Kit was loyal, but he was like me . . ." Dunlay, *Kit Carson and the Indians,* p. 229.

345 he "had the utmost firmness and the best of common sense . . ." Ibid., p. 232.

345 Carson "then approached and in a mild manner . . ." Ibid., p. 233.

347 "The mountains here are full of Indians, . . ." Hall, *Sibley's New Mexico Campaign,* p. 40.

347 he looked "like a horned frog." Donald Frazier, "Long Marches and Short Rations," in Carrol and Sebastian, *Fort Craig,* p. 102.

348 "Our leaders were crazy . . ." Sabin, *Kit Carson Days,* p. 687.

349 The precise terms and arrangements of their servitude . . . Dunlay, *Kit Carson and the Indians,* p. 201.

349 "in truth but a more charming name for a species of slavery . . ." Davis, *El Gringo,* p. 232.

354 "fell so hard as to almost peel the skin off your face." Josephy, *The Civil War in the American West,* p. 60.

356 "a widely acknowledged reputation for the spectacular." Jerry Thompson, *Desert Tiger: Captain Paddy Graydon and the Civil War in the Far Southwest.*

358 "You've come too far from home hunting a fight . . ." Taylor, *Bloody Valverde,* p. 39.

358 "had given his allegiance to country rather than to state." Ibid., p. 50.

358 cut out a large piece of his own tongue . . . Josephy, *The Civil War in the American West,* p. 69.

359 "one of the most gallant and furious charges . . ." Taylor, *Bloody Valverde,* p. 70.

360 "fought full of courage and almost in a frenzy, . . ." Jacqueline Meketa, *Legacy of Honor: The Life of Rafael Chacon,* p. 175.

362 "could not understand the signals to retreat . . ." Ibid., p. 338.

Chapter 38 The Sons of Some Dear Mother

363 "If we can subsist our men and horses, . . ." Hall, *Sibley's New Mexico Campaign,* p. 74.

364 "too intimate an acquaintance with 'John Barley Corn.' " Edrington and Taylor, *The Battle of Glorieta Pass,* p. 115.

365 "Those of you who volunteered . . . were doubtless deceived . . ." Hall, *Sibley's New Mexico Campaign,* p. 81.

368 "By the grace of God and these two revolvers, . . ." Reginald Craig, *The Fighting Parson,* p. 40.

369 "something of an epic." Alvin Josephy, *The Civil War in the American West,* p. 77.

371 "On they came to . . . certain destruction, . . ." Ibid., p. 80.

373 "You are right on top of them, Major." Marc Simmons, *The Little Lion of the Southwest,* p. 184.

374 "lost all sense of humanity." Edrington and Taylor, *The Battle of Glorieta Pass,* p. 95.

375 "We pierced the Confederate vitals and drew . . . the life blood." Ibid., p. 89.

376 "We have been crippled . . ." Josephy, *The Civil War in the American West*, p. 85.

377 "a further connection might result in my assassination." Edrington and Taylor, *The Battle of Glorieta Pass*, p. 107.

378 "We do not want to take any unfair advantage . . ." Hall, *Sibley's New Mexico Campaign*, p. 132.

379 "chasing a shadow in a barren land." Ibid., p. 150.

379 "Any cause that men sustain to death . . ." Ibid., p. 135.

Chapter 39 The Round Forest

380 "truly frightful . . . This death list is not made up of a few lives lost . . ." Gerald Thompson, *The Army and the Navajo: The Bosque Redondo Reservation Experiment, 1863–1868*, p. 10.

380 "there is now no choice between . . . extermination or their removal . . ." Dunlay, *Kit Carson and the Indians*, p. 267.

383 "utterly ignorant of everything beyond their corn fields . . ." Aurora Hunt, *Major General James H. Carleton, 1814–1873*, p. 146.

384 if Carleton had "never had to function as God . . ." C. L. Sonnichsen, *The Mescalero Apaches*, p. 97.

384 Born in 1814, the son of a shipmaster . . . My biographical sketch of Carleton is primarily drawn from Hunt, *James H. Carleton.*

385 When happiness lived up this way . . . David Barker poem is quoted in ibid., p. 28.

386 "I cannot but think that good tales . . ." Letter from Dickens to Carleton is printed in full in ibid., p. 31.

387 "a fine companion and a perfect gentleman." Ibid., p. 71.

388 his heart "would pant with impatience . . ." Ibid., p. 85.

388 "Judging from the way they go on . . . there will be a broad stream . . ." Ibid., p. 91.

389 the sunlight "seeming to cover with flashing diamonds . . ." James Henry Carleton, *The Battle of Buena Vista*, p. 56.

390 "the Battle of Buena Vista . . . the greatest ever fought . . ." Ibid., p. 158.

391 "I presume courage was oozing from his fingertips, . . ." Carson, *Autobiography*, p. 142.

391 "I understood them to say . . . they could easily kill me . . ." Ibid., p. 143.

392 "I've done you no injury, . . ." Ibid.

392 "I have many friends among the soldiers . . ." Ibid., p. 144.

396 "Carson is justly celebrated as the best tracker . . ." Dunlay, *Kit Carson and the Indians*, p. 168.

Chapter 40 Children of the Mist

398 the tragedy that became known as the Mountain Meadows Massacre . . . For further reading on the massacre see Will Bagley, *Blood of the Prophets*; Sally Denton, *American Massacre*; and J. P. Dunn, *Massacres of the Mountains*.

398 It was . . . "horrible to look upon: Women's hair, in detached locks . . ." James Carleton, *Special Report on the Massacre at Mountain Meadows*, p. 36, a copy of which I viewed at the Library of Congress.

399 "Murderers of the parents and despoilers of their property . . ." Ibid., p. 34.

400 "They are an ulcer upon the body-politic . . ." Ibid., p. 39.

402 "driven from their fishing and hunting grounds, . . ." Gerald Thompson, *Edward F. Beale and the American West*, p. 56.

402 "that which was accomplished by a few poor priests . . ." Ibid.

402 "Either the whole Indian race . . . must be exterminated . . ." Ibid., p. 65.

403 "could be transformed from a state of semi-barbarism, . . ." Ibid.

403 "When I came here this time" . . . "some new remedy must be adopted." James Carleton, "To the People of New Mexico," December 16, 1864, a copy of which I viewed at the Library of Congress.

404 "the Pecos . . . contains much unhealthy mineral matter." Thompson, *The Army and the Navajo*, p. 14.

404 "The only peace that can ever be made with them . . ." Ibid., p. 28.

405 "the Navajo Wars will be remembered . . ." Ibid.

407 "An Indian . . . is a more watchful and wary animal than a deer . . ." Dunlay, *Kit Carson and the Indians*, p. 237.

410 "Do not despise New Mexico, as a drain . . ." Dunlay, *Kit Carson and the Indians*, p. 262.

412 "All Indian men of that tribe are to be killed . . ." C. L. Sonnichsen, *The Mescalero Apaches*, p. 110.

412 "Your weapons are better than ours . . ." Ibid., p. 113.

414 "I am sorry that I am obliged to dissolve our Official conexion, . . ." Dunlay, *Kit Carson and the Indians*, p. 247.

414 "they are unable to support themselves by the chase . . ." Carson testimony in United States, *Condition of the Indian Tribes*, pp. 96–98.

415 "Indians generally learn the vices and not the virtues . . ." Ibid.

415 "In all cases of locating reservations . . ." Dunlay, *Kit Carson and the Indians*, p. 186.

416 "an hereditary warfare" that had "always existed." Ibid.

Chapter 41 General Orders No. 15

418 "The Utes . . . are very brave, and fine shots, . . ." Lynn Bailey, *Bosque Redondo*, p. 38.

419 "We have no faith in your promises. You can have no peace . . ." Lawrence Kelly, *Navajo Roundup*, p. 18.

420 "For a long time past, the Navajo Indians have murdered and robbed . . ." For the full text of General Orders No. 15, see ibid., p. 22.

420 *"Make a note of this"* . . . "You will send me a weekly report . . ." Ibid., p. 35.

421 "Much is expected of you, . . ." Dunlay, *Kit Carson and the Indians*, p. 279.

421 "thermometer past endurance." Raymond Lindgren, ed., "A Diary of Kit Carson's Navajo Campaign, 1863–1864," *New Mexico Historical Review* (July 1946): 226–46.

422 "With straining eyes and beating hearts . . ." Ibid., p. 229.

422 "The troops sometimes accused him of cowardice . . ." Dunlay, *Kit Carson and the Indians*, p. 278.

422 "must have been an *hombre grande*." Lindgren, "Diary of Kit Carson's Navajo Campaign," p. 230.

423 "Major Cummings left the command alone" . . . "result of rash bravery." Dunlay, *Kit Carson and the Indians*, p. 278.

424 "They have no stock . . . and were depending . . . on the corn . . ." Kelly, *Navajo Roundup*, p. 42.

425 "communicating with them—through the barrels of my Rifles." Dunlay, *Kit Carson and the Indians*, p. 291.

426 "murder, alcoholism, embezzlement, . . ." Kelly, *Navajo Roundup*, p. 15.

427 "There can be no other talk on the subject." Dunlay, *Kit Carson and the Indians*, p. 283.

428 "I have not the authority to grant you a leave." Ibid., p. 290.

428 "*as soon as* you have secured one hundred captive . . ." Kelly, *Navajo Roundup*, pp. 69–70.

Chapter 42 Fortress Rock

431 "A frightened feeling had settled among the Navajo people, . . ." Ruth Roessel, ed., *Navajo Stories of the Long Walk Period*, p. 127.

432 "this thrusting fin . . . the place of ultimate refuge." David Roberts, *A Newer World*, p. 266.

432 "You can go to the safe place until the soldiers are gone . . ." Roessel, *Navajo Stories of the Long Walk Period*, p. 45.

433 *Come dress your ranks . . . Bold Johnny Navajo*. Hunt, *James H. Carleton*, p. 284.

433 "all that is connected with this canon [canyon] will cease to be a mystery . . ." Kelly, *Navajo Roundup*, p. 95.

435 "When will you have sense?" . . . "Can't you try and quit whiskey . . ." Dunlay, *Kit Carson and the Indians*, p. 294.

436 "jumped about on the ledges, like Mountain Cats, . . ." Kelly, *Navajo Roundup*, p. 104.

436 "in an almost famishing condition, half-starved and naked." Ibid.

437 "two Buck Indians and one Squaw who obstinately persisted . . ." Ibid.

437 the people "were instructed to stay quiet . . ." Roessel, *Navajo Stories of the Long Walk Period*, p. 45.

437 "Kit Carson—a very pure White Man." Ibid., pp. 43–51.

438 "no damage was done except with the tongue." Kelly, *Navajo Roundup*, p. 104.

438 Working through the night, they filled gourd after gourd . . . I heard two slightly differing versions of this story during my visits to Canyon de Chelly. See also Roberts, *A Newer World*, p. 268.

440 "If you do not come in by then, my soldiers will hunt you up . . ." Kelly, *Navajo Roundup*, p. 98.

440 "we believed this was a war of extermination." Ibid.

443 "They are arriving almost hourly . . ." Dunlay, *Kit Carson and the Indians*, p. 297.

443 *"Killed, 23. Prisoners, 34. Voluntarily surrendered,* **200 souls . . ."** Ibid., p. 296.

443 **"a hundred campfires sparkling amongst the hills . . ."** Lynn Bailey, *Bosque Redondo,* p. 55.

444 **the "crowning act in a long life spent fighting the savages . . ."** Kelly, *Navajo Roundup,* p. 108.

445 **"An enemy he could neither outwit nor outfight . . ."** Dunlay, *Kit Carson and the Indians,* p. 344.

445 **"The state of my health warns me . . ."** Ibid.

Chapter 43 *The Long Walk*

446 **"I have nothing to lose but my life, . . ."** Locke, *The Book of the Navajo,* p. 369.

447 **"protégés of the United States . . ."** Hunt, *James H. Carleton,* p. 282.

448 **"The exodus of this whole people from the land of their fathers . . ."** Kelly, *Navajo Roundup,* p. 128.

449 **"Carleton rules the land."** Hunt, *James H. Carleton,* p. 304.

451 **"supply their wants, settle their disputes, stand between them . . ."** Dunlay, *Kit Carson and the Indians,* p. 319.

452 **"every promise however trifling . . ."** Ibid. p. 320.

452 **"not the position I contemplated occupying."** Ibid., p. 323.

453 **"nocturnal forays . . . were the cause of serious . . . complaint."** Thompson, *The Army and the Navajo,* p. 61.

455 **The nuns named her Mary Carleton in his honor.** Hunt, *James H. Carleton,* p. 338.

456 **"lost their lives in crude attempts at abortion."** Thompson, *The Army and the Navajo,* p. 81.

457 **"The cursed insects seem to devour all the grain . . ."** Ibid., p. 92.

458 **this "visitation from God."** Ibid., p. 57.

Chapter 44 *Adobe Walls*

459 **had "held high carnival . . ."** Capt. George Pettis, *Kit Carson's Fight with the Comanche and Kiowa Indians,* Historical Society of New Mexico 12 (1908): 7.

459 **"You cannot imagine a worse state of affairs . . ."** Dunlay, *Kit Carson and the Indians,* p. 325.

459 **"We have been greatly embarrassed . . ."** Ibid., p. 327.

460 **"his face seemed haggard and drawn with pain . . ."** Ibid., p. 341.

460 **Whether this story is actually true . . .** For unskeptical accounts of Carson's Comanche encounter, see Lavender, *Bent's Fort,* p. 167; and Vestal, *The Happy Warrior,* pp. 108–11.

462 **"You know where to find the Indians, . . ."** Dunlay, *Kit Carson and the Indians,* p. 329.

462 **"Their groans and howlings became almost intolerable, . . ."** Pettis, *Kit Carson's Fight,* p. 11.

464 **"severe charges" . . . "with their bodies thrown over the sides, . . ."** Ibid., p. 21.

465 "Throw a few shell into that crowd over thar." Ibid., p. 19.
466 "repeatedly charging my command from different points . . ." Dunlay, *Kit Carson and the Indians*, p. 332.
467 "had it not been for the two cannon, this Thanksgiving . . ." Edward Sabin, *Kit Carson Days*, p. 746.
468 "It was impossible for me to chastise them further . . ." Dunlay, *Kit Carson and the Indians*, p. 334.
468 "I had serious doubts for the safety of my rear." Sabin, *Kit Carson Days*, p. 744.
469 "exactly in the style the Indians understood . . ." Thelma Guild and Harvey Carter, *Kit Carson: A Pattern for Heroes*, p. 255.
469 "a brilliant affair" . . . "another green leaf to the laurel . . ." Sabin, *Kit Carson Days*, p. 748.
470 Without provocation, Chivington attacked Black Kettle's village . . . For further reading on the Sand Creek Massacre, I recommend Stan Hoig, *The Sand Creek Massacre*; Patrick Mendoza, *Song of Sorrow: Massacre at Sand Creek*; Bob Scott, *Blood at Sand Creek*; and Bruce Cutler, *The Massacre at Sand Creek*.
470 "Jis to think of that dog Chivington . . ." Dunlay, *Kit Carson and the Indians*, p. 391.

Chapter 45 The Condition of the Tribes

471 The Navajos . . . "will upbraid us for having taken their birthright . . ." Hunt, *James H. Carleton*, p. 282.
472 "The whole animal, including . . . head and pluck, . . ." Ibid., p. 280.
472 "Tell them . . . to be too proud to murmur . . ." Ibid., p. 285.
472 "You must pardon me, for suggesting all these details . . ." Ibid., p. 280.
473 "My God and my mother live here in the west . . ." Locke, *The Book of the Navajo*, p. 369.
473 "If he attempts to escape, he will be shot down." Ibid.
474 "must kill all Male Indians found outside the Reservation . . ." Thompson, *The Army and the Navajo*, p. 118.
475 "Let me tell you what we think." C. L. Sonnichsen, *The Mescalero Apaches*, p. 8.
476 "saturated with animal and vegetable impurities." Thompson, *The Army and the Navajo*, p. 80.
478 "Knowing him as a bear-hunter and an Indian fighter . . ." Dunlay, *Kit Carson and the Indians*, p. 346.
478 "I came to this country in 1826 . . ." Carson testimony recorded in United States, *Condition of the Indian Tribes: Report of the Joint Special Committee*, pp. 96–98.
479 "an hereditary war . . ." Ibid.
480 "In their appointed time . . . God wills that one race of men . . ." Carleton, quoted in Thompson, *The Army and the Navajo*, p. 158.
481 "this man Carleton, who has so long lorded it amongst us." Thompson, *The Army and the Navajo*, p. 122.
482 "like steel filings around a lodestone." Ibid., p. 131.

Chapter 46 Crossing Purgatory

483 a bottle of opium distilled in a syrup . . . Marc Simmons, *Kit Carson and His Three Wives*, p. 140.

483 "He begged me not to let him suffer such tortures . . ." Henry R. Tilton, *The Last Days of Kit Carson*, p. 7.

484 "With the hero for my auditor . . ." Ibid., p. 6.

484 "as wild and untamed as a brood of Mexican mustangs . . ." Simmons, *Kit Carson and His Three Wives*, p. 130.

484 "I fear I've not done right by them." Dunlay, *Kit Carson and the Indians*, p. 388.

484 he sent William and Charles . . . to be outfitted with new hats. Simmons, *Kit Carson and His Three Wives*, p. 144.

485 "Oh, call me Kit and be done with it." Ibid., p. 128.

485 "My damn luck—thar's the difficulty." Ibid., p. 133.

485 "I am now quite old and worn out . . . and hardly my own master." Ibid., p. 137.

486 "Gentlemen, that thar may be true, . . ." Dunlay, *Kit Carson and the Indians*, p. 406.

487 "General, I'm not so sure the Great Spirit means for us . . ." Ibid., p. 415.

488 an aneurysm can also be a symptom of syphilis . . . Ibid., p. 407.

488 "You called your Lord Jesus . . ." Jessie Fremont, *The Will and the Way Stories*, pp. 46–47.

488 "I'm alive yet!" . . . "I must get home, and I think I can do it." Ibid.

489 "the tumor, pressing on the pneumogastric nerves . . ." Tilton, *The Last Days of Kit Carson*, p. 5.

489 "He just seemed to pine away after mother died." Simmons, *Kit Carson and His Three Wives*, p. 142.

490 "Doctor, *compadre, adios!*" Tilton, *The Last Days of Kit Carson*, p. 7.

490 "This is the last of the general." Ibid.

490 "He had in him a personal courage . . . like lightning from a cloud." Edward Sabin, *Kit Carson Days*, p. 805.

Epilogue: In Beauty We Walk

494 It was running headlong toward the west. A prominent story in the oral history of the Navajos, another account of Barboncito's ceremony can be found in Gerald Thompson, *The Army and the Navajo*, p. 152.

494 "Kit Carson was a good type of a class of men most useful in their day . . ." Dunlay, *Kit Carson and the Indians*, p. 418.

495 "I found the Bosque a mere spot of grass . . ." Thompson, *The Army and the Navajo*, p. 140.

495 "The Commissioners are here now for the purpose . . ." My account of the discussion between Sherman and Barboncito is taken from United States, *Proceedings of the Great Peace Commission of 1867–1868*, pp. 121–24.

495 "It appears to me . . . that the General commands . . . as a god." Ibid.

496 "We do not want to go to the right or left . . ." Ibid.

497 "We wondered if it was *our* mountain, . . ." Thompson, *The Army and the Navajo*, p. 140.

SELECTED BIBLIOGRAPHY

BOOKS

Abel, Annie Heloise. *Official Correspondence of James S. Calhoun, While Indian Agent at Santa Fe and Superintendent of Indian Affairs in New Mexico*. Washington, DC: Government Printing Office, 1915.

Acrey, William P. *Navajo History: The Land and the People*. Shiprock, NM: Department of Curriculum Materials Development, 1994.

Allie, Stephen J. *All He Could Carry: U.S. Army Infantry Equipment, 1839–1910*. Leavenworth, KS: Leavenworth Historical Society, 1991.

Altshuler, Constance Wynn. *Cavalry Yellow & Infantry Blue: Army Officers in Arizona between 1851 and 1886*. Tucson: Arizona Historical Society, 1991.

Alvord, Lori Arviso, and Elizabeth Cohen Van Pelt. *The Scalpel and the Silver Bear: The First Navajo Woman Surgeon Combines Western Medicine and Traditional Healing*. New York: Bantam Books, 1999.

Armer, Laura Adams. *In Navajo Land*. New York: David McKay Company, 1962.

Armstrong, Nancy M. *Navajo Long Walk*. Niwot, CO: Roberts Rinehart Publishers, in cooperation with the Council for Indian Education, 1994.

Baars, Donald L. *Navajo Country: A Geology and Natural History of the Four Corners Region*. Albuquerque: University of New Mexico Press, 1995.

Bacon, Melvin, and Daniel Blegen. *Bent's Fort: Crossroads of Cultures on the Santa Fe Trail*. Palmer Lake, CO: Filter Press, 1995.

Bagley, Will. *Blood of the Prophets: Brigham Young and the Massacre at Mountain Meadows*. Norman: University of Oklahoma Press, 2002.

Bahti, Mark. *A Guide to Navajo Sandpaintings*. Tucson: Rio Nuevo Publishers, 2000.

———. *Spirit in the Stone: A Handbook of Southwest Indian Animal Carvings and Beliefs*. Tucson: Rio Nuevo Publishers, 1999.

Bailey, Garrick, and Roberta Glenn Bailey. *A History of the Navajos: The Reservation Years*. Santa Fe: School of American Research Press, 1986.

Bailey, Lynn R. *Bosque Redondo: An American Concentration Camp*. Pasadena: Socio-Technical Publications, 1970.

———. *Bosque Redondo: The Navajo Internment at Fort Sumner, New Mexico, 1863–1868*. Tucson: Westernlore Press, 1998.

———. *The Captive Years: Slave Taking as a Source of the Navajo Wars, 1846–1868*. Los Angeles: Corral of Westerners, 1963.

———. *If You Take My Sheep: The Evolution and Conflicts of Navajo Pastoralism, 1648–1668*. Pasadena: Westernlore Press, 1980.

———. *Indian Slave Trade in the Southwest*. Los Angeles: Westernlore Press, 1966.

————. *The Long Walk: A History of the Navajo Wars, 1846–1868*. Pasadena: Western-lore Press, 1964.

Bass, Florence. *Stories of Early Times in the Great West*. Indianapolis: Bobbs-Merrill, 1927.

Basso, Keith H., and Morris E. Opler, eds. *Apachean Culture History and Ethnology*. Tucson: University of Arizona Press, 1971.

Beasley, Conger, Jr. *Canyon de Chelly: The Timeless Fold*. Arcata, CA: Sweetlight Books, 1988.

Beck, Peggy V., Anna Lee Walters, and Nia Francisco. *The Sacred Ways of Knowledge, Sources of Life*. Tsaile, AZ: Navajo Community College Press, 1996.

Bell, William A. *New Tracks in North America: A Journal of Travel and Adventure Whilst Engaged in the Survey for a Southern Railroad to the Pacific Ocean During 1867–1868*. Albuquerque: Horn and Wallace, 1965.

Benton, Thomas H. *Thirty Years View: A History of the Working of the American Government, 1820 to 1850, Part Two*. New York: D. Appleton and Company, 1856.

Bighorse, Tiana. *Bighorse the Warrior*. Tucson: University of Arizona Press, 1990.

Blake, Michael. *The Holy Road*. New York: Random House, 2001.

Blomberg, Nancy J. *Navajo Textiles: The William Randolph Hearst Collection*. Tucson: University of Arizona Press, 1988.

Bodine, John J. *Taos Pueblo: A Walk through Time*. Santa Fe: Lightning Tree, 1977.

Bohrer, Vorsila L., and Margaret Bergseng. *An Annotated Catalogue of Plants from Window Rock, Arizona*. Window Rock, AZ: Navajoland Publications, 1963.

Bowers, Janice Emily. *100 Roadside Wildflowers of the Southwest Woodlands*. Tucson: Southwest Parks and Monuments Association, 1987.

Brewerton, George Douglas. *Overland with Kit Carson: A Narrative of the Old Spanish Trail in '48*. New York: Coward-McCann, 1930.

Brown, David E. *The Grizzly in the Southwest*. Norman: University of Oklahoma Press, 1985.

Brown, Dee. *Bury My Heart at Wounded Knee: An Indian History of the American West*. New York: Pocket Books, 1970.

Brown, Kenneth A. *Four Corners: History, Land, and People of the Desert Southwest*. New York: HarperCollins, 1995.

Bruchac, Joseph. *Navajo Long Walk: The Tragic Story of a Proud People's Forced March from Their Homeland*. Washington, DC: National Geographic Society, 2002.

Brugge, David M. *The Navajo-Hopi Land Dispute: An American Tragedy*. Albuquerque: University of New Mexico Press, 1994.

————. *Navajos in the Catholic Church Records of New Mexico, 1694–1875*. Window Rock, AZ: Research Section, Parks and Recreation Department, The Navajo Tribe, 1968.

————. *Zarcillos Largos: Courageous Advocate of Peace*. Window Rock, AZ: Navajo Parks Publications, 1970.

Brugge, David M., J. Lee Correll, and Editha L. Watson. *Navajo Bibliography*. Window Rock, AZ: Navajo Tribal Museum, 1967.

Bulow, Ernie. *Navajo Taboos*. Gallup, NM: Buffalo Medicine Books, 1991.

Caperton, Thomas J., and LoRheda Fry. *Old West Army Cookbook, 1865–1900* (1974).

Carleton, James Henry. *The Battle of Buena Vista*. New York: Harper and Brothers, 1848.

Carmony, Neil B., ed. *The Civil War in Apacheland. Sergeant George Hand's Diary: California, Arizona, West Texas, New Mexico, 1861–1864.* Silver City, NM: High-Lonesome Books, 1996.

Carroll, Charles, and Lynne Sebastian, eds. *Fort Craig: The United States Fort on the Camino Real: Collected Papers of the First Fort Craig Conference.* Socorro, NM: New Mexico Bureau of Land Management, 2000.

Carson, Kit. *Kit Carson's Autobiography.* Edited by Milo Milton Quaife. Lincoln: University of Nebraska Press, 1966.

Carson, Phil. *Fort Garland Museum: A Capsule History and Guide.* Denver: Colorado Historical Society, 2005.

Carter, Harvey Lewis. *Dear Old Kit: The Historical Christopher Carson, with a New Edition of the Carson Memoirs.* Norman: University of Oklahoma Press, 1968.

Carter, Jack L. *Trees and Shrubs of New Mexico.* Boulder, CO: Johnson Books, 1997.

Cassidy, James J., Jr., Bryce Walker, and Jill Maynard. *Through Indian Eyes: The Untold Story of Native American Peoples.* Pleasantville, NY: Reader's Digest Association, 1995.

Chaffin, Tom. *Pathfinder: John Charles Frémont and the Course of American Empire.* New York: Hill and Wang, 2002.

Chavez, Fray Angelico. *But Time and Change: The Story of Padre Martinez of Taos, 1793–1867.* Santa Fe: Sunstone Press, 1981.

Chronic, Halka. *Roadside Geology of New Mexico.* Missoula, MT: Mountain Press, 1987.

Clark, Bonnie. *The Women of Boggsville.* Denver: Colorado Historical Society.

Clark, Laverne H. *They Sang for Horses: The Impact of the Horse on Navajo and Apache Folklore.* Tucson: University of Arizona Press, 1966.

Clarke, Dwight L., ed. *The Original Journals of Henry Smith Turner: With Stephen Watts Kearny to New Mexico and California, 1846–1847.* Norman: University of Oklahoma Press, 1966.

———. *Stephen Watts Kearny: Soldier of the West.* Norman: University of Oklahoma Press, 1961.

Cobos, Rubén. *A Dictionary of New Mexico & Southern Colorado Spanish.* Santa Fe: Museum of New Mexico Press, 2003.

Colton, Ray C. *The Civil War in the Western Territories: Arizona, Colorado, New Mexico, and Utah.* Norman: University of Oklahoma Press, 1959.

Connell, Evan S. *Son of the Morning Star: Custer and the Little Bighorn.* New York: North Point Press, 1984.

Cooke, Philip St. George. *Conquest of New Mexico and California in 1846–1848.* Chicago: Rio Grande Press, 1964.

Correll, J. Lee. *Sandoval: Traitor or Patriot.* Window Rock, AZ: Navajo Nation, 1970.

———. *Through White Man's Eyes: A Contribution to Navajo History—A Chronological Record of the Navajo People from the Earliest Times to the Treaty of June 1, 1868.* Window Rock, AZ: Navajo Heritage Center, 1979.

Craig, Reginald S. *The Fighting Parson: A Biography of Col. John M. Chivington.* Tucson: Westernlore Press, 1959.

Cremony, John C. *Life among the Apaches.* San Francisco: A. Roman Company, 1868.

Crosby, Molly. *The American Plague: The Untold Story of Yellow Fever, the Epidemic that Shaped our History.* New York: Berkley Hardcover, 2006.

Crutchfield, James A. *Tragedy at Taos: The Revolt of 1847.* Plano: Republic of Texas Press, 1995.

Cullum, George W., comp. *Biographical Register of the Officers and Graduates of the United States Military Academy.* Boston: Houghton, Mifflin and Company, 1891.

Cutler, Bruce. *The Massacre at Sand Creek.* Norman: University of Oklahoma Press, 1995.

Dale, Edward Everett. *The Indians of the Southwest: A Century of Development under the United States.* Norman: University of Oklahoma Press, 1949.

Dary, David. *The Santa Fe Trail: Its History, Legends, and Lore.* New York: Penguin Books, 2000.

Davis, W. W. H. *El Gringo.* Lincoln: University of Nebraska Press, 1982.

Decker, Peter R. *"The Utes Must Go!": American Expansion and the Removal of a People.* Golden, CO: Fulcrum Publishing, 2004.

Del Castillo, Richard Griswold. *The Treaty of Guadalupe Hidalgo: A Legacy of Conflict.* Norman: University of Oklahoma Press, 1990.

Denton, Sally. *American Massacre: The Tragedy at Mountain Meadows, September 1857.* New York: Alfred A. Knopf, 2003.

DeVoto, Bernard. *The Year of Decision: 1846.* New York: Truman Talley Books, 1942.

A Diary of Kit Carson's Navajo Campaign, 1863–1864. Edited by Raymond Lindgren. San Marino, CA: Ritch Collection, Huntington Library, 1946.

Dobyns, Henry F., and Robert C. Euler. *The Navajo Indians.* Albuquerque: Center for Anthropological Studies, 1977.

Downs, James F. *The Navajo.* Prospect Heights, IL: Waveland Press, 1972.

Dunlay, Tom. *Kit Carson and the Indians.* Lincoln: University of Nebraska Press, 2000.

Dunn, J. P. *Massacres of the Mountains: A History of the Indian Wars of the Far West.* New York: Harpers, 1886.

Durand, John. *The Taos Massacres.* Elkhorn, WI: Puzzlebox Press, 2004.

Dutton, Bertha P. *American Indians of the Southwest.* Albuquerque: University of New Mexico Press, 1983.

Dyk, Walter. *Son of Old Man Hat: A Navajo Biography.* Lincoln: University of Nebraska Press, 1938.

Edrington, Thomas S., and John Taylor. *The Battle of Glorieta Pass: A Gettysburg in the West, March 26–28, 1862.* Albuquerque: University of New Mexico Press, 1998.

Edwards, Frank S. *A Campaign in New Mexico.* Readex Microprint, 1966.

Eisenhower, John S. D. *So Far from God: The U.S. War with Mexico, 1846–1848.* New York: Random House, 1989.

Ellis, Florence Hawley. *An Anthropological Study of the Navajo Indians.* New York and London: Garland Publishing, 1974.

Emory, William. *Lieutenant Emory Reports.* Edited by Ross Calvin. Albuquerque: University of New Mexico Press, 1951.

Estabrook, Emma Franklin. *Givers of Life: American Indians as Contributors to Civilization.* Albuquerque: University of New Mexico Press, 1931.

Estergreen, Marian Morgan. *Kit Carson: A Portrait in Courage.* Norman: University of Oklahoma Press, 1962.

Farb, Peter. *Man's Rise to Civilization as Shown by the Indians of North America from Primeval Times to the Coming of the Industrial State.* New York: E. P. Dutton, 1968.

Faris, James C. *Navajo and Photography.* Salt Lake City: University of Utah Press, 2003.

Faust, Patricia L. *Historical Times Illustrated Encyclopedia of the Civil War.* New York: Harper & Row, 1986.

Fehrenbach, T. R. *Comanches: The History of a People.* New York: Random House, 1974.

Fergusson, Erna. *Dancing Gods: Indian Ceremonials of New Mexico & Arizona.* Albuquerque: University of New Mexico Press, 1931.

Folsom, Franklin. *Indian Uprising on the Rio Grande: The Pueblo Revolt of 1680.* Albuquerque: University of New Mexico Press, 1996.

Forbes, Jack. *Apache, Navaho and Spaniard.* Norman: University of Oklahoma Press, 1960.

Frazier, Donald S., ed. *The United States and Mexico at War: Nineteenth-Century Expansionism and Conflict.* New York: Simon & Schuster Macmillan, 1998.

Frazier, Ian. *Great Plains.* New York: Farrar, Straus and Giroux, 1989.

————. *On the Rez.* New York: Farrar, Straus and Giroux, 2000.

Freiberger, Harriet. *Lucien Maxwell: Villain or Visionary.* Santa Fe: Sunstone Press, 1999.

Frémont, Jessie Benton. *The Will and the Way Stories.* Boston: D. Lathrop Company, 1891.

Frémont, John C. *Memoirs of My Life.* New York: Cooper Square Press, 2001.

————. *Report of the Exploring Expedition to the Rocky Mountains: In the Year 1842, and to Oregon and North California in the Years 1843–44.* Santa Barbara: Narrative Press, 2002.

Frink, Maurice. *Fort Defiance and the Navajos.* Boulder: Pruett Press, 1968.

Fugate, Francis L., and Roberta B. Fugate. *Roadside History of New Mexico.* Missoula, MT: Mountain Press Publishing Company, 1989.

Gardner, Mark L. *Bent's Old Fort: National Historic Site.* Tucson: Southwest Parks and Monuments Association, 1998.

Garrard, Lewis H. *Wah-to-yah and the Taos Trail.* Norman: University of Oklahoma Press, 1955.

George, Isaac. *Heroes and Incidents of the Mexican War: Containing Doniphan's Expedition.* San Bernardino: Borgo Press, 1985.

Gerow, Peggy A. *Guardian of the Trail: Archaeological & Historical Investigations at Fort Craig.* Santa Fe: Bureau of Land Management, 2004.

Gerson, Noel B. *Kit Carson: Folk Hero and Man.* Garden City: Doubleday, 1964.

Gibson, George Rutledge. *Journal of a Soldier under Kearny and Doniphan, 1846–1847.* Philadelphia: Porcupine Press, 1974.

Gillmor, Frances, and Louisa Wade Wetherill. *Traders to the Navajos: The Story of the Wetherills of Tayenta.* Albuquerque: University of New Mexico Press, 1953.

Gilpin, Laura. *The Enduring Navaho.* Austin: University of Texas Press, 1974.

Goodman, James M. *The Navajo Atlas: Environments, Resources, People and History of the Diné Bikeyah.* Norman: University of Oklahoma Press, 1986.

Goodwin, Grenville. *The Social Organization of the Western Apache.* Tucson: University of Arizona Press, 1969.

Gordon-McCutchan, R. C., ed. *Kit Carson: Indian Fighter or Indian Killer?* Niwot: University Press of Colorado, 1996.

Grant, Campbell. *Canyon de Chelly: Its People and Rock Art.* Tucson: University of Arizona Press, 1977.

Gregg, Josiah. *Commerce of the Prairies.* Norman: University of Oklahoma Press, 1954.

Guild, Thelma S., and Harvey L. Carter. *Kit Carson: A Pattern for Heroes.* Lincoln: University of Nebraska Press, 1984.

Haile, Berard, O.F.M. *Navajo Coyote Tales.* Lincoln: University of Nebraska Press, 1984.

Halaas, David Fridtjof, and Andrew E. Masich. *Halfbreed: The Remarkable True Story of George Bent.* Cambridge, MA: Da Capo Press, 2004.

Haley, J. Evetts. *Charles Goodnight, Cowman and Plainsman.* Norman: University of Oklahoma Press, 1949.

Hall, Martin Hardwick. *Sibley's New Mexico Campaign.* Albuquerque: University of New Mexico Press, 2000.

Hané, Hwéeldi Baa. *Oral Histories of the Long Walk.* Lake Valley, NM: Lake Valley Navajo School, 1989.

Hardwick, William. *Authentic Indian-Mexican Recipes.* Fort Stockton, 1993.

Hart, E. Richard. *Pedro Pino: Governer of Zuni Pueblo, 1830–1878.* Logan: Utah State University Press, 2003.

Haynes, Sam W. *James K. Polk and the Expansionist Impulse.* New York: Addison Wesley Longman, 2002.

Hazen-Hammond, Susan. *Timelines of Native American History through the Centuries with Mother Earth and Father Sky.* New York: Berkley Publishing Group, 1997.

Heffernan, William Joseph. *Edward M. Kern: The Travels of an Artist-Explorer.* Bakersfield, CA: Kern County Historical Society, 1953.

Heitman, Francis B. *Historical Register and Dictionary of the U.S. Army.* Washington, DC: Government Printing Office, 1965.

Henderson, Alice Corbin. *Brothers of Light: The Penitentes of the Southwest.* Santa Fe: William Gannon, 1977.

Henry, Jeanette, ed. *The Indian Historian.* San Francisco: American Indian Historical Society, 1976.

Herr, Pamela. *Jessie Benton Frémont.* Norman: University of Oklahoma Press, 1987.

Herr, Pamela, and Mary Lee Spence, eds. *The Letters of Jessie Benton Frémont, 1824–1902.* Urbana and Chicago: University of Illinois Press, 1993.

Heyman, Max L. *Prudent Soldier: A Biography of Major General E. R. S. Canby, 1817–1873.* Glendale: Arthur H. Clark, 1959.

Hillerman, Tony. *Coyote Waits.* New York: HarperCollins, 1990.

———. *Talking God.* New York: HarperCollins, 1989.

Hine, Robert V. *Edward Kern and American Expansion.* New Haven, CT: Yale University Press, 1962.

Hoffman, Virginia, and Broderick H. Johnson. *Navajo Biographies.* Vols. 1 & 2. Rough Rock, AZ: Navajo Curriculum Center Press, 1974.

Hoig, Stan. *The Sand Creek Massacre.* Norman: University of Oklahoma Press, 1980.

Hordes, Stanley M. *To the End of the Earth: A History of the Crypto-Jews of New Mexico.* New York: Columbia University Press, 2005.

Horgan, Paul. *The Centuries of Santa Fe.* New York: E. P. Dutton, 1965.

———. *Great River: The Rio Grande in North American History.* Hanover, NH: University Press of New England, 1984.

Houk, Rose. *Navajo of Canyon de Chelly.* Tucson: Southwest Parks and Monuments Association, 1995.

Hughes, John T. *Doniphan's Expedition: Containing an Account of the Conquest of New Mexico*. Chicago: Rio Grande Press, 1962.

Hughes, Patrick J. *Fort Leavenworth: Gateway to the West*. Newton, KS: Mennonite Press, 2000.

Hunt, Aurora. *Major General James H. Carleton, 1814–1873*. Glendale: Arthur H. Clark, 1958.

Hyde, George E. *Life of George Bent, Written from His Letters*. Norman: University of Oklahoma Press, 1968.

Irving, Washington. *The Adventures of Captain Bonneville: Digested from His Journals*. New York: Stackpole Books, 2001.

Iverson, Peter. *Diné: A History of the Navajos*. Albuquerque: University of New Mexico Press, 2002.

———. *The Navajo Nation*. Albuquerque: University of New Mexico Press, 1983.

Jahoda, Gloria. *The Trail of Tears: The Story of the American Indian Removals, 1813–1855*. New York: Wings Books, 1975.

James, Thomas. *Three Years among the Indians and Mexicans*. Chicago: Rio Grande Press, 1962.

Jamison, Bill. *Santa Fe: An Intimate View*. Santa Fe: Milagro Press, 1982.

Johnson, Broderick H., ed. *Stories of Traditional Navajo Life and Culture by Twenty-two Navajo Men and Women*. Tsaile, AZ: Navajo Community College Press, 1977.

Jones, Charles, ed. *Look to the Mountain Top: Contemporary Authors Reveal Our True Indian Heritage*. San Jose: Times Mirror Company, 1972.

Josephy, Alvin M., Jr. *The Civil War in the American West*. New York: Vintage Books, 1991.

Judge, James. *New Light on Chaco Canyon*. Santa Fe: School of American Research, 1984.

Julyan, Robert. *The Place Names of New Mexico*. Albuquerque: University of New Mexico Press, 1972.

Kavanagh, Thomas W. *The Comanches: A History, 1706–1875*. Lincoln: University of Nebraska Press, 1996.

Keleher, William Aloysius. *Turmoil in New Mexico, 1846–1868*. Santa Fe: Rydal Press, 1952.

Kelley, Klara B., and Francis Harris. *Navajo Sacred Places*. Bloomington: Indiana University Press, 1994.

Kelly, Lawrence C. *Navajo Roundup: Selected Correspondence of Kit Carson's Expedition against the Navajo, 1863–1865*. Boulder: Pruett Press, 1970.

Kessell, John L. *Kiva, Cross, and Crown: The Pecos Indians and New Mexico, 1540–1840*. Tucson: Southwest Parks and Monuments Association, 1987.

Kluckhohn, Clyde, and Dorothea Leighton. *The Navajo*. Cambridge, MA: Harvard University Press, 1946.

Kluckhohn, Clyde, Lucy Wales Kluckhohn, and Willard Williams Hill. *Navajo Material Culture*. Cambridge, MA: Harvard University Press, 1971.

Kosik, Fran. *Native Roads: The Complete Motoring Guide to the Navajo and Hopi Nations*. Tucson: Rio Nuevo Publishers, 1996.

Kupke, William A. *The Indian and the Thunderwagon*. Fort Sumner, NM: Fort Sumner State Monument, 1989.

La Farge, Oliver. *Laughing Boy*. Boston: Houghton Mifflin, 1929.

———. *Santa Fe: The Autobiography of a Southwestern Town*. Norman: University of Oklahoma Press, 1959.

Lamar, Howard R., ed. *The New Encyclopedia of the American West*. New Haven, CT: Yale University Press, 1998.

Langellier, John P. *Redlegs: The U.S. Artillery from the Civil War to the Spanish-American War, 1861–1898*. London: Greenhill Books, 1998.

———. *Terrible Swift Sword: Union Artillery, Cavalry and Infantry, 1861–1865*. London: Greenhill Books, 2000.

Launius, Roger D. *Alexander William Doniphan: Portrait of a Missouri Moderate*. Columbia: University Press of Missouri, 1997.

Lauritzen, Jonreed. *The Battle of San Pasqual*. New York: G. P. Putnam's Sons, 1968.

Lavender, David. *Bent's Fort*. Lincoln: University of Nebraska Press, 1954.

———. *Climax at Buena Vista*. Philadelphia: University of Pennsylvania Press, 1966.

———. *The Southwest*. Albuquerque: University of New Mexico Press, 1980.

Leach, Nicky J. *The Guide to National Parks of the Southwest*. Tucson: Southwest Parks and Monuments Association, 1992.

Limerick, Patricia Nelson. *The Legacy of Conquest: The Unbroken Past of the American West*. New York: W. W. Norton, 1987.

Linford, Laurance D. *Navajo Places: History, Legend, and Landscape*. Salt Lake City: University of Utah Press, 2000.

Link, Martin A. *Hwelte*. Window Rock, AZ: Navajo Tribal Museum, 1971.

Locke, Raymond Friday. *The Book of the Navajo*. Los Angeles: Mankind Publishing, 1976.

Mabery, Marilyne. *El Malpais National Monument*. Tucson: Southwest Parks and Monuments Association, 1990.

MacCarter, Jane Susan. *New Mexico Wildlife Viewing Guide*. 2d ed. Helena: Falcon Press, n.d.

Magoffin, Susan Shelby. *Down the Santa Fe Trail and into Mexico: The Diary of Susan Shelby Magoffin, 1846–1847*. Edited by Stella M. Drumm. Lincoln: University of Nebraska Press, 1982.

Makepeace, Anne. *Edward S. Curtis: Coming to Light*. Washington, DC: National Geographic Society, 2002.

Mansfield, Joseph K. *Mansfield on the Condition of the Western Forts, 1853–1854*. Norman: University of Oklahoma Press, 1962.

Marks, Paula Mitchell. *In a Barren Land: American Indian Dispossession and Survival*. New York: William Morrow, 1998.

Marszalek, John F. *Leaders of the American Civil War: A Biographical and Historiographical Dictionary*. Westport, CT: Greenwood Press, 1998.

Marti, Werner H. *Messenger of Destiny: The California Adventures, 1846–1847, of Archibald H. Gillespie, U.S. Marine Corps*. San Francisco: John Howell-Books, 1960.

Matthews, Washington. *Navajo Legends*. Salt Lake City: University of Utah Press, 1994.

Mayes, Vernon O., and Barbara Bayless Lacy. *Nanise': A Navajo Herbal Guide: One Hundred Plants from the Navajo Reservation*. Tsaile, AZ: Navajo Community College Press, 1989.

McCarthy, Cormac. *Blood Meridian*. New York: Vintage Books, 1985.

Mclean, Kim. *Casa Rinconada*. Tucson: Southwest Parks and Monuments Association, 1995.

————. *Chetro Ketl.* Tucson: Southwest Parks and Monuments Association, 1995.

————. *Pueblo Bonito.* Tucson: Southwest Parks and Monuments Association, 1996.

McMurtry, Larry. *The Colonel and Little Missie: Buffalo Bill, Annie Oakley, and the Beginnings of Superstardom in America.* New York: Simon & Schuster, 2005.

————. *Oh What a Slaughter: Massacres in the American West, 1846–1890.* New York: Simon & Schuster, 2005.

McNeley, James Kale. *Holy Wind in Navajo Philosophy.* Tucson: University of Arizona Press, 1981.

McNierney, Michael, ed. *Taos 1847: The Revolt in Contemporary Accounts.* Boulder: Johnson Publishing, 1990.

McNitt, Frank, ed. *Navaho Expedition: Journal of a Military Reconnaissance from Santa Fe, New Mexico, to the Navaho Country, Made in 1849 by Lieutenant James H. Simpson.* Norman: University of Oklahoma Press, 1964.

McNitt, Frank, *The Indian Traders.* Norman: University of Oklahoma Press, 1962.

————. *Navajo Wars: Military Campaigns, Slave Raids and Reprisals.* Albuquerque: University of New Mexico Press, 1972.

Meketa, Jacqueline Dorgan. *Legacy of Honor: The Life of Rafael Chacón, a Nineteenth-Century New Mexican.* Albuquerque: University of New Mexico Press, 1986.

Mendoza, Patrick M. *Song of Sorrow: Massacre at Sand Creek.* Denver: Willow Wind Publishing, 1993.

Miller, Darlis A. *The California Column in New Mexico.* Albuquerque: University of New Mexico Press, 1982.

Mindeleff, Cosmos. "Navaho Houses," in *The Seventeenth Annual Report.* Washington, DC: Bureau of Ethnology, 1897.

Mitchell, James R. *Gem Trails of New Mexico.* Baldwin Park, CA: Gem Guides, 2001.

Mitchell, Marie. *The Navajo Peace Treaty of 1868.* New York: Macon and Lipscomb Publishers, 1973.

Momaday, N. Scott. *House Made of Dawn.* New York: HarperCollins, 1966.

Moore, Lucy. *Into the Canyon: Seven Years in Navajo Country.* Albuquerque: University of New Mexico Press, 2004.

Morand, Sheila. *Santa Fe Then and Now.* Santa Fe: Sunstone Press, 1998.

Morris, Don P. *Early Navajo Sites in Cañon de Chelly.* Unpublished manuscript. Tucson: Western Archaeological Center, n.d.

Moulton, Candy. *Everyday Life among the American Indians, 1800 to 1900.* Cincinnati: Writer's Digest Books, 2001.

Murphy, Dan. *El Morro National Monument.* Western National Parks Association, 2003.

Nabokov, Peter. *Indian Running: Native American History & Tradition.* Santa Fe: Ancient City Press, 1981.

————. *Native American Testimony.* New York: Penguin Books, 1978.

Neihardt, John G. *Black Elk Speaks.* Lincoln: University of Nebraska Press, 1932.

Newcomb, Franc Johnson. *Hosteen Klah: Navajo Medicine Man and Sand Painter.* Norman: University of Oklahoma Press, 1964.

Noble, David Grant, ed. *Houses Beneath the Rock: The Anasazi of Canyon de Chelly and Navajo National Monument.* Santa Fe: Ancient City Press, 1986.

Noble, David Grant, and Richard B. Woodbury. *Zuni and El Morro Past & Present.* Santa Fe: School of American Research, 1993.

O'Bryan, Aileen. *Navaho Indian Myths.* New York: Dover Publications, 1993.

Ogle, Ralph Hedrick. *Federal Control of the Western Apaches, 1848–1886*. Albuquerque: University of New Mexico Press, 1940.

Parkman, Francis, Jr. *The Oregon Trail*. Oxford: Oxford University Press, 1996.

Parsons, Elsie Clews. *Taos Tales*. New York: Dover Publications, 1996.

Pearce, T. M., ed. *New Mexico Place Names: A Geographical Dictionary*. Albuquerque: University of New Mexico Press, 1965.

Pettis, Capt. George H. *Personal Narratives of the Battles of the Rebellion: Kit Carson's Fight with the Comanche and Kiowa Indians*. Santa Fe: Historical Society of New Mexico, 1908.

Pettit, Jan. *Utes: The Mountain People*. Boulder: Johnson Books, 1990.

Phillips, Catharine Coffin. *Jessie Benton Frémont: A Woman Who Made History*. Lincoln: University of Nebraska Press, 1995.

Pike, David. *Roadside New Mexico: A Guide to Historic Markers*. Albuquerque: University of New Mexico Press, 2004.

Pratt, Boyd C., and Dan Scurlock. *Llano, River, and Mountains: The Southeast New Mexico Regional Overview: Volume 1: Historic Overview*. Fort Sumner, NM: Fort Sumner State Monument, 1989.

Preston, Douglas. *Cities of Gold: A Journey across the American Southwest*. Albuquerque: University of New Mexico Press, 1992.

———. *The Royal Road: El Camino Real from Mexico City to Santa Fe*. Albuquerque: University of New Mexico Press, 1998.

———. *Talking to the Ground: One Family's Journey on Horseback across the Sacred Land of the Navajo*. New York: Simon & Schuster, 1995.

Price, Peter. *The Battle of San Pasqual Dec. 6, 1846 & the Struggle for California*. San Diego: Pembroke Publishers, 1990.

Pritzker, Barry M. *A Native American Encyclopedia: History, Culture, and Peoples*. New York: Oxford University Press, 2000.

Reid, Robert Leonard. *America, New Mexico*. Tucson: University of Arizona Press, 1998.

Rittenhouse, Jack D. *New Mexico Civil War Biography*. Houston: Stage Coach Press, 1961.

Roberts, David. *In Search of the Old Ones: Exploring the Anasazi World of the Southwest*. New York: Simon & Schuster, 1996.

———. *A Newer World: Kit Carson, John C. Frémont, and the Claiming of the American West*. New York: Simon & Schuster, 2000.

———. *Once They Moved Like the Wind: Cochise, Geronimo, and the Apache Wars*. New York: Simon & Schuster, 1993.

Robinson, Jacob. *Sketches of the Great West: A Journal of the Santa Fe Expedition*. Portsmouth, NH: Portsmouth Journal Press, 1848.

Roessel, Robert A., Jr. *Pictorial History of the Navajo: From 1860 to 1910*. Rough Rock, AZ: Navajo Curriculum Center, 1980.

Roessel, Ruth, ed. *Navajo Stories of the Long Walk Period*. Tsaile, AZ: Navajo Community College Press, 1973.

Roosevelt, Theodore. *Thomas H. Benton*. New York: Houghton, Mifflin and Company, 1887.

Royce, Josiah. *California: A Study of the American Character*. Berkeley: Heyday Books, 2002.

Rutledge, Lee A. *Campaign Clothing: Field Uniforms of the Indian War Army, 1866–1871*. Tustin, CA: North Cape Publications, 1998.

Ruxton, George Frederick. *Life in the Old West*. Edited by LeRoy R. Hafen. Norman: University of Oklahoma Press, 1951.

Ryan, John P. *Fort Stanton and Its Community*. Las Cruces, NM: Yucca Tree Press, 1998.

Sabin, Edwin LeGrand. *Kit Carson Days, 1809–1868: Adventures in the Path of Empire*. Chicago: A. C. McClurg, 1914.

Salzmann, Zdenek, and Joy M. Salzmann. *Native Americans of the Southwest: The Serious Traveler's Introduction to Peoples and Places*. Boulder: Westview Press, 1997.

Sando, Joe S. *Pueblo Profiles: Cultural Identity through Centuries of Change*. Santa Fe: Clear Light Publishers, n.d.

Sapir, Edward. *Navajo Texts*. Iowa City: University of Iowa Press, 1942.

Schroeder, Albert H. *The Changing Way of Southwestern Indians: A Historic Perspective*. Glorieta, NM: Rio Grande Press, 1973.

Scott, Bob. *Blood at Sand Creek: The Massacre Revisited*. Caldwell, ID: Caxton Printers, 1994.

Seigenthaler, John. *James K. Polk*. New York: Henry Holt, 2003.

Seymour, E. L. D., ed. *The Garden Encyclopedia: A Complete, Practical and Convenient Guide to Every Detail of Gardening*. New York: W. H. Wise, 1936.

Sherry, John W. *Land, Wind, and Hard Words: A Story of Navajo Activism*. Albuquerque: University of New Mexico Press, 2002.

Shinkle, James D. *Fifty Years of Roswell History, 1867–1917*. Roswell: Hall-Poorbaugh Press, 1965.

———. *Fort Sumner and Bosque Redondo Indian Reservation*. Roswell: Hall-Poorbaugh Press, 1965.

Shoumatoff, Alex. *Legends of the American Desert: Sojourns in the Greater Southwest*. New York: HarperCollins, 1997.

Simmons, Marc. *Kit Carson and His Three Wives*. Albuquerque: University of New Mexico Press, 2003.

———. *The Last Conquistador: Juan de Oñate and the Settling of the Far Southwest*. Norman: University of Oklahoma Press, 1991.

———. *The Little Lion of the Southwest: A Life of Manuel Antonio Chaves*. Athens: University of Ohio Press, 1973.

———. *New Mexico: An Interpretive History*. Albuquerque: University of New Mexico Press, 1988.

———. *The Old Trail to Santa Fe: Collected Essays*. Albuquerque: University of New Mexico Press, 1996.

Simmons, Marc, and R. C. Gordon-McCutchan. *The Short Truth about Kit Carson and the Indians*. Taos: Columbine Printing, 1993.

Simmons, Virginia McConnell. *The San Luis Valley: Land of the Six-Armed Cross*. 2d ed. Niwot, CO: University Press of Colorado, 1999.

Smith, George Winston, and Charles Judah, eds. *Chronicles of the Gringos: The U.S. Army in the Mexican War, 1846–1848: Accounts of Eyewitnesses and Combatants*. Albuquerque: University of New Mexico Press, 1962.

Sonnichsen, C. L. *The Mescalero Apaches*. Norman: University of Oklahoma Press, 1958.

Spicer, Edward H. *Cycles of Conquest: The Impact of Spain, Mexico, and the United States on the Indians of the Southwest, 1533–1960.* Tucson: University of Arizona Press, 1962.

Stanley, F. E. V. *Sumner.* Borger, TX: Jim Hess Printers, 1969.

———. *The Jicarilla Apaches of North Mexico.* Pampa, TX: Pampa Print Shop, 1967.

Starr, Kevin. *Americans and the California Dream, 1850–1915.* New York: Oxford University Press, 1973.

Steele, Thomas J., and Rowena A. Rivera. *Penitente Self-Government: Brotherhoods and Councils, 1797–1947.* Santa Fe: Ancient City Press, 1985.

Stegner, Page. *Winning the West: The Epic Saga of the American Frontier, 1800–1899.* Hong Kong: Free Press, 2002.

Stern, Theodore. *The Klamath Tribe: A People and Their Reservation.* Seattle: University of Washington Press, 1965.

Stone, Irving. *Immortal Wife: The Biographical Novel of Jessie Benton Fremont.* Chicago: Consolidated Book Publishers, 1954.

Supplee, Charles, and Douglas and Barbara Anderson. *Canyon de Chelly: The Story behind the Scenery.* KC Publications, 1990.

Taylor, John. *Bloody Valverde: A Civil War Battle on the Rio Grande, February 21, 1862.* Albuquerque: University of New Mexico Press, 1965.

Terrell, John Upton. *The Navajos.* New York: Weybright and Talley, 1970.

The Editors of *National Geographic. The World of the American Indian.* Washington, DC: National Geographic Society, 1974.

Theisen, Gerald. *A Study Guide to New Mexico History.* Santa Fe: Museum of New Mexico Press, n.d.

Thomas, David Hurst. *Skull Wars: Kennewick Man, Archaeology, and the Battle for Native American Identity.* New York: Basic Books, 2000.

Thompson, Gerald E. *The Army and the Navajo: The Bosque Redondo Reservation Experiment, 1863–1868.* Tucson: University of Arizona Press, 1976.

———. *Edward F. Beale & the American West.* Albuquerque: University of New Mexico Press, 1983.

Thrapp, Dan L. *The Conquest of Apacheria.* Norman: University of Oklahoma Press, 1967.

Thybony, Scott. *Canyon de Chelly National Monument.* Tucson: Western National Parks Association, 1997.

———. *The Hogan: The Traditional Navajo Home.* Tucson: Western National Parks Association, 1999.

Tiller, Veronica E. Velarde. *The Jicarilla Apache Tribe.* Lincoln: University of Nebraska Press, 1983.

Tilton, Henry R. *The Last Days of Kit Carson.* Grand Forks: Holt Printing Company, 1939.

Trafzer, Clifford E. *Anglo Expansionists and Navajo Raiders: A Conflict of Interests.* Tsaile, AZ: Navajo Community College Press, 1978.

———. *Navajos and Spaniards.* Tsaile, AZ: Navajo Community College Press, 1978.

Turner, Frederick W., III. *The Portable North American Indian Reader.* New York: Viking Press, 1973.

Twitchell, Ralph Emerson. *The Story of the Conquest of Santa Fe, New Mexico, and the Building of Old Fort Marcy.* Santa Fe: Historical Society of New Mexico, 1929.

Underhill, Ruth M. *The Navajos*. Norman: University of Oklahoma Press, 1956.

Utley, Robert M. *Fort Union National Monument*. Washington, DC: National Park Service, 1962.

———. *The Indian Frontier of the American West, 1846–1890*. Albuquerque: University of New Mexico Press, 1984.

———. *A Life Wild and Perilous: Mountain Men and the Paths to the Pacific*. New York: Henry Holt, 1997.

Utley, Robert, and Wilcomb E. Washburn. *Indian Wars*. Boston: Houghton Mifflin, 1977.

Van Valkenburgh, Richard. *Diné Bikéyah*. Window Rock, AZ: Department of the Interior, 1941.

Vestal, Stanley. *Kit Carson: The Happy Warrior of the Old West*. Boston: Houghton Mifflin, 1928.

———. *The Old Santa Fe Trail*. Lincoln: University of Nebraska Press, 1939.

Waldman, Carl. *The North American Indian*. New York: Checkmark Books, 1985.

Wall, Leon, and William Morgan. *Navajo-English Dictionary*. New York: Hippocrene Books, 1958.

Wallace, Ernest, and E. Adamson Hoebel. *The Comanches: Lords of the South Plains*. Norman: University of Oklahoma Press, 1952.

Ward, Geoffrey C. *The West: An Illustrated History*. Boston: Little, Brown, 1996.

Waters, Frank. *The Book of the Hopi*. New York: Ballantine Books, 1970.

Weber, David J. *On the Edge of Empire: The Taos Hacienda of Los Martinez*. Santa Fe: Museum of New Mexico Press, 1996.

———. *Richard H. Kern: Expeditionary Artist in the Far Southwest, 1848–1853*. Albuquerque: University of New Mexico Press, 1985.

Weigle, Marta. *The Penitentes of the Southwest*. Santa Fe: Ancient City Press, 1970.

Wenger, Gilbert R. *The Story of Mesa Verde National Park*. Mesa Verde National Park, CO: Mesa Verde Museum Association, 1980.

Werner, Michael S. *Encyclopedia of Mexico: History, Society & Culture*. Chicago: Fitzroy Dearborn Publishers, 1997.

White, John Manchip. *Everyday Life of the American Indian*. New York: Holmes & Meier Publishers, 1979.

White, Lonnie T. *Chronicle of a Congressional Journey: The Doolittle Committee in the Southwest, 1865*. Boulder: Pruett Publishing, 1865.

White, William. *Encyclopedia of Civil War Biographies*. Armonk, NY: Sharpe Reference, 2000.

Wilson, Chris. *The Myth of Santa Fe: Creating a Modern Regional Tradition*. Albuquerque: University of New Mexico Press, 1997.

Wilson, John P. *Fort Sumner, New Mexico*. Portales: Museum of New Mexico Monuments Division, n.d.

Wilson, John Philip. *Military Campaigns in Navajo Country, Northwestern New Mexico, 1800–1846*. Santa Fe: Museum of New Mexico Press, 1973.

Wissler, Clark. *Indians of the United States*. New York: Doubleday, 1940.

Zolbrod, Paul G. *Diné Bahané: The Navajo Creation Story*. Albuquerque: University of New Mexico Press, 1984.

Zollinger, Norman. *Meridian: A Novel of Kit Carson's West*. New York: Forge Books, 1998.

ARTICLES, MONOGRAPHS, LETTERS, AND OTHER PAPERS

Abel, Annie Heloise. "Indian Affairs in New Mexico under the Administration of William Carr Lane. From the Journal of John Ward." *New Mexico Historical Review* 16 (April 1941): 206–32.

Amsden, Charles. "The Navajo Exile at Bosque Redondo." *New Mexico Historical Review* 8 (January 1933): 31–52.

Bancroft, Hubert H. "The Works of Hubert Howe Bancroft." *History of Arizona and New Mexico* (1890): 17.

Barbour, Barton H. "Kit Carson and the 'Americanization' of New Mexico." *New Mexico Historical Review* 77(2) (Spring 2002): 115.

Bender, A. B. "Frontier Defense in the Territory of New Mexico, 1846–1853." *New Mexico Historical Review* 9(3) (July 1934).

———. "Frontier Defense in the Territory of New Mexico, 1853–1861." *New Mexico Historical Review* 9(4) (October 1934).

———. "Military Posts in the Southwest." *New Mexico Historical Review* 16(2) (April 1941).

Benton, Thomas H. "Domestic Politics: The Tariff and Slavery." *American Statesmen* (1972).

Brewer, Sallie Pierce. "The Long Walk to Bosque Redondo as Told by Peshlakai Et-sidi." *Museum of Northern Arizona Museum Notes* 9(11) (May–June 1937): 55–62.

Brown, Sharon A., and Josina Martinez. "Long Walk News." *National Park Service Study News* (2003).

Brugge, David M. "Documentary Reference to a Navajo Naach'id in 1840." *Ethnohistory* 10(2) (1963).

Carson, Alvar W. "Hispanic Settlements on Indian Land." *El Palacio* 85(1) (1979).

Castel, Albert. "The Life of a Rising Son, Pt. 1: The Failure." *Civil War Times* 4 (July 1979).

———. "The Life of a Rising Son, Pt. 2: The Subordinate." *Civil War Times* 12 (August 1979).

———. "The Life of a Rising Son, Pt. 3: The Conqueror." *Civil War Times* 10 (September 1979).

Chaput, Donald. "Generals, Indian Agents, Politicians: The Doolittle Survey of 1865." *Western Historical Quarterly* 3 (July 1972): 269–82.

Commissioner of Indian Affairs. "Appropriation for the Navajo Indians." House Executive Document 1, 40th Cong., 2d sess.

———. "Annual Report of the Commissioner of Indian Affairs." Washington, DC: Government Printing Office, 1865.

———. "Annual Report of the Commissioner of Indian Affairs." Washington, DC: Government Printing Office, 1866.

———. "Annual Report of the Commissioner of Indian Affairs." Washington, DC: Government Printing Office, 1867.

Correll, J. Lee. "Ganado Mucho—Navajo Naat'aani." *Navajo Times* (November 30, 1967): 24–27.

Danziger, Edmund J. "The Steck-Carleton Controversy in Civil War New Mexico." *Southwestern Historical Quarterly* 74(2) (October 1970): 189–203.

Fort Canby. "Memorandum of Events at Fort Canby September 9–12, 1863." Records of United States Army Continental Commands (1821–1920).

Fort Defiance. "Reminiscences of Fort Defiance, New Mexico, 1860." *Journal of the Military Service Institution of the U.S.* (1883): 14.

Gardner, Mark L. "Tragedy in Taos: Bloody Rebellion of 1847 Haunts New Mexico's History." *New Mexico Magazine* (October 2000): 32.

Gregory, Herbert E. "The Navajo Country, a Geographic and Hydrogeographic Reconnaissance of Parts of Arizona, New Mexico, and Utah." U.S. Geological Survey Professional Paper (1916): 93.

Greiner, John. "Private Letters of a Government Official in the Southwest." *Journal of American History* 3 (1909): 551–54.

Gwyther, George A. "An Indian Reservation." *Overland Monthly* (December 1970): 10.

Heib, Louis A. "Alexander M. Stephen and the Navajos." *New Mexico Historical Review* 79(3) (Summer 2004): 353.

Heyman, Max L. "On the Navajo Trail: The Campaign of 1860–1861." *New Mexico Historical Review* 26 (January 1951): 44–64.

Hutton, Paul. "Why Is This Man Forgotten?" *True West: Celebrating the American West* (March 2006): 24.

Jenkins, Myra Ellen, and Ward Allen Minge. "Record of Navajo Activities Affecting the Acoma–Laguna Area, 1746–1910." New Mexico State Records Center and Archives (typed manuscript), 1974.

Jett, Stephen C. "The Destruction of the Navajo Orchards in 1864: Captain John Thompson's Report." *Arizona and the West* 16 (Winter 1974): 365–78.

Kappler, Charles J., ed. "Indian Laws and Treaties II." Senate Executive Document 452, 57th Cong. 1st sess.

Kelly, Lawrence C. "Where Was Fort Canby?" *New Mexico Quarterly Review* 42 (January 1967): 49–62.

Kemrer, Meade, and Donald Graybill. "Navajo Warfare and Economy, 1750–1868." *Western Canadian Journal of Anthropology* 2(1) (1974).

Kessell, John L. "General Sherman and the Navajo Treaty of 1868: A Basic Expedient Misunderstanding." *Western Historical Quarterly* 12 (July 1981): 251–72.

Lindgren, Raymond E., ed. "A Diary of Kit Carson's Navaho Campaign, 1863–1864." *New Mexico Historical Review* (July 1946): 226–46.

Lyon, William H. "History Comes to the Navajos: A Review Essay." *American Indian Culture and Research Journal* 11(3) (1987): 75–92.

Magers, Pamela C. "Settlement in Cañon del Muerto." Unpublished Ph.D. dissertation. Tucson: University of Arizona, 1976.

Mangiante, Rosal. "History of Fort Defiance, 1851–1900." Unpublished Master's thesis. Tucson: University of Arizona, 1950.

Mangum, Neil C. "Old Fort Wingate in the Navajo War." *New Mexico Historical Review* 66 (October 1991): 393–412.

Mann, Charles C. "1491." *Atlantic Monthly* 289(3) (March 2002): 41.

Marino, C. C. "The Seboyetanos and the Navahos." *New Mexico Historical Review*, n.d.

Matson, Daniel S., and Albert H. Schroeder, eds. "Cordero's Description of the Apache: 1796." *New Mexico Historical Review*, n.d.

McNitt, Frank. "Fort Sumner: A Study in Origins." *New Mexico Historical Review* 45 (April 1970): 101–17.

Miller, Darlis A. "General James Henry Carleton in New Mexico." Master's thesis. Las Cruces: New Mexico State University, 1970.

————. "Los Piños, New Mexico: Civil War Post on the Rio Grande." *New Mexico Historical Review* 62 (January 1987): 1–32.

Moody, Marshall D. "Kit Carson, Agent to the Indians in New Mexico, 1853–1861." *New Mexico Historical Review* 28 (January 1953): 1–20.

Morris, Earl H. "Exploring the Canyon of Death." *National Geographic* 48 (1925): 263–300.

Murphy, Lawrence R. "Master of the Cimarron: Lucien B. Maxwell." *New Mexico Historical Review* 55(1) (January 1980).

————. "Rayado: Pioneer Settlement in Northeastern New Mexico, 1848–1857." *New Mexico Historical Review,* XLVI: 1.

Navajo People. "Removal of the Navajo and Ute Indians." House Executive Document 308, 40th Cong., 2d sess.

Neary, John. "It's Hard to Believe One Man Held Sway over All This Land." *Smithsonian* (July 1995): 44.

Niederman, Sharon. "Ol' Max Evan: Writing the Western Wave." *Crosswinds Weekly* (October 2004): 12.

Osburn, Katherine Marie Birmingham. "The Navajo at Bosque Redondo: Cooperation, Resistance, and Initiative, 1864–1868." *New Mexico Historical Review* 60 (October 1985): 399–413.

Reeve, Frank D. "Albert Franklin Banta: Arizona Pioneer, Part II." *New Mexico Historical Review* 17 (July 1952): 200–252.

————. "Early Navajo Geography." *New Mexico Historical Review* 31 (October 1956): 290–309.

————. "Federal Indian Policy in New Mexico, 1858–1880" (in three parts). *New Mexico Historical Review* 12, 13, 14 (July 1937–July 1938).

————. "The Government and the Navajos, 1846–1858." *New Mexico Historical Review* 14 (January 1939): 82–114.

————. "Navajo Foreign Affairs, 1795–1846." *New Mexico Historical Review* 46, 47 (April–June 1971): 101–32, 223–51.

————. "Navajo–Spanish Wars, 1680–1720." *New Mexico Historical Review* 33 (July 1958): 205–32.

————. "A Navajo Struggle for Land." *New Mexico Historical Review* 21 (January 1946): 1–21.

"Reminiscences of Early Days in New Mexico." *Albuquerque Evening Herald,* June 11, 1922.

Reynolds, Gretchen. "No Bed, No Breakfast." *Metropolis* (November 1999): 134.

Rister, Carl Coke. "Harmful Practices of Indian Traders of the Southwest, 1865–1876." *New Mexico Historical Review* 6 (July 1931): 231–48.

Roberts, David. "The Long Walk to Bosque Redondo." *Smithsonian* (December 1997): 46.

Russell, Inez. "Filling in the Blanks the Winners Left Empty." *Taos Revistado* (February 2, 2006).

————. "State's Collective Conscience Comes Clean about Long Walk." *Santa Fe New Mexican,* June 2005, B1, B4.

Salmon, Roberto M. "The Disease Complaint at Bosque Redondo." *Indian Historian* 9(3) (1976).

Schroeder, Albert H. "Navajo and Apache Relationships West of the Rio Grande." *El Palacio* 7(3) (Fall 1963): 5–23.

Secretary of War. Letter from the Secretary of War Relative to the Unsuitableness of the Bosque Redondo Reservation. House Executive Document 248, 40th Cong., 2d sess.

Simmons, Marc. "A Good Deed by Carson Went Largely Unnoticed." *Santa Fe New Mexican* (n.d.), C1, C5.

———. "Horse Race at Fort Fauntleroy: An Incident of the Navajo Wars." *La Gaceta* 5 (3) (1970).

———. "Navajos Have Long History of Rich Lore." *Santa Fe New Mexican,* November 29, 2003, B1, B5.

———. "The Tragic, Controversial 'Long Walk' of the Navajos." *Santa Fe New Mexican* (n.d.), B1, B4.

Smalling, Wes. "The Long Walk." *Santa Fe New Mexican,* September 25, 2005, C1, C3.

Spano, Susan. "Trails of the Ancients: Navajos Weave Hues of Land into Famed Rugs." *The Commercial Appeal,* June 16, 2002, F1, F4.

Stewart, Ronald D. "An Adobe Post on the Pecos." *El Palacio* (1971): 4.

Sunseri, Alvin R. "Sheep Ricos: Sheep Fortunes in the Aftermath of the American Conquest, 1846–1861" (n.p.; 1977): 1.

Taylor, Morris. "Ka-ni-ache." *Colorado Magazine* 43 (1966–67): 275–302.

Thompson, Gerald E. "To the People of New Mexico, General Carleton Defends the Bosque Redondo." *Arizona and the West* 14 (Winter 1972): 347–66.

Thompson, John. "The Destruction of Navajo Orchards in 1864." *Arizona and the West* 16(4) (Winter 1974): 365.

Tietz, Jeff. "Fine Disturbances: To Track Someone, You Have to Learn How to See." *The New Yorker.* November 29, 2004.

Trafzer, Clifford E. "Defeat of the Lords of New Mexico: The Navajo-Apache Wars." *Military History of Texas and the Southwest* 9 (1971): 215–25.

———. "Mr. Lincoln's Army Fights the Navajos, 1862–1864." *Lincoln Herald* 77 (1975): 148–58.

———. "Politicos and Navajos." *Journal of the West* (1974): 13.

United States. Senate Report No. 64, 31st Cong., 1st sess. Washington, DC: Government Printing Office, 1850.

———. *Proceedings of the Great Peace Commission of 1867–1868.* Washington, DC: Institute for the Development of Indian Law, 1975.

———. *Treaty Between the United States of America and the Navajo Tribe of Indians, With a Record of the Discussions That Led to Its Signing.* Las Vegas: KC Publications, 1868.

———. Joint Special Committee. *Condition of the Indian Tribes: Report of the Joint Special Committee Appointed Under Joint Resolution of March 3, 1865, with an Appendix.* Washington, DC: Government Printing Office, 1867.

Unrau, William E. "The Civil War Career of Jesse Henry Leavenworth Montana." *Magazine of Western History* 12 (April 1962): 74–83.

Usher, John P. *Report on the Navajo Indians.* House Executive Document 65, 38th Cong. 1st sess.

Van Valkenburgh, Richard. "Captain Red Shirt." *New Mexico Magazine* (July 1941): 44–45.

———. "Navajo Naataani." *The Kiva* (January 1948): 13.

Waldrip, William I. "New Mexico during the Civil War." *New Mexico Historical Review* 28 (July–October 1953): 163–82, 251–90.

Walker, Henry P. "Soldier in the California Column: The Diary of John W. Teal." *Arizona and the West* 13 (Spring 1971): 33–82.

Wallen, Henry Davis. "Prisoners without Walls." *El Palacio* 74(1) (Spring 1967).

Watkins, T. H. "Hawk High over Four Corners." *National Geographic* 190(3) (1996): 80.

Widdison, Jerold Gwayn. "Historical Geography of the Middle Rio Puerco Valley, New Mexico." *New Mexico Historical Review* 34 (October 1959): 248–84.

Witherspoon, Gary. "Sheep in Navajo Culture and Social Organization." *American Anthropologist* 75(5) (1973).

Woodard, Arthur. "Sidelight on Fifty Years of Apache Warfare." *Arizoniana* (Fall 1961): 2.

Worchester, Donald E. "The Navajo during the Spanish Regime in New Mexico." *New Mexico Historical Review* 26 (April 1951): 101–18.

Zollinger, Norman. "Ambushed: The Late 20th Century Attack on Kit Carson." *Book Talk: New Mexico Book League* 27(3) (July 1998).

ACKNOWLEDGMENTS

The following museums and historical sites proved to be of tremendous value to my research: the Kit Carson Home and Museum in Taos, New Mexico; Hacienda de los Martinez in Taos; the Bosque Redondo Memorial in Fort Sumner, New Mexico; the Navajo Nation Museum and Library in Window Rock, Arizona; the Canyon de Chelly National Monument in Chinle, Arizona; Bent's Old Fort National Historical Site in La Junta, Colorado; Sutter's Fort State Historic Park in Sacramento, California; the Frontier Army Museum in Fort Leavenworth, Kansas; and the National Museum of the American Indian in Washington, D.C.

I made six trips to the remarkable Navajo Nation. While there, I greatly benefited from the scholarly insights and warm generosity of the Roessel family—Ruth, Bob, Monty, and Mary—who, among other kindnesses, invited me to what has to have been the coldest Yeibichei ceremony ever held. At Canyon de Chelly, I must thank the estimable Adam Teller, professional guide and interpreter, and traditional Navajo storyteller, with whom I had the good fortune to tour the canyon by horse, foot, and Jeep.

I gained valuable insights from many Western scholars (both academic and non), a few of whom I'd like to acknowledge here: Marc Simmons, without question the most erudite—not to mention prolific!—scholar of the American Southwest; Howard Lamar, the gray eminence of all Western studies and my college dean at Yale; John Farr of the Kit Carson Museum, a priceless resource; Scott Smith of the Bosque Redondo Museum, whose knowledge of the Long Walk literature is unparalleled; and John Carson, great-grandson of Kit

Carson, unofficial keeper of the family flame and (may I add) a dead ringer for the man himself.

Thanks to Dave Byrnes and the whole crew at CD Café who saw me through many dark hours and left me alone in my perfectly hideous piss-yellow thrift shop chair. Thanks as well to the good folks at Yaddo for a lifesavingly productive fellowship. I also thank the late great Shelby Foote, the first writer I ever met as a kid growing up in Memphis, who taught me what narrative history should aspire to be.

The editors at *Outside* magazine have been good to me all these years, and have smiled on this project in a number of ways. From the House of "O," I must especially thank Hal Espen, Mary Turner, Alex Heard, and Jay Stowe.

Two friends and esteemed colleagues—Kevin Fedarko and Laura Hohnhold—read earlier drafts of my manuscript with much care and made astute suggestions for improvement. Other readers who offered valuable critiques include Dennis Romero, Davant Latham, Will Hobbs, Joe and Mary Neihardt, and Mack and Marnie Goodwin.

I was fortunate to have the formidable Alyssa Brandt as my research assistant and "charge d'affaires" in the early going—she led the way. Others who helped me with various phases of my research include Grayson Schaffer, Kevin Kennedy, Jason Nyberg, Link Sides, Michael Gerber, and Charles Bethea. Thanks to Robin Wiener, Verena Schwarz, and Munson Hunt for helping us keep the home fires burning, and to Christine Pride, my lifeline at Doubleday.

A final thank you goes to Sloan Harris, my loud-shirted friend, and a wise counsel to all denizens of the pain cave; to the intrepid Bill Thomas at Doubleday, who sees things others can't; and to my amazing family—Griffin, Graham, McCall, and Anne Almighty, for whom the mantra always applies: Times that are good, goodness that is timely.

INDEX

ART CREDITS

Title page: *Canyon de Chelly* by Edward S. Curtis. © Christie's Images/CORBIS.

"This may be the best road trip you'll ever take—full of strange visions, hilarious detours, and sudden beauty in unlikely places."
—Burkhard Bilger, staff writer at The New Yorker

AMERICANA
Dispatches from the New Frontier

For more than fifteen years, Hampton Sides has traveled the continent exploring the America that thrives just behind the surface of our mainstream culture. In this collection of thirty pieces, we follow Sides as he crashes the redwood retreat of an apparent cabal of powerful military-industrialists, drops in on the Indy 500 of bass fishing, and joins a giant techno-rave at the lip of the Grand Canyon. We meet a diverse gallery of American visionaries—from the impossibly perky founder of Tupperware to Indian radical Russell Means to skateboarding legend Tony Hawk. We retrace the route to the historic Bataan Death March with veterans from Sides's acclaimed World War II epic, *Ghost Soldiers*. Sides also examines the nation that has emerged from the ashes of September 11, recounting the harrowing journeys of three World Trade Center survivors and deciding at the last possible minute not to "embed" on the Iraqi frontlines with the U.S. Marines. *Americana* gives us a sparkling mosaic of our country today, in all its wild and poignant charm.

Nonfiction/978-1-4000-3355-3

"*More than any monument,* Ghost Soldiers *is the memorial both prisoners and liberators deserve.*"
—The Seattle Times

GHOST SOLDIERS
The Epic Account of World War II's Greatest Rescue Mission

On January 28, 1945, 121 hand-selected U.S. troops slipped behind enemy lines in the Philippines. Their mission: March thirty rugged miles to rescue 513 POWs languishing in a hellish camp, among them the last survivors of the infamous Bataan Death March. A recent prison massacre by Japanese soldiers elsewhere in the Philippines made the stakes impossibly high and left little time to plan the complex operation. Sides vividly re-creates this daring raid, offering a minute-by-minute narration that unfolds alongside intimate portraits of the prisoners and their lives in the camp. Sides shows how the POWs banded together to survive, defying the Japanese authorities even as they endured starvation, tropical diseases, and torture. Harrowing, poignant, and inspiring, *Ghost Soldiers* is the mesmerizing story of a remarkable mission. It is also a testament to the human spirit, an account of enormous bravery and self-sacrifice amid the most trying conditions.

History/World War II/978-0-385-49565-3

ANCHOR BOOKS
Available at your local bookstore, or visit
www.randomhouse.com